WRITERS
Literary Lives in Focus

foreword by Goffredo Fofi

contrasto

via Nizza, 56
00198 Rome, Italy

Translated from the Italian *Scrittori*
by Grace Crerar-Bromelow and Clare Costa

Photo editing
Franca De Bartolomeis

Editor
Alessia Tagliaventi

Design and Layout
Tania Russo

Quality control
Barbara Barattolo

ISBN 978-88-6965-525-8

Jacket image by Richard Avedon
Truman Capote, New York, October 10, 1955

The writers' biographies were contributed by the following

Maria Baiocchi 18, 28, 30, 34, 36, 40, 48, 50, 80, 82, 104, 106, 110, 116, 118, 122, 126, 128, 136, 140, 152, 154, 156, 158, 160, 178, 190, 196, 202, 208, 216, 220, 222, 224, 228, 238, 248, 250, 264, 274, 280, 280, 292, 398, 300, 316, 330, 342, 354, 376, 378, 386, 394, 408, 424, 442, 444, 456, 472, 476, 480, 486, 488, 492, 496, 500

Guia Boni 16, 22, 24, 42, 52, 62, 68, 84, 94, 102, 114, 164, 168, 170, 186, 194, 204, 226, 258, 260, 262, 290, 320, 336, 344, 350, 366, 372, 374, 384, 402, 434, 464, 466, 468, 474

Goffredo Fofi 8, 10, 60, 76, 88, 88, 146, 150, 184, 198, 234, 236, 282, 296, 302, 312, 338, 346, 352, 362, 422

Carlo Mazza Galanti 54, 96, 98, 100, 134, 162, 180, 212, 240, 242, 244, 270, 304, 332, 340, 358, 370, 388, 392, 404, 412, 414,420, 436, 450, 462, 482, 484

Alessandra Mauro 26, 92, 142, 174, 182, 192, 272, 306, 322, 324, 326, 356, 398, 400, 410, 428, 440, 452, 454, 478

Isabella Pedicini 20, 44, 46, 58, 66, 72, 108, 112, 120, 130, 144, 172, 176, 218, 252, 284, 288, 294, 334, 368, 380, 382, 406, 426, 432, 490, 502, 504

Alessia Tagliaventi 12, 14, 32, 38, 56, 64, 70, 74, 78, 86, 90, 124, 132, 148, 166, 188, 200, 206, 214, 230, 232, 254, 256, 266, 268, 278, 278, 286, 308, 310, 314, 318, 328, 348, 360, 364, 390, 396, 416, 418, 430, 438, 446, 448, 458, 460, 470, 494, 498, 506

Anna Tagliavini 210

CONTENTS

AS YOU SEE ME

Goffredo Fofi

The portrait has always been at the heart of the great history of painting. Its purpose has been, partly, to celebrate the external appearance of the person being represented – normally a prominent figure in a society, establishment, circle, situation or family. Who judges this prominence is another question; the choice is most often made by the patron who has commissioned the artist to 'immortalize' an individual, though occasionally the artist may select a subject he or she considers worthy of being portrayed regardless of the rank or milieu to which they belong. Yet also (and ever more frequently)the portrait represents more than external appearance – it seeks to interpret and somehow present the intimate life, the originality and uniqueness of the person being portrayed. Over time, photography has stolen many functions away from painting but, as can be seen clearly in art, media and everyday life, photography has most particularly made portraiture its own.

From the second half of the nineteenth century through to the first decades of the twentieth, photography placed itself in direct competition with painting; not solely in the field of portraiture, although it was there that the competition was most obvious. Inevitably, photographers strove to make portraits of the greatest figures of their time, and more than that, they sought to define their very essence. Photographers searched for the feature or expression that made clear the subject's humanity, while also capturing minute details that displayed how life and history had left their mark – the details that when presented to the world can both distil and evoke the era.

In a photographer's successes we see instantly what they saw, something all the more authentic for being almost hidden: the vexations, hopes, joys, desires, frustrations, worries, ambitions, defeats, or simply thoughtlessness and indifference. We see what, if anything, they have chosen to live for. When portraying famous artists, writers or philosophers, commercial aims are secondary to a great photographer's ambition to demonstrate his or her ability: talented photographers have always wanted to capture something more than simply a likeness. Just as journalism developed into a medium that not only related but also enquired, photographers, too, began attempting to capture the originality, the difference and the qualities of these artists that marked them out from their contemporaries. It is fascinating to see how great photographers have portrayed great painters – virtually robbing them of their own job, and setting themselves up in direct competition – but no less fascinating to see what they have attempted with writers.

In their own art, writers do not show us a momentary flash or what truly 'is'. They reconstruct. They invent. To express themselves, they exchange images for words – arguably the most widely available of all artists' media. The tools of their trade have always been technically simple and relatively commonly available: the stylus, the pen (in ancient times it was a reed or a goose quill) and the typewriter. Some writers still prefer to write in longhand but for most the utility of the modern computer has won out, although word-processing software is still very simple compared to the complexities of graphic-design or music-editing programs. Computers have made the work of writing so much faster that they may even end up influencing it by encouraging a certain hurriedness and lack of reflection.

There is a distance between photographer and writer that does not exist between two artists who work only with visual media. When a photographer makes an image of, say, a film- or theatre-director, it seems to me that there is often some level of antagonism or complicity in the encounter because both artists 'work with images'. However, when making an image of a writer, if the photographer wishes to use his or her talent to the fullest to create something that is well judged and thus of lasting value, he or she must have a knowledge of the writer's works (and both of the worlds he has described and how he has described them). What's more, the individual holding the camera must have agreat curiosity about them; otherwise the photographs that he or she takes may have nothing to say, or may say something only through luck or accident.

Environment is vitally important. All great writers are the bearers of a unique vision, something specific to their origin and upbringing. When the masters of the image confront the masters of the word, their media are so different from one another that they must work to select and create the image. The photographer bears a weighty responsibility. He must distinguish the more self-absorbed traits of the subject – What it is that the writer wishes to communicate about him- or herself? How does he want to be seen? – and present them in a way that is at once both honest and challenging to the writer.

In the best instances, we can see in the photograph that the writer (although not just the writer, of course) has discovered something about him- or herself that he or she was unaware of, or had not reflected upon sufficiently. The photographer is someone who knows how to see, and through the photographs in *Writers* the reader will also often discover something previously unrevealed about the artists depicted.

It is because of this that many of the photographs in this book allow us to understand the writers we love (or perhaps detest) better: we see their doubts; we see their vanity; often we grasp more about their work. Whatever we see, it is thanks to the photographer–artist that we have this opportunity to judge and either absolve or condemn. We may also accept with a smile that no one is perfect and no one exempt from some degree of narcissism.

Literature in the twentieth century saw great changes that stemmed from how artists and intellectuals perceived the historic changes of their times. From this era of enormous transformations, the literature we inherit, however incomplete, is an epic of the ways in which humanity views itself and its history, its rights and its duties. Those hundred years saw two world wars; a seemingly never-ending stream of regional conflicts; revolutions that began with great hopes but have led to dictatorships; the financial and political divisions within our planet becoming entrenched; the wars of liberation from colonial rule in Asia, Africa and Latin America; thirty 'glorious' years of reconstruction and development in Europe; the growth and collapse of the Soviet Empire; and the global spread of the American way of life with all its alienating, homogenizing consequences; the response of different fundamentalisms; the end of the civilization of steel, in turn replaced by the digital boom; the unprecedented dominance of big finance and of world economies; the religion of money and its all-powerful high priests supplanting politics; and ongoing ecological crises that over the next hundred years may take on apocalyptic proportions.

These changing interrelationships within the world may have brought us closer together, yet they have also become the means by which market forces exert ever greater control over the creation, marketing and sale of art – books in particular. As we enter the new century, venturing into the territory in which a book such as this can come into being, it is not hard to see that the digital revolution has had a significant effect on photography, too. Quite simply, it has cancelled out many of its most creative pathways, and not just its most traditional ones. We may view this as the death of the noble art of photography, or possibly the start of an evolution that will prove to be so radical that it may produce modes of expression with barely any connection to the forms that preceded it.

At the turn of the twentieth century, in which the core of this book lies, there were many writers, particularly Marcel Proust, James Joyce and Italo Svevo, who breathed new life into literature with revolutionary novels. Our selection brings together the great writers of yesterday with those of today, who for the most part have lived through the changes mentioned, and variously accepted them, discussed them or fought against them as they searched for their own path. They have extracted experience and knowledge from these events and turned it into revolutionary novels of their own.

Of course, we could include only a small selection of photographers and writers; we cannot represent the true scope of talent that has existed across the globe. One thing we can be certain of is that anyone who picks up this book will quickly discover that some photographers and writers are missing, probably some of those who he or she considers to be among the greatest! For reasons of space we have chosen to include mainly novelists and poets, and have had to leave out most essayists and playwrights. There have been so many great writers who have left their mark on the world, and so many great photographers who have left us portraits to treasure, that it is in reality a near-impossible task. What is clear from this selection is the immense skill of the photographers who observed writers, captured them and presented them to history. The artists we cannot see in the photographs have contributed just as much to our curiosity and our memories as those we can see.

CHINUA ACHEBE

[Albert Chinualumogu Achebe] born Ogidi, Nigeria, 1930; died Boston, Massachusetts 2013

by Beowulf Sheehan

New York, 2008

International critics and intellectuals from every African county had no doubts: Achebe was one of the greatest African writers of the twentieth century. A Nigerian of the Igbo people, he wrote *Things Fall Apart*, the masterpiece that the world had been waiting for; a great novel that was able to express the contradictions of black Africa as it travelled from colonial rule to a hard and difficult, and sometimes tragic, independence. The old world, with its faiths, values and tribal distinctions, had been all but eroded away by colonialism, which had flooded the continent with new weapons, new beliefs and new manners. In doing so, colonizers destroyed a culture that had been built up over centuries. These sudden changes to the continent's foundations are what Achebe confronted in *Things Fall Apart* (1958), *No Longer at Ease* (1960) and *Arrow of God* (1964). The first of these novels has a lasting resonance because, better than any other work of literature, it has helped us understand a history and a culture undergoing an often violent change, a change that was not sought but imposed from outside.

Although widely regarded as the 'father of modern African literature', Achebe disliked the title, saying: 'I don't want to be singled out as the one behind it because there were many of us – many, many of us.' But the 'many' also tended to consider him peerless among them, a masterful writer who knew how to focus their history through events and characters – each recognizable as true to the life of the vast continent. For much of the twentieth century, and the times that came before, conquerors and oppressors had primarily told the story of Africa and its people. But now there were African voices: inspiring authors able to depict the clash between a past and a present, as well as to see the political difficulties to come. As well as Achebe, writers such as his fellow Nigerian Wole Soyinka and the Kenyan writer Ngũgĩ wa Thiong'o chose to retain and reuse the languages of their colonizers. Books such as *Things Fall Apart* are now key texts on university reading lists across the world, challenging the descendants of those who may have been involved or complicit with colonial activities to ask themselves about their own identity and the rights of peoples. These are just some of the great questions posed by African literary culture.

Achebe explained that he wrote because 'The story is our escort; without it, we are blind,' for 'It is only the story that outlives the sound of war-drums and the exploits of brave fighters.' His short stories, poetry, essays, autobiography and historical analysis brought profundity and complexity to African literature. Father of modern African literature or not, there was no one quite like Achebe.

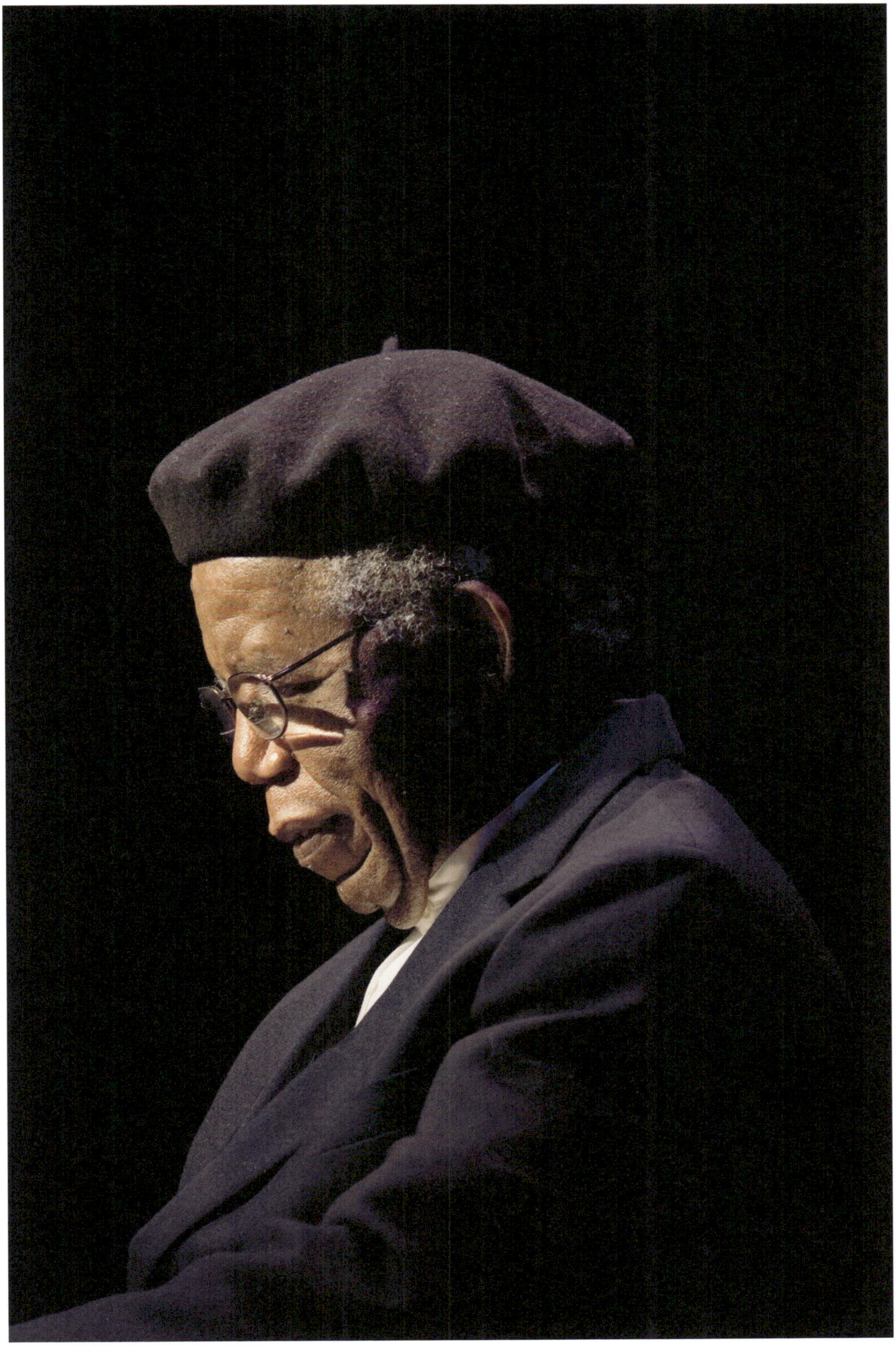

ZHONG ACHENG

[Ah Cheng] born Beijing, 1949

by Alberto Cristofari

Rome, 2003

Novelist, screenwriter and artist Zhong Acheng, who also writes under the pseudonym Ah Cheng, was born in 1949, the year that marked the birth of the new Chinese nation under the leadership of Mao Zedong. When Acheng was a young child, his father, a prominent film critic, was sent to the countryside along with many other students and intellectuals to be 're-educated' through the experience of hard manual labour, a strategy that also removed potential activists from the cities, where the new government feared political unrest might continue. This practice was a core tenet of the Cultural Revolution that would leave a devastating legacy on an entire generation. As a teenager Acheng himself was sent to work in Shanxi Province and Inner Mongolia. Thanks to the vitality of youth, he was not destroyed by this experience, and emerged with a heightened awareness of the contradictions inherent in the social and political system in which he had grown up.

In the late 1970s Acheng returned to Beijing and began writing screenplays and exhibiting his paintings and drawings with an avant-garde collective that included the artists Li Shuang and Ai Weiwei. As the political winds continued to shift he wrote the three short novels that formed his landmark 'King' cycle: *The King of the Trees*, *The Chess Master* and*The King of Children* (1984–85). By this time he was in his thirties, sufficiently mature and reflective to recount the darker experiences his youth.

What's more, the trilogy has kept its critical significance over the years. Chinese and international readers were struck not just by Acheng's portrayal of a hard day-to-day existence and the brutal confrontation between ideals and reality, but also by his skilful blending of the rhythms of classical literature with the immediacy of colloquial language. Alongside Mo Yan's *Red Sorghum* Acheng's novels are among the most famous in the late-twentieth-century renaissance in Chinese literature known as the *xungenpai* ('seeking roots') movement, aimed at addressing the loss of traditional heritage during the Cultural Revolution.

In the late 1980s Acheng spent several years in exile in the USA, working manual jobs and continuing to write short stories and essays. Following his return to China, he established his international reputation as a screenwriter, producing scripts for Chinese films including *Springtime in a Small Town* (2002) and *The Go Master* (2006).

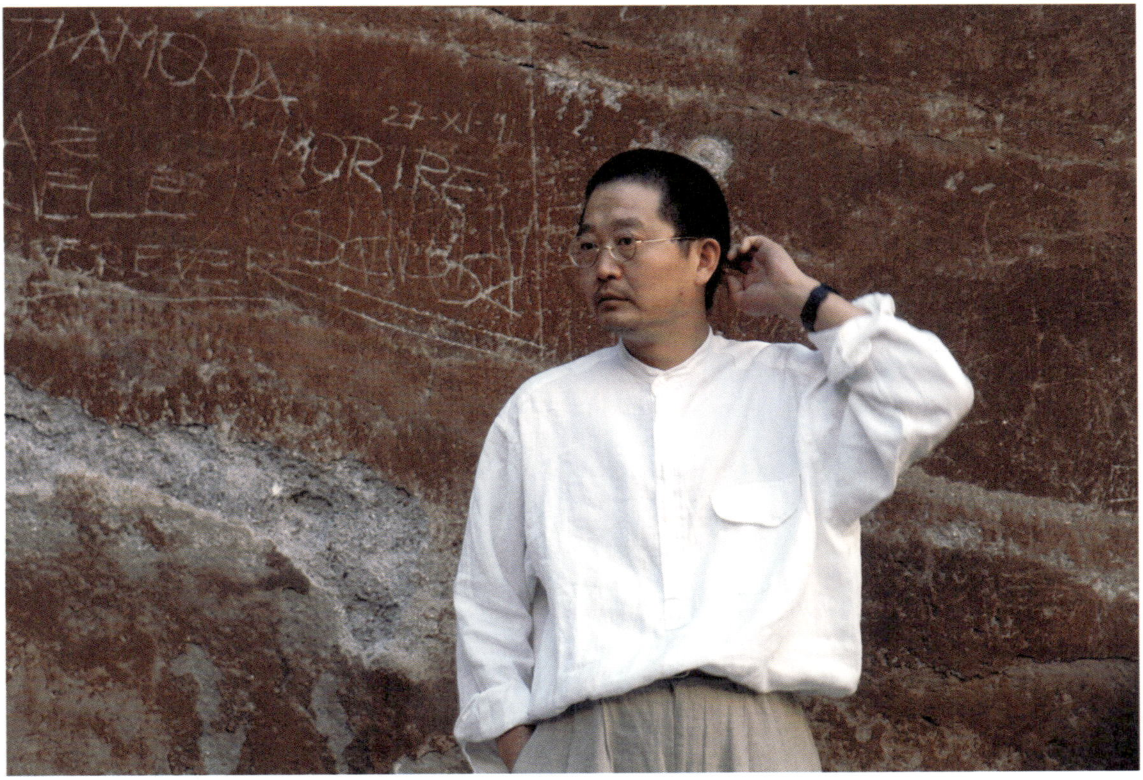
MORIRE

ANNA AKHMATOVA

[Anna Andreevna Gorenko] born Odessa, Ukraine, 1889; died Moscow, 1966

by Moisei Nappelbaum

St Petersburg, 1924

In this image of Anna Akhmatova, her aristocratic face brings to mind a Renaissance portrait. Moisei Nappelbaum (who also took the first official portrait of Lenin) photographed her in profile, which was so splendidly irregular that, as she told an acquaintance, she showed it off with pride. It was an object of fascination for many portraitists, who were struck by the commanding and mysterious femininity of a woman who demanded to be called a 'poet'; the label of 'poetess', she felt, was far too restrictive. The Italian artist Modigliani, who knew Akhmatova in Paris, was particularly fascinated by her. Although he never asked her to sit for him, he executed sixteen portraits of the writer from memory and then sent them to her in Russia. Unfortunately, with the exception of a single work, which she guarded jealously, the paintings were lost during the Russian Revolution.

Both Akhmatova's poetry and her life are eloquent and painful testimonies to the events that mark the history of Russia in the twentieth century. After her marriage to the poet Nikolai Gumilev, Akhmatova was involved in the formation of the Acmeist movement, which was opposed to Symbolism and loosely associated with Futurism. Her first collection of verses, *Evening*, was published in 1912. She spent the following years travelling in Europe and writing poetry.

In 1921 Gumilev was accused of being involved in a subversive monarchist conspiracy and was shot. Although he and Akhmatova had divorced some years earlier, the latter was still the ex-wife of a counter-revolutionary poet. Furthermore, her poetry had never adhered to the spirit of renewal that Socialism was intended to bring to art. She thus found herself alone in a Russia that was clearly becoming hostile to her: the government condemned her as a decadent poet and banned the publication of her work. In 1938 her only son was arrested and sent to a gulag labour camp, his only (presumed) guilt being that he carried his father's name.

During these painful years Akhmatova wrote *Requiem*, a devastating poem that, although it could not be published (it first appeared in print in Germany in 1963), was circulated in manuscript form and gained an enormous following. Her words represented a bitter attack on Stalin's dictatorship. However, at the outbreak of the Second World War, in order to bolster the Russian people's sense of patriotism, Stalin himself considered turning to the nation's cultural treasures for help – including Akhmatova. She spoke on Radio Leningrad while the city was under siege, sending out a strong and dignified message to its women. It was only in 1977, eleven years after her death, that her fellow citizens were able to read *Requiem* and *Poem without a Hero*, a complex analysis of the age in which she had lived, in a Soviet magazine.

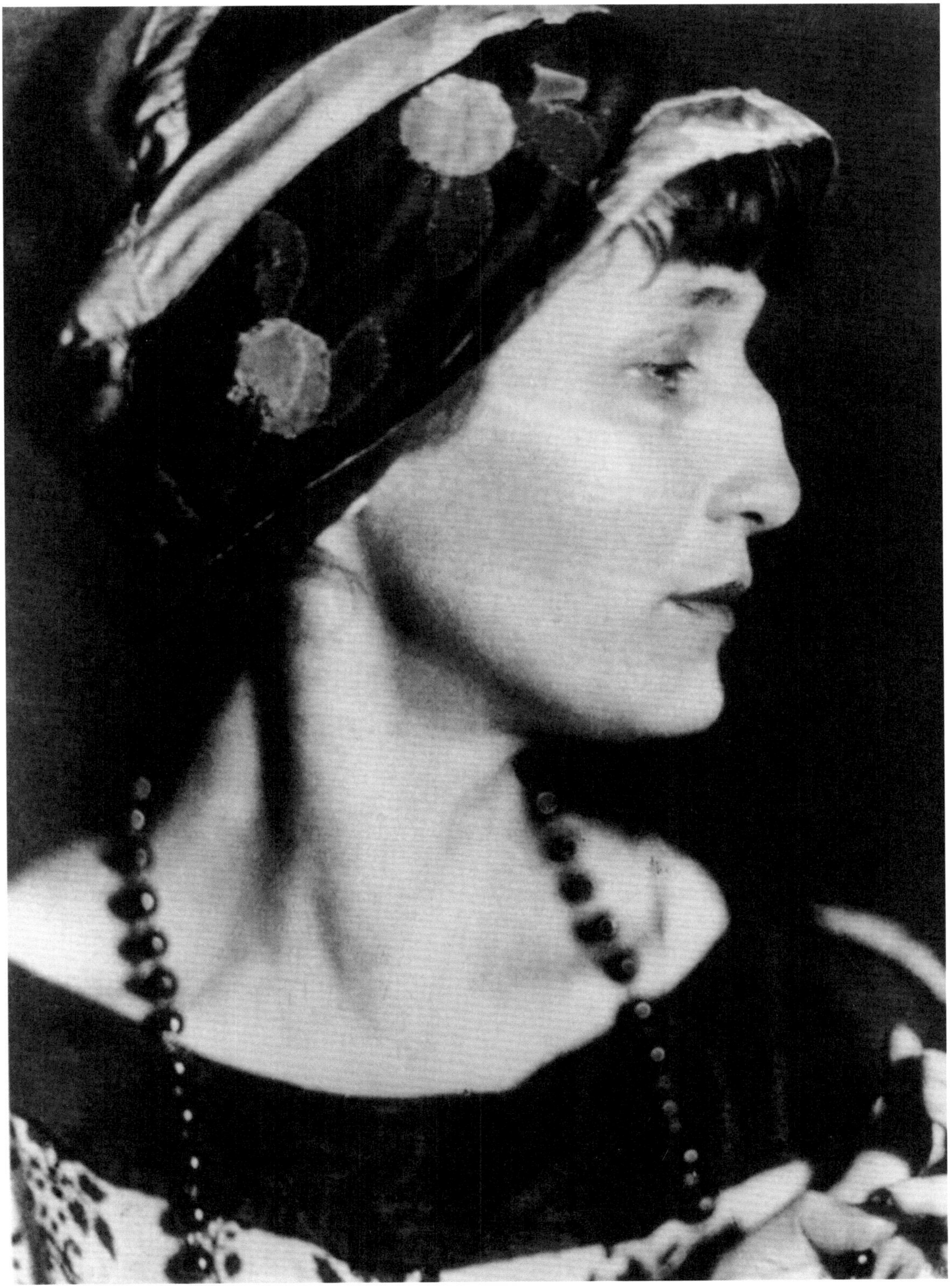

ADONIS

[Ali Ahmad Sa'id Isbir] born al-Qassabin, Syria, 1930

by Abbas

Paris, 1991

Our identity, Adonis maintains, is neither fixed nor inherited. Just like a poem, it is a creation that is conveyed, perhaps above all, through words; and it begins with the word that indicates our name. Adonis is the pen name of Ali Ahmad Sa'id Isbir, who was born into a farming family in a small village near the port of Latakia in north-west Syria. He did not receive a conventional schooling, but grew up immersed in a culture in which poetry is a popular and traditional form of expression. At the age of fourteen, he won a scholarship to study at the Lycée Français in Tartus by reading one of his poems to the president of the newly established Republic of Syria, greatly impressing him. When he was seventeen, the poet decided to change his name to that of a Greek god of beauty, in order to alert prospective publishers of his work to his pre-Islamic and pan-Mediterranean influences. It was his first act of rebirth.

His second was to go into exile. In 1956, having spent six months in jail for being a member of the Syrian National Socialist Party, Adonis moved to Beirut and became a Lebanese citizen. There, he became the leader of a modernist literary revolution that had an enormous impact on Arabic poetry. He founded influential journals, translated Western poets, embraced colloquial Arabic in his writing and raised his voice in opposition to Arab nationalism and the use of poetry as propaganda. For him, literature always had to be in revolt in order to be true to itself. He confirmed this view in the book-length poem *This Is My Name* (1970), his deeply felt reflection on the Arab forces' defeat by Israel in the Six Day War of 1967, and in *The Book of Siege* (1985), which was prompted by the Israeli invasion of Lebanon in 1982.

In 1985 Adonis left Beirut for Paris. This portrait of him was taken by the Iranian photographer Abbas, another expatriate living in voluntary exile in the French capital. Abbas also has his own special relationship with words: in *Iran Diary: 1971–2002* (2002), he retells the story of the Iranian Revolution and the history of his country in the form of a personal journal illustrated with his own photographs. Working just with words, says Adonis, cannot change society, for in order to do so, 'you have to change its structures – family, education, politics. That's work art cannot do.' But, he adds, what poetry is truly able to do is to change the 'relationship between things and words, so a new image of the world can be born'.

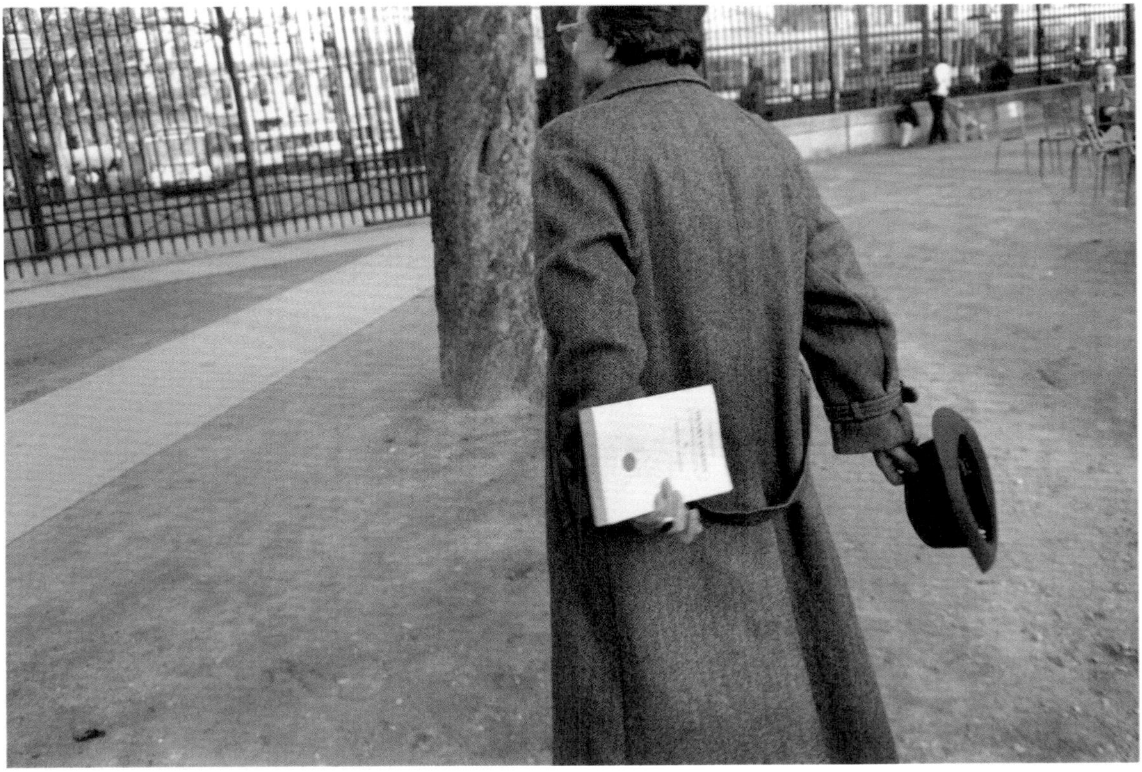

JORGE AMADO

born Itabuna, Brazil, 1912; died Salvador, Brazil, 2001

by René Burri

Salvador, Brazil, 1966

In many ways, Jorge Amado's Brazil is the eastern state of Bahia, where he was born and grew up. It is described in his novels as if it had been created by his own pen, and as if it were he who had introduced it to the rest of the world. Amado was the first Brazilian writer to achieve a global reputation. His early period of political engagement culminated in *The Bowels of Liberty* (1954), a trilogy that focuses on the lives of the Brazilian working classes (peasants, fishermen, manual labourers), the raising of their political consciousness and the moment of their rebellion. However, by the time he had completed his next novel, *Gabriela, Clove and Cinnamon* (1958), he had begun to temper his political views.

In 1955, just a few months before the 20th Congress of the Communist Party of the Soviet Union denounced Stalin's crimes, Amado decided to leave the Brazilian Communist Party. In the late 1950s, Brazil had reasons to feel positive: Juscelino Kubitschek's election as president, an economic boom, the construction of the model city of Brasília and the music of Tom Jobim all seemed to presage a better future. It was in this optimistic atmosphere that Amado wrote *Gabriela, Clove and Cinnamon*, giving life to a series of unforgettable female characters, including Dona Flor, Tereza Batista and Tieta do Agreste. However, he was immediately accused of populism, which he had always sought to avoid, and critics did little to hide their suspicions of his motives. In response, Amado argued that he had not abandoned his political commitment, but instead had introduced a new ingredient into his prose: a sense of humour allied to kindness and sympathy.

It is nonetheless true that the class struggle was no longer at the heart of Amado's novels; however, this did not mean that he had left it behind altogether. His vision of Brazilian society had perhaps become less polarized, but this allowed him to be more incisive and far-reaching. His prose – mellow, sensual, captivating, filled with musicality and shot through with humour – was no longer placed at the service of a single people, but at that of the whole world under the banner of fraternal solidarity.

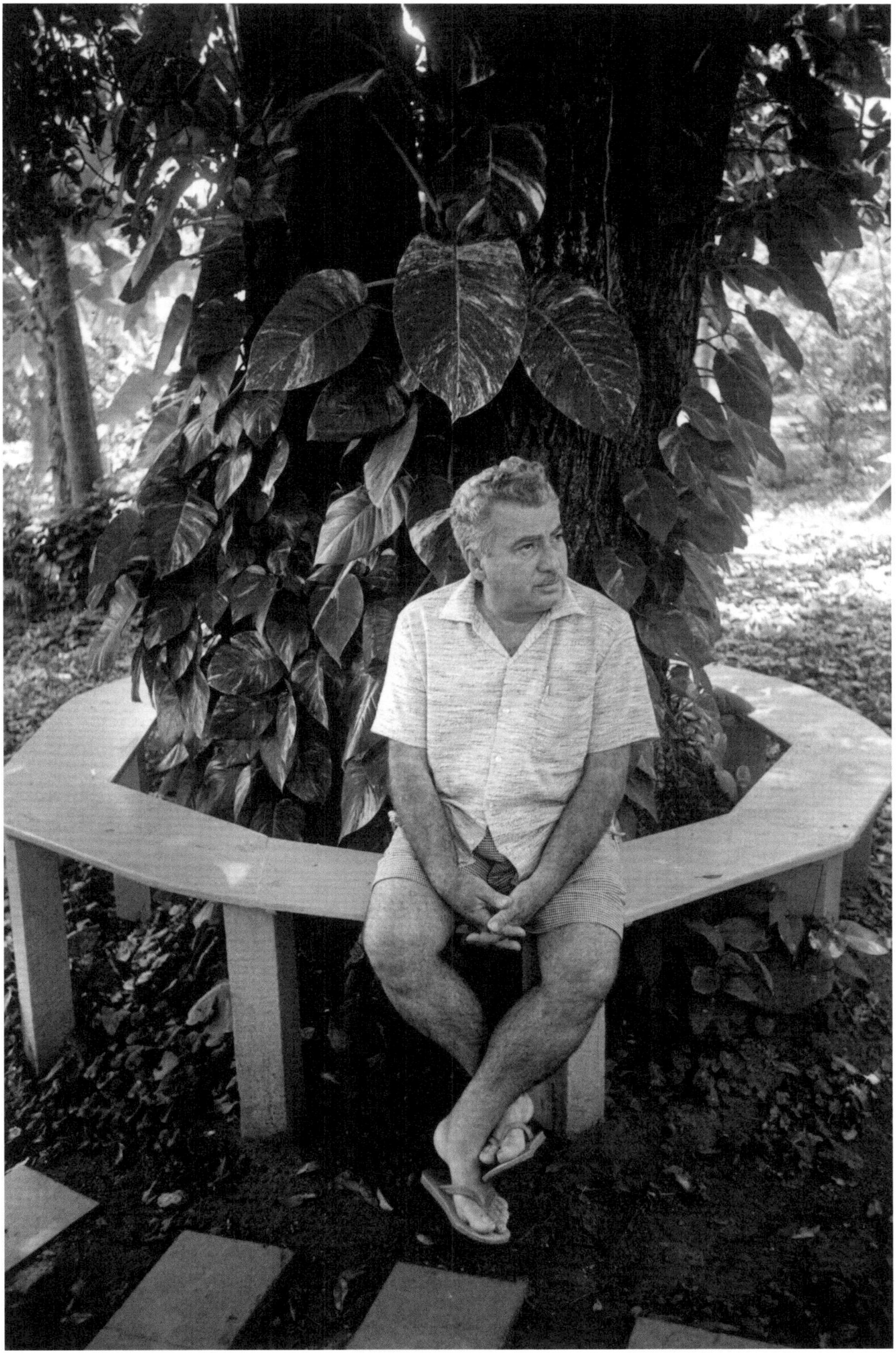

MARTIN AMIS

born Swansea, UK, 1949

by Lord Snowdon

London, 1978

Both Martin Amis and his debut novel, *The Rachel Papers* (1973), make a cameo appearance in *Sweet Tooth* (2012), a novel by Amis's fellow writer Ian McEwan. In McEwan's book, the aspiring writer Tom Haley is left in the shadows while Amis steals the limelight during a public reading of *The Rachel Papers*. Amis succeeds in making the audience laugh heartily, while Tom's literary efforts are far less well received.

Despite the light-hearted nature of this cameo, Amis – the son of the English writer Kingsley Amis – has a reputation for being a serious and forbidding individual, loved and loathed in equal measure. Indeed, since the publication of *The Rachel Papers*, which earned him the Somerset Maugham Award in 1974, he has enjoyed a somewhat tempestuous relationship not only with the press but also with publishers, the adjudicators of literary prizes and the general public.

Much of Amis's writing is centred around the excesses and absurdities of modern society, which he exposes through the use of satire and caricature. In the 1980s and 1990s he won great critical acclaim for his 'London' trilogy (*Money*, 1984; *London Fields*, 1989; and *The Information*, 1995), which was noted for its bleak and cynical portrayal of human nature, and even gave rise to a new genre: 'dirty realism'.

However, since the publication of *London Fields*, which was itself the subject of controversy owing to the way in which its female characters are portrayed, each of Amis's books has divided critics and readers alike, sometimes provoking polemical reactions. In 1997 he published his first work of crime fiction, *Night Train*. His novel of 2003, *Yellow Dog*, received some particularly harsh criticism, especially from his fellow writers. Likewise, *The Pregnant Widow* (2010) and *Lionel Asbo: State of England* (2012) were given somewhat lukewarm receptions. But whatever his standing with the critics, Amis is widely regarded as one of the most important and influential stylists of his generation, noted for his linguistic and narrative innovations: 'I don't want to write a sentence that any guy could have written.'

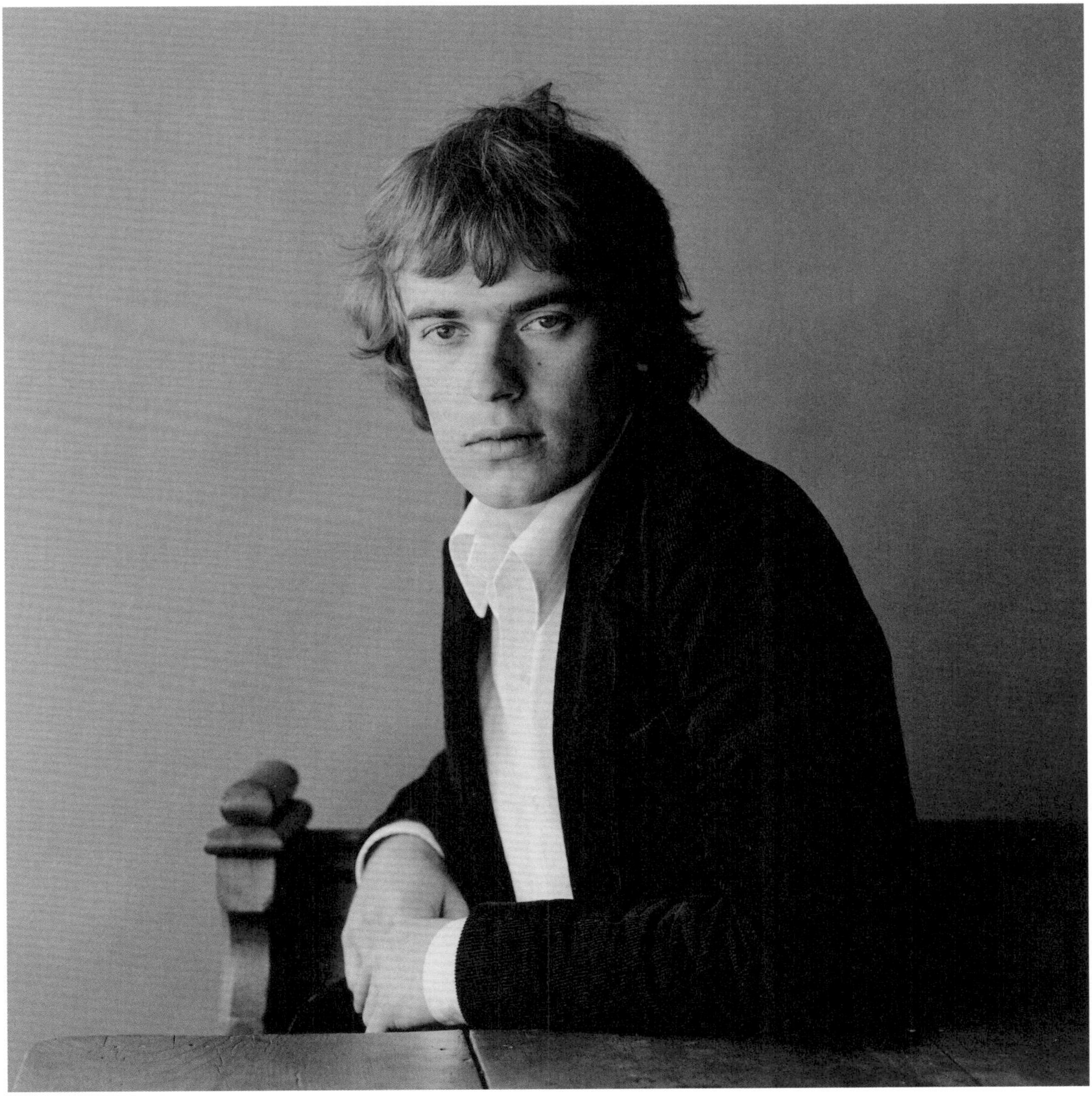

GUILLAUME APOLLINAIRE

[Guillaume Albert Wladimir Alexandre Apollinaire de Kostrowitzky] born Rome, 1880; died Paris, 1918

by Pablo Picasso

Paris, 1910

Guillaume Apollinaire's first collection of poetry, *Spirits* (1913), was the product of fifteen years of work and reflection. Noted for the richness of its tone and for the variety of its expressive forms, the book mixes experimentalism with poetry of rare simplicity, free verse with almost classical rhyme schemes, and factual descriptions with elegiac rhythms – all of which would prove to be essential features of Apollinaire's verse.

Apollinaire was the illegitimate son of a former Italian military officer and a Polish noblewoman. At the age of nineteen, after studying in Monaco, Nice and Cannes, he arrived in Paris. There, in order to earn a living, he wrote *feuilletons* (newspaper gossip columns) and erotic stories. He also attended avant-garde salons, befriended Pablo Picasso and the French writer Alfred Jarry, and took part in contemporary debates. Apollinaire was a supporter of Fauvism and Cubism, among other avant-garde artistic movements; he wrote his own Futurist manifesto, *The Futurist Anti-tradition* (1913) and, in a volume entitled *The Cubist Painters* (1913), collected together his writings in defence of modern art. At the outbreak of the First World War Apollinaire volunteered for military service, referring to the conflict as 'a great spectacle'. In 1916, however, he was wounded in the head, an injury that required a complicated surgical procedure.

In addition to poetry, Apollinaire wrote prose – including *The Poet Assassinated* (1916), a collection of short stories inspired by his experiences on the Western Front – and a play, *The Breasts of Tiresias* (first performed 1917). He had a deep appreciation of the graphic arts and found a new, visual way of approaching language, using the words of a poem to form the shape of the subject of the poem. A collection of these ideograms, in which he also used overlapping lines of dialogue and linked fragments of text taken from a variety of sources, was published under the title *Calligrammes* in 1918. He was working on a range of new projects when he died unexpectedly that same year, struck down by the Spanish influenza epidemic that had spread throughout Europe.

Picasso, who took this photograph in his studio in 1910, met Apollinaire for the first time in the Café Fox on the rue d'Amsterdam. They became great friends, and the poet was soon admitted to 'la bande à Picasso', a group of intellectuals and artists who often met in the artist's home and studio.

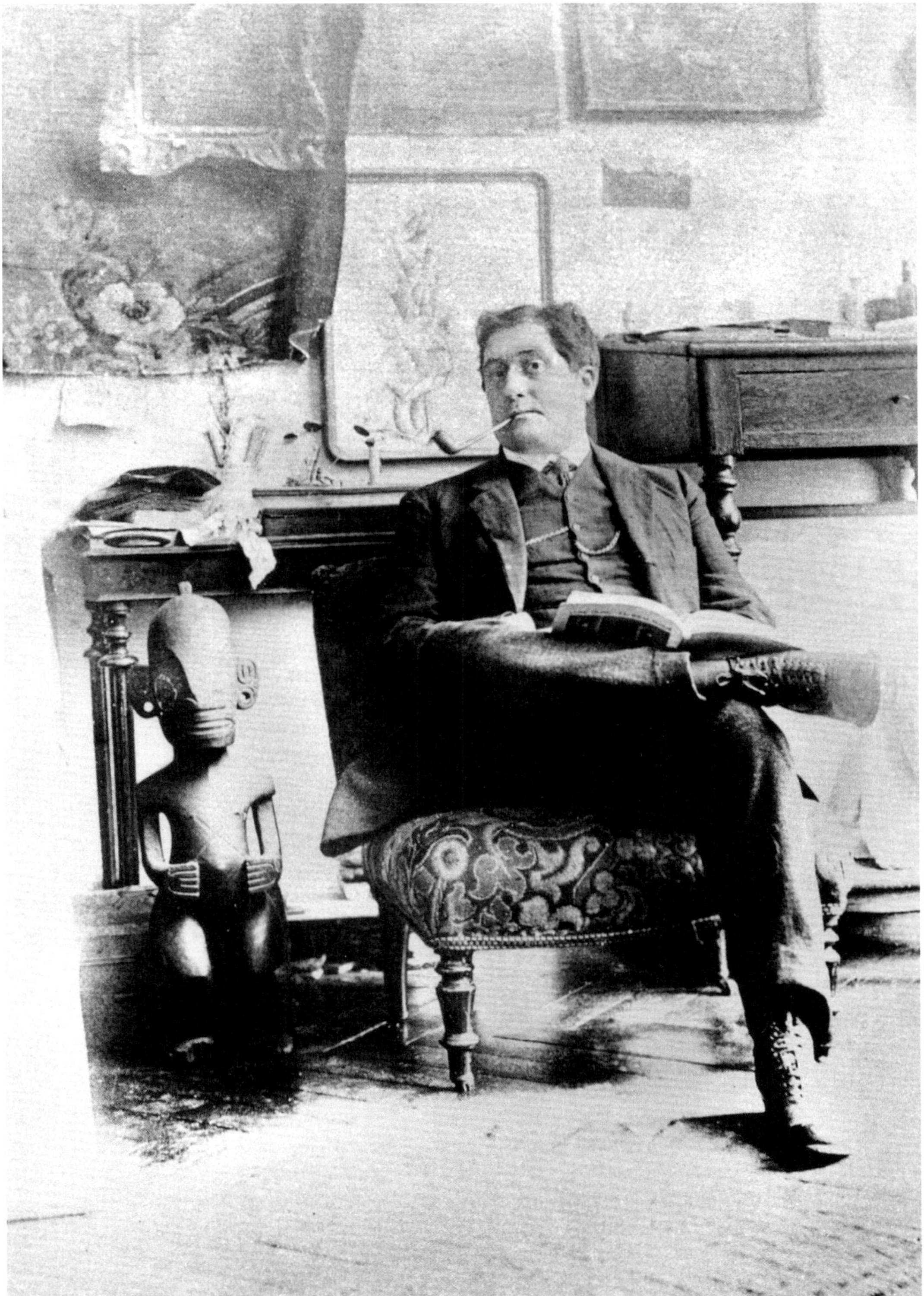

ROBERTO ARLT

born Buenos Aires, 1900; died Buenos Aires, 1942

by Véronique Pestoni

Buenos Aires, c. 1938

Largely self-taught after leaving school at the age of eight, Roberto Arlt was a literary pioneer in portraying the chaotic urban environment of Buenos Aires in the wake of the waves of immigration that poured into the Argentine capital from 1870 onwards. The son of two such immigrants (his father was a Prussian from what is now Poznan, Poland; his mother an Italian from Trieste) Arlt focused on the plight of the many Italian, German and Spanish citizens who had seen the possibility of social advancement in Argentina, but whose hopes had been dashed by the financial crash of 1929. The figure of the petty bourgeois who has been defeated in his aspirations, yet still tries to do his best, was consequently a central figure in his novels.

Arlt's writing was distinguished by its expressionistic use of the vernacular, transcending the division between written and spoken language. As Arlt explained, 'I write in an "idiom" that cannot properly be called Castilian, but rather *porteño* ... to celebrate how the people speak, in their agile, picturesque and changeable way that engages all our sensibilities. This lexicon, which I call an idiom, will be triumphant in our literature despite the indignation of the purists, who are not and will not be read by anyone.' Arlt was the first literary figure to include elements of lunfardo, the underworld dialect of Buenos Aires, which he had studied in philological articles written while he was working as a newspaper crime correspondent. Arlt's characters are united by their failed attempts to recover a status of which they feel they have been unjustly deprived. His semi-autobiographical *The Mad Toy* (1926) tells the story of the misadventures of Silvio Astier, a roguish school leaver whose attempts at social climbing in four different occupations at the turn of the century end in the humiliation not only of being socially downgraded, but also of dishonouring himself by a betrayal. Many of characters in *The Seven Madmen* (1927), *Los lanzallamas* (The flame-throwers, 1931) and *El amor brujo* (Bewitching love, 1932) embody the discontent of the middle classes and their failed attempts to escape their destiny. An acute observer of the class struggle, Arlt became a model for other Latin American writers such as Julio Cortázar, Ernesto Sábato, Ricardo Piglia and Roberto Bolaño.

Arlt's literary reputation also encompasses his journalistic output. The articles he published in the Argentine newspaper *El Mundo* were collected in a volume entitled *Aguafuertes porteñas* (Etchings from Buenos Aires, 1933) followed by *Aguafuertes españolas* (Etchings from Spain, 1936) written as he travelled through Spain and North Africa as the Spanish Civil War was unfolding. These articles were not just fine examples of journalistic writing, reflecting Arlt's ear for the vernacular, but were also accompanied by his own photography.

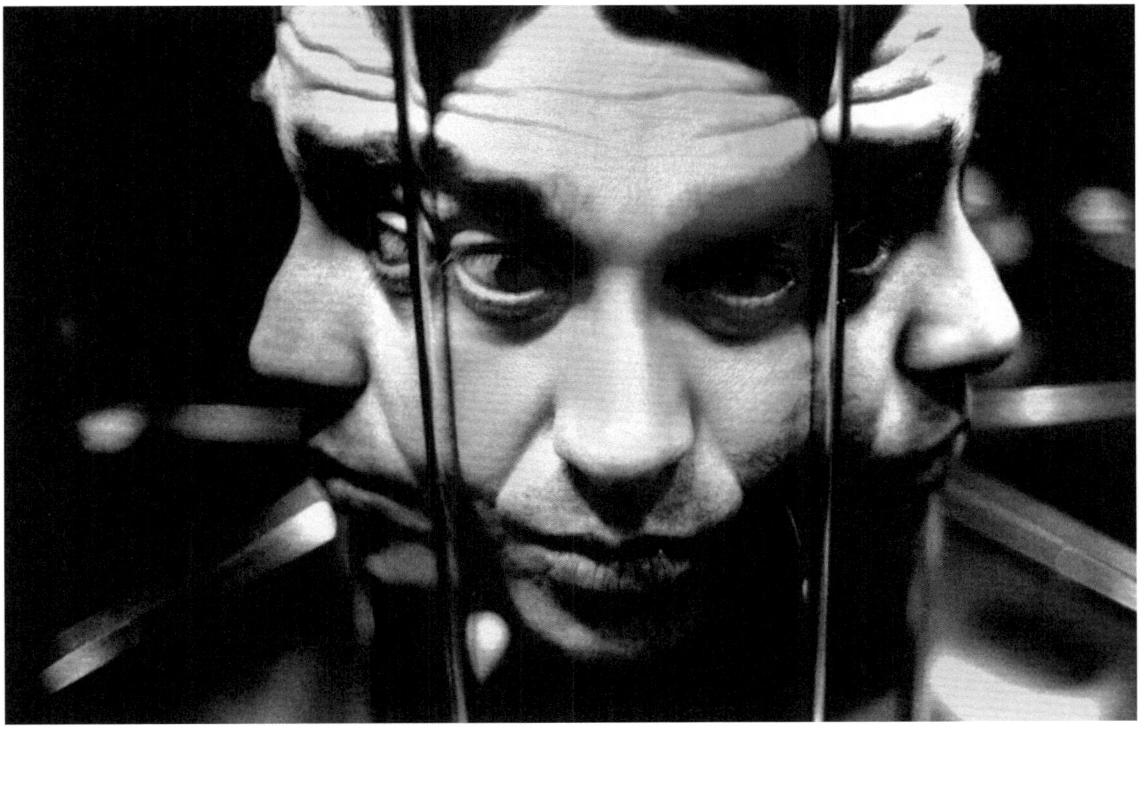

MIGUEL ÁNGEL ASTURIAS

born Guatemala City, Guatemala, 1899; died Madrid, 1974

by Henri Cartier-Bresson

Paris, 1967

In 1967 Miguel Ángel Asturias was awarded the Nobel Prize for 'his vivid literary achievement, deep-rooted in the national traits and traditions of Indian peoples of Latin America'. Throughout his career, Asturias – poet, novelist, playwright, journalist and diplomat – allied himself with the oppressed and downtrodden of society.

Asturias's first work of fiction, completed while he was living in Paris, was the short-story collection *Legends of Guatemala* (1930), in which he rewrites several ancient Mayan myths in a modern and poetic vein. The dreamlike Surrealism of this work marked the development of a style that hovered between fantasy and reality. While still in Paris, Asturias wrote *The President* (1946), a ruthless critique of life under two of Guatemala's dictators – Manuel Estrada Cabrera and Jorge Ubico y Castañeda – and of the damage caused by dictatorial regimes in general. In *Men of Maize* (1949) Asturias recounts the struggle between the Maya Indians (who, according to Maya tradition, believed that their flesh was made of corn) and the *maiceros*, the planters who were stripping the forests bare to line their own pockets.

Asturias's 'Banana' trilogy comprises the novels *Strong Wind* (1950), *The Green Pope* (1954) and *The Eyes of the Interred* (1960), all of which focus on the exploitation of the indigenous peoples working on the banana plantations by foreign companies. The period between the first and second books of the trilogy coincided with the rule of Guatemalan president Jacobo Arbenz (1951–54). This enlightened politician promised to restore land to the peasants in a programme of agrarian reform, but the USA, fearing the spread of Communism in South America, overturned his government in a CIA-backed coup. Asturias was forced to live in exile, first in Argentina, where he wrote the caustic collection of stories *Weekend in Guatemala* (1956), and later in Europe, where he rewrote further Maya legends in *The Mulatta and Mr Fly* (1963).

Henri Cartier-Bresson photographed Asturias in Paris, where he served as the Guatemalan ambassador to France for a number of years. Cartier-Bresson believed that all photographic portraits should try to convey the 'inner silence' of the subject.

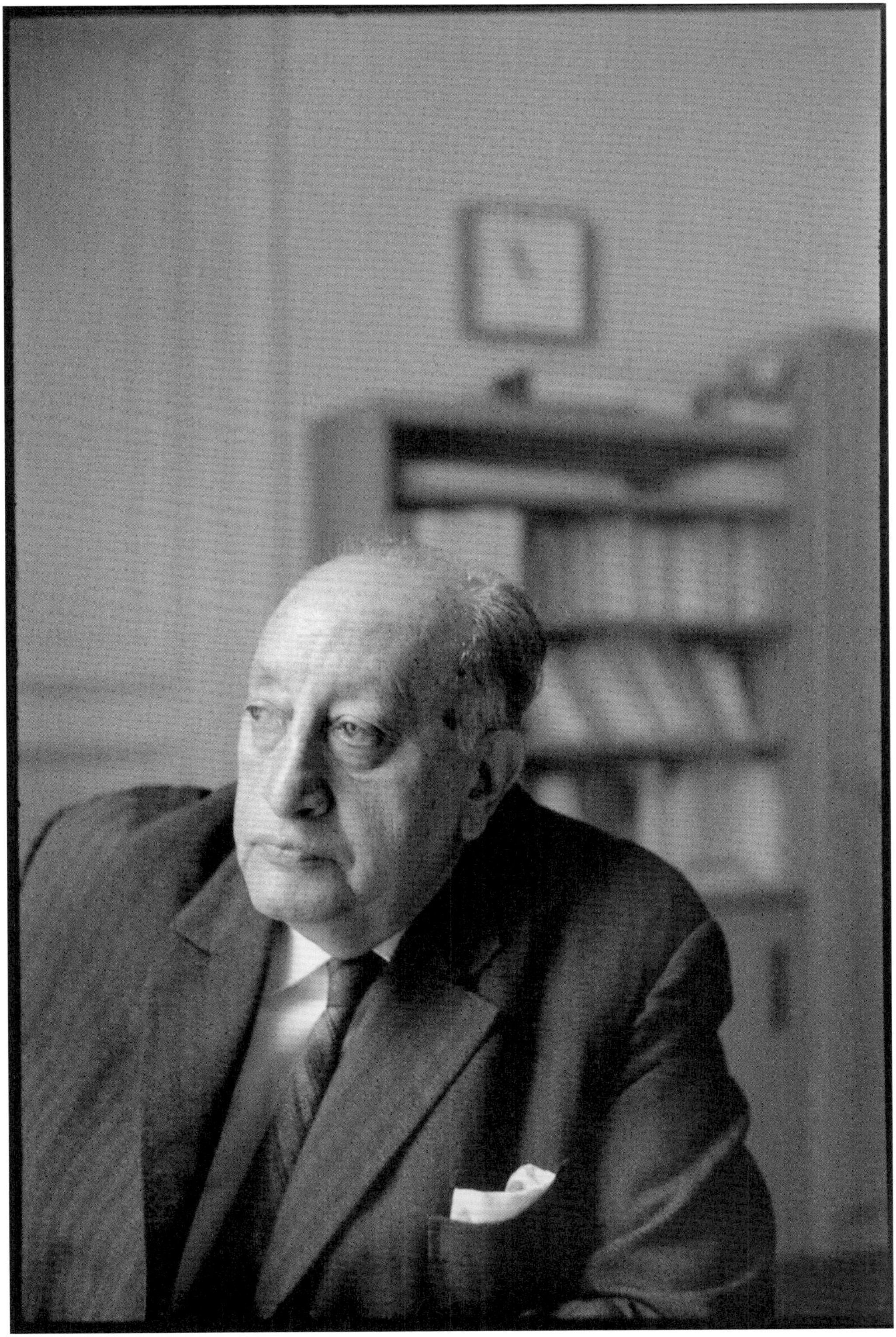

MARGARET ATWOOD

born Ottawa, 1939

by Sandy Nicholson

Toronto, 2003

A message on the homepage of Margaret Atwood's website reads: 'Welcome readers! I am very pleased that you are interested in my writing, and I hope this site helps you to find what you are looking for. Happy reading and best wishes!' The warmth of this message of welcome is a clear indication of the kind of writer Atwood is: one who is interested in her readership and their opinions.

Born in Ottawa, Atwood grew up in northern Ontario, Quebec and Toronto. Her father was an entomologist, and she spent part of her childhood living with her family amid the forests of eastern Canada, an experience that would later inform her writing. An avid reader, she began writing stories at an early age, and has since produced a wealth of novels, short stories, poetry, critical essays, literary essays and political commentaries. Despite the dystopian nature of some of her books, Atwood uses her writing as a means of examining the past and of exploring and understanding an increasingly complex present. Her work is rich, visionary and inquisitive, and marked by a compassionate and ironic sensibility.

Atwood's most famous books include *The Handmaid's Tale* (1985), *Alias Grace* (1996), *The Blind Assassin* (2000), *Oryx and Crake* (2003) and *The Year of the Flood* (2009). In these and other works she explores themes such as the role and rights of women, the effects of one's surroundings and environment, the Canadian literary world and the irrational side of human nature. In addition to working in the genres already mentioned, she has produced children's books, television scripts, science fiction and fantasy. It is her lightness of touch as a writer that enables her to move between genres in this way, but without losing her characteristically critical and intelligent voice. Regardless of genre, Atwood's aim is to help readers make sense of themselves and their place in the world.

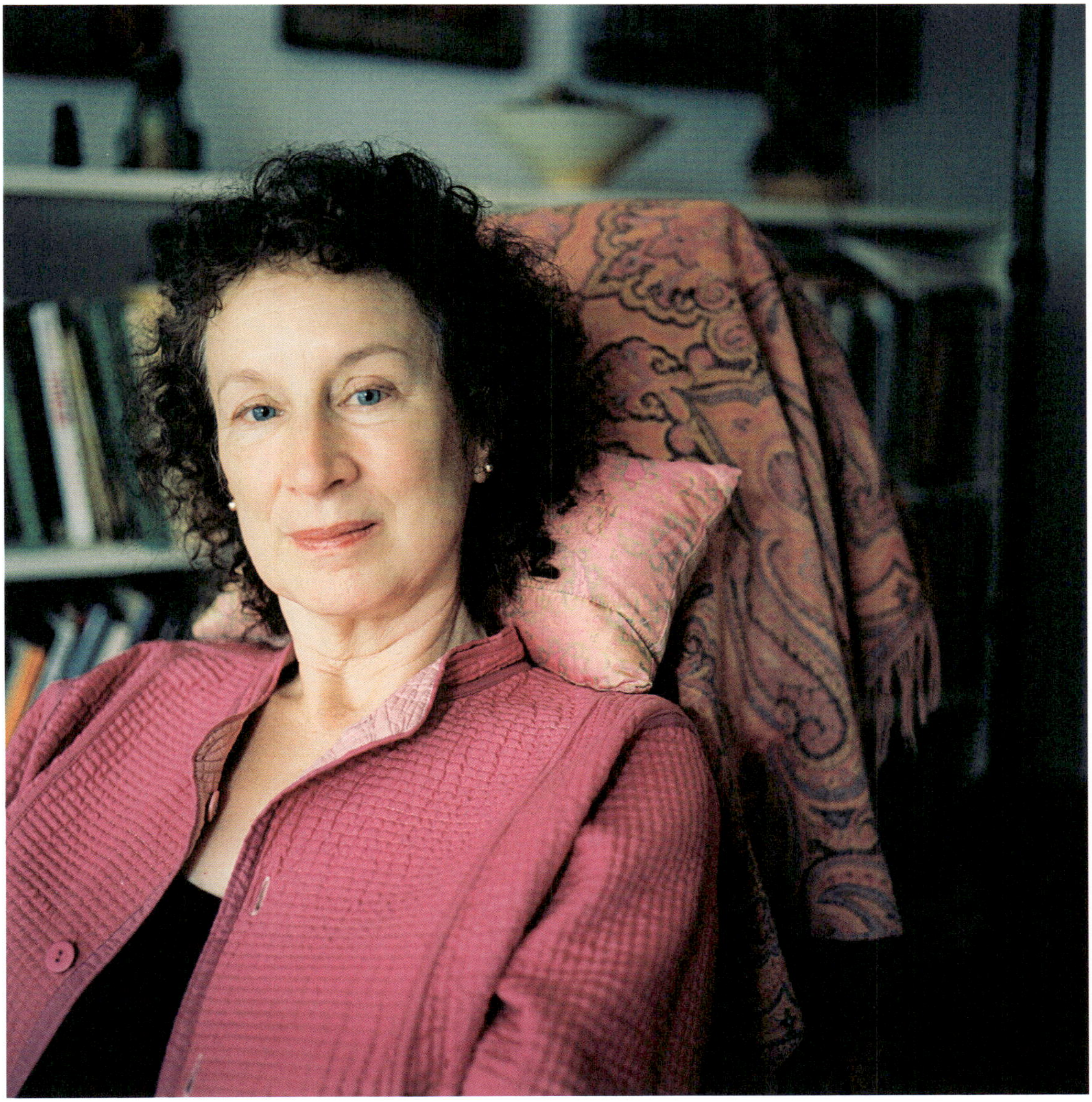

W. H. AUDEN

born York, UK, 1907; died Vienna, 1973

by Richard Avedon

New York, 1960

Wystan Hugh Auden is arguably one of the most inventive poets ever to have lived, in terms of style, form and content. In addition to an exceptionally wide-ranging collection of poems, he produced essays, reviews, screenplays, opera libretti and other musical collaborations. No single book can be deemed representative of his poetic voice. Anyone beginning their exploration of Auden's *oeuvre* by reading *Another Time* (1940), for example, a collection that contains the well-known poems 'Funeral Blues' and 'O tell me the truth about love', might infer that he was a poet who wrote only about love, albeit with a hefty dose of irony. Yet love was just one of several different themes he addressed during the many phases of his prolific career.

Auden wrote his first poetry while he was an adolescent, mainly imitating the Romantics and then T. S. Eliot, whom he admired greatly. In 1925 he entered Christ Church, Oxford, where he became the driving force behind a group of poets and intellectuals that included Christopher Isherwood, Cecil Day-Lewis, Louis MacNeice and Stephen Spender. It was during this period that he began to concentrate seriously on writing poetry, and his first book, entitled simply *Poems*, was published in 1930 with the help of Eliot himself, who accepted it for publication by Faber & Faber. A revised edition of *Poems* appeared in 1933 with seven of the original poems replaced.

Auden went through several incarnations as a poet, using a multitude of styles, and with varying religious and political affiliations. During this long process of evolution, he often dismissed his previous poetry as insincere, or ceased to identify with it altogether. His early poetry was more heavily charged and rebellious, but then began to employ a more colloquial language. By the 1950s he was dividing his time between New York and Italy, and his poetic voice became more reflective and philosophical. Towards the end of the 1960s he was producing some of his most vivid and energetic work, as can be seen in *City without Walls* (1969). Although his poetic style was continually shifting, he was constant in his friendships and love affairs. He had a long relationship with Isherwood, and then for many years what he called a 'marriage' to the American poet and librettist Chester Kallman.

In Richard Avedon's photograph of Auden, taken on a snowy day in New York, the poet appears as a charismatic figure, wrapped up against the cold but with a determined look on his face.

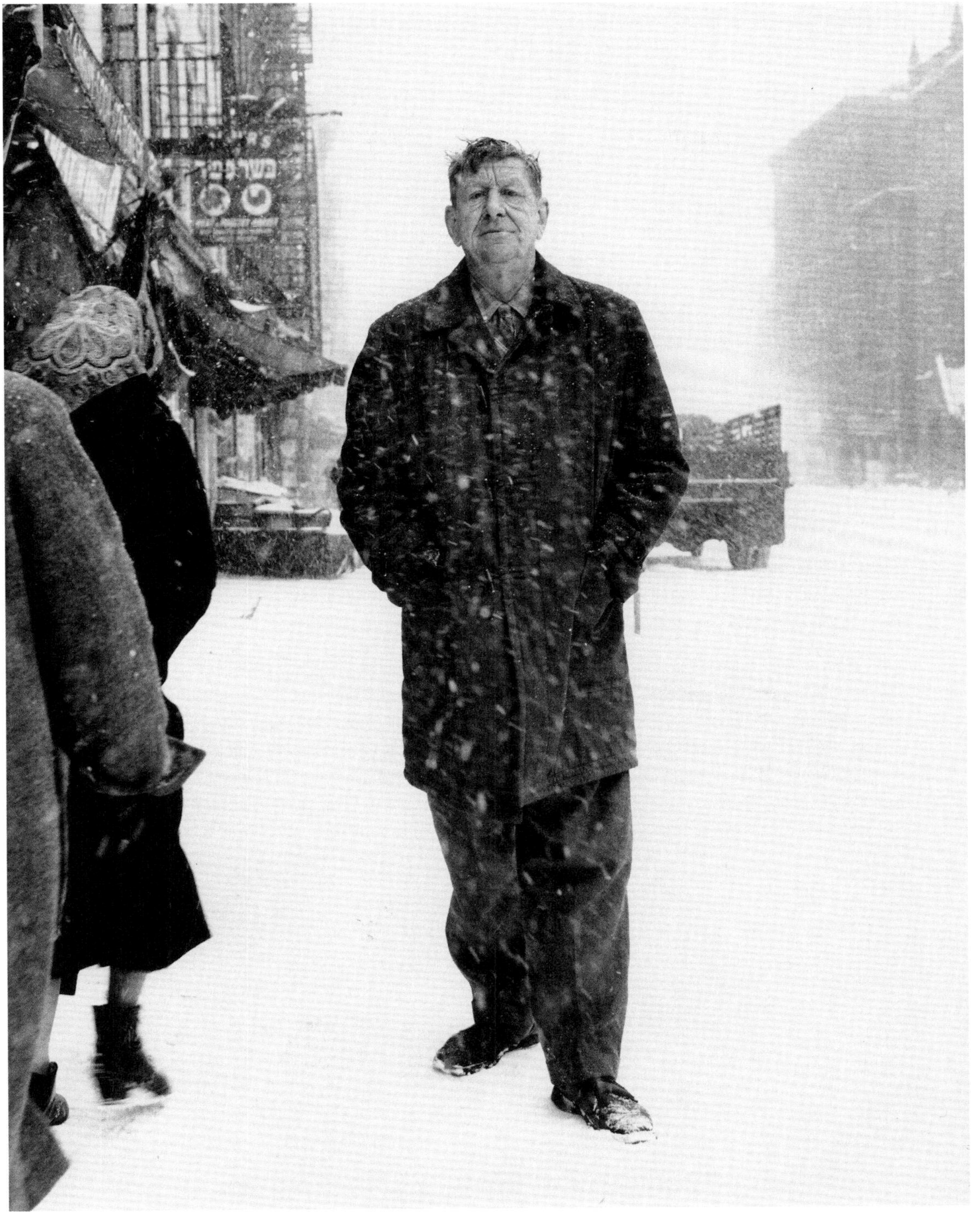

PAUL AUSTER

born Newark, New Jersey, 1947

by Bruce Davidson

New York, 1994

When he was a teenager, Paul Auster was out playing with some friends in a wood when they got caught in a storm. In order to reach the safety of a clearing, they had to get through a barbed-wire fence: 'The boy in front of me was directly under the fence when lightning struck it. He was killed instantly ... If you see that when you are fourteen years old, you begin to sense that the world is a lot less stable than you thought it was. Life is not neatly boxed.'

Auster's books are full of such events – acts of chance and coincidence that have the potential to turn one's life upside down, never to be the same again. Indeed, Auster uses the word 'fluke' to describe the circumstances in which he met his second wife, the writer Siri Hustvedt. His breakthrough as a writer came with *City of Glass* (1985), the first book of his *New York Trilogy* (*City of Glass*; *Ghosts*, 1986; and *The Locked Room*, 1986). This success was followed by a series of cult novels dealing with not only coincidence but also the nature of reality and the search for identity, including *Moon Palace* (1989), *Mr Vertigo* (1994), *The Book of Illusions* (2002) and *The Brooklyn Follies* (2005).

Few authors have divided the critics to such an extent as Auster. More popular in Europe than at home, he has been praised for a style of writing that encompasses absurdism and existentialism, while also being criticized for 'fake realism', 'shallow scepticism' and a 'postmodern disassembly' that is 'grindingly explicit' (James Wood, 'Shallow Graves', *New Yorker*, 30 November 2009). Similarly polarized opinions greeted his second work of autobiography, *Winter Journal* (2012), published thirty years after his first, *The Invention of Solitude* (1982), which was triggered by the death of his father.

At one point in *Winter Journal*, Auster describes himself as 'the lone person ... a silent man cut off from the rest of the world, day after day sitting at his desk for no other purpose than to explore the interior of his own head'. The many photographs that have been taken of the writer over the years, including Bruce Davidson's portrait, seem to confirm this image of an intense and inscrutable character, absorbed in the process of self-analysis.

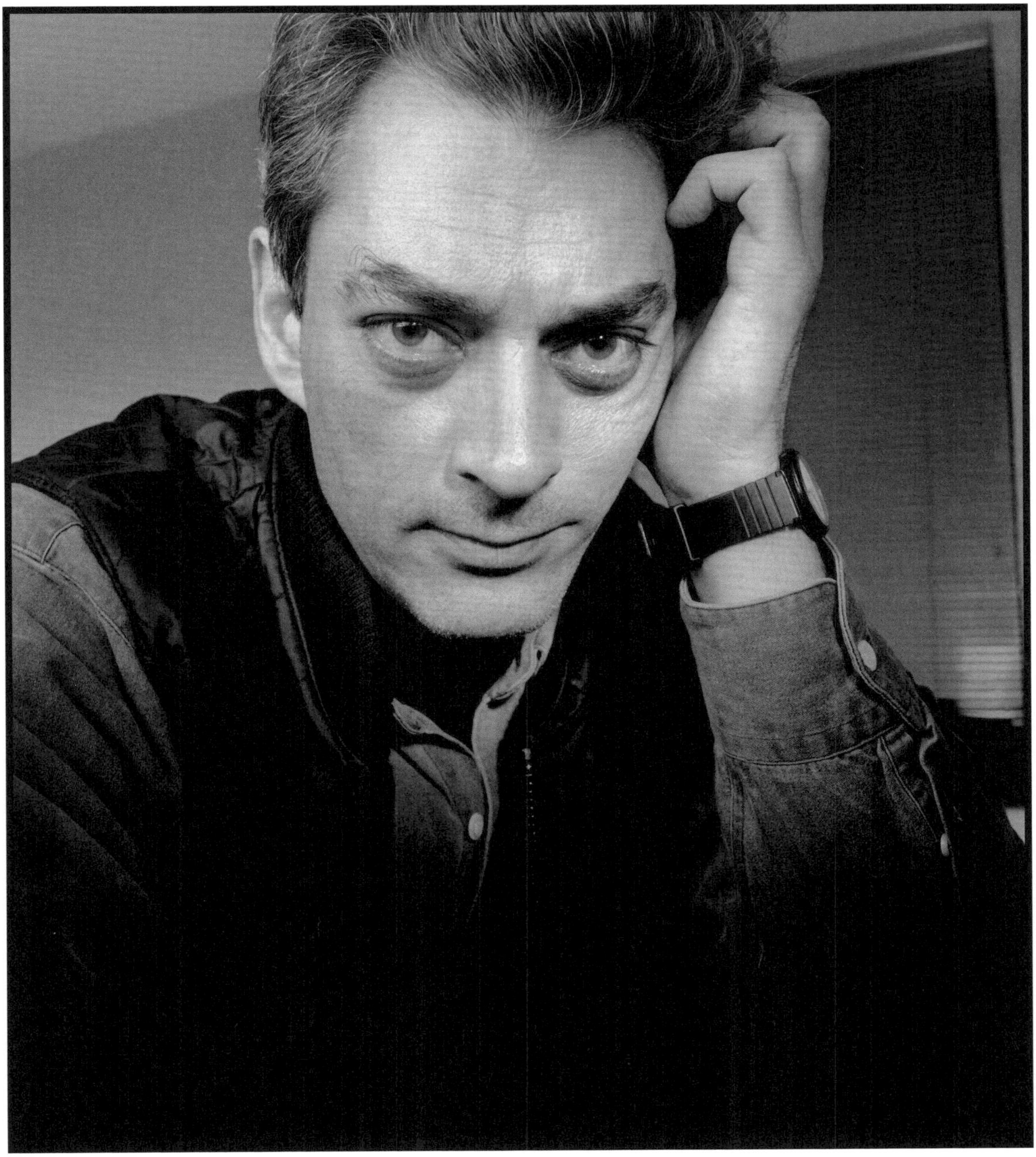

INGEBORG BACHMANN

born Klagenfurt, Austria, 1926; died Rome, 1973

by Herbert List

Rome, 1954

Ingeborg Bachmann ended up in Rome almost by accident. This was in 1953, when she was twenty-seven years old, and she remained in the city for the rest of her life. It was there, in the Campo de' Fiori, that Herbert List took this photograph of her. List was a German photographer in love with the Mediterranean, Bachmann the Austrian 'poetess-philosopher', one of the most complex female voices of the twentieth century. As she herself recalled, one event in particular helped to shape her world view and literary concerns: the occupation of her native city, Klagenfurt, by German troops when she was just twelve years old.

Despite studying philosophy and writing both poetry and fiction, Bachmann experienced a difficult relationship with words, in which reality and language no longer seemed to relate to each other. However, the struggle to give form to her voice was for her both an ethical imperative and an act of rebellion against a patriarchal world. In her novel from 1971, *Malina*, a father has a dream in which he tries to tear out the heroine's tongue in order to deprive her of her right to words and self-assertion, to everything that is most human within her. Bachmann's own life was marked by passionate and stormy love affairs, all of which were based on a dynamic of dominance and dependence. Writing, although it also caused her pain, remained her one means of coping with the events of her life, and her work retains a sense of optimism.

In 1961, after several years of producing no poetry, Bachmann published the lyric poem 'Your Words'. In an interview she declared: 'For five years I could not risk writing a poem, I did not want to write any more. … I still know so little poetry, but among the few things that I do know is suspicion. Suspicion of self-importance, suspicion of words, of language. I've often told myself, we should analyse this suspicion – because one day perhaps it will give birth to something new.' Suspicious of the inadequacy of words, the poet abandoned poetry in favour of a new experiment in prose: a cycle of novels entitled *Manners of Death*. However, by 1973 she had completed only the first book, *Malina*, and in October of that year she succumbed to the effects of a fire in her bedroom (caused, it was concluded, by a lit cigarette). Two further novels in the cycle, *The Book of Franza* and *Requiem for Fanny Goldmann*, remained unfinished.

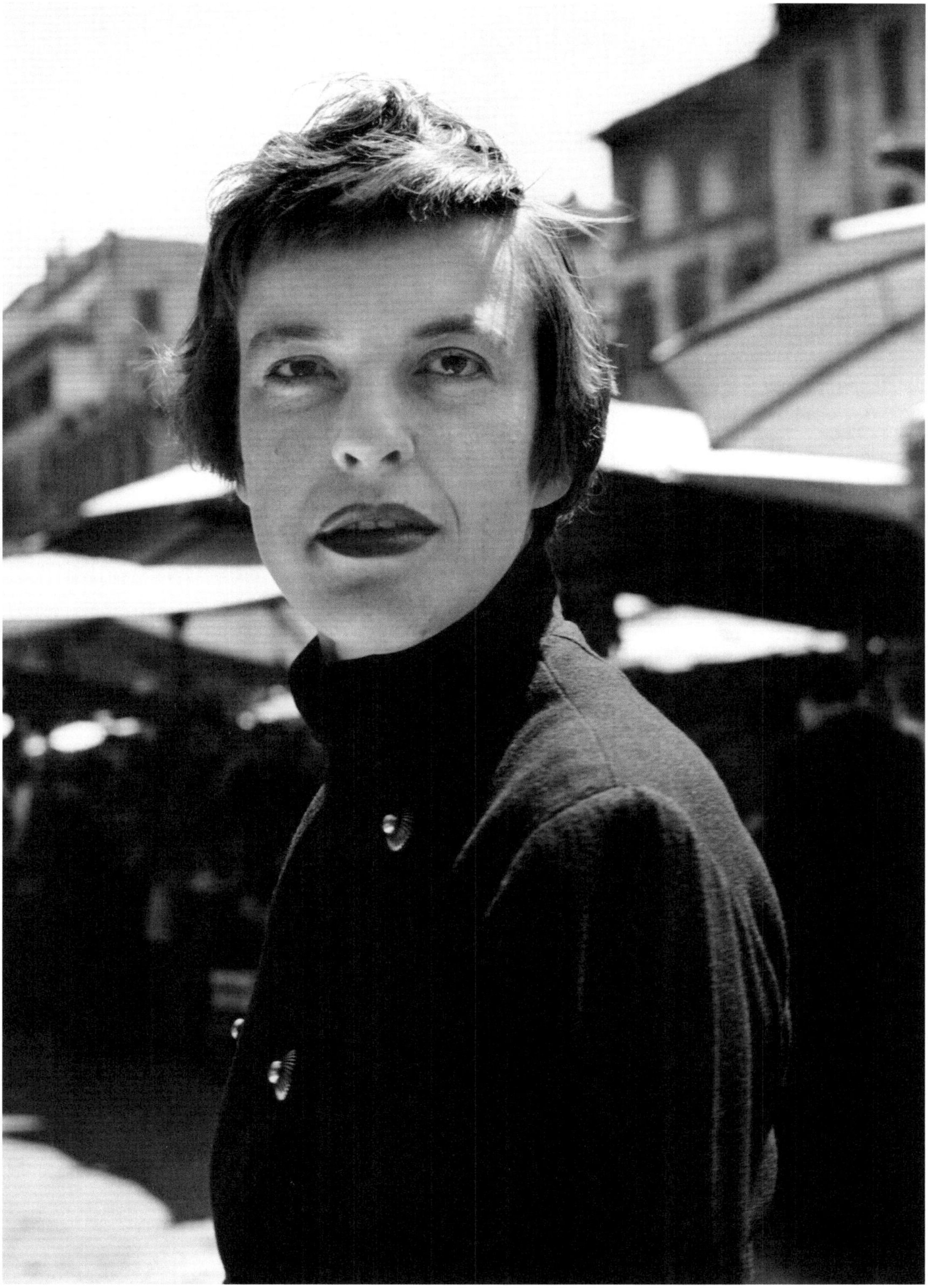

JAMES BALDWIN

born New York, 1924; died Saint-Paul-de-Vence, France, 1987

by Ara Güler

Paris, 1974

James Baldwin had to grow up fast. New York's Harlem neighbourhood could be a rough place for children, and when Baldwin was still young, his mother, who had divorced Baldwin's father, married a stern and forbidding preacher. The stepfather treated the boy with unusual harshness. The couple had many children, whom James, as the eldest, was often required to look after. He was barely nineteen years old when tuberculosis took away the only father he had ever known – it happened on the same day that the family's youngest child was born and the Harlem Riot of 1943 took place.

Despite his responsibilities, Baldwin not only managed to support himself and to study during childhood, but also, by the tender age of fourteen, already enjoyed greater success as a preacher than had his stepfather. Baldwin's experience in the pulpit left a profound impression on him but (precocious as he was in everything) he was also quick to lose his faith. By seventeen, he already considered it as an experience that had come to an end: it was, he said, like 'being in the theatre', although later on it did stand him in good stead when writing his dramatic tales. During this period, he also began to spend time in Greenwich Village. It was there he learned that a black man could also be an artist. He started to write essays, short stories and autobiographical fragments that were later collected in *Notes of a Native Son* (1955) and in other compilations, such as *Nobody Knows My Name* (1961).

His real breakthrough came in 1948, when, conscious of being doubly discriminated against in his own land, both for being black and for being homosexual, Baldwin travelled to Paris on a study scholarship that he had received thanks to the author Richard Wright. He thus began his transatlantic commuting between France and the USA, which he continued for the rest of his life. Baldwin also became famous with the publication of his first – and most celebrated – novel, *Go Tell It on the Mountain* (1953). It had decidedly autobiographical themes, as he explained: 'I had to deal with what hurt me most. I had to deal, above all, with my father.' His next work, *Giovanni's Room* (1956), considered the subject of homosexuality.

Through his essays and later novels, Baldwin became a standard-bearer in the civil rights battles that raged across USA at the end of the 1950s and in the 1960s. His written pieces (above all, his 1963 essay collection *The Fire Next Time*) touched the hearts of readers of all colours. *The Fire Next Time* sold more than a million copies, and Baldwin appeared on the cover of *Time* magazine. Although the assassination of Martin Luther King Jr and the events of the 1970s eroded his faith in the possibility of the improvement of the condition of black people, and his final works were far less successful than his earlier ones, we have not grown tired of his voice, his writings or his teachings.

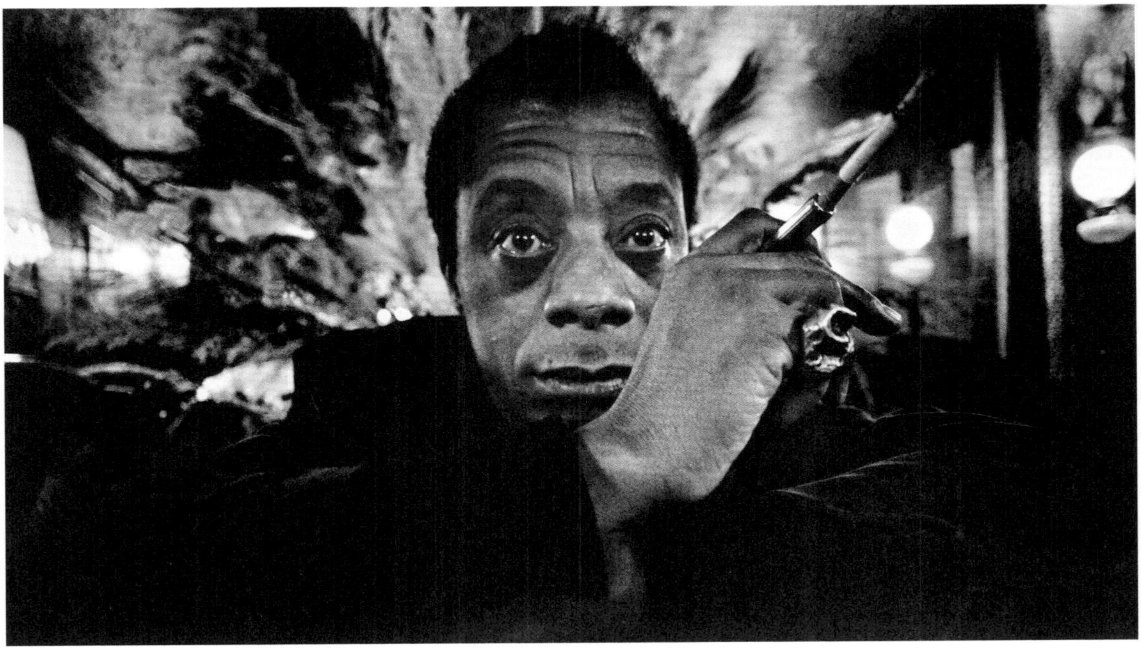

J. G. BALLARD

born Shanghai, 1930; died Shepperton, Surrey, UK, 2009

by David Levenson

Shepperton, Surrey, UK, 1988

James Graham Ballard was the acknowledged master of 'New Wave' science fiction, a writer who, once stories about adventures in outer space had been rendered obsolete by Sputnik and NASA, preferred to take the genre in radical new directions. This did not prevent him, however, from making predictions at least as well as, or even better than, many of the more traditional science fiction writers. But for Ballard, prophecy was not an end in itself; rather, it was a kind of 'collateral effect' of his study of the human mind. Ballard freed science fiction from the pulp tradition of the 1950s, and made it the genre par excellence for the strain of postmodern literature that focuses on contemporary psychopathologies.

Ballard imagined often terrifying worlds not so very different from our own. His disaster scenarios stripped human behaviour bare, revealed our basest instincts, took us beyond the limits of our neuroses and glorified pornography – not only the pornography of sex but also that of violence and atrocity. In 1964 Ballard's wife died suddenly of pneumonia, and, left with three small children to look after, he began to place his characters in extreme situations to see if they could cope. His apocalyptic 'quadrilogy of the elements', *The Wind from Nowhere* (1961), *The Drowned World* (1962), *The Drought* (1965) and *The Crystal World* (1966), envisioned four different ways in which the world could end, while his urban trilogy from the 1970s, *Crash* (1973), *Concrete Island* (1974) and *High Rise* (1975), abandoned outer space in order to analyse the inner space of its characters.

David Levenson's photograph of Ballard pictures him in front of a copy of *The Violation*, a painting by the Belgian artist Paul Delvaux. The original was destroyed during the Second World War, but the writer commissioned a reproduction from the painter Brigid Marlin. According to Ballard, Delvaux's visionary world consists of bizarre external landscapes propelled by powerful psychic forces, and numerous references to Delvaux's art can be found in Ballard's *oeuvre*. In an interview with the *Guardian*, Ballard claimed that Surrealism and psychoanalysis were central to his work.

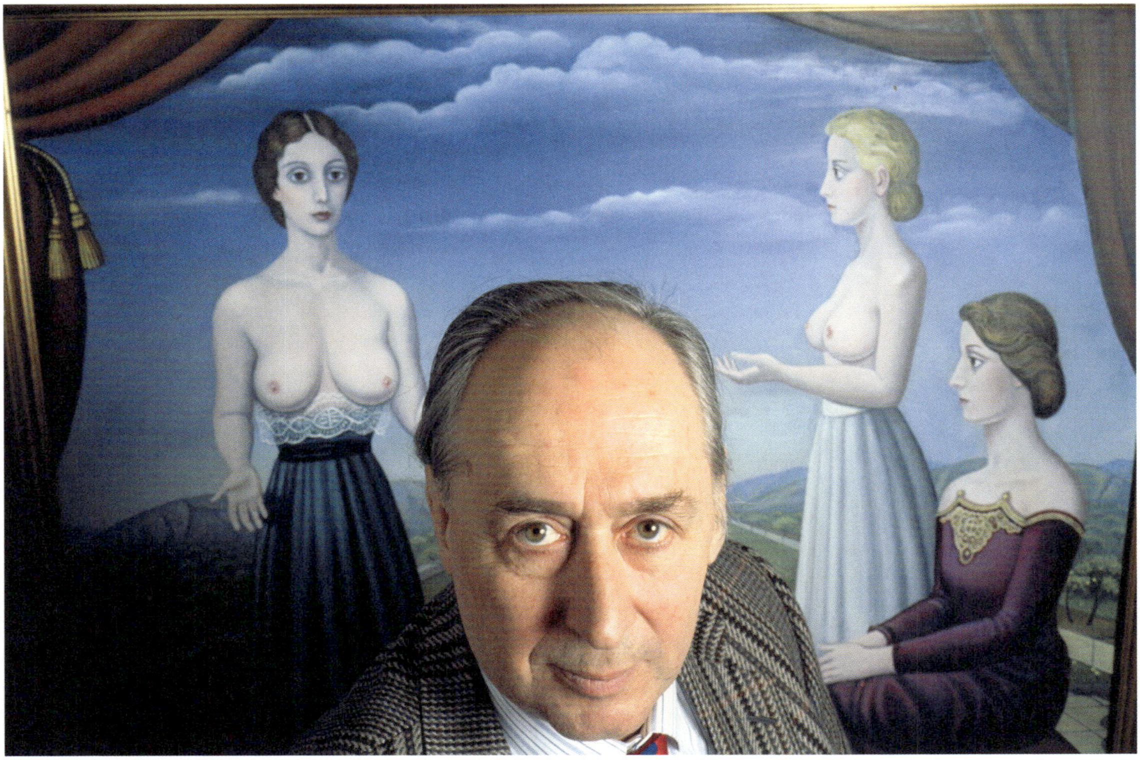

ALESSANDRO BARICCO

born Turin, Italy, 1958

by Roberto Koch

Turin, Italy, 1997

When, in 1991, Alessandro Baricco published his first novel, *Lands of Glass*, it sent a shockwave through the world of Italian literary criticism. For some, it was a wave of pleasure, for others surprise, and for still others hostility. The book certainly did not pass unnoticed, achieving remarkable success.

Baricco was then thirty-three years old, with the demeanour of a rebel and an indisputable talent for storytelling. His literary success grew, and he became a public figure. Throughout the 1990s he appeared on television to talk about not only literature but also classical music. Wearing jeans and a pullover, he would tell the viewers about the works of J. D. Salinger, Joseph Conrad and Gustave Flaubert, the language of the Italian writer Carlo Emilio Gadda and the music of Rossini. His speech, just like his writing, overflows with a passion for narrative, invention and storytelling. In 1993 he published his second novel, *Ocean Sea*; this was followed by *Silk* (1996) and *City* (1999). Each of these books divided the critics and fascinated the reading public.

In addition to writing novels, Baricco has contributed articles to newspapers, given public readings and produced screenplays and such pieces for the theatre as *The Legend of 1900* (1994). He is also the co-founder of the Scuola Holden, a creative-writing school named after Salinger's most famous character. Baricco's writing, made up of short phrases and brief pieces of dialogue, is anything but minimal, immersing the reader in the pleasure of discovering a story. Some accuse him of flaunting his literary talents, while others, such as the Italian writer Fernanda Pivano, are more complimentary: 'Baricco is certainly highly professional, and is also a talented poet, especially as, more than writing, he seems to recall stories of nineteenth-century spirituality, which are delightful. But these nineteenth-century preciosities are in reality an American style. It is something that he can do to perfection, keeping us all riveted to the page; and it is his pages that sometimes seem like an end in themselves, as they are miniature gems of imagination and invention, bound together by a narrative scheme that once again, or so it seems to me, is reminiscent of that same American style.'

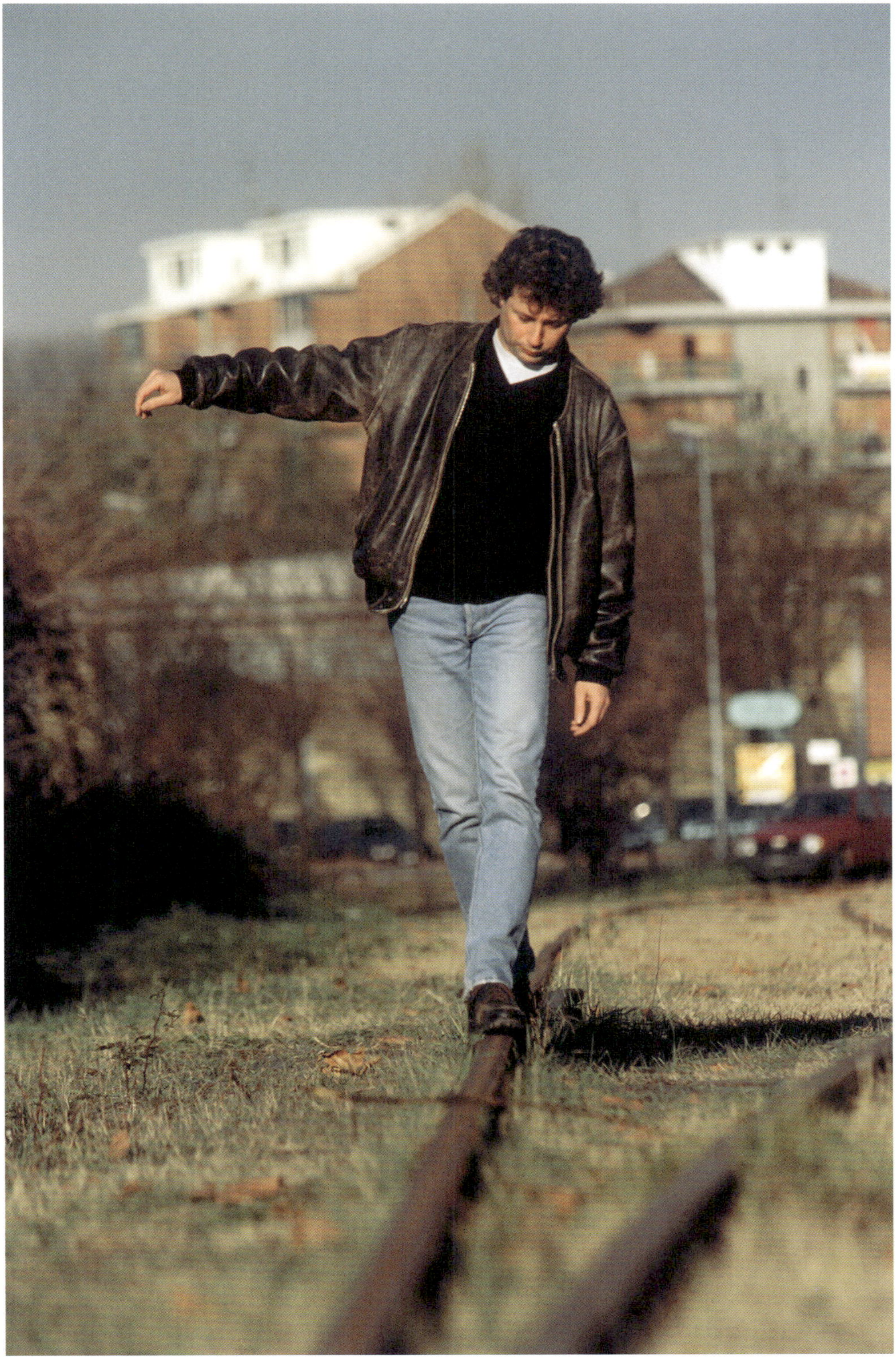

JULIAN BARNES

born Leicester, UK, 1946

by Jillian Edelstein

London, 1991

Following a deeply autobiographical debut (*Metroland*, 1980) and a novel of jealousy and vendetta (*Before She Met Me*, 1982), Julian Barnes found fame with *Flaubert's Parrot* (1984). Centred around the protagonist's (and its author's) love of the great French writer, this experimental and unusual work is characterized by a complex but rigorous structure and multiple points of view. Almost thirty years later, Barnes was awarded the Man Booker Prize (having been shortlisted on three previous occasions) for *The Sense of an Ending* (2011), an intense meditation on the ambiguous and elusive nature of memory and identity.

Barnes has received numerous other awards, not only in Britain but also especially in France; indeed, he is the only author to have won both the Prix Médicis, for *Flaubert's Parrot*, and the Prix Femina, for *Talking It Over* (1991). His work is also distinguished by its breadth and scope, from the comedy of manners that is *Talking It Over* to the blending of fictional and historical narratives in *A History of the World in 10½ Chapters* (1989) and *Arthur and George* (2005), a historical thriller based on an actual episode from the life of Arthur Conan Doyle. Barnes has also published several volumes of short stories and non-fiction, including collections of his journalism and essays, and is a noted critic.

In the 1980s Barnes adopted the persona of Dan Kavanagh, an Irish immigrant to USA (as we can read on 'his' website) and the author of four hard-boiled detective novels featuring a bisexual ex-cop as the main character. Barnes has also translated the work of the French writer Alphonse Daudet and a German-language graphic novel by Volker Kriegel; he has even played Georges Simenon in a radio series for the BBC about Commissaire Maigret. Despite this prolificacy, Barnes remains protective of his privacy, preferring to tell stories about himself through the medium of his books.

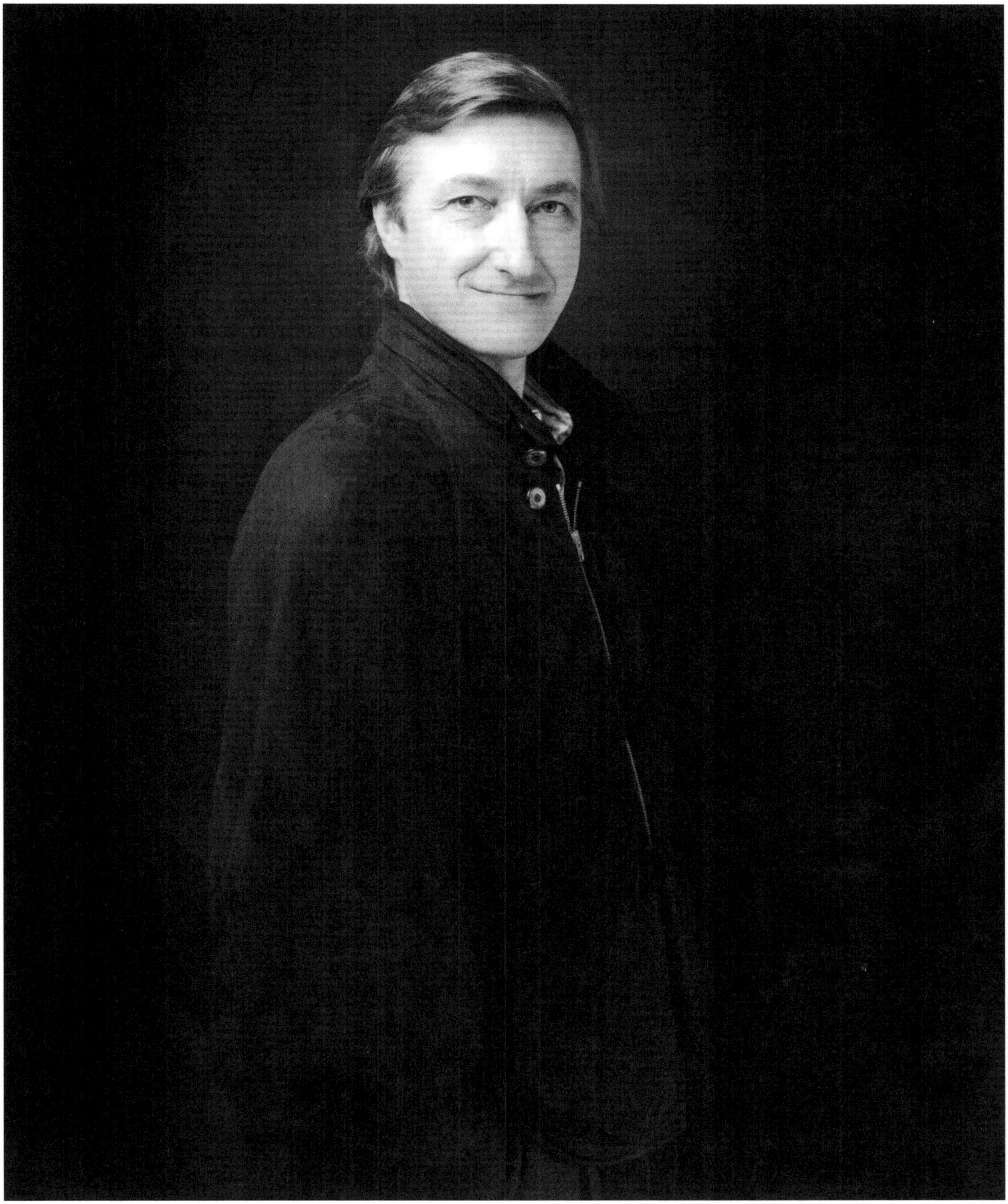

PÍO BAROJA

[Pío Baroja y Nessi] born San Sebastían, Spain, 1872; died Madrid, 1956

unknown photographer

Madrid, c. 1955

Pío Baroja was born into a well-to-do Basque family. He trained as a doctor, but soon left the profession, pronouncing himself ill-suited to the work. The experience did, however, provide him with the material for his first collection of short stories, *Vidas sombrías* (Sombre lives). Published in 1900, it immediately attracted the attention of intellectuals and writers such as Miguel de Unamuno and José Ortega y Gasset. Although the door of the literary world had opened for him, he was restless and began to travel throughout Europe.

The aspect of Baroja's writing that had most interested Unamuno, and which would become a characteristic of his work, was his ability to observe reality objectively and honestly, while plumbing its psychological depths. Each different level of society was subjected to the same level of scrutiny. Such authenticity is evident in *Memorias de un hombre de acción* (Memoirs of a man of action, 1913–34), a series of twenty-two novels of varying length depicting the life of the nineteenth-century Spanish insurgent Eugenio de Aviraneta.

In his work, Baroja exploits the freedom of the writer to retell history from the perspective of minor characters, thereby putting a different slant on events. At times he employs an abrupt, almost disjointed style, creating a fragmentary and impressionistic literary landscape. He was an ideological rebel, an individualist and a pessimist who offered his characters little hope of redemption; indeed, in many cases they seem to be passive victims, propelled helplessly along by a chain of events over which they have almost no control. In 1936, following the outbreak of the Spanish Civil War, Baroja went into exile in France, returning to Spain in 1939. His work has influenced a number of writers, both at home and abroad, most notably Camilo José Cela and Ernest Hemingway.

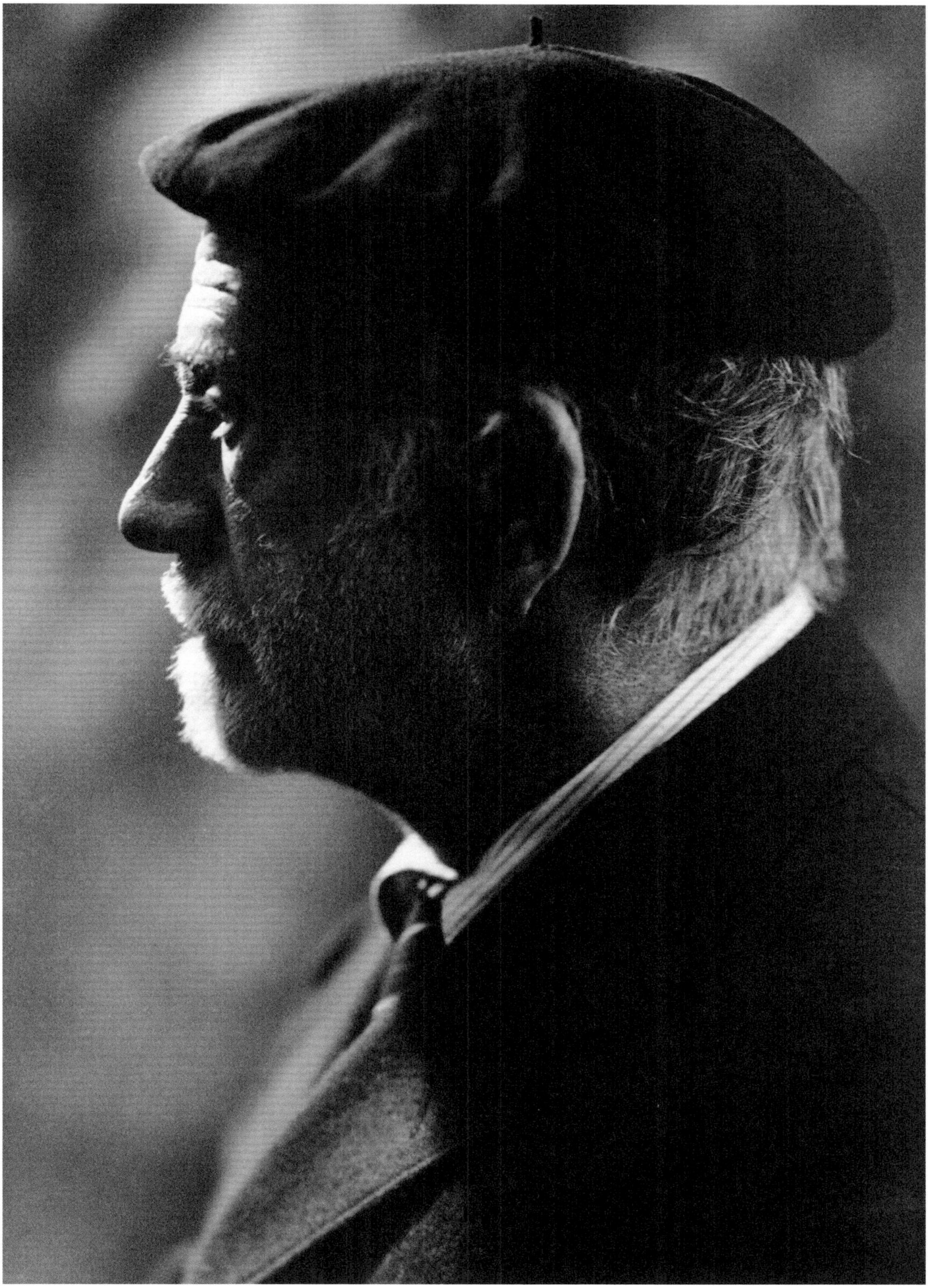

GEORGES BATAILLE

born Billom, France, 1897; died Paris, 1962

by René Saint Paul

Paris, c. 1961

The novels attributed to Pierre Angélique, Lord Auch and Louis Trente are in fact the work of the French writer Georges Bataille, who chose to publish several books under these pseudonyms. A poet of the dark corners of the soul, of the uncomfortable, Bataille was also an intellectual, a philosopher and an anthropologist committed to exploring the subjects closest to his heart: eroticism, transgression and the sacred.

One of Bataille's most celebrated novels is *Story of the Eye* (1928), a synthesis of mysticism and eroticism centred around the sexual exploits of a pair of teenage lovers. The story is told in a series of vignettes, each of which is linked by the human eye. Roland Barthes, one of Bataille's most attentive readers, has noted how, within the narrative, the eye is treated as interchangeable with eye-shaped objects such as eggs, bulls' testicles and the sun. He also notes the metaphorical use of liquids, including tears, urine, milk and egg yolks, and how these, too, are linked to the eye, eggs and other ovoid objects. In this and other works, Bataille uses such devices to challenge the conventional use of language.

Story of the Eye also displays the influence of the Marquis de Sade, Surrealism and Friedrich Nietzsche. Indeed, it was Bataille who, with *On Nietzsche* (1945), re-established the respectability of Nietzschean thought by freeing it from its Fascist interpretations and from the accusations that it had nurtured Nazism. In the early 1930s Bataille became a member of the Democratic Communist Circle, together with French writers and philosophers such as Raymond Queneau and Simone Weil. Bataille was at his most politically active at this time, writing articles for the anti-Fascist magazine *La Critique sociale* and setting up various communitarian projects, including the College of Sociology (with the French intellectual Roger Callois) and the Society of Collective Psychology. However, the death of his lover Colette Peignot in 1938 and the outbreak of the Second World War caused Bataille to withdraw from such activities. He also began to develop a more inward-looking, almost mystical style of writing, choosing to concentrate on his interior experiences, a tendency for which he was heavily criticized by Jean-Paul Sartre.

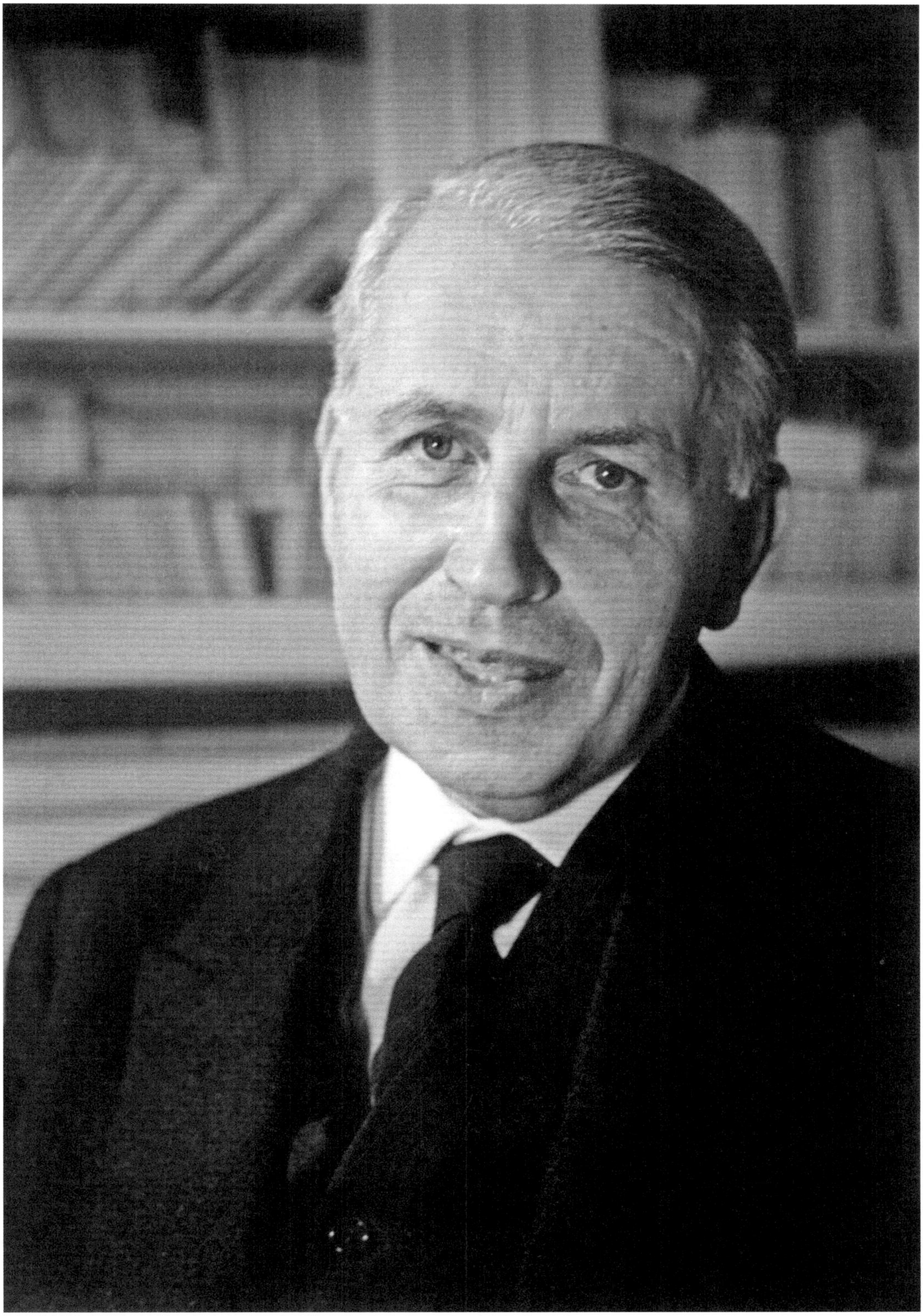

SIMONE DE BEAUVOIR

born Paris, 1908; died Paris, 1986

by Henri Cartier-Bresson

Paris, 1947

‘Two images of me are current: I am a madwoman, an eccentric. ... My morals are extremely dissolute. ... I have assiduously practiced every vice, my life is a perpetual orgy, etc. Or flat heels, tight bun, I am a chieftainess, a lady manager, a schoolmistress (in the pejorative sense given to this word by the right). I spend my existence with books and sitting at my worktable, pure intellect. ... Apparently a combination of these two portraits involves no contradiction. ... The fact is that I am a writer – a woman writer, which doesn’t mean a housewife who writes but someone whose whole existence is governed by her writing.’

Simone de Beauvoir shared her life, love and existentialist philosophy with Jean-Paul Sartre. In 1945 the pair founded the magazine *Les Temps modernes*, which became an important forum for cultural debate among the French intelligentsia, promoting the idea that the engagement of intellectuals was essential in combatting the crisis of values that had been precipitated by the destruction wrought in the Second World War.

De Beauvoir’s own writing encompassed novels, including the *The Mandarins* (1954), which won the Prix Goncourt, as well as essays and short stories on political and ideological themes ranging from colonialism, Communism and the role of intellectuals, to her profound and original examination of human existence. Fundamental to this was her analysis of the condition of being female, which she investigated, in particular, in her treatise *The Second Sex* (1949). This book has become a point of reference for many feminist movements, most importantly for its argument that a woman’s role in society should not be treated as a biologically determined destiny, demonstrating how many different historical and cultural influences have contributed to inequalities in the hierarchical relationship between the sexes. ‘One is not born, but rather becomes, a woman,’ was de Beauvoir’s motto. When de Beauvoir died in Paris in 1986, the French philosopher and writer Élisabeth Badinter wrote, ‘Women, you owe her everything!’

In this image taken by Henri Cartier-Bresson on the rue Victor Schoelcher in Montparnasse, where the writer lived from 1955 until 1986, de Beauvoir wears her hair scraped back and exudes a prophetic, schoolmistress-like air, even though forced into the bottom corner of the framing.

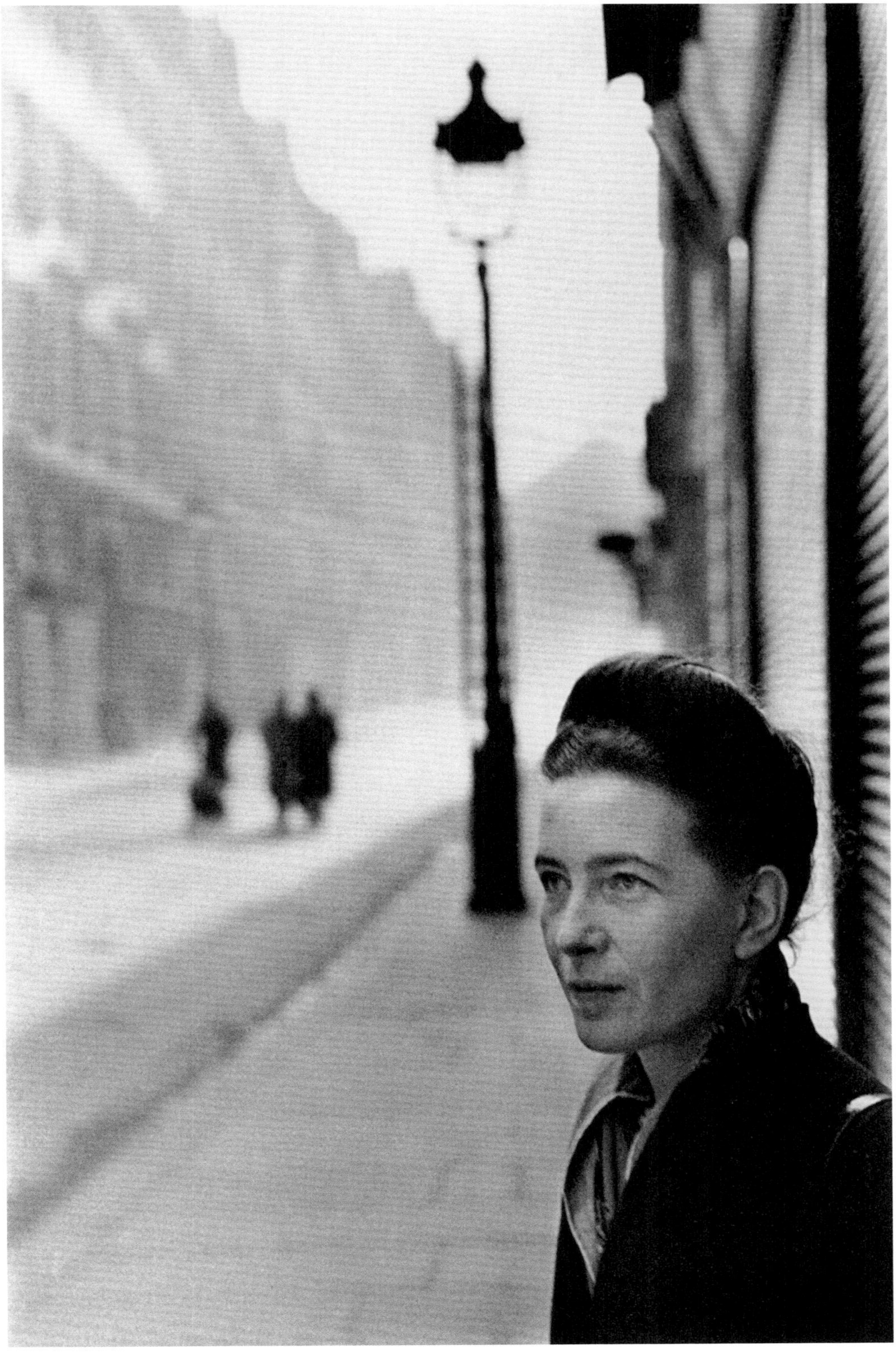

SAMUEL BECKETT

born Foxrock, Ireland, 1906; died Paris, 1989

by Henri Cartier-Bresson

Paris, 1964

On 5 January 1938 Samuel Beckett, who by that time had settled permanently in Paris, was stabbed in the chest when he refused the approaches of a pimp touting for business. He suffered a perforated lung and was almost killed. In court, Beckett asked his attacker to explain why he had stabbed him. The man, who was known as Prudent, replied: 'I do not know sir. I'm sorry.' Beckett dropped the charges, feeling a degree of sympathy for the man. The existence of a world shaped by such apparently random, meaningless acts would inform one of Beckett's best-known works, *Waiting for Godot* (1952). Noted for its bleak, minimalist tone and mix of futility and black humour, the play was heralded as a masterpiece of the Theatre of the Absurd.

Beckett was born into a middle-class Protestant family in Foxrock, near Dublin. He was a shy boy, but excelled at school and soon showed evidence of possessing a great intellect, albeit a subversive one. As a young man he was anxious to escape both the dreary bourgeois environment of Dublin and his turbulent relationship with his mother. It was during his first stay in Paris that he began to write, inspired by his friend James Joyce, for whom he acted as secretary. In contrast to Joyce, Beckett developed a minimalist style, paring down language to its barest elements, and juxtaposing the use of sound and silence. Today he is widely regarded as one of the twentieth century's most influential writers, the author of not only plays but also novels, poetry and short stories. In 1969 he was awarded the Nobel Prize 'for his writing, which – in new forms for the novel and drama – in the destitution of modern man acquires its elevation'.

In this photograph of Beckett by Henri Cartier-Bresson, the writer looks as though he is about to slip out of the frame. His sharp features are etched with lines, while his penetrating gaze is lost in the middle distance.

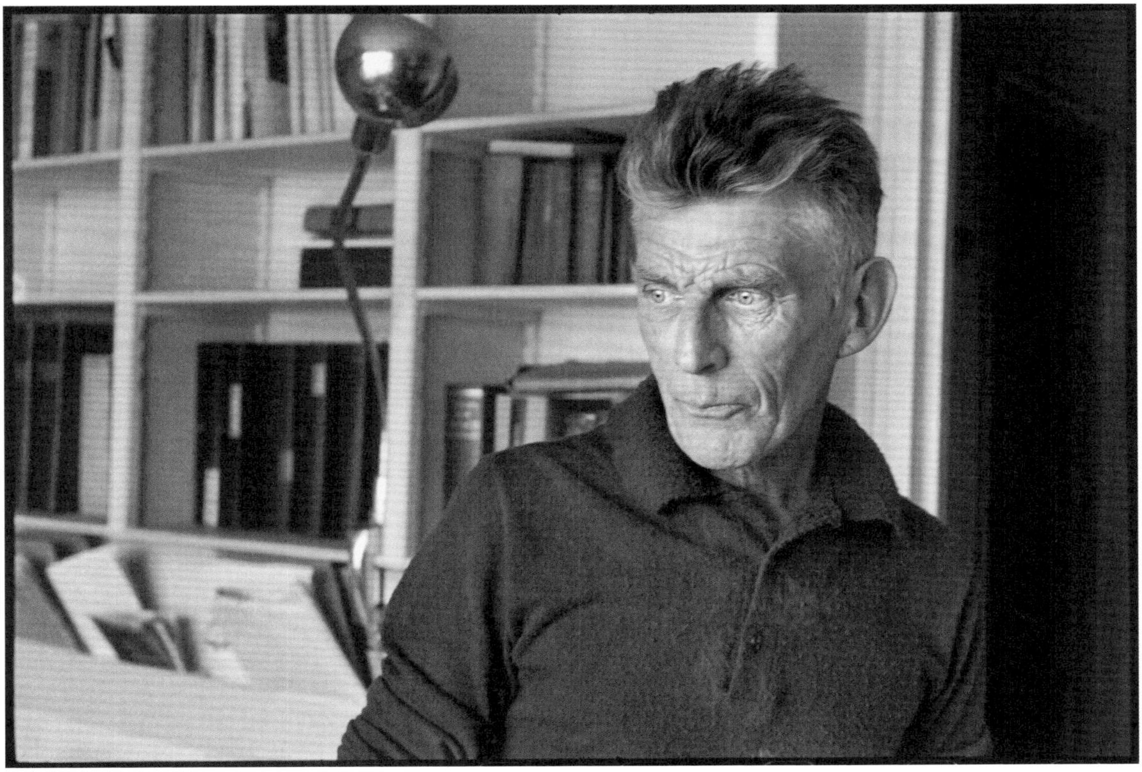

SAUL BELLOW

born Lachine, Quebec, 1915; died Brookline, Massachussetts, 2005

by Ferdinando Scianna

Capri, Italy, 1984

This photograph was taken on the occasion of Saul Bellow's receipt of the prestigious Malaparte Literary Award in Capri in 1984. The location was the cloister of the fourteenth-century Certosa di San Giacomo, a Carthusian monastery located in the east of the island. At this stage in his life Bellow had published more than a dozen books, including novels, short-story collections and works of non-fiction, and was the winner of three National Book Awards and one Pulitzer Prize. By the time of his death in 2005, he had added significantly to each of these tallies, but the essence of the author and his work remained constant throughout.

Widely regarded as one of the most significant authors of the twentieth century, Bellow wrote over a period of some sixty years. He published his first novel, *Dangling Man*, in 1944, and his last, *Ravelstein*, in 2000; this was followed by a collection of short stories in 2001. His writing is characterized by an ironic yet compassionate tone, observing with an acute eye the tribulations of his characters as they make their way through life. His breakthrough as a writer came with *The Adventures of Augie March* (1953), a picaresque novel that won the National Book Award for Fiction in 1954.

The character with whom Bellow is most often identified is the protagonist of *Henderson the Rain King* (1959), a troubled, middle-aged man who sets off to Africa in an attempt to fill his spiritual void. Among Bellow's many other memorable characters are the protagonists of *Herzog* (1964), an obsessive-compulsive writer; *Mr Sammler's Planet* (1970); *Humboldt's Gift* (1975); and *Ravelstein* (2000), a portrait of his great friend the philosopher Allan Bloom. The individual is central to Bellow's writing, even in his later, more pessimistic works, and his characters are often engaged in a struggle to find their place in the world without forsaking their identity or integrity. To quote Albert Corde in *The Dean's December* (1982), they are fighting against the 'big-scale insanities of the twentieth century'.

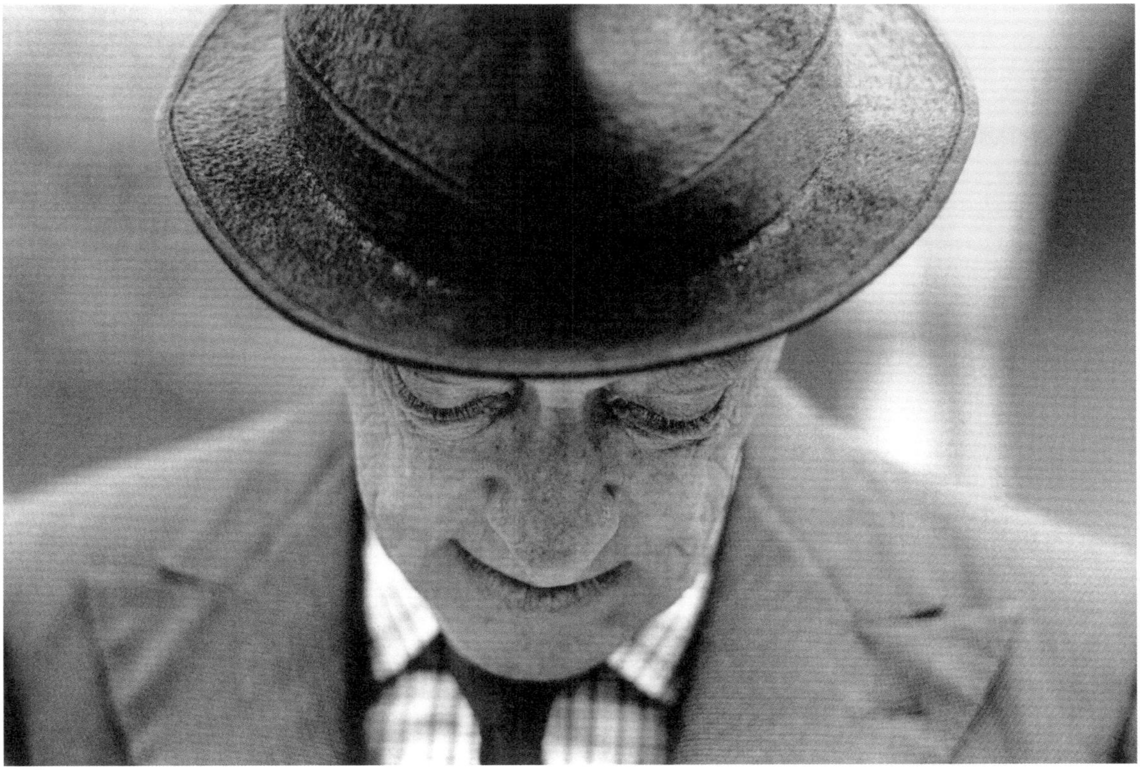

JUAN BENET

born Madrid, 1927; died Madrid, 1993

by Sigfrid Casals

Madrid, 1980

Juan Benet was both a writer and an engineer, two professions that, on the face of it, have little in common. However, Benet was able to inhabit the borderlands that exist between these two worlds: 'For science, the possibility of contradiction must not exist, and wherever it occurs is where scientific discourse ends. But for a man of letters, this same point is the beginning of his shadow zone, his field of work, his source of stimulus and inspiration.'

Benet wrote his first novel, *Return to Región* (1967), at the age forty. He had no intention of becoming a full-time writer, and never gave up his work as an engineer. Benet's debut marked the arrival of a fresh and innovative voice in Spanish literature, characterized by many of the features of the modern novel: complexity, fractured narrative time and formal experimentation. Región, his fictional region of Spain located amid mountains and desert, became the setting for a series of novels, including a trilogy (*Return to Región*; *A Meditation*, 1969; and *A Winter Journey*, 1972) and *Rusty Lances* (1983).

With its own precise topography, Región was an allegory of a Spain consumed by civil war and then suffocated by Franco's dictatorship, a region caught in a moment of forgetfulness and resignation: 'The people of Región have opted to forget their own history: very few must conserve a true idea of their parents, of their first steps, of a golden age of adolescence that ended suddenly in a moment of shock and resignation.' In addition to creating Región, Benet challenged his readers with his complex but rigorous prose, presenting them with a style of writing that was new to Spain. In *A Meditation*, for example, he employed what he called his 'lifeline of continuous literature', writing the whole novel in a single paragraph. Likewise, *A Winter Journey* is punctuated by his own marginalia, while his detective story, *The Air of a Crime* (1980), provocatively fails to arrive at a solution.

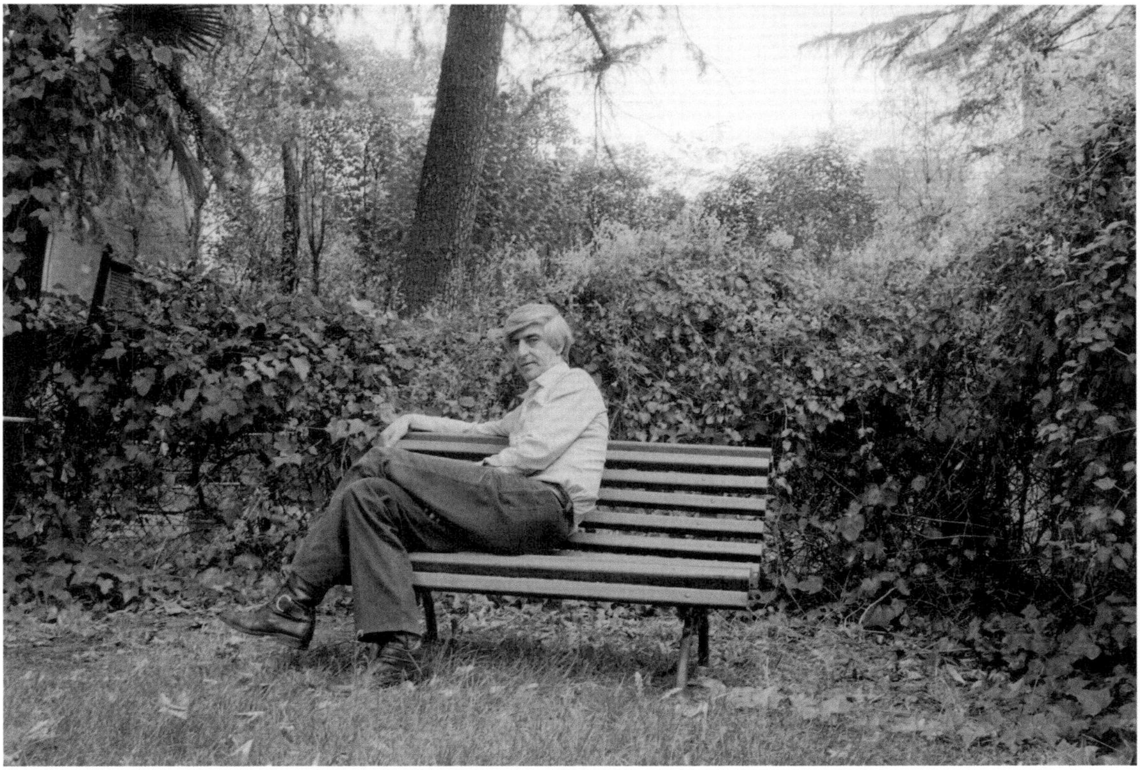

TAHAR BEN JELLOUN

born Fez, Morocco, 1944

by Bruno Barbey

Draa Valley, Morocco, 2000

Tahar Ben Jelloun began his literary career in the 1960s, working with the seminal journal *Anfas/Souffles* headed by the charismatic Moroccan poet Abdellatif Laabi. In 1971 he left Morocco following King Hassan II's introduction of a policy of Arabic-language instruction at Mohammed V University in Rabat, where he was teaching philosophy, and moved to Paris, where he completed a doctorate in psychiatric social work. His academic research inspired him to write his first major novel, *La Reclusion solitaire* (Solitary imprisonment, 1976), which was based on the existential condition of African migrants in Europe, drawing on fictionalized versions of his patients' case histories.

Ben Jelloun has never concealed his open opposition to the Moroccan monarchy's authoritarian rule, nor ceased to comment on the social and economic problems in his country that have arisen in the wake of decolonization. A prolific writer, his works have been translated into many languages and include poetry, theatrical pieces and essays, but he first achieved international success with his novel *The Sand Child* (1985), the story of a Moroccan girl who from birth is forced by her father to live as a boy, followed by the sequel *The Sacred Night* (1987), which was the first book by an Arab writer to be recognized by the prestigious Prix Goncourt. The search for identity forms the central theme of Ben Jelloun's writing, both in relation to the metamorphoses that his country of origin has undergone and to the cultural rootlessness that is a product of migration. His social engagement is made clear by the numerous strong public stances he has taken (most recently with regard to Nicolas Sarkozy's xenophobic policies and the events behind the Arab Spring) and his highly successful books of popular essays, in particular *Racism Explained To My Daughter* (1998), a vibrant dialogue with a ten-year-old girl about racial discrimination. Ben Jelloun's novels are filled with fabulous images, and have a powerful lyric tension and prose style influenced by the Arab tradition of oral storytelling. His interweaving of Eastern and Western elements; political reflection and popular storytelling; and metaphysical poetry and literary realism has made him one of the most significant figures in the post-colonial renaissance of Moroccan literature.

This portrait was taken in the Draa Valley by the Moroccan photographer Bruno Barbey. Ben Jelloun and Barbey jointly published a book of photographs and poetry dedicated to Ben Jelloun's native city of Fez in 1999.

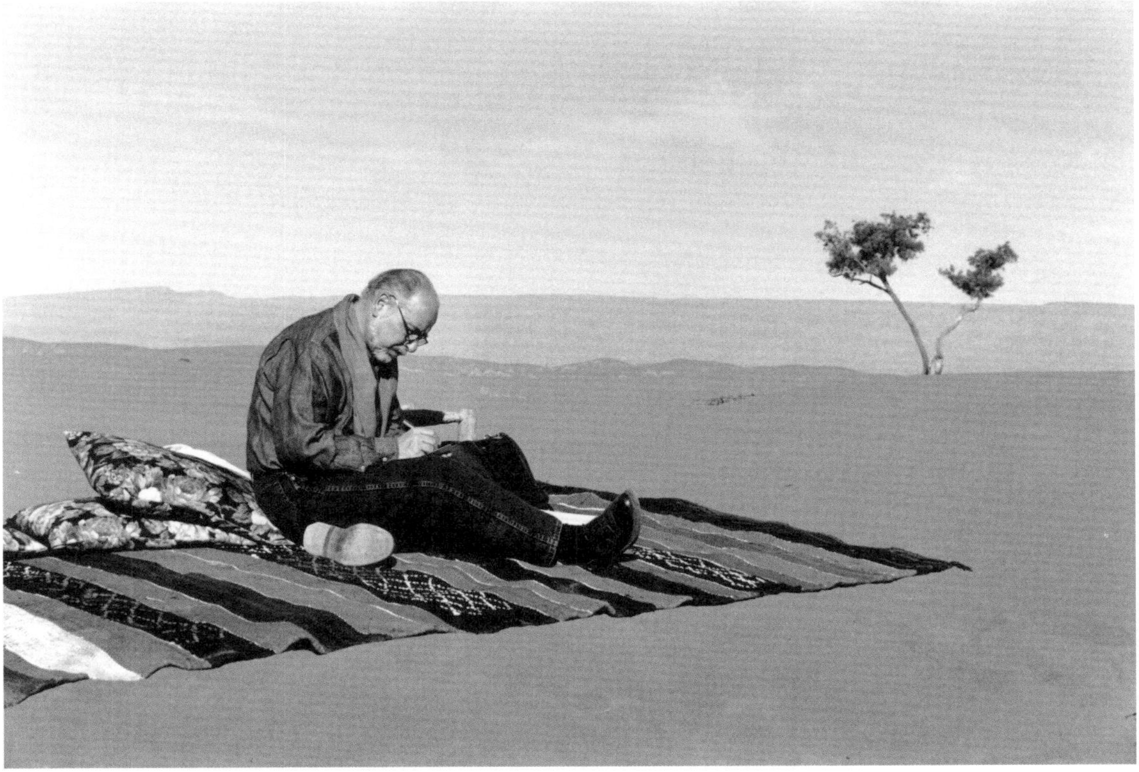

THOMAS BERNHARD

born Heerlen, the Netherlands, 1931; died Gmunden, Austria, 1989

by Helmut Baar

Maria Saal, Austria, 1958

Thomas Bernhard's life was one of rebellion and resistance. He railed against everything: his mother, his education, his country, his chronic illness and even death itself. With the publication of each of his books came a flood of criticism, controversy and even libel action. This did not deter him, however, from his ruthless exposition of all that he found ridiculous and distasteful – especially in his native Austria – in such novels as *Old Masters: A Comedy* (1985), the final book of his 'Arts' trilogy (*The Loser*, 1983; *Woodcutters*, 1984; and *Old Masters*). The acute suffering of his childhood and youth are documented in his autobiography, originally published in five volumes and later issued as *Gathering Evidence* (1985). If anything, his experience of such ordeals seemed to strengthen his will.

Bernhard was born in 1931 to a father he never knew, and a mother who appeared not to care for him very much. It was his maternal grandfather, an author, who took the boy under his wing and nurtured his artistic talents. In 1938 his family moved to Germany, where Bernhard was bullied at school for being Austrian. Prompted by his unhappiness and suicidal thoughts, his mother sent him to a National Socialist boarding school in Salzburg, where life became even more intolerable. *Die Ursache* (An indication of the cause, 1975), the first volume of his autobiography, is a damning indictment of the education system, Salzburg and its inhabitants.

In 1947 Bernhard left boarding school and started work as a grocer's apprentice in a poor area of Salzburg. The straightforward, physical nature of the work seems to have suited him, bringing him a degree of peace. He also took solace in his passion for music, particularly the violin and singing. However, the tuberculosis from which he had suffered since childhood made a career as a singer impossible. For a while his illness proved life-threatening, but he was determined to recover his health and defy the doctors' prognosis, an episode he recounts in *Der Atem. Eine Entscheidung* (Breath: a decision, 1978), the third volume of his autobiography. Following a brief period as a journalist, he devoted his renewed energy to becoming a writer.

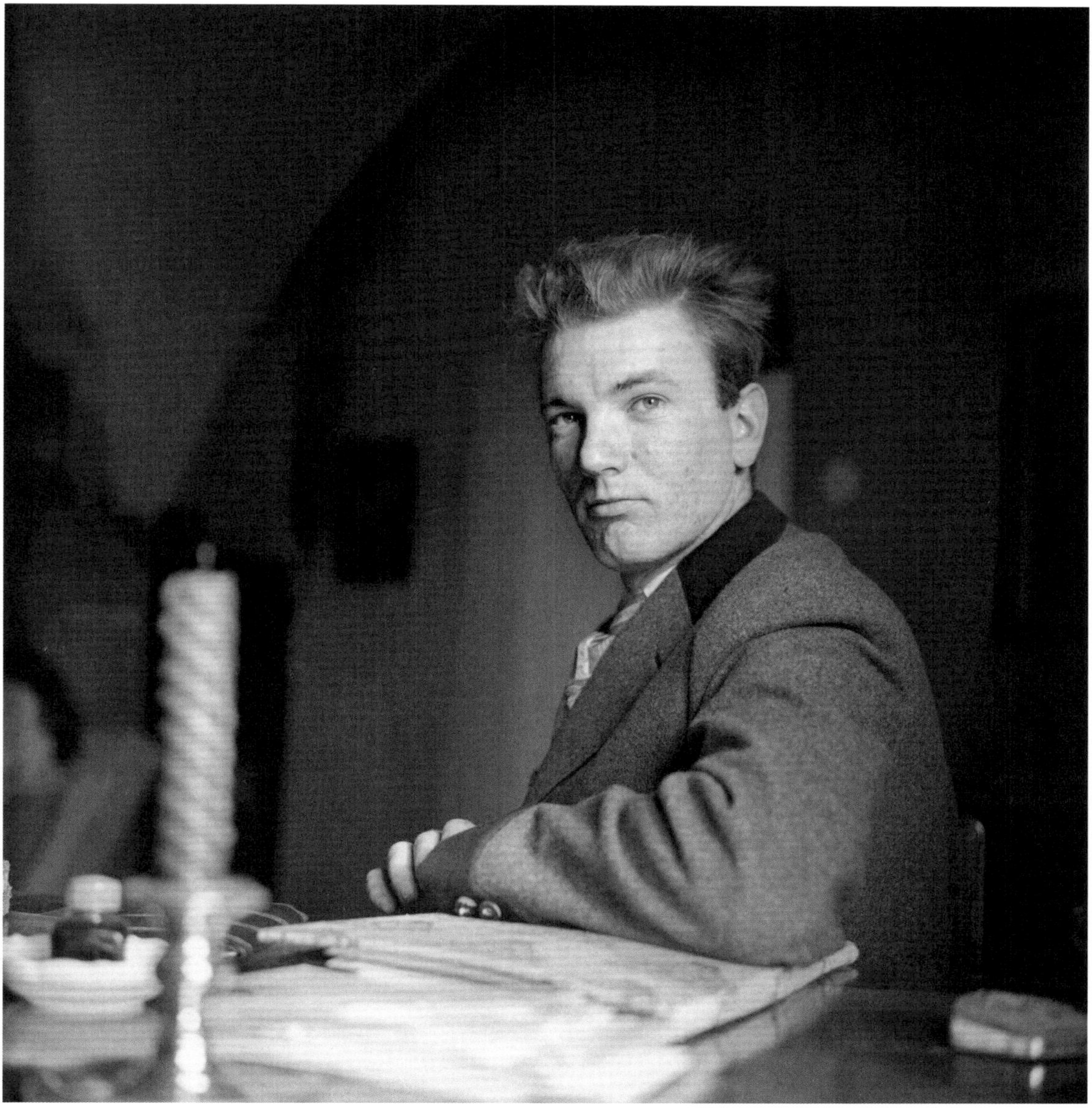

KARAN BLIXEN

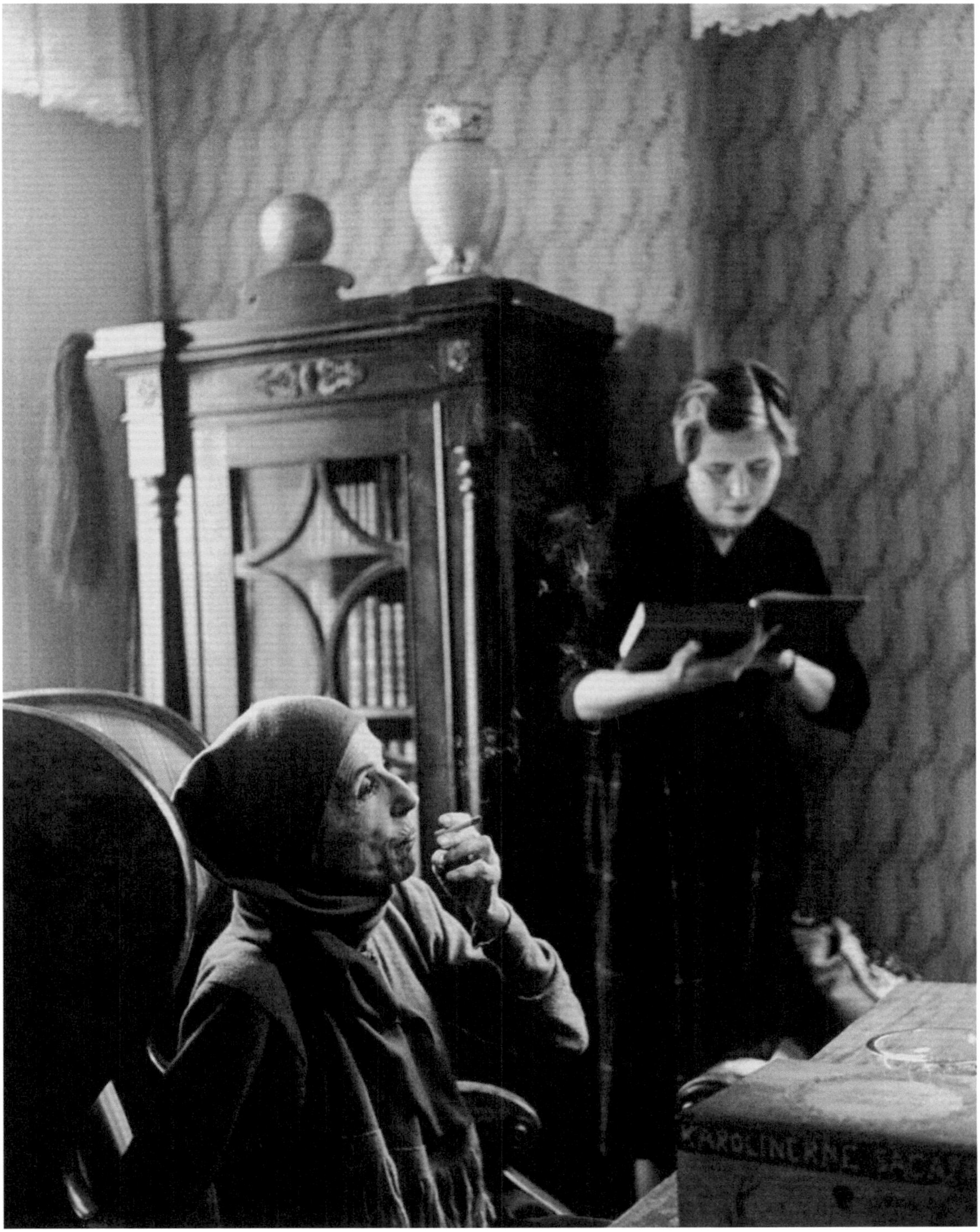

ALEXANDER BLOK

[Alexander Alexandrovich Blok] born St Petersburg, 1880; died St Petersburg, 1921

by Moisei Nappelbaum

Moscow, 1919

It was his *Stikhi o prekrasnoi Dame* (Verses on the fair lady, 1904), published when he was twenty-three years old, that made Alexander Blok famous. He was a young man of exquisite sensibility from a bourgeois background who married Lyubov Mendeleev, a daughter of the famous chemist Dmitri Mendeleev. In these early poems, the Fair Lady – his wife – symbolized Sophia, the spirit of 'Eternal Femininity' who pervaded all of reality according to the philosopher Vladimir Solovyov.

These poems clearly linked Blok with the beliefs of the Russian Symbolist poets, although his association with this movement was short-lived. He marked his break with the group in a play entitled *A Puppet Show* (1906), which mocked both its members and himself, and in the poem 'The Unknown Woman' (1906), in which the spirit of femininity, though still mystical, returned as a kind of prostitute in a low tavern.

The influence of Symbolism did not disappear completely from his later works. From 1907 onwards, he wrote a number of cycles of poems set against the background of St Petersburg; these verses were, at first, somewhat opaque, filled with metaphysics and musicality, and gradually became darker as they touched on the insecurity and mediocrity of the world.

The Rose and the Cross (1913) was a drama set in the brutal past of medieval knights. The sense of unease and menace that it emphasized resurfaced in Blok's two great poems from the period of the Russian Revolution, 'The Scythians' (1918) and 'The Twelve' (1918). Both works combine violence and mysticism to capture a sense of the radical change Russian society was undergoing. Both, too, are filled with powerful images, such as the barbarian Scythians dominating the West, and the twelve avenging Apostles led by a warlike Christ figure, invisible in the snowstorm raging around them. Blok was the greatest exponent of Russian Symbolism, and his visionary approach – with all its contradictions – allowed him to express the limits, inadequacies and difficulties of describing the new times, the new uncertainties and the new fears.

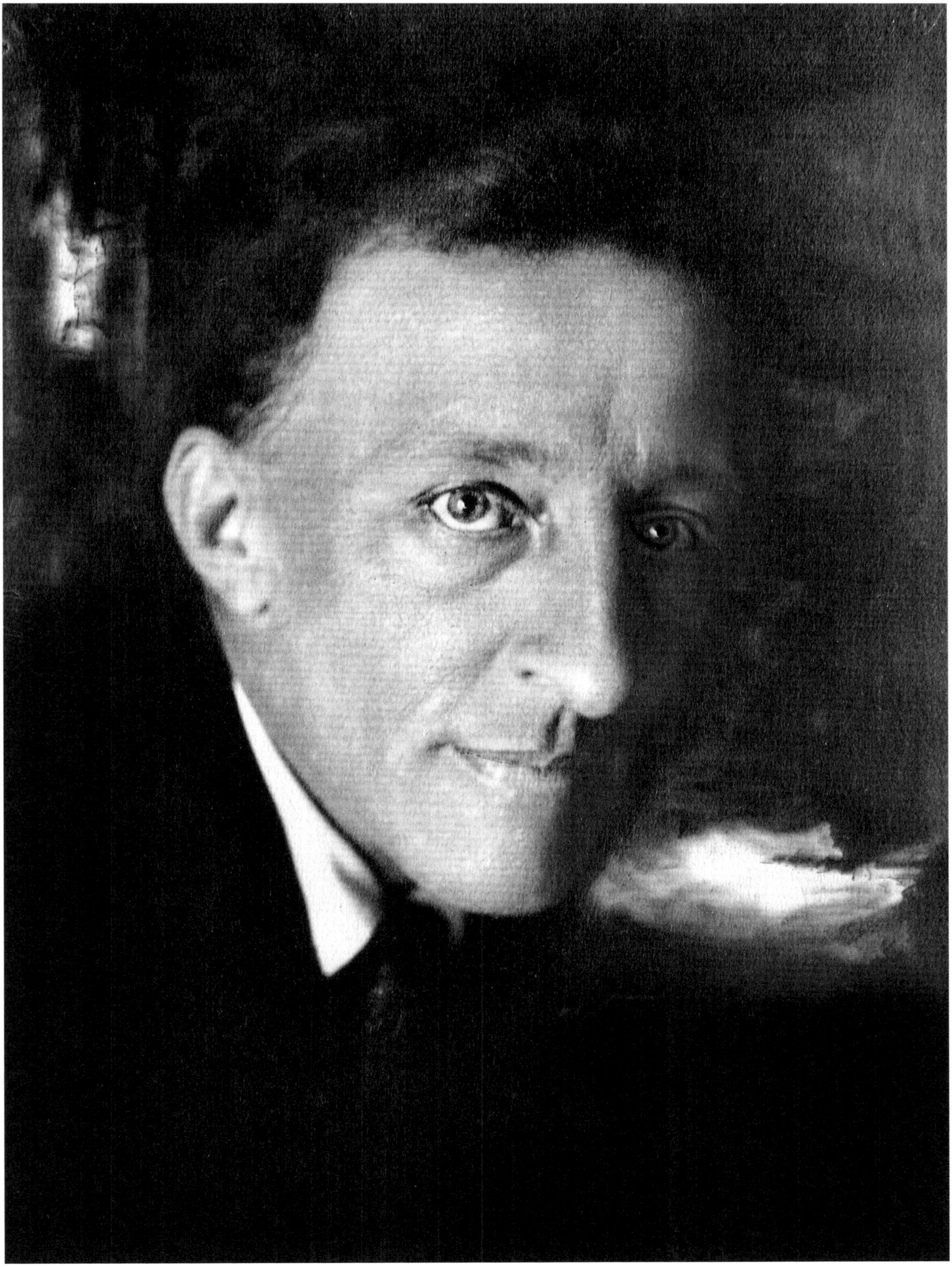

ROBERTO BOLAÑO

born Santiago, Chile, 1953; died Barcelona, Spain, 2003

by Jerry Bauer

unknown location, 2003

'I was born in 1953, the year that Stalin and Dylan Thomas died. In 1973, I was detained for eight days by the military, which had staged a coup in my country, and in the gym where the political prisoners were held I found an English magazine with pictures of Dylan Thomas's house in Wales. I had thought that Dylan Thomas died poor, but the house looked wonderful, almost like a fairytale cottage in the woods. There was no story about Stalin. But that night I dreamed of Stalin and Dylan Thomas: the two of them were at a bar in Mexico City, sitting at a little round table, a table for arm wrestling, but instead of wrestling they were competing to see who could hold his liquor better. The Welsh poet was drinking whisky and the Soviet dictator was drinking vodka. As the dream went on, however, I was the only one who seemed to feel queasier and queasier, ever closer to the verge of nausea.'

Chilean writer Roberto Bolaño, who had lived in Mexico since the age of fifteen, returned to his homeland in 1972 to support Salvador Allende's socialist movement but was imprisoned following Augusto Pinochet's coup shortly thereafter, and freed only when he was recognized by two former school friends who were working as prison guards. Bolaño's recounting of the grim incident is typical of both the man and his writing: an amalgam of dream and reality, expressed with humour and innocence through a terse writing style and peculiar images that do not try to conceal the bad side of the world.

Following his ill-fated sojourn in Santiago, Bolaño returned to Mexico City and eventually drifted to Spain, where he settled first in Barcelona and then in Blanes. With his friend Mario Santiago, a fellow poet, he was instrumental in founding the Infrarealist movement, which took its inspiration from Dadaism, in reaction to what Bolaño regarded as the irritatingly self-righteous and uncritical nature of the mainstream Latin American literary scene.

Bolaño's novels often have an unconventional structure, as in *Nazi Literature in the Americas* (1996), his darkly comic faux literary encyclopedia of imaginary fascist authors, and *The Savage Detectives* (1998), the story of two poets in search of a Mexican poet called Césarea Tenajero, which is narrated by more than forty different characters. *2666* (2004), which explores the unsolved murders of hundreds of women in 'Santa Teresa' in Mexico (modelled on Ciudad Juárez), through five stories encompassing a similarly wide range of characters and settings, was published posthumously and awarded the National Book Critics Circle Award for Fiction in 2008. Ironic and satirical, the influence of Bolaño's prose style can be seen in Spanish writer Javier Cercas's *Soldiers of Salamis* (2001), in which Bolaño himself appears as a character.

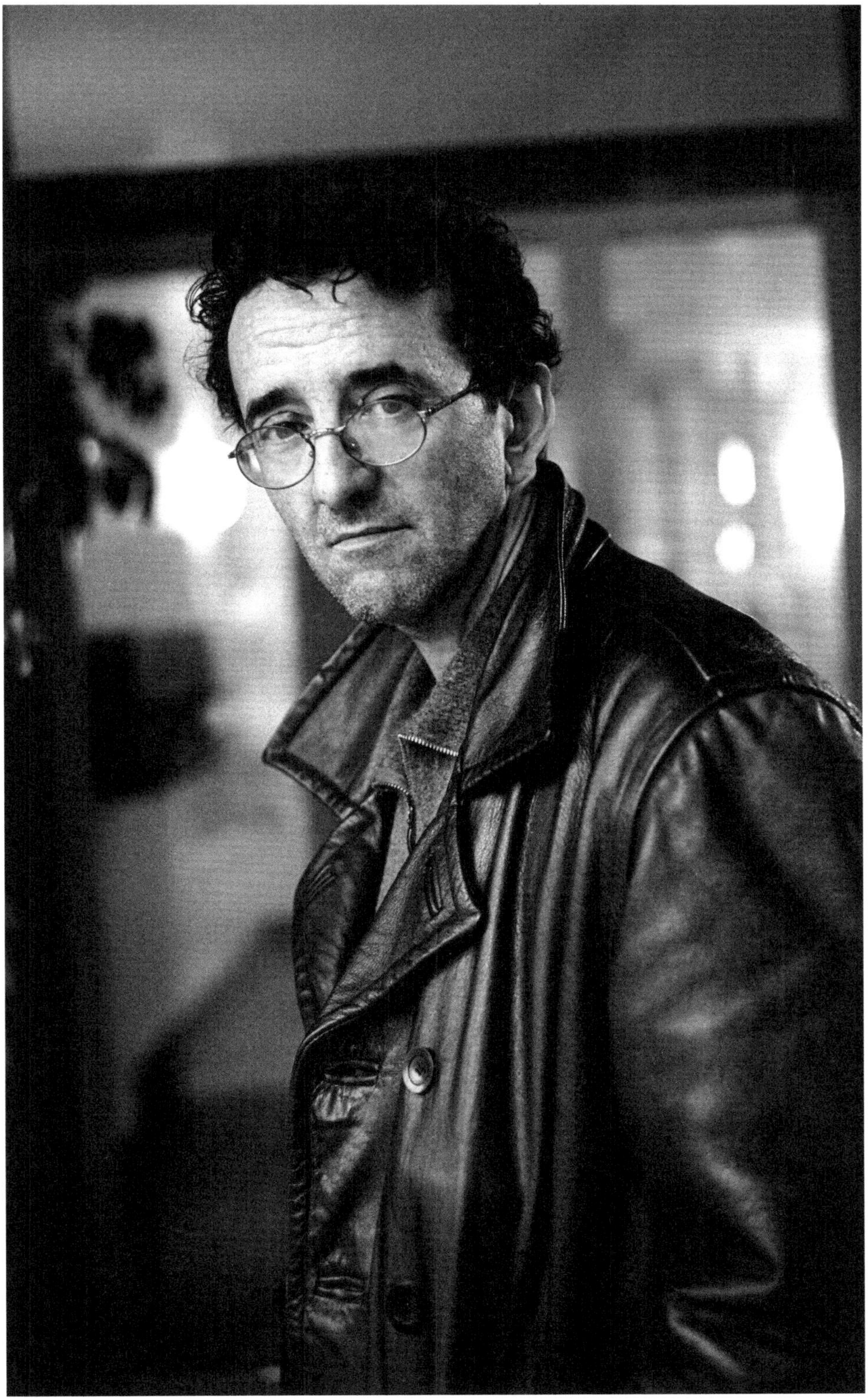

HEINRICH BÖLL

born Cologne, Germany, 1917; died Langenbroich, Germany, 1985

by Isolde Ohlbaum

Bornheim-Merten, Germany, 1981

Heinrich Böll was awarded the Nobel Prize in 1972. In 'An Essay on the Reason of Poetry', a Nobel lecture given by Böll in May 1973, the German author states: 'Art is always a good hiding-place, not for dynamite, but for intellectual explosives and social time-bombs.' Literature, in short, is never innocuous, and art really can bring about change since it continues to have the capacity to startle people out of their complacency.

Böll was one of the most lucid and caustic voices of dissent in post-war Germany. He developed this voice through his short stories, novels and numerous articles and essays, all of which were written in his sparse, sarcastic, cutting style. He began to write after the Second World War, during which he had fought as an infantry soldier on the Western Front and later on the Eastern Front, in both Russia and Romania. This experience clearly left an indelible mark on the writer, while also providing the impetus behind his work. He was a peace activist; an anti-nuclear campaigner; a religious man, albeit fiercely anti-clerical; and a defender of the rights of Russian socialist dissidents. For Böll, political militancy went hand in hand with literature; he was a writer who was never afraid of provoking debate.

Disgusted by the capitalism and consumerism of post-war Germany, he castigated his country's superficial concerns in a series of debunking satires. In *The Clown* (1963), a highly political novel, his critique extended to an open attack on the power of the Church. His radical views, instead of marginalizing him, made him a literary phenomenon. His quarrel with ecclesiastical authority led to his decision to take public leave of the Catholic Church in 1972 – the year in which he received the Nobel Prize.

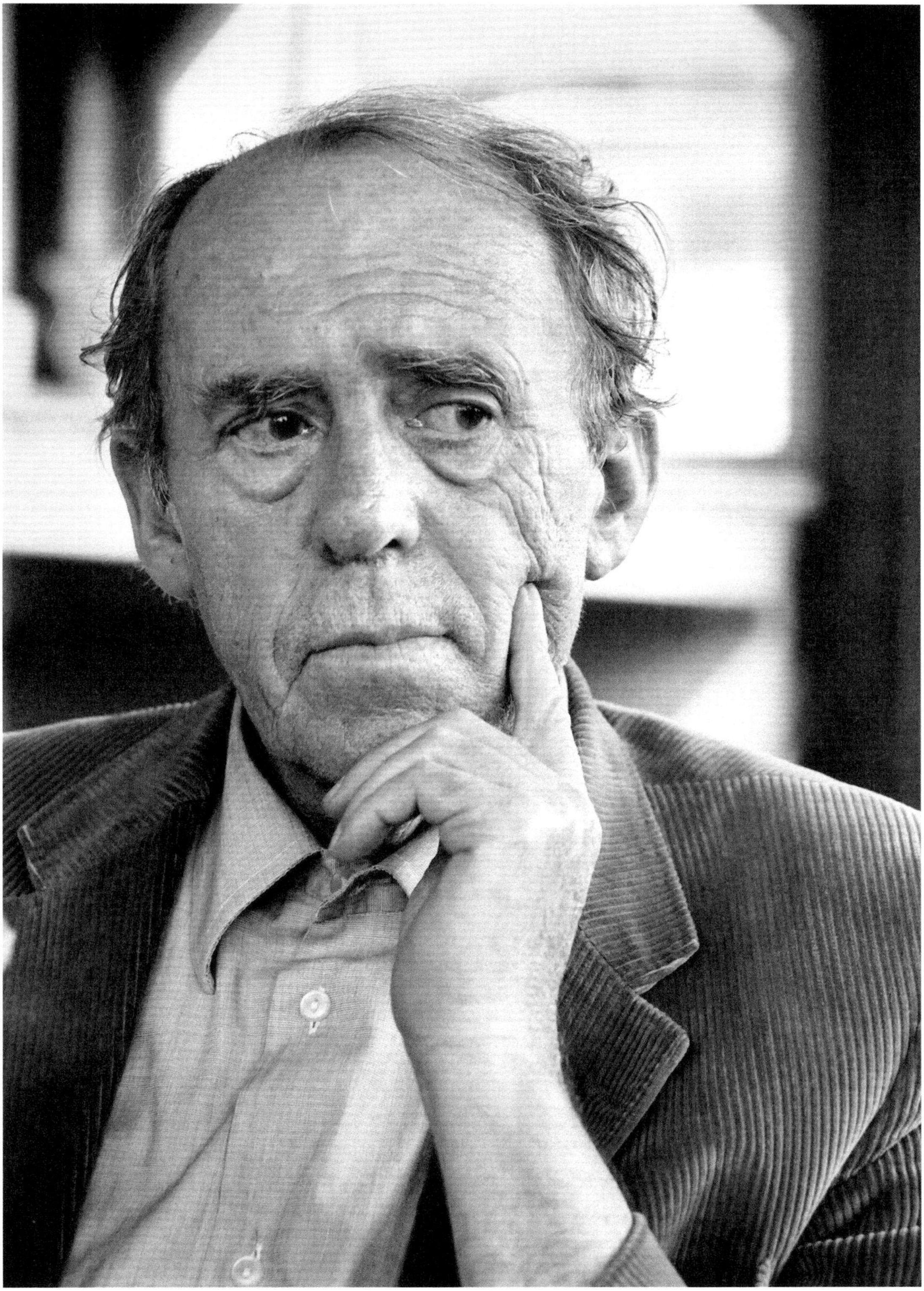

YVES BONNEFOY

born Tours, France, 1923

by Martine Franck

Céreste, France, 1989

Yves Bonnefoy is a multi-award-winning poet, translator, essayist, art historian and critic, and is a professor of poetry at the Collège de France. In all his many artistic activities, he has tried to give poetry the means to make the world complete. The poetic use of words can deconstruct the concepts that language exploits to represent things and living beings. It allows it to pass from the abstract nature of ideas to concrete reality. It is not by chance that *Anti-Platon* (Anti-Plato, 1962) is the title of one of his most important collections of poems. A word, when freed from its conceptuality, can bring its subject closer to living reality and deepen its presence, revealing its own finiteness and that of the world around it. If the word carries fixed associations, abstract models that ignore the reality of individuals, then that word becomes dangerous. The poet must struggle against any such tendencies.

Bonnefoy had a brief literary apprenticeship with André Breton's Surrealists in Paris in the 1940s – an influence apparent in his earliest published work – although he left the group after only a few years as he did not share its leader's interest in magic and the occult. But it was with *On the Motion and Immobility of Douve* (1953), a collection of poems centred on a beloved woman called 'Douve', that he found his own unique poetic voice. Bonnefoy's rich and varied literary output constantly engages with living languages and the figurative arts. He has a great passion for the Renaissance and considers Italy the land of images par excellence, its architecture and paintings creating a theatre in which nostalgia for the infinite and a perception of the finite come together.

For Bonnefoy, even visual artists – who use images rather than words as a language – run the risk of reflecting only the surface of reality. For this reason, Bonnefoy considers the great masters of photography, such as Walker Evans and Henri Cartier-Bresson, who struggled against their instrument even as they used it, to have been true poets. Accompanied by Cartier-Bresson, Martine Franck visited the writer at his home in Provence and took this photograph; another picture taken during this session shows Cartier-Bresson drawing a portrait of his friend Bonnefoy.

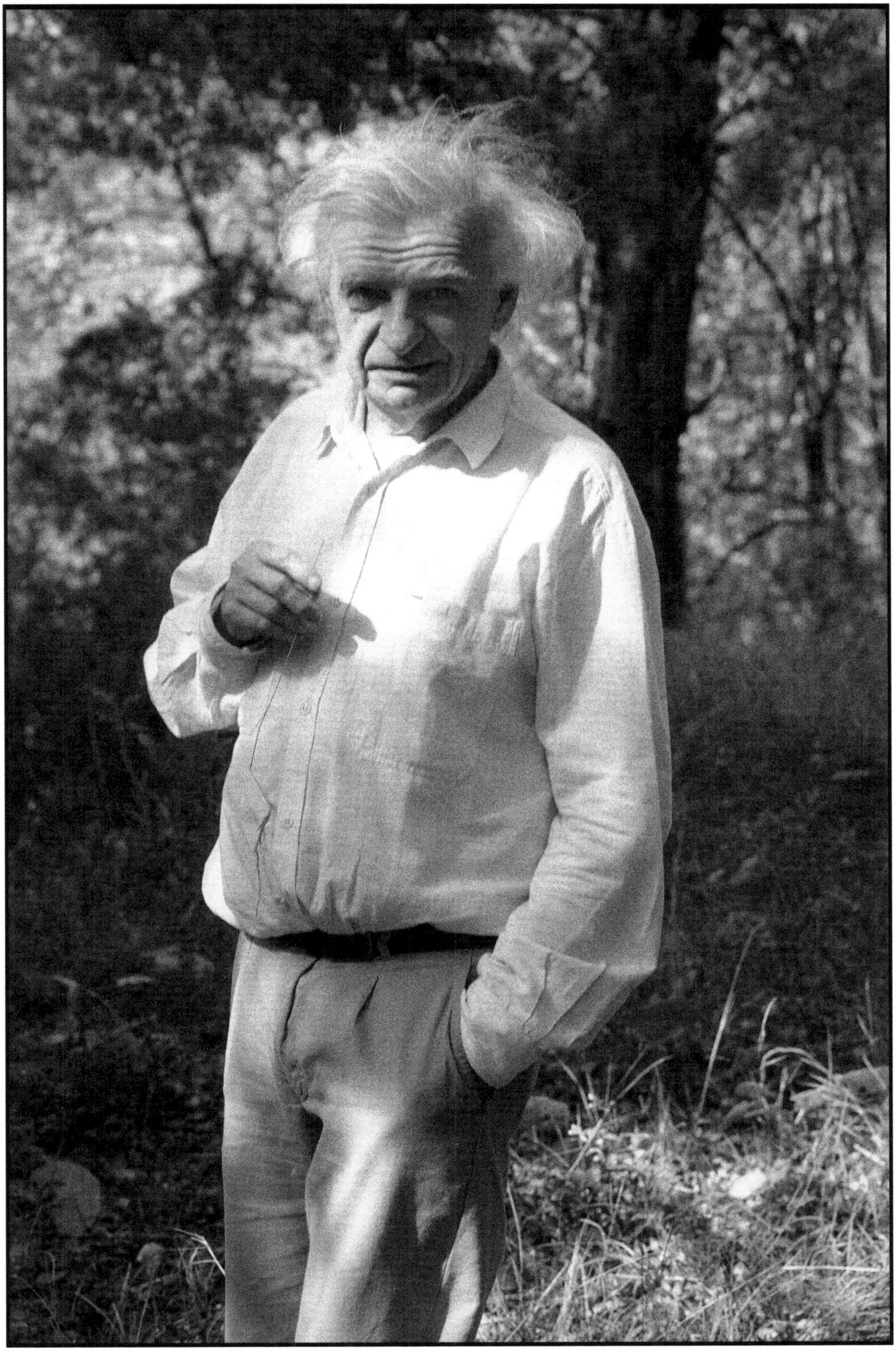

JORGE LUIS BORGES

born Buenos Aires, 1899; died Geneva, 1986

by Ferdinando Scianna

Palermo, Italy, 1984

Thousands of pages have been written in an attempt to explain Jorge Luis Borges's *oeuvre*, in particular his prose work, such as his short stories from the 1940s that revolutionized literature in his native Argentina and beyond. Although poetry was his first love, it was through such stories that Borges initially came to prominence. His first published story was 'The Man from the Pink Corner' (1933), in which the main character was the Buenos Aires underworld of the *guapos* (street gangs). But it was in 'The Approach to al-Mu'tasim' (1935) that the elements that would come to characterize his writing first became apparent: the ambiguity between narrative and non-narrative elements, and the labyrinthine structure of his metaphysical reflections.

Borges's literary coming of age is said to be marked by the short story 'Pierre Menard, Author of the *Quixote*' (1939), in which the author brings together paradox and congruity by demolishing and reconstructing a classic work of literature. Pierre Menard rewrites Cervantes's *Don Quixote* word for word, but the result is something entirely new. In its subject matter and blurring of the line between fiction and non-fiction, Borges's story contains many of the preoccupations of his later work, in particular the cyclical nature of time and the relationship between fiction, truth and identity.

Double images, fragments, falsifications, irony, a pared-down and precise language, perfectly balanced plot structures and references to other works were just a few of the ingredients that made Borges a universal writer. However, his interest in the questions with which humanity has struggled for centuries was seasoned by a sceptical wit and modesty. According to Borges, '[Stories] are the irresponsible sport of a shy sort of man who could not bring himself to write short stories, and so amused himself by changing and distorting (sometimes without aesthetic justification) the stories of other men.'

The Italian photographer Ferdinando Scianna took this portrait of Borges in Palermo, on the terrace of a seaside hotel: 'It was a dazzlingly bright day. Spring, which had been very bizarre that year, even in Sicily, seemed to have made an exception for Borges. He seemed to drink in the particular fragrance of the air, and said that he felt that the sky had to be ultra-blue. He turned towards the sun, whose light he could no longer see, but whose warmth he felt, and he began to declaim: "'A sweet colour of oriental sapphire' … Dante, Purgatory, First Canto," he explained with a timid smile.'

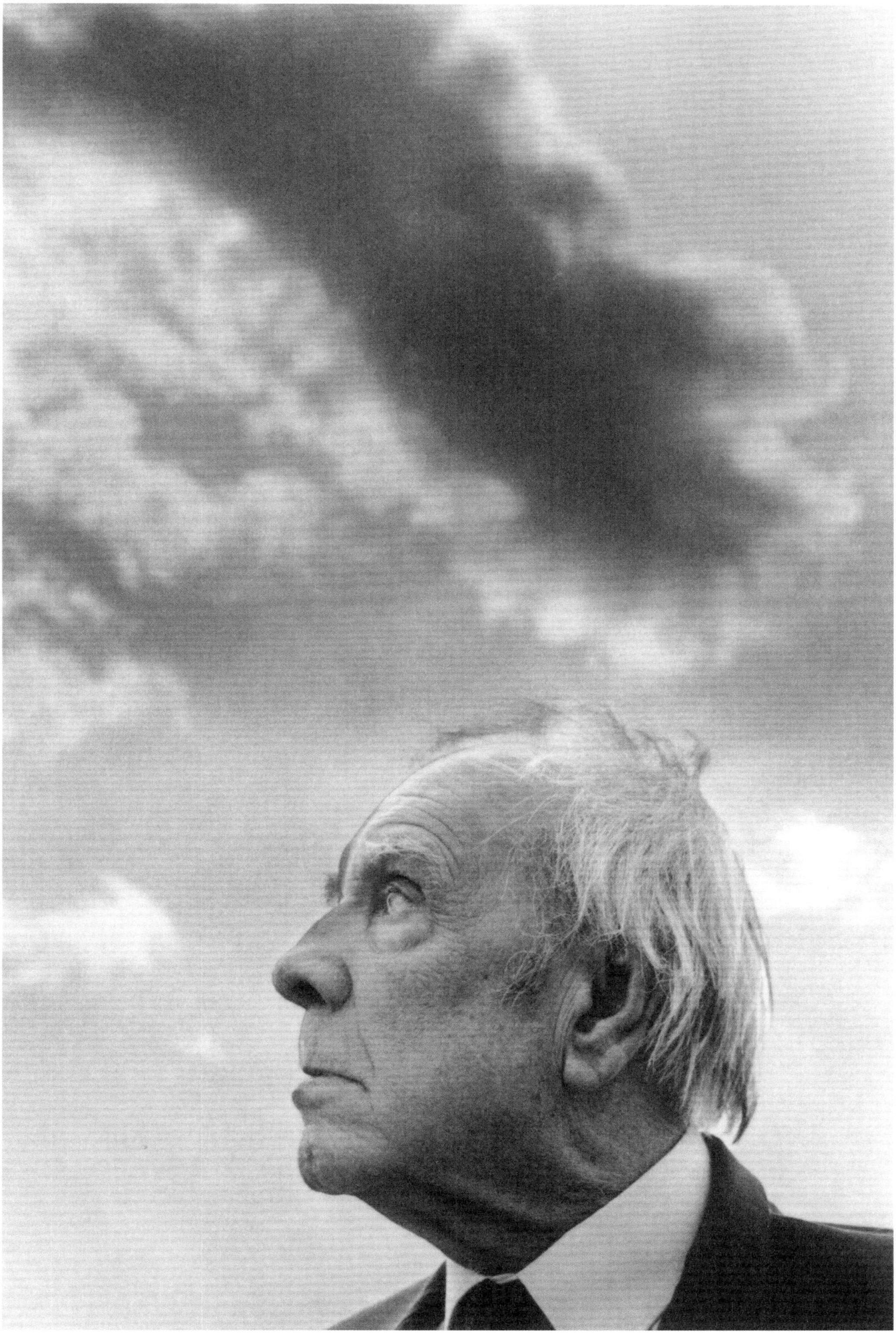

BERTOLT BRECHT

born Augsburg, Germany, 1898; died Berlin, 1956

by 'Chim' (David Seymour)

Paris, 1936

In the wake of the 1933 arson attack on the Reichstag – an event seen as pivotal in the establishment of Nazi Germany – Bertolt Brecht went into exile. Among the leading German intellectuals of the day, Brecht was regarded by the Nazi government as one of its principal detractors.

At the time of his exile, Brecht was the famous and renowned author of *The Threepenny Opera*. Performed for the first time in 1928 in Berlin, it depicted a world of derelicts and the sub-proletariat with the express intention of provoking the small-minded bourgeois audience. However, much to the author's disappointment, it was precisely this audience that decreed it a great success. Brecht was undeterred. He continued to experiment and to develop his theory of 'epic theatre', seeking to eliminate any emotional identification, any sense of rapture, in his audience. He had no use for a group of entranced spectators; rather, he wanted to provoke discussion, to force the observer to take a stance. Art had to denounce the horror of capitalism, rip away its mask and point to a better future. Brecht could not limit himself to interpreting the world – he had to change it.

In 1930, despite a picket of young Nazis attempting to prevent the audience from entering the auditorium, Brecht's *Rise and Fall of the City of Mahagonny* was performed in the Neues Theater in Leipzig. Among the theatre-goers that evening was a very young David-Szymin, a Polish art student who, just a few years later, as the photographer 'Chim' (David Seymour), would take Brecht's photo in Paris. By the time Brecht had completed writing *Saint Joan of the Stockyards* (1929–31), however, there was no time left for it to be staged. By then, the Nazis were on the point of taking power, and Brecht's works were disappearing from theatre playlists.

Brecht spent the first part of his exile in Denmark, where he remained until 1939. It was during these years that he wrote, among other works, *Fear and Misery of the Third Reich* (1935–38) and *Mother Courage and Her Children* (1938–39). This period also saw him produce some of his best poetry, which was collected as *The Svendborg Poems* (1939). Brecht's exile then took him to Sweden, Finland and, ultimately, the USA, where he remained for several years. When he returned to Berlin in 1949, he was poor and almost forgotten, but he was not a man to accept his fate quietly. Shortly after his return he produced a memorable staging of *Mother Courage*, with his second wife, the actress Helene Weigel, taking the role of 'Mother'. Together, they founded the Berliner Ensemble, and the value of Brecht's theatre became recognized around the world.

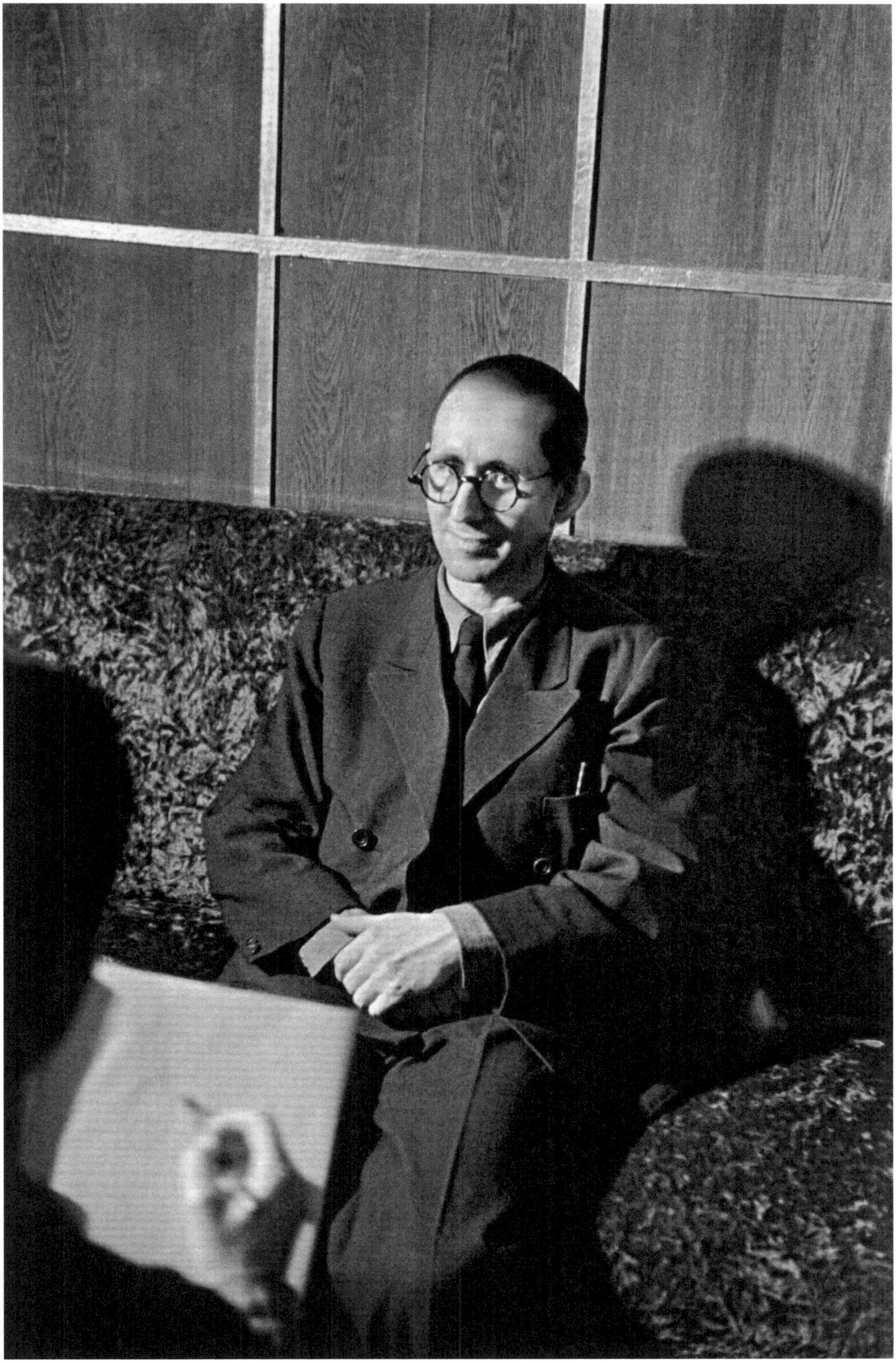

ANDRÉ BRETON

born Tinchebray, France, 1896; died Paris, 1966

by Burt Glinn

Paris, 1958

'There is no use in being alive if one must work', says the eponymous protagonist of André Breton's novel *Nadja* (1928), in a line that neatly captures the philosophy of both the principal character and the author himself. In common with *Communicating Vessels* (1932) and *Mad Love* (1937), *Nadja*, Breton's autobiographical and visionary text, interweaves Surrealism ('psychic automatism', as he termed it) with Paris, the city most associated with the revolutionary artistic movement. Its streets and squares, flea markets, shop windows and sprawling nightlife not only provided a setting for *Nadja* but also formed the fertile ground from which the Surrealist aesthetic sprang. Breton set out to define the new movement in his *Surrealist Manifesto* of 1924, and in the magazine he founded in the same year, *La Révolution surréaliste*, which also included contributions from artists and writers such as Antonin Artaud, Joan Miró, Raymond Queneau and René Magritte.

Breton arrived in Paris in 1907. Six years later he began studying medicine, but was more interested in poetry and the figurative arts, composing verses that he sent to the writer Paul Valéry. Together with a fellow medical student, Louis Aragon, who shared his passion for both the visual arts and literature, Breton began to explore the cultural side of Paris. In 1915, having been conscripted into the French army, he started reading Arthur Rimbaud and Alfred Jarry, and wrote his first prose poem, 'Age', while working in a military hospital in Nantes. It was, however, not until his break with Dadaism in the early 1920s that he became a leading figure of Surrealism, one of the most significant avant-garde artistic movements of the twentieth century.

Breton's politics, first anarchistic and then Communist, were always clear-cut. A close friend of Leon Trotsky, he later broke with the Communist Party because of his opposition to the idea of art as propaganda; he also voiced his horror at both Nazism and Stalinism. When Hitler invaded Poland in 1939, triggering the Second World War, Breton was recalled to the French medical corps. The following year, he brought out his *Anthology of Black Humour*, but its distribution was interrupted: German troops had entered Paris, and his name was on a list of known Communists.

Breton left Europe in 1941, travelling first to the Caribbean and then to New York, where he launched the Surrealist magazine *VVV*, despite refusing to learn English. When the war ended, he was able to return to his beloved Paris. Burt Glinn's photograph shows him in his home on the rue Fontaine in the Pigalle district, surrounded by the extraordinary collection of objects that he had gathered throughout his life, such as sculptures, books, photographs, primitive masks, precious manuscripts and the many works of art created by his friends.

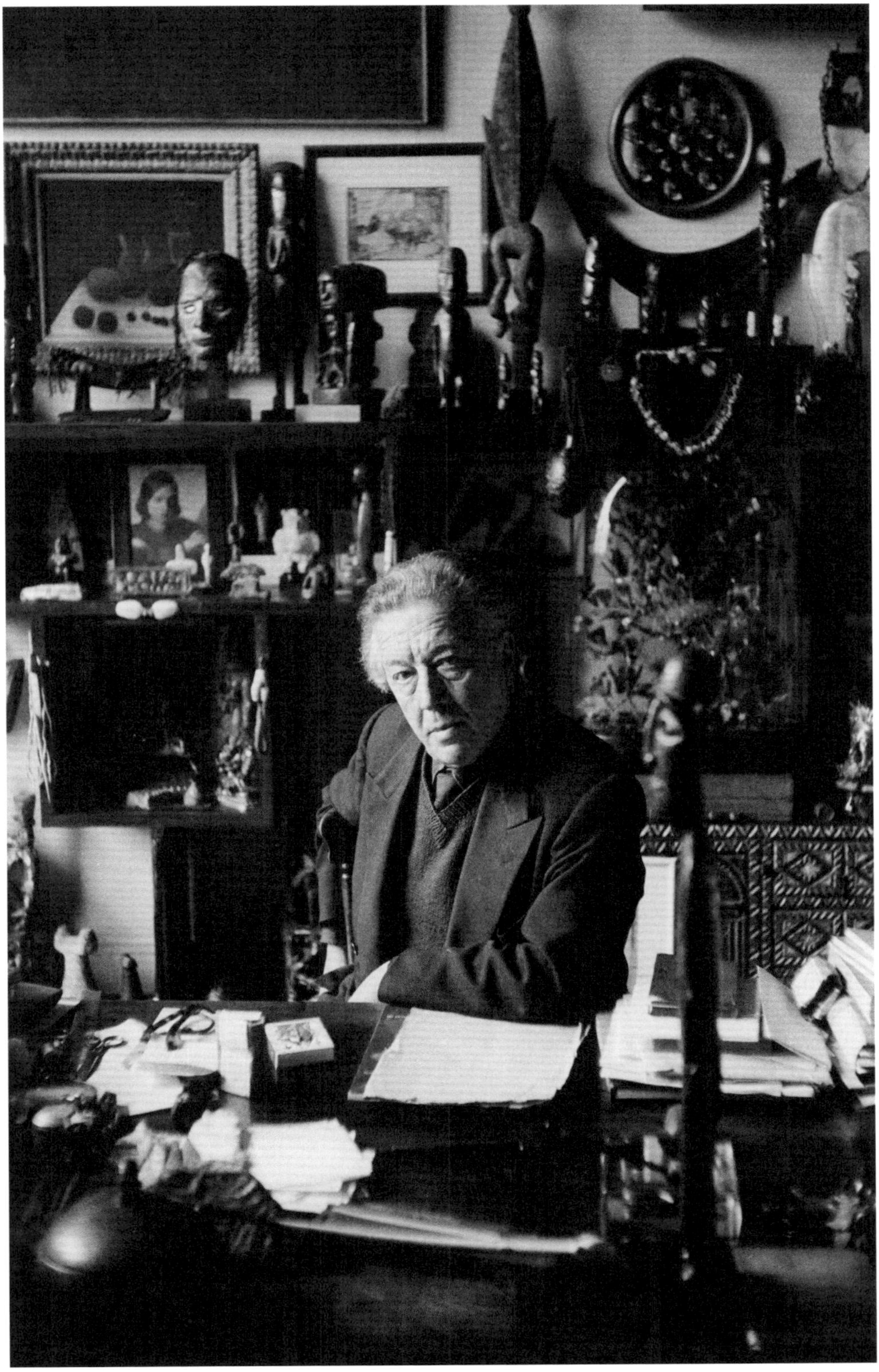

HERMANN BROCH

born Vienna, 1886; died New Haven, Connecticut, 1951

unknown photographer

Vienna, 1937

In 1938, following the occupation and annexation of Austria by Nazi Germany, Hermann Broch was arrested by the Gestapo. Locked up in a prison cell, from which he was convinced he would never emerge alive, the Austrian writer found himself reflecting on the figure of Virgil. Broch had already produced a short radio broadcast on the Roman poet, but it was while in prison that he found the main theme for *The Death of Virgil* (1945), one of his foremost works. It seems that, in the solitude of his cell, Broch prepared for death by telling himself the story of the Roman poet's last day. Combining reality, hallucinations, poetry and prose, Broch's novel is a solo piece, a grand interior dialogue conducted in the third person over a period of eighteen hours. But this is no novel of escape into the mythical past: Broch's Virgil is a man of the twentieth century, an artist and a desperate fugitive.

Broch belonged to a group of German-language writers who saw all around them the inexorable signs of the end of the Austro-Hungarian Empire and the rise of Nazi rule. In common with Thomas Mann and Robert Musil, Broch was an interpreter of his own times and an experimenter with the form of the novel. What interested Broch were man and his place in the world, and in Virgil he found the perfect subject with which to explore the end of an era while at the same time expressing his conviction that it was only through literature that one could truly understand the human condition.

Before pursuing a full-time career as a writer, Broch had worked in his father's textile mill. In 1927, however, he had sold the family firm in order to study mathematics, philosophy, psychology and sociology, subjects that allowed him to pursue a theme in which he was particularly interested: the psychology of the masses. Broch made his literary debut with *The Sleepwalkers* (1931–32), a trilogy on the corrupt nature of modern society. He was released from the Gestapo prison thanks to the assistance of a group of friends, including James Joyce, who then helped him move to the USA, where he became an American citizen and professor of German at Yale University. It was also in the USA that he finally completed *The Death of Virgil*.

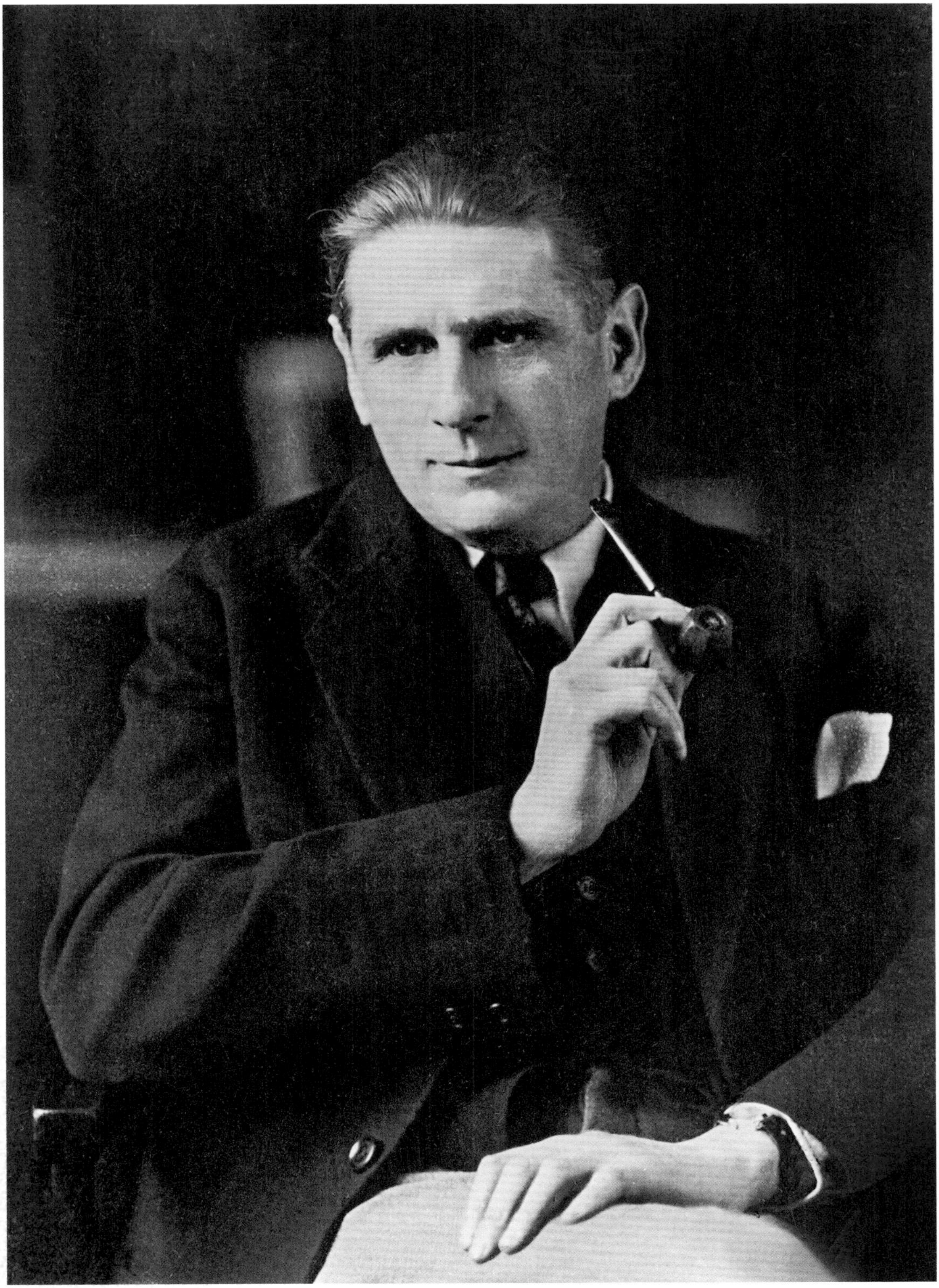

JOSEPH BRODSKY

born St Petersburg, 1940; died New York, 1996

by Giorgia Fiorio

Massachusetts, 1995

As a teenager, Joseph Brodsky began publishing his poems in a underground magazine devoted to *samzidat*, the secret reproduction of censored publications. Established Russian poets, such as Anna Akhmatova, who had survived the previous state purges, immediately recognized his lyrical gifts, and his poems were avidly read by a younger generation disenchanted with the Soviet cultural diet. Brodsky himself was inspired by the seventeenth-century metaphysical poet John Donne, and by T. S. Eliot, who had himself been influenced by Donne.

Despite the gradual demise of Stalinism, Brodsky still managed to fall foul of the Soviet authorities in the early 1960s and in 1964 was sentenced to five years of forced labour on a charge of 'social parasitism' for his anti-government writings. He served only eighteen months, however, as his sentence was commuted following pressure from leading cultural figures around the world. He continued to write, and many of his works were published abroad, including *A Stop in the Desert,* which was translated into English in 1970. Finally in 1972 he was 'invited' to leave the country, which he did, never to return. He settled in New York, where he published a new collection of poems entitled *Roman Elegies* (1989), containing frequent classical allusions, and a book of essays called *Less Than One* (1986), many of which were dedicated to his favourite poets, including Akhmatova, Marina Tsvetaeva, Thomas Hardy, Robert Frost, Rainer Maria Rilke, Eugenio Montale, Konstantino Kavafis and W. H. Auden.

Like fellow émigré Vladimir Nabokov, he wrote both in Russian and in English, and devoted many pages to the experience of living in exile and working in two different languages. Prominent themes in his writing include the impossibility of rooting oneself in the present, shifting landscapes, emotional and geographical displacement, and the enduring power of beauty to sustain the human spirit. In 1987, by then well known on both sides of the Atlantic, he was awarded the Nobel Prize. Four years after his death, his *Collected Poems in English, 1972–1999* (2000) was published. He is buried in Venice, a place he described evocatively in his essay collection *Watermark* (1989).

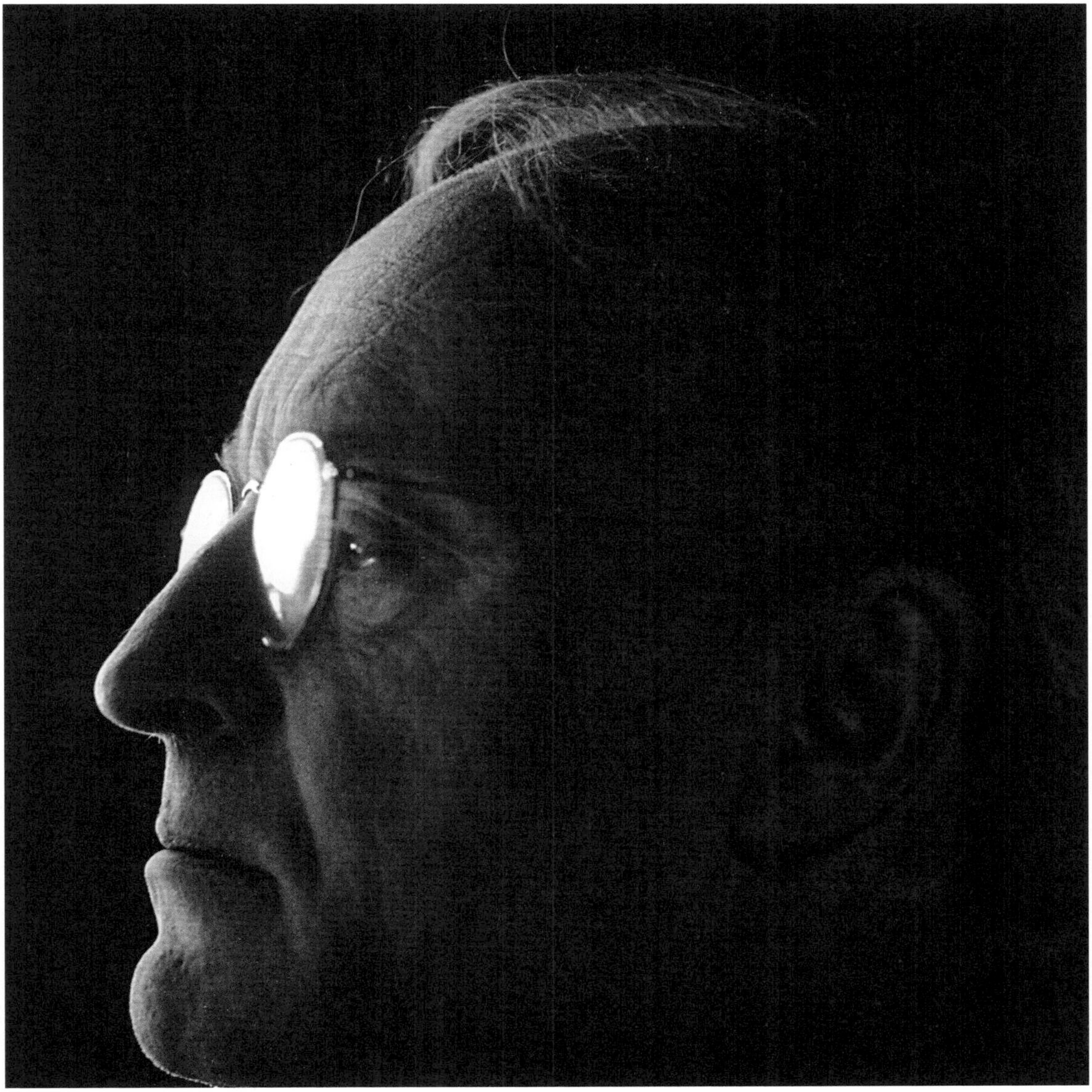

MIKHAIL BULGAKOV

born Kiev, Ukraine, 1891; died Moscow, 1940

unknown photographer

Moscow, 1926

The Master and Margarita, widely regarded as Mikhail Bulgakov's masterpiece, features one of the most bizarre creations of twentieth-century literature, Professor Woland: 'He looked slightly over forty. Crooked sort of mouth. Clean-shaven. Dark hair. Right eye black, left eye for some reason green. Eyebrows black, but one higher than the other. In short – a foreigner.' In fact, the professor turns out to be Satan in the guise of a gentleman. Arriving in Moscow, he proceeds to turn the lives of its inhabitants upside down.

Written between 1928 and 1940, *The Master and Margarita* was finally published in 1967. Fearing the censorship of the Soviet authorities, Bulgakov burned the first draft and had to rewrite it from memory. Yet for a brief period he was one of Stalin's favourite authors. Stalin was said to have seen his play *The Day of the Turbins* (1925–26) fifteen times, hailing it as a 'demonstration of the overwhelming force of Bolshevism'. However, the tide of fortune was to turn against Bulgakov, and by the late 1920s his works had been censored by the authorities for being anti-proletariat and reactionary, while he himself was accused of being in the pay of the 'new bourgeois'. Out of his earlier respect for the writer, Stalin permitted Bulgakov to continue to work as a theatre director and librettist, but he was forbidden to publish anything. He wrote to Stalin in desperation, saying that for him, 'not being able to write is tantamount to being buried alive'. He continued to write in secret, not knowing whether anyone would ever read his work.

Set in a hallucinatory and grotesque world, *The Master and Margarita* represents a fierce critique of Stalin's regime. Satan disguised as Woland steps into a city populated by bureaucrats, fools and over-privileged classes, and from that moment on its characters, including minor functionaries and members of the theatrical and literary circles of Moscow, are overtaken by unexpected, tragicomic events. The only characters ultimately to attain peace, through a Faustian encounter with Woland, are the Master, a marginalized writer whose drama about Pontius Pilate has been refused publication by the authorities, and his unhappy lover, Margarita.

After its publication, the Italian writer Eugenio Montale described the book as a 'novel-poem', reasoning that 'a show that introduces innumerable characters, a book in which an almost cruel realism is interwoven with the most exalted of themes, that of the Passion, could not have been conceived of by anything other than a truly poetic imagination.'

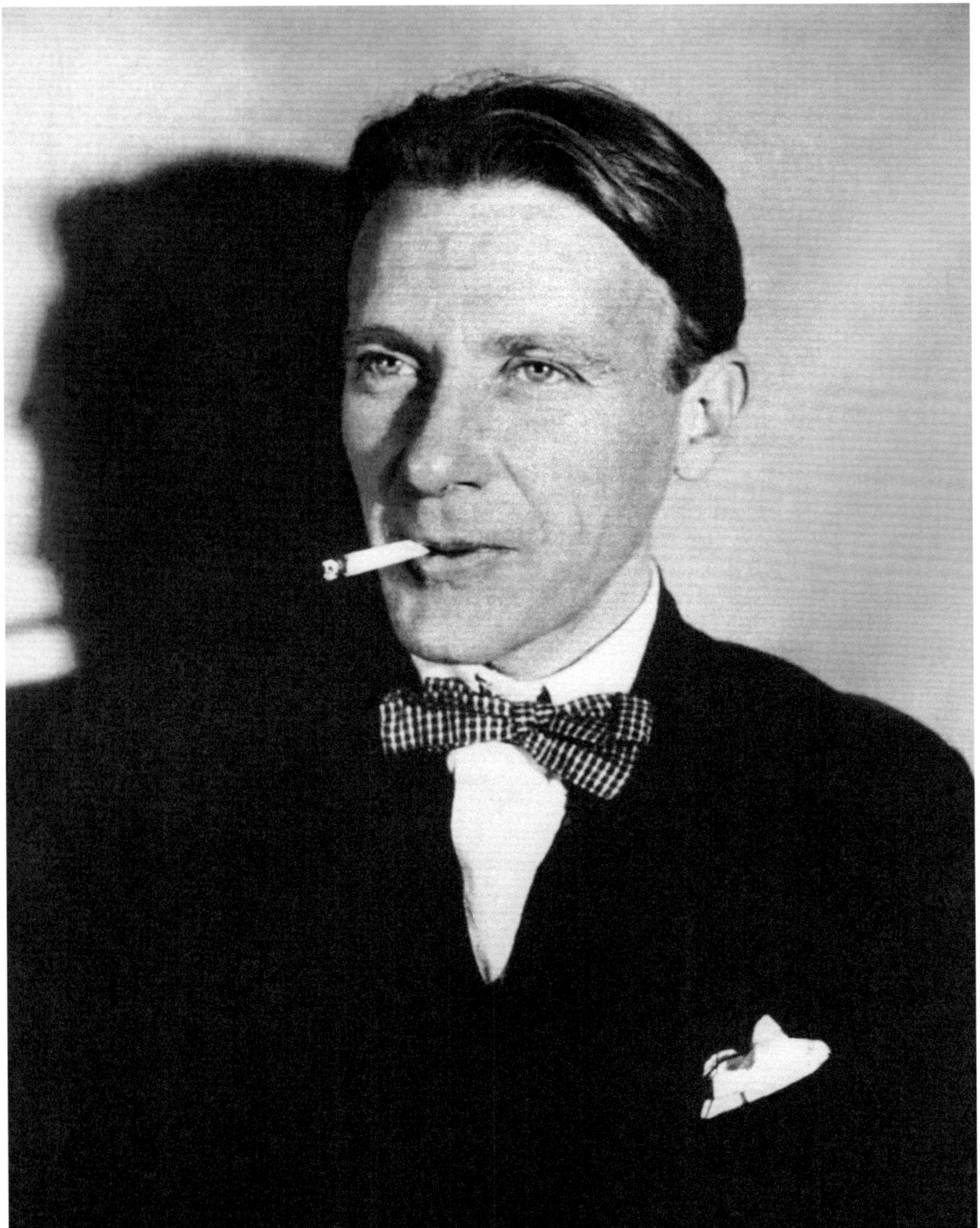

ANTHONY BURGESS

[John Anthony Burgess Wilson] born Manchester, UK, 1917; died London, 1993

by Martine Franck

Monte Carlo, 1985

Although by 1959 Anthony Burgess had produced three novels, he was far from being a full-time writer. Since 1954 he had lived with his wife, Lynne, in Malaya, where he worked as an education officer in the colonial service, but problems with his health forced him to return to England. The diagnosis was inauspicious: he had a brain tumour and just a year to live. Burgess, however, believed it was his duty to care and provide for his wife, who by then had become an alcoholic. There were two things he could do: compose music – his original ambitions had been musical – and write books. Music did not earn him any money, and books only slightly more. Nevertheless, he threw himself into writing, and by the end of 1962 he had completed a further seven novels. Even when it became clear that his brain was perfectly healthy, he continued to write at breakneck speed.

Among Burgess's first ten novels was one that was destined to change his life. *A Clockwork Orange* (1962) could never have passed unnoticed; indeed, its innovative use of language and challenging themes caused an immediate sensation. Almost a decade later, Stanley Kubrick's film version of 1971 would bring him global fame. Burgess's fortune was made, although it was too late for Lynne, who had died of cirrhosis of the liver in 1968. Life with his new Italian wife and son, however, was now secure.

Burgess continued to produce an uninterrupted flow of novels, critical essays and musical works. In 1973, in an interview in the *Paris Review,* he declared: 'It has been a sin to be prolific only since the Bloomsbury group … made it a point of good manners to produce, as it were, costively. … I've always written with great care and even some slowness. I've just put in rather more hours a day at the task than some writers seem able to.' Thanks to such discipline, by the time of his death in 1993 he had produced more than two hundred musical compositions; innumerable critical works, including a seminal study on James Joyce; and thirty-three novels, among them his Enderby quartet, the black comedy *M/F* (1971), an imagined biography of his father's family called *Abba Abba* (1977), a homage to George Orwell entitled *1985* (1978) and, above all, *Earthly Powers* (1980), which many consider to be his masterpiece.

Martine Franck, a Magnum photographer and creator of many memorable portraits of writers and artists, took this photo of Burgess in Monte Carlo. A used cup and saucer and a half-drunk glass of wine sit on the table before him as he smokes a cigar, a thoughtful expression on his face.

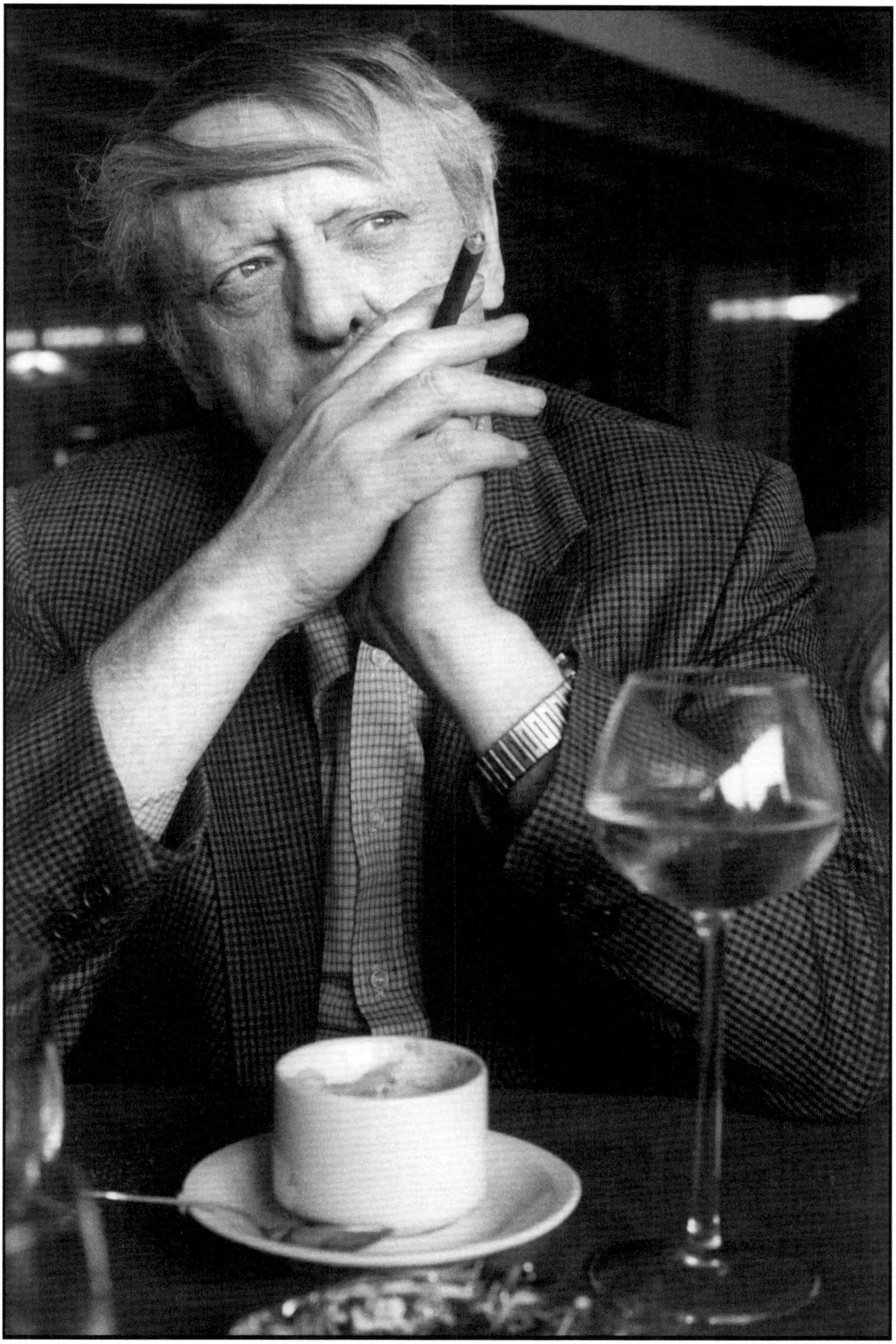

WILLIAM S. BURROUGHS

born St Louis, Missouri, 1914; died Lawrence, Kansas, 1997

by Mario Ruiz

New York, 1987

In 1943 William Seward Burroughs met the young writers Allen Ginsberg and Jack Kerouac, with whom he would later form the Beat Generation. At that time, however, he had no intention of becoming a writer himself. He was estranged from his family, who struggled to accept his homosexuality and drug dependency, and was living a marginal existence, often in trouble with the law over his use of heroin and morphine. In 1951, however, his life took a decisive turn: on a trip to Mexico City he shot and killed his wife, in circumstances that have remained unclear. He managed to avoid a jail sentence, and eventually took refuge in Tangier, Morocco. Although he had dabbled with writing since the mid-1940s, it was the tragic death of his wife that compelled him finally to become a writer of serious intent.

Tangier at the time was a cultural centre much visited by members of the American avant-garde, and Burroughs was soon joined by Kerouac and Ginsberg, who found him almost buried beneath a pile of disordered pages. Armed with a typewriter, his friends took control of the situation, putting his work into some kind of order and sending it off to the publishers. The result was *The Naked Lunch* (1959), and sudden fame. It was the launch of a literary career characterized by linguistic innovation and imagination, at times exploring the realms of science fiction, at others retreating to the dreamlike, visionary state of the 'Red Night' trilogy (*Cities of the Red Night*, 1981; *The Place of the Dead Roads*, 1983; and *The Western Lands*, 1987). His works have influenced the literary genre of cyberpunk, as well as authors such as J. G. Ballard and William Gibson, and the musicians Tom Waits and Kurt Cobain.

After the death of his friend Brion Gysin in the late 1980s, Burroughs's attention turned once again to painting. His favourite technique was to place cans or bottles of paint in front of the canvas and shoot them with a gun. The results became known as his 'shotgun paintings', and in 1987 they were exhibited for the first time in a gallery in New York. It was there that Burroughs was photographed by Mario Ruiz.

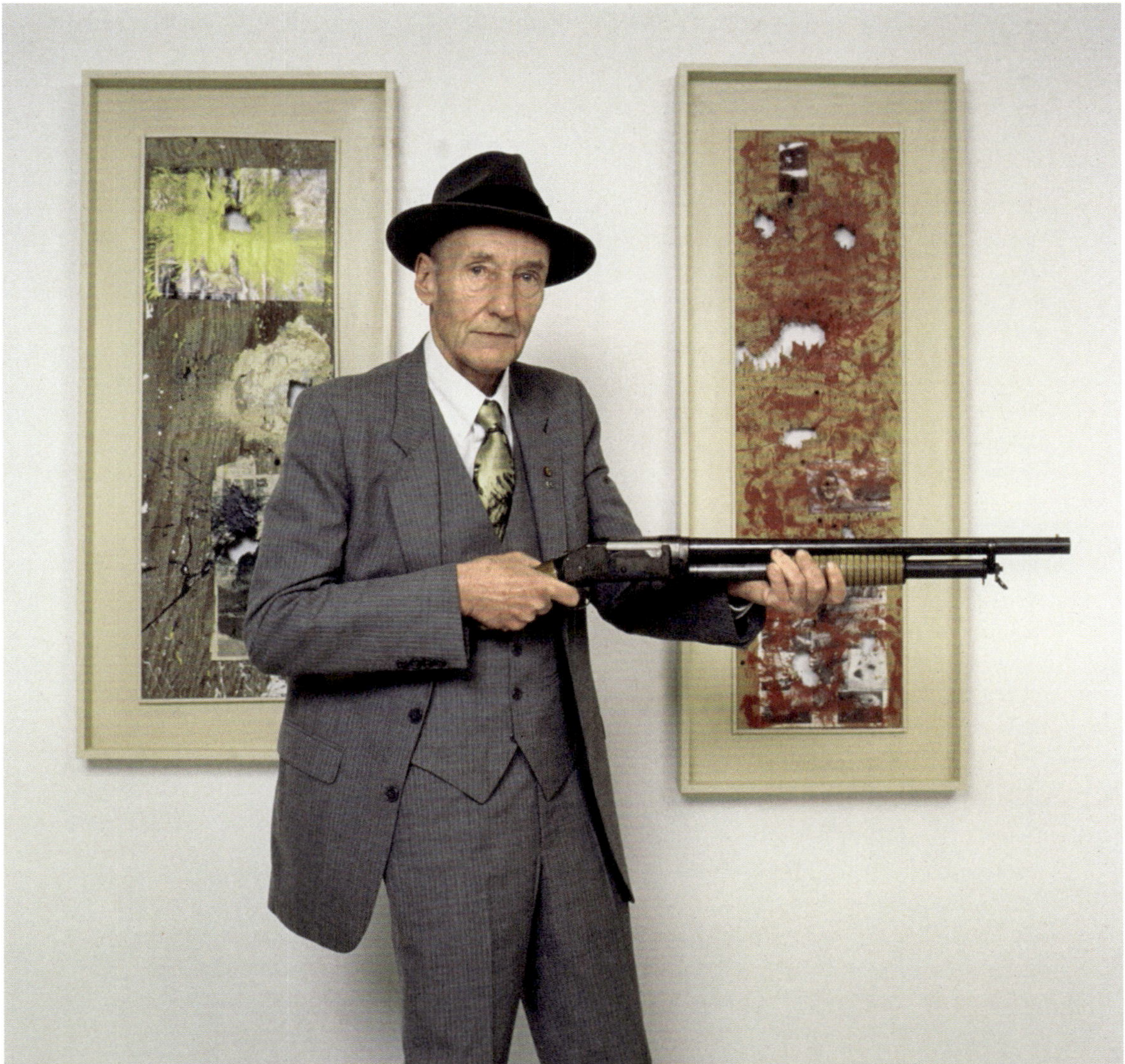

GUILLERMO CABRERA INFANTE

born Gibara, Cuba, 1929; died London, 2005

by Isolde Ohlbaum

Hamburg, Germany, 1989

The Cuban writer Guillermo Cabrera Infante was a committed enemy of totalitarianism. He first opposed the regime of former Cuban president Fulgencio Batista, who seized power for a second time in 1952 following a military coup, and later that of Fidel Castro. In 1965, however, having spent three years working as a cultural attaché in Brussels, he went into exile.

Cabrera Infante was born in Gibara, a town in the Oriente province of Cuba. In 1941 he moved with his family to Havana, where he studied medicine before deciding to pursue a literary career, initially writing about the cinema. In the 1950s he fell out of favour with the Batista regime and was forced to write under the pseudonym G. Caín (using a surname formed from the first two letters of each part of his actual surname). Initially a supporter of Fidel Castro and the Cuban Revolution of 1959, he was appointed director of the National Council of Culture and made deputy director of the newspaper *Revolución*, with special responsibility for its literary supplement. However, his relationship with the regime deteriorated when he led a campaign against the banning of a film made by his brother and Orlando Jiménez Leal. It was at this point that he was sent to Brussels. Following his decision to go into exile, he moved first to Madrid and then to London, where his literary career began in earnest.

In 1967, the same year in which Gabriel García Márquez's *One Hundred Years of Solitude* appeared, Cabrera Infante published *Three Trapped Tigers*, the story of three young men living in Havana in 1958. Cabrera Infante described the book as 'a gallery of voices, almost a museum of Cuban speech, in which generations to come could hear their ancestors'. Taking the form of a personal hymn to a much-loved city, a summing up of Cuban life told through the voices of its various characters, the book is characterized by unusual punctuation, teasing word games (as in its tongue-twister of a title) and formal experimentation. In the autobiographical novel *Infante's Inferno* (1979), Cabrera Infante examines the sexual character of the Cuban people before the revolution through the erotic adventures of a provincial adolescent who comes to live in the capital city. *Mea Cuba* (1991) is a collection of the author's political essays. Its title, an echo of the Latin phrase *mea culpa*, expresses how the author's feelings of guilt for having left Cuba are inextricably linked with the guilt of the land that forced him to go into exile.

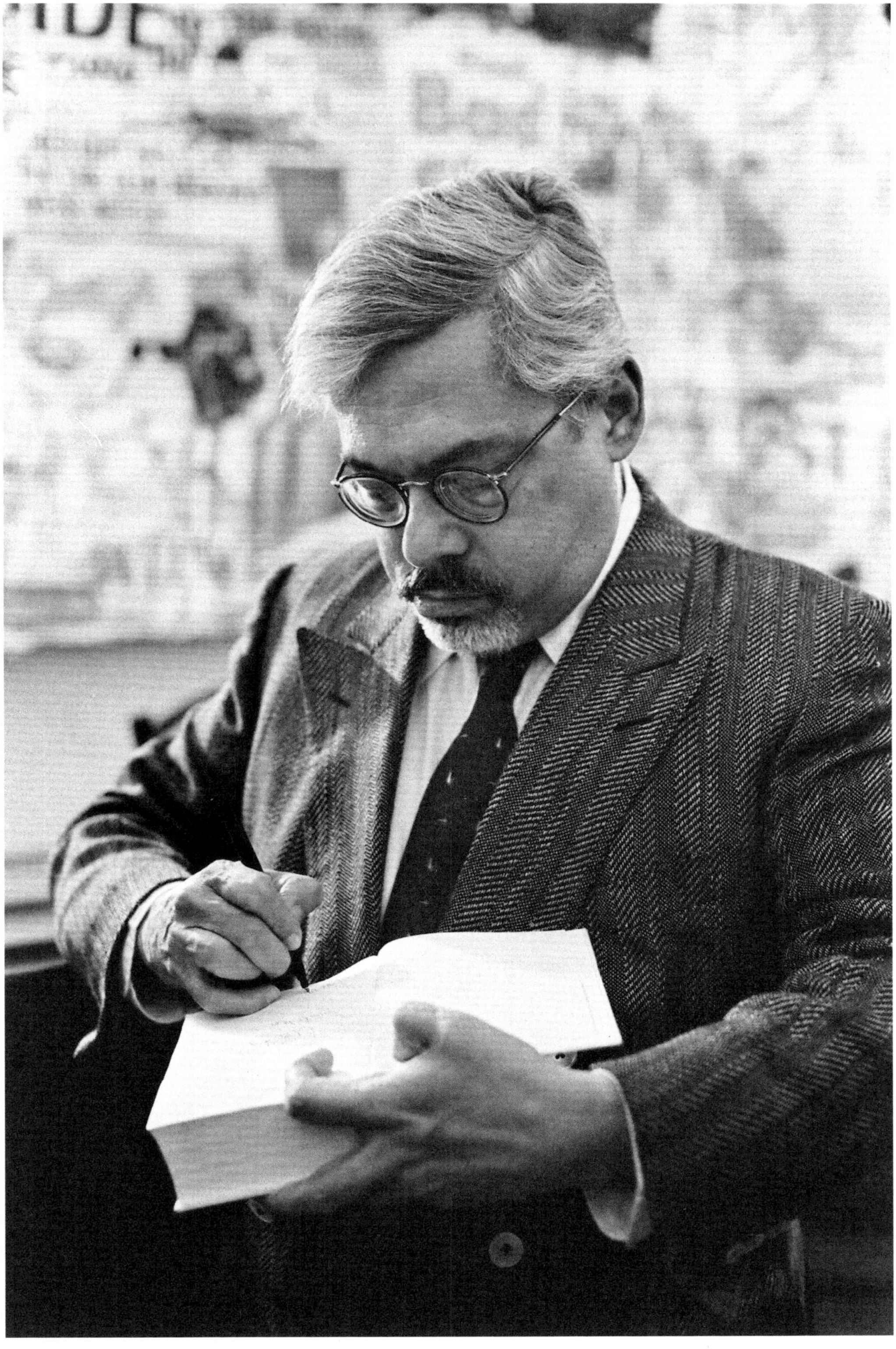

ITALO CALVINO

born Santiago de Las Vegas, Cuba, 1923; died Siena, Italy, 1985

by Gianni Giansanti

Rome, 1984

At the heart of Fedora, the city of grey stone from Italo Calvino's novel *Invisible Cities* (1972), there is a building made of metal with a glass sphere in every room. Inside each of these spheres is a bright blue city, a model of a different Fedora. In common with his fictitious city, Calvino himself had many faces, an idea expressed in Gianni Giansanti's photographic portrait of the writer.

As was the case for many authors of Calvino's generation, neo-Realism was his first interest. Inspired by his involvement in the Italian Resistance during the Second World War, he felt it was his duty to create stories inspired by his recent experiences. He began with *The Path of the Nest of Spiders* (1947), a coming-of-age novel set amid the fight against Fascism. In the years that followed, however, Calvino began to explore the limits of Realism and of his own imagination, experimenting with form and narrative structure in such short-story collections as *Cosmicomics* (1965) and *t zero* (1967). By this time, language had become more political, and Calvino, who was politically engaged himself, was happy to explore the way in which language could be given alternative meanings. He was, above all, a writer who loved to try new things, combining different genres and eventually developing a narrative form akin to a logic exercise or a game of chess.

As his intellectual and cultural stature grew, his prose became lighter and more elusive. In 1984 Calvino was invited to give a series of six lectures at Harvard University during the following academic year. He became obsessed by the writing of these lectures. Choosing the new millennium as his subject, he decided to dedicate his first lecture to the idea of lightness. With reference to his own work, he wrote: 'I have tried to remove weight, sometimes from people, sometimes from heavenly bodies, sometimes from cities; above all I have tried to remove weight from the structure of stories and from language.' The subjects of his other lectures were quickness, exactitude, visibility, multiplicity and consistency. However, the lectures were never delivered: in September 1985, just one month before he was due to leave for the USA, Calvino died of a cerebral haemorrhage.

Following his death, Calvino's lecture notes were collected into a seminal book, *Six Memos for the Next Millennium* (1988), which was both a recapitulation of a life spent reflecting on literature and a series of lucid proposals for the new millennium.

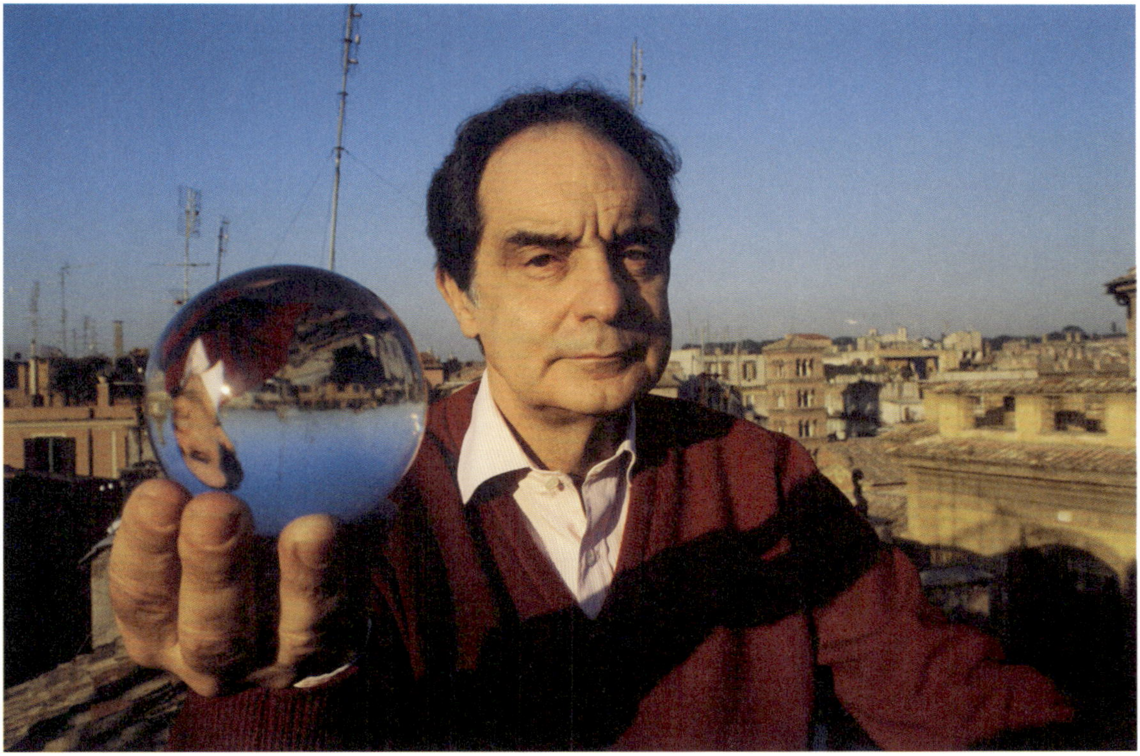

ALBERT CAMUS

born Dréan, Algeria, 1913; died Villeblevin, France, 1960

by Henri Cartier-Bresson

Paris, 1944

Albert Camus's importance has grown steadily as humankind has slowly become conscious of, and has been compelled to accept, its own fundamental inadequacy. This inadequacy is seen most clearly when humankind attempts to resolve the dilemmas that arise from its existence and the nature of human society. His writing speaks of both the Absurd and the need for human solidarity – necessities if humanity is to live and accept life.

The protagonist of *The Stranger* (1942) is an outsider who believes in nothing other than himself; he is a stranger to the world, and follows his own logic in an extreme, even heroic way. Conversely, the protagonists of Camus's multi-layered novel *The Plague* (1947) – which tells the story of a shared disaster, an inexplicable epidemic – learn that by suffering together it is possible to find meaning. The decision of the protagonists to defy the arbitrary, unpredictable plague is echoed in Camus's book-length essay *The Rebel* (1951), which encapsulated his whole philosophical approach with its famous motto: 'I rebel – therefore we exist.'

During the Second World War and the immediate post-war period, existentialism arose from the background of global tragedy to emerge as the dominant contemporary philosophy, and Camus became a beacon for many young writers, artists and militants. His radical position, culturally and politically, led him to criticize both Western capitalism and the Soviet Union, and precipitated breaks with friends, such as Jean-Paul Sartre.

Camus was also the author of several plays, including *Caligula*, which he began in 1938 (although it would not be published until 1944), and *The Just Assassins* (1950). He died aged forty-six in a car accident, three years after being awarded the 1957 Nobel Prize. *The First Man*, an incomplete autobiographical novel and his final masterpiece, was published posthumously in 1994. Despite his early death, Camus's reputation and his influence have continued, the persistent popularity of his work suggesting that the human conditions it examined are just as fundamental and relevant today.

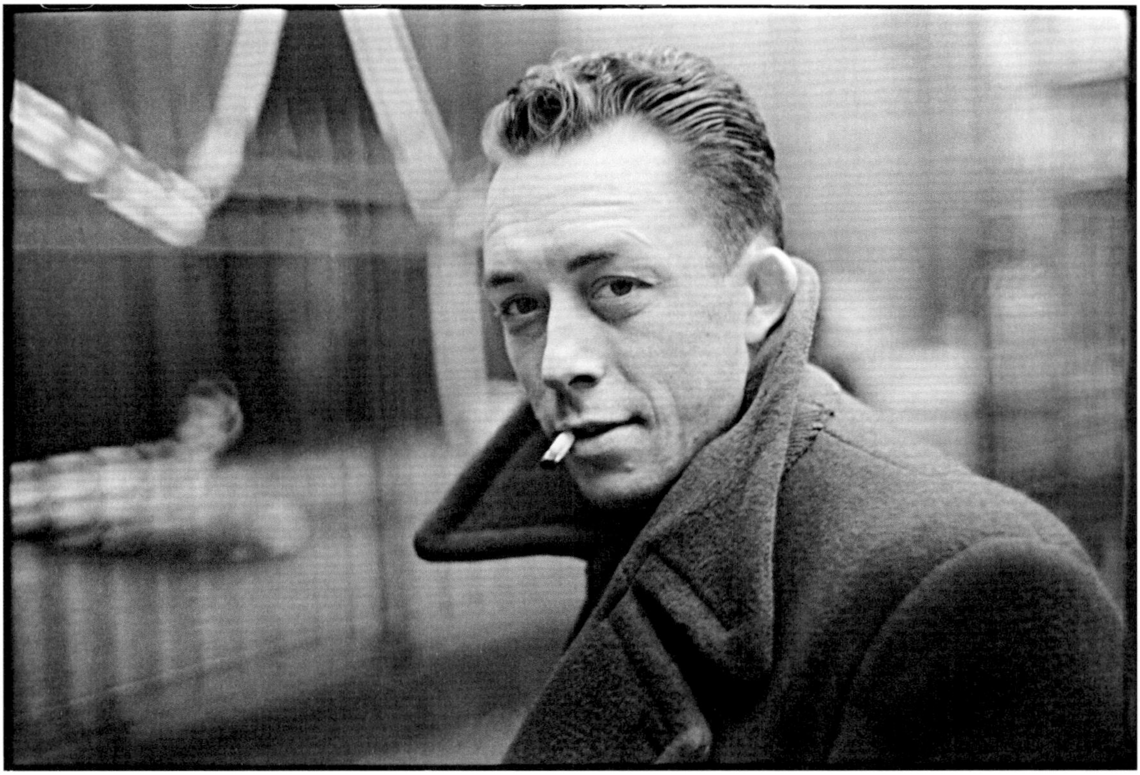

ELIAS CANETTI

born Ruse, Bulgaria, 1905; died Zurich, 1994

by Isolde Ohlbaum

Munich, 1978

In *The Tongue Set Free* (1977), the first volume of his memoirs, Elias Canetti remembers the city of his birth, Ruse in Bulgaria, as a melting pot of peoples, cultures, languages and religions. He was born there to a Sephardic family, and his mother tongue was the ancient Castilian of Spain's Jewish population. His memoir also embraces the other places in the writer's life, from Paris and London to Zurich, Manchester and Vienna. Canetti could speak several languages, but it was in German that he became one of the greatest authors of the twentieth century. His first book arrived with something of a bang, or rather a bedazzlement, as the original German title, *Die Blendung* (The blinding), indicates.

Translated into English as *Auto-da-Fé*, Canetti's novel was published in 1935 after a period of four years in which the former chemistry student had had his manuscript rejected by every publisher to whom he had sent it. As he himself recalls, the first thing he did once it had been printed was to send a copy to the German novelist Thomas Mann; after a few days it was returned to Canetti with a note explaining that, at the moment, '[Mann's] strength was not sufficient to the task' (the German acquired a copy a short time later and became one of Canetti's most enthusiastic admirers). *Auto-da-Fé* is an extremely powerful book, a grotesque and tragic human comedy of contemporary psychoses. As the Italian writer Claudio Magris has said, '*Auto-da-Fé* has all the ugliness of great books that concede nothing, do nothing to soften our anxiety or avoid death, do not round off any corners and hit you like a fist; it is one of the greatest books written on the fiendish nature of the twentieth century and of life itself.'

Such praise alone would have been enough for the work to win the Nobel Prize and secure Canetti's reputation as a writer, but during the years in which the book was being published, he began to reflect on another subject, an enigma that obsessed him throughout his life: the gravitational pull exercised by the crowd and its relationship with power. *Crowds and Power* appeared in 1960 after some thirty years of work and proved to be not only a great sociological and anthropological essay but also a profoundly poetic and literary work. In 1981 Canetti finally received the Nobel Prize, 'for writings marked by a broad outlook, a wealth of ideas and artistic power'.

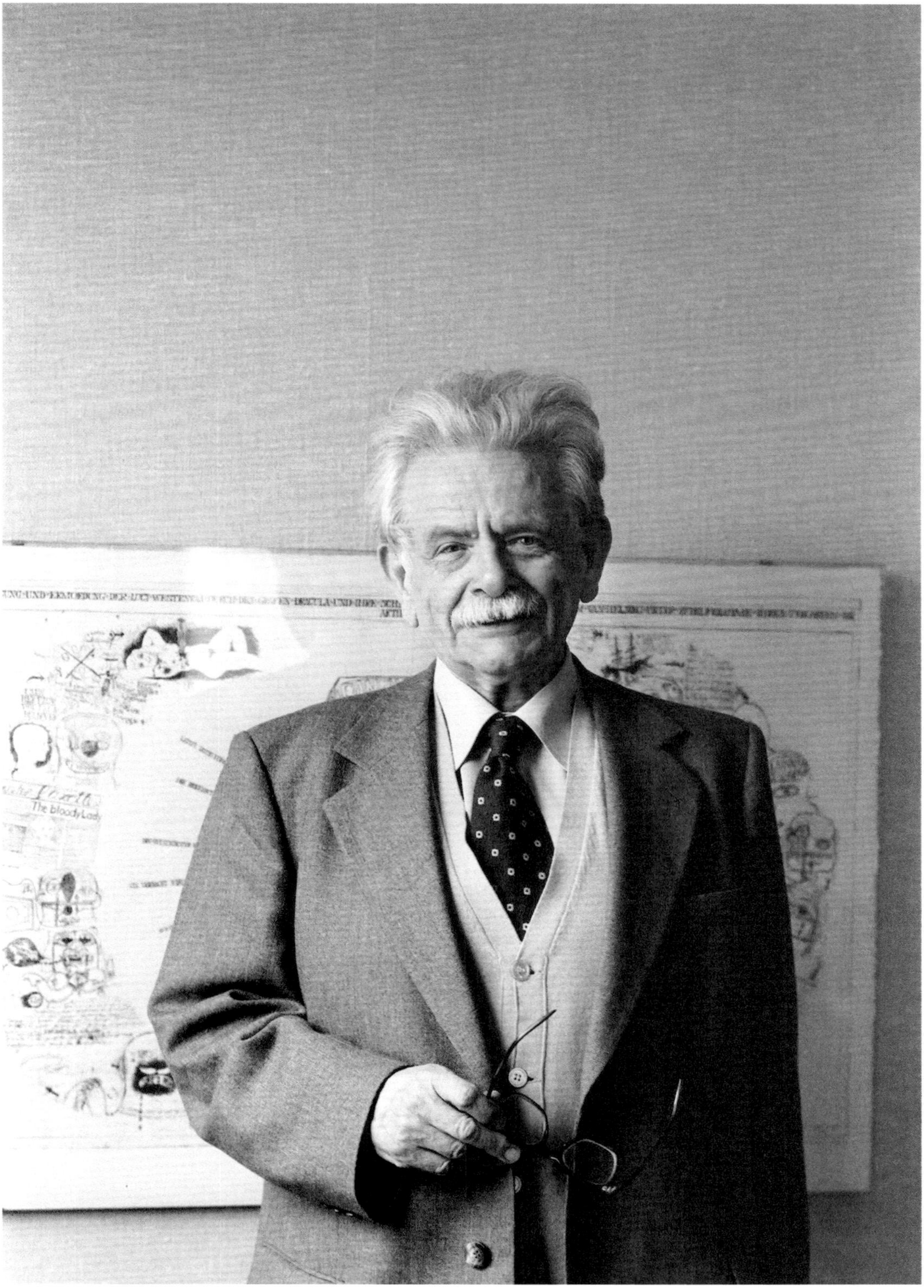
The bloodyLady

TRUMAN CAPOTE

[Truman Streckfus Persons] born New Orleans, Louisiana, 1924; died Bel Air, Los Angeles, 1984

by Richard Avedon

New York, 1955

Abandoned by his father and left to live with relatives by his mother, Truman Capote experienced an unhappy childhood. His first novel, *Other Voices, Other Rooms*, was an attempt to exorcise the demons of the past. It was published in 1948, by which time Capote had been living in New York for several years, having moved there to live with his mother and her second husband. The deprivations of his childhood had led him to seek solace in literature from an early age, and he began writing fiction while still a child. As he grew older he became something of an eccentric and a loner, although more by circumstance than by choice. A second novel, *Grass Harp* (1951), was also dedicated to his childhood, in particular the tree house he had loved as a boy.

In New York Capote invented a new identity for himself, taking on his stepfather's surname. He was clearly a very gifted writer, and in the mid-1940s he produced a string of short stories for such magazines as *Atlantic Monthly* and *Harper's Bazaar*. He styled himself as a dandy and a socialite, and was a great favourite among actors and singers. His most famous work is arguably *Breakfast at Tiffany's* (1958), although the Holly Golightly of the novel is a rather different character from the one immortalized by Audrey Hepburn in the film adaptation of 1961. The ending of the film was also rewritten, to give it a more positive slant.

In 1966 Capote published *In Cold Blood*, a fictionalized account of the true-life murder of an entire Kansas family by two ex-convicts. Capote spent several years in Kansas interviewing all those involved in the case, including local residents and investigators, in an attempt to understand what drove the murderers to commit the crime. The book, which first appeared as a four-part serial in the *New Yorker*, gave rise to a new genre of literature: the 'non-fiction novel', or work of faction. It is widely acknowledged as one of the best books of its type ever written.

In 1959 Capote collaborated with the photographer Richard Avedon on the book *Observations*, a collection of photographs of some of the twentieth century's most famous figures. In the preface, Capote describes Avedon as 'a man with gifted eyes', and this is clearly evident in this photograph of the writer. It is a dreamlike, elegant and feminine portrait, reflecting Capote's enigmatic and ambiguous character.

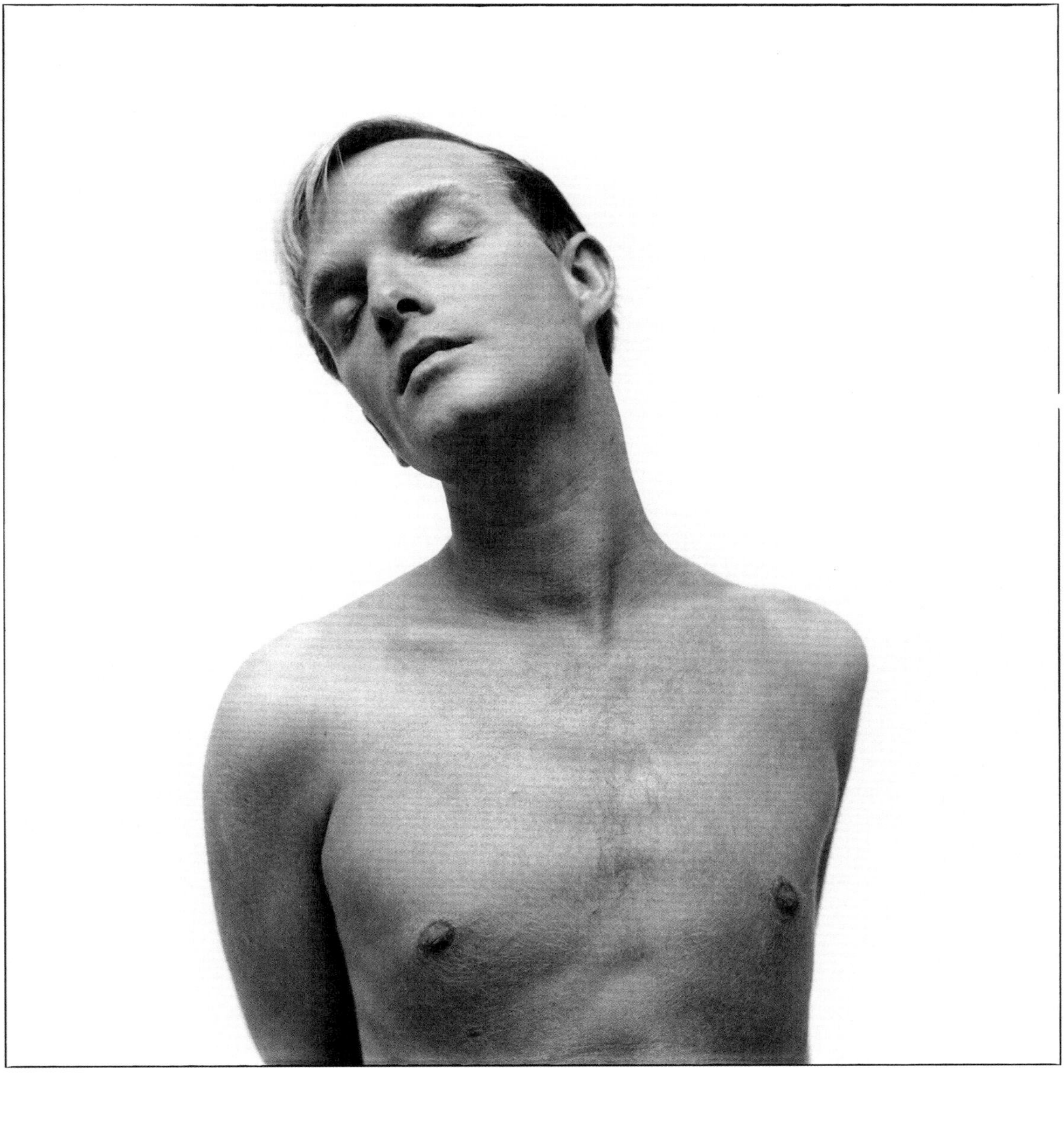

ALEJO CARPENTIER

born Lausanne, Switzerland, 1904; died Paris, 1980

by Sara Facio

Paris, 1968

With a French father and a Russian mother, Alejo Carpentier's family had an international outlook even before moving to Cuba. At the age of seventeen, he began to write for newspapers, contributing articles on literature, music and the theatre. Carpentier soon became involved in political activities and, in 1928, after several months in prison, he left Cuba for France, where he joined the Surrealist movement. A later journey to Mexico allowed him to discover Latin America, which he described as 'the magical reality'.

Carpentier did not see it as the writer's role to invent the fantastical, but rather to describe the magical reality that surrounded him or her – and this led the author to rediscover and rework the mythology of Latin America. This process included inventing words and adapting narrative forms to fit a continent whose story has always been told in other people's terms. The style he chose was baroque; a style that had been imported by the continent's colonizers but that had subsequently been reinterpreted in a regional mode. The baroque could include everything, from the real to the marvellous and the magical. According to Carpentier, the Americas were the only place where different eras still coexisted.

This explains why Carpentier's characters inhabit worlds that are simultaneously real and marvellous, their stories interweaving diverse periods and epic adventures. The protagonist of *The Lost Steps* (1953), for example, is a musician who takes part in an expedition up the Orinoco in a search for indigenous instruments. The voyage is also a journey back in time, back to the world's infancy, back towards magical reality. A similar concept plays out in *Journey to the Seed* (from the 1958 'War of Time' trilogy), in which the main character travels back through his life, past deathbed, past childhood, to his mother's womb. Carpentier combines his baroque style with music in *Baroque Concerto* (1974). In this tale, a wealthy eighteenth-century Mexican nobleman sets out for the *carnivàle* in Venice; the first stage of his journey takes him to Havana, and he then travels on to Spain and finally to Venice where he meets Vivaldi, Handel and Scarlatti. The novel's blend of epochs, costumes, colours and sounds reaches a crescendo in a frenzied baroque concert.

Argentinian photographer Sara Facio, who has photographed many of the greatest exponents of Latin American culture, took this picture. It shows Carpentier walking through Paris's elegant Étoile district, where he was working as an adviser on cultural affairs at the Cuban embassy.

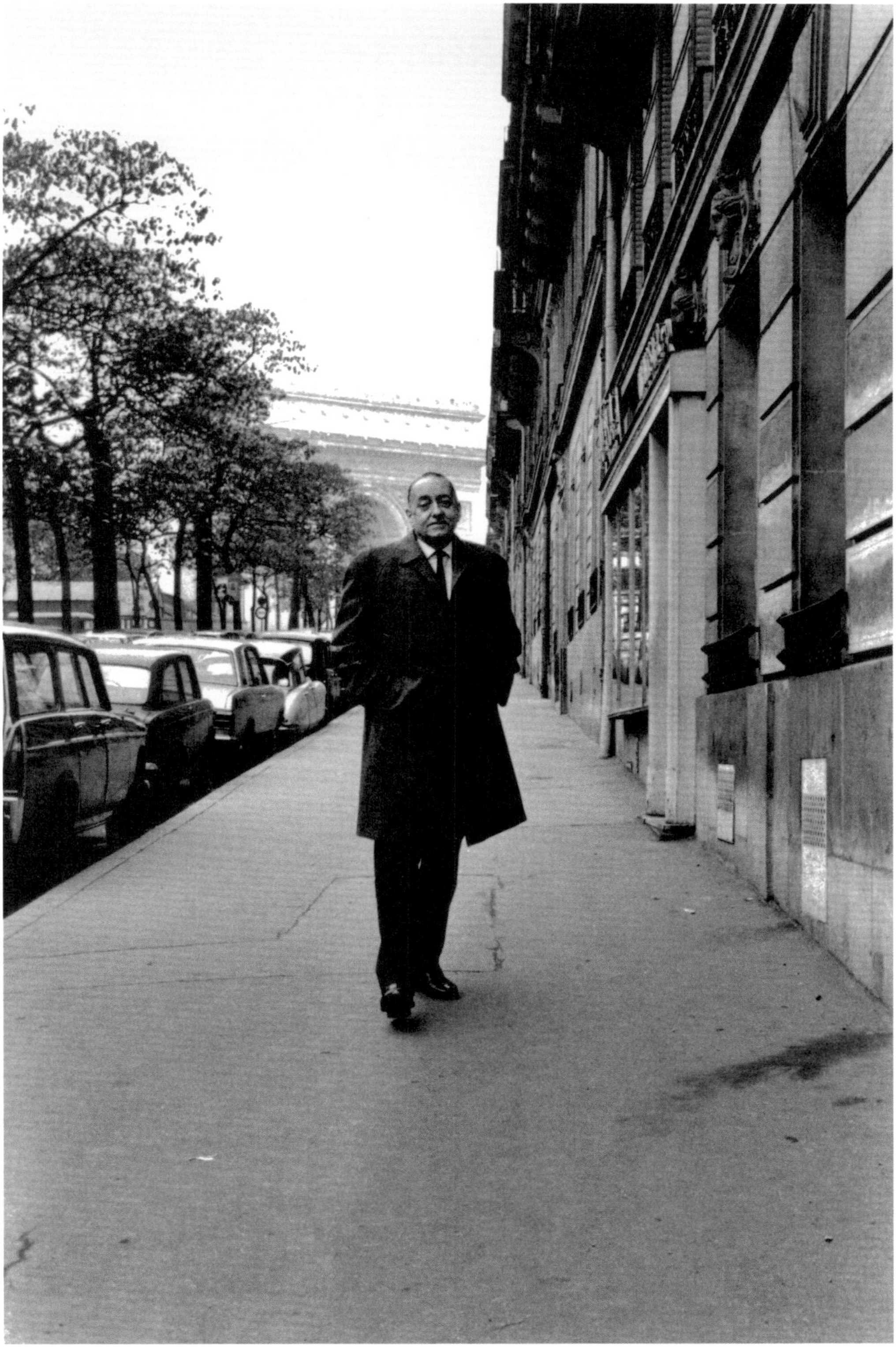

EMMANUEL CARRÈRE

born Paris, 1957

by Lise Sarfati

Paris, 2004

After producing several impressive but rather structurally orthodox works, which included *The Moustache* (1986) and *Class Trip* (1995), Emmanuel Carrère changed direction with *The Adversary* (2000), setting off down a path that has led to him being acknowledged as one of the greatest French writers of the last few decades. Together with Michel Houellebecq, he is possibly the only author who has been able to unite both public and critical opinion so successfully. By using novelistic framing and journalistic reconstruction to tell the story of Jean-Claude Romand – the notorious mass murderer imprisoned in 1996 for having killed his family – *The Adversary* walks a fine line between fiction and reality.

Carrère employed the same technique in his subsequent books, beginning with *A Russian Novel* (2007), an account of his own life and the story of his family constructed from a journal he had been keeping in Russian (Carrère is of Russian descent on his mother's side); the text was originally published in *Le Monde,* under the title *L'usage du Monde* (The way of the World). *In Other Lives but Mine* (2009), Carrère intertwines the tragedy of the tsunami that devastated South East Asia in 2004 and the death of his partner's sister from cancer. Finally, *Limonov* (2011), perhaps his best book to date, tells the story of Eduard Limonov, an eccentric Russian writer and political dissident who, after many mishaps, has ended up leading an ambiguous anti-Putinist movement made up of resurgent nationalists and youthful rebels. With each successive work, Carrère has succeeded in reviving an interest in dramatic storytelling in the form of elegant, sophisticated literature.

In her portrait of Carrère, the French photographer Lise Sarfati has placed the writer in the centre of the frame. He is depicted – as he often portrays his own characters – within a bare, almost banal domestic setting, his hands resting in his pockets. The image has asense of frozen action, as if it were a still taken from a slightly faded video, creating a sense of alienation.

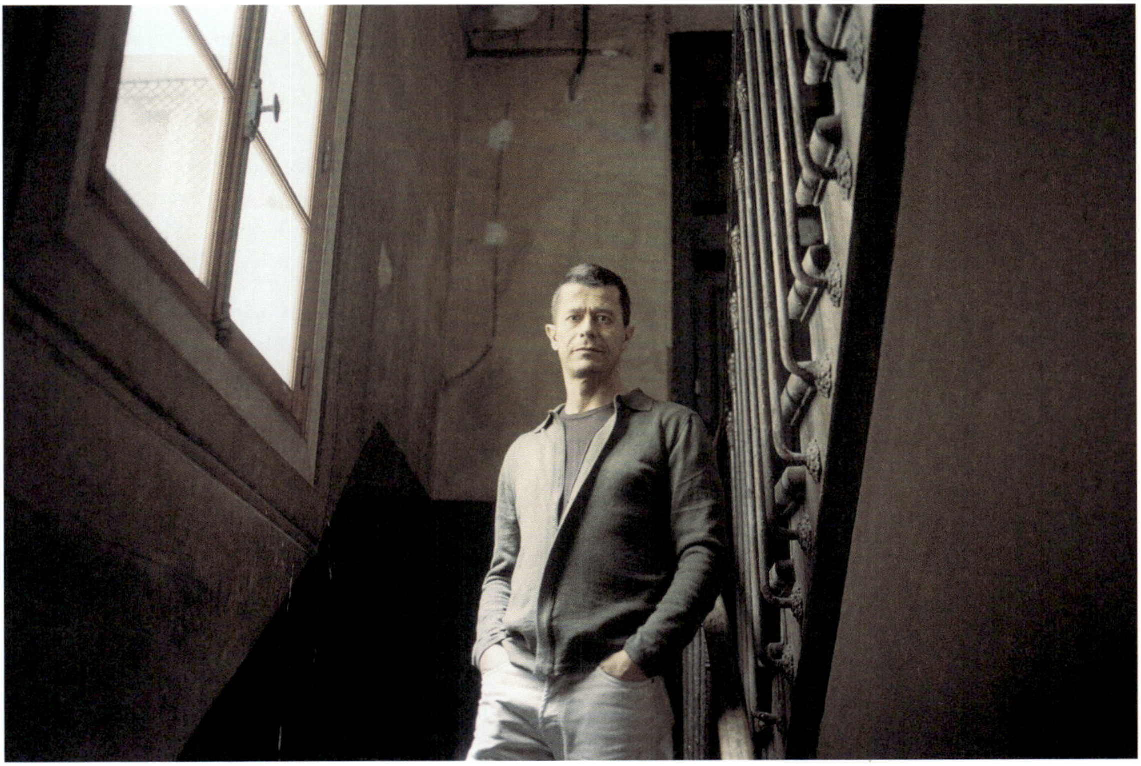

RAYMOND CARVER

born Clatskanie, Oregon, 1938; died Port Angeles, Washington, 1988

by Bob Adelman

Port Angeles, Washington, 1984

Raymond Carver's literary career was shaped by a life full of drama. His adolescent years were marked by a sense of inadequacy, financial hardship, alcoholism and a troubled marriage that would end in divorce – all experiences that he would later draw on in his writing. In the last ten years of his life, he liberated himself from alcohol dependency and married his second wife, the writer Tess Gallagher. He died aged only fifty, having published a relatively small but highly significant body of work, including short-story collections and volumes of poetry. Today he is regarded as one of the major voices of American literature, a writer who helped to breathe new life into the short story. *The Times* dubbed him 'the American Chekhov'.

Carver grew up as an unhappy, overweight child in a rough, working-class family, and turned to alcohol in his teenage years. He married his first wife, Maryann Burk, when he was just nineteen (she was sixteen and pregnant), and was the father of two children by the time he was twenty-one. He had a variety of casual jobs, but suffered from depression and recurrent bouts of alcoholism. In his few moments of serenity he would write, an endeavour in which he was encouraged by Maryann, who bought him his first typewriter and suggested he attend a creative writing course taught by John Gardner, writer and professor at Chico State University, California. It was there that Carver began to develop his characteristically minimalist style. Drawing on the heritage of Ernest Hemingway's laconic, precise prose, he perfected an incisive and poetic narrative tone with which to convey American provincial life. Robert Altman adapted several of his short stories for the film *Short Cuts* (1993), one of the most memorable portraits of life in the USA at the end of the millennium.

In 1984 the photographer Bob Adelman created a photographic biography of the writer entitled *Carver Country*, which details aspects of his life in and around his home in Port Angeles, on the Pacific coast of Washington State.

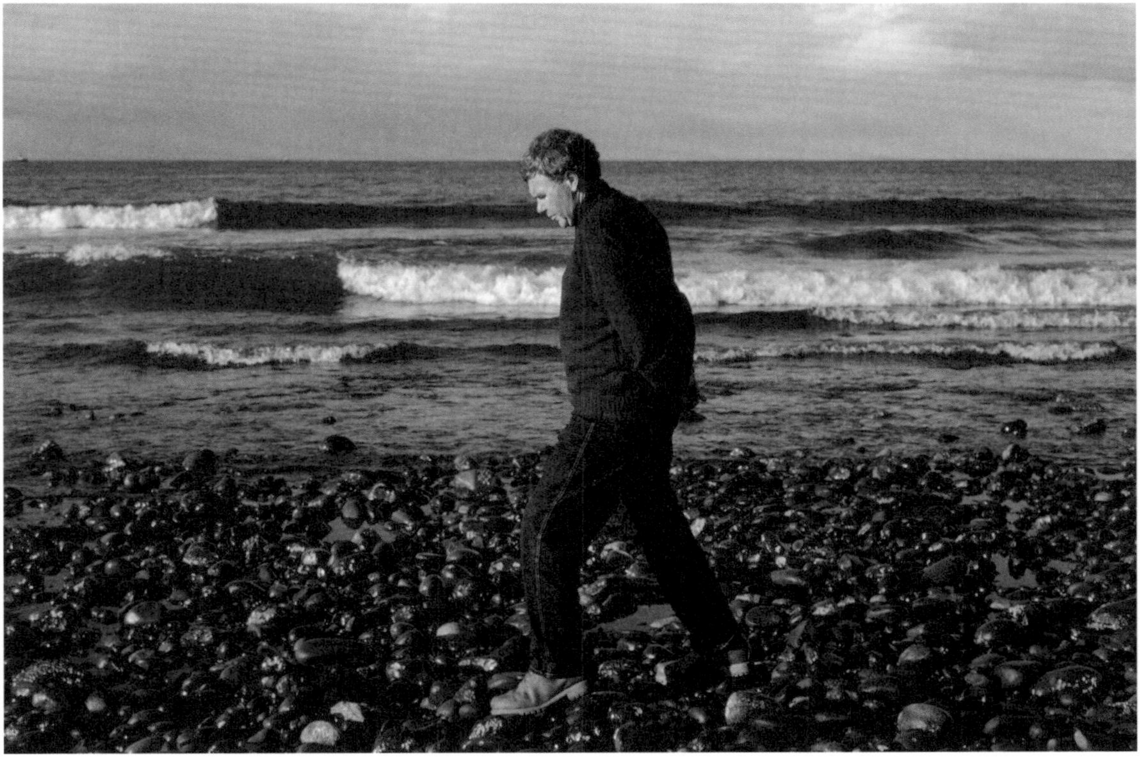

LOUIS-FERDINAND CÉLINE

[Louis-Ferdinand Destouches] born Courbevoie, France, 1894; died Meudon, France, 1961

by Bernard Lipnitzki

Meudon, France, c. 1955

Louis-Ferdinand Céline spent much of his childhood in the 2nd arrondissement of Paris, on a dingy shopping street known as Passage Choiseul, where his mother worked as a lace-maker. This microcosm of daily life had a profound effect on the young Céline, who would later become one of the greatest French writers of the twentieth century.

Céline was a man of contrasts and extremes. A qualified doctor, he devoted much of his writing to the Parisian underclass, while his early medical articles not only show a concern for the health of the working classes but also openly support the sanitary inspection of factories. However, his first novel, *Journey to the End of the Night* (1932), the story of an unsavoury slum doctor during and after the First World War, earned him the reputation of a right-wing misanthrope. He was also responsible for writing many strongly anti-Semitic pamphlets during the 1930s, and was convicted of collaboration with the Nazis during the Second World War.

Many attempts have been made to understand both Céline and his work. Some have suggested that he may have suffered from an obsessive and psychotic need to cure all the ills of the world, or that he was some kind of mythomaniac driven by a need for scandal and controversy, intent only on mocking the human race. Others have insinuated that he was simply a disagreeable character, whose Fascist tendencies were the result of an outmoded, bourgeois attitude, somewhat detached from reality. Whatever his personal inclinations, as a writer he is widely credited for his stylistic innovation and modernizing use of language and punctuation, and both *Journey to the End of the Night* and *Death on Credit* (1936) have secured him a place in literary history.

Although better known as a fashion photographer, Bernard Lipnitzki took this photograph of Céline in 1955, at his house in Meudon, in the suburbs of Paris. The house lies at the top of a small hill, and was bought by the writer on his return to France from Denmark, where he had been living in exile since the end of the Second World War. He shared the house with his wife, Lucette, a parrot named Toto and three dogs.

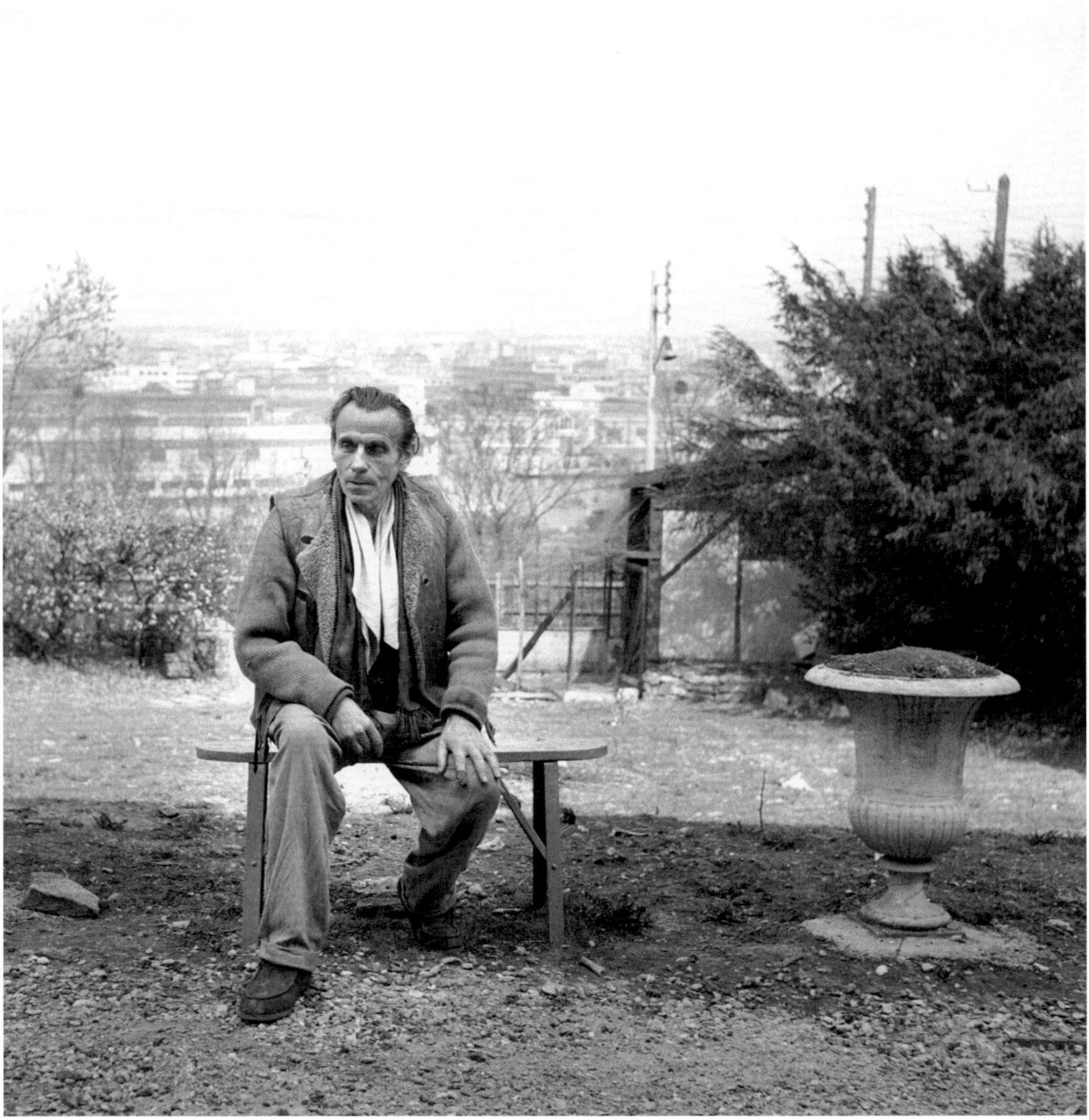

JAVIER CERCAS

born Ibahernando, Spain, 1962

by Geraint Lewis

Edinburgh, UK, 2011

For some, the history of Spain in the twentieth century is closely associated with those individuals whom the German writer Hans Magnus Enzensberger defined as 'the heroes of retreat': men and women who are distinguished by having taken courageous decisions in the face of adversity. This is the position from which Javier Cercas re-examines Spain's past, taking his inspiration from real personalities in the hope of bringing about a sense of closure.

Cercas's fifth novel, *Soldiers of Salamis* (2001), was inspired by a true, although minor, incident that took place towards the end of the Spanish Civil War, when the Republicans were in disarray. Rafael Sánchez Mazas, a Spanish writer and a leader of Franco's right-wing Falange, had been found by a Republican soldier after escaping from a firing squad, but the soldier decided not to give the writer away, thus saving his life. In Cercas's novel, a journalist begins to investigate this incident by concentrating on the soldier whose gesture of clemency had allowed a leading figure of Franco's government to live. The journalist is determined to give a name to the man who made this choice, but, above all, he wants to ask him 'what he thought that morning, in the forest, after the execution, when he recognized Sánchez Mazas and looked him in the eye. To ask him what he saw in those eyes. Why he spared him, why he didn't give him away.'

Similar questions of motivation lie at the heart of *The Anatomy of a Moment* (2009), Cercas's non-fiction account of the attempted *golpe*, or coup, of 23 February 1981. At 6.31 p.m. that day, 350 members of the Spanish parliament were taken hostage by a faction of the Civil Guard led by Lieutenant Colonel Antonio Tejero Molina. The politicians quickly took cover under their desks, with the exception of three men: the prime minister, Adolfo Suárez; his deputy, Manuel Gutiérrez Mellado; and the leader of the Communist Party, Santiago Carrillo. Suárez had remained standing in symbolic defence of democracy and its institutions, although there was nothing in his political career to suggest that he would ever have behaved in this way. In an act of measured reflection, Cercas's book centres on this moment of defiance and investigates what prompted such a courageous gesture.

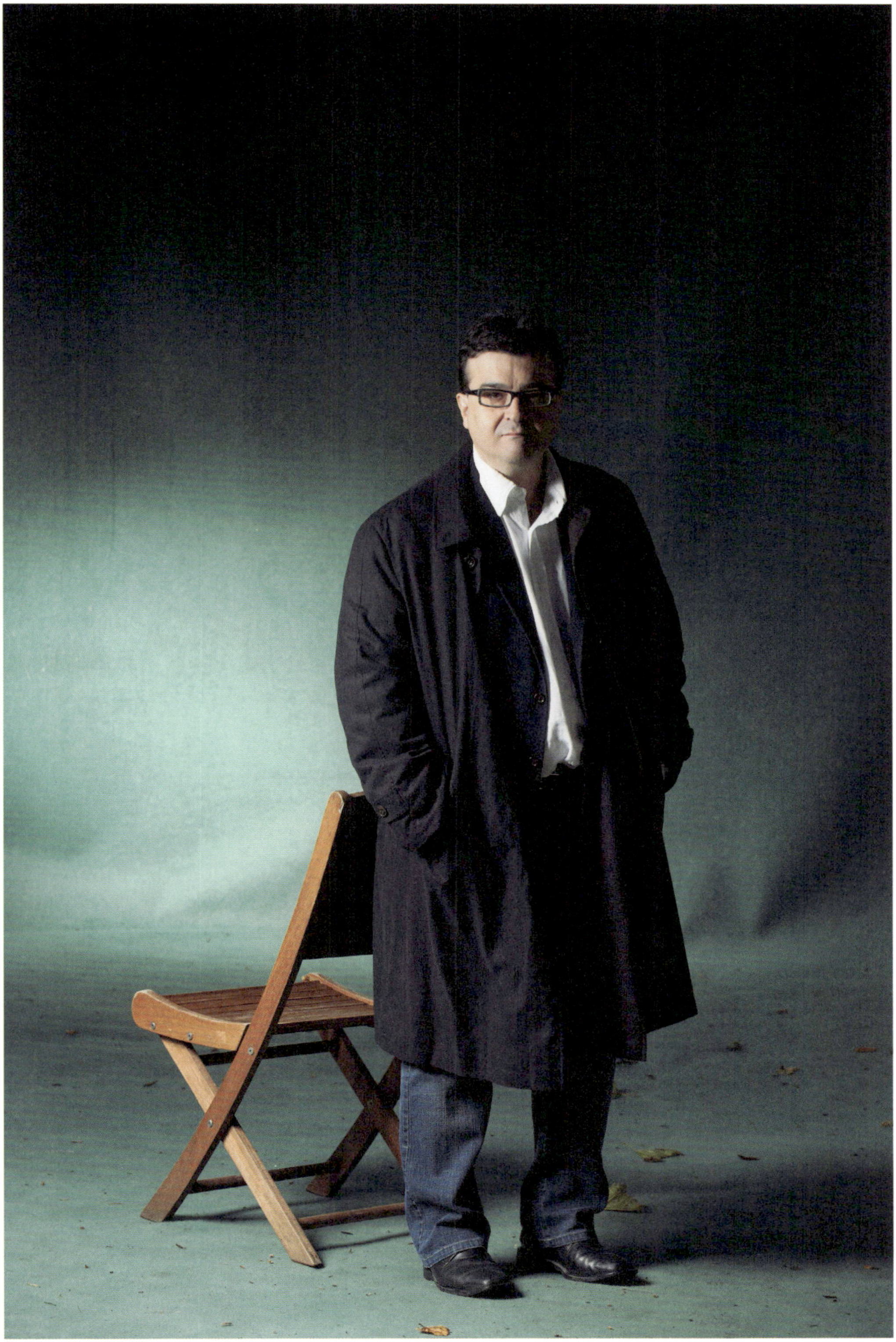

RAYMOND CHANDLER

born Chicago, 1888; died La Jolla, California, 1959

by George Platt Lynes

La Jolla, California, c. 1947

In 1932 Raymond Chandler was dismissed from his executive position at an oil company on account of behaviour that was deemed unacceptable, and had included alcoholism and regular absences. While looking for a new job, he started reading the popular pulp fiction magazine *Black Mask*, in which he discovered the work of Dashiell Hammett. Inspired to create his own private detective, Philip Marlowe, he thus became one of the founding members of the hard-boiled school of detective fiction, along with Hammett and James M. Cain. Chandler himself inspired many writers, including Chester Himes, Elmore Leonard and James Ellroy, as well as film directors such as Howard Hawks and Quentin Tarantino. Indeed, the cinematic adaptations of his books, together with those of the work of the American writer Cornell Woolrich, were instrumental in shaping the film noir genre.

Chandler wrote a total of seven books of detective fiction, including *The Big Sleep* (1939), *Farewell, My Lovely* (1940) and *The Long Goodbye* (1953), as well as numerous short stories and an important essay on the genre entitled 'The Simple Art of Murder' (1944). He also wrote a number of screenplays, but did not take the film business too seriously: 'If my books had been any worse, I should not have been invited to Hollywood, and if they had been any better, I should not have come.' Chandler set most of his stories in Los Angeles, his home for many years, prompting the American writer S. J. Perelman to describe him as 'the major social historian' of the city. It was also the place where he met and fell in love with Cissy Pascal, a married woman eighteen years his senior. His mother, Florence, disapproved of the relationship, and although Cissy had divorced her husband, it was not until after Florence's death that she and Chandler felt able to marry. They stayed together until Cissy's death in 1954, an event that devastated the author and led to severe bouts of depression and alcoholism. He died in La Jolla, on the Californian coast, in 1959.

George Platt Lynes took this photograph of Chandler on the beach near his home in La Jolla. Lynes was a great fan of literature, and in his youth he had approached Chandler with the idea of putting together a series of photographs of writers and artists for an exhibition in New Jersey. Shortly thereafter he had become a commercial photographer for *Harper's Bazaar*, but he continued to photograph his favourite writers throughout his career.

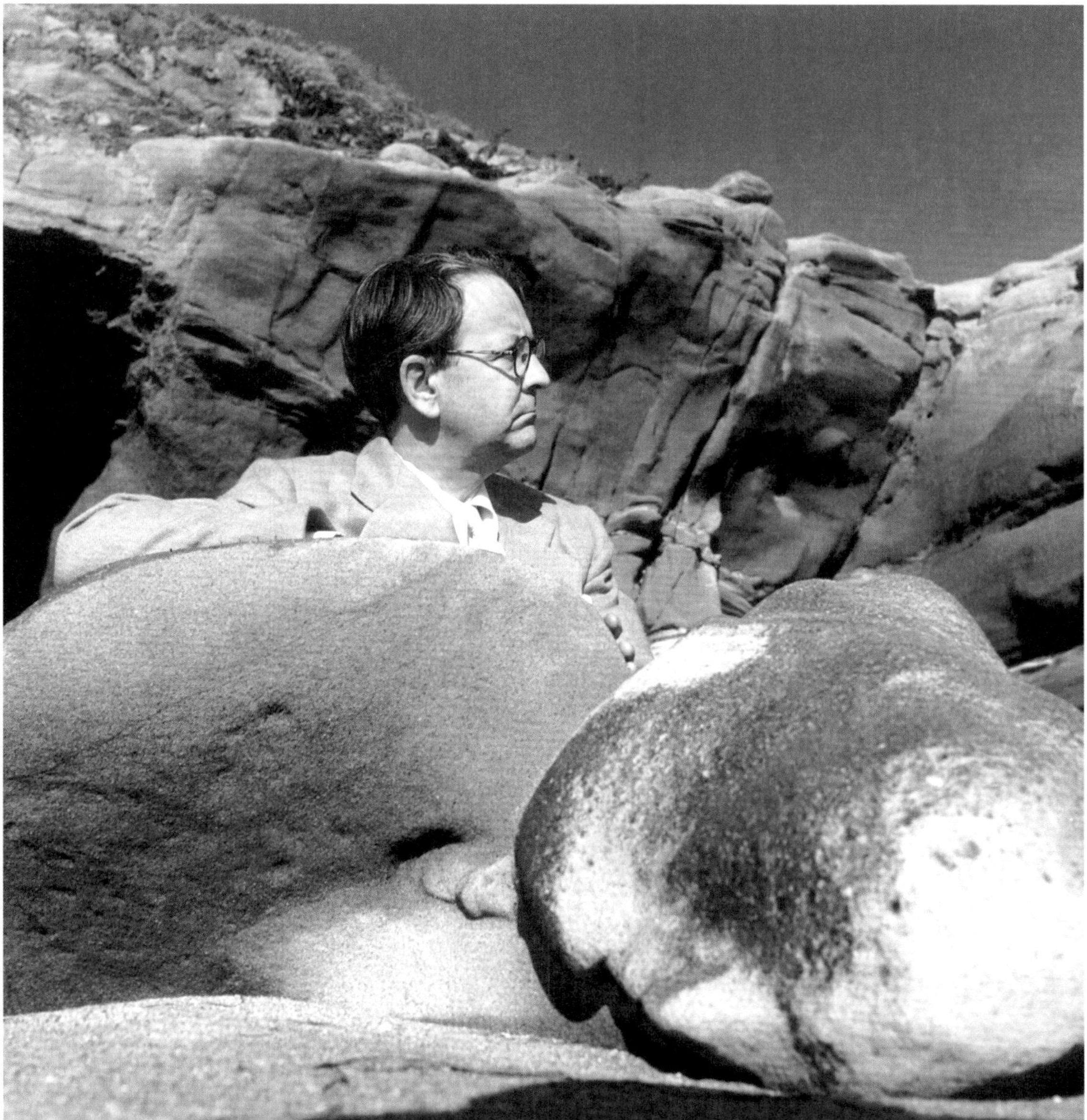

BRUCE CHATWIN

born Sheffield, UK, 1940; died Nice, France, 1989

by Lord Snowdon

London, 1982

In 1972, when Eileen Gray – the noted architect and designer whom Bruce Chatwin had come to interview for the *Sunday Times* – challenged him to go to Patagonia on her behalf, she could not have imagined that he would accept her challenge quite so readily. Nor could she have foretold that this journey, and the book that tells its story, *In Patagonia* (1977), would mark such an important change of fortune in the life of her interviewer, setting him on the road to becoming a renowned travel writer.

Before working for the *Sunday Times*, which sent him to the Great Wall of China, the Soviet Union and almost anywhere to interview the most famous personalities of the day, Chatwin had become an expert on Impressionist art while working for Sotheby's, and had studied archaeology at the University of Edinburgh. Above all, however, he was a great storyteller and traveller – with a particular interest in nomads – combining reportage, diary entries and fiction in his books, most notably *The Songlines* (1987) and *What Am I Doing Here* (1989), as well as *In Patagonia*. Chatwin was also a travel photographer, and a selection of his photographs and notebooks, edited by David King and Francis Wyndham, was published in 1993.

It was Chatwin's willingness to mix reportage and reinvention that often drew criticism from the subjects of his books, who complained that they did not always recognize themselves in his tales. Arguably, this is what made his narratives so fascinating, and he is often seen as the heir to the great travellers of yesteryear who embellished and enriched the accounts of their journeys. Lord Snowdon's famous portrait of Chatwin the adventurer, a rucksack on his back and rugged walking boots slung over his shoulder, has played a significant role in shaping how we remember the writer today. It is also an enduring icon of a nomadic lifestyle and of travelling as an existential human necessity.

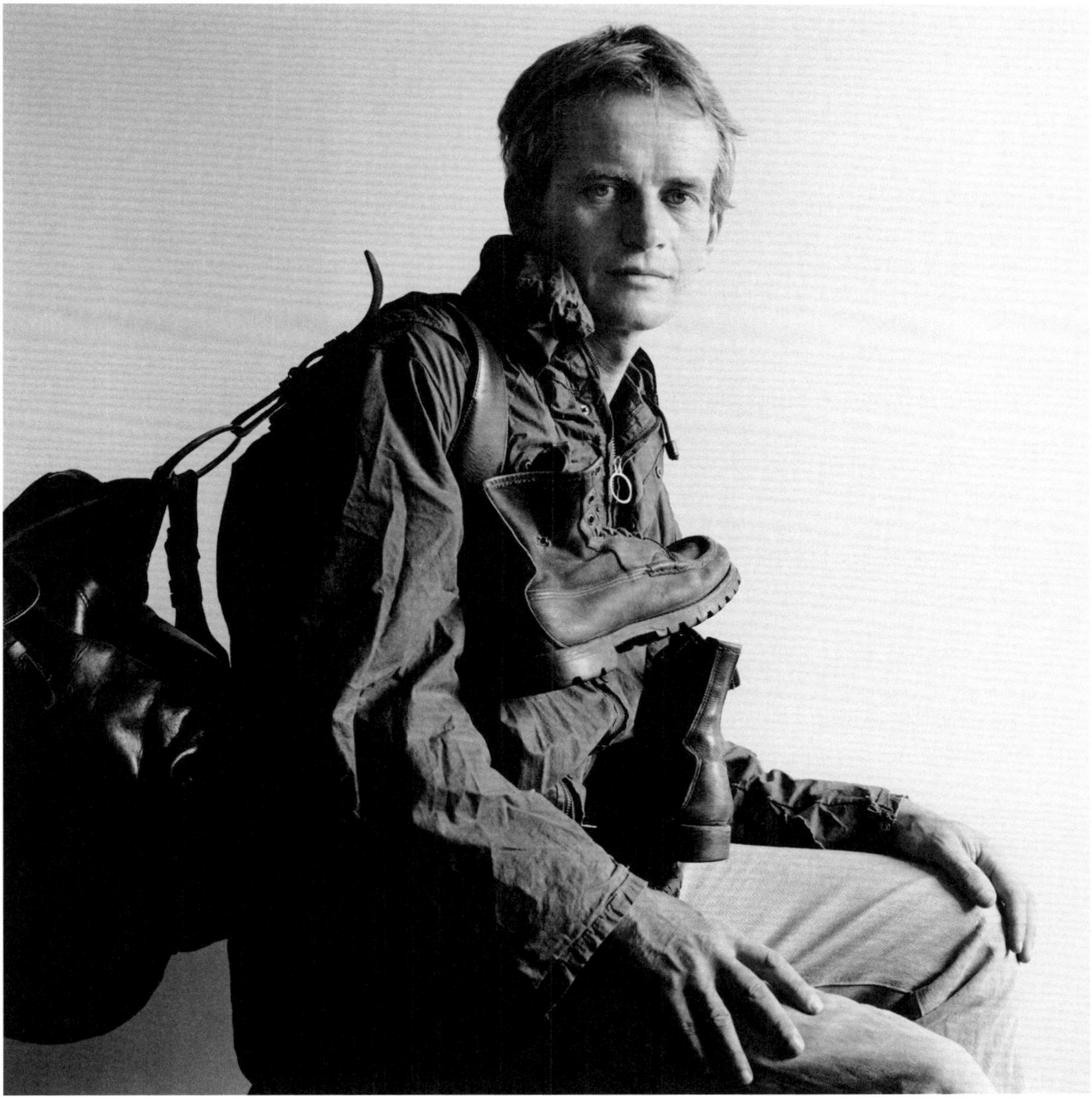

JEAN COCTEAU

born Maisons-Laffitte, France, 1889; died Milly-la-Forêt, France, 1963

by Herbert List

Paris, 1944

Jean Cocteau, a habitué of the most exclusive salons of Paris in the early decades of the twentieth century, and friend to all the major artists of the period, from Pablo Picasso and André Derain to Matisse and Amadeo Modigliani, was an extraordinarily versatile individual with a great expressive capacity. Variously a poet, a dramatist, an essayist, a scriptwriter, a designer, a novelist, a librettist and an actor, he was a key member of the avant-garde without ever truly belonging to any particular movement.

In 1917 Cocteau scandalized the entire audience of the Théâtre du Châtelet in Paris with the premier of his ballet *Parade* (1917). Performed by the Ballets Russes, it featured music composed by Erik Satie and costumes designed by Picasso. Cocteau considered it a riotous success: the shock caused by the highly unconventional nature of the performance had shattered every aesthetic taboo. His challenging ideas remained unaltered in *Orpheus*, his play of 1927.

Cocteau's life contained its own share of drama, including the suicide of his father when he was nine years old, the early death of his close friend Raymond Radiguet in 1923, his dependency on opium and his stay in a clinic in Saint-Cloud, during which time he wrote his most successful novel, *Les Enfants terribles* (1929). In his work in cinema, which corresponds with the final stages of his poetic development, he combined his Surrealist background with a hallucinatory realism. The influence of this combination can be seen to a certain extent in the work of the New Wave film-makers, and more precisely in Roberto Rossellini's film *L'Amore* (1948), the second part of which is based on Cocteau's play *The Human Voice* (1930).

In Herbert List's photograph of Cocteau, the writer is standing in front of the door to his apartment on the rue de Montpensier in Paris, a cigarette between his fingers. The profile on the door is that of a melancholy Orpheus, drawn by Cocteau himself.

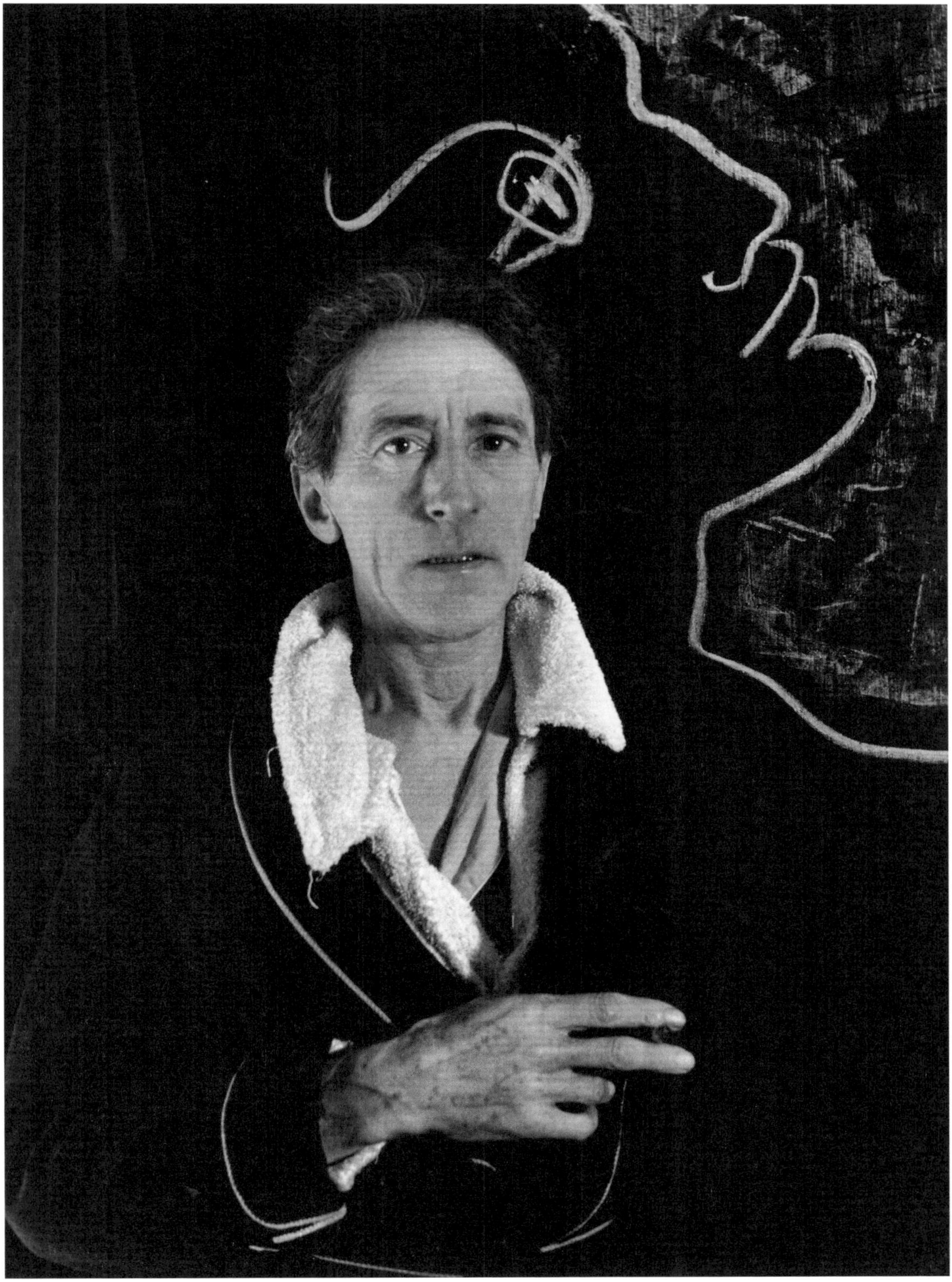

J. M. COETZEE

born Cape Town, South Africa, 1940

by Steye Raviez

Amsterdam, 1997

Each of John Maxwell Coetzee's protagonists is engaged in his or her own personal battle with evil and its multiple incarnations. To find salvation they must follow a path back to humanity and grasp to an unshakeable ethical idea. Ultimately, they all end up with a keen awareness of life and a painful perception of themselves and of their place in the world. Yet, paradoxically, they all find an answer to their loneliness, mortality and unhappiness by accepting something other than themselves. It is in this discovery – that it is possible to give something to someone else, even to an animal – that relief comes, that hope is kindled.

Suffering and its acceptance lie at the heart of Coetzee's universe. They are themes present in *Dusklands* (1974) and *Waiting for the Barbarians* (1980), on which Philip Glass based his 2005 opera of the same name. They are present, too, in *Life & Times of Michael K* (1983), *The Master of Petersburg* (1994) and *Disgrace* (1999). Coetzee is also interested in using his writing to explore the form of the novel and of the essay. Works in this vein include *Elizabeth Costello* (2003), published the year in which he won the Nobel Prize; *Diary of a Bad Year* (2007); and his trilogy of semi-autobiographical novels comprising *Boyhood: Scenes from Provincial Life* (1997), *Youth: Scenes from Provincial Life II* (2002) and *Summertime* (2009). In the last of these, Coetzee challenges ideas of both memory and justice through imaginary interviews with people he has known. In each of his literary utterances, whether in the form of a novel, an essay, a thesis or a character, Coetzee has been sustained by the unshakeable moral force of those who claim the right to bear witness. This was true even in Apartheid-era South Africa, which did not spare Coetzee from censure, and which the writer left only after the end of white rule.

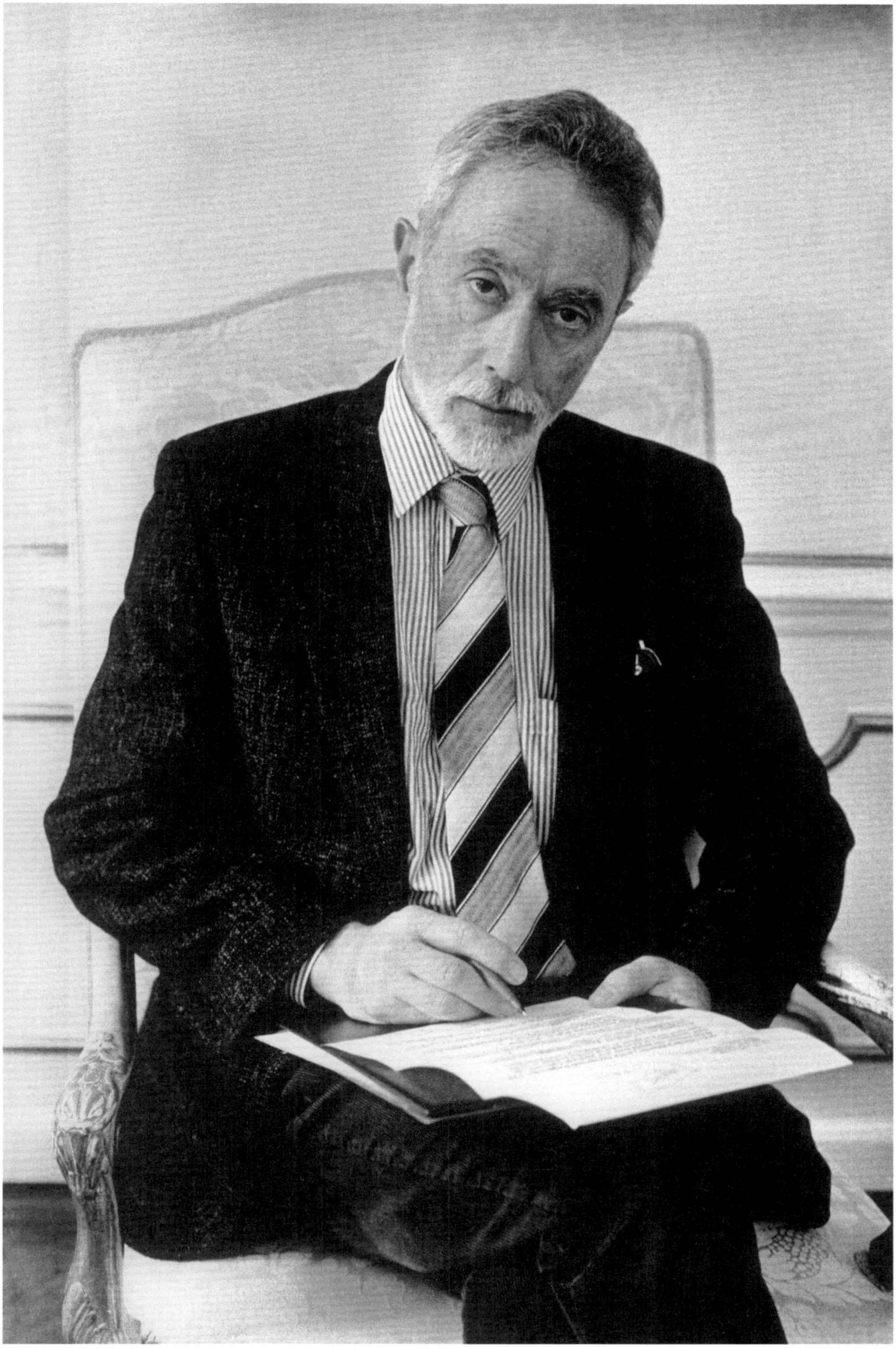

COLETTE

[Sidonie-Gabrielle Colette] born Saint-Sauveur-en-Puisaye, France, 1873; died Paris, 1954

by Herbert List

Paris, 1949

Sidonie-Gabrielle Colette (better known simply as Colette) embodied the euphoric and sparkling spirit of the belle époque, and over the years became a veritable living monument of French culture in the first half of the twentieth century. She was a writer, music-hall artiste, journalist, editor, playwright, theatre critic, screenwriter, film critic and seller of cosmetics and beauty products. Often to be found at the centre of scandals caused by her uninhibited relationships with persons of both sexes in the demi-monde of Paris, Colette also married three times and had a lover thirty years her junior. Even if she held the feminists of her period in contempt, in both her life and work she showed herself to be a free, emancipated and non-conformist woman, always ready to challenge conventions and to overturn as many taboos relating to women as possible.

Colette's first books (a series of four coming-of-age novels published between 1900 and 1903) investigated human emotions with both wisdom and irreverence. The works followed the protagonist, Claudine, through the (occasionally salacious and homoerotic) adventures and fantasies of school, adolescence and marriage. These early books concentrating on the story of Claudine were published under the name of her first husband, Henry Gauthier-Villars (also known as Willy), a Parisian bon viveur who financed authors prepared to write novels and novellas for him. Colette was one of these ghostwriters, and due to the outrageous success of the books she had written for him, she was gradually able to move out of her husband's shadow. After they divorced in 1910, she became a star in the French cultural firmament, appearing at society events and participating in theatrical tours.

A woman with a revolutionary sensibility who refused to be restricted by the rules of bourgeois existence, Colette imbued all the characters in her novels with the same passion for life and desire for freedom that drove her own extraordinary vivacity. In later life her mobility became severely limited by arthritis, so the writer spent her final years in her bedroom in the Palais-Royal, propped up on the divan, which she called her *zattera* (raft).

Throughout this period Colette never lost heart and never stopped working, writing or receiving her friends. The great photographer Herbert List also paid her a visit and took several photographic portraits of her. In this image, Colette is seated at her writing desk and fixes the camera with a penetrating stare, while the backlighting seems to transform her hair into a crown.

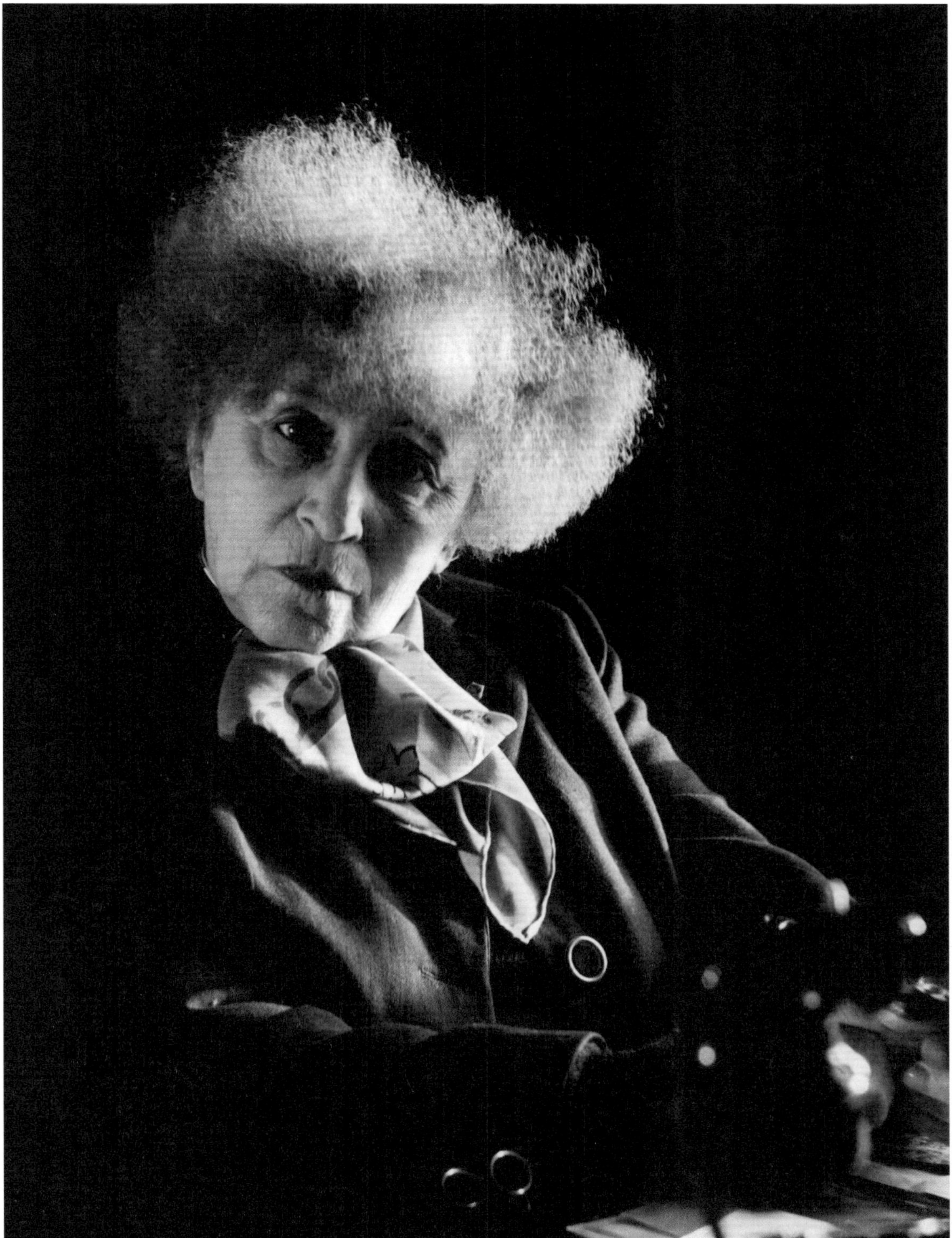

JULIO CORTÁZAR

[Julio Florencio Cortázar Descotte] born Brussels, 1914; died Paris, 1984

by Sara Facio

Paris, 1967

In the 1950s, while living in Paris, the Belgian-born Argentine writer Julio Cortázar worked as a translator for UNESCO, producing Spanish-language versions of the work of writers such as Daniel Defoe and Marguerite Yourcenar. He also translated the work of Edgar Allan Poe, whose influence may be seen in much of Cortázar's own writing, in which surreal, unpredictable, startling or supernatural events are introduced into apparently normal situations.

In 'House Taken Over', which appeared in Cortázar's first collection of short stories, *Bestiary* (1951), a middle-aged brother and sister discover that their house has been taken over by a group of unidentified individuals. Variously interpreted as a delusion on the part of the protagonists, a comment on the nature of solitude and a reference to the government of Argentine president Juan Domingo Perón from which Cortázar fled in 1951, the work creates a sense of unease in the reader, who is left to contend with the uncertain nature of reality and the human psyche.

Cortázar's masterpiece is widely considered to be the novel *Hopscotch* (1963). The book begins with a set of instructions for the reader. They may read it in a linear fashion, from the first to the last chapter, or by 'hopscotching' between chapters according to a 'table of instructions' provided by the author; readers may also choose their own individual paths through the book. Described as an anti-novel, it turns all the traditional elements and structures of storytelling and narrative upside down, affording the role of protagonist to the reader.

Cortázar, who was unafraid to challenge convention, took risks not only in his writing but also in his life. He demonstrated against Argentina's right-wing politics, and was an eloquent supporter of the Sandinistas, to whom he donated the royalties of his last books. He was also an admirer of Che Guevara, who is referenced in one of his poems: 'I had a brother / we never saw each other / but that doesn't matter. / I had a brother / who walked through the mountains / while I was sleeping. / I loved him in my own way / I took his voice / as free as water.'

The Argentine photographer Sara Facio took this photograph of Cortázar in the French capital. 'On that afternoon in Paris', she recalls, 'I took rolls and rolls of pictures, then I chose this one because I liked it and I sent it to him by mail and he replied that he loved it and that he wanted to make it his official portrait, and so he did.'

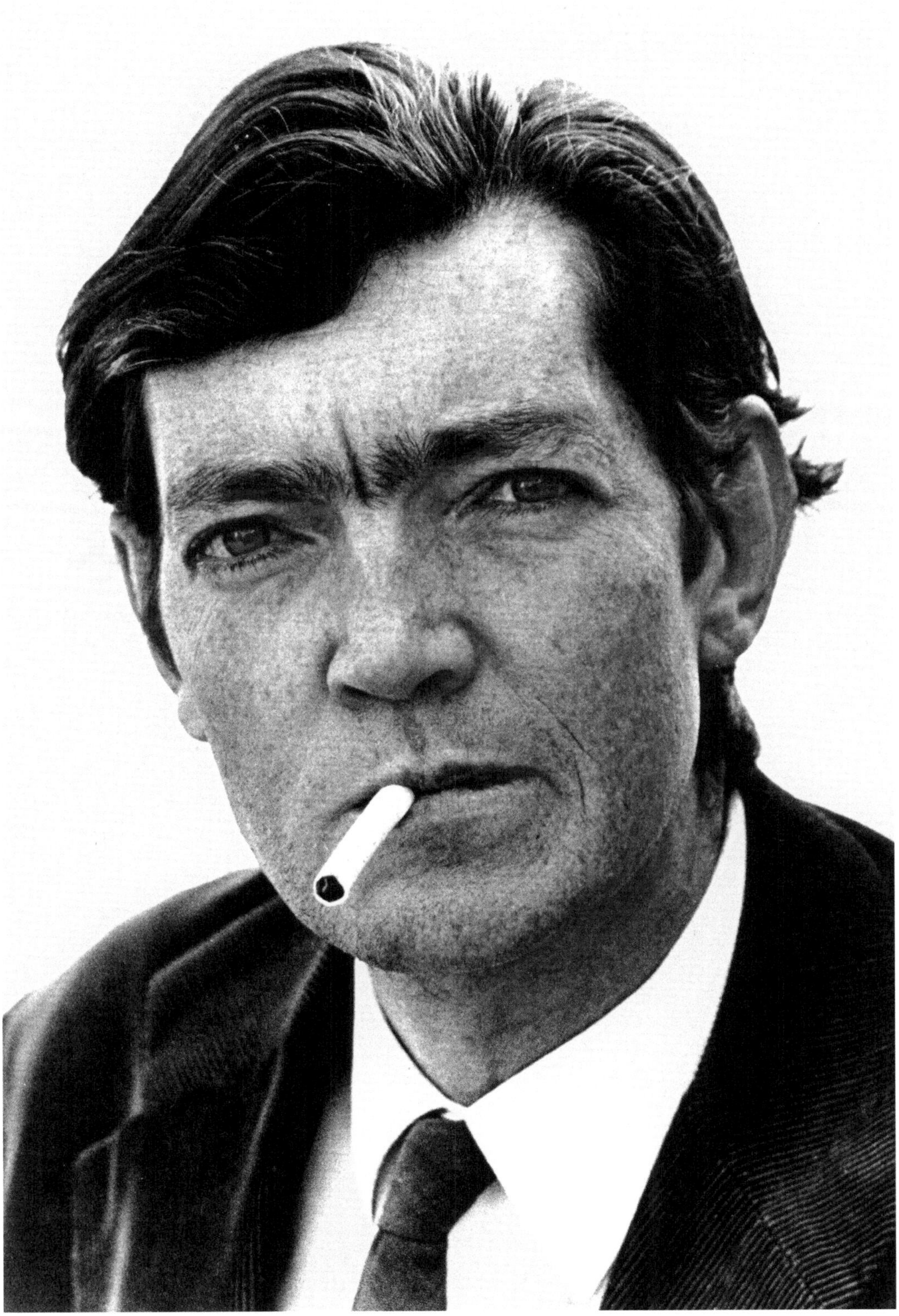

E. E. CUMMINGS

[Edward Estlin Cummings] born Cambridge, Massachusetts, 1894; died North Conway, New Hampshire, 1962

unknown photographer

Cambridge, Massachusetts, 1920

One of the most important American poets of the twentieth century, Edward Estlin Cummings made his debut with a work of prose, the novel-memoir *The Enormous Room* (1922), which deals with his dramatic experiences during the First World War. As a volunteer ambulance driver on the Western Front in 1917, Cummings was unjustly accused of espionage and imprisoned for more than three months in a French military detention camp. The following year, however, he was able to return to the USA and his real love, poetry, which he had dabbled in since childhood.

In 1923 Cummings published his first collection, *Tulips and Chimneys*, in which the stylistic experimentation that would become his trademark was already present: his innovative syntactical structures; his use of the 'visual' juxtaposition of words, which takes precedence over grammatical conventions; punctuation marks located in unexpected and apparently absurd positions; his refusal to use capital letters; the graphic arrangement of his verses; and erotic content. His poetic playfulness underwent an abrupt about-face in 1926, however, when his father was killed in a traffic accident, which also left his mother gravely injured. His work began to display existentialist themes, including an awareness of mortality and a celebration of nature, which he expressed through his highly painterly poetic style. During the long periods he spent in Paris, where he attended Gertrude Stein's literary salon, he began to combine classical themes and formal avant-gardism with linguistic experimentation within canonical forms such as the sonnet.

A contract with *Vanity Fair* in 1926 allowed Cummings not only to travel but also to concentrate on his painting and poetry, and in 1931 he published a selection of his art, *CIOPW* (an acronym of the media he had used: charcoal, ink, oil, pencil and watercolours). Together with Stein, the most important influences on Cummings's poetry were Ezra Pound and Pablo Picasso. Written by 'an author of pictures, a draughtsman of words', as Cummings described himself, his poems often take the form of graphic compositions, surreal fusions of neologisms and word play. All his collections, among them *XAIPE: Seventy-One Poems* (1950), *Poems, 1923–1954* (1954), *95 Poems* (1958) and *73 Poems* (1963), bear witness to his desire to travel down new roads, provoking astonishment and controversy. But the real wonder is that, despite being animated by Dadaist irreverence, Futurist vehemence and Surrealist fantasy, Cummings was able to create what to many is an oxymoron: popular experimental poetry.

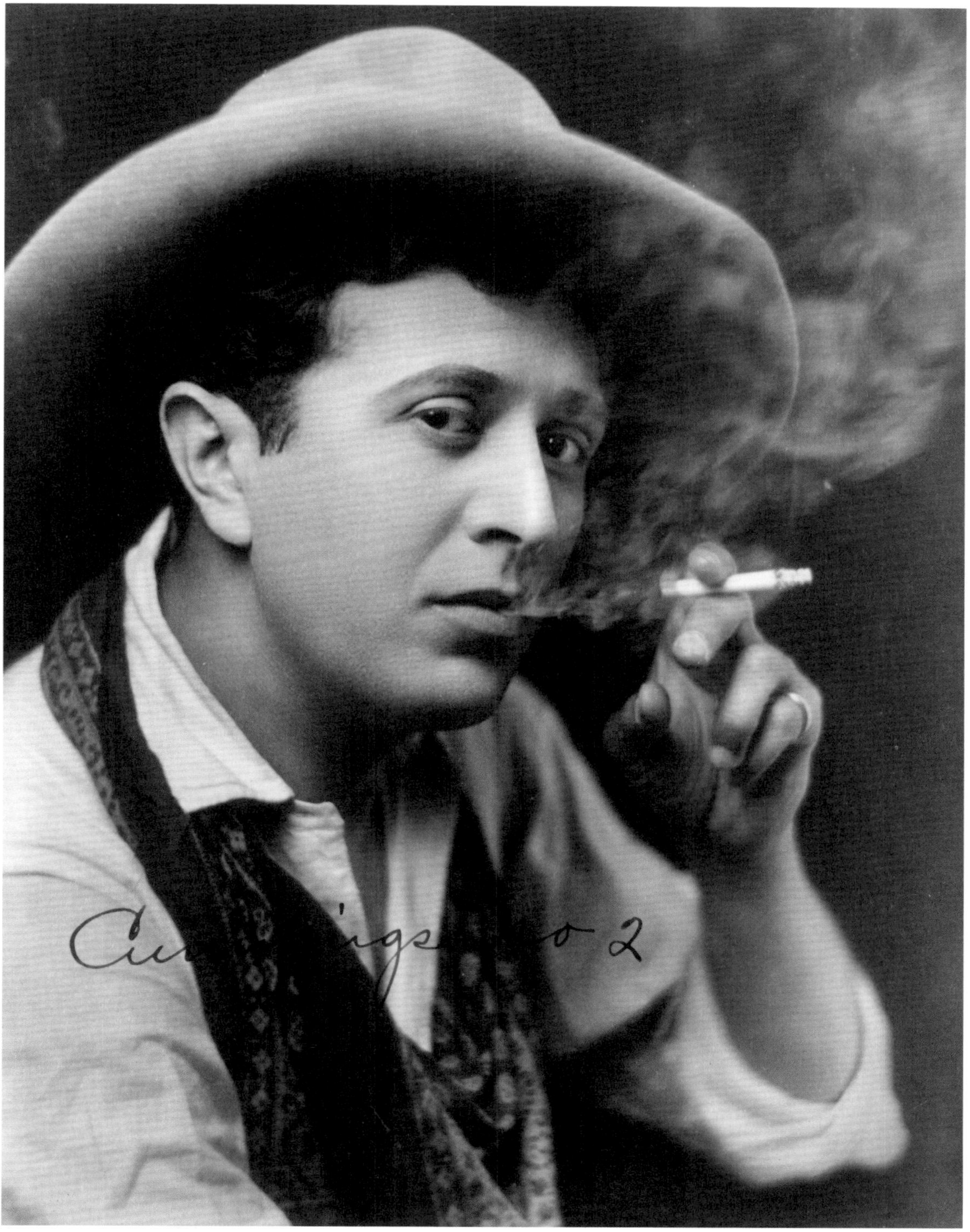

DON DELILLO

born New York, 1936

by Sophie Bassouls

Paris, 1992

Born in the Bronx to Italian parents who had emigrated to the USA at the beginning of the twentieth century, Don DeLillo had no notion of writing a novel until he was approaching his thirties. He hated school ('I slept for four years', he has said of his time there) but loved European cinema ('Probably the movies of Jean-Luc Godard had a more immediate effect on my early work than anything I'd ever read'). It wasn't until he was eighteen, while working as a playground attendant one summer, that he discovered the likes of William Faulkner, Ernest Hemingway and, above all, James Joyce: 'It was through Joyce that I learned to see something in language that carried a radiance, something that made me feel the beauty and fervor of words, the sense that a word has a life and a history.'

During the 1960s DeLillo worked in advertising, as a copywriter for Ogilvy & Mather, but left his post after just a few years: 'I quit my job just to quit. I didn't quit my job to write fiction. I just didn't want to work anymore.' But start writing he did. His first novel, *Americana* (1971), took him four years to complete, but by 1978 he had produced a further five, including *End Zone* (1972), *Ratner's Star* (1976) and *Running Dog* (1978). While each of these works received favourable reviews, they were known only to a small but loyal following.

It was the 1980s that saw DeLillo produce the novels that would raise his public profile and establish him as one of the great figures of American letters. *White Noise* (1985), for example, a fierce and caustic reflection on intellectualism, consumerism, man-made disasters and the nature of violence and power, is arguably one of the most important books of the late twentieth century; indeed, it is regarded as a landmark novel by many younger writers, including Zadie Smith, Jonathan Franzen and Dave Eggers. In *Libra* (1988) DeLillo revisited the assassination of John F. Kennedy, exploring the position of the novelist in a society dominated by the power of the media and by the violence of power itself. Similar themes reappeared in his first novel of the 1990s, *Mao II* (1991), a grandiose, postmodern work. After something of a pause, DeLillo produced *Underworld* (1998), the book for which he is perhaps best known.

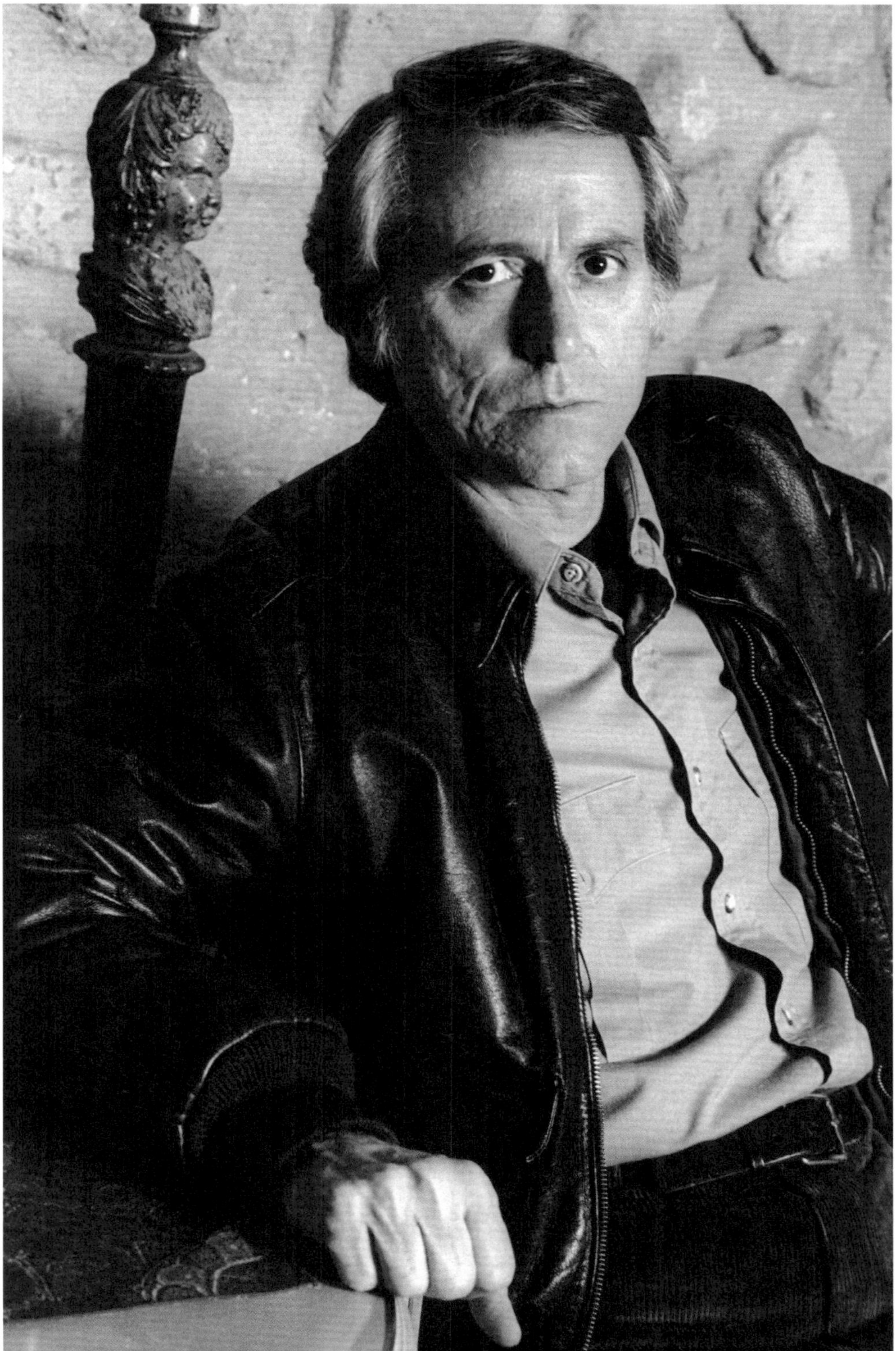

ANITA DESAI

born Mussoorie, India, 1937

by Leonard Freed

Rome, 2000

The Indian writer Anita Desai, born to a German mother and a Bengali father, describes her country of origin as being suspended between two poles: a highly traditional one and another that wants to be part of the modern world. The conflict this creates for the individual does not always involve political parties or factions but it does impose the impossible question: how to move forwards and improve one's own life, without losing touch with one's roots?

The India of Desai's novels is not a place of spirituality and mysticism – the stereotype that has attracted so many Europeans for years. Rather, it is a contradiction: a country with problems caused by poverty and degradation but that has a great capacity for development nonetheless. Desai's attention is especially drawn to the plight of Indian women, who are among some of the most oppressed individuals on the planet. It is a difficulty with which she can identify.

She herself has experienced troubles stemming from her engagement in an activity that, in short, is simply not expected of women in Indian society: being a writer. Until the 1980s and 1990s the only socially acceptable roles for females were daughter, wife and mother. Since then, the social status of women has undergone considerable changes, and, most recently, extraordinary movements have arisen to protest the violence and abuse directed against women.

These difficult themes – conflict and control, East and West – are often explored Desai's writings. In *Fasting, Feasting* (1999), for example, she sets out two models of family that are only superficially opposed: the American family and the Indian family. Both structures exercise control to prevent their members from achieving any freedom – one through its excesses, and the other through its deprivation. Despite confronting these issues with characteristic style and drawing on a wide linguistic inheritance, the writer's language is always focused on simplicity. She believes language must be like glass, transparent so that the reader can see what is behind it.

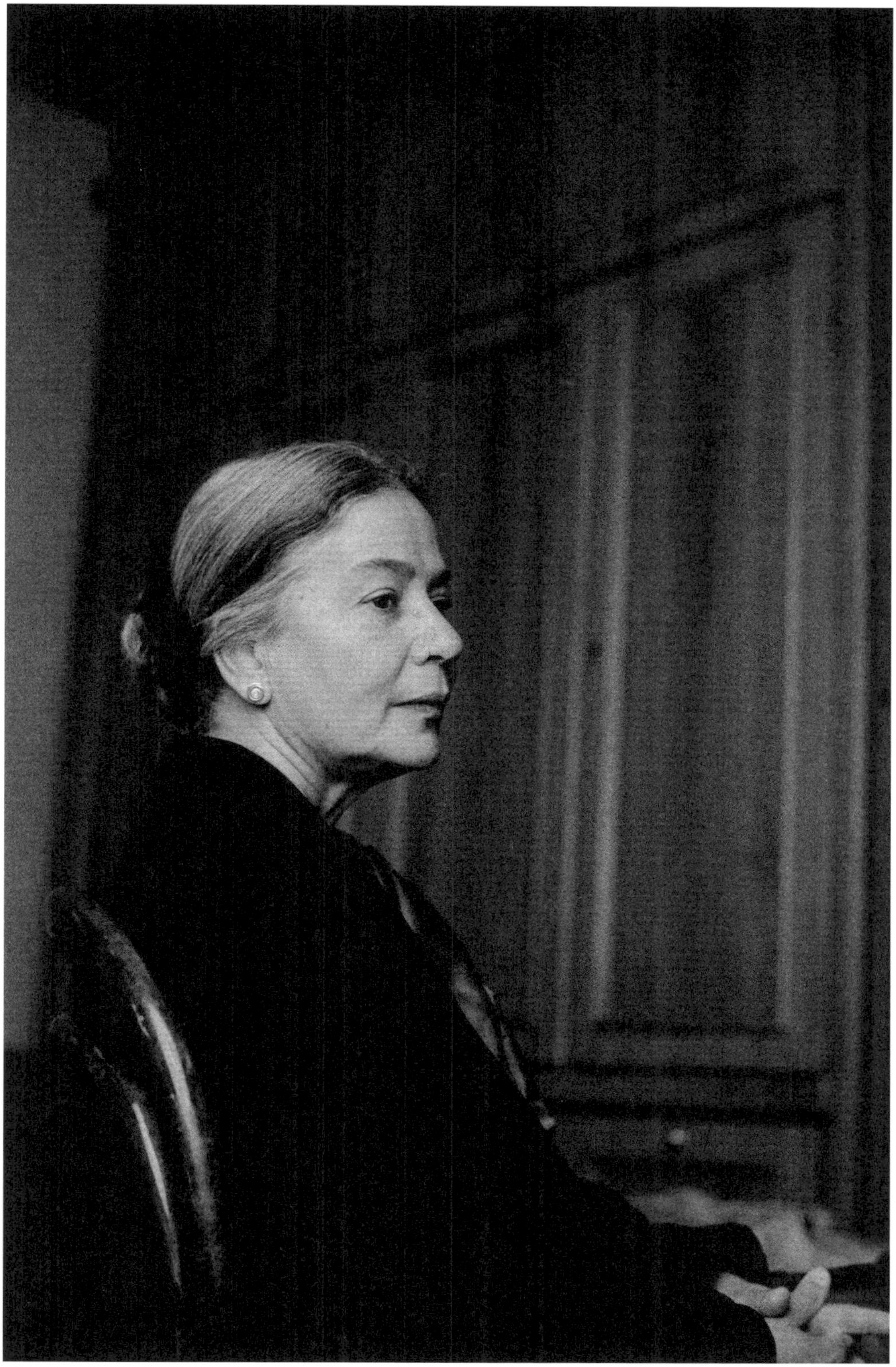

PHILIP K. DICK

born Chicago, 1928; died Santa Ana, California, 1982

by Niki Sublime

unknown location, 2006

It seems impossible that a writer of the calibre of Philip K. Dick, who exerted such an enormous influence on so many of his contemporaries, who raised such profound existential questions and wrote so elegantly about them, should have remained comparatively unknown during his lifetime. Yet throughout his career Dick struggled financially and the only major prize he ever received was a Hugo Award for his novel *The Man in the High Castle* (1962). He eventually had to break into more mainstream literary genres to escape the marginalization that had condemned science fiction writers to second-rate publications that were completely ignored by the critics. It is largely due to Dick that science fiction is now recognized, at least at its best, as a genre uniquely able to anticipate and investigate the existential questions that still torment humanity in the twenty-first century: what is 'real' and what is 'human'; what distinguishes an android from a human being; the nature of time itself and its manipulation; and the relationship between insanity and our capacity to perceive reality.

Cinema also owes a great debt to Dick, starting with the celebrated film *Blade Runner* (1982), directed by Ridley Scott, which was adapted from Dick's novel *Do Androids Dream of Electric Sheep?* (1968) and finally propelled him into the pantheon of great writers. More recently there has been a film version of Dick's *Minority Report* (1956), while *The Matrix* films make explicit reference to his work, in particular to *Ubik* (1969) and to some of his essay collections. Would Dick have had a different life, or written different books, if he had been successful during his lifetime? Would he have left us his final, dark masterpieces, such as *A Scanner Darkly* (1977)? This is the sort of question to which only science fiction can provide answers.

This amusing photomontage, created by Niki Sublime and posted on the Flickr website, takes its inspiration from an actual incident. In 2005, David Hanson, an artist who specializes in the creation of androids, accidentally left the head of a robot modelled on Philip K. Dick in the overhead luggage compartment of an aeroplane bound for San Francisco. The sophisticated software installed in the robotic head allowed it to carry on conversations, recognize faces and to quote passages of the writer's work. This expensive object, valued at US$25,000, was recovered in 2010 during an anti-software piracy police raid in St Petersburg, Russia. It seems that Dick's computerized head was being used as a portable hard drive to transport pirated films and video games from Russia to South America.

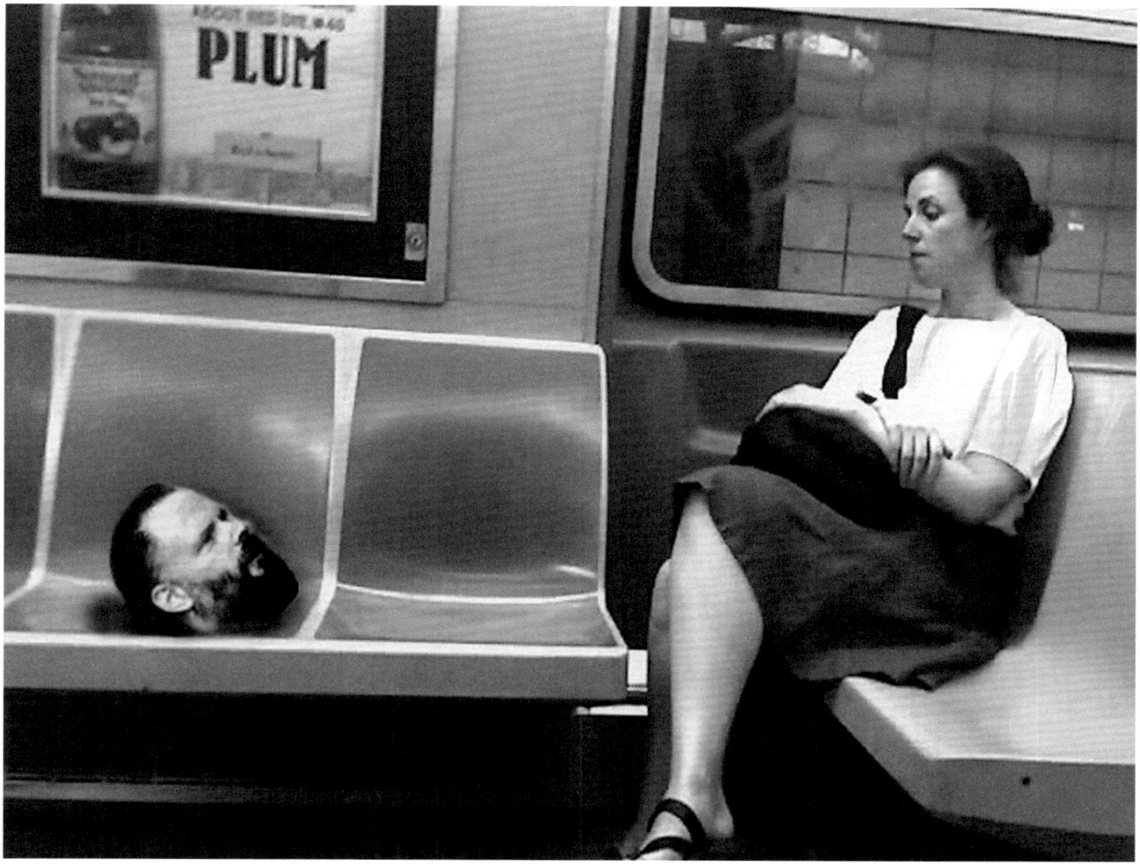
PLUM

ALFRED DÖBLIN

born Szczecin, Poland, 1878; died Emmendingen, Germany, 1957

by Herbert List

Berlin, 1950

When he left Germany in 1933 to escape the Nazi regime, Alfred Döblin was one of the most famous writers in the country and a serious contender for the Nobel Prize. On his return in 1945, no one remembered him. His death in 1957 passed almost unnoticed; the only tributes paid to him were those of the writer Günter Grass, who regarded him as one of his mentors. It took another twenty years for him to be rediscovered.

Döblin, who was born to Jewish parents in Poland, experienced terrible poverty during his childhood. Having been abandoned by his father, he moved with his mother and four siblings to Berlin. Döblin's lifelong ideological militancy had its roots in these years of pitiful destitution in the city's slums. He nonetheless completed his studies and became a psychiatrist, practising his profession in a poor part of the city. He maintained his passion for literature throughout his medical studies, and before the onset of the First World War he had already established himself as one of the most innovative writers on the Berlin literary scene. In 1910 he began contributing to the Expressionist journal *Der Sturm*, and in 1915 he published *The Three Leaps of Wang Lun*, a work that Bertolt Brecht considered fundamental to his own literary development.

Döblin's writing career culminated in 1929 with the publication of his most famous work, *Berlin Alexanderplatz*. Its popular and critical success was remarkable. Writers such as Walter Benjamin recognized the innovative nature of a prose text constructed using a montage technique. Döblin exploited the language of the city itself – its slums, its adverts, its popular songs and its chaotic streets – in order to compose an epic portrait of modern life. Berlin, for him, was not only his home but also the archetypal city and a microcosm of the world. In the meantime, the Nazi Party had begun its rise to power, and, as a radical socialist, Döblin reacted strongly to the signs of the coming dictatorship. When his fears were realized, however, he was forced to leave his beloved Berlin to save his own life. He returned after the war, and it was there, in 1950, that Herbert List, another famous German who had been forced into exile, photographed him seated at his writing desk, a composed yet rather stern expression on his face.

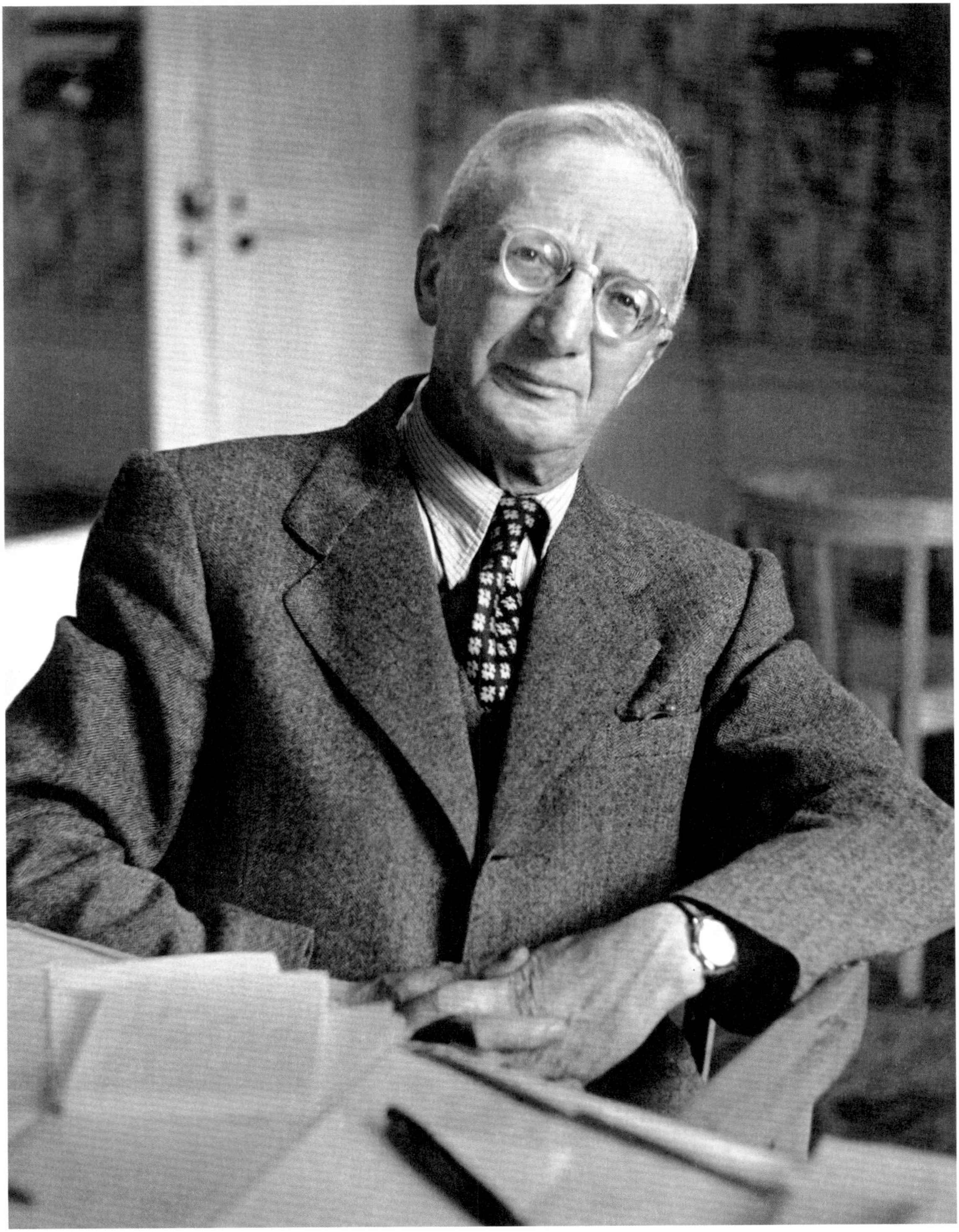

JOHN DOS PASSOS

born Chicago, 1896; died Baltimore, Maryland, 1970

by Philippe Halsman

New York, 1948

It was not until John Dos Passos was sixteen years old that his father, a successful lawyer, acknowledged his paternity. Nevertheless, Dos Passos received an excellent education, which allowed him to graduate from Harvard University and to travel to Europe with a private tutor. In July 1917, impatient with USA's reluctance to enter the First World War, he enlisted in the French ambulance service so that he could be close to the conflict. His experience of the war formed the basis of his first major novel, *Three Soldiers* (1921), a powerfully anti-militaristic book that established him as the 'anti-Fitzgerald'. The two writers had been born in the same year, and both had their first significant books published in the early 1920s, but their trajectories would turn out to be very different – with the social commitment of the one being in sharp contrast to the jazz sensibility of the other.

Dos Passos's dedication to Communism grew in the years that followed. He also produced his most significant works during this period: *Manhattan Transfer* (1925) and *U.S.A.* (1936), a trilogy consisting of *The 42nd Parallel* (1930), *1919* (1932) and *The Big Money* (1936).Dos Passos worked with the Marxist magazine *New Masses*, fought on behalf of Nicola Sacco and Bartolomeo Vanzetti, two Italian immigrants and suspected anarchists whose execution for murder has since been described as unjust, and travelled to Russia to learn more about socialism.

In 1936, shortly after the publication of *The Big Money*, Dos Passos was described by Jean-Paul Sartre as 'the greatest writer of our times'. However, in the years that followed, Dos Passos's faith in Communism began to wane. He had gone to fight against Franco in Spain and had seen many things of which he did not approve. Above all, he was horrified at the suspicious circumstances surrounding the death of his Spanish translator, José Robles – circumstances that clearly pointed to Soviet guilt. It was because of this incident that he left *New Masses* (which had described *The Big Money* as 'Trotskyist agitprop') for the conservative *National Review*. Philippe Halsman took this portrait of the writer in 1948, the year in which the Magnum photographer received American citizenship after having fled German-occupied France.

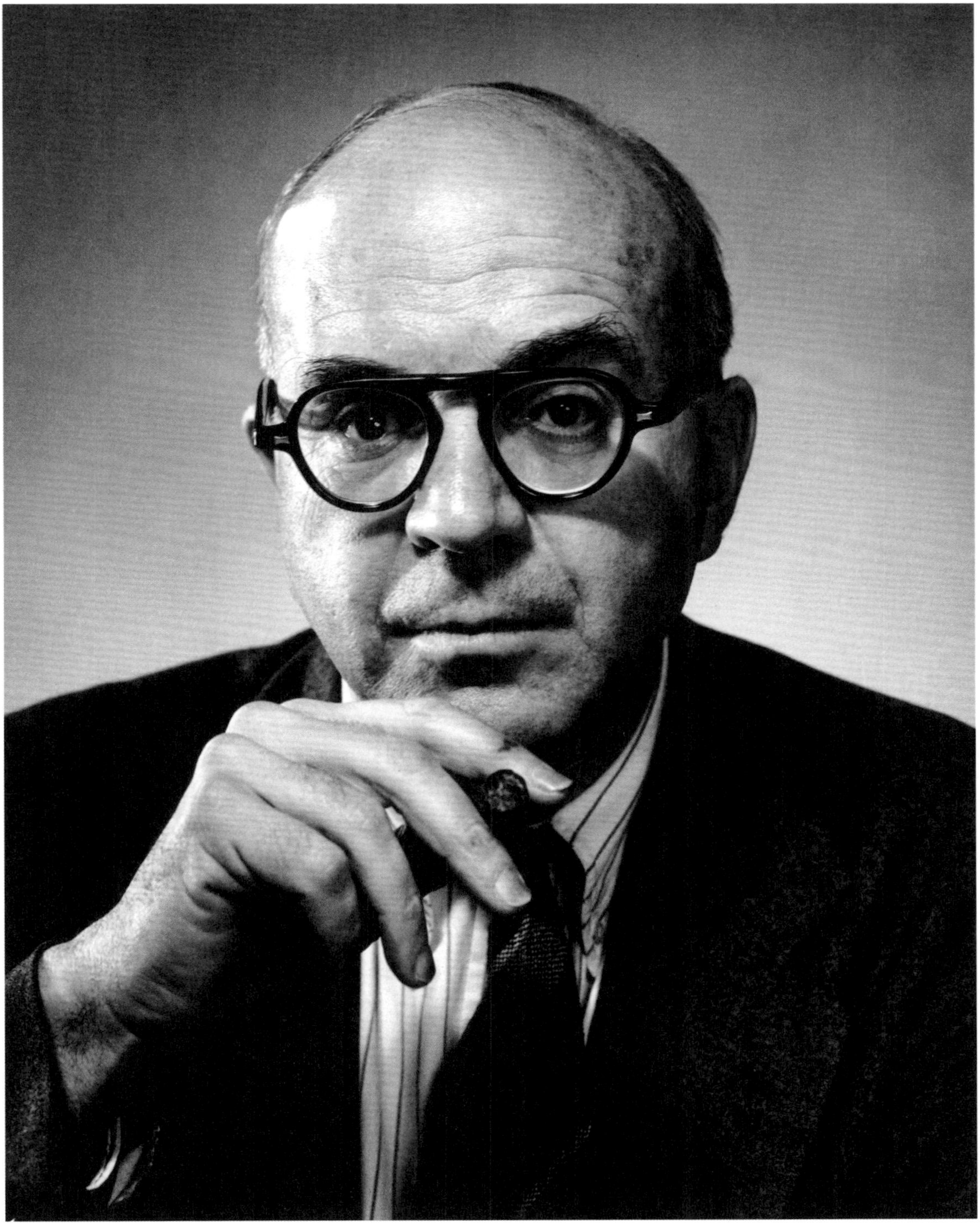

THEODORE DREISER

born Terre Haute, Indiana, 1871; died Hollywood, California, 1945

by Carl Van Vechten

New York, 1933

The protagonists of Theodore Dreiser's most famous novels, *Sister Carrie* (1900) and *An American Tragedy* (1925), are both ruthless fortune hunters prepared to cast morality aside in pursuit of their goals. Dreiser himself came from a poor family, and was brought up a strict Catholic. In later life he would become politically active, campaigning against social injustice.

Although he was also an accomplished journalist and essayist, it is Dreiser's works of fiction for which he is best remembered. His first novel, *Sister Carrie*, is regarded as a milestone in American literature. At the time, however, it was not widely promoted by its publishers, who were apprehensive about the immoral behaviour of its heroine, and sales were poor. The fact that it did not sell well failed to deter Dreiser and he embarked on a lengthy trilogy featuring the magnate Frank Cowperwood (*The Financier*, 1912; *The Titan*, 1914; and *The Stoic*, 1947, published posthumously).

Dreiser's first commercial success was *An American Tragedy*, a lucid critique of the American dream. Inspired by an actual criminal case, the novel tells the story of Clyde Griffiths, another fortune hunter determined to get on in life. When he sees the opportunity of marrying a wealthy woman, he hatches a plan to murder his pregnant girlfriend while making it look like an accident. Although the narrative is deliberately uncertain regarding the final circumstances of her death, Clyde is convicted of murder and sentenced to death by electric chair. Dreiser portrays Clyde as both criminal and victim of the workings of capitalism. The novel provides a vivid depiction of the USA at the beginning of the twentieth century, and was influential in the development of post-war literature.

Carl Van Vechten took this portrait of Dreiser in New York in 1933. The photographer had initially worked as a journalist and arts critic for the *New York Times*, as well as publishing several novels and works of non-fiction. His interest in photography emerged in the 1930s, when he started taking photographs of actors, writers, musicians, artists and dancers. He often photographed them spontaneously, against improvised backgrounds, focusing on the face to capture the essence of his subject's character.

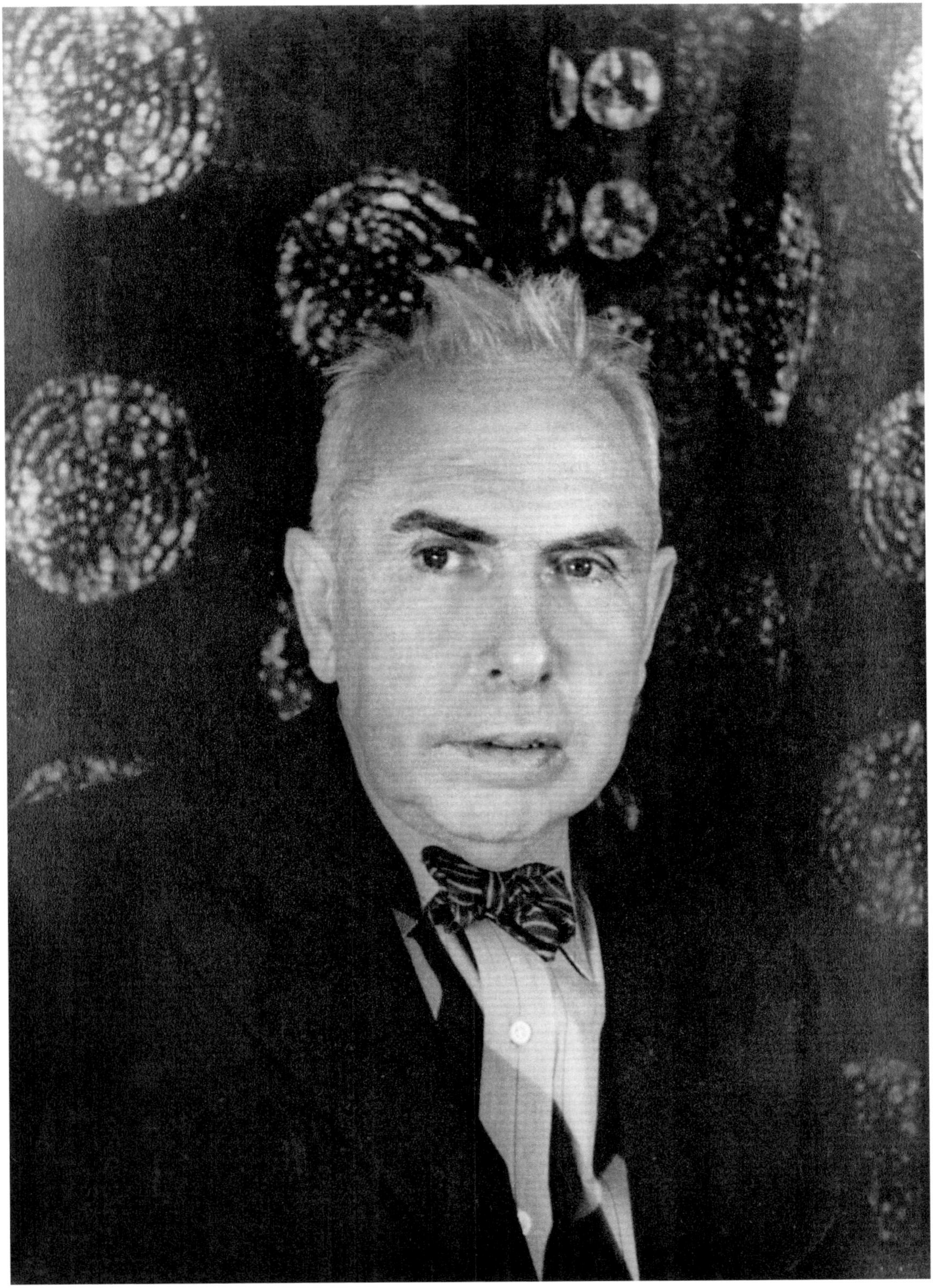

MARGUERITE DURAS

born Saigon, 1914; died Paris, 1996

by Robert Doisneau

Par s, c. 1955

The opening part of Marguerite Duras's autobiographical novel *The Lover* (1984) features a visually striking episode: a fifteen-year-old girl, her hair in plaits, a boyish cap on her head and gold-coloured shoes on her feet, is leaning on the railings of a ferry crossing the Mekong River. As she gazes into the distance she is approached by a rich young Chinese man, almost thirty years of age. This encounter proves to be the beginning of an illicit and explosive love affair between a young French girl of humble origins and the son of a wealthy businessman who is heir to a fortune.

Based on the turbulent experiences of Duras's adolescence, *The Lover* reads like a series of photographic images, as if the author were sorting through a box of old photographs and placing them in chronological order. Together they tell the story of her formative years in French Indochina, now Vietnam, including her affair with an older Chinese man. The book opens with a photographic-like description of the now mature author's face as she embarks on her story. Such images run throughout the novel, each one an attempt to capture a moment of time.

An extremely visual writer, Duras later turned to film. In the late 1950s and early 1960s she wrote the screenplays for *Hiroshima Mon Amour* (1959) and *The Long Absence* (1960), directed by Alain Resnais and Henri Colpi, respectively, and adapted one of her own novels for the cinema: *Moderato Cantabile* (1958), filmed as *Seven Days ... Seven Nights* (1960) by Peter Brook. Often dissatisfied with the results, Duras took to directing films herself. Her first film as director, *La Musica* (1967), confirmed her ability to switch from the printed page to the silver screen.

The French photographer Robert Doisneau, who took this photograph of Duras sitting outside a cafe on the rue Saint-Benoît in Paris, saw photography as a way to 'fix time, preserve youth'. However, he was also aware of its limitations: 'It is a crazy business. Time always ends up winning.'

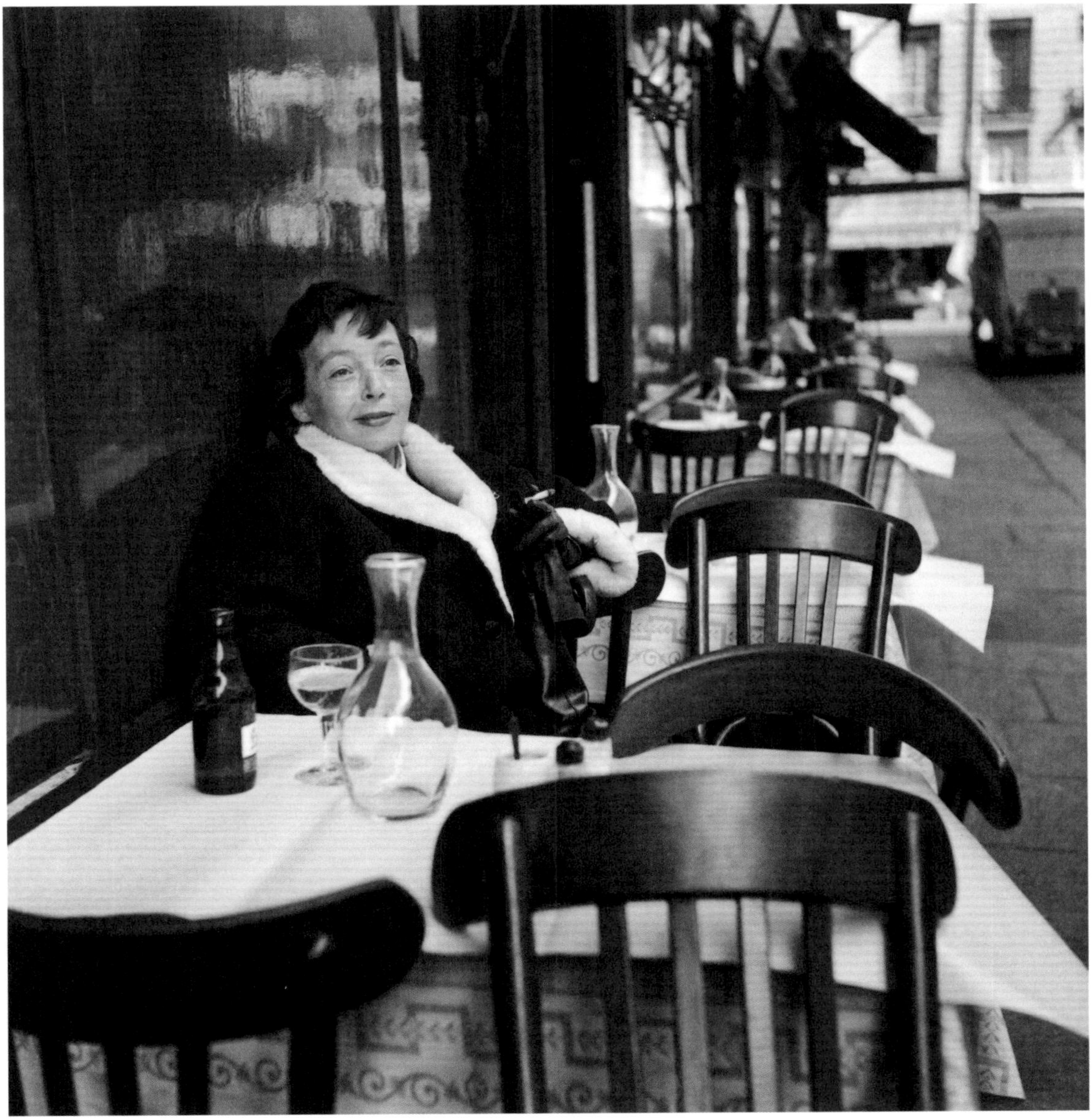

FRIEDRICH DÜRRENMATT

born Konolfingen, Switzerland, 1921; died Neuchâtel, Switzerland, 1990

by Henri Cartier-Bresson

Neuchâtel, Switzerland, 1966

In 1946, after five years of studying philosophy intermittently, Friedrich Dürrenmatt gave up university altogether to immerse himself in the theatre and to concentrate on writing. As Dürrenmatt himself put it: '[I wrote] my first piece instead of a dissertation with the title "The Tragic in Kierkegaard", not actually because I thought it better to write total nonsense than partial nonsense, but because I came to believe that one can think not only in philosophy, but also on the stage.' The result was his comedy *It Is Written*. On the evening of its premier at the Theater Kanton Zürich in 1947, the audience, 'instead of yawning, started whistling', and Dürrenmatt felt certain he had made a promising start.

Dürrenmatt's work, both his theatrical pieces and his novels, is informed by the Greek myths and tales from the Old Testament that his father, a protestant minister in Bern, had read to him when he was a child. His first comedy, which had caused such a scandal and ensured his notoriety, was followed by his first novel, *The Judge and His Hangman* (1950), the story of a detective's lifelong pursuit of a career criminal. Within the framework of a police investigation, Dürrenmatt offers the reader something more profound: a study of crime and punishment, of guilt and innocence, although it is often hidden by satirical touches and flashes of humour.

In *The Execution of Justice*, a novel that he began writing in the 1950s and which was eventually published in 1985, Dürrenmatt turns his attention to the failings of the Swiss legal system and the nature of justice. The problems at the heart of such a system, Dürrenmatt suggests, have their origins in human behaviour, a subject that he was committed to investigating through his work. In 1969, in the middle of the sensation caused by the first moon landing, Dürrenmatt said: 'To penetrate the basic human predicament is more important than to fly to the moon, which is nothing but an escape from the Earth and thereby an escape from man. Literature arrests man, makes him its subject, just as physics makes nature its subject.'

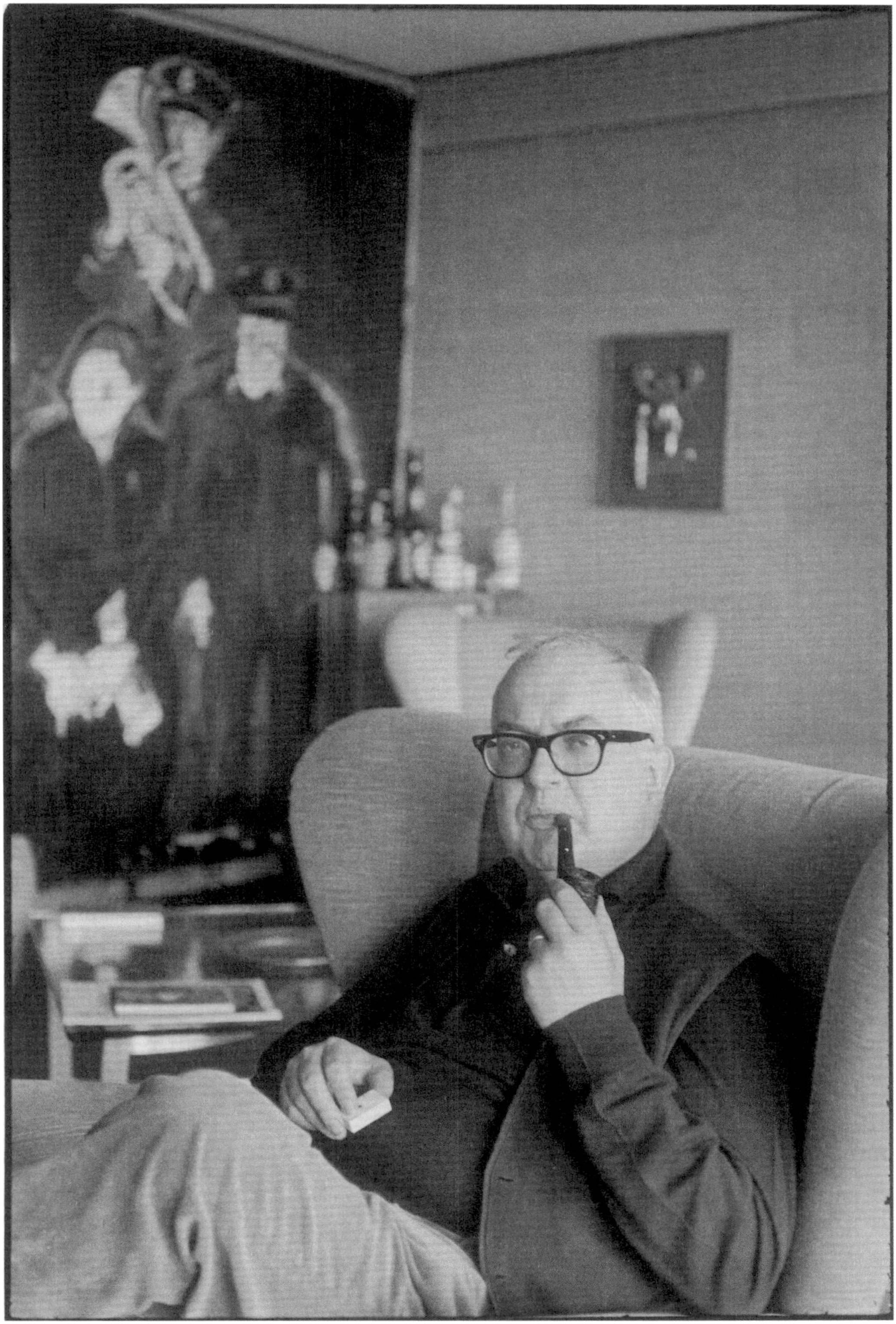

UMBERTO ECO

born Alessandria, Italy, 1932

by Roberto Koch

Bologna, Italy, 1987

Author of one of the most popular Italian-language novels of recent years, *The Name of the Rose* (1981), Umberto Eco is adamant that academics and intellectuals should not closet themselves away in their ivory towers. He is himself an academic credited with the advancement of social studies and the introduction of the study of semiotics in Italian universities. Driven by an astonishing intellect and an insatiable curiosity, his interests are extremely wide-ranging, encompassing subjects such as medieval aesthetics, the language spoken by the Smurfs and, in an essay entitled 'Phenomenology of Mike Bongiorno', the communication style of an American-born Italian quiz-show host. He is widely respected both in academic circles and by the general public, and has written for many international publications.

Eco has always been interested in linguistic experimentation. He was a member of avant-garde Italian literary movement Group '63 and of Oulipo (an acronym of Ouvroir de Littérature Potentielle, or 'Workshop of Potential Literature'), during which time he translated Raymond Queneau's *Exercises in Style* (1947). He is one of the greatest exponents of the labyrinthine construction typical of the postmodern novel, as can be seen not only in his metaphysical thriller *The Name of the Rose* but also in *Foucault's Pendulum* (1988), a complex book involving esoteric references, a conspiracy theory and a mysterious order descended from the Knights Templar. Generally acknowledged as a 'difficult' read, it is rumoured to boast the greatest discrepancy between the number of copies sold and the number actually read.

Nevertheless, over the years Eco has continued to write novels and works of non-fiction that have been highly acclaimed by critics and the general reader alike. In many ways, he has himself become one of the figures from popular culture that he studies and writes about in his work.

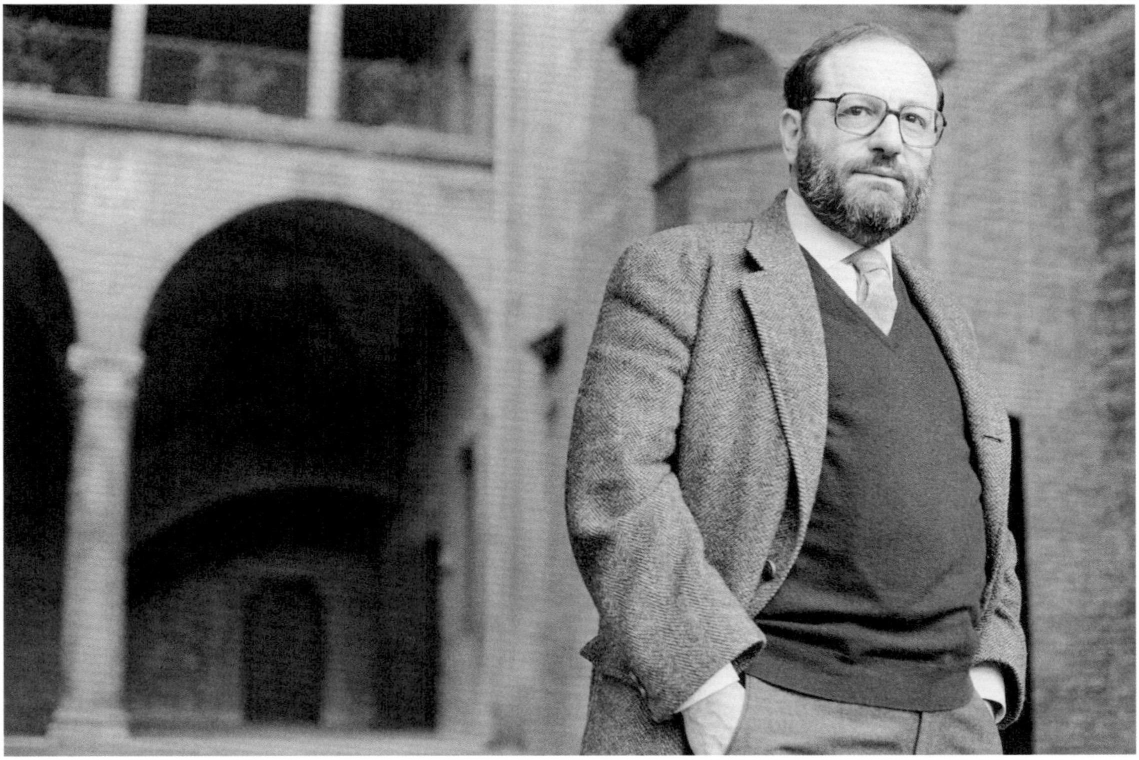

T. S. ELIOT

born St Louis, Missouri, 1888; died London, 1965

by Lord Snowdon

London, 1958

Noted for his powerful yet delicate poetry and his exposition of the spiritual crisis at the heart of modern society, Thomas Stearns Eliot was one of the most influential literary figures of the twentieth century. He defined himself as 'classicist in literature, royalist in politics, and anglo-catholic [*sic*] in religion'. Born in the USA, he was educated at Harvard, the Sorbonne and Merton College, Oxford. He settled in London in 1915, where he lived for the rest of his life, later becoming a British citizen. Following Eliot's decision to devote his life to literature, his father had cut him off without a penny, so he struggled financially for a number of years, at one point selling his early volumes of poetry to his friends.

In June 1915 Eliot married Vivienne (known as Vivien) Haigh-Wood; their union, however, would not be a happy one. She had a history of emotional and physical problems, and was later committed to a psychiatric hospital, where she died of a heart attack in 1947. In the early years of their marriage she was briefly involved with the philosopher Bertrand Russell, who had offered her and Eliot the use of his London flat. Between 1919 and 1921 Eliot himself experienced a series of crises, including the death of his father and a nervous collapse brought on by Vivien's illness and financial concerns. Yet despite such setbacks, this period saw the production of some of Eliot's finest poetry, including *The Waste Land* (1922) and, later, the *Four Quartets* (1935–42). In 1948 Eliot was awarded the Nobel Prize. Towards the end of his life he married his secretary, Valerie Fletcher, and found a degree of happiness that had eluded him for most of his life. As Valerie noted, he 'obviously needed a happy marriage. He wouldn't die until he'd had it.'

Unlike many photographers, Lord Snowdon does not try to establish a rapport with his subjects: 'I don't want people to feel at ease. You want a bit of edge. There are quite long, agonized silences. I love it. Something strange might happen. I mean, taking photographs is a very nasty thing to do. It's very cruel.' This sense of unease and slight uncertainty is clearly present in his portrait of Eliot.

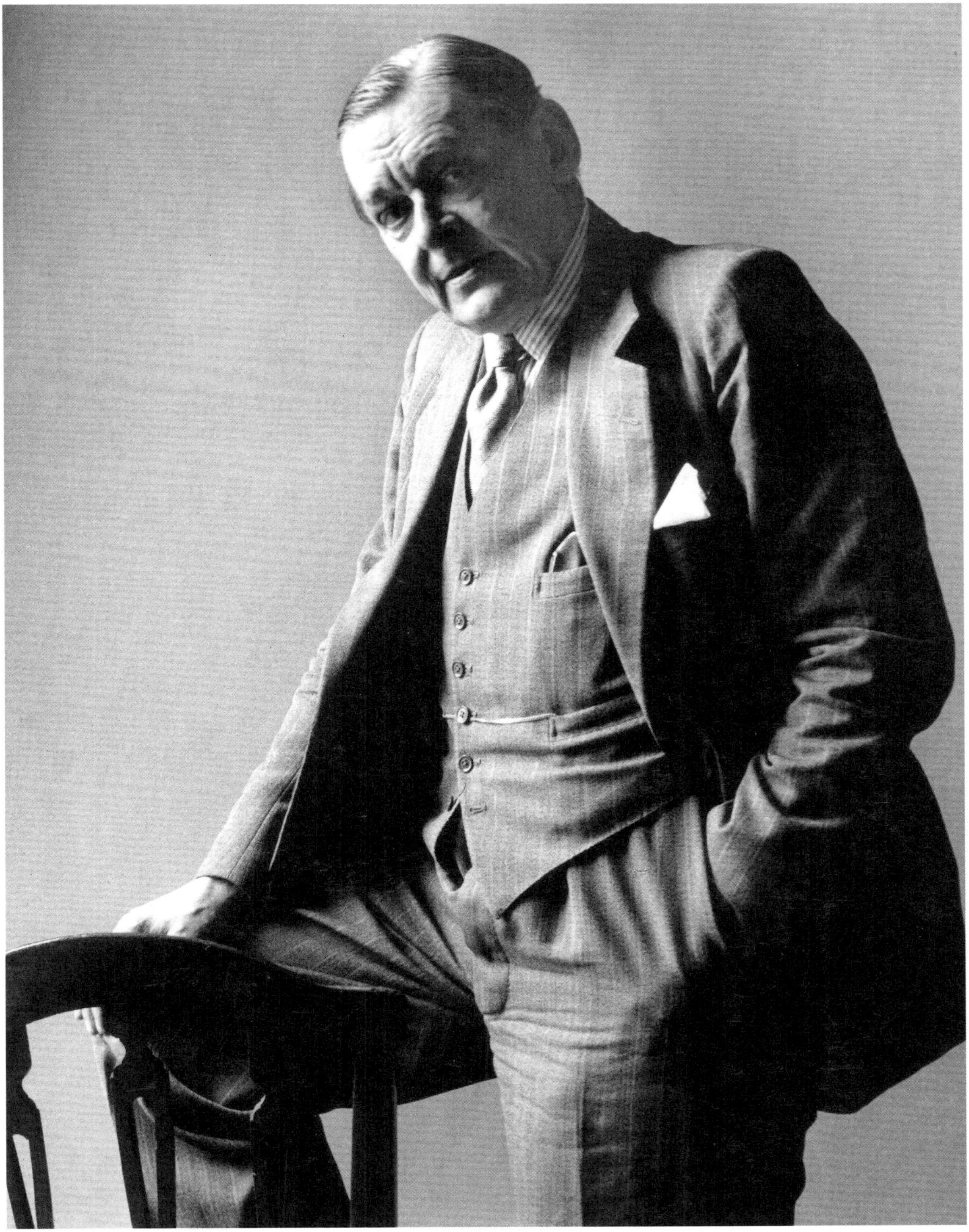

BRET EASTON ELLIS

born Los Angeles, 1964

by Debra Hurford Brown

London, 2010

Bret Easton Ellis is perhaps best known as the writer who, in his early twenties, was able to describe better than anyone else the lives of rich American post-adolescents in the 1980s: young people from wealthy families who spend their time attending opulent parties, consuming alcohol and cocaine and indulging in anonymous sex and brief affairs. Such are the characters who inhabit *Less Than Zero*, his debut novel from 1985, and its meta-narrative sequel, *Imperial Bedrooms* (2010), which was set and published twenty-five years later. Immersed in brilliant colours and the cultural myths of the period, the 'MTV generation' of *Less Than Zero* reappears in Ellis's second novel, *The Rules of Attraction* (1987), set on a university campus and told through a complex interweaving of first-person narrators.

Ellis's third novel, and his most controversial novel to date, *American Psycho* (1991), enjoyed a success directly proportional to the number of its critics and the size of the wave of indignation it provoked. The story of Patrick Bateman, a young businessman and serial killer, is a pitiless portrayal of the psychotic behaviour of a wealthy Manhattanite, and includes a catalogue of unmediated atrocities. A disturbing and violent social critique of the pathological vacuity of a certain American way of life spent drunk on money and wholly immersed in pop culture, *American Psycho* was a publishing phenomenon that reverberated around the world.

If in his early novels Ellis employed an almost Raymond Carver-like minimalism, the writing in his later books moved closer to the more ambiguous territory of metafiction. *Glamorama* (1998), a fiercely sarcastic depiction of the world of fashion, of the cult of the image and ofthe exhibitionist hedonism of American yuppies, transforms itself into a visionary and surreal story of a terrorist plot. In *Lunar Park* (2005), the partly autobiographical story of a fictional Bret Easton Ellis, the confusion of the novel's narrative threads morphs into a fantastical tale with disturbing, thriller-like resonances. And while the sophisticated twists of plot and deliberate wrong-footings of *Imperial Bedrooms* divided the critics, Ellis's ability toreinvent himself and to push the limits of his own imagination has certainly contributed to making him one of the leading figures of contemporary American literature.

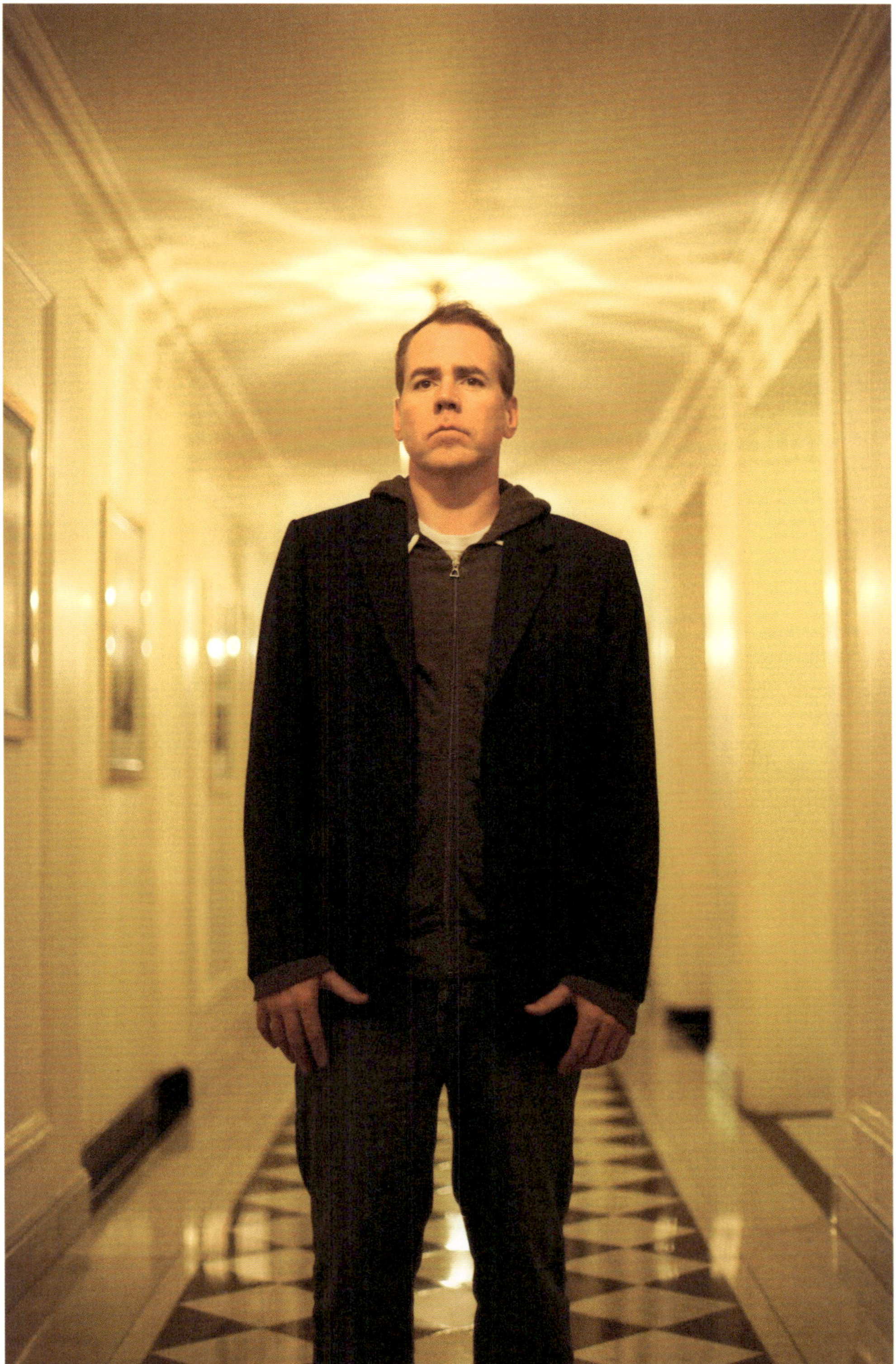

RALPH ELLISON

born Oklahoma City, Oklahoma, 1914; died New York, 1994

by Gordon Parks

New York, 1948

Ralph Waldo Ellison, the grandson of a slave and the son of a construction worker, was born in Oklahoma City in 1914. He was orphaned at just three years old, but, thanks to his musical talent and a scholarship, Ellison was able to attend the Tuskegee Institute where he studied piano and trumpet. Music and audio technology remained lifelong interests that would later influence his writing style. He then went on to study art in New York, working odd jobs to make ends meet, and began writing book reviews, essays and short stories for magazines. He was one of the founders of the *Negro Quarterly*, and edited and contributed articles to several American Communist publications until becoming disillusioned with the movement during the Second World War, an experience that would partially inspire his first novel.

Richard Wright was the first person to encourage Ellison to write, but it was only with the moral and material support of his second wife, the photographer Fanny McConnell, that he was able to dedicate himself to writing and rewriting his novel *Invisible Man* (1953) for seven years. It was to be a landmark work in the awakening of the urban African-American consciousness, with its searing portrayal of racism in the urban north of the USA, rather than in the rural South. Despite the National Book Award and overwhelming public acclaim the book received when it was published, Ellison considered it only as a rough approximation of what he wanted to achieve. He subsequently worked for more than forty years on his second novel, and, although he completed more than two thousand pages, he never considered it finished, and did not publish it during his lifetime; it appeared in fragmentary form under the title *Juneteenth* (1999) only after the writer's death. Although incomplete, it is still a work of extraordinary power, interweaving the voices of its characters with a jazz sensibility, creating a grand fresco of African American and Southern history and culture. While working on his second novel, Ellison published two collections of essays, *Shadow and Act* (1964), and *Going to the Territory* (1986). During this period he also lectured in Europe and taught at Bard College, Rutgers University and Yale University. In 1975 he was elected to the American Academy of Arts and Sciences.

Ellison was photographed in Harlem, New York City, by Gordon Parks, who was the first black photographer to work for *Life* magazine, and who produced an extraordinary photo-documentary feature for the magazine shortly after the publication of *Invisible Man* that explored the novel's themes and social issues.

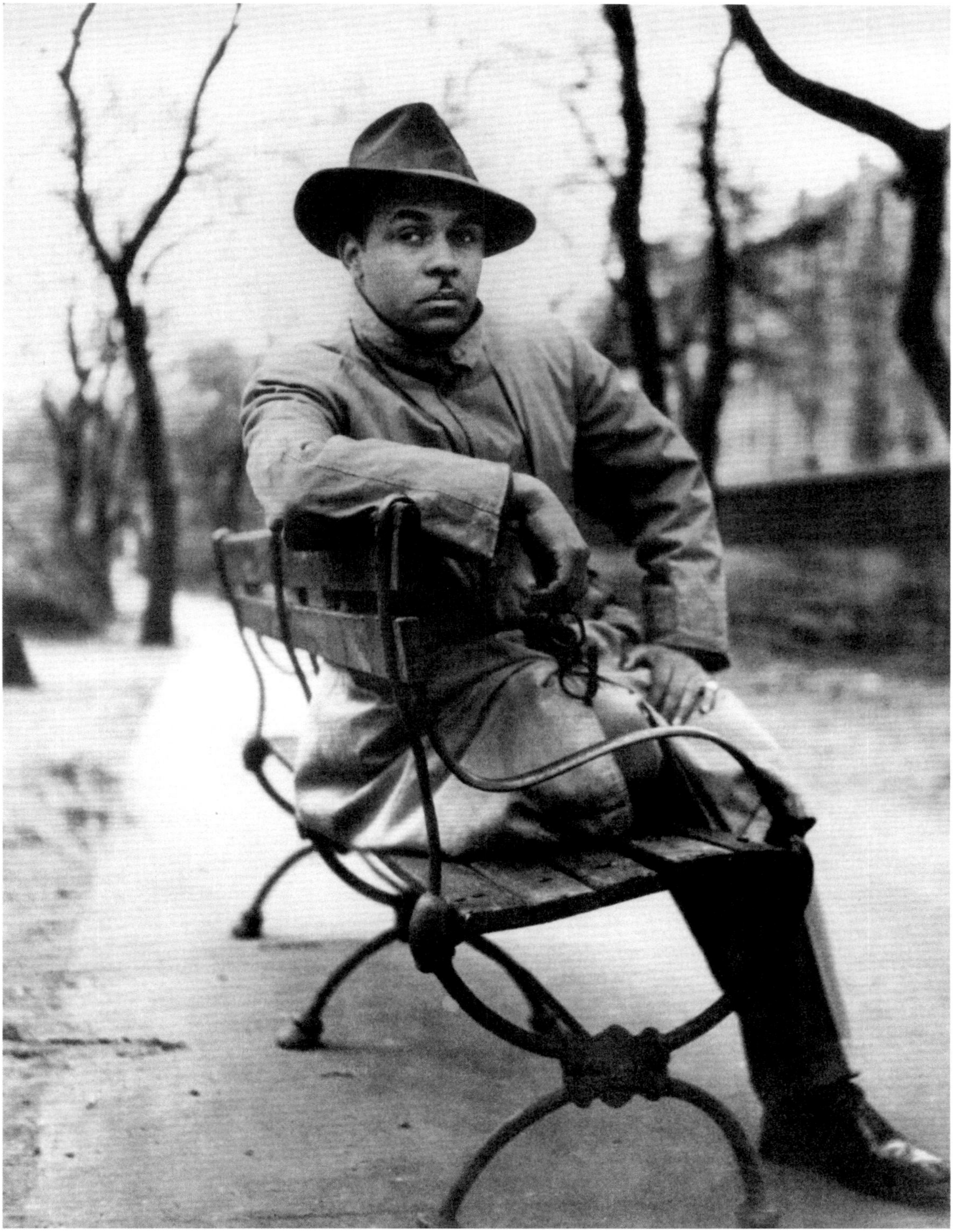

JAMES ELLROY

born Los Angeles, California, 1948

by Bruce Gilden

Connecticut, 1991

There is no better example of how life and fiction can sometimes become intertwined than in the case of James Ellroy. Author of the 'L.A. Quartet' (*The Black Dahlia*, 1987; *The Big Nothing*, 1988; *L.A. Confidential*, 1990; and *White Jazz*, 1992) and of the 'American Underworld Trilogy' (*American Tabloid*, 1995; *The Cold Six Thousand*, 2001; and *Blood's A Rover*, 2009), Ellroy the man is as captivating and complex as any of his books.

Born Lee Earle Ellroy in Los Angeles in 1948, he was just ten years old when his parents divorced. His mother was killed a short time later in a crime that remains unsolved; this tragic event would have a lasting impact on both his life and his work. As an avid reader of crime fiction, he developed a youthful fascination with murder cases after reading *The Badge* by Jack Webb. Among the many gruesome cases documented in the book was the murder and mutilation of Elizabeth Short, known later as the *Black Dahlia*, in 1947. The case had excited a great deal of morbid attention in the inhabitants of post-war Los Angeles, and it captivated the imagination of a young Ellroy, who would later use it as the basis of one of his most successful books.

If his early life was difficult, Ellroy's late adolescence was even more tumultuous: he ran away from home, faked a nervous breakdown to escape from the army, took drugs and travelled around the USA, during which time he was arrested repeatedly for vagrancy. Eventually, he found redemption in writing. In an interview with the film-maker, writer and artist Matthew Caron, Ellroy described himself in characteristically direct terms: 'I'm a straight-ahead, hard-charging, religious right-wing heterosexual American, out of another era. I do not think the world is going to blow up. I do not think America is a demon. I think America will prevail in the world of geopolitics. I'm a nationalist, a militarist, a capitalist and a Christian. People find this shocking. I feel no need to justify my opinions. I'm happy and obsession suits me. I have remained fixed on very few things in my lifetime and I've profited from it. I'm very good at turning shit into gold.'

Bruce Gilden, heir to the aggressive and caustic style of street photography pioneered by such photographers as 'Weegee' (Arthur Fellig), directs a very penetrating stare at the world. His photograph of Ellroy, lit by the harsh light of an unshaded bulb, resembles a police mugshot.

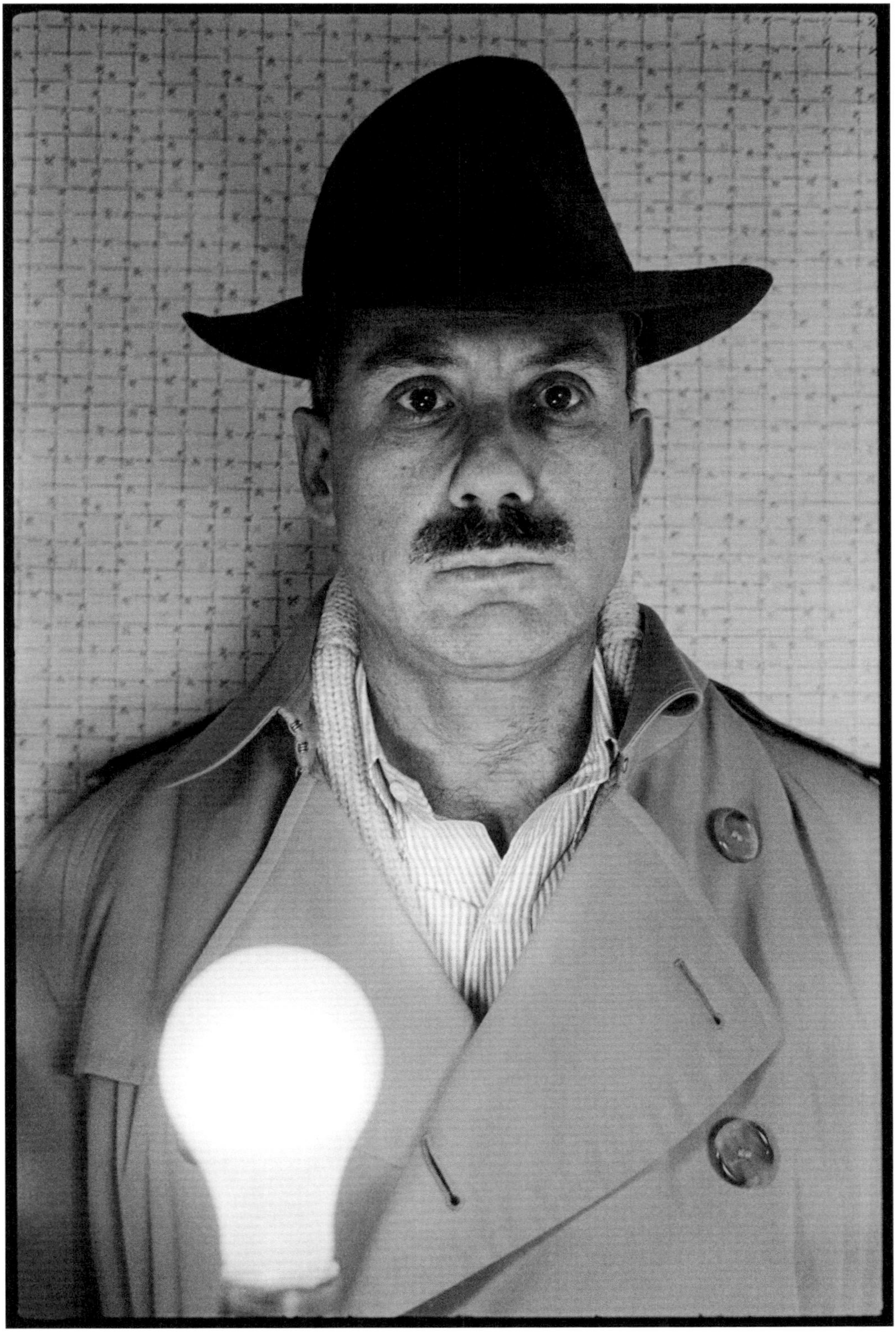

PAUL ÉLUARD

[Eugène Émile Paul Grindel] born Saint-Denis, France, 1895; died Charenton-le-Pont, France, 1952

by Robert Doisneau

Paris, c. 1947

In 1924 Paul Éluard went missing from the Paris scene. Presumed dead, he had in fact set off on a voyage to the Pacific without telling anyone he was leaving. A poet and a prominent exponent of Surrealism, he had disappeared in the hope of placating his inner demons. He would return to France seven months later, eager to reassume his position among the Parisian avant-garde.

Éluard had been an adherent of Surrealism from its infancy, leaving the Dada movement in order to join forces with André Breton and others. He participated in the production of *cadavres exquis* (literally, 'exquisite corpses'), drawings created by means of collaborative game-playing among members of the Surrealist movement, and wrote verses to accompany the photographs taken by Man Ray for the book *Les Mains Libres* (1937). A master of language, Éluard was able to blend the quirks of Surrealism with the linguistic heritage of the past, combining different idioms, patterns of speech and proverbs. His poetry revolved around the subject of love as the supreme human experience.

Éluard's personal life was marked by a number of crises. His first marriage, to the enigmatic Gala (Elena Ivanovna Diakonova), ended when she left him for Salvador Dalí, for whom she had posed on several occasions. His second marriage, to the model Nusch (Maria Benz), was a much happier affair, and provided him with the inspiration for his most passionate love poetry. In 1942, inspired by the events of the Spanish Civil War, Éluard enlisted in the French Communist Party. From that point on, his poetry took on a more political slant. Love was still the central theme, but as an expression of solidarity rather than of physical passion. During the Second World War he participated actively in the French Resistance, and was involved in the production of secret broadcasts and the printing of underground books and newspapers. His poem 'Liberté' (1942) is a love song to freedom in all its forms.

Éluard was also a great lover of art, as can be seen in this photograph of the poet by Robert Doisneau. Taken in Éluard's house, it shows several paintings by some of the most famous artists of the period, including Dalí's portrait of Nusch, painted in 1941.

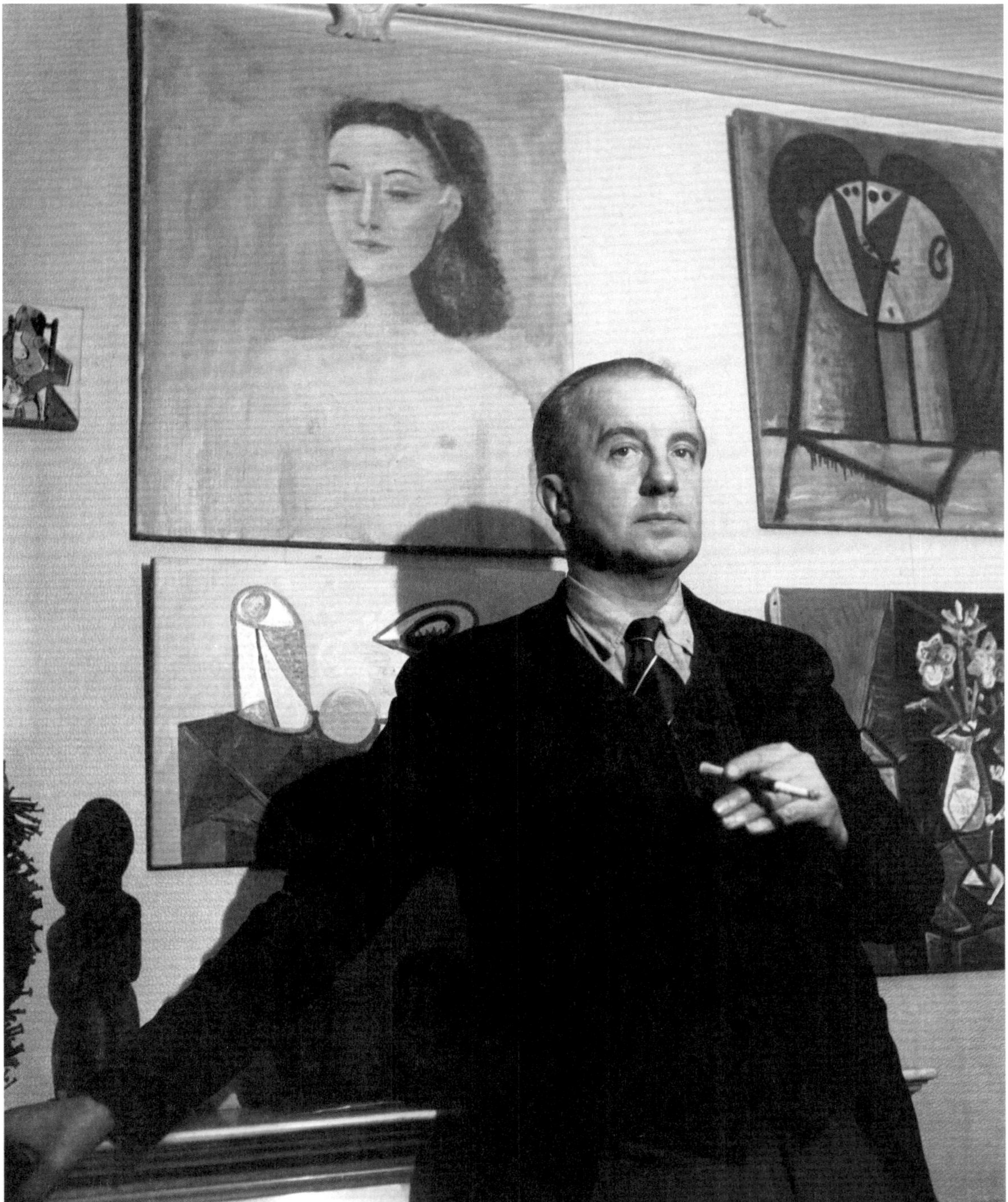

P. O. ENQUIST

[Per Olov Enquist] born Hjoggböle, Sweden, 1934

by Isolde Ohlbaum

Munich, 2009

Per Olov Enquist has established himself as one of the most significant names in a literature that can be defined as 'postmodernist', but has ancient roots that set it apart from the mainstream cannon of modern literature. A journalist, novelist and playwright he has also worked in television, exploiting its narrative possibilities with great skill. He has been relentless in telling the story of the confrontation between religious and psychological concerns in both individuals and society as a whole, and in examining the nature of social control. He regards the present through the lens of history and tells its story through the dilemmas of a past that has become etched into the very character of modern society.

Enquist's work deliberately blends documentary research and invention, focusing on historical personalities and events that he considers to be important for understanding our times. In one of his many plays, *The Night of the Tribades* (1975), he portrayed the great Swedish writer August Strindberg's conflicted and neurotic relationships with women and with society. Another play, *Rain Snakes* (1981), evoked the life of Hans Christian Andersen. Along similar lines, Enquist adapted the script for the film *Hamsun* (1996), about the treasonous conduct of Norwegian Nobel laureate Knut Hamsun during the Second World War, from a novel by Thorkild Hansen. Enquist's novels are also largely inspired by famous individuals and historical events: the story of the eighteenth-century showman scientist Franz Anton Mesmer in *The Magnetist's Fifth Winter* (1964); the struggle of manual labourers in an early twentieth-century timber mill in *The March of the Musicians* (1978); the Swedish Pentecostal revivalists at the start of the nineteenth century in *Lewi's Journey* (2001); the Danish royal court in the eighteenth century – the 'Century of Enlightenment', which for Enquist is the basis of all the contradictions of modern times – in *The Visit of the Royal Physician* (1999); and even Marie Curie and Jean-Martin Charcot's scientific experiments in *The Book About Blanche and Marie* (2006). The novel in which the author may have revealed most about himself, however, was *Captain Nemo's Library* (1990), in which the protagonist of Jules Verne's novel comes to the narrator's assistance in his attempt to understand both the world and himself, asserting that there 'are only three types of people: executioners, victims and traitors'.

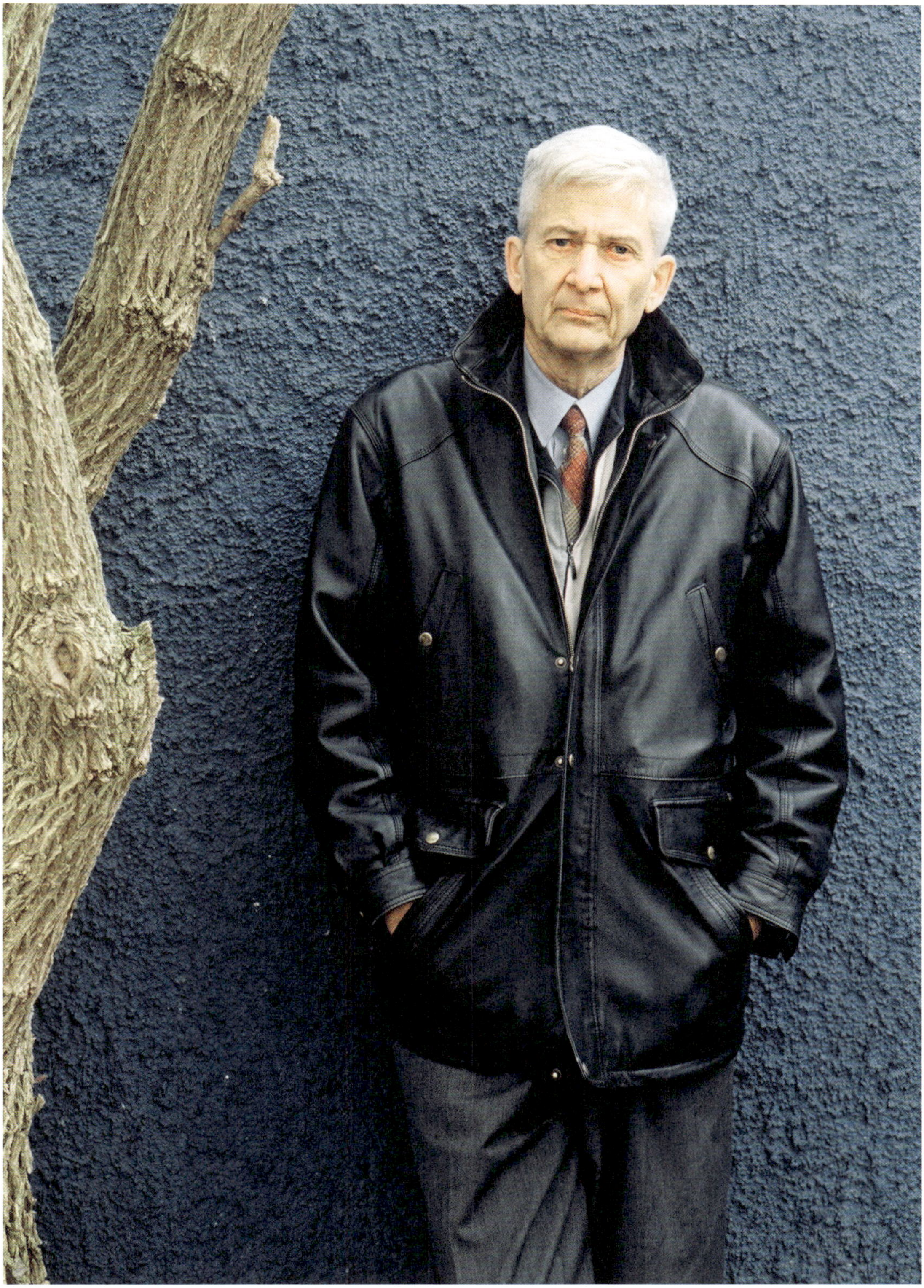

HANS MAGNUS ENZENSBERGER

born Kaufbeuren, Germany, 1929

by René Burri

Munich, 1960

The work of Hans Magnus Enzensberger is characterized by civic engagement, moral indignation, irony and anti-conformism. The writer himself is harder to categorize: over the years he has been a poet, a novelist, a philosopher, an essayist, a journalist, a translator, an editor, a literary critic, a political analyst and an activist. One of the most original voices of post-war Germany, he is also a writer capable of transforming mathematics into a fable-like, fantastical universe (*The Number Devil*, 1997). His ethical and civic impulses can be seen in his early poetry collections *Defence of the Wolves Against the Lambs*(1957) and *The Country's Tongue* (1960), in which he criticized the instinct of the German people to be submissive in the face of authority and fought against the language that he had inherited.

Enzensberger's childhood and adolescence coincided not only with the Third Reich but also with the difficulties experienced by post-war Germany, which struggled to confront its Nazi past and chose instead to celebrate its economic successes. In the 1960s Enzensberger channelled some of his anger into his essays; in the collection *Details* (1964), he focuses his criticism on the power and conformity of the media. It was during this period, while living in a Berlin still divided into East and West, that the writer got to know René Burri. The Magnum photographer was engaged in documenting Germany's post-war recovery; images from this project were later published as *The Germans* (1962).

In 1972 Enzensberger published one of his most accomplished novels, *The Short Summer ofAnarchy*, which uses both a documentary style and oral history to reconstruct the life of the Spanish anarchist Buenaventura Durruti. Enzensberger was a militant figure during this period, and not only in principle: in 1965 he was one of the founders of *Kursbuch*, a radical left-wing magazine; in 1967 the radical collective Kommune 1 established its first headquarters in his Berlin flat; and in 1968 he moved to Cuba to analyse its socialist Marxist society, concluding that it had failed. Europe now seemed to him to be one of the best places to live, and in 1989 he published *Europe, Europe* (1989), a collection of his travel diaries and studies of seven European countries and their cultures.

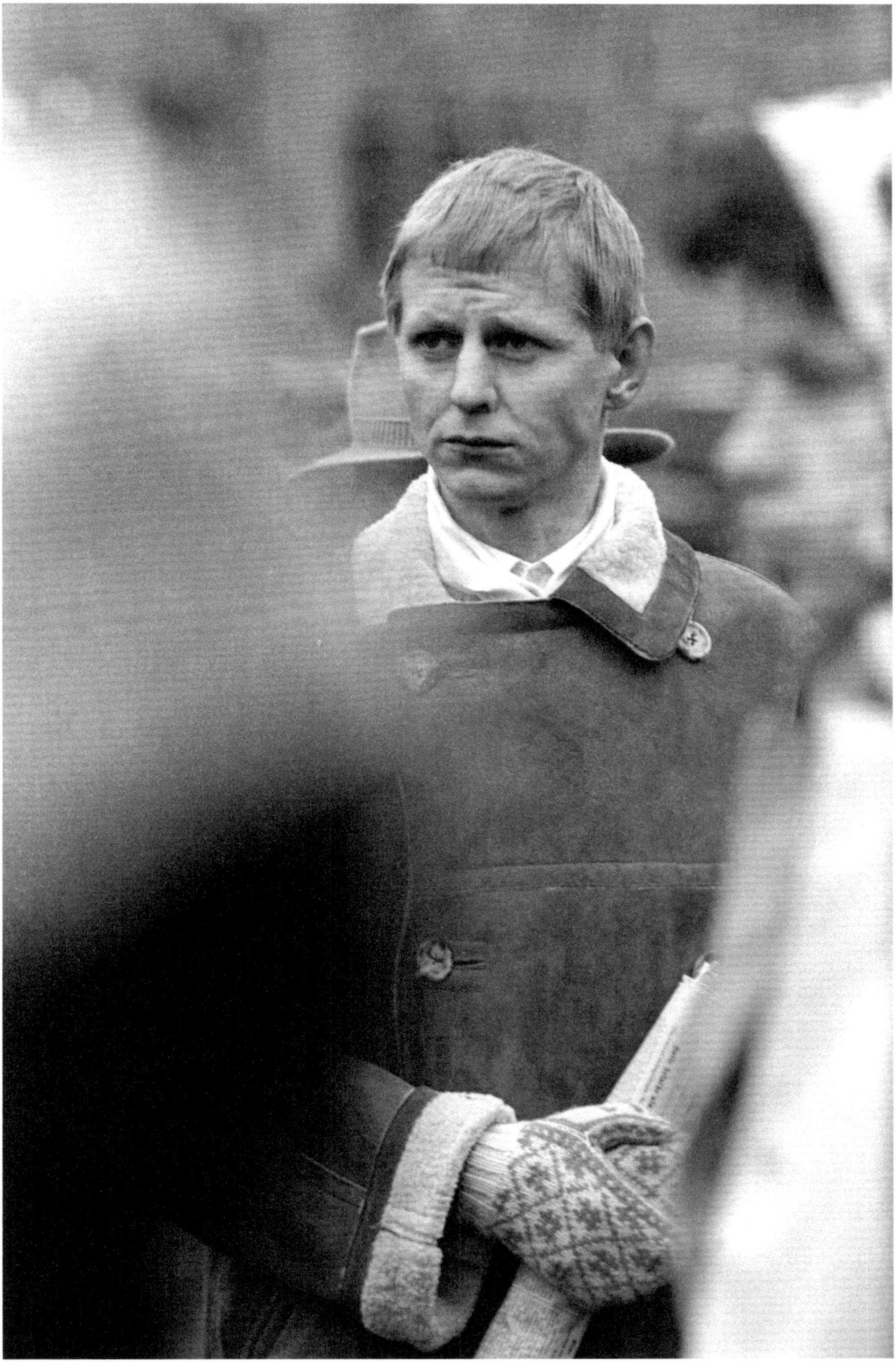

SERGEI ESENIN

born Konstantinovo, Russia, 1895; died St Petersburg, 1925

unknown photographer

Russia, 1914

Sergei Esenin, born in a farming village in Russia, became renowned as the bard of the peasants, although he was equally fascinated by the excitement of the new and the 'mud-filled cities' in which the artistic life of his changing times blossomed. The 'new' in this case was the Bolshevik revolution, in which he believed wholeheartedly. Artistically, however, he sought to sing new songs that were rooted in an ancient and vital rural tradition.

Emerging as a writer in the St Petersburg milieu of Alexander Blok and the Russian Symbolists, Esenin excited the passionate admiration of poetry lovers – who were not restricted to the middle classes – with the violence of his imagery in the poems 'Inonija' and 'Transfiguration' (both 1918), his enthusiasm for violence in *Confessions of a Hooligan* (1920) and his lyrical treatment of it in *Tavern Moscow* (1924), with its nostalgic sympathy for underworld figures of the past. Together with his lover Anatoly Mariengof, a fellow poet, Esenin was recognized as a founder of the Imagist movement. *Pugachev* (1921), his verse drama about a peasant revolt against the Empress Catherine the Great, a story that had previously been recounted by Alexander Pushkin, invoked biblical themes that bordered on the blasphemous and recklessly ignored the new political orthodoxies. Following the first wave of the revolution, Esenin had become disillusioned with the Soviet regime as the interests of peasants were increasingly sacrificed in the name of modernity and industrial factory production was given the central role in the new economy. This disillusionment was expressed in final works such as *Anna Snegina* (1925), in which he told the story of his own life, while in *The Black Man* (1925, published posthumously), he donned the guise of a clown as bizarre and sorrowful as his own verses.

Esenin was only thirty years old when he committed suicide, devastated by alcoholism – but he had lived every moment of his life with maximum possible intensity, and was as famous for his literary bohemianism, his many journeys, his romantic relationships with men and his three marriages (one of them to the celebrated American dancer Isadora Duncan) as he was for his writing. Although the image of Esenin the man often overwhelms that of Esenin the poet, this contradiction was the root of his originality, and his signature juxtaposition of sweetness and violence a mark of his boundless vitality

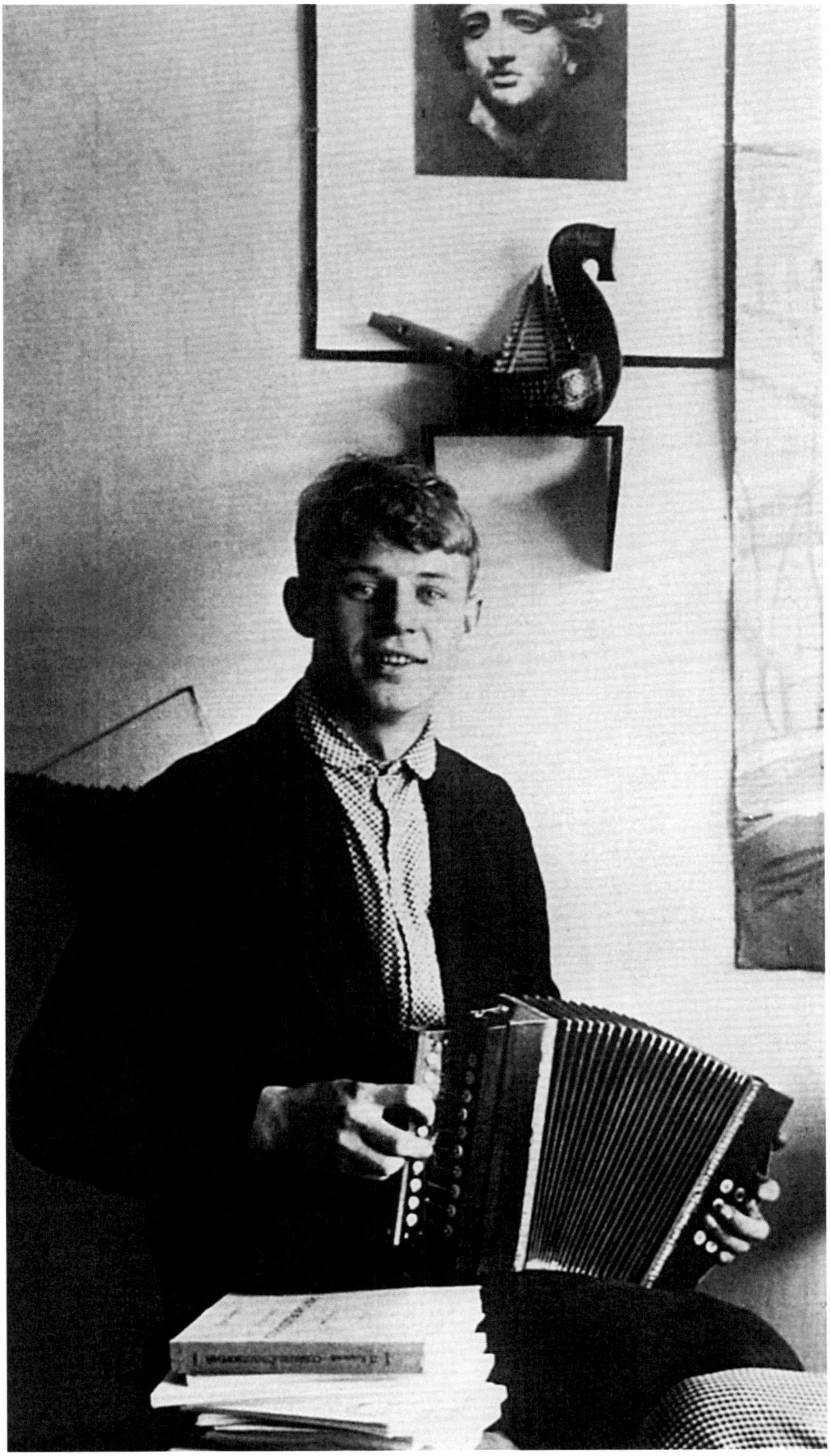

JOHN FANTE

born Denver, Colorado, 1909; died Los Angeles, 1983

unknown photographer

Los Angeles, 1950s

'Fante was my god,' declared Charles Bukowski on several occasions, and it is Bukowski who can be credited with helping John Fante to achieve the recognition he deserved. In 1978 Bukowski was at the height of his fame, while Fante remained 'criminally neglected'. Despite the publication of *The Brotherhood of the Grape* in 1977, he had almost been forgotten, until Bukowski managed to convince his own publisher, Black Sparrow Books, to reprint Fante's forgotten works, beginning with *Ask the Dusk* (1939) in 1980.

John Fante was born the son of impoverished immigrants from Abruzzi, Italy. His initial forays into the literary world met with success, especially the saga of his alter-ego Arturo Bandini. *Wait Until Spring, Bandini* was published in 1938, and the following year he wrote *Ask the Dust,* which was equally well received by the critics. His subsequent novel, *The Little Brown Brothers*, was rejected by the publisher, however, which resulted in a crisis of confidence for Fante. He did not write again until 1952, when *Full of Life* was published successfully and met with approval. During his years of desolation and frustration he had resorted to drinking and gambling, both of which had taken their toll on his spirits and his health.

After the publication of *Full of Life*, Fante enjoyed a fruitful period writing mainly screenplays and short stories, though with the exception of *The Brotherhood of the Grape* (1977) all his works from this period were published posthumously, most notably *1933 Was a Bad Year* (1985) and *West of Rome* (1986), which contained the two novellas *My Dog Stupid* and *The Orgy*. Another period of inactivity and self-doubt followed, but encouraged by the intervention of Bukowski, Fante resumed his writing once again in 1979, despite the physical problems caused by diabetes. He dictated to his wife what was to be his last novel, *Dreams from Bunker Hill*, which was published by Black Sparrow Books in 1982. Fante died in May 1983, too early to see the republication of *Wait Until Spring, Bandini* a few months later or to enjoy the resurgence of enthusiasm for his books that occurred during the 1990s and the start of the second millennium.

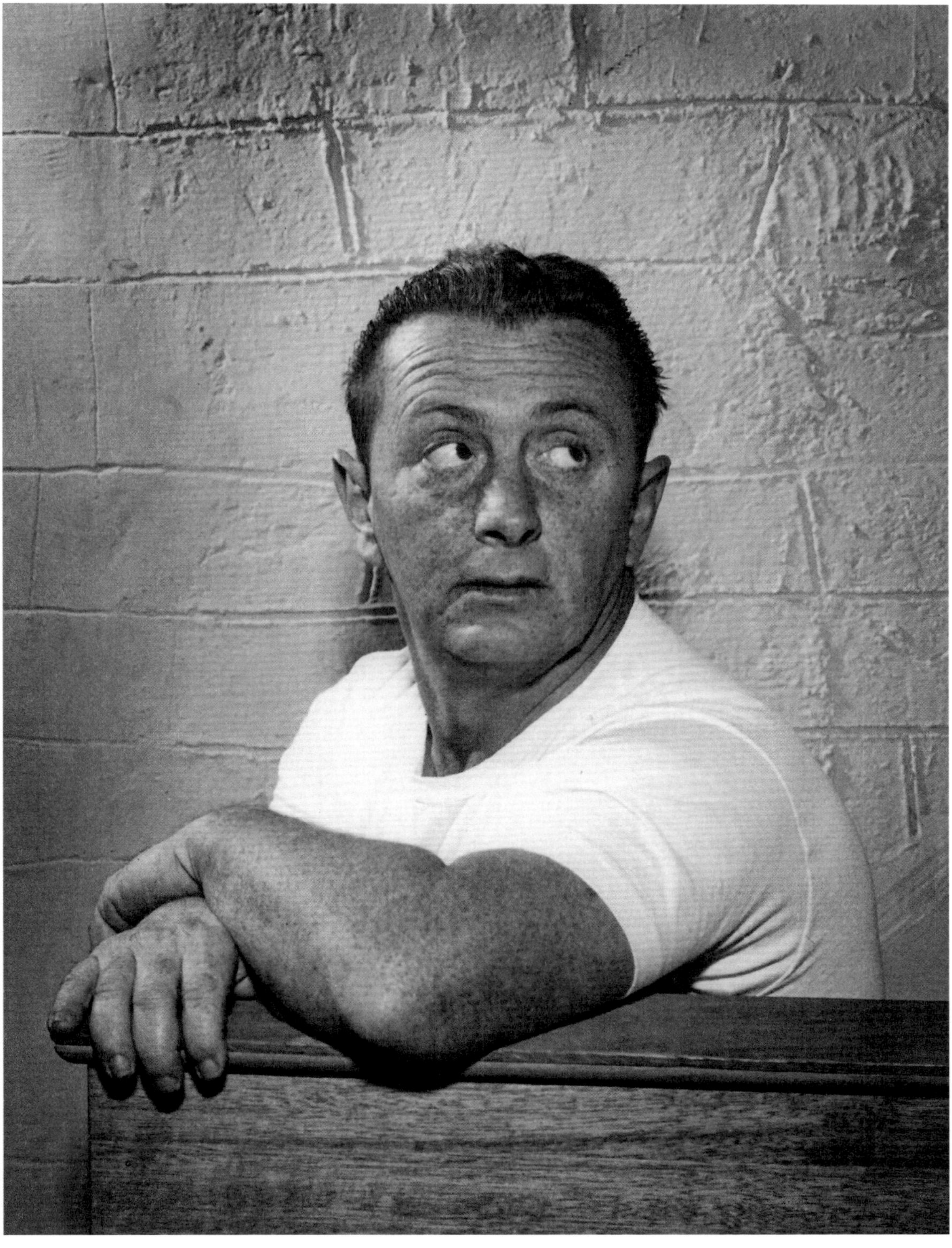

WILLIAM FAULKNER

born New Albany, Mississippi, 1897; died Oxford, Mississippi, 1962

by Henri Cartier-Bresson

Oxford, Mississippi, 1947

While working as a journalist in New Orleans, William Faulkner met the American novelist and short-story writer Sherwood Anderson, who at that time was at the height of his career. Anderson encouraged Faulkner in his desire to be a writer, and agreed to present the manuscript of his first book to his own publishers, on the condition that he did not have to read it himself. Faulkner's manuscript was accepted for publication, and the result, *Soldiers' Pay* (1926), would prove to be the debut novel of one of the greatest writers of the twentieth century.

Faulkner's life was marked by financial hardship and recurrent bouts of alcoholism. In 1918 the great love of his life, Estelle Oldham, whom he had met while still a teenager, was forced into a more prestigious marriage by her parents, and she and Faulkner were not able to marry until 1929, after her divorce from her first husband. That year also saw the publication of *Sartoris*, the first of Faulkner's novels set in Yoknapatawpha, a fictional county based on the writer's childhood memories and the stories he had been told about the South. It also addresses the tensions between black and white, poverty and decadence, and the past and the present.

Towards the end of 1929 Faulkner published what he described as his favourite book, *The Sound and the Fury*, the story of the decline of an old Southern family It is a groundbreaking novel, noted for its innovative structure and use of narrative techniques such as stream of consciousness. Thereafter, Faulkner's quest for new modes of expression and fresh subject matter led to a succession of highly accomplished novels, including *As I Lay Dying* (1930), *Light in August* (1932) and *Absalom! Absalom!* (1936). However, it was only with the publication of *Sanctuary* (1931), a more sensational work written to attract sales, that Faulkner began to receive the critical attention he was due. His status as one of the foremost modernists of his era was confirmed in 1949 when he was awarded the Nobel Prize.

Henri Cartier-Bresson photographed Faulkner relaxing with his dogs among the trees surrounding Rowan Oak, the neoclassical house in Oxford, Mississippi, that he had bought and restored in the 1930s.

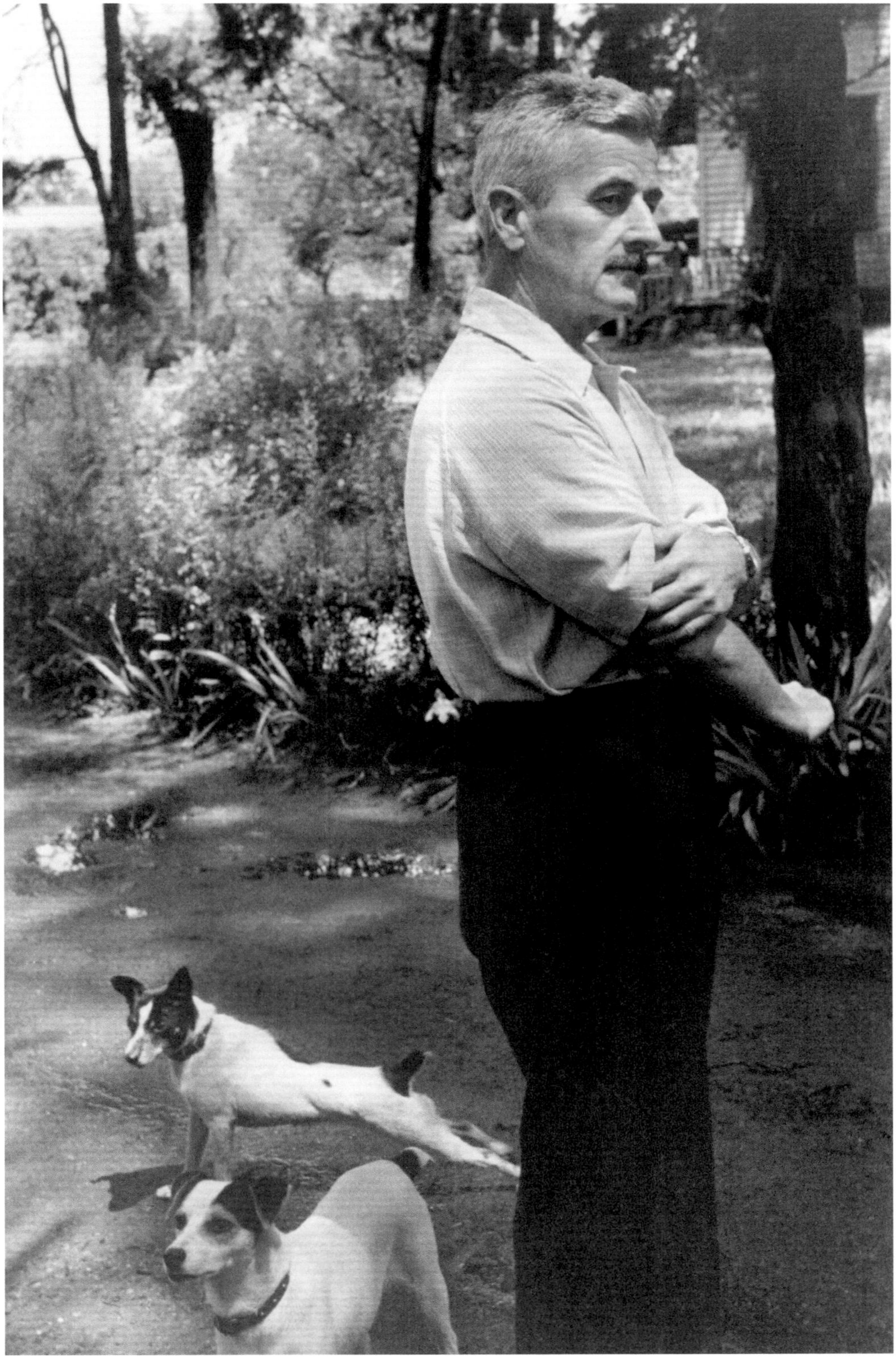

F. SCOTT FITZGERALD

born St Paul, Minnesota, 1896; died Hollywood, California, 1940

unknown photographer

Paris, 1925

There is no other writer (with the exception, perhaps, of Ernest Hemingway) who has elicited the same degree of fascination, or who has been so completely identified with the characters and settings of his novels, as Francis Scott Fitzgerald. *The Beautiful and Damned* (1922), *Tales of the Jazz Age* (1922) and *The Great Gatsby* (1925) sum up an entire era in their titles alone.

Literature had been Fitzgerald's passion since his youth, and he neglected his studies at Princeton University in favour of his writing. In 1917, while still an undergraduate, he enlisted in the US Army and was sent to a training camp in Montgomery, Alabama. It was at a nearby country club that he met Zelda Sayre. Although she initially accepted his proposal of marriage, she later rejected him. Determined to convince her that he could make something of himself, Fitzgerald resumed work on the novel that would become the runaway literary sensation of 1920. *This Side of Paradise* was an immediate best-seller; it was a breath of fresh air, an insider's view of the exciting and liberated world of the post-First World War flapper generation.

This, then, was the Jazz Age, and Fitzgerald and Zelda, by now husband and wife, were living life to the full. They moved to Paris and then to the French Riviera, continuing the high living and big spending that they had begun in New York. Fitzgerald wrote short stories to support their expensive lifestyle; *The Great Gatsby* (1925), widely considered Fitzgerald's finest work, was also written in this period. His relationship with Zelda proved extremely difficult, and in the early 1930s she began to show signs of the mental illness that would eventually lead to her death in a psychiatric hospital. The strain of their marriage, together with the atmosphere of decadence and desperation that pervaded the Jazz Age, manifested itself in his fourth novel, *Tender Is the Night* (1934). Towards the end of the 1930s Fitzgerald developed serious health problems but continued to write, producing screenplays in Hollywood. It was there that he died from a heart attack, leaving his final novel, *The Last Tycoon* (1941), unfinished.

Taken by an unknown photographer, this photograph of the Fitzgeralds at Christmas perhaps reflects some of the tensions underlying their family life. We see a bourgeois interior, a Christmas tree festooned with decorations, and Fitzgerald, Zelda and their daughter, Frances (known as 'Scottie'), performing a dance step together. Their gestures, however, seem self-conscious, the expressions in their eyes and their forced smiles betraying their unease.

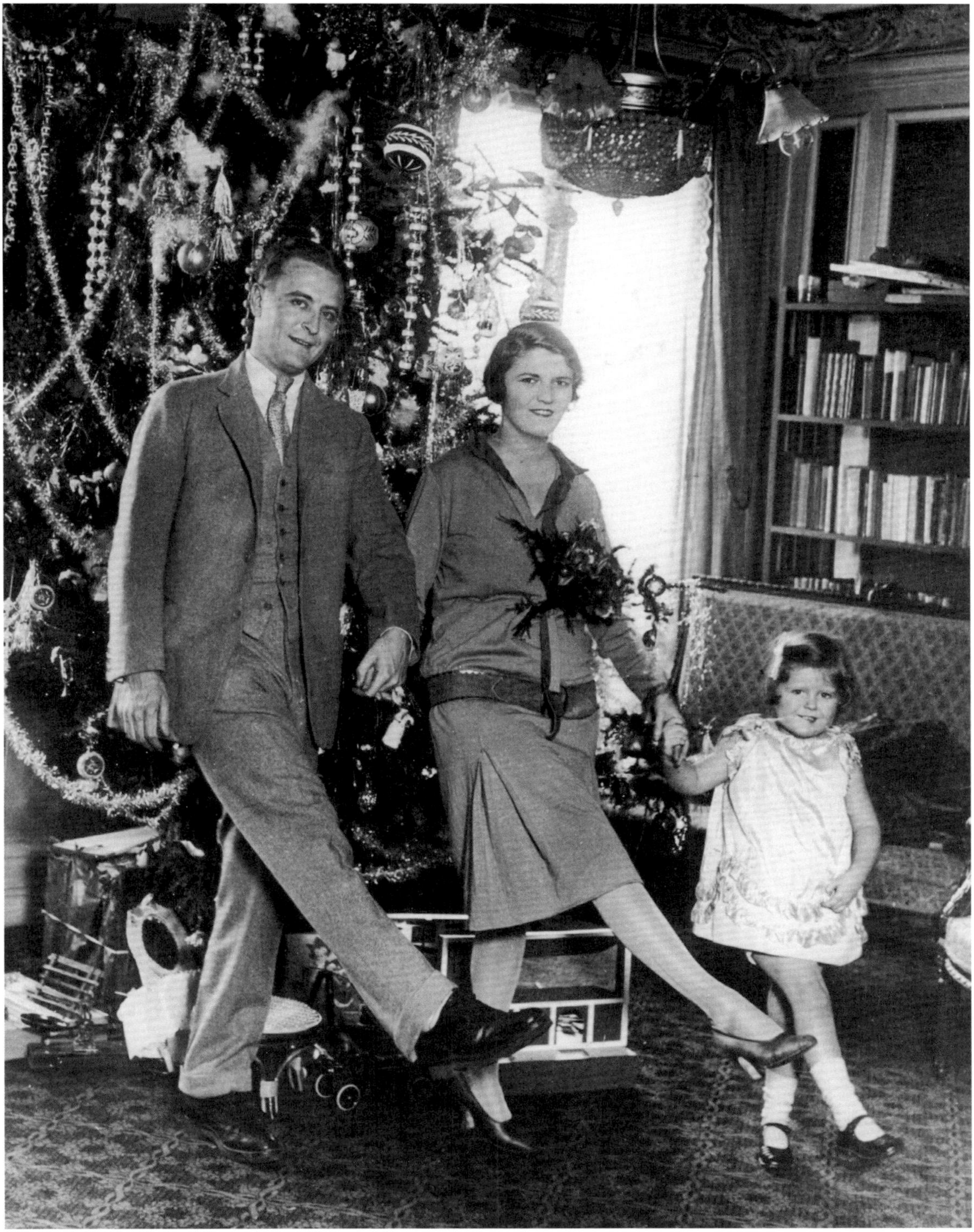

JONATHAN SAFRAN FOER

born Washington DC, 1977

by Peter Rigaud

New York, 2006

After graduating from Princeton University in 1999, Jonathan Safran Foer travelled to the Ukraine to investigate further the subject of his undergraduate thesis: the life of his maternal grandfather, a Jew who had been saved from the Holocaust by a woman whose photograph his mother still preserved. His adviser for his thesis had been the American writer Joyce Carol Oates, who, having also been his tutor for an introductory creative-writing course at Princeton, was quick to recognize his potential. Although the journey revealed nothing new about his grandfather's story, it did give Safran Foer the idea for a novel, *Everything Is Illuminated* (2002). Written in just ten weeks, but edited over the course of three years, the book was an immediate success, winning numerous prizes and awards. It also made him one of the most high-profile authors of the new millennium.

Safran Foer's second novel followed in 2005. *Extremely Loud and Incredibly Close* tells the story of Oskar Schell, a young boy whose father was killed in the terrorist attacks of 11 September 2001. Oskar travels around New York City in search of the lock into which a mysterious key, the last trace he has of his father, will fit. The novel's critical reception was somewhat ambivalent, as was perhaps inevitable after such a brilliant debut. His next book, *Eating Animals* (2009), was a work of non-fiction, an investigation into intensive farming methods, animal rights and our modern relationship with food.

In addition to his novels and *Eating Animals*, Safran Foer has written numerous short stories, articles and essays. In 2010 he published *Tree of Codes*, an artwork in the form of a book. To create it, he physically removed series of words from his favourite book, *The Street of Crocodiles* (1934) by Bruno Schulz, thereby producing a new story. Peter Rigaud's photograph of the author was taken not long after the publication of *Extremely Loud and Incredibly Close*. Behind Safran Foer, part of the Manhattan skyline is visible, still scarred by the absence of the Twin Towers.

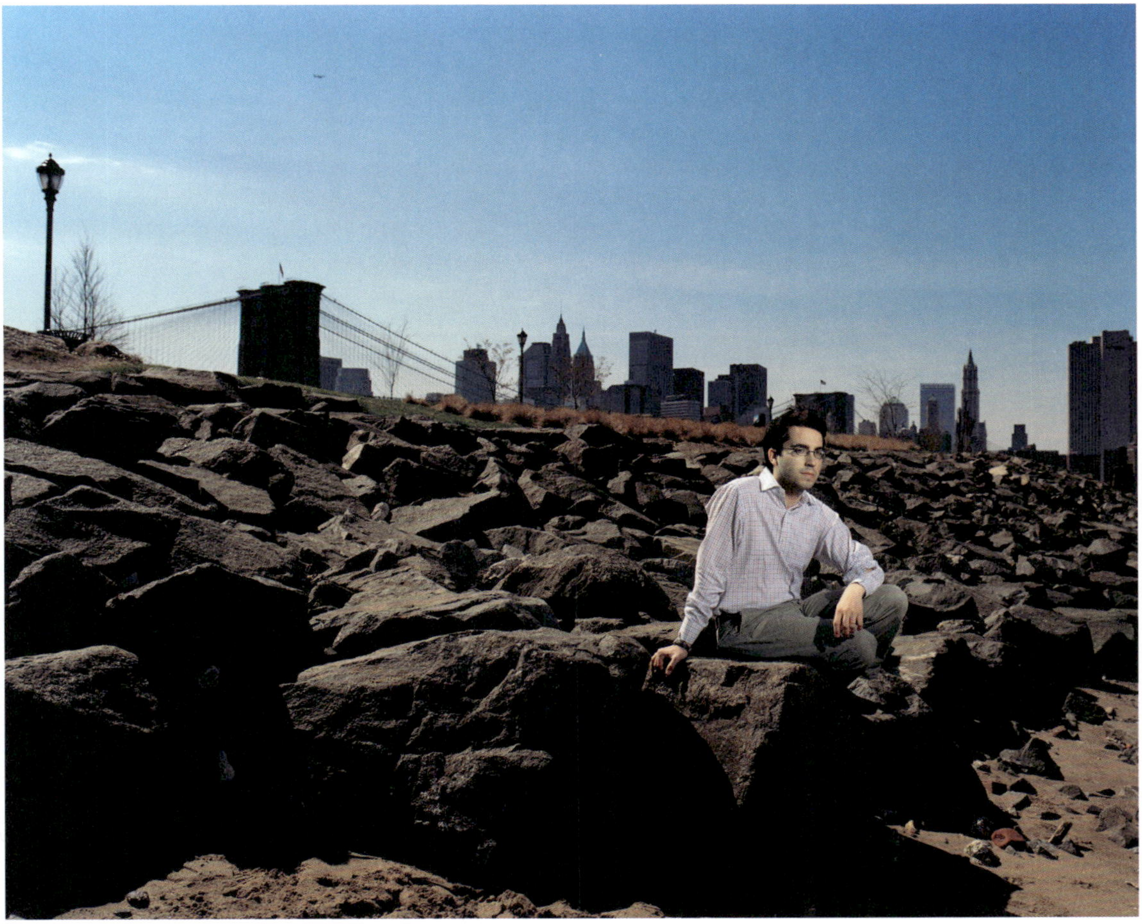

JANET FRAME

born Dunedin, New Zealand, 1924; died Dunedin, New Zealand, 2004

by Jerry Bauer

London, c. 1963

Between the ages of nineteen and twenty-seven, Janet Frame was periodically incarcerated in a mental hospital. While behind its walls she – believing herself to be abnormal – felt protected. From the very start her life had been a catalogue of personal disasters: her childhood was overshadowed by the death of her two sisters and it was made more difficult by her own very unusual, imaginative and extremely fragile personality. This led her to be diagnosed (a misdiagnosis, it would emerge) as a schizophrenic and undergo electroconvulsive therapy. Frame was scheduled to have a lobotomy because of her 'illness'; however, the timely success of her first collection of short stories, *The Lagoon and other Stories* (1951), which won the Hubert Church Prose Award, led to the procedure being cancelled.

After Frame was released, it was Frank Sargeson (born Norris Frank Davey), the master of New Zealand storytelling, who encouraged her to go on writing – even offering her lodgings in a shed on his property. So it was that in 1957 she published her first novel, *Owls Do Cry*. From this time onwards she began to travel, spending seven years in England before returning to New Zealand, and leaving her homeland again only to make several trips to USA. Throughout this period she carried on writing, producing titles such *Faces in the Water* (1961), *The Edge of the Alphabet* (1962) and *Scented Gardens for the Blind* (1963), which were mostly about her own appalling history and the many different experiences she had faced behind the walls of the institution. The three volumes of her autobiography – *To the Is-Land* (1982), *An Angel at My Table* (1984) and *The Envoy from Mirror City* (1985) – prove, if proof were needed, that writing really can save your life.

Her stories are chilling portraits of a pitiless war: a war waged between the interior world of fragile and sensitive people and the external world. During these encounters sensitive individuals feel, and – except in extremely rare cases such as her own – often are, irredeemably lost. Her pages are populated by epileptics, the mentally ill and artists, but it was her most autobiographical novels that brought her to wider public attention, especially after Jane Campion chose to make *An Angel at My Table* (1990), a film that examined Frame's experiences.

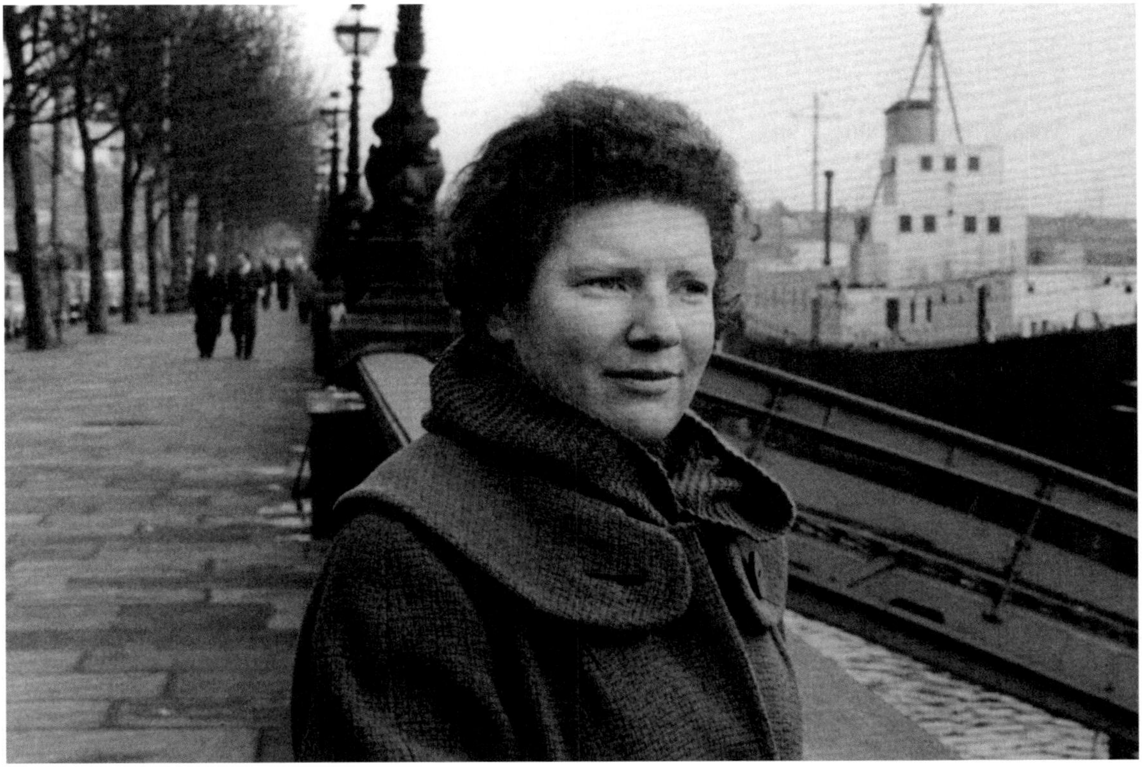

JONATHAN FRANZEN

born Western Springs, Illinois, 1959

by Marion Ettlinger

New York, 1996

Jonathan Franzen enjoyed high-profile free publicity in 2010 when US President Barack Obama was photographed exiting a bookstore with a copy of Franzen's novel *Freedom* (2010) and Oprah Winfrey made the novel a selection for her influential book club, inviting the author to appear on her television chat show. That same year *TIME* magazine featured Franzen on its front cover, a rare accolade for a novelist (only J. D. Salinger, Vladimir Nabokov, Toni Morrison, James Joyce and John Updike have been so honoured). The cover photograph was accompanied by the caption 'Great American Novelist', a phrase that generated controversy, for Franzen is one of those authors over whom opinion seems perpetually divided. His harshest critics accuse him of being an easy read, lacking the depth and substance of fellow American authors David Foster Wallace or Don DeLillo, and of skimming over the reality of the American middle classes. Others, perhaps in the majority, see in him a writer who explores the relationships and power struggles of Middle America and the characteristics of the American psyche with compassion, offering an interesting and thought-provoking cross-section of human life.

Despite the perpetual debate, there is no doubt that Franzen will go down in history as the author who best documented the life of the American middle classes in the Bush era, with their personal and professional successes and failures, social tensions, generational conflicts and overriding sense of unease at living in a world of political, social and economic uncertainty. *The Corrections,* the book that first made him famous, was published in 2001. In the intervening nine years before the publication of *Freedom*, he established a reputation as a controversial and acute essayist, tackling issues such as consumerism and the technological revolution. He has published two collections of essays: *How To Be Alone* (2002) and *Farther Away* (2012).

Marion Ettlinger has photographed writers, particularly American ones, for almost thirty years. This shot captures something of the ambiguity surrounding the figure of Franzen, with a clever juxtaposition of light and dark, and studied elegance. It is an accurate reflection of the public persona of this author, who would nonetheless prefer to remain private.

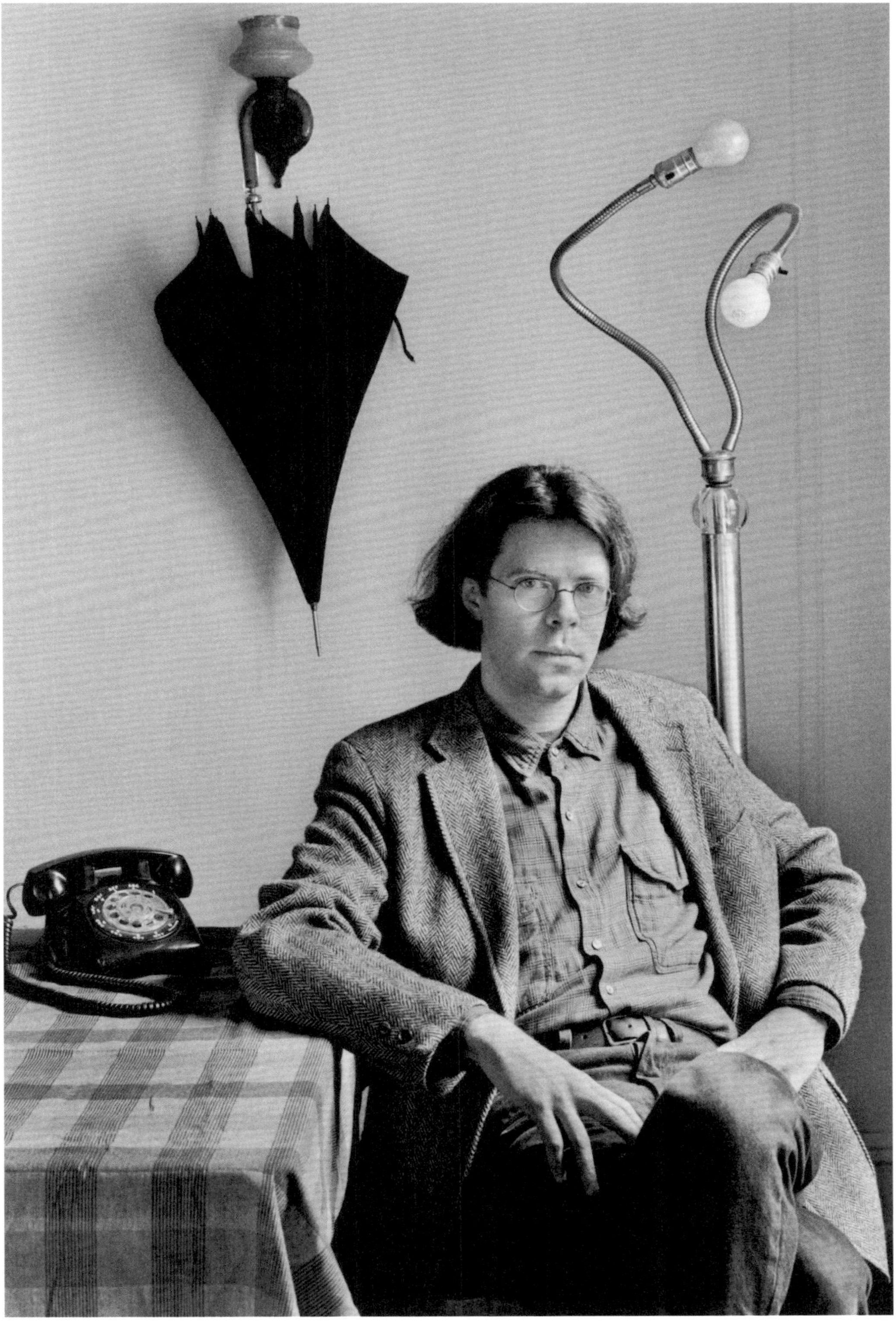

CARLOS FUENTES

born Panama City, Panama, 1928; died Mexico City, Mexico, 2012

by Inge Morath

Mexico, 1960

The Mexican writer Carlos Fuentes spent much of his early life travelling, at first with his family – his father was a diplomat – and then on his own as he followed his father into the diplomatic service. At the same time, his artistic career was travelling along the parallel lines of literature and cinema; in the 1960s, he wrote several screenplays with Gabriel García Márquez.

Fuentes's writing revolves around his interest in history and Latin America's search for an identity; it is also characterized by linguistic and formal experimentation. The narrative in *Where the Air Is Clear* (1958), a book in which the principal character is arguably Mexico City itself, takes the form of a fragmentary collage. In *The Death of Artemio Cruz* (1962), the eponymous narrator retraces the past and the present at the moment of his own death; by alternating between different time periods in this way, Fuentes examines how a young revolutionary could have become a corrupt and powerful man. *Our Land* (1975), considered one of the greatest works of Latin American storytelling, is a historical epic, beginning in the Spain of the Catholic Monarchs and ending in the twentieth century. Fuentes continued to experiment in his more mature works, such as *Destiny and Desire* (2008), in which the severed head of Josué Nadal becomes a symbol of violence in Mexico: 'I'm one of fifty decapitated heads this week, the seventh today, and the only one in the past three and a quarter hours.' Fuentes was nominated for the Nobel Prize in Literature numerous times.

Magnum photographer Inge Morath portrayed many of the twentieth century's greatest artists and writers from the 1950s onwards. Her familiarity with many of her subjects allowed her to imbue her images with a sense of intimacy. Here, the Mexican writer's sensitive and slightly melancholy gaze seems to have been captured not during a formal photo session, but in a moment of quiet reflection.

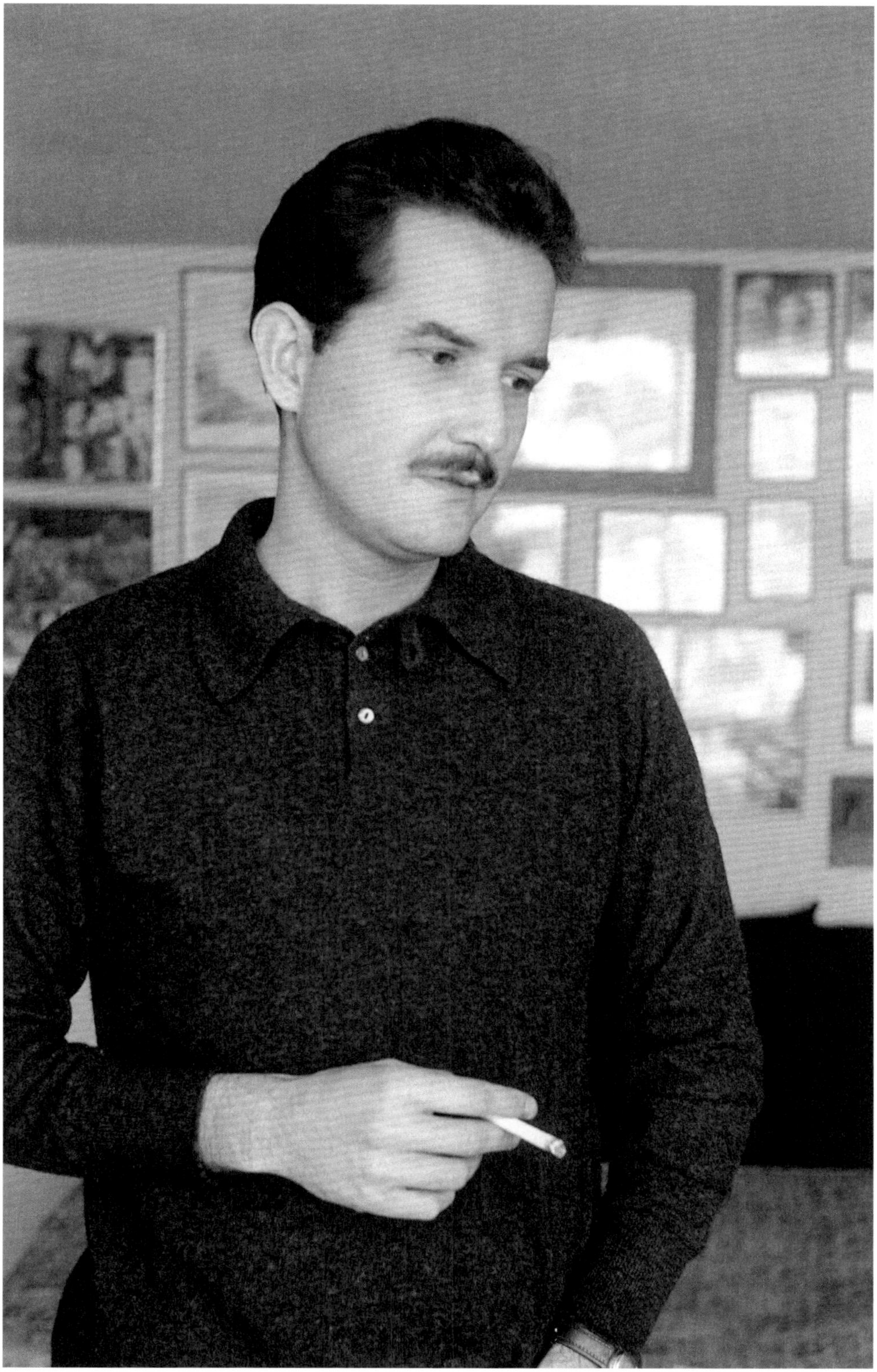

CARLO EMILIO GADDA

born Milan, Italy, 1893; died Rome, 1973

unknown photographer

Rome, 1960

When examining a writer who placed autobiography at the heart of his extraordinary literary production, it seems only fitting to begin with some biographical details. Born in Milan in 1893, Carlo Emilio Gadda learned a great deal observing the mores of his once well-off, middle-class family, and in later work no one, not even himself, was spared from the derisive unmasking of pretensions. It was his father's unfortunate investments (which included the construction of a villa in Brianza that Gadda detested) and subsequent death that reduced the family's circumstances. Gadda unwillingly became an engineer to please his Hungarian mother.

With the onset of the First World War, Gadda, aged twenty-two, travelled to the front filled with nineteenth-century notions of heroism, patriotism and faith in progress. He sought redemption through action, but what he found was quite different. He described this experience in his war diaries using his most withering language. Rather than heroes, he found: 'Napoleons over our heads and scum behind our backs.' He was taken prisoner at Caporetto and although this defeat weighed heavily on his soul and future, it had an explosive effect on his literary output. Living in a world in which he had seen war led him to question the power of words, and fiercely denounce the condition of being a favourite son and yet a man without qualities, incapable of heroism.

When his mother died in 1936, Gadda sold the villa in Brianza, banked the profits, gave up working as an engineer once and for all and started writing full-time. Between 1938 and 1941 he produced one of the great masterpieces of Italian literature, *Acquainted With Grief* (published in 1963). The novel is set in the imaginary country of Maradagàl, which, despite supposedly being in South America, greatly resembled the town of Brianza under Fascist rule. In this work an engineer called Gonzalo Pirobutirro – the author's alter ego – suffers from neurasthenia, and goes on to fulminate against the mentality, behaviour and language of his social group.

At the end of the Second World War, Gadda's Commissario Ingravallo arrived, a detective attempting to make sense of a reality that tended to remain more than a little muddled. Ingravallo (yet another of the author's alter egos) tries unsuccessfully to unravel the tangled problem of *That Awful Mess on the Via Merulana* (1957). Although nothing is resolved and no conclusion is reached, Gadda's baroque murder mystery shook the foundations of contemporary Italian literature.

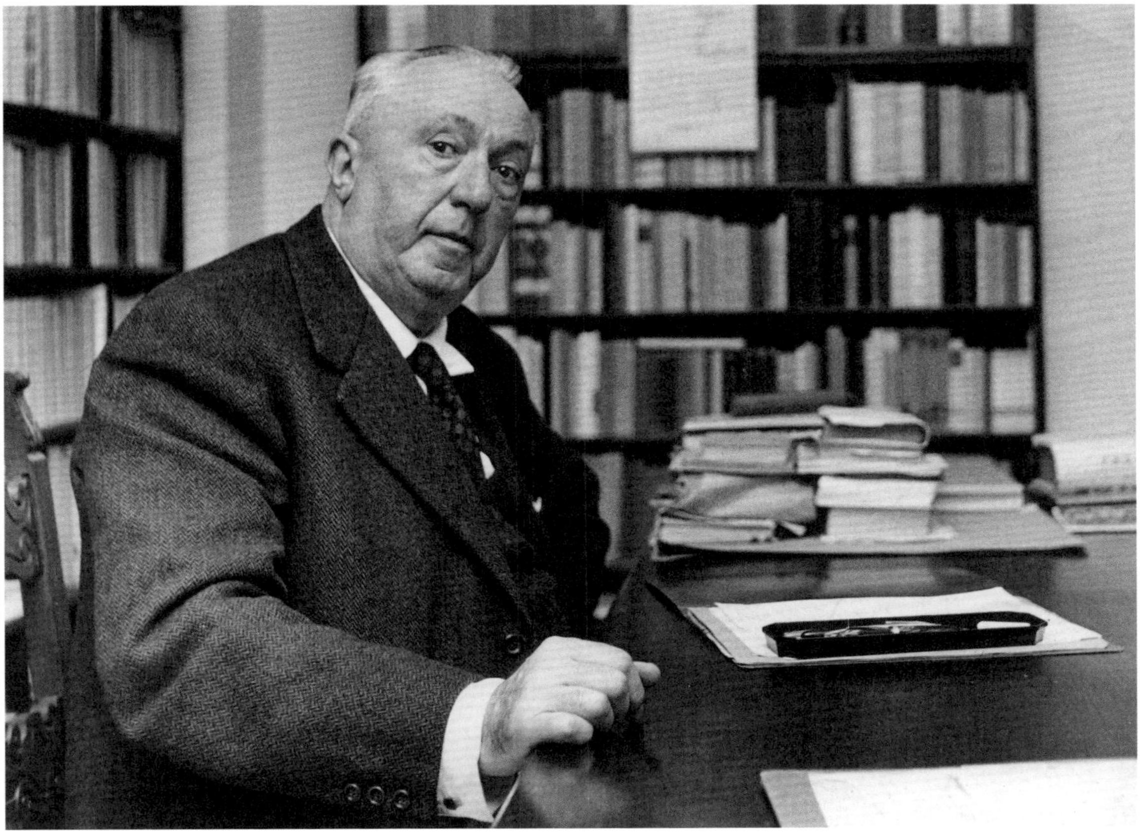

FEDERICO GARCÍA LORCA

born Fuente Vaqueros, Spain, 1898; died Víznar, Spain, 1936

by 'Chim' (David Seymour)

Madrid, 1936

'What a poet! I have never seen grace and genius, a winged heart and a crystalline waterfall, come together in anyone else as they did in him. Federico García Lorca was the extravagant *duende* [mysterious force, akin to 'soul' and authenticity]; his was a magnetic joyfulness that generated a zest for life in his heart and radiated it like a planet.' This is how Pablo Neruda remembered him, yet García Lorca's dates of birth and death coincided with two terrible events in recent Spanish history: the loss of its last colonies, and the end of the Republican dream.

Born in Andalusia, García Lorca moved to Madrid in 1919. There he spent time with Rafael Alberti, Salvador Dalí and Luis Buñuel. Two years later he published *Libro de poemas* (Book of poems, 1921) in which his mature lyric style could already be glimpsed. It blossomed later in *Songs* (1927) when his popular spontaneity was combined with his sophisticated style and his rediscovery of Andalusian folklore. His poems in *Gypsy Ballads* (1928) depicted the world of the Gypsies, who for him symbolized spontaneity and a lost innocence.

In 1932 the Republican government made García Lorca director of the experimental travelling theatre La Barraca (literally 'The Shack'), with a commission to take the classic works of the Spanish stage to the most remote parts of the country. García Lorca saw this as the concrete realization of his dream of culture made available to all. After travelling to Argentina and Uruguay, he returned to Spain at the time when Rafael Alberti and Jose Bergamín were secretary and president of the Alliance of Anti-Fascist Intellectuals. García Lorca felt sympathy for the movement, and in 1935 he signed the anti-Fascist manifesto. This portrait was taken in Madrid by David Seymour at the start of July 1936.

García Lorca had returned to Granada after the start of the war, but felt himself to be in danger. He was arrested one day in August 1936 and shot in cold blood. The lament that he had written in 1935 for the bullfighter Ignacio Sánchez Mejías took on sinister, prophetic tone: 'At five in the afternoon. / It was exactly five in the afternoon. / A boy brought the white sheet / *at five in the afternoon.* / A basket of lime already prepared / *at five in the afternoon.* / The rest was death, and death alone / *at five in the afternoon.*'

This photograph of García Lorca was lost until 2007, when it was rediscovered among the images in the famous 'Mexican suitcase', which contained more than 4,000 negatives taken by Robert Capa, Gerda Taro and Seymour himself during the Spanish Civil War.

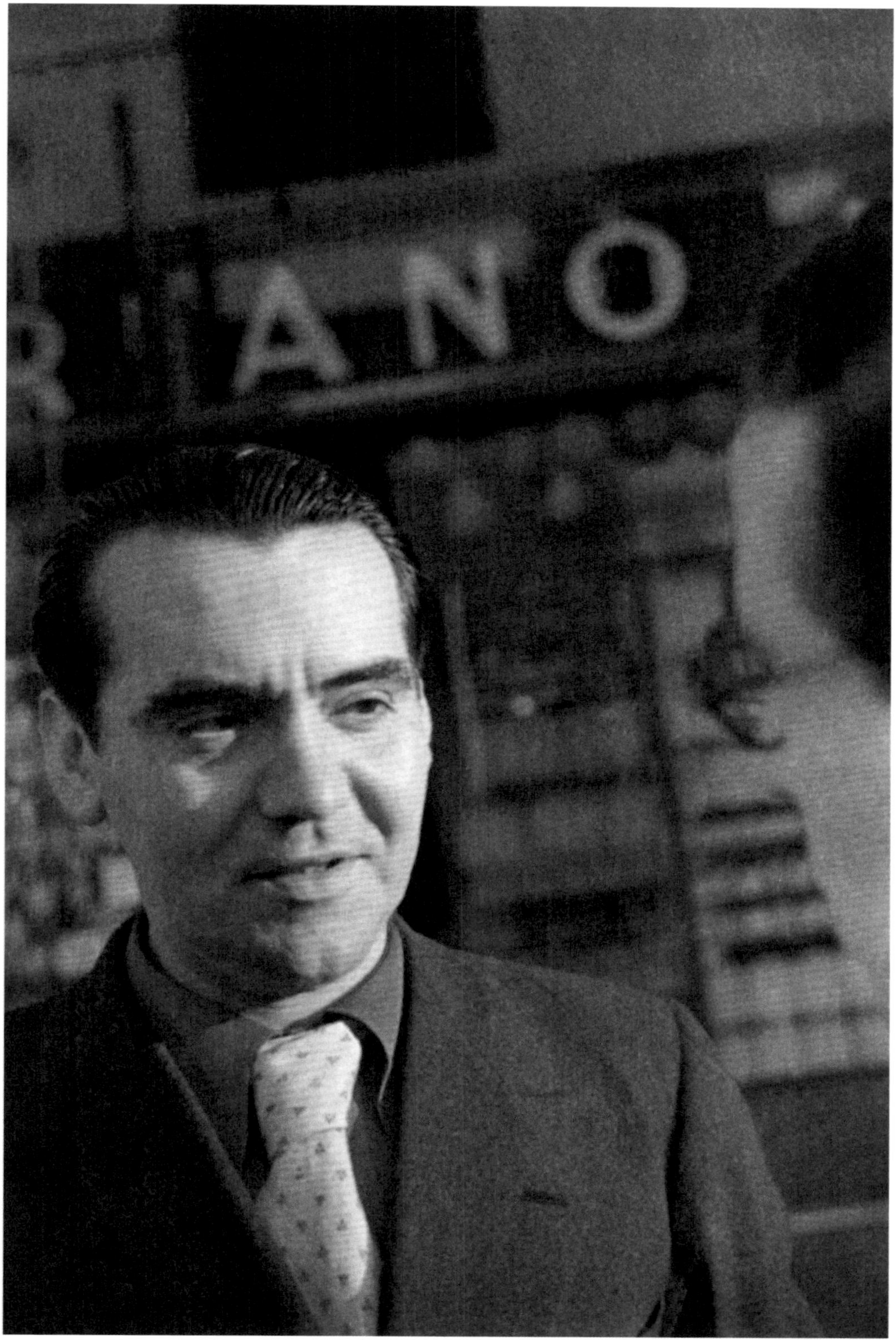
RIANO

GABRIEL GARCÍA MÁRQUEZ

born Aracataca, Colombia, 1928; died Mexico City, 2014

by Isabel Steva Hernández

Colombia, 1975

In 1982 Gabriel García Márquez was awarded the Nobel Prize for 'his novels and short stories, in which the fantastic and the realistic are combined in a richly composed world of imagination, reflecting a continent's life and conflicts'. In his acceptance speech, 'The Solitude of Latin America', García Márquez chose to focus on the region's apparent isolation from the West as a consequence of the latter's inability to comprehend the real Latin America, exemplified by a tendency to think of it as being inhabited by 'haunted men and historic women, whose unending obstinacy blurs into legend'. This link between solitude and the Latin American experience is one that García Márquez had already explored in the novel that made him famous, *One Hundred Years of Solitude*, which was published in Buenos Aires in 1967.

García Márquez has always rejected the tag of 'magical realism', preferring instead the term 'sorrowful realism': behind physical reality, he argues, there is always another poetic reality that is tangible and not magical. *One Hundred Years of Solitude* tells the multi-generational story of the Buendía family, whose members live in Macondo. Once a happy place, the town has since been destroyed by civil wars, by the banana plantation owners, by poverty and by the coming of the railway. It stands as a metaphor for the whole of Latin America, for a region that, before it was carved up first by its colonizers and then by its dictators, had been an earthly paradise. The story itself is told with explosive narrative force.

With *One Hundred Years of Solitude*, García Márquez brought about a renaissance in novel writing. It is this very book that the writer has placed on his head in Isabel Steva Hernández's photograph of him. The image seems to echo the great iconographic tradition in which saints and famous people are portrayed with the specific attributes that make them universally recognizable. However, in Hernández's anti-mythologizing image, García Marquez seems almost bent over under the weight of his work, his gaze directed towards the camera and his readers.

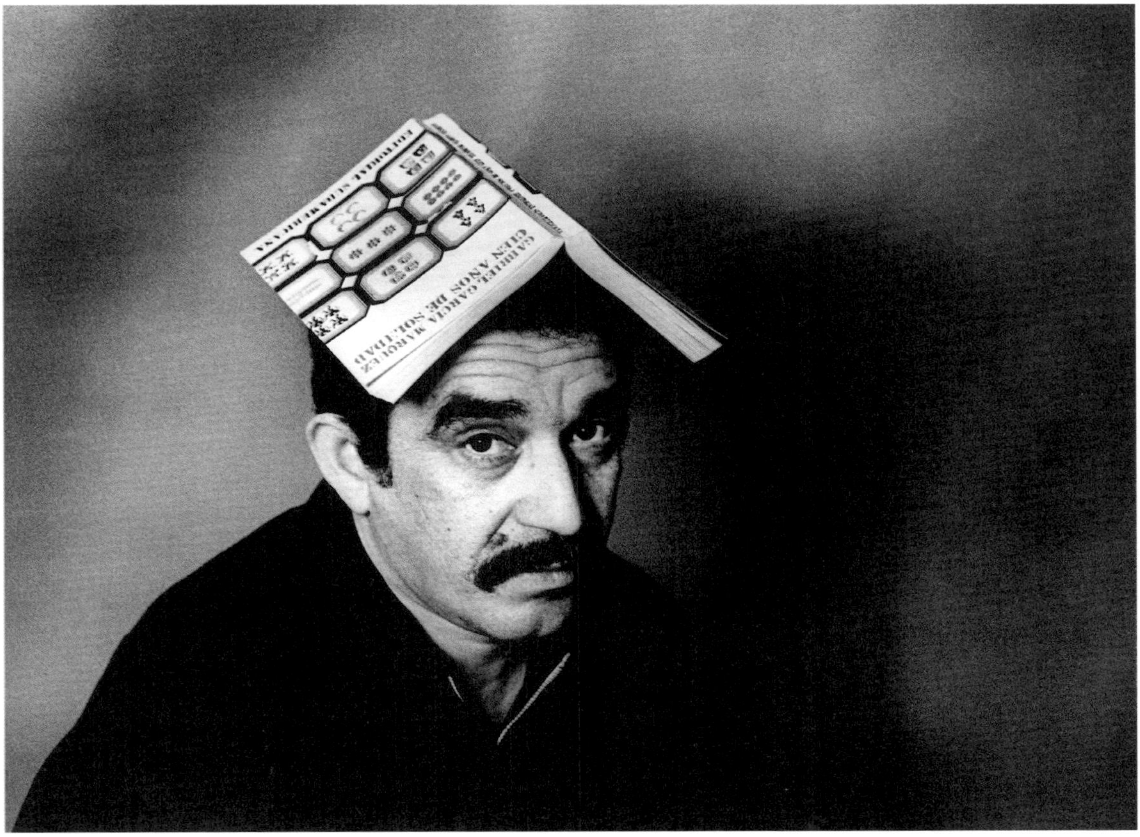
GABRIEL GARCIA MARQUEZ
CIEN AÑOS DE SOLEDAD
EDITORIAL SUDAMERICANA

JEAN GENET

born Paris, 1910; died Paris, 1986

by Leonard Freed

New Haven, Connecticut, 1970

In this photograph of Jean Genet, taken by Leonard Freed while the photographer was documenting the civil rights movement in the USA, the French writer is seen participating in a demonstration held by the Black Panther Party at Yale University. In his search for echoes of the civil uprisings of May 1968 in France and elsewhere, Genet was always ready to agitate on behalf of radical political groups, such as Yasser Arafat's Palestinian Liberation Organization. Genet also dedicated his last book, *Prisoner of Love* (1986), to the theme of political activism.

Genet wrote his first novel, *Our Lady of the Flowers* (1944), while in prison. It was actually this period of incarceration that allowed him to dedicate himself to writing. The lives of his fellow prisoners provided him with inspiration, while the prison walls offered him some protection from the conformism and hypocrisy that he perceived in modern society: 'Prison offered me the first consolation, the first peace, the first friendly fellowship: I experienced them in the realm of foulness.'

Genet's life was both complicated and fascinating, alternating between crime and literature. Having been left by his mother in a children's home, from where he was later adopted, he spent time as an inmate in various prisons, a soldier in the French Foreign Legion, a beggar, a petty thief and a prostitute. However, he was also a passionate writer, poet and dramatist, and his literary talents were soon recognized by both Jean Cocteau and Jean-Paul Sartre. The latter made him the subject of a book, *Saint Genet: Actor and Martyr* (1952) which, although it brought him notoriety, also had the unfortunate effect of temporarily blocking his creativity.

Genet was an insatiable explorer of artistic forms. In 1950 he directed a short film, *A Song of Love*, which tells the story of the frustrated desires of a group of prisoners and the sadism of their guards through powerfully contrasting imagery, without the use of dialogue. In the early 1980s the German director Rainer Werner Fassbinder paid homage to Genet with a film version of his novel *Querelle of Brest* (1947), a story of sailors, the sea and murder set in the titular French port.

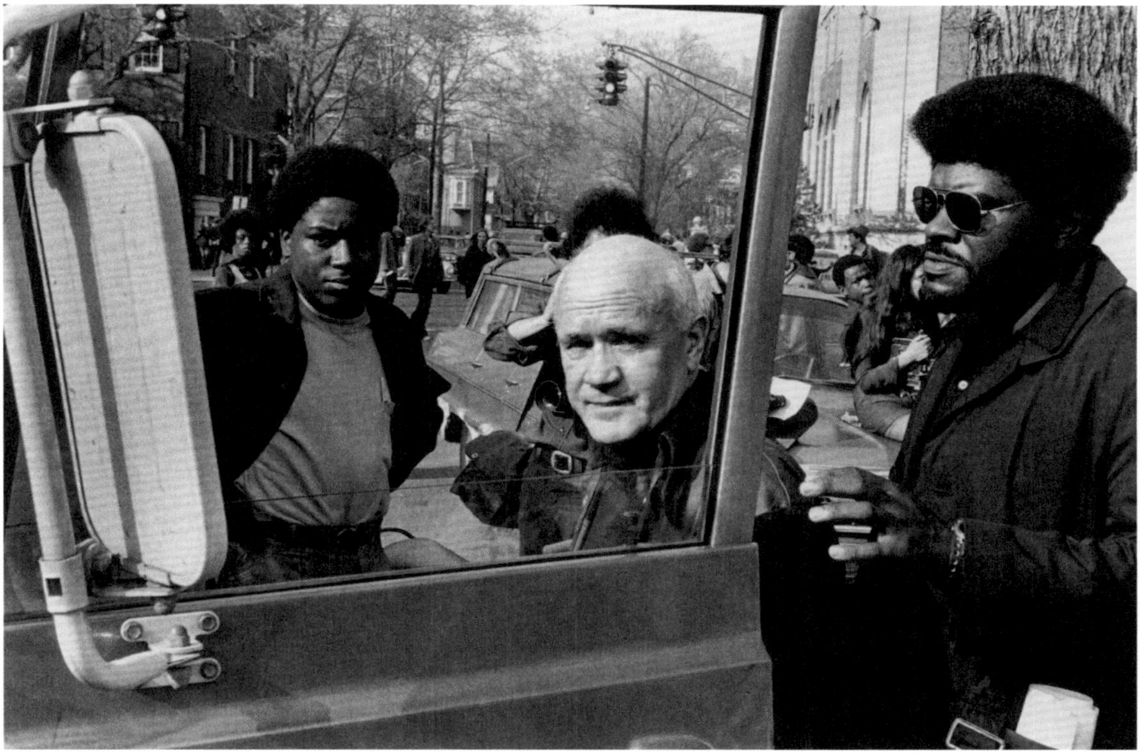

AMITAV GHOSH

born Calcutta, India, 1956

by Sophie Bassouls

Paris, 1990

Born in Calcutta in 1956, Amitav Ghosh grew up moving between India, Bangladesh, Sri Lanka and Iran. His captivating stories encompass multitudes of major and minor characters, often speaking a variety of languages and exhibiting different behaviours and psychologies. It is within these differences that his complex fiction – and sometimes even a genuine, painful and cruel history – exists.

In *The Shadow Lines* (1988), the story of an adolescence lived out between an Indian reality and imagination; *The Calcutta Chromosome* (1955), an extraordinary science fiction mystery; and in *The Glass Palace* (2000), which traces the impact of colonialism in India and Burma, readers will discover Ghosh's talent for evoking a broad sweep of historical narrative and his capacity for writing richly on a multicultural level. In the more recent and ambitious 'Ibis' trilogy (2008–) these qualities combine with a storyline of unprecedented complexity.

The story is set during the nineteenth century, a period of British dominance over the Indian subcontinent during which the colonizers decided to transform the lush region of Bihar into a monoculture dedicated solely to the profitable production of opium. This opium was then transported to the port of Calcutta and from there it was sent on by ship to Canton to be sold in China. Opium was the trigger for a war fought in the name of freedom of trade, and the resulting treaties imposed on the Asian continent had terrible and long-lasting consequences. The trilogy charts the journey of a dubious cargo of men and merchandise carried by the double-masted schooner *Ibis*. Their journey over the ocean and beyond tells the cruel story of the Opium Wars in intricate historical detail that informs, astonishes and enthrals.

Ghosh chooses the Indian Ocean as the focal point for his study of the continent of Asia, its people and its history. His writing draws on the ocean as both a metaphor and a fluid region in which culture, commerce, colonialism and conflict combine.

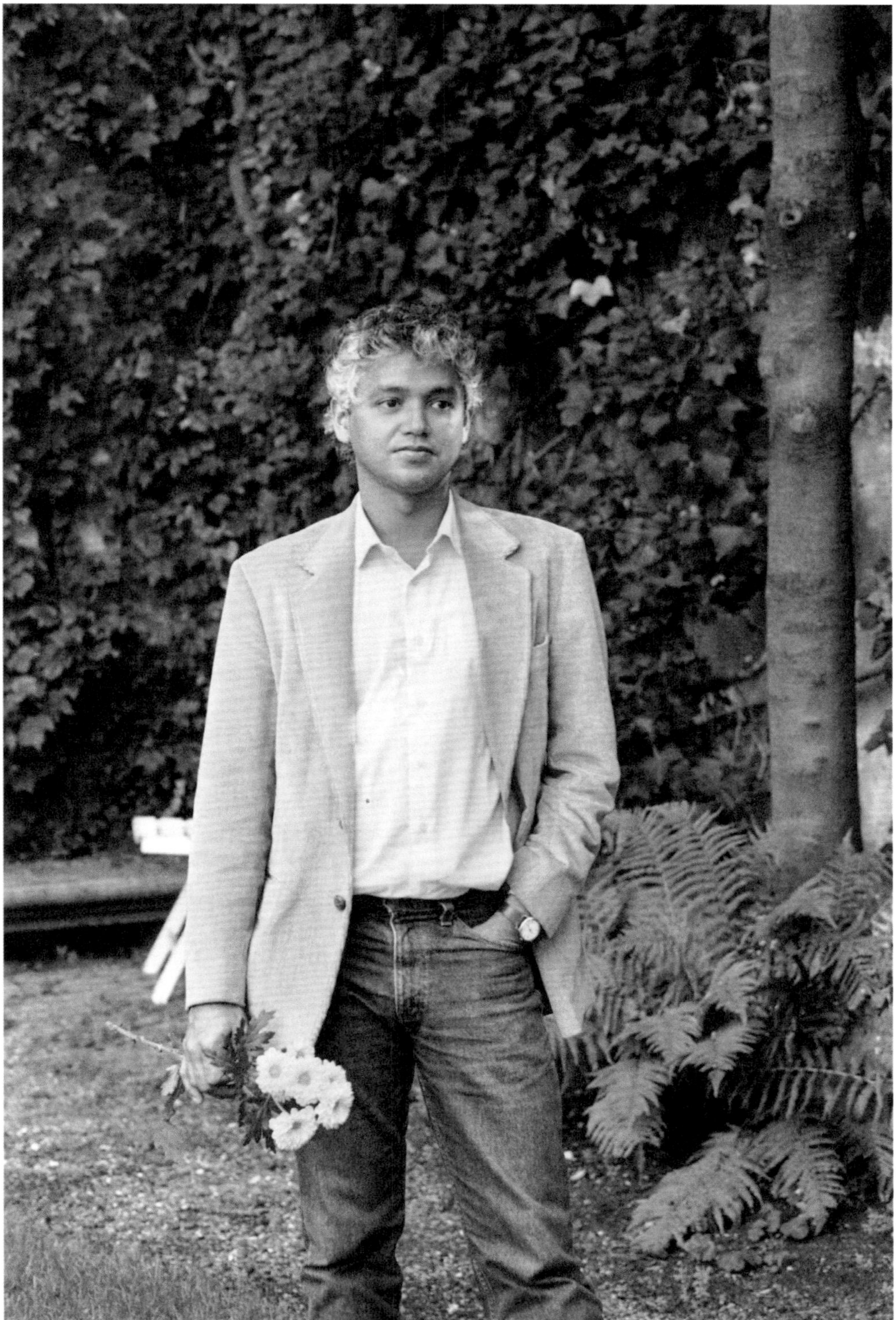

ANDRÉ GIDE

born Paris, 1869; died Paris, 1951

by Gisèle Freund

Paris, 1939

André Gide was born in Paris in 1869 to a Calvinist father who taught law at the University of Paris, and a Catholic mother who expressed her love for him by insisting he receive a severe and repressive education. 'Families, I hate you! Shut-in homes, closed doors, jealous possessors of happiness,' was the writer's harsh comment on his experience of family life.

His first literary efforts, *The Notebooks of André Walter* (1891) and *Traité du Narcisse* (Treatise of Narcissus, 1892), were produced under the influence of Stéphane Mallarmé's Symbolism, as Gide found himself drawn to the religious mysticism of this aesthete's early work. Thereafter, frequent changes in his cultural allegiances arose, according to the author, from his *disponibilité* – literally, 'availability'. This readiness to live life in such a way as to be free to experience everything was a fundamental component of his personality – and in sharp contrast to the strict education he had received. The religious code he had inherited should have meant that homosexuality was unthinkable for Gide, but instead he openly declared his sexual orientation.

Up until the First World War, Gide's works were filled with glorification of the life freed from moral obligation (most notably in his 1902 novel, *The Immoralist*, considered one of the most celebrated and scandalous texts of the last century), but during the war he experienced a profound religious crisis. Soon afterwards, his views swiftly underwent yet another change, and he again declared his right to earthly happiness in both art and life.

Gide expanded his vision to encompass a more general human condition and denounced the exploitation of countries colonized by European nations. He supported the idea of Communism as a way of liberating people from such oppression, but, after having observed the severe limitations of the Stalinist reality, rejected it again. What remained – a profound faith in human beings and a desire to struggle against conformism and prejudice – led to Gide's being awarded the Nobel Prize in Literature in 1947.

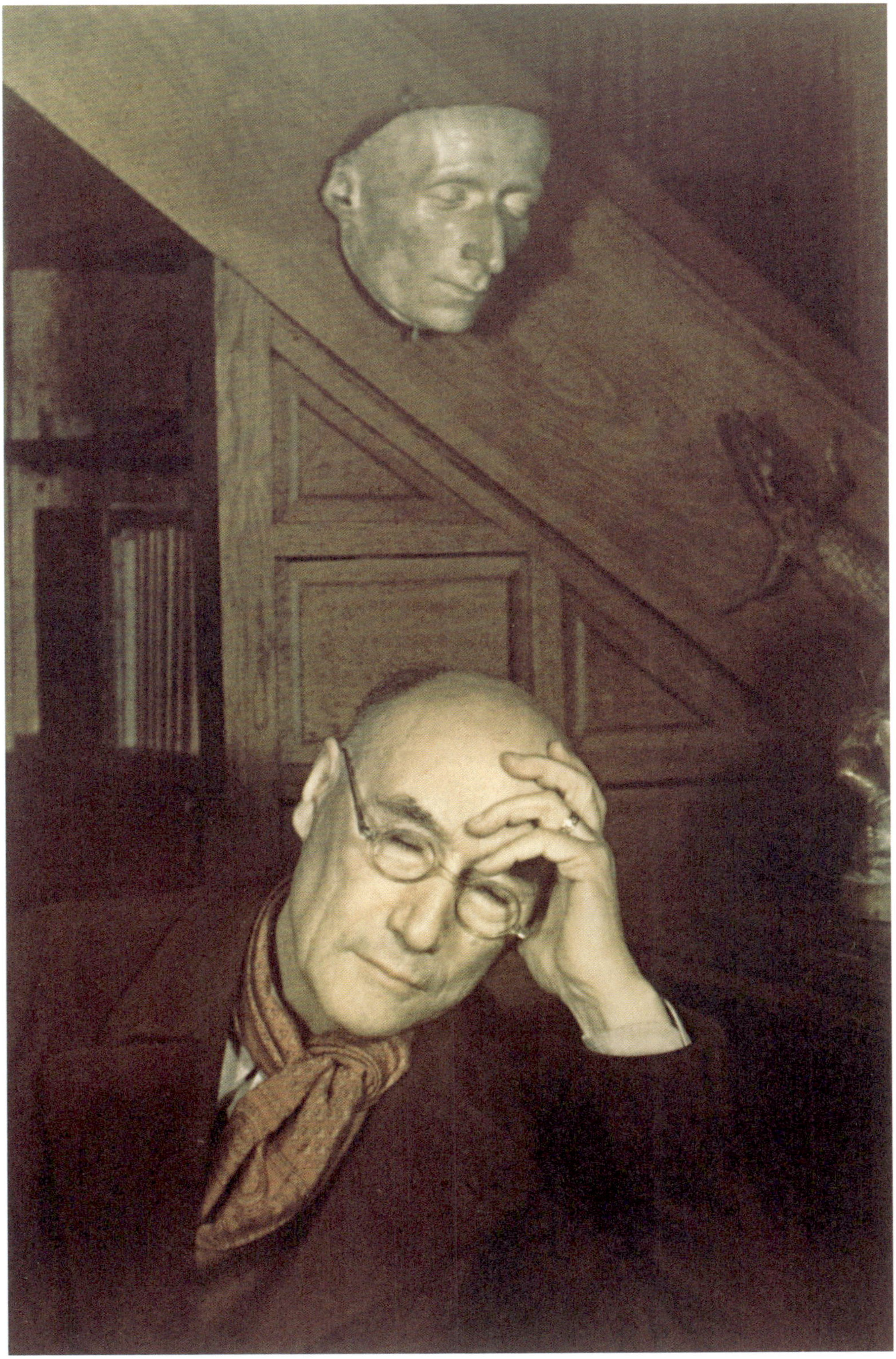

ALLEN GINSBERG

born Newark, New Jersey, 1926; died New York, 1997

by Richard Avedon

New York, 1963

In 1948, the year in which T. S. Eliot was awarded the Nobel Prize, Allen Ginsberg was living through what he would later call his 'Blake vision', an auditory hallucination that he tried to re-create many times with the assistance of various pharmaceuticals. It has been said that while the world was heaping praise on Eliot, a radically new generation of poets and writers was emerging. This was the Beat Generation, the members of which would go on to exercise an unprecedented influence on the youth of the second half of the twentieth century. The birth of this movement was the Six Gallery reading, a poetry reading in a San Francisco gallery in October 1955 – the moment when the so-called San Francisco Renaissance, which included writers such as Gregory Corso, Jack Kerouac, William S. Burroughs and Neal Cassady, announced itself to the world. It was also at this reading that Ginsberg, the true soul of the event, presented his poem *Howl* for the first time.

The first line of *Howl* – 'I saw the best minds of my generation destroyed by madness' – instantly became synonymous with the Beat movement. In 1957 an obscenity trial triggered by the poem turned into a cause célèbre in defence of the First Amendment. However, the roots of Ginsberg's poetry lay primarily in his childhood: his father, Louis, had read writers such as Emily Dickinson, John Milton and Edgar Allan Poe to him when he was young (his education was later expanded dramatically by his discovery of Walt Whitman). He was also greatly influenced by the mental fragility of his mother, Naomi, to whom he dedicated his masterpiece, a lengthy and tormented autobiographical poem entitled *Kaddish for Naomi Ginsberg (1894–1956)* (1961).

San Francisco soon became too restrictive for the Beats, and Ginsberg, together with his companion Peter Orlovsky, Corso and Burroughs, moved first to Paris and then to London. Ten years after the Six Gallery event, Ginsberg created a similar 'happening' in London's Royal Albert Hall in front of an audience of some seventeen thousand fans. By now the Beat Generation had begun to stifle him. He reached out by forming friendships with counter-culture figures such as Timothy Leary and Bob Dylan, and continued his tireless search for spiritual meaning, which eventually led him to Krishnaism. He also formed links with the hippy movement and became an icon for entire generations of young people.

Richard Avedon's striking photograph of Ginsberg depicts him holding a position that Buddhists call *abhaya mudra*: a symbolic gesture indicating reassurance and detachment from fear.

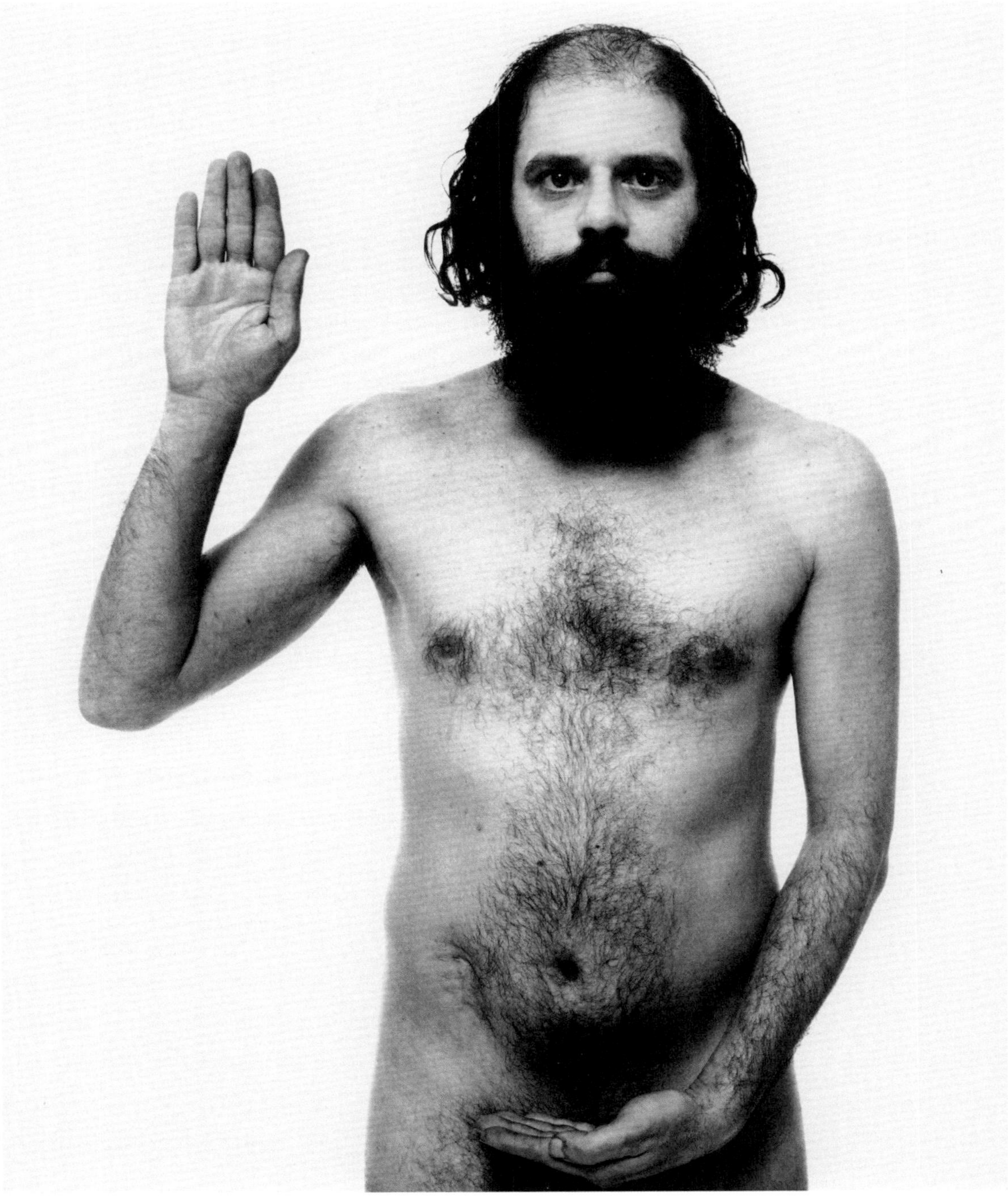

WITOLD GOMBROWICZ

born Maloszyce, Poland, 1904; died Vence, France, 1969

by Sophie Bassouls

Vence, France, 1967

Hailed as one of the greatest Polish writers of the twentieth century, Witold Gombrowicz is also one of the most brilliant and eccentric characters to have influenced the development of Western literature. He spent twenty-five years of his life in Argentina, having arrived there on what was supposed to have been a brief visit when the Nazis invaded Poland, thereby preventing his return. Apart from references in his diaries, little of that experience is discernible in his writing. His novels revolve instead around his personal obsessions.

Ferdydurke (1937), arguably his most popular novel, has been described by the Czech writer Milan Kundera as 'one of the three or four great novels written after Proust's death'. It tells the story of a thirty-year-old man who is transported back to school, where he finds himself trapped in the persona of a young boy. Described as a philosophical satire of the immaturity inherent in both institutions and individuals, it was also interpreted as a critique of the Polish authorities, and was subsequently banned.

It was not until the 1980s that Gombrowicz's books could circulate once again in his homeland, but from the 1960s onwards they had been read and appreciated in the rest of Europe by critics, writers and intellectuals alike. Over the years, the tone of his writing grew darker, and he became obsessed with the search for form and meaning. His last novel, *Cosmos* (1965), examines the fragility of human nature in the face of the chaos of existence. He is acclaimed for his originality, imagination and innovation, while his works represent some of the most important experimental novels of the twentieth century.

Over the course of her career the French photographer Sophie Bassouls *has* taken more than three thousand photographs of writers and artists. Her portraits of such individuals are characterized by their informality, as can be seen here in her photograph of Gombrowicz at home in Vence, where he spent the last years of his life.

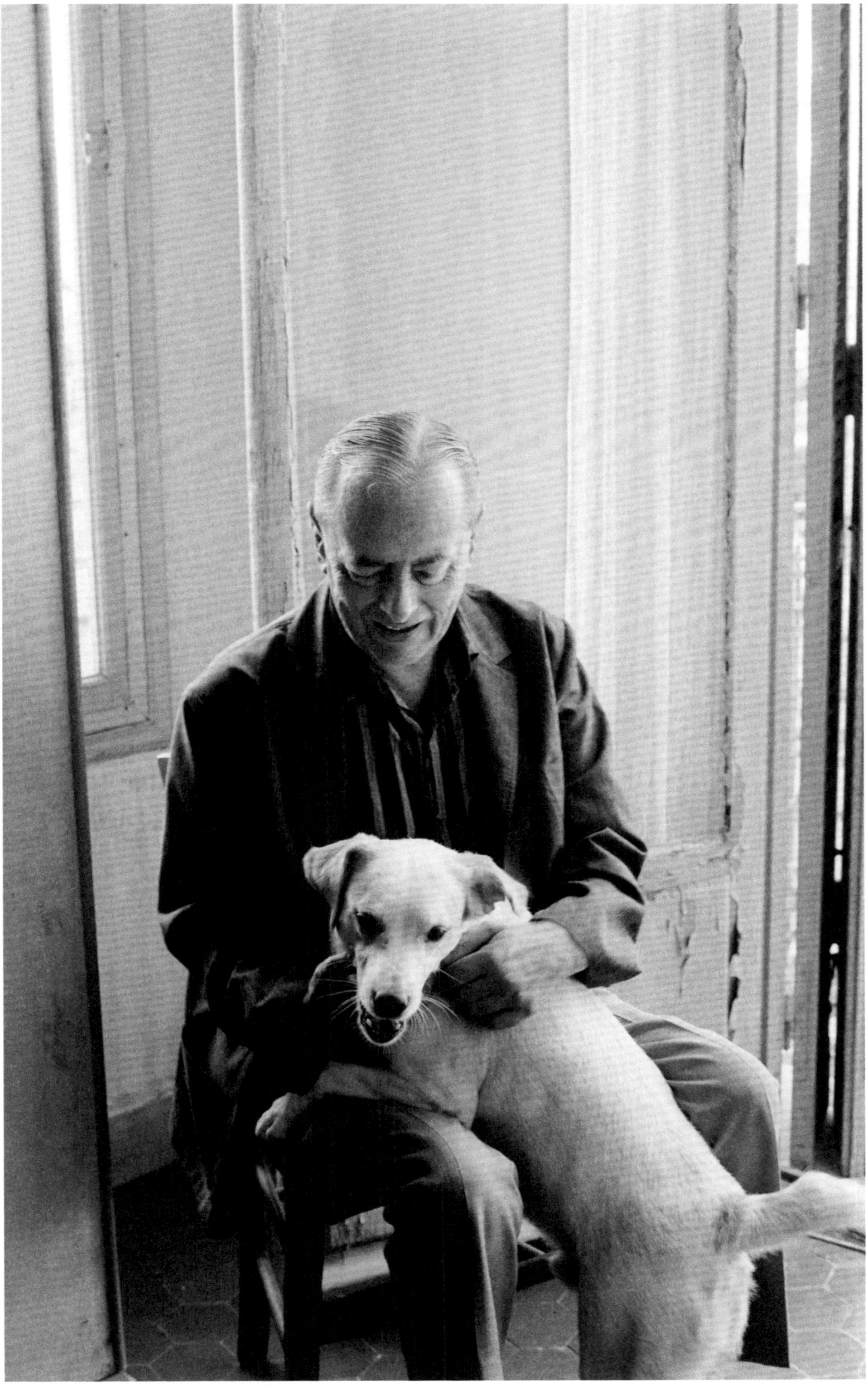

NADINE GORDIMER

born Springs, South Africa, 1923

by Graham Jepson

London, 2009

Nadine Gordimer's third novel, *Occasion for Loving* (1963), serves as an apt introduction to the writer's *oeuvre*. Set in South Africa, the book revolves around Jessica and Tom Stilwell, a white, well-educated, middle-class couple whose tranquil lives are turned upside down by the arrival of Ann Davis, twenty-two years old and married to the Jewish musicologist Boaz Davis. Ann embarks on an illicit love affair with a talented black artist, Gideon Shibalo. The novel explores the themes of racial and political tension, convention, tolerance, intellectual and emotional intelligence and the cost of personal happiness in a country paralysed by apartheid.

Gordimer was born in Springs, a city in the Gauteng province of South Africa. Her father was originally from Lithuania, and her mother from England. Apart from brief periods in the USA, she has never left her homeland. Her work is characterized by an almost classical style and solid narrative structures, but her particular skill lies in her ability to indulge in complex introspection without compromising the objective narrative voice. She has the great capacity to reproduce reality, in all its social and emotional complexity, with unnerving precision.

For many years Gordimer was a tireless campaigner for the abolition of apartheid, and her writing has confronted the difficulties experienced by the diverse peoples of South Africa in their search for an identity. In such works as *The Lying Days* (1953), *The Late Bourgeois World* (1966), *Burger's Daughter* (1979) and *The House Gun* (1998), she addresses the moral, social and psychological tensions caused by South Africa's now defunct system of racial segregation. Against an intensely descriptive background, she highlights the personal dramas of her characters and their struggle for liberty, using South Africa's story as a metaphor for a more universal journey towards freedom and equality. In 1991, Gordimer was awarded the Nobel Prize. The Swedish Academy described her as a writer who has been 'of very great benefit to humanity'.

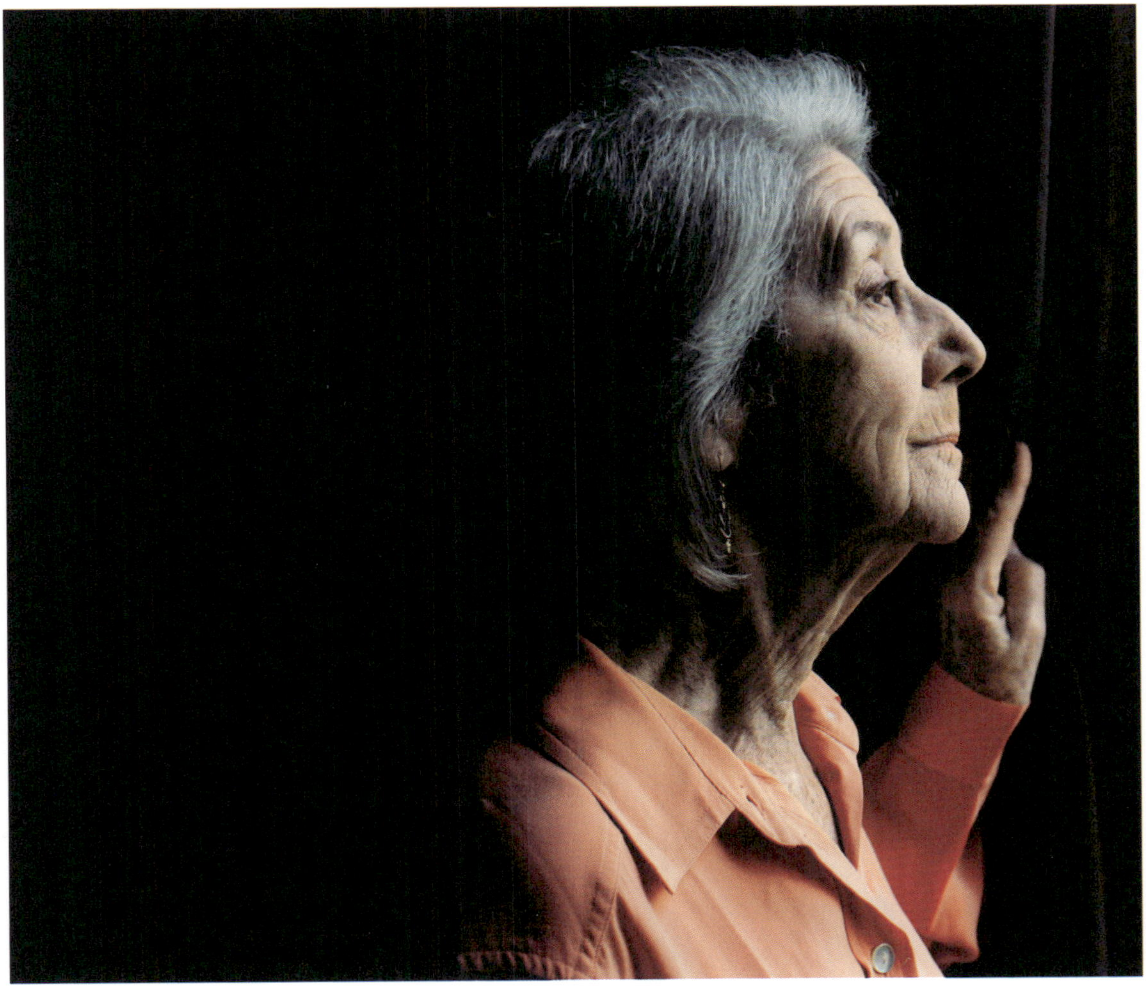

MAXIM GORKY

[Alexei Maximovich Peshkov] born Nižnij Novgorod, Russia, 1868; died Moscow, 1936

unknown photographer

unknown location c. 1900

Today it is difficult to imagine the importance of Maxim Gorky's role in Russian and Soviet literary history, and the fame that surrounded him in the Western world towards the end of the nineteenth century and in the first few decades of the twentieth century. At one time he was even compared to such literary giants as Victor Hugo and Leo Tolstoy. His prodigious output of stories, novels and dramas, and in particular his opposition to the Tsarist regime, meant that he became a favourite of influential leaders such as Vladimir Lenin, elevating him to a status that outstripped his actual artistic capabilities as a writer.

Gorky was brought up by his grandparents, and largely self-taught. The experiences of his early life are described in his autobiographical works *My Childhood* (1913–14), *In the World* (1916) and *My Universities* (1923). His first writings were picaresque, sentimental and romantic in nature, heavily influenced by the weighty figures of Tolstoy, Fyodor Dostoevsky and Anton Chekhov. Although Gorky never achieved the grandeur and moral strength of those authors, his works possess a certain strength and conviction. Many of them drew on his unusual life experiences as a vagabond drifting across Russia. He described the plight of peasants, sailors, woodcutters, and all the outcasts of society with great passion. This period of personal enlightenment and the sense of solidarity it gave him fuelled the revolutionary spirit that later came to define his works. *The Mother* (1907), written following the revolution of 1905, was a popular and highly influential novel; during this period Gorky also wrote plays, including *The Lower Depths* (1902), noted for its social realism. In the 1920s he wrote *The Artamanov Business* (1927) and *The Life of Klim Samgin* series (1927–36), lengthy tomes that are now little read, though they do provide an accurate portrayal of the Russian bourgeoisie of the day.

Following the bloody revolution of 1905, Gorky moved to Capri, ostensibly for the benefit of his health, and did not return to Russia until 1913, when the political situation had calmed. In 1921, during the Russian Revolution, he again fled the country, this time to Germany and Czechoslovakia. Although initially hostile to the Bolsheviks, Gorky was subsequently won over by them and in 1924 again returned to his homeland, where he was hailed as a national hero for his 'proletarian' literature.

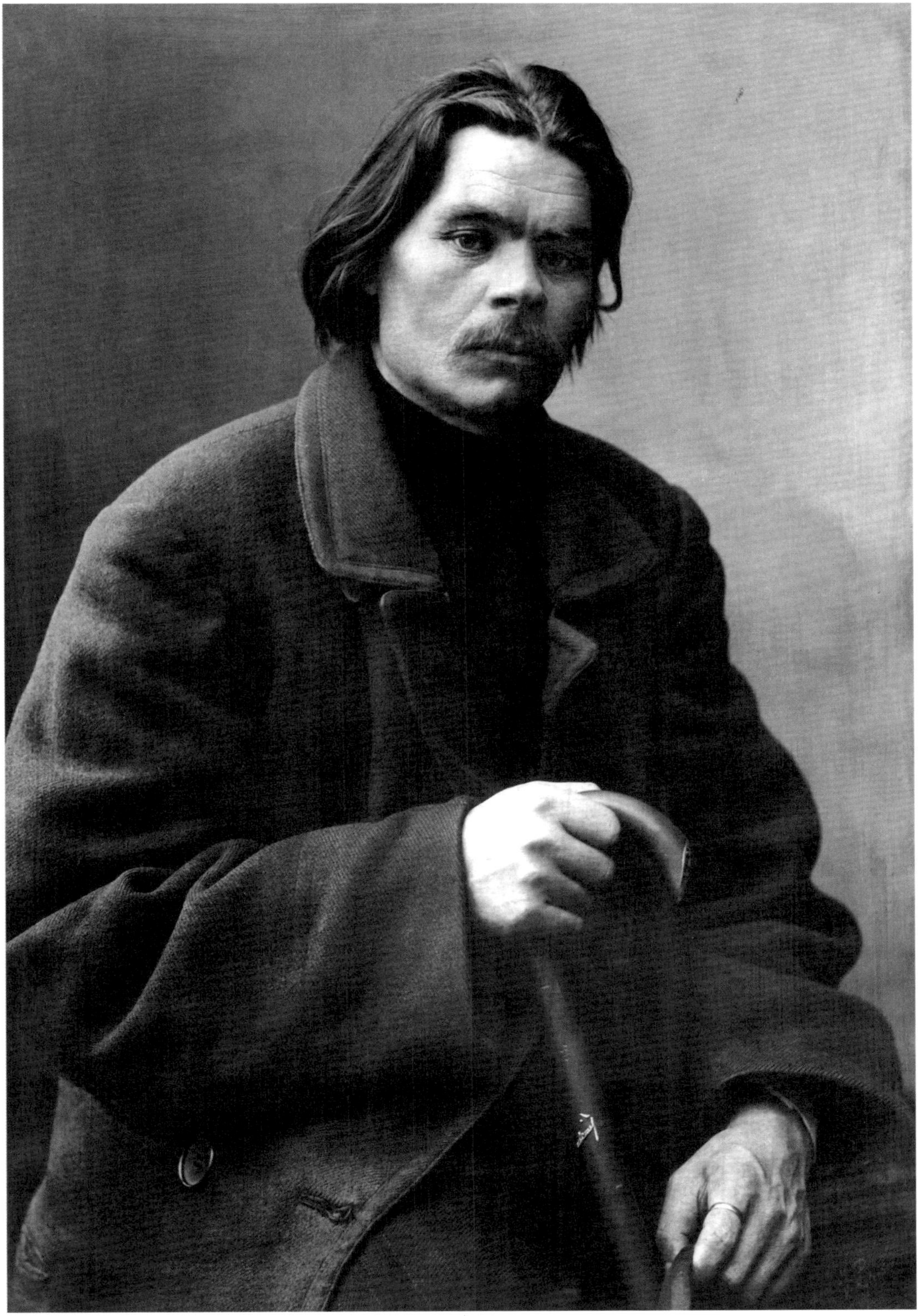

JUAN GOYTISOLO

born Barcelona, Spain, 1931

by Isabel Steva Hernández

Paris, 1976

With such novels as *The Young Assassins* (1954) and *Duel in Paradise* (1955), Juan Goytisolo was able to breathe new life into the Spanish novel under Franco's stifling dictatorship, which regularly criticized his works or withdrew them from sale. This suppression of his work led him to choose voluntary exile in France in 1956.

After a period in Paris during which he produced no work and suffered a personal and artistic crisis, Goytisolo returned to writing with his 'Álvaro Mendiola' trilogy: *Marks of Identity* (1966), *Count Julián* (1970) and *Juan the Landless* (1975). The second book in the trilogy was not only a homage to the legendary Count Julián of Ceuta, who opened thegates of Spain to the Moorish invaders in the eighth century, but also ventured to make certain claims on behalf of the values of Islamic Arab culture. Goytisolo has long sought a bridge between the Arab and Western worlds, and after living in Marrakesh he became interested in promoting dialogue between Morocco and Europe.

Even after the end of Franco's rule, Goytisolo continued to strike a critical note in his writing, examining the world through subjects such as Marxism, war and religion. In *The Marx Family Saga* (1993), he imagined Karl Marx brought back to life and sitting on his sofa in front of the television, channel-hopping and watching his ideology collapse in real time. War itself is the principal character in both *Sarajevo Notebook* (1993), a collection of articles he wrote for the Spanish newspaper *El País*, and *Landscapes of War* (1996). Religion, meanwhile, is the subject of *A Cock-eyed Comedy* (2000), his satire on the Catholic Church and its secret society, Opus Dei.

As Goytisolo has said, it is his self-imposed exile and outsider status that have allowed him to examine the world from a more objective point of view, to be 'Castilian in Catalonia, Frenchified in Spain, Spanish in France, a Latin in North America, *nesrani* in Morocco and a Moor everywhere. As a result of my wanderings, I would soon become that rare species of writer not claimed by anybody, alien and opposed to groupings and categories.'

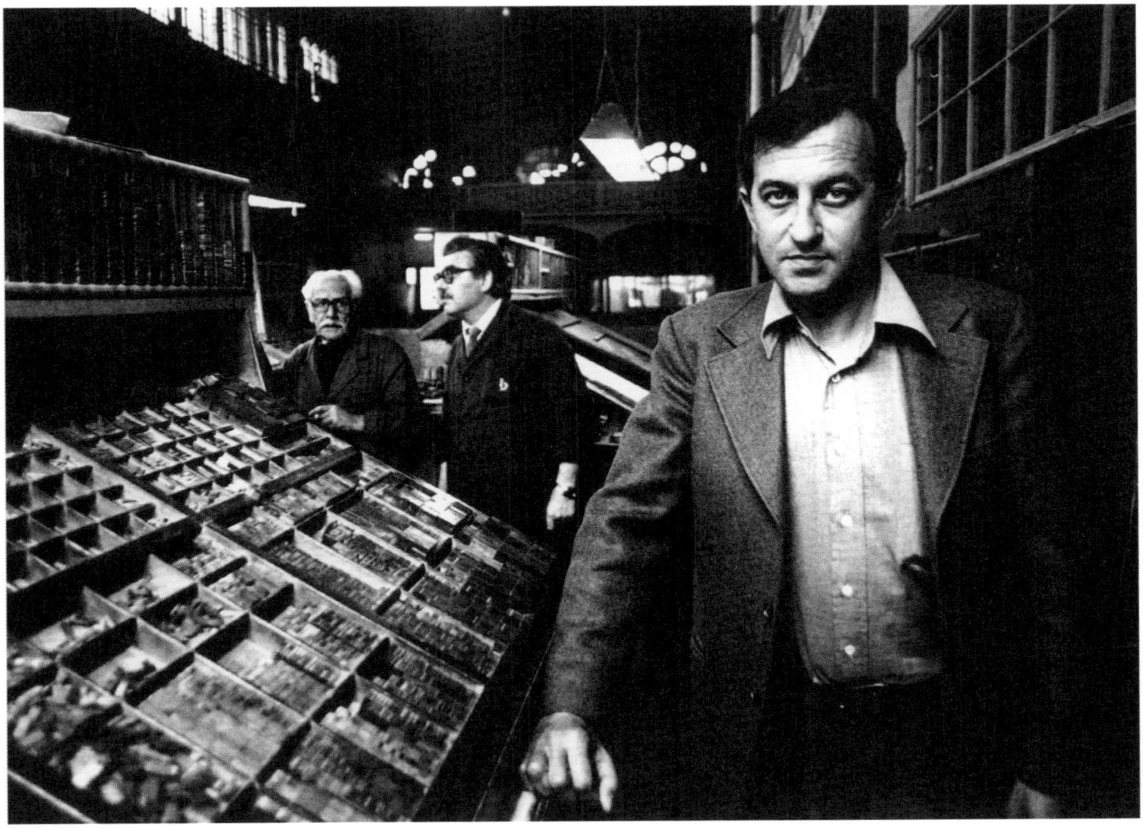

GÜNTER GRASS

born Gdansk, Poland, 1927

by René Burri

Berlin, 1961

Günter Grass's debut novel, *The Tin Drum*, appeared in 1959. A picaresque and baroque farce in which the life of the central character, Oskar Matzerath, runs parallel to the rise and fall of Nazi Germany, the book immediately placed Grass among the literary greats. The sins of the Nazi past were an integral part of the German national identity in the difficult post-war years, and the country's best voices could not avoid confronting the Holocaust. In the visionary universe of *The Tin Drum*, Grass also found space for his surreal Onion Cellar club, where people go in order to be able to cry, although they are sometimes silenced by the enormity of the past.

Forty years later, with the award of the Nobel Prize in Literature, Grass was confirmed as the voice of the moral conscience of the German nation. *Peeling the Onion* (2006), the first volume of his controversial memoirs, begins in 1939, when the German army invaded Poland and the fighting of the Second World War swept across the area around Danzig (now Gdansk), the city in which Grass was born in 1927. At the age of ten, in common with many German boys of the period (Grass's father was an ethnic German), Grass joined the Jungvolk, a feeder organization for the Hitler Youth. In 1944, at the age of seventeen, he volunteered for submarine service but was assigned to a panzer division. The war was virtually over, however, and he was captured almost immediately and placed in an American prisoner-of-war camp.

It was only with the publication of *Peeling the Onion* that Grass revealed that, in 1944, he had in fact been conscripted into the Waffen SS. His admission provoked considerable outrage, eliciting accusations of hypocrisy and calls for him to return his Nobel Prize. Grass responded by saying that it had been decades before he felt able to describe his own life, and that investigating one's past is a painful process: it has to be peeled away, layer by layer, like an onion. The Swiss photographer René Burri took this picture of him in the guise of a mythological animal, as provocative and wild as some of his own writing.

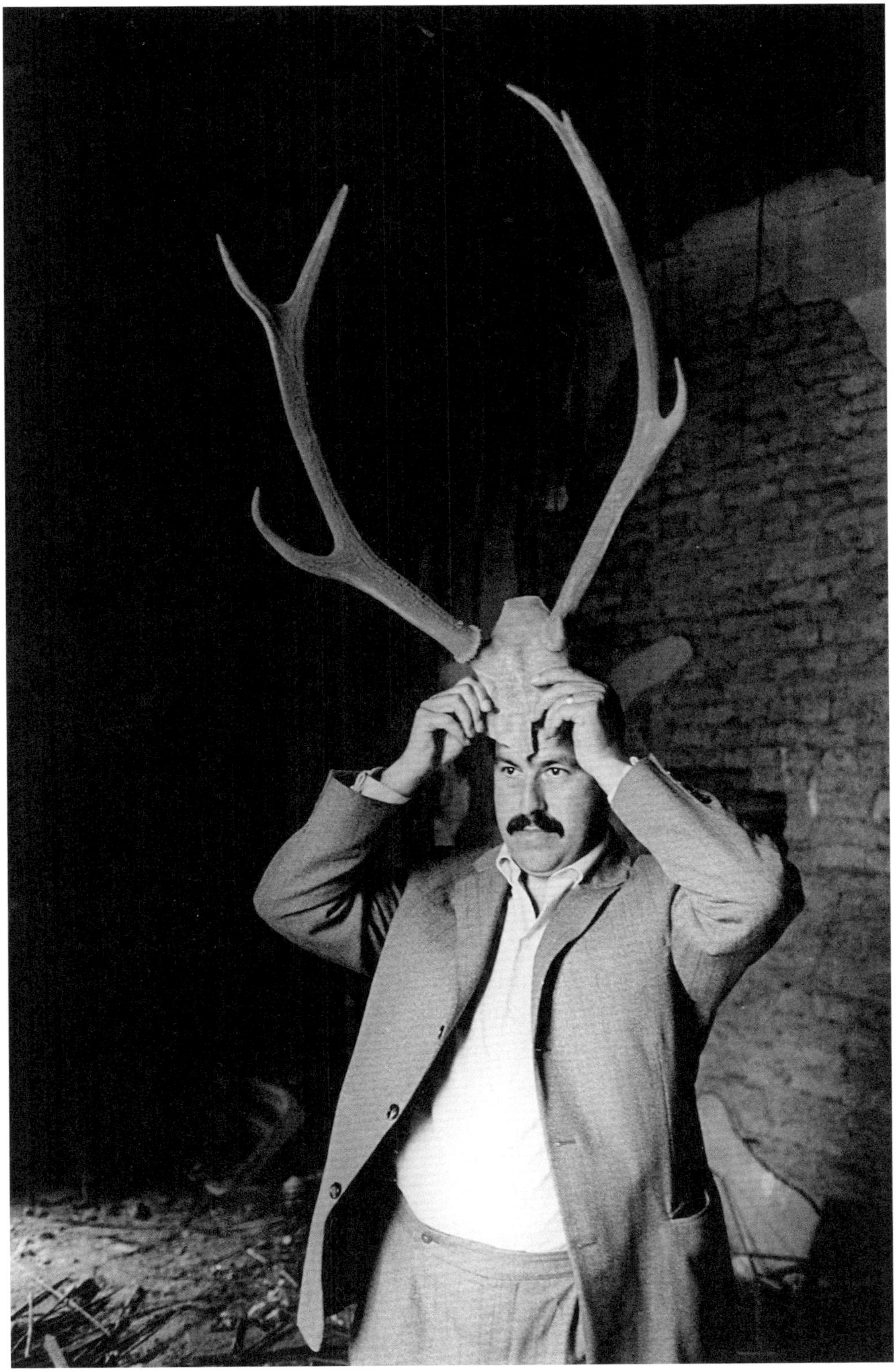

GRAHAM GREENE

born Berkhamsted, Hertfordshire, UK, 1904; died Corseaux, Switzerland, 1991

by Larry Burrows

[right] with Carol Reed, London, 1951

Although Graham Greene – novelist, playwright, spy – converted to Catholicism in his early twenties, he saw himself not as a Catholic writer but as a writer who was also a Catholic. Religious themes, ethical dilemmas and questionable morals lie at the heart of many of his works, and not just his so-called Catholic novels: *Brighton Rock* (1938), *The Power and the Glory* (1940), *The Heart of the Matter* (1948) and *The End of the Affair* (1951). They can also be found in his stories of espionage and exoticism, both imagined and experienced first-hand, which are enlivened by his subtle and diffuse interweaving of truth and fiction in *The Quiet American* (1955), *Our Man in Havana* (1958) and *The Human Factor* (1978). His spy novels are the product of, and hold up a mirror to, a world divided up into good and evil by the Cold War; they may even have been shaped by the bipolar disorder from which Greene appears to have suffered.

Greene was criticized by the Vatican for *The Power and the Glory*. The novel tells the story of an alcoholic Catholic priest with several children who exposes himself to great physical danger in order to celebrate mass and administer the sacraments in the revolutionary and anti-clerical atmosphere of Mexico in the 1930s. In the end, the priest is seized and dies a martyr's death. The author reacted to the criticism by claiming that he no longer had any control over the work; it had appeared around the world in various translations, and he couldn't possibly remove any incriminating passages now. In a private audience with Pope Paul VI, Greene was offered reassurance and told not to attach any importance to the affair. In recalling this criticism from the Church in the preface to a later edition of the book, Greene asks himself if any other totalitarian state would ever have treated him so gently.

In this photograph by Larry Burrows, Greene is pictured with Carol Reed, who directed three adaptations of his novels: *The Fallen Idol* (1948), *The Third Man* (1949) and *Our Man in Havana* (1959). In each case, Greene himself either wrote or co-wrote the screenplay.

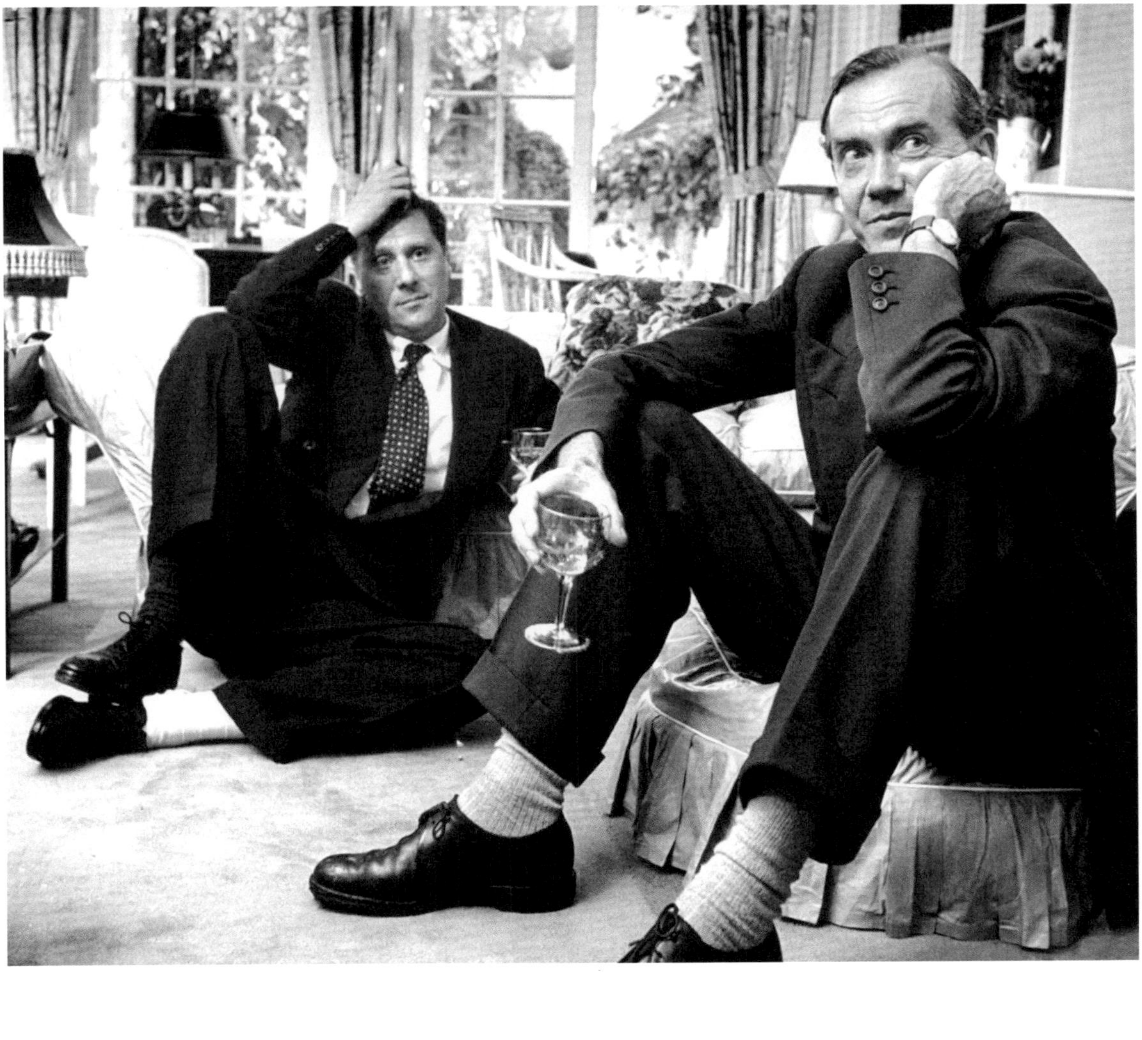

DAVID GROSSMAN

born Jerusalem, 1954

by Cato Lein

Stockholm, 2011

He has a Palestinian mother, a Jewish father of Polish descent, and was born in Jerusalem. Even in its most basic biographical details, David Grossman's life reads like a condensed version of the complex make-up of the state of Israel.

A prodigiously talented child (by the age of ten he had already planned and directed his own radio programmes), he has since become one of the most sensitive voices in international literature and has turned much of his own life – and the echoes that reverberate through his life from his country at large – into literary metaphor. It is practically impossible not to take part in political life in a city like Jerusalem, and Grossman has not withdrawn into himself. He has taken sides, pointing out a route towards tolerance and negotiation; he has also clashed with those in power.

When confronted with such a dramatic reality, literature can have a redeeming role; it can help readers find a personal dimension in shattered lives, etched by pain. In *See Under: Love* (1986) the horror of the Holocaust is told through the stories and imagination of a child, using a technique of intersecting time frames. *The Book of Intimate Grammar* (1991) and *Someone to Run With* (2000) both also feature young protagonists caught in the early phases of constructing their own identities. But Grossman is capable of taking an adult's perspective, too, as in *Be My Knife* (1998), or a delightfully feminine one, as in *To the End of the Land* (2008), creating flawlessly realized emotional worlds for his characters.

In 2006, Grossman's twenty-year-old son Uri was killed in the war in Lebanon by an anti-tank missile fired during an operation carried out by the Israeli army. A few days earlier, Grossman and several other Israeli intellectuals had asked the government to commit itself to a ceasefire as the basis of potential negotiations. With the tangled knot of history that informs his present life with its undeniable weight of sorrow, the difficulty of living in his country and his decision to live come what may, Grossman faces his choices with courage and confirms the supremacy of literature as a paradigm for going forward.

He explains: 'The secret fascination and greatness of literature, the secret of which always pushes you towards it with enthusiasm and the desire to find refuge and significance, resides in the fact that literature continually re-creates for us the tragedy of the individual when faced with the statistics of the masses. It is the individual on whom history is written, and it is the individual who will read that very history.'

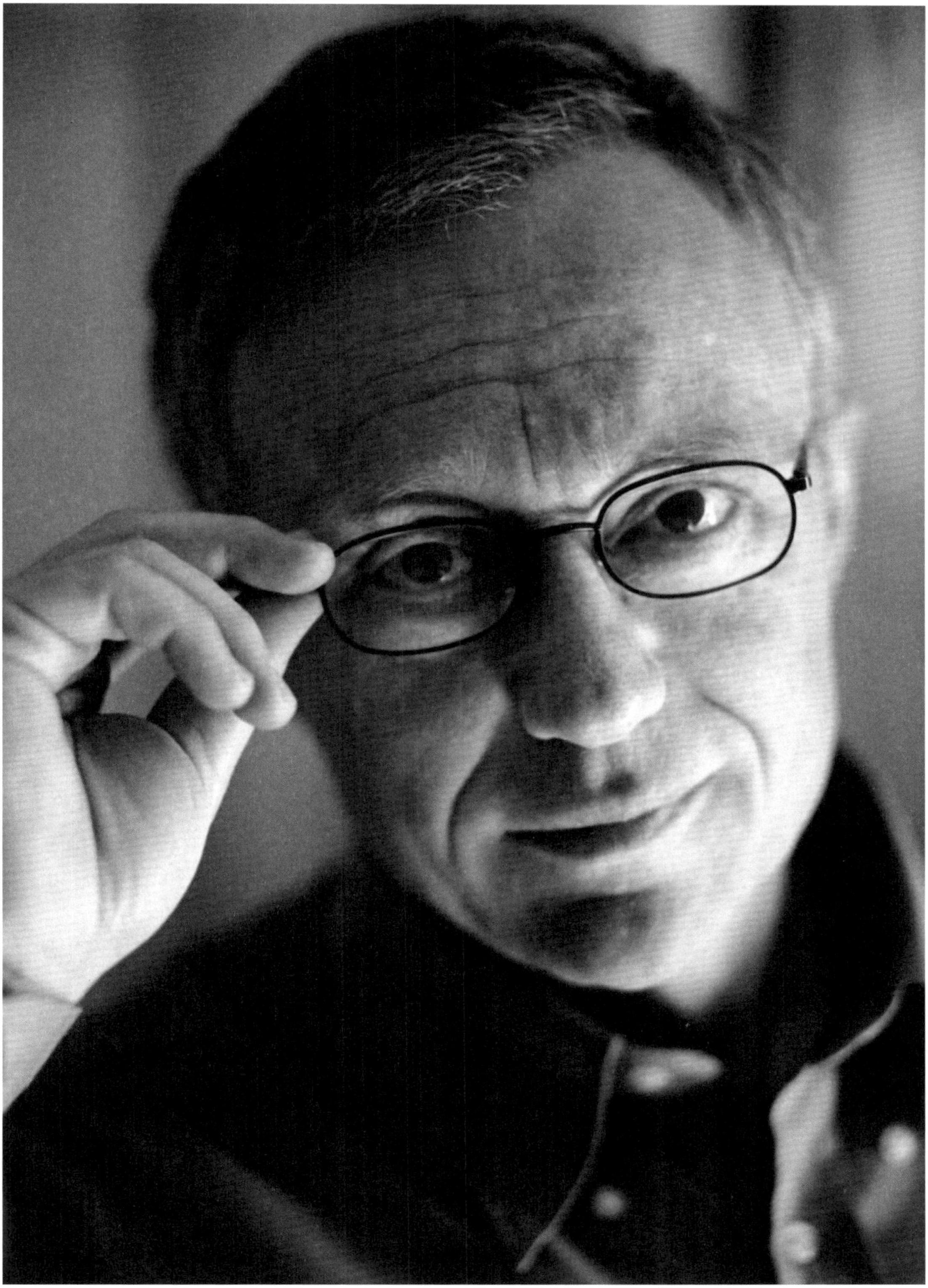

JOÃO GUIMARÃES ROSA

born Cordisburgo, Brazil, 1908; died Rio de Janeiro, 1967

by Eugênio Silva

Sertão de Minas Gerais, Brazil, 1952

The Devil to Pay in the Backlands (1956) is the epic of Brazilian letters, a novel of existential themes and enchanted and enchanting prose. Its heroes, Riobaldo and Diadorim, are joined together in an ambiguous brotherhood: 'That overpowering friendship ... Let him be near me and I lacked for nothing. Let him frown or look sad and I would lose my peace of mind'. The novel's geographical boundaries mark out the *sertão* (semi-arid region) of Minas Gerais, a state in eastern Brazil: 'The *sertão* is where the strong and the shrewd call the tune. God himself, when he comes here, had better come armed!'. Its story, related by Riobaldo in flashbacks to an unknown interlocutor, tells of the struggles between the bands of *jagunços* (mercenaries): 'there are people in this hateful world who kill others just to see the faces they make as they die ... A *jagunço* is a man who has halfway given up already.'

With its onomatopoeia, internal rhymes, archaic vocabulary, colloquialisms and neologisms, the novel echoes the musicality of the *sertão*. Here, language is being used not simply to describe nature, but to experiment with it and to re-create it. 'When I write,' the author once said, 'I repeat that which I've already lived. And for those two lives, only one lexicon will not suffice.' Under the banner of myth, dreams and madness, Guimarães Rosa's characters ride out like medieval knights, like modern heroes from an ancient time, into a no-man's-land where honour, life and death, and God and the Devil are intertwined.

An extremely cultured doctor and diplomat who could speak numerous languages, Guimarães Rosa travelled through the *sertão* in 1952 taking notes on everything he encountered, including its dialects and costumes. *The Devil to Pay in the Backlands* began as a story intended for his collection *Corps de Ballet* (1956), but it soon became something much greater: an anthem to a place and its people; an encyclopaedia of the *sertão*. Eugênio Silva, a photographer for the *O Cruzeiro* magazine, accompanied the writer on several of his journeys into the *sertão*. In Brazil, his photographs of these expeditions are at least as famous as Guimarães Rosa's novel.

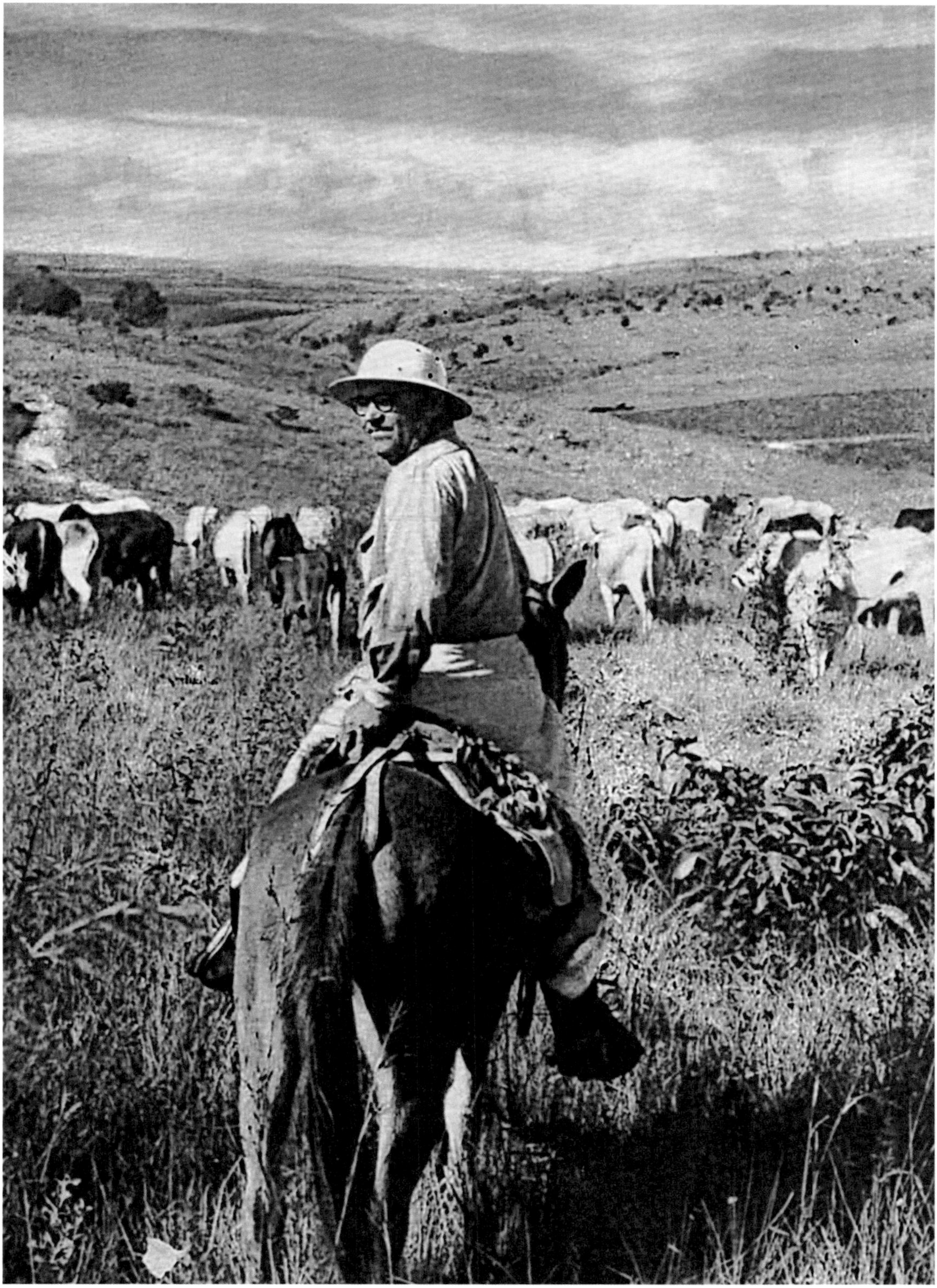

DASHIELL HAMMETT

born Lexington Park, Maryland, 1894; died New York, 1961

unknown photographer

New York, c. 1930

Before publishing his first story, 'The Road Home' (1922), in the magazine *Black Mask*, Dashiell Hammett had performed a variety of jobs, including driving an ambulance in the First World War. Most significant in terms of his later career, however, was his job in San Francisco as a detective for the Pinkerton National Detective Agency.

Hammett's collaboration with *Black Mask*, the most important pulp fiction magazine of the 1920s and 1930s, inspired him to achieve greater things. Although he went on to publish several more stories, their quality was far from good. The format did not allow for anything more ambitious, which Hammett, having begun to explore the philosophy of Charles Sanders Peirce and the 'real' literature of William James, felt he was able to write. But it so happened that in 1926 the magazine came under the control of an imaginative and inspired new editor, Joseph Shaw. Together, the two men revolutionized the world of the detective story, removing it from the parlours described by the American novelist S. S. Van Dine and taking it out into the street, where it belonged.

Hammett's breakthrough came with *Red Harvest* (1929), but it was with *The Maltese Falcon* (1930), featuring his most famous creation, Sam Spade, that he set the standard for tough, realistic works of detective fiction. Hammett's golden age was relatively short-lived, also producing *The Glass Key* (1931) and his last, great masterpiece *The Thin Man* (1934), which he dedicated to the love of his life, the playwright Lillian Hellman. In addition to his writing, Hammett's life was marked by alcoholism, illness and political engagement; the last of these cost him six months in jail when in 1951 he was accused of 'anti-American' activities and subsequently blacklisted. He is, however, primarily remembered as a great writer and the author of a highly influential body of work. André Malraux recommended him to his fellow French author André Gide, while the film director John Huston compared him to William Faulkner and considered him better than Ernest Hemingway. Raymond Chandler, meanwhile, his most illustrious successor, recognized him to be the master of the genre: 'Hammett gave murder back to the kind of people that commit it for reasons, not just to provide a corpse.'

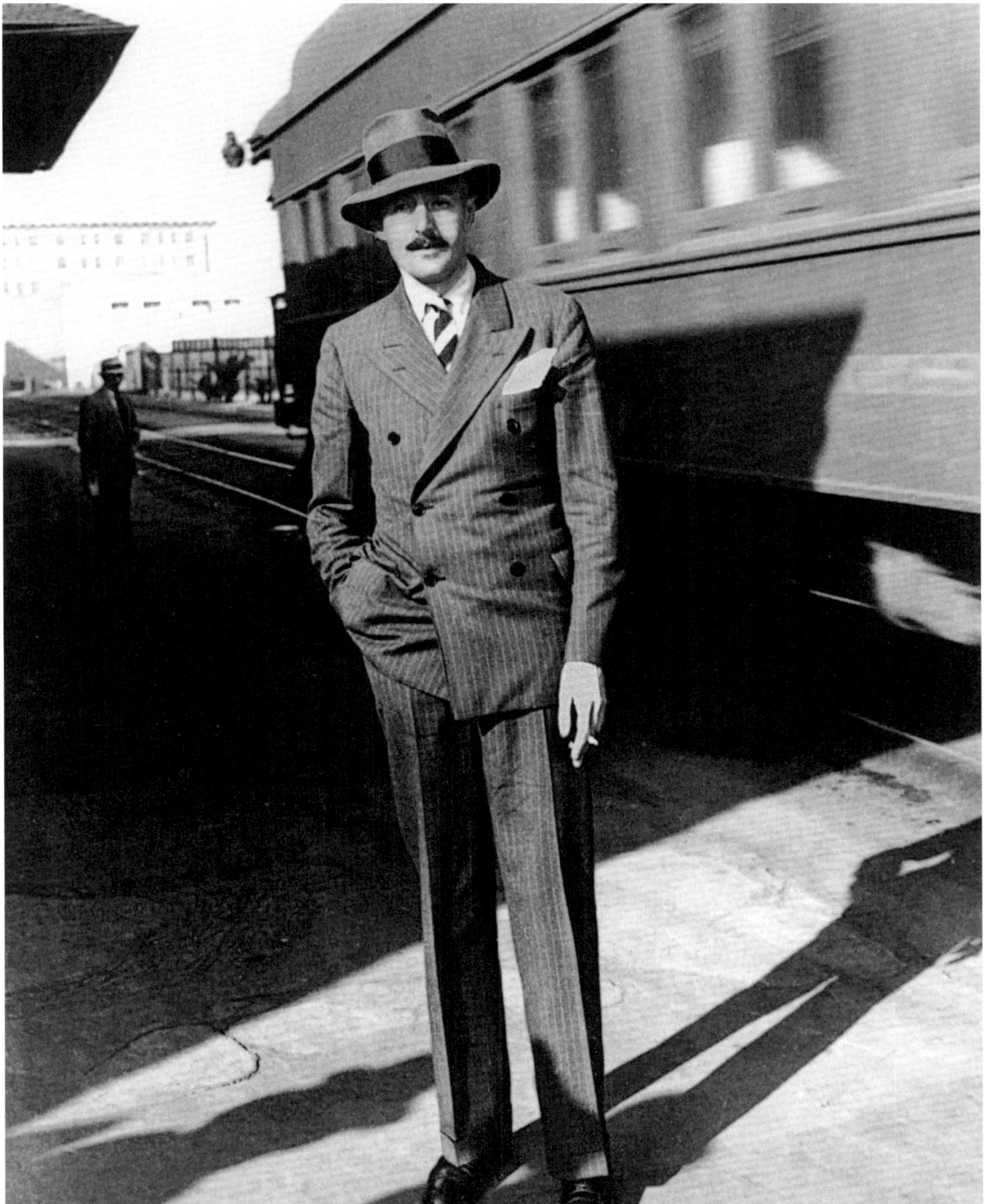

KNUT HAMSUN

born Lom, Norway, 1859; died Grimstad, Norway, 1952

by Anders Beer Wilse

Grimstad, Norway, 1930

Knut Hamsun's life spanned almost a century, and witnessed the struggles of the latter half of the nineteenth century, and the brutalities of world wars and dictatorships in the first half of the twentieth century. He experienced the inadequacies of a bourgeois democratic system that failed to safeguard liberty and social justice. He was a contemporary of many key figures, most notably Friedrich Nietzsche, whose works influenced him greatly, and fellow nonconformists August Strindberg and Fyodor Dostoevsky. Other prominent contemporaries included Sigmund Freud, Marcel Proust, James Joyce and Franz Kafka. In 1920 he was awarded the Nobel Prize. His epic novel *Growth of the Soil* (1917), is sympathetically narrated account of a courageous couple living in the wilds. Many of his other works are more painful and penetrating, such as the semi-autobiographical novel *Hunger* (1890), which became popular at the turn of the century. It is written in the first person and deals with the torments of starvation, the failure of the established order, and the role of the conscience, interwoven with elements of the mysterious, as a homeless writer searches for food in the streets of Oslo.

Hamsun grew up in poverty and was starved and abused by an uncle who took him in at the age of nine. After escaping from the situation as a teenager, he worked at various manual jobs to survive and spent several years travelling in the USA, which left mixed impressions on him, later chronicled in *The Cultural Life of Modern America* (1889). He was deeply attached to his native Norway, and his novels frequently contrasted the beauty and strength of its scenery with the weakness and decay of its society. He wrote in an individual and anarchistic vein, laying bare the hypocrisy inherent in the institutions around him. His major works include: *Pan* (1894), *Victoria* (1898), *Under the Autumn Star* (1906) and its sequel *A Wanderer Plays On Muted Strings* (1909), the *Wayfarers* cycle (1927–33), and *Ringen Sluttet* (The ring is closed, 1936), his penultimate work.

Disgusted with democracy, he embraced Nazism during the Second World War, and after the fall of Hitler was put on trial and committed to a psychiatric hospital. Thomas Mann described him as 'full of hatred for civilization, the common life, industrialism, intellectualism etc. … and so vehemently anti-English as to betray his fatherland.' But he also recognized in Hamsun 'a fascinating case of conservative social criticism, some might even say reactionary, and the finest quality of artistry.'

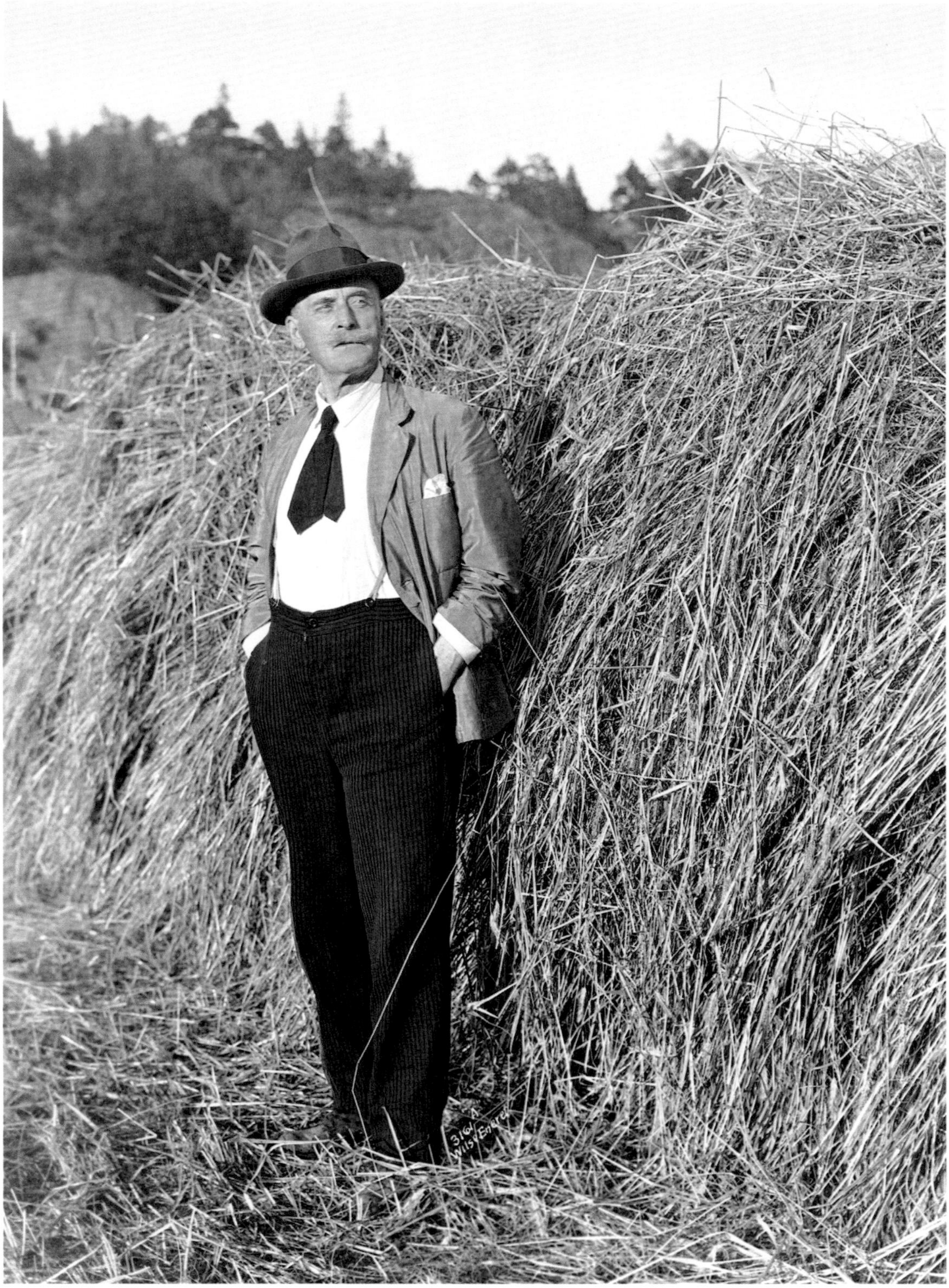
3161 A
Wilse Eneret

PETER HANDKE

born Griffen, Austria, 1942

by Patrick Zachmann

Paris, 2008

In 1966, the annual meeting of Group 47, the influential literary association of German writers, was held in Princeton, New Jersey. Several members of the group were there, including Günter Grass, Peter Weiss, Ingeborg Bachmann and Peter Handke. Handke was only twenty-four at the time, and relatively unknown, but he already had strong opinions and a combative spirit. When it was his turn to speak, he launched an attack on the group, accusing it of being 'descriptively impotent' and removed from reality. With only one book to his name (*The Hornets*, 1966), many saw this outburst as nothing more than a publicity stunt, but when his next work was published shortly afterwards, a play entitled *Offending the Audience* (1966) , it was clear that he had become the *enfant terrible* of the contemporary literary scene. This status was soon confirmed by the publication of plays such as *Self-accusation* (1966) and *Kaspar* (1967).

Handke has experimented with many forms of writing, ranging from plays, novels and short stories to poetry and screenplays, and collaborating with Wim Wenders on the film *Wings of Desire* (1987). He frequently incorporates elements from his own life in his work, including, in *A Sorrow Beyond Dreams* (1972), the suicide of his mother. After learning of the event from the local newspaper, he began writing the book in an attempt to understand not only her death but also her life, but even this work of personal catharsis was written in an anti-conformist vein. In the 1990s he provoked controversy with his attitude to the war in Yugoslavia, writing a short story that promoted Serbian interests and defended the actions of Slobodan Miloševič.

Since 1991 Handke has lived in Chaville, on the outskirts of Paris, surrounded by books and trees. As this photograph by Magnum photographer Patrick Zachmann shows, his books are not neatly lined up on bookshelves, but stand in piles wherever there is space. Visitors to the house also talk of his collections of various objects, as well as quantities of pens and pencils. There is no sign of a computer.

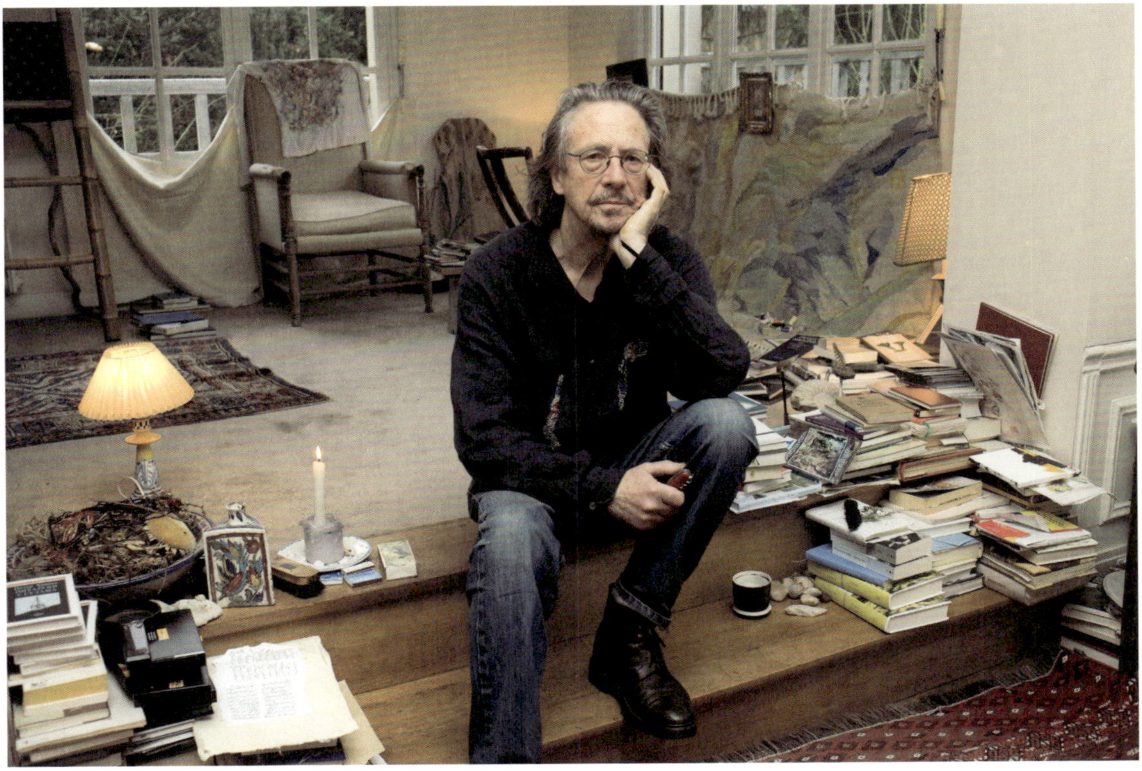

ERNEST HEMINGWAY

born Oak Park, Illinois, 1899; died Ketchum, Idaho, 1961

by Robert Capa

Sun Valley, Idaho, 1940

By 1925 Ernest Hemingway was a veteran of the First World War, having volunteered with an ambulance unit on the Italian front, and a former correspondent for the *Toronto Star*. He was also a young writer who, with only a few stories to his name, had just signed a contract with a well-respected publisher, Boni & Liveright. It was during this time that he met F. Scott Fitzgerald, who introduced him to his editor at Charles Scribner's Sons, Maxwell Perkins, one of the most important literary editors of the era. According to some accounts, in order to release himself from his contract with Boni & Liveright so that he could move to Scribner's, Hemingway dashed off a short novel mocking the work of another more important author in Boni & Liveright's stable, his own friend Sherwood Anderson. Boni & Liveright duly rejected the novella, *The Torrents of Spring* (1926), and terminated his contract (Hemingway later denied that he had written the book for this reason). He was thus free to transfer to Scribner's, taking with him his idea for a 'real' novel, one that would gain him a reputation as an authentic writer: *The Sun Also Rises* (1926).

Hemingway's relationship with Scribner's was perhaps the only constant in the life of a man famed not only for his literary accomplishments but also for his desire to experience life in all its extremes. Indeed, his move to Scribner's proved to be a landmark in his literary career. Under Perkins's guidance, he produced a series of works that would cement his position as a giant of twentieth-century literature, following *The Sun Also Rises* with *A Farewell to Arms* (1929), *For Whom the Bell Tolls* (1940) and *The Old Man and the Sea* (1952), for which he won the Pulitzer Prize. The Nobel Prize followed in 1954 ('too late', as he apparently commented), after which he wrote little; several works were published posthumously, however, including volumes of selected journalism and his *Selected Letters* (1981).

Robert Capa, Hemingway's great friend, took this photograph of the writer while he was out hunting in Sun Valley, Idaho. Hemingway had purchased a house in nearby Ketchum in 1959, and it was there, on 2 July 1961, that he took his own life.

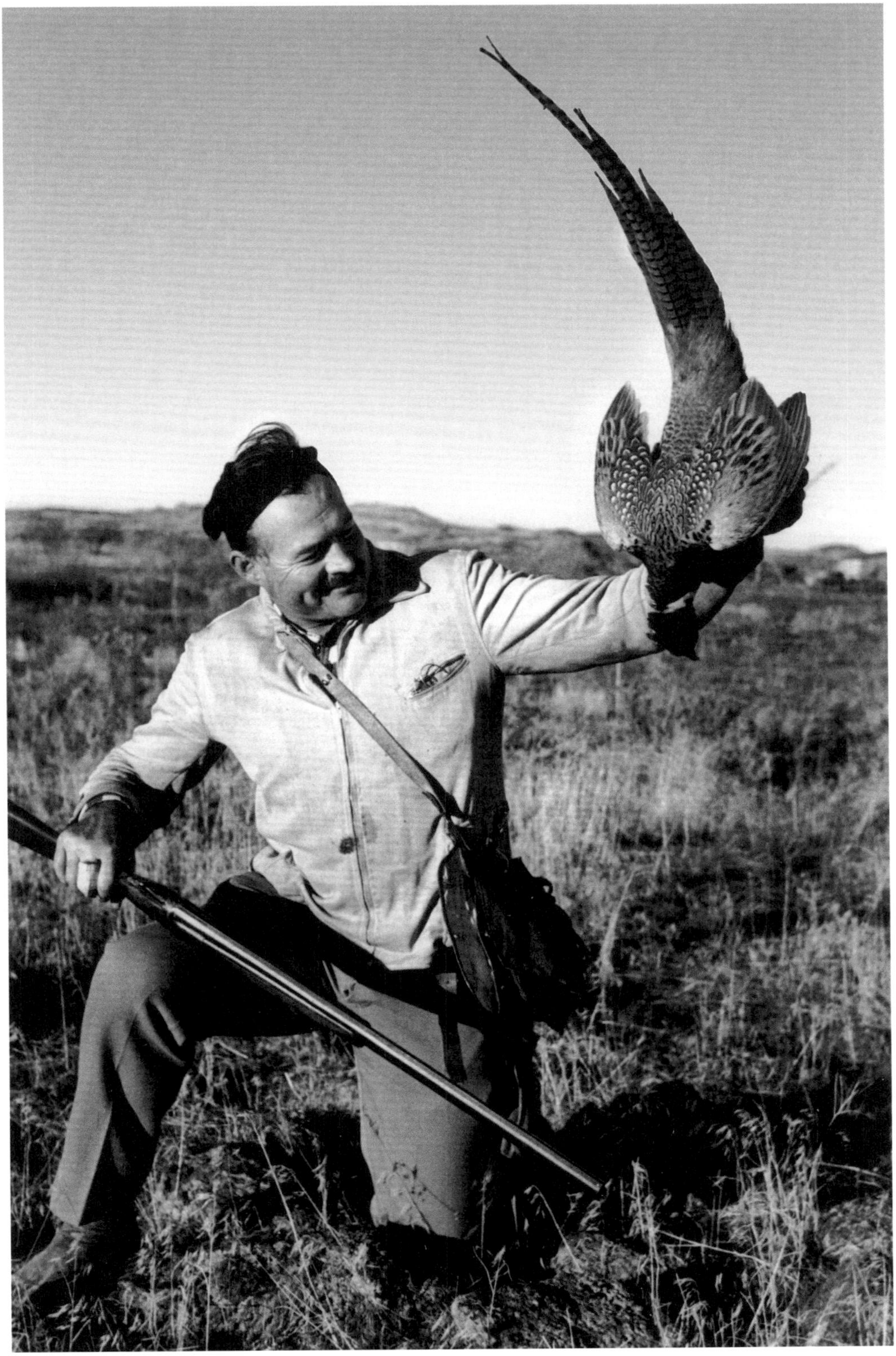

MIGUEL HERNÁNDEZ

born Orihuela, Spain, 1910; died Alicante, Spain, 1942

by 'Chim' (David Seymour)

Spain, 1936

As a child, Miguel Hernández had to help his father with his work as a herdsman; eventually, however, the pull of literature and writing became too great. Initially he devoured the classics, soon progressing to his contemporaries, such as the Spanish poet Juan Ramón Jiménez. It would take a love affair, and a blossoming friendship with Pablo Neruda, to free him from other influences, help him find his own voice as a poet and develop the perfect combination of spontaneity and craftsmanship. The poetry of his collection *Unceasing Lightning* (1936) lived up to the *poesía sin pureza* (poetry without purity) that Neruda had encouraged in him: it was passionate, shimmering and full of nervous energy.

When the Spanish Civil War broke out in 1936, Hernández enlisted in the 'Fifth Regiment', a Republican militia, in defence of Madrid. The following year he fought in the Battle of Teruel, and his poems became so popular that they were printed on postcards and distributed to the soldiers in the trenches. This photograph by 'Chim' (David Seymour) shows the poet declaiming his verses to his fellow soldiers. The photograph came to light only in 2007, when a series of missing Spanish Civil War negatives by Seymour, Robert Capa and Gerda Taro were found in three cardboard boxes sent from Mexico, the so-called 'Mexican Suitcase'.

The anthology *Viento del pueblo* (Wind of the people, 1937) represents the apex of Hernández's development as a poet. The verses resonate with the appalling suffering and desolation of war, and with vivid depictions of the blood-soaked earth. The collection includes an elegy to the poet Federico García Lorca, with whom Hernández had been friends: 'A poet dies, and creation feels the hurt and dying inside.' In 1939 Hernández was on the verge of publishing *El hombre acecha* (Man is a hunter), dedicated to Neruda, when the Spanish Republic crumbled and he was forced to flee to Portugal to escape Fascist reprisals.

In Portugal, Hernández was arrested by the police and handed over to the Spanish Civil Guard. From that moment on he was forced to endure a life behind bars, and was transferred from one prison to another. At one point he was condemned to death, but this sentence was subsequently commuted to life imprisonment. Weak and in deteriorating health, he continued to write verses whenever he could, works that were later published in the collection *Cancionero y romancero de ausencia* (Songs and ballads of absence, 1958). The force of resistance in these poems – terse meditations on key words such as home, bed, blood and heart – is still tangible, despite the specific historical circumstances in which they were written.

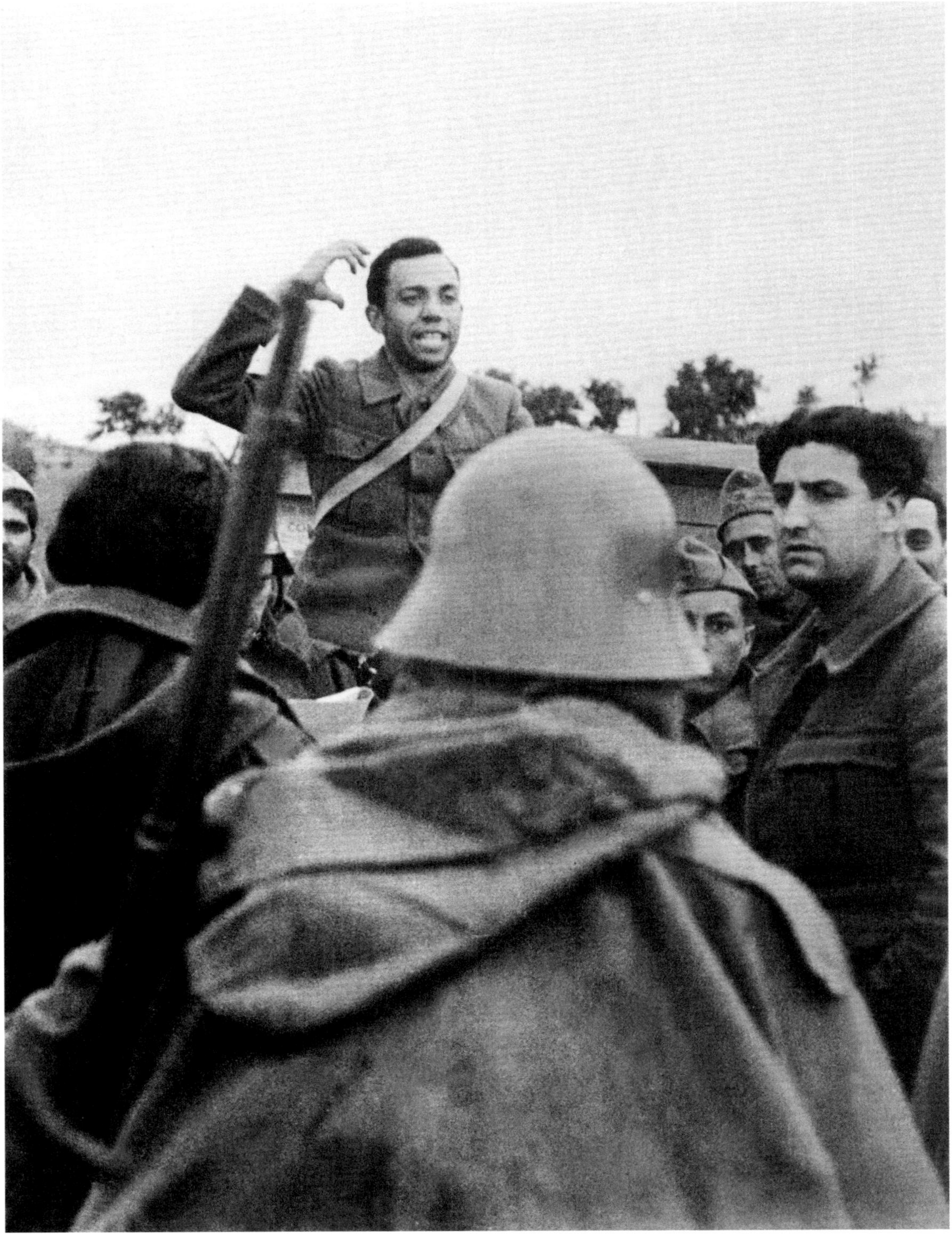

HERMANN HESSE

born Calw, Germany, 1877; died Montagnola, Switzerland, 1962

by Gisèle Freund

Montagnola, Switzerland, 1950s

Herman Hesse was a cosmopolitan from the provinces. He was born in a little town in the Black Forest; his maternal grandfather had been a famous missionary in India and his family lived according to strict Lutheran Pietist principles. Hesse spent the majority of his youth in boarding schools, including the theological seminary at Maulbronn Abbey, in which he later set his novel *Beneath the Wheel* (1906). His time at Maulbronn marked the beginning of a personal crisis: having displayed his rebellious character by temporarily escaping from the seminary, he was later sent to various corrective institutions. During this period, his anger at the authoritarianism of the education system and the repressive mechanisms of the family were expressed in a series of letters. After completing his studies he served as an apprentice to a mechanic; this was followed by a period working in book and antique shops in Tübingen and Basel. Throughout his life, a quest for liberty remained central to his existence.

Hesse was a committed pacifist, and at the outbreak of the First World War he was one of the few intellectuals who did not participate in the general enthusiasm for the conflict; indeed, his anti-nationalist stance drew considerable public criticism and personal attack. He was an intransigent anti-Fascist and an early critic of the Nazis, and in 1923 he gave up his German citizenship to become a Swiss national.

His love of travelling took him to the Indian subcontinent in 1911. Although he found neither the idealized India that his grandfather had told him about nor his desired inner peace, thejourney did bring him closer to Buddhist and Hindu spirituality; it also resulted in one of his most famous books, *Siddhartha* (1922), which in the 1960s became the bible of an entire generation of young people. During the Second World War he wrote *The Glass Bead Game* (1943) and in 1946 he was awarded the Nobel Prize.

The German-born French photographer Gisèle Freund took this portrait of Hesse in Switzerland in the 1950s. Freund was a great lover of literature and, from the 1930s onwards, photographed some of the most influential writers of the time.

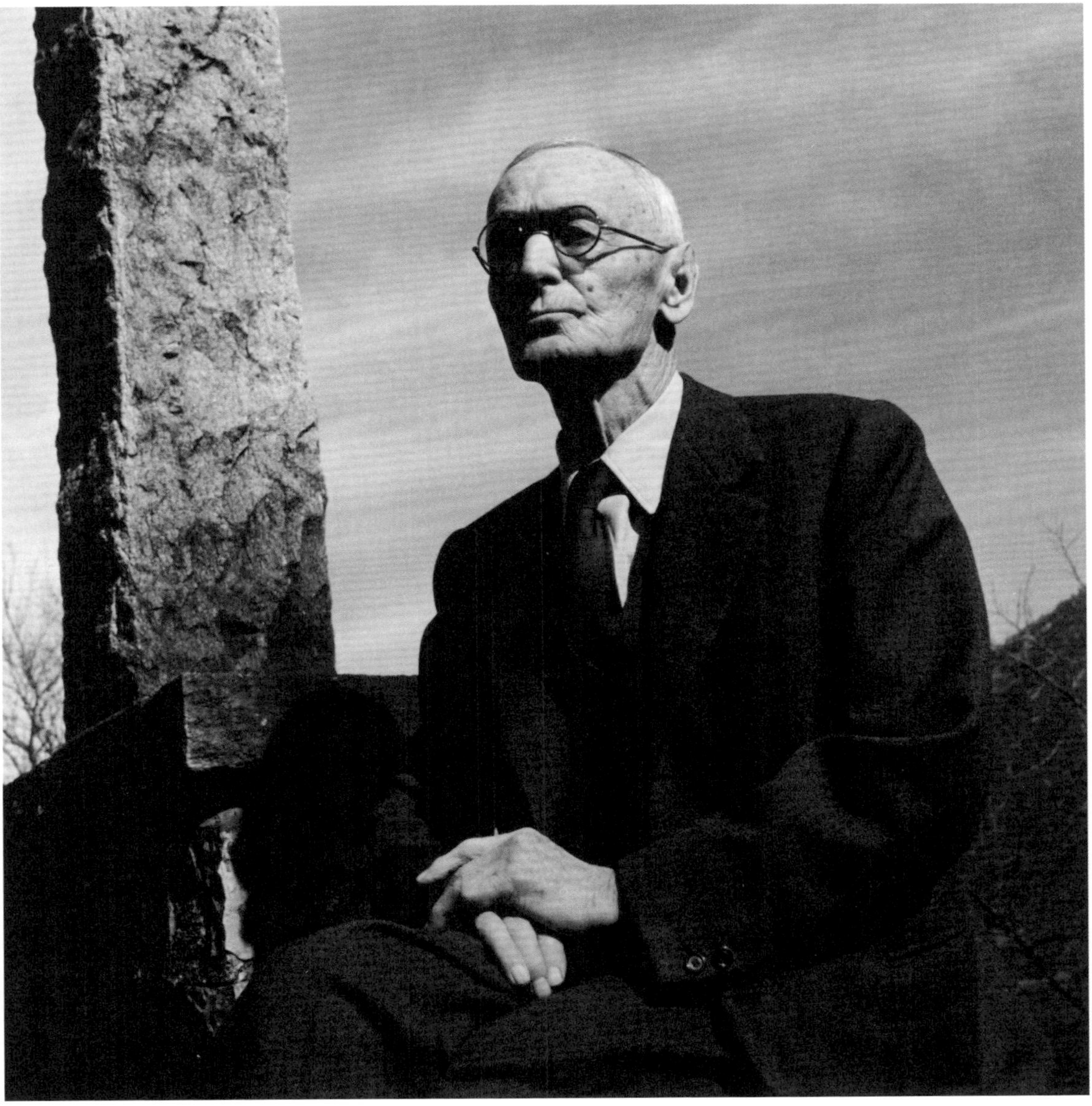

PATRICIA HIGHSMITH

[Mary Patricia Plangman] born Fort Worth, Texas, 1921; died Locarno, Switzerland, 1995

by Martine Franck

Fontainebleau, France, 1974

In the early hours of 1 January 1947, at the age of twenty-six, Patricia Highsmith wrote in her journal: 'My New Year's Eve Toast: to all the devils, lusts, passions, greeds, envies, loves, hates, strange desires, enemies ghostly and real, the army of memories, with which I do battle – may they never give me peace.'

All too aware of the demons that fuelled her writing, Highsmith led an extremely troubled life. Her childhood was marked by a destructive love–hate relationship with her mother, who, when Highsmith was twelve years old, left her with her grandmother for a year. To such childhood traumas can be added her hatred of her own homosexuality and a strange obsession with psychoses, in particular schizophrenia and pyromania. An alcoholic and a misanthrope, she preferred the company of cats to that of people, and was often photographed in the presence of her beloved pets. She was also unafraid of being politically controversial, showing clear tendencies towards anti-Semitism and racism. However, out of this turmoil came an unnerving ability to expose the deepest neuroses of modern life in her writing.

Her first book, *Strangers on a Train*, was published in 1950. The following year it was adapted into a film by Alfred Hitchcock, the success of which helped to establish her reputation as a writer of dark and often disturbing psychological thrillers and crime fiction. Her greatest and most complex creation was the character of Tom Ripley, to whom she devoted five novels. Through this cold and ruthless anti-hero, Highsmith explored themes such as homosexuality, morality, sociopathic behaviour and empathy. The first book in which he appears, *The Talented Mr Ripley* (1956), also addresses the issue of identity, with Ripley murdering a wealthy heir and taking on his identity and lifestyle.

According to Graham Greene, with whom Highsmith frequently corresponded, all of her books bear rereading, with some new discovery to be made each time. In addition to *Strangers on a Train*, many of her novels have attracted the attention of film-makers, including René Clair, Wim Wenders, Anthony Minghella and Liliana Cavani. Of the five Ripley novels (*The Talented Mr Ripley*; *Ripley Underground*, 1971; *Ripley's Game*, 1974; *The Boy Who Followed Ripley*, 1980; and *Ripley Under Water*, 1991), the first three have been made into films.

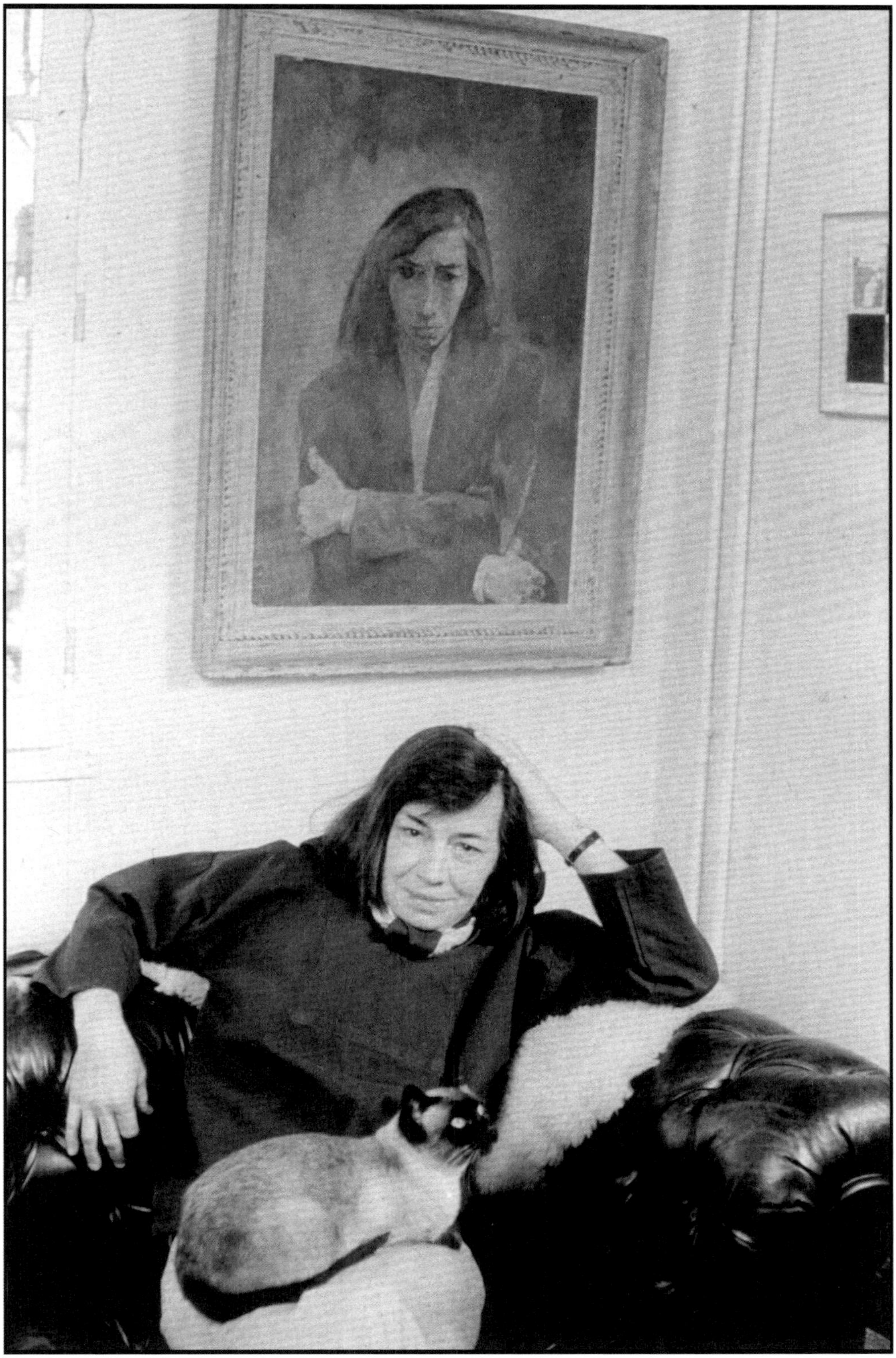

NICK HORNBY

born Redhill, Surrey, UK, 1957

by John Angerson

London, 2002

According to Nick Hornby, the most significant influences on his early literary career were the writers Anne Tyler, Raymond Carver, Richard Ford and Lorrie Moore. However, equal credit must surely go to Arsenal Football Club, of which he has been an ardent fan for most of his life. Indeed, the club functions as a central character in Hornby's debut novel, the autobiographical *Fever Pitch* (1992), which was an immediate success. On his official website, he also lists the club's former ground in Highbury, north London, as one of the venues of his education (subject: football/facts of life); the other is the University of Cambridge (English).

After the success of *Fever Pitch*, which received the William Hill Sports Book of the Year award, Hornby's life changed dramatically. Having worked as an English teacher, he was now able to devote himself to writing full-time. What followed was a string of best-selling novels, including *High Fidelity* (1995), *About a Boy* (1998) and *A Long Way Down* (2005), as well as short stories, screenplays and works of non-fiction. He has also had a successful career as a journalist, writing about his other great passion: contemporary music. In 2002 he published *31 Songs*, a collection of essays on the music that has had the greatest impact on his life.

Hornby's popularity as a writer owes a great deal to his direct and unvarnished style, much in the vein of one of his inspirations, Anne Tyler. His obsession with Arsenal has remained constant, to the extent that he still lives in the shadow of the club's ground (now the state-of-the-art Emirates Stadium), much to the amazement of his fellow writer and friend Zadie Smith: 'Every English writer needs their corner that is forever England – but only a few brave men choose to make that corner Highbury. Who would have thought the square mile around Arsenal's stadium could be a suitable surrogate for the whole wide world.'

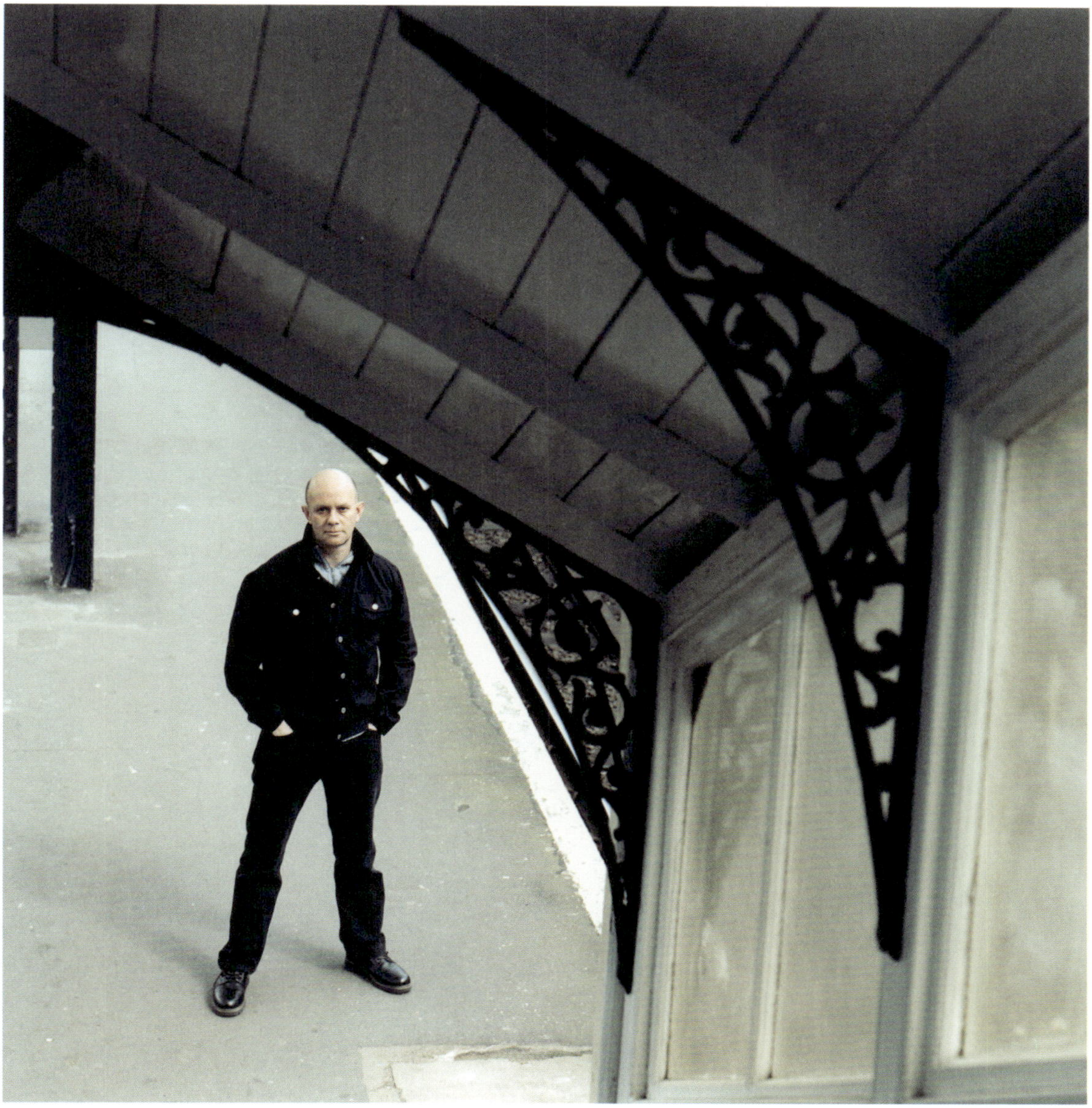

MICHEL HOUELLEBECQ

[Michel Thomas] born French island of Réunion, 1958

by Martine Franck

Paris, 1998

As the new millennium approached, Michel Houellebecq seemed to be the writer that the world had been lacking: a European writer who could formulate a credible cynicism and express harsh realities through a well-crafted and accessible style of prose. There was a need for someone who could give a legitimate voice to the darkest thoughts of several generations who had wrestled with their own consciences in isolation. Houellebecq fitted the bill perfectly. In his works he rails against the evils of modern society and the miseries of the human condition. He writes about the latent sense of alienation within social relationships, the loneliness of the human race now wedded to technology, and the general resignation of a society obsessed with sex. All these issues are discussed in a tone of fatalism, and the only sparks of life are to be found in the vehemence of the prose itself.

The subjects of Houellebecq's novels include the dullness of the office environment (*Whatever*, 1994), the tormented lives of two brothers who have abandoned themselves to reckless hedonism (*Atomised*, 1998) and the development of new-age beliefs in response to a life spent behind a computer screen (*The Possibility of an Island*, 2005). In *The Map and the Territory* (2010), in which the writer ingenuously describes his own death, he revisits the style of eighteenth and nineteenth-century novels. Houellebecq has also published a number of volumes of poetry, including *The Pursuit of Happiness* (1992) and *The Meaning of the Fight* (1996).

Outside the realms of literature Houellebecq is an incisive polemicist, writing articles – many of which are in the same controversial vein as his fiction – for newspapers and magazines. He is reluctant to make public appearances, and after living in Ireland for a while moved to Spain, where, as he himself puts it, he is 'immersed in reading'. In this photograph he appears lost in thought, preoccupied with unknown concerns. The picture was taken in 1998, the year of the publication of *Atomised*, the novel that established his international reputation.

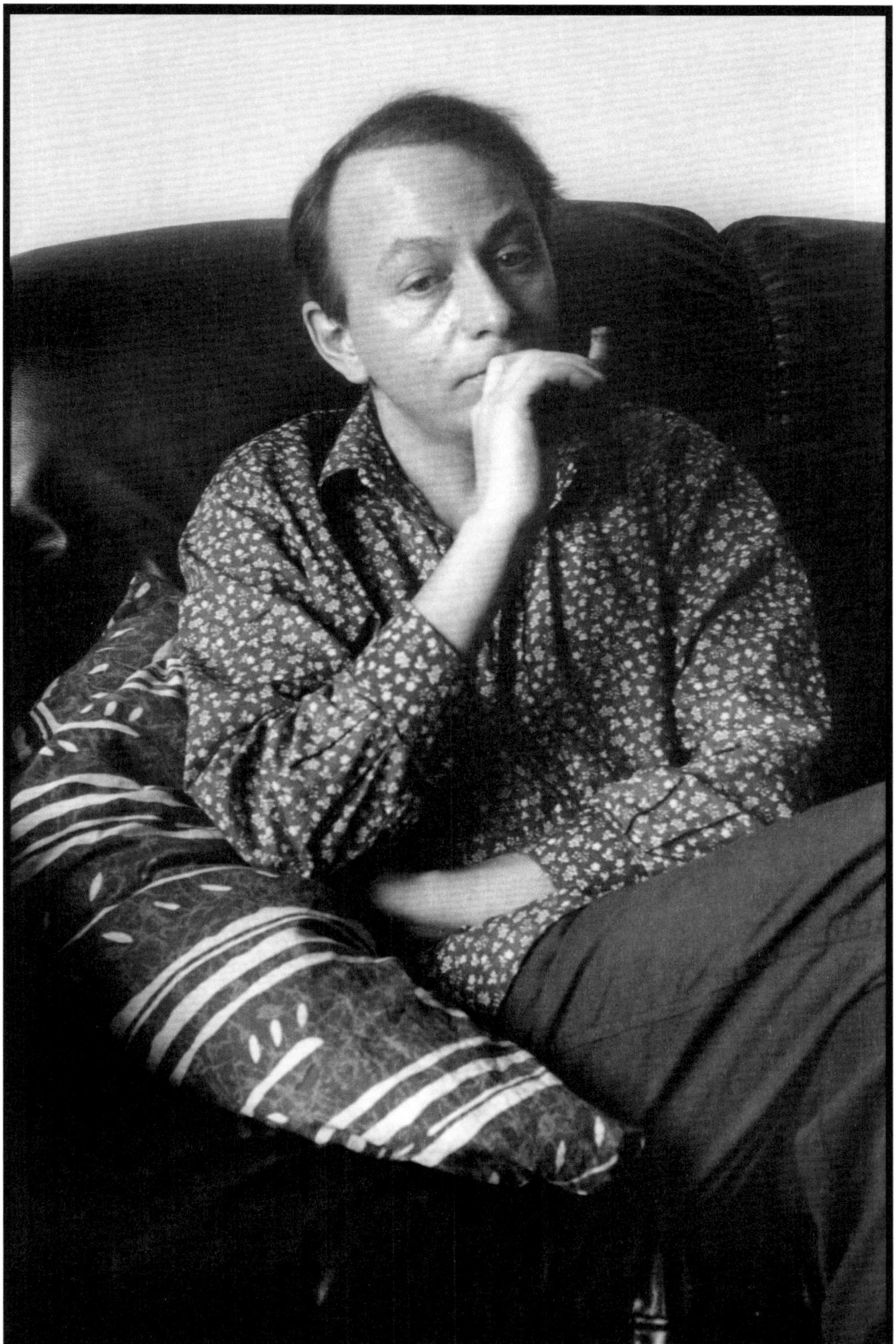

BOHUMIL HRABAL

born Brno, Czech Republic, 1914; died Prague, 1997

by Ulf Andersen

Paris, 1995

A description of Bohumil Hrabal is perhaps best made by Hrabal himself: 'I alternated regularly, not just in my life, but also in my writing, between being a fragile Pierrot and a hard ruffian. But be careful! I have always been more than Pierrot; I only became a ruffian so that my text could thunder out. Just as [Russian writer] Veniamin Kaverin taught me: write in a way that the overseers cannot do, that the astonished reader should take his head in his hands, that the editor should laugh and cry, lose his glasses and quarrel with his wife.'

Hrabal was both a hardened Pierrot – the stock pantomime character with the sad, white-painted face – and, to borrow the title of his novel of 1973, a gentle barbarian. An outsider and a great drinker, he learned about life and literature from books, from the people he met in the taverns of Prague and from the characters he encountered in one of his many odd jobs, which included notary's clerk, railway worker, underwriter for an insurance agency, travelling salesman, steelworker, telegraphist, stagehand and labourer in a warehouse for wastepaper. It is likely that one of these jobs provided the inspiration for Miloš, the young railwayman protagonist of *Closely Watched Trains* (1965), as well as for Hanta, the elderly and obsessive collector of books in *Too Loud a Solitude* (1977), a perceptive study on the theme of the permanence of ideas.

Many of Hrabal's stories and novels are autobiographical, drawing on his rich and varied experiences. His characters are humble workers, anarchists, anti-heroes, poets, misfits and eccentrics who use their imagination to bring colour to the greyness of everyday life. In the aftermath of the Prague Spring of 1968, the Communist government imposed a total ban on Hrabal's works. However, his stories continued to be published in underground editions, and their distribution was such that he became recognized as a great writer both in Czechoslovakia and beyond.

In 1997 the writer fell to his death from a fifth-floor window of a Prague hospital where he was recovering from orthopaedic treatment. It was said that he was trying to feed the birds, although the exact reason for his fall remains uncertain. Whatever the circumstances, his passing marked the loss of arguably the greatest writer in the Czech language of the last century.

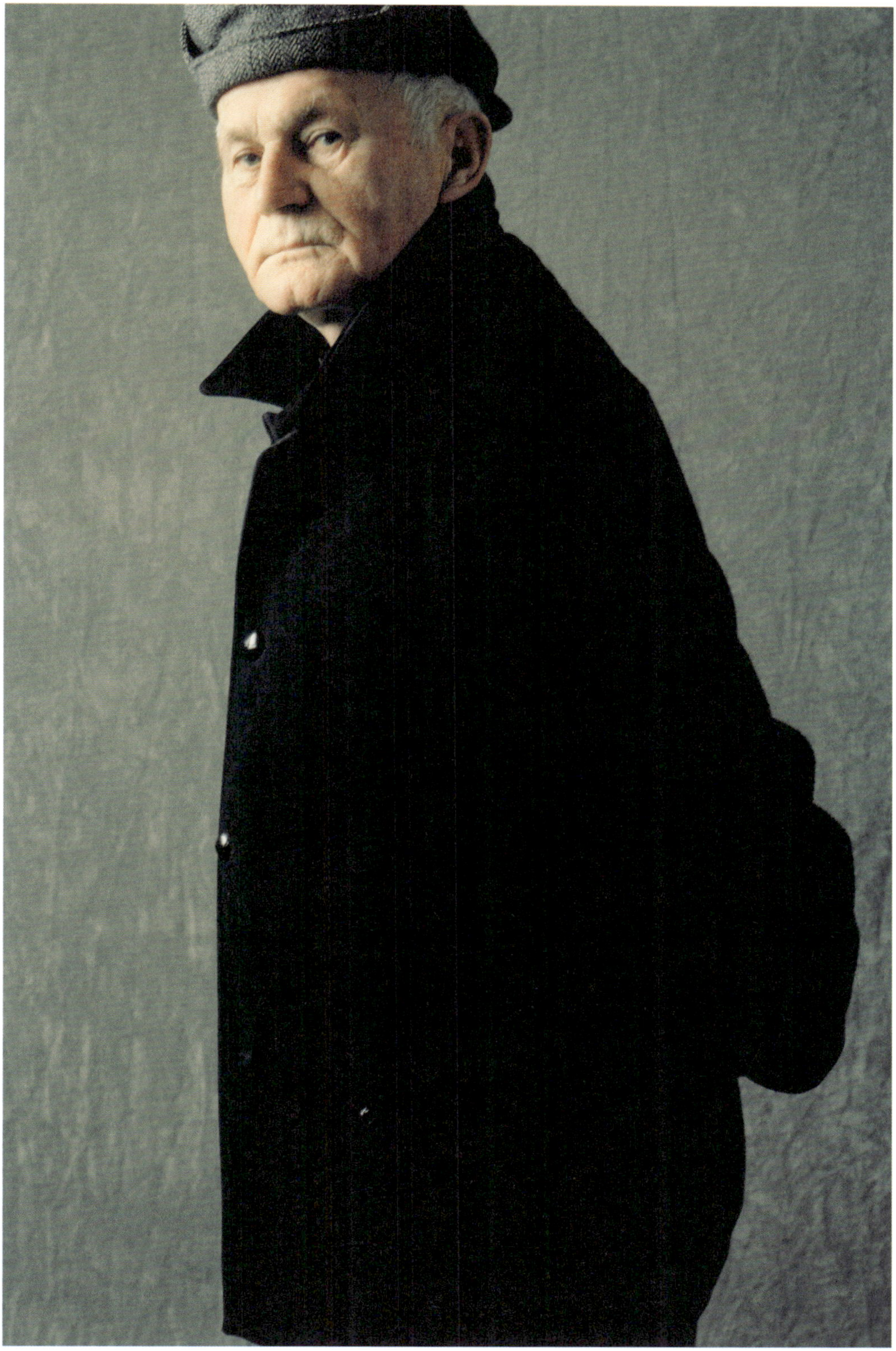

ALDOUS HUXLEY

born Godalming, Surrey, UK, 1894; died Los Angeles, 1963

by Philippe Halsman

New York, 1958

It was not a precocious literary talent that drove Aldous Huxley to writing, but an eye infection that left him almost blind and prevented him from completing his medical studies or enlisting in the army at the outbreak of the First World War. He was, however, able to read literature at Balliol College, Oxford, and later to teach at Eton, where George Orwell, who was to become the most important inheritor of Huxley's dystopian vision, was one of his pupils. Huxley's first novel, *Crome Yellow*, was published in 1921. The popularity of this country-house satire was surpassed a decade later by a very different book, the darkly ironic *Brave New World* (1932), in which the ruling deity is called Ford, human beings are mass-produced, and the words 'mother' and 'father' are terrible insults.

In 1937 Huxley moved to the USA, eventually settling in California, where he said the clear, bright air aided his eyesight. However, his art suffered as his health recovered, and the success of *Brave New World* was not to be repeated. He nevertheless continued to write in a number of genres, and in the 1950s he combined his interest in mysticism and parapsychology with his experiments with synthetic hallucinogens (he was an enthusiastic user of such drugs and an early advocate for their legalization) to produce *The Doors of Perception* (1954), an autobiographical account of his use of mescaline. Huxley died in Beverly Hills on 22 November 1963, after having been administered a large dose of LSD by his wife, Laura, at his own request. She described his passing as the 'most beautiful death'.

The photographer Philippe Halsman took this portrait of Huxley as part of his 'Jump' series: a light-hearted collection of photos of famous people leaping into the air in front of his camera. For Halsman, the series was not about achieving a spectacular effect, but about a new way of confronting the age-old challenge posed by portraiture: 'When you ask a person to jump,' he explained, 'his attention is mostly directed toward the act of jumping, and the mask falls, so that the real person appears.'

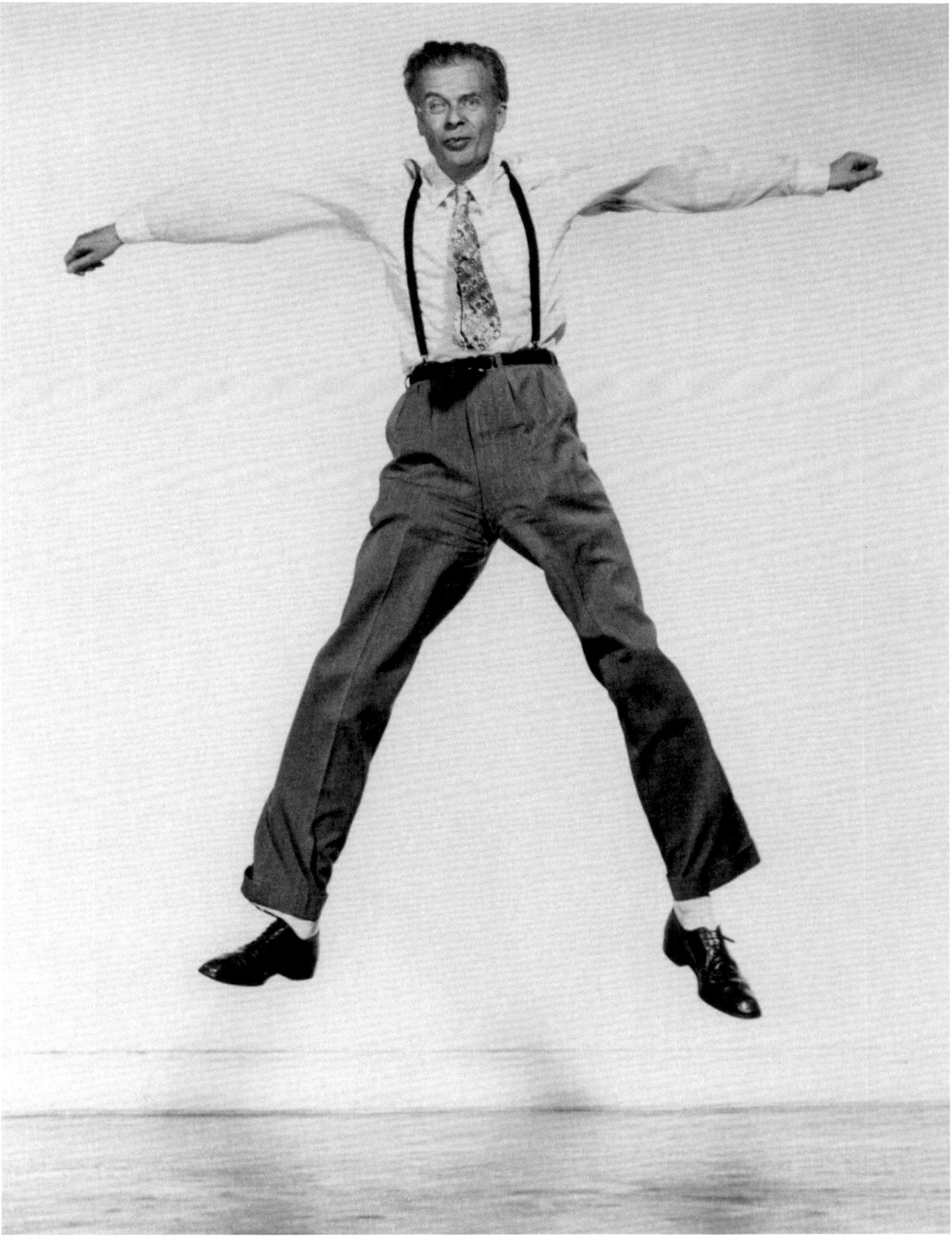

EUGÈNE IONESCO

born Slatina, Romania, 1909; died Paris, 1994

by Henri Cartier-Bresson

Paris, 1971

Henri Cartier-Bresson's portrait of Eugène Ionesco neatly captures the man and the author in a single image, hinting at the qualities for which the Romanian-born French playwright is best remembered: his sense of humour and his ability to use nonsense to explore the human condition. Ionesco, as one of the fathers of the Theatre of the Absurd, created a dramatic style characterized by his abandonment of a logical narrative and his use of nonsensical dialogue that is both concise and verbose, and which makes us laugh even while the tragic events of the performance work themselves out on stage. To some degree, it is language itself, with all its conventional codes, that is being critiqued.

Even the house in which Cartier-Bresson photographed Ionesco seems to hint at the claustrophobic setting of *The Bald Soprano*, the *anti-pièce* (anti-play) first performed in May 1950 at the Théâtre des Noctambules in Paris. It was a complete fiasco, but this did not deter Ionesco; indeed, five years later the play became an enormous success. Set in a bourgeois drawing room, *The Bald Soprano* directly critiques the vacuity of the characters' conversations through the incongruities and hesitancies in their dialogue, overturning accepted distinctions between the ordinary and the absurd.

In the 1930s Ionesco had been a talented young member of the Romanian avant-garde, and he began his literary career as a writer of poetry and criticism. One of his first works was *No* (1934), a collection of essays criticizing many of his fellow writers. His encounter with theatre was quite unexpected: he had decided to learn English, and as he copied out phrases from a textbook he soon noticed the utter banality of such statements as 'the ceiling is high' and 'there are seven days in the week'. It is precisely this sort of statement that Mrs Smith directs at Mr Smith in the first scene of *The Bald Soprano*, thus beginning the ironic and incisive analysis of the human psyche and social conventions that runs throughout Ionesco's theatre.

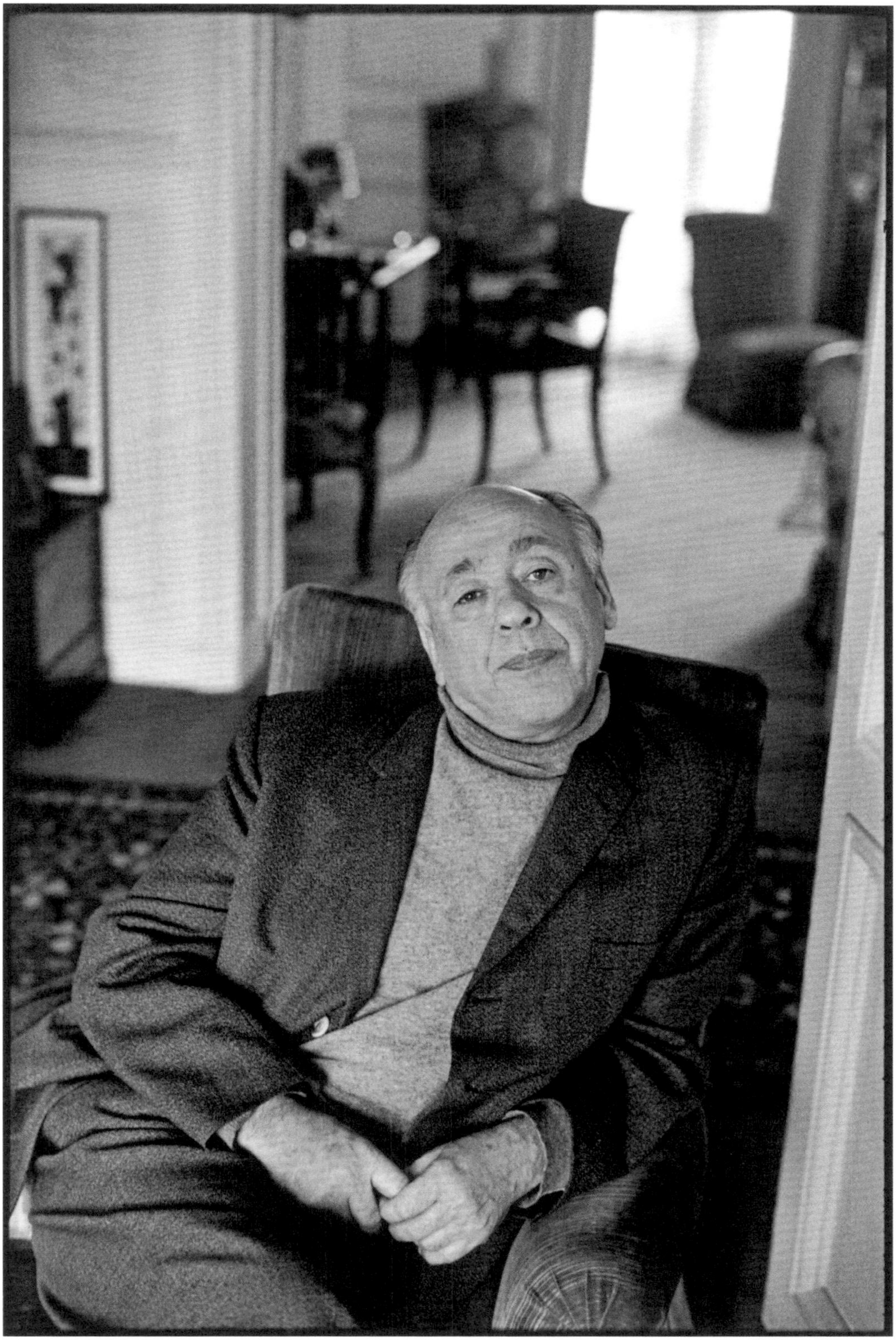

CHRISTOPHER ISHERWOOD

born High Lane, Greater Manchester, UK, 1904; died Santa Monica, California, 1986

by George Platt Lynes

California, 1939

Christopher Isherwood was born into a life of wealth and privilege. His rejection of this world, however, began at an early age; it later found its greatest expression when he left the University of Cambridge prematurely, having deliberately failed his exams. In 1925 Isherwood became reacquainted with W. H. Auden, whom he had known at preparatory school, and through him was introduced to Stephen Spender. Together, the three men would form one of the most innovative literary groups of the time. In 1929 Isherwood followed Auden to Weimar-era Berlin, where, in the city's liberal atmosphere, he was able to live openly as a homosexual. His experiences of this period are reflected in his novel *Goodbye to Berlin* (1939). It was also in Berlin that he met Heinz Neddermeyer, a young German with whom he fell in love. The two spent much of the 1930s travelling in Europe, evading the attentions of the German military authorities.

The 1930s also saw a number of collaborations between Isherwood and Auden, including *Journey to a War* (1939), an account of their travels in China during the Sino–Japanese War of 1937–45. This traumatic experience gave rise to Isherwood's pacifism. In January 1939 the two men emigrated to the USA, with Auden settling in New York and Isherwood in Los Angeles. There he found work as a screenwriter for Metro Goldwyn Mayer and, following his encounter with the Indian mystic and philosopher Swami Prabhavananda, became one of the leading figures in the Vedanta Society, an experience he recounts in *Ramakrishna and His Disciples* (1965). His final novel, *A Single Man* (1964), describes a day in the life of a British professor, who resembles Isherwood and, like him, is an outsider in the USA. Described by the novelist Edmund White as the founding text of modern gay storytelling, the book was written following Isherwood's temporary separation from the great love of his life, the painter Don Bachardy.

James J. Berg, the author of various essays on Isherwood's life and work, has noted that Bachardy and Isherwood were perhaps one of the few gay couples of the period who were happy to be photographed together. As a consequence, they attracted many of the most celebrated photographers of the day, including Cecil Beaton, Horst P. Horst and George Platt Lynes, who took this portrait of Isherwood.

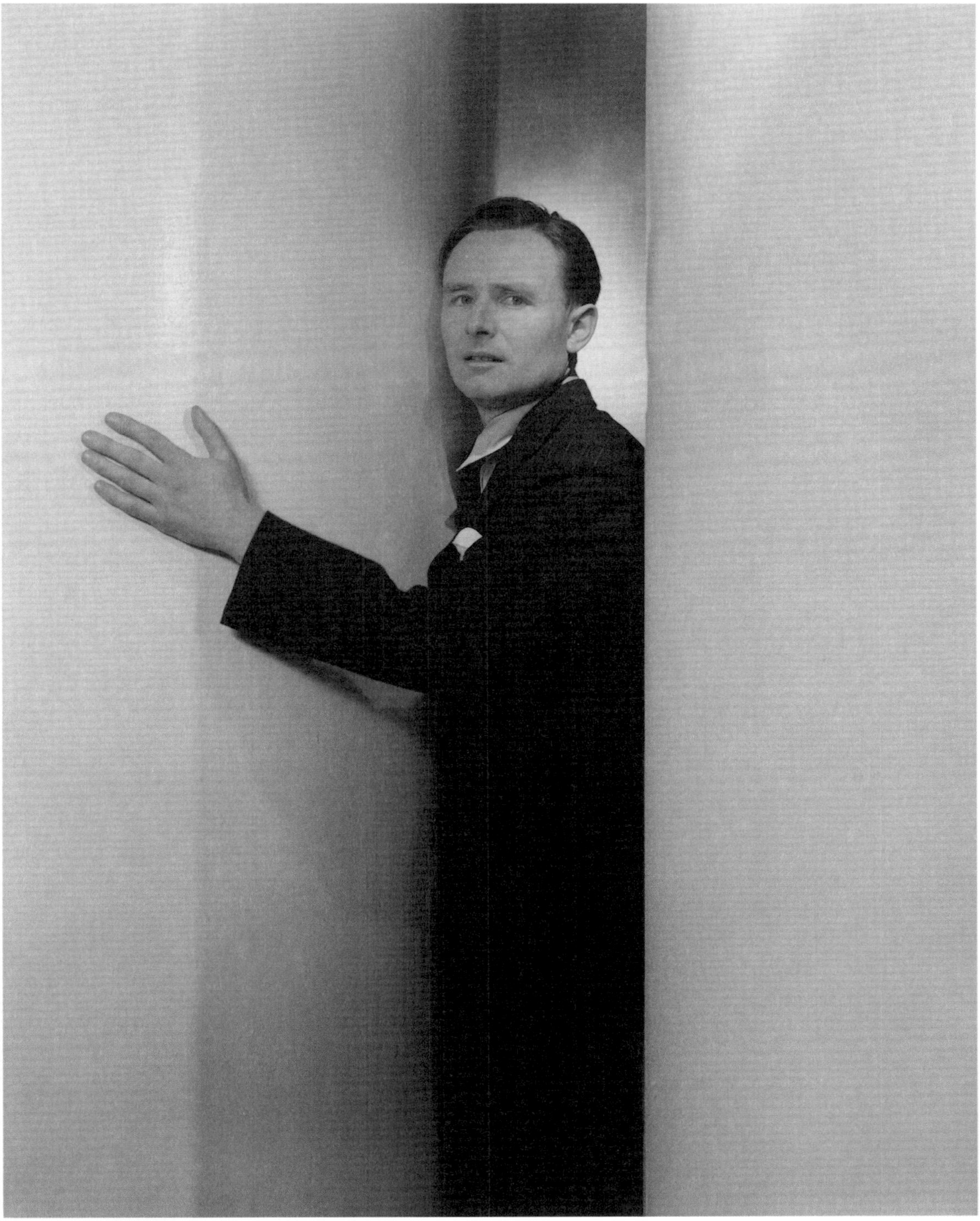

KAZUO ISHIGURO

born Nagasaki, Japan, 1954

by Sophie Bassouls

Paris, 1990

Born in Japan, Kazuo Ishiguro moved to England with his family when he was five years old, for what was intended to be only a temporary stay. In the end they remained in the country, and Ishiguro went on to become one of the most distinguished writers in the English language.

After graduating from the University of Kent in 1978, Ishiguro attended the University of East Anglia's renowned creative writing course, founded by Malcolm Bradbury and Angus Wilson. Ishiguro's first two novels, *A Pale View of the Hills* (1982) and *An Artist of the Floating World* (1986), feature Japanese characters and settings. However, his next novel, *The Remains of the Day* (1989), was quintessentially English in both setting and tone. According to the author, this change of focus reflected his realization that the essence of what he wanted to write about was universal, and not tied to a specific place or time. Central to much of his work are the themes of memory, loss and mortality.

In 1993 *The Remains of the Day*, in which a long-serving butler at an English country house looks back at his life and his relationship with a former housekeeper, was made into a film directed by James Ivory. A further screen success came in 2010 with the adaptation of Ishiguro's sixth novel, *Never Let Me Go* (2005), a dystopian tale that chronicles the lives of a community of clones bred for organ donation.

French photographer Sophie Bassouls is well known for her portraits of both writers and artists. On her website she describes the selection and creative processes behind one of her collections of writers' portraits: 'I have read them, followed them and pursued them. I have felt respect for them, affection, admiration, sometimes irritation, but above all curiosity. That is what drove me to these encounters; then a hope arose, sometimes attained, of creating an image which would reveal ideas and words by capturing a face.'

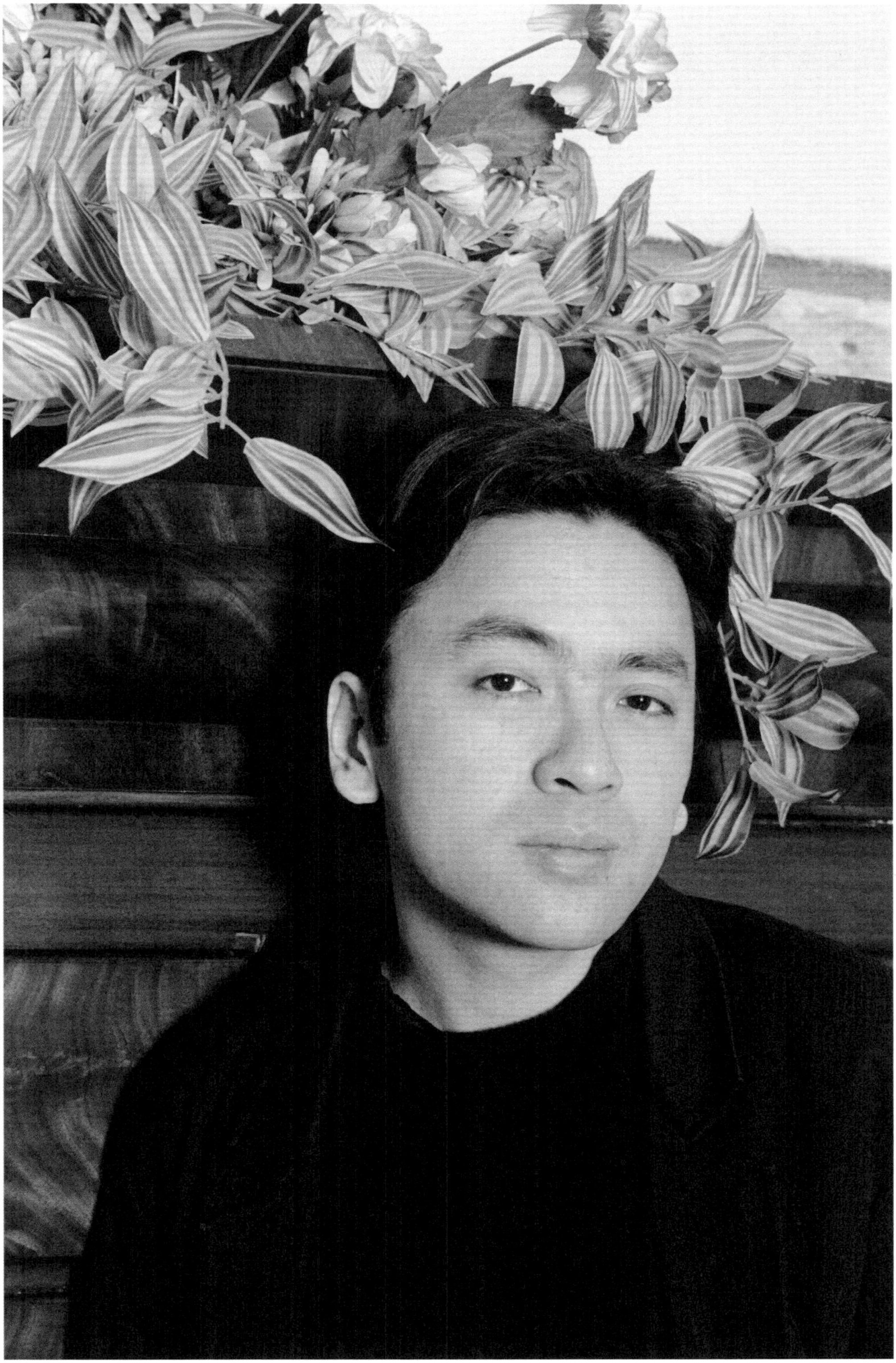

HENRY JAMES

born New York, 1843; died London, 1916

by E. O. Hoppé

London c. 1880

Henry James was exposed to a wide range of cultural influences from an early age. Together with his brother (William, the future philosopher and psychologist), James accompanied his parents on their extended travels in Europe. It was on such trips that he not only learned different languages and discovered different cultures, but also developed his taste for a refined form of decadence that he juxtaposed in many of his works with the slightly coarse yet genuinely fresh American world view. James's 'intellectual commuting' continued throughout his life. In an existence almost entirely free of any major life-changing events (he never married, and was even able to keep his presumed homosexuality quiet), his movement between the USA and Europe was a constant feature of his life, almost until the end. In 1875 he decided to set up home in Europe (Paris in particular, and later London), but this did not prevent him from returning to the USA for long periods of time. It was only in 1911 that he left the USA for good, and he did not apply to become a British citizen until the year before his death.

The contrast between a charming yet corrupt Europe and a robust but rather unrefined USA was a theme that ran through all his works, from *Daisy Miller* (1879) and *Portrait of a Lady* (1881) to the 'supernatural' novella *The Turn of the Screw* (1898) and the great works of his late period, such as *The Ambassadors* (1903). But to focus on James's interest in the conflict between the Old and New worlds would be misleading. The author of some twenty novels – others of note include *The Bostonians* (1886), *The Princess Casamassima* (1886), *The Wings of the Dove* (1902) and *The Golden Bowl* (1904) – and of more than one hundred short stories, James laid the basis for contemporary storytelling in the USA and beyond. His psychological excavation of his characters, the prominence of their interior development in relation to the exterior development of the plot, the substitution of a circumscribed and subjective point of view for the omniscient narrator, and the introduction of elements of psychoanalysis are all features of the finest twentieth-century literature.

The German-born English photographer E. O. Hoppé opened his photographic studio inLondon in 1907, and within a few years he had become a highly successful and well-regarded portraitist. Some of the most important artistic and literary figures of the era passed in front of his camera, and James was no exception. Hoppé portrayed the writer in profile, allowing the light to illuminate his somewhat distant expression.

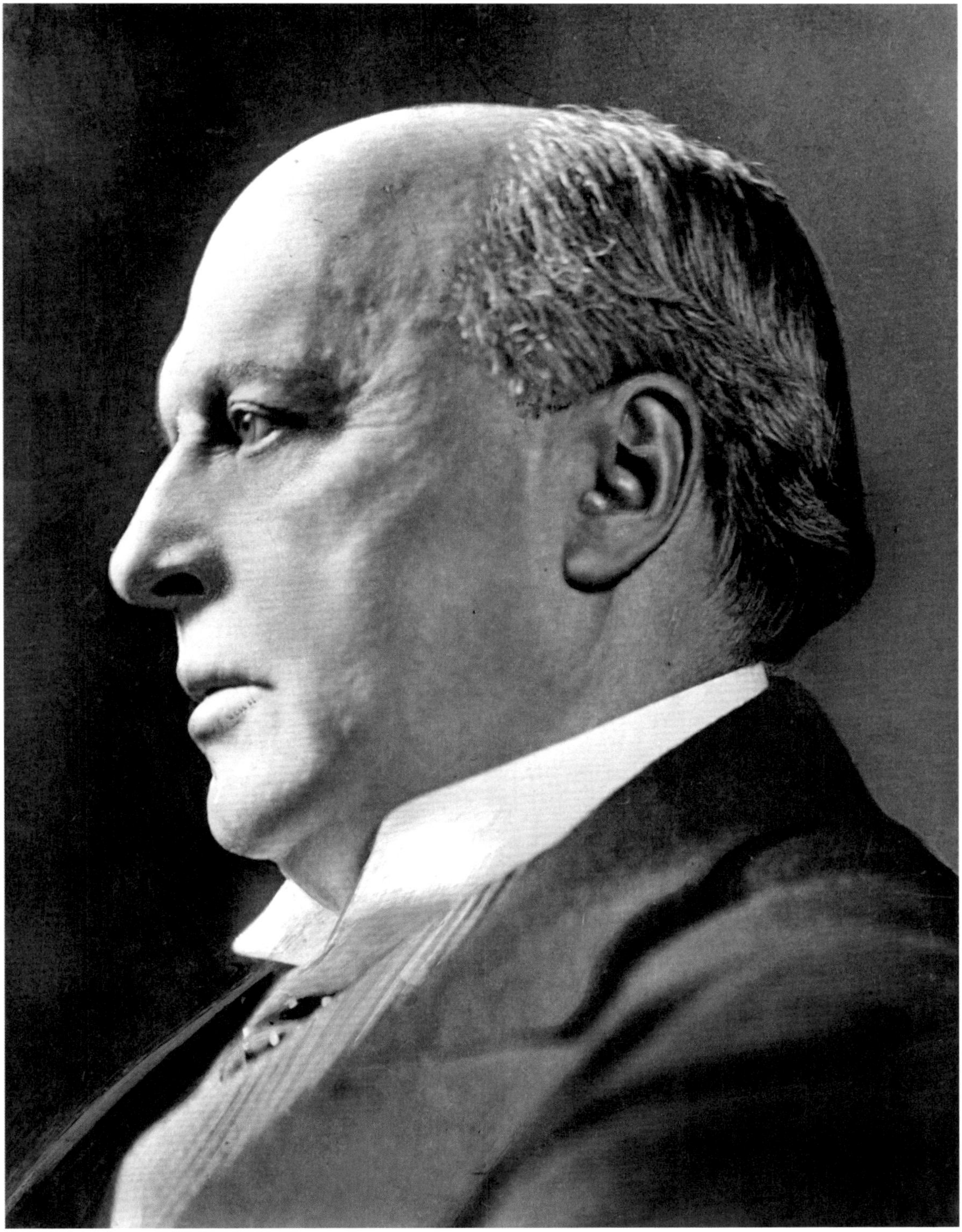

JUAN RAMÓN JIMÉNEZ

born Moguer, Spain, 1881; died San Juan, Puerto Rico, 1958

unknown photographer

Riverdale, Marylanc, c. 1950

Juan Ramón Jiménez described himself as a 'universal Andalusian', a modest epithet for an accomplished poet and winner of the 1956 Nobel Prize in Literature. He was very attached to his childhood home: 'Moguer. Mother and siblings. The clean and welcoming nest.' His adult life, however, was characterized by travel: initially to Madrid, where his first collections of poetry, *Ninfeas* (Waterlilies, 1900) and *Almas de violeta* (Violet souls, 1900) were published; and then to the USA in pursuit of his sweetheart, Zenobia Cambrubí Aymar. The couple were married, and she remained his lifelong companion. The transatlantic voyage kindled in him a fascination with the sea as muse, which he explored in *Diary of a Newlywed Poet* (1917), and inspired him to develop the concept of 'pure poetry', in which he envisaged verses flowing as freely as the waves around him. 1914 saw the publication of his most famous work, *Platero and I*, dedicated to a donkey that had been his faithful childhood companion in Moguer. The work conveys a sense of searching for a concrete sense of existence, and contains a series of reflections on nature, social reality and the cruelty of mankind.

In 1936 Jimenéz and his wife left Spain for Puerto Rico and Cuba, later moving to the USA where he taught Spanish literature at the University of Miami and the University of Maryland before settling permanently in Puerto Rico. Following his exile from Spain, Jimenéz began a process of soul-searching and seeking God, expressing himself in language whose neologisms are symptomatic of an existential crisis, perhaps most intensely in the poems of the collection *Animal de fondo* (Animal from the deep, 1949). During this period he also became obsessed with the question of the role of a poet in a time of war. He concluded that his own role was to rally public opinion in the USA, where he collected donations and compiled the material for his monumental *Guerra en España: Prosa y Verso 1936–1954* (War in Spain: prose and verse 1936–1954), which was published posthumously in 1985 and is now considered one of the greatest works written about the Spanish Civil War.

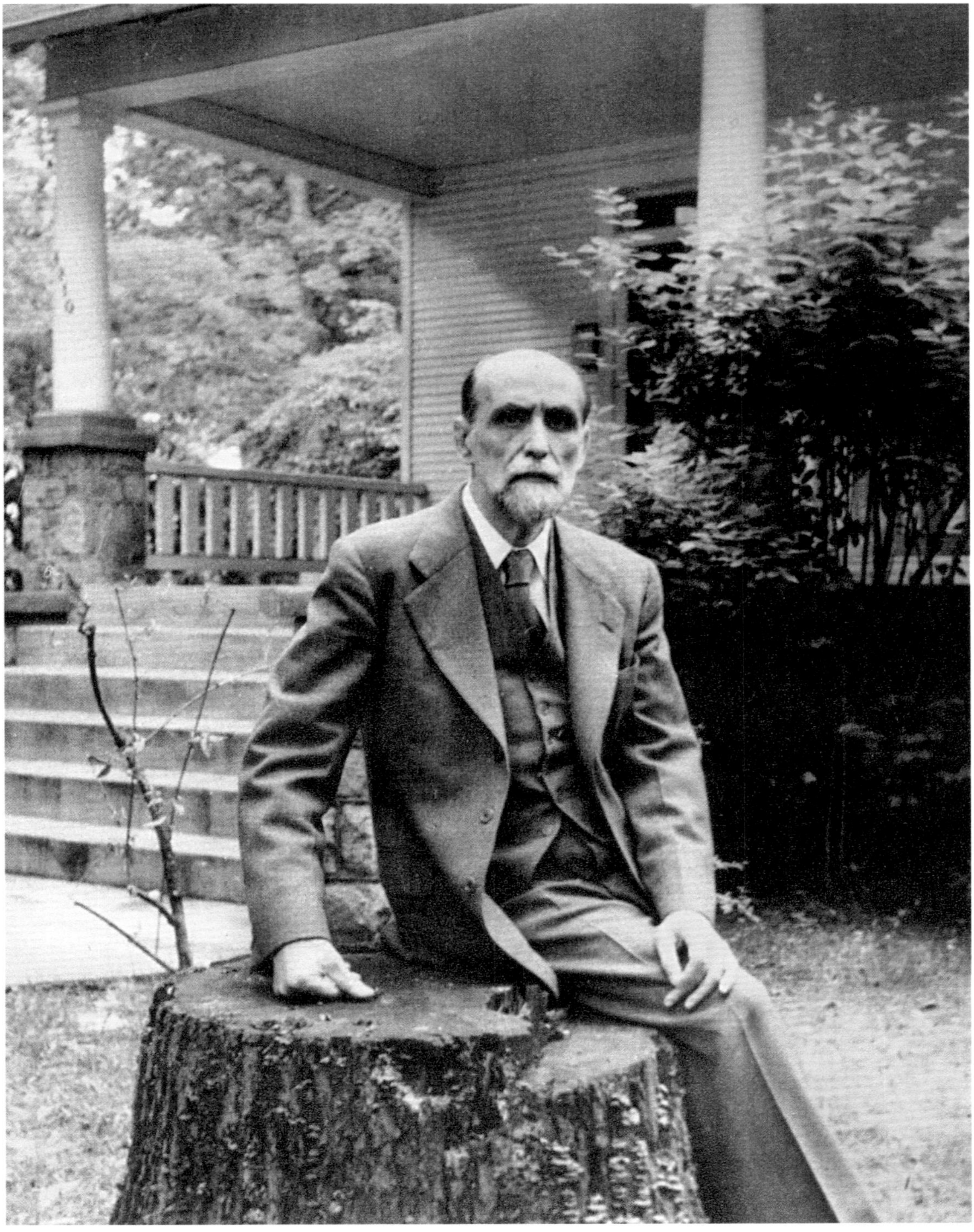

JAMES JOYCE

born Dublin, 1882; died Zurich, 1941

by Gisèle Freund

Paris, 1939

On 16 June each year, known as 'Bloomsday', Dublin is filled with the voices of Leopold Bloom, Molly Bloom and Stephen Dedalus. In a celebration of the events of *Ulysses* (1922) and of its principal characters, these voices ring out from every corner, just as they had emerged in the pages of James Joyce's groundbreaking book: a chronicle of Leopold Bloom's passage through Dublin on 16 June 1904.

Born into a Catholic family in the city of Dublin, Joyce spent much of his life escaping – from the restrictions of his city, his family and religion. After leaving Ireland he lived in France, Italy and then Switzerland, often in poverty; while living in Trieste, he taught English to help make ends meet. Having already published a collection of short stories, *Dubliners* (1914), and the largely autobiographical *A Portrait of the Artist as a Young Man* (1914–15), Joyce wrote *Ulysses* amid the rise of the avant-garde and the growing interest in the subconscious. Dismissed by Virginia Woolf as the work of a 'queasy undergraduate scratching his pimples', the book is widely regarded as one of the most significant and influential in the English language; indeed, Joyce's pioneering use of interior monologue, or 'stream of consciousness', marked a turning point in twentieth-century literature. Together with the later *Finnegans Wake* (1939), *Ulysses* revolutionized the form and structure of the novel and pushed language and linguistic experimentation to their limits.

It was a commission from *Life* magazine that brought Gisèle Freund to Joyce's home in the rue Edmond-Valentin in Paris. The writer, however, was extremely guarded in his welcome: he had a fear of colour photography and was worried about the lights being too bright for his eyes, and when he bumped into a light shortly before the start of the photo session he accused Freund of trying to kill him. The entire shoot was a disaster, but Freund managed to convince Joyce to try again the next day. Eventually, as he later recalled to his friends, he was won over by her persistence: 'Gisèle is stronger than the Irish. I didn't want to be photographed in colour, but she took possession of me, not once but twice!'

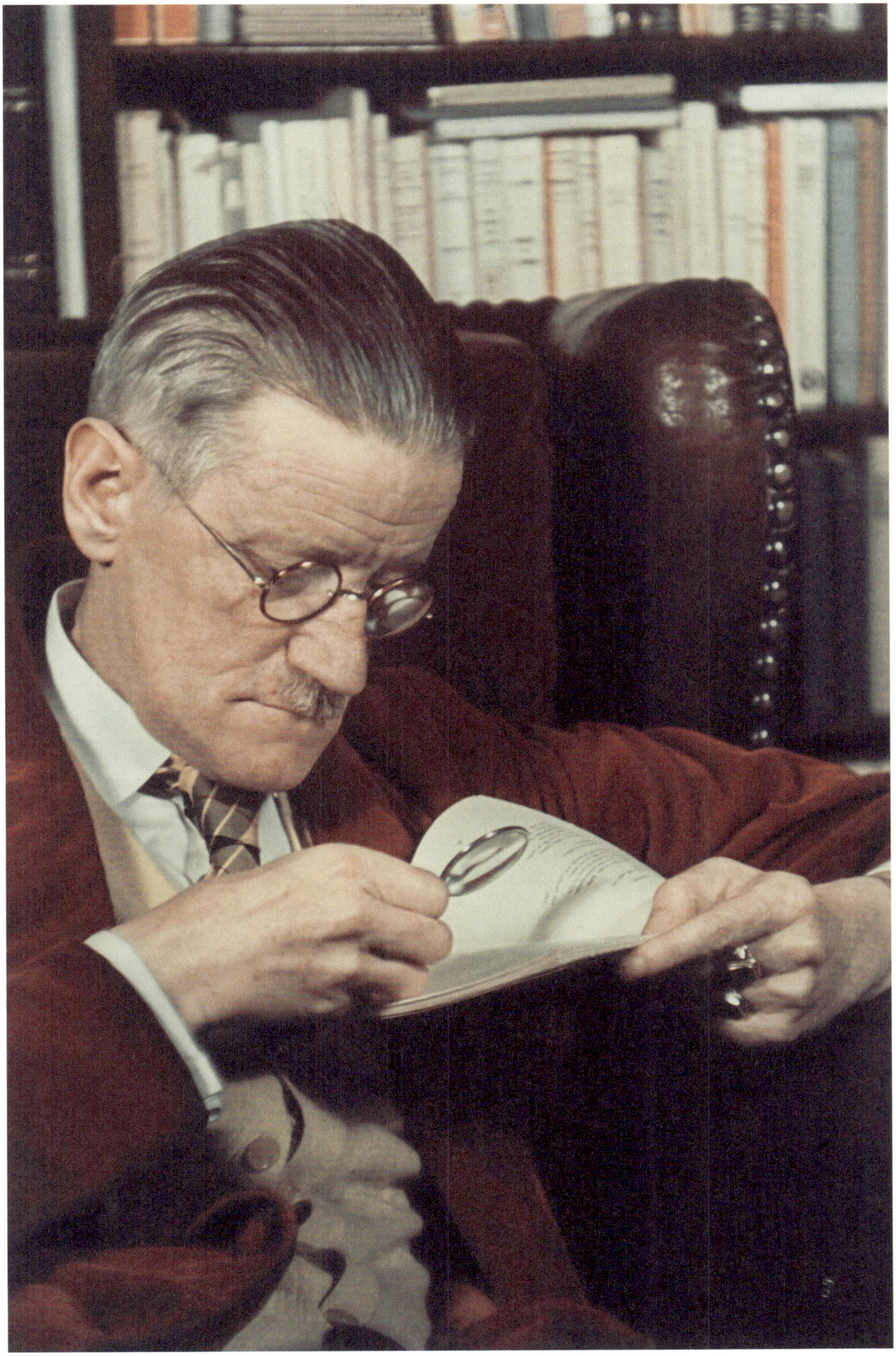

ISMAIL KADARE

born Gjirokaster, Albania, 1936

by Richard Kalvar

Paris, 1991

In *The General of the Dead Army* (1963), Ismail Kadare's first novel, a general and a military chaplain are commissioned by the Italian government to carry out a delicate task: they must repatriate the bodies of the Italian soldiers who fell in Albania during the Second World War. Over the course of the novel, this task reveals itself to be increasingly complicated. The general finds himself having to travel to every corner of Albania, carrying with him not only the bodies of the fallen soldiers but also all the memories, hatred and horrors associated with the conflict. Published when Kadare was just twenty-six years old, the book was a great success, bringing him both national and international acclaim (in 1983 it was adapted into a film by Luciano Tovoli, with Marcello Mastroianni in the role of General Ariosto).

Kadare studied literature at the University of Tirana, and began postgraduate work at the Maxim Gorki Literature Institute in Moscow, although he was forced to leave the latter when relations between Albania and the Soviet Union became strained. Kadare's attitude towards Enver Hoxha, the Communist leader of Albania from 1944 to 1985, was considered by many to be highly ambiguous. In 1970 Kadare became a member of the People's Parliament of Albania, a position that gave him the freedom to travel and to be published abroad. However, following the publication of 'The Red Pashas' (1975), a satirical poem seen as criticizing the authorities, the Albanian Writers' Union forced him to go through a process of 'self-criticism' and prevented him from publishing for the next three years.

Kadare's books explore subjects such as the history of the Balkans and the Communist experiment in Albania, often using classical mythology as a filter through which to analyse contemporary events. In *The Palace of Dreams* (1981), Kadare sets an allegory of totalitarianism in the capital of the Ottoman Empire. The Albanian authorities accused him of hiding political themes behind its layers of history and folklore, however, and banned its publication. In 1990 Kadare sought political asylum in France. He is portrayed here by the Magnum photographer Richard Kalvar, who uses unusual framing and a mixture of inaction and motion to give his portrait of the writer a sense of unfamiliarity.

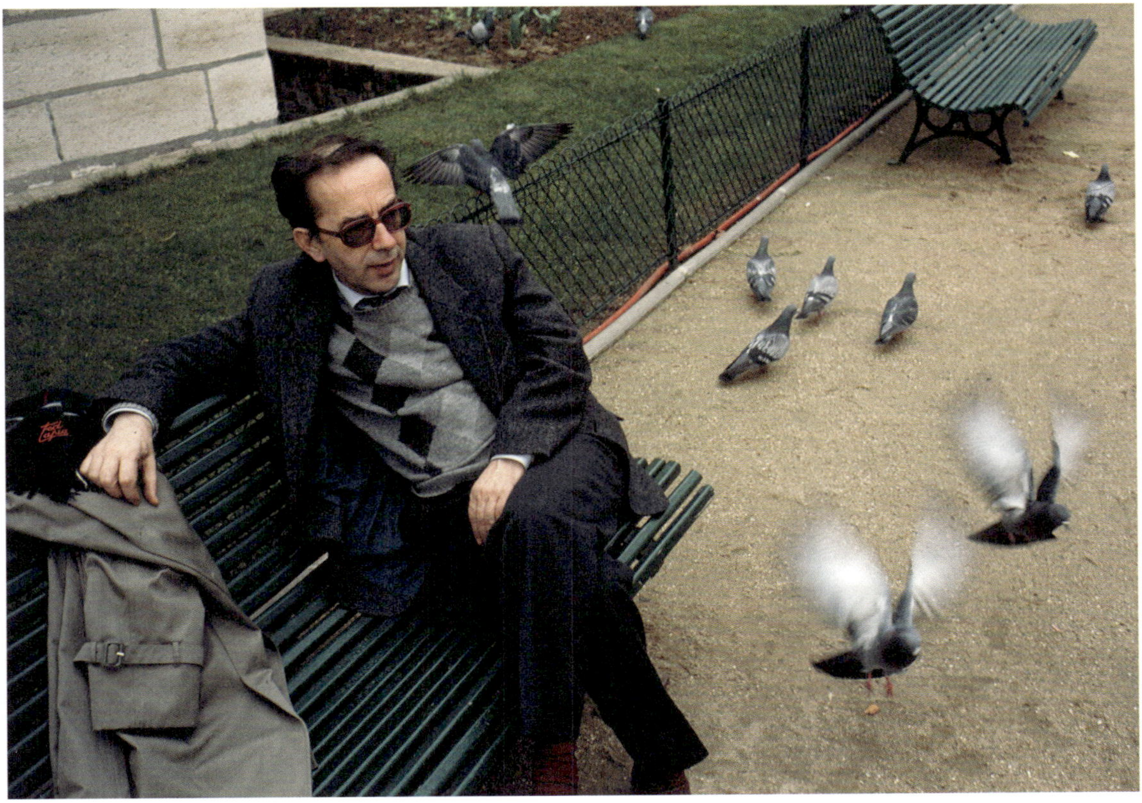

FRANZ KAFKA

born Prague, 1883; died Kierling, Austria, 1924

unknown photographer

unknown location, c. 1923

In the majority of photographs of Franz Kafka, his gaze seems both profound and enigmatic. The German-speaking Jewish author fixed the same insistent gaze on the whole of reality throughout his life, producing in his work an unflinching examination of the human condition in an increasingly complex world.

Kafka, who started life as an insurance clerk, published only a few of his stories during his lifetime, and asked his friend and literary executor, the author and composer Max Brod, to destroy his work following his death. Brod ignored this request, however, thus saving for posterity some of the twentieth century's most affecting and unsettling literature. Kafka's writing is extremely visual and his language eerily objective. The city of *The Trial* (1925) is made up of low-ceilinged rooms, labyrinthine apartment blocks and gloomy offices in which we can almost feel the dust on the furniture. The inns in the village in *The Castle* (1926) have the whiff of soup and beer about them, and everything is described with such precision that the reader even becomes aware of the smell of the cold. Yet the power of Kafka's stories lies in their menacing combination of the banal and the fantastical and the familiar and the unfamiliar.

Among the works Kafka did publish during his lifetime are the short stories 'The Metamorphosis' (1915) and 'In the Penal Colony' (1919). In these and other stories, as well as in his novels, Kafka examines what it means to be an individual faced with an enigmatic reality, leaving numerous questions unresolved; indeed, many of his stories were left open-ended or unfinished. In *The Trial,* Joseph K. struggles against the irrational behaviour of an incomprehensible power, and at the end of his futile struggle he asks himself exhaustedly: 'Where was the judge he had never seen? Where was the High Court he had never reached? He raised his hands and spread out all his fingers.' This small act of K.'s before he is condemned to death is one of Kafka's most eloquent gestures.

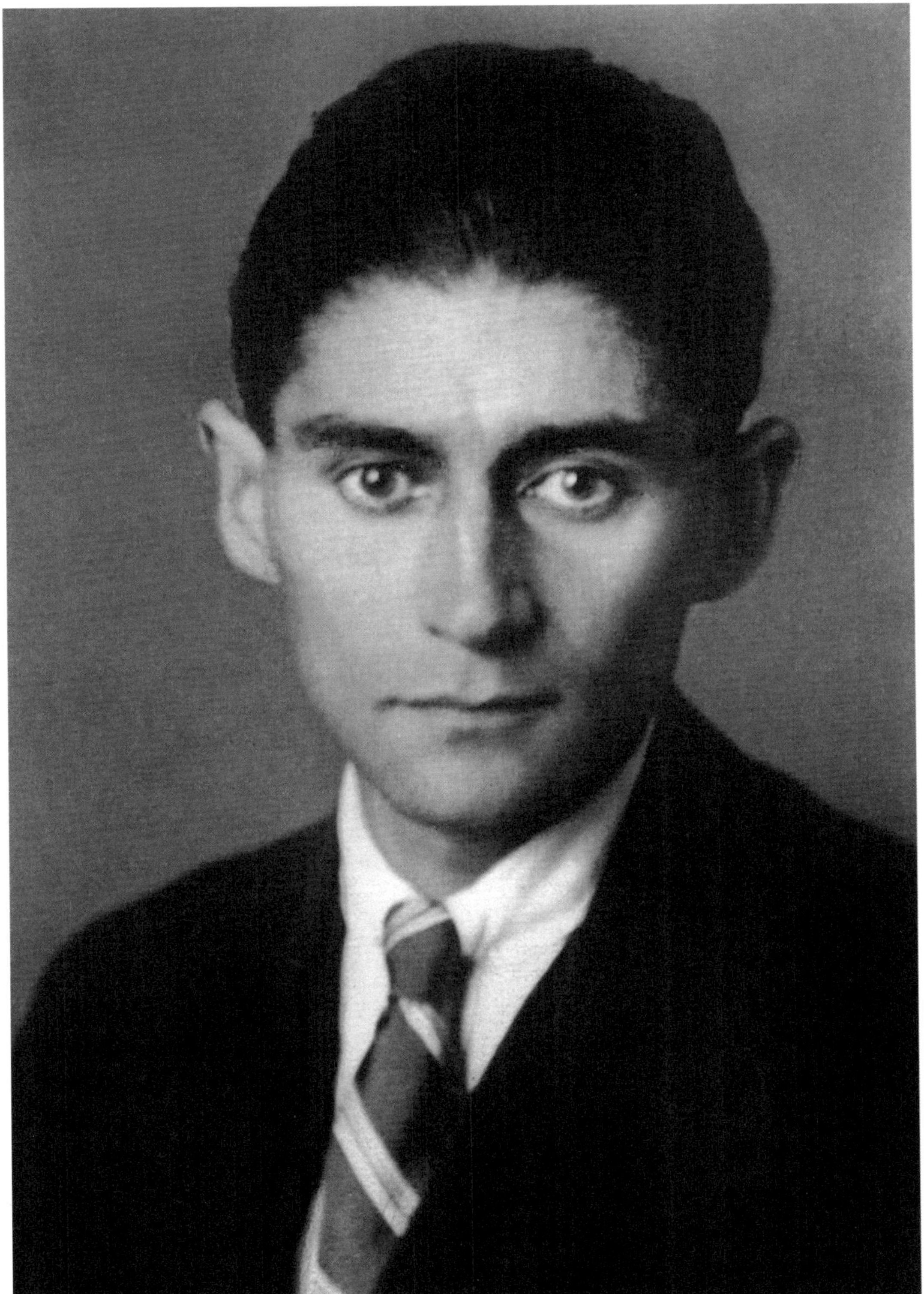

KONSTANTINOS P. KAVAFIS

born Alexandria, Egypt, 1863; died Alexandria, Egypt, 1933

unknown photographer

unknown location, c. 1900

His family had originally come from Constantinople; as their fortunes fluctuated Konstantinos P. Kavafis moved with them between a number of other cities, including Liverpool, UK, before finally settling in the Egyptian city of Alexandria. It was this melting pot of many cultures, the great gateway between Africa and Europe, that Kavafis would celebrate all throughout his life.

He worked as a civil servant in order to survive but in personal life was an isolated figure who spent his time reading the classics – ancient Greek, but also Latin, Arabic and European literature – and pursuing passionate love affairs. A homosexual, he sang of his male lovers in a style that was drawn from classical literature. His other themes included the Greek language, which for him contained the memory of all kinds of ancient nuances; the beauty of the physical body; the fragile nature of human encounters and the fleeting nature of pleasure. The ineluctable passage of time, which corrupts and consumes everything, lay at the heart of his poetry. It was partly because of its homoerotic tone that his work was slow to be appreciated and recognized, and some regarded his subject matter with a degree of displeasure. These verses were so personal, yet so universal when one considers human love and sexuality beyond the simple definition of type.

Kavafis also wrote other poems, often examining historical themes; they represented the fruit of his cultured background and his capacity for reflecting on a past in which he saw collective events as being dynamic but not separate from the experience of the individual. These unforgettable poems – which in some cases, such as lines from 'Waiting for the Barbarians' (first printed in 1904) have become almost proverbial – concentrate on what was inevitable and recurrent in ancient history and what, by extension, forms part of every history: concepts of violence, tyranny and the decay of civilizations, originating both outside the state and within it. He read 'great' history as being essentially not so very different from the mundane and the personal.

It was in only 1935, two years after Kavafis's death, that his poems were collected together and became more widely appreciated. They were soon translated out of modern Greek and numbered among the finest examples of twentieth-century poetry. Once considered by some to be the most controversial of the modern Greek poets, Kavafis is now said to be one of the greatest. When one thinks of his work as a deep reflection on the history of nations and the human condition, on the precarious nature of civilization, on happiness and peace, and on the existence of each individual, such an elevation seems only right.

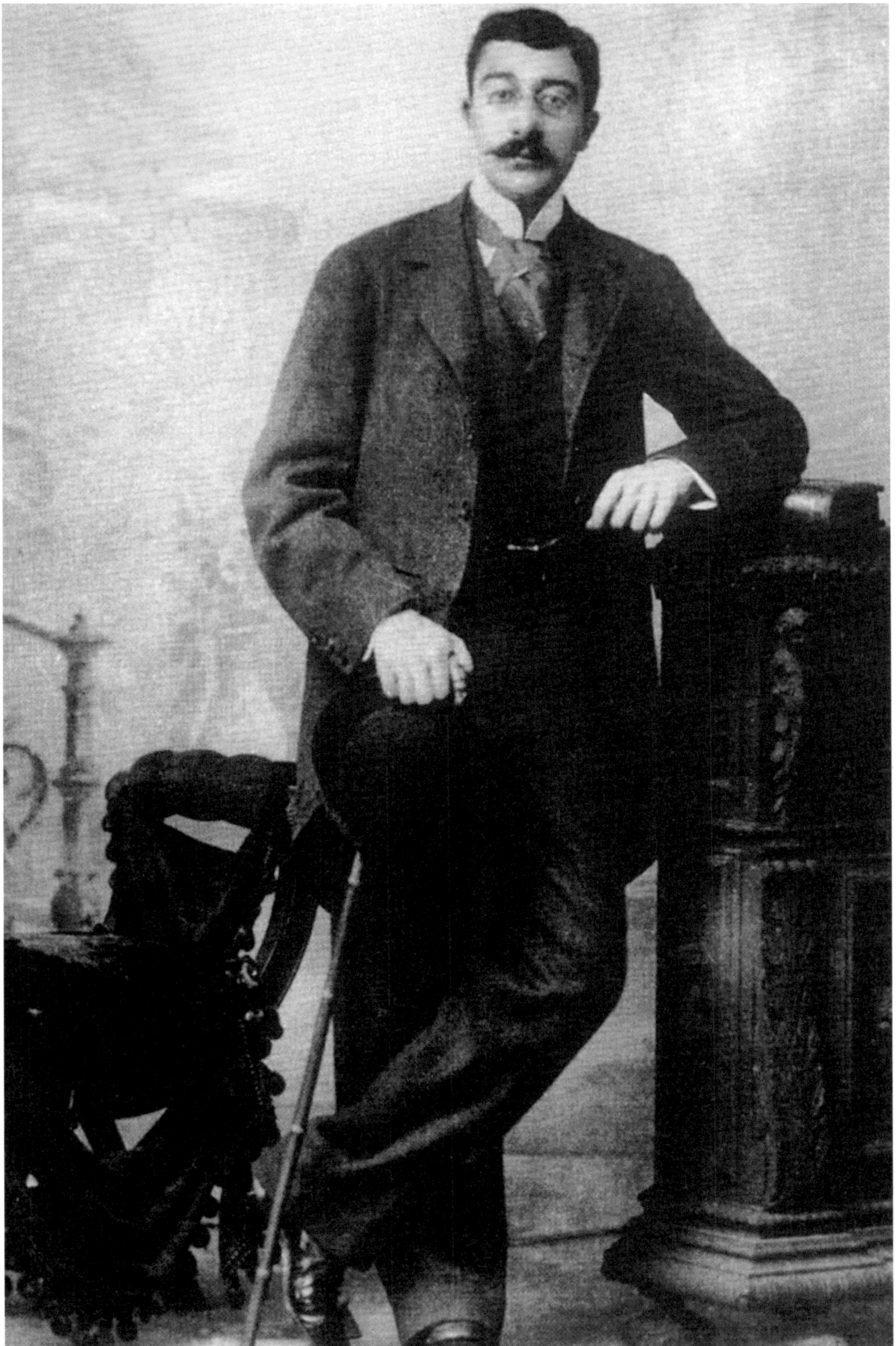

YASUNARI KAWABATA

born Osaka, Japan, 1899; died Zushi, Japan, 1972

by Yousuf Karsh

Japan, 1969

In 1968 Yasunari Kawabata became the first Japanese author to be awarded the Nobel Prize in Literature. Kawabata established his literary reputation in 1926 with the short story 'The Dancing Girl of Izu', which centres around a depressed student who meets a young female dancer on a walking trip down the Izu Peninsula. His first novel, *Snow Country* (published in instalments, 1935–47), tells the story of the doomed love affair between a wealthy, Westernized ballet aficionado from Tokyo and a provincial geisha at an inn in a hot-spring town in the mountains. In *Thousand Cranes* (1952), the very Japanese art of the tea ceremony becomes a profound metaphorical reflection in the midst of a multi-generational love triangle marred by suicide. *The Sound of the Mountain* (published in installments, 1949–54) is a novel about a family dominated by a father figure. *The House of the Sleeping Beauties* (1961) is rather more explicit in its eroticism than Kawabata other novels. Kawabata's aesthetic theories are expressed perhaps most clearly in his *Palm-of-the-Hand Stories* (published in two vols, 1988 and 1998), which were written over a number of years and are short, sometimes even very short, and pared-down, elliptical and highly evocative in their language.

Kawabata's refinement appeared excessive to many critics. He paid great attention to the most subtle psychological and erotic sensations, crafting allusive language and rarefied, atmospheric settings with an elegant classicism, firmly convinced that only the ephemeral could be beautiful and meaningful. It was claimed in some circles that the decision to award Kawabata the Nobel Prize was in compensation for the committee having failed to award the prize to Junichiro Tanizaki, considered the greatest Japanese writer of the century, and who had died three years earlier. Others, however, view Kawabata as themost Japanese of Japanese writers. In his Nobel acceptance speech, entitled 'Japan, the Beautiful and Myself' (1968) he praised his country's aesthetic traditions and its appreciation of a type of 'sad beauty'.

Shortly after the prize had been awarded, the great Armenian-born portraitist Yousuf Karsh photographed Kawabata smiling and holding an example of his extensive collection of antique Haniwa funerary statuettes. Karsh later recalled of his meeting with Kawabata, 'In his seaside home, this gentle author's every movement, his every utterance was like the subtle, precise beauty of his beloved Japan.'

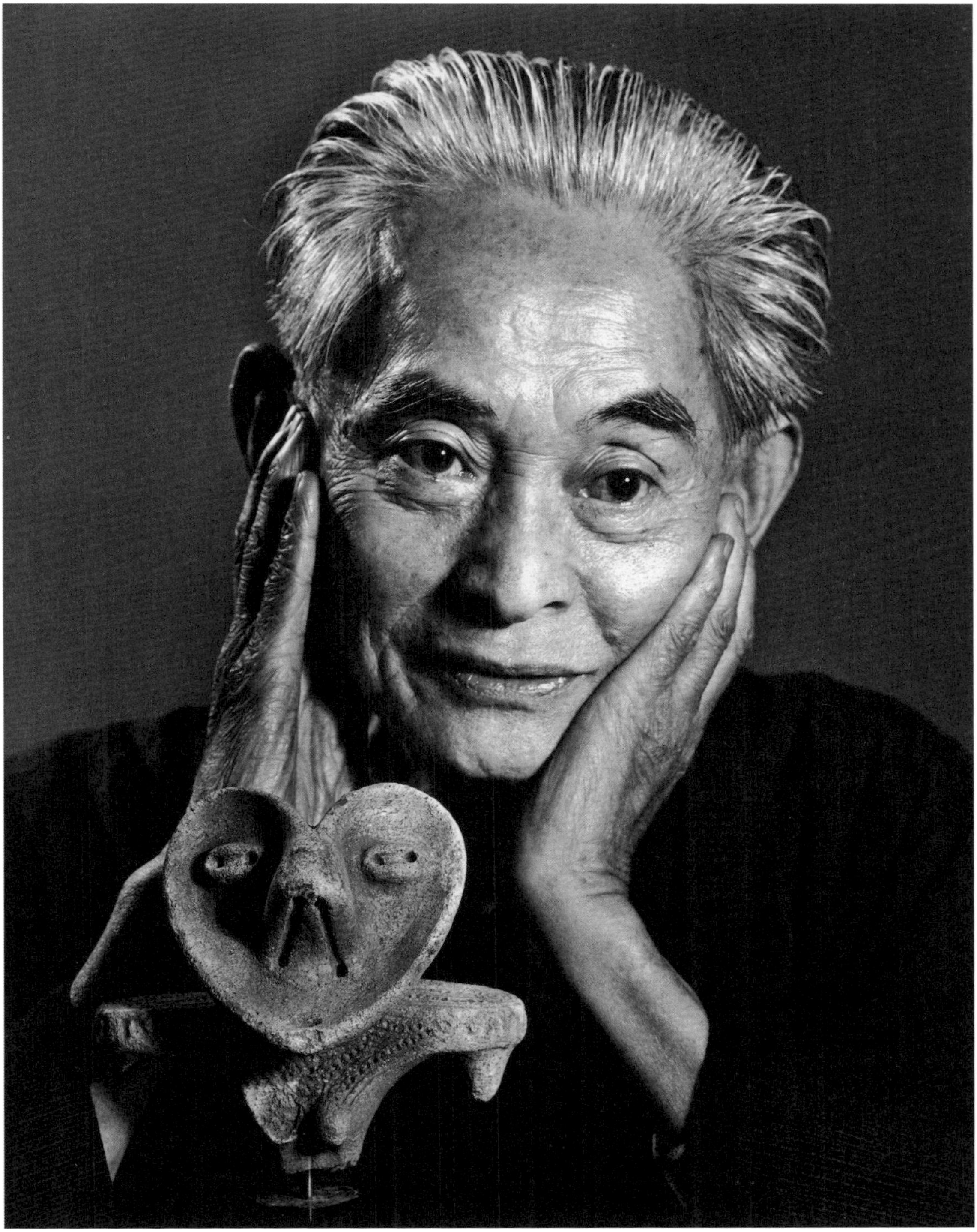

JACK KEROUAC

[Jean-Louis Kerouac] born Lowell, Massachusetts, 1922; died St Petersburg, Florida, 1969

by Elliott Erwitt

New York, 1953

If asked to summarize *On the Road*, Jack Kerouac's seminal novel from 1957, few of us would describe it as a story about two Catholic buddies roaming the country in search of God. But this was precisely the definition that the author himself gave in an interview. Perhaps the ultimate iconic writer, Kerouac became the unofficial spokesperson for the Beat Generation, a group of rebellious American writers who experimented with drugs and alcohol with the same, breezy self-confidence with which they dabbled in religion and mysticism, pacifism and violence, and sex and erotic art.

Kerouac was born into a family of Catholic French Canadians in a small industrial town in Massachusetts. A scholarship took him to Columbia University in New York but he dropped out before completing his studies. It was at this time, however, that he was exposed to the work of some of the great figures of American literature, among them William Saroyan, John Dos Passos and Thomas Wolfe. The last of these had a notable influence on Kerouac's first novel, *The Town and the City* (1950).

After serving in the Second World War, Kerouac had a life-changing encounter with some of the major figures of the Beat Generation, including William Burroughs, Allen Ginsberg and, in particular, Neal Cassady. Cassady became his 'buddy', and the two of them set off on a series of journeys across the USA that would form the basis of Kerouac's most famous novel. In common with some of his other books, however, *On the Road* struggled to find an audience, owing not only to its controversial content but also to its unconventional use of language. Kerouac had begun to experiment with what he called his 'spontaneous prose': an attempt to use words to convey the immediacy of experience.

Kerouac continued with such experiments until the end of his life, but they were never fully understood by either his public or his critics. The opprobrium attracted by almost all his books (with the exception of *The Dharma Bums*, 1958) took its toll. By the 1960s he was both the most famous author of his time and an alcoholic; indeed, it was his heavy drinking that eventually led to his death. Elliott Erwitt's photograph of Kerouac remembers the writer as a slightly mysterious yet elegant young man, the lighting and lowered perspective giving him an enigmatic quality.

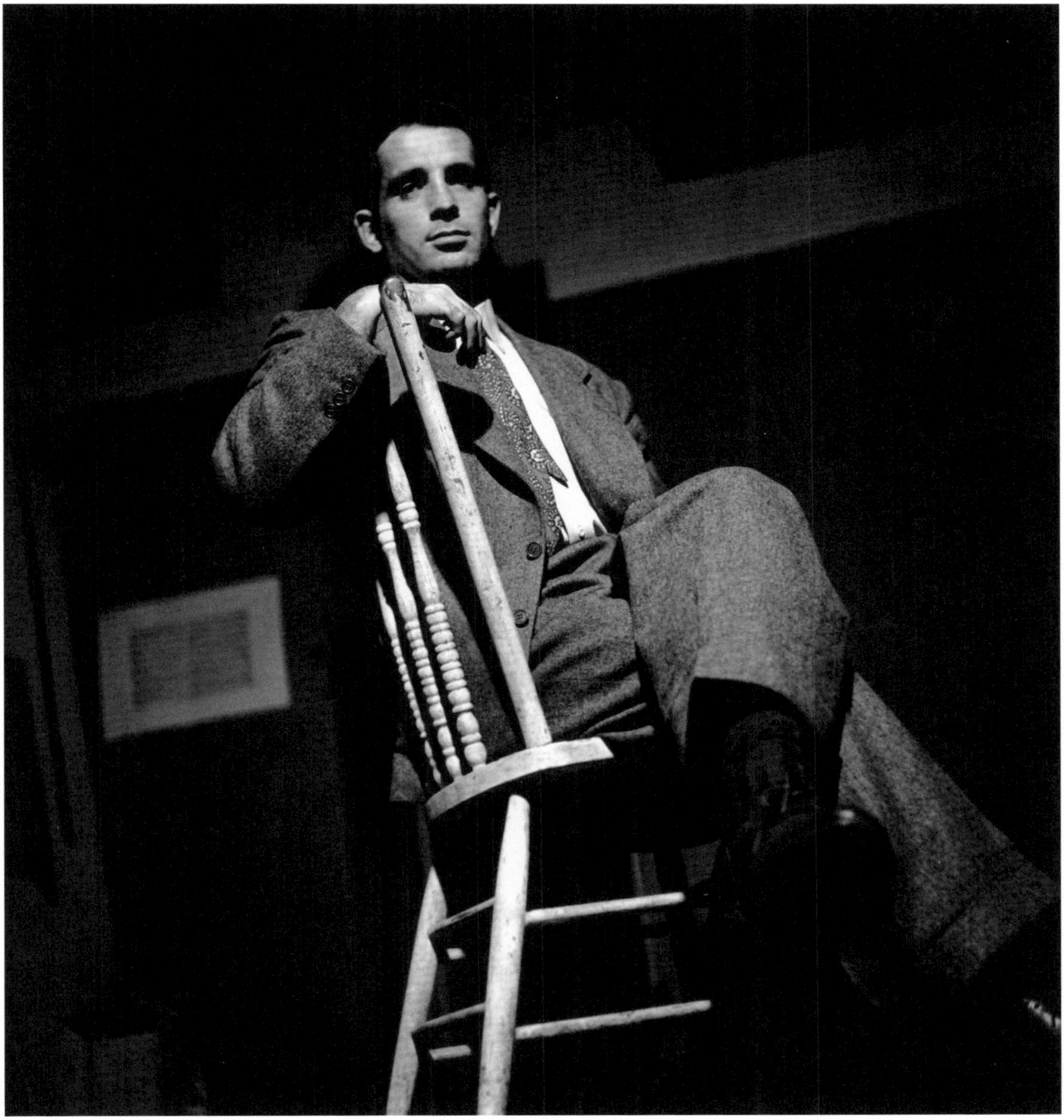

STEPHEN KING

born Portland, Maine, 1947

by Ted Thai

Bangor, Maine, 1986

Pictured sitting astride a motorbike in front of the gates of his home in Maine, Stephen King, already a financially successful author in 1986, grins into Ted Thai's camera. Today, having sold more than 350 million books, Stephen King is one of the world's best-selling authors of all time, with a literary output so prolific that at one point he even adopted the pseudonym of Richard Bachman in order to have the option of publishing even more books each year without overexploiting his own name.

King was born in Maine and raised by his mother after his father left the family when he was a young child. Unable to find a job as a teacher after graduating from university, he worked in an industrial laundry to support his family and wrote short stories for magazines to bring in extra income. His fortunes were transformed overnight when his debut novel *Carrie* (1974) received a lucrative paperback contract, and the novel that followed, *Salem's Lot* (1975), was a success. King's ability to produce plot-driven narratives that please both a mass audience and more discerning readers has made him one of the greatest living authors of quality popular literature. A self-declared heir to writers of classic science fiction and horror such as Edgar Allen Poe and H. P. Lovecraft, he has also found inspiration in the Californian writer Richard Matheson, who, like King himself, is a master in moving seamlessly between different genres and subjects.

King has reflected on his career and writing both in his non-fiction book *On Writing* (1999) and in a fictional setting in the thriller *Misery* (1987). The latter is one of his most original novels, with its disturbing and grotesque portrayal of the blackmail-like relationship that binds a highly successful author to his audience. His books have been made into films by many important directors, such as Brian De Palma (*Carrie*), Stanley Kubrick (*The Shining*), John Carpenter (*Christine*) and David Cronenberg (*The Dead Zone*).

King's imagination seems to maintain an almost telepathic contact with the collective subconscious of our times. Whether powerful and weighty works of fantasy such as *IT* 1986), *The Stand* (1987) and the novels of the *Dark Tower* series (1982–2012), or stories in which the 'sociological' element is more prominent, such as *The Running Man* (1981, written as Richard Bachman) and the apocalyptic *Cell* (2006), in which humans undergo a regression to violence controlled by the global cell-phone network, King's books skilfully evoke the violence, anxieties and disturbing spectres that stalk our contemporary world.

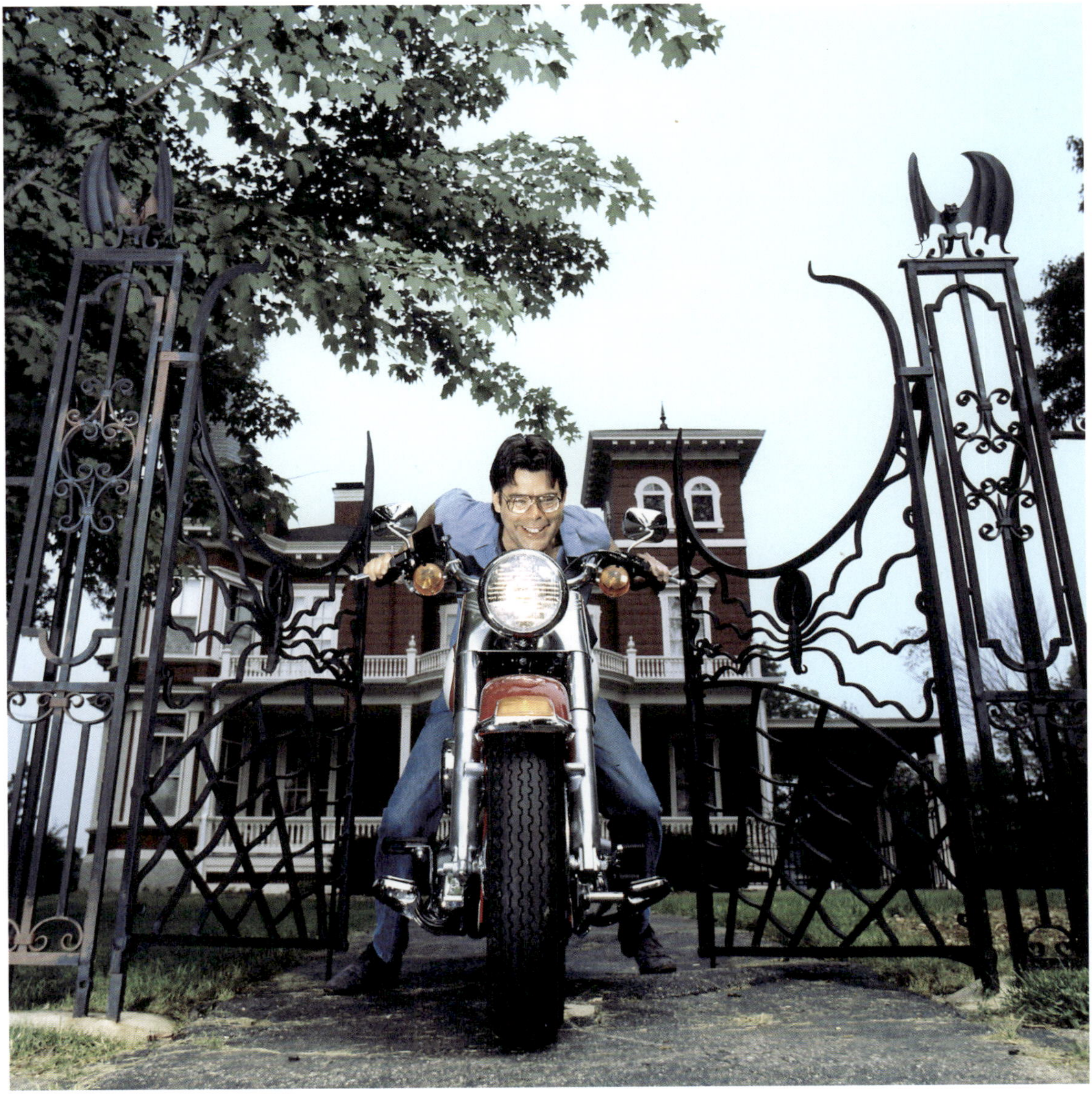

AGOTA KRISTOF

born Csikvánd, Hungary, 1935; died Neuchâtel, Switzerland, 2011

by Isolde Ohlbaum

Solothurn, Switzerland, 2005

Physically slight, an intense and somewhat sad expression behind her large spectacles, modest in her dress and as tough and straightforward as the words she used in her books: this was the image by which Agota Kristof was known – first in the Francophone media and then in the rest of the world – when it became clear that her debut novel, *The Notebook* (1986), was the product of a unique and exceptional literary mind. This short work later became the first volume of her 'Twins' trilogy (*The Notebook*; *The Proof*, 1988; and *The Third Lie*, 1991), the story of Lucas and Claus and the disordered world they inhabit that also functions as an allegory of the political history of twentieth-century Europe and of war, totalitarianism and exile.

Kristof's life was touched by all these experiences. Born in Hungary, she left her native country in 1956 with her husband and four-month-old daughter following the Soviet Union's violent suppression of the Hungarian Revolution. From Austria they travelled on to French-speaking Switzerland, to the town of Neuchâtel, where the writer spent the rest of her life pining for her homeland. Literature became the only form of resistance open to her, theonly way she could come to terms with her sudden abandonment of the wider family, the country and the people to whom she belonged. She began writing while working in a watch factory, where, as she later explained, the sounds made by the machinery inspired her to compose her first poems in her native tongue. She continued to write in Hungarian for several years before she felt ready to write in French. In its extremely dry, pared-down style, her writing still carried traces of a distinct foreignness. She confronted her adopted language with a degree of diffidence, feeling that the French language is an 'enemy language', because 'it is killing my mother tongue'.

Kristof published several pieces for the theatre: short, autobiographical narratives in which traces of her lost world are preserved in the form of ironic and melancholic fragments. It is, however, for her trilogy that she is remembered as a major European writer of the last century, and perhaps as the last great interpreter of the twentieth century's sense of alienation, working very much in the tradition of Franz Kafka. Such overtones can be found in her laconic style, her characters' elusive identities and the sombre nature of their destinies.

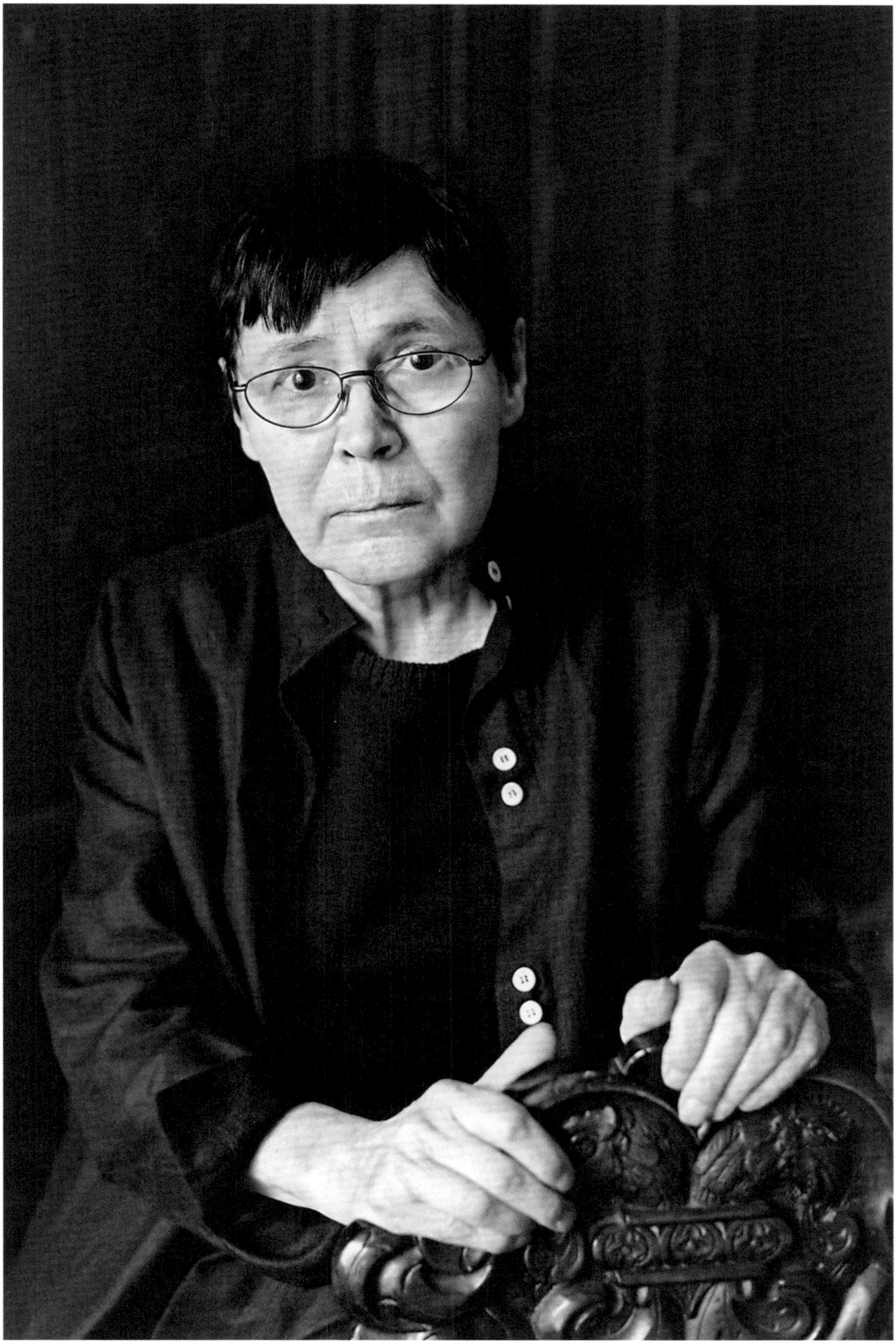

MILAN KUNDERA

born Brno, Czech Republic, 1929

by Ferdinando Scianna

Rennes, France, 1981

Czech writer Milan Kundera is widely regarded as one of the most important European novelists of the last fifty years. Kundera's writing attracted international attention well before the publication of *The Unbearable Lightness of Being* (1984), the bestselling novel that made him famous. His first novel to be published in his homeland was *The Joke* (1967), which was quickly translated into French after the failed 'Prague Spring' of 1968 and subsequently celebrated as a protest against Soviet totalitarianism. In 1975 Kundera moved to Paris and wrote *The Book of Laughter and Forgetting* (1979) and *Immortality* (1990). His books, now banned in Czechoslovakia, were translated into French under the watchful eye of the author. In the 1990s he began to write in his adopted language, however, beginning with the novel *Slowness* (1995).

Kundera's stories alternate between the sentimental and the incisive, and are characterized by frequent philosophical digressions. The characters he portrays are deeply rooted in their historical contexts, and through them he explores the nature of the human condition. For Kundera, writing is less about politics than it is about philosophy, particularly existentialism. He discusses issues of universal relevance, setting them within the context of his own cultural experience, which has encompassed both Soviet Communism and consumerist democracy. 'The experience of Communism', he once said, 'seems to me an excellent introduction to the modern world in general.'

Kundera strictly limits his public appearances, and since 1985 has given only written interviews. Ferdinando Scianna, who took this photograph of the author, was a frequent visitor at Kundera's house during his time in Paris. He recounts this anecdote: 'He could never bear, in the prose of certain journalists, to be turned into a ventriloquist's dummy. One evening he telephoned me with an odd proposal. An important literary magazine had asked him for an interview, and he had asked them if I could conduct the interview. "But I want to write it," he added, "the questions as well as the answers. Would you mind doing that?" I replied that it would be an honour. It was certainly the best interview I have ever done.'

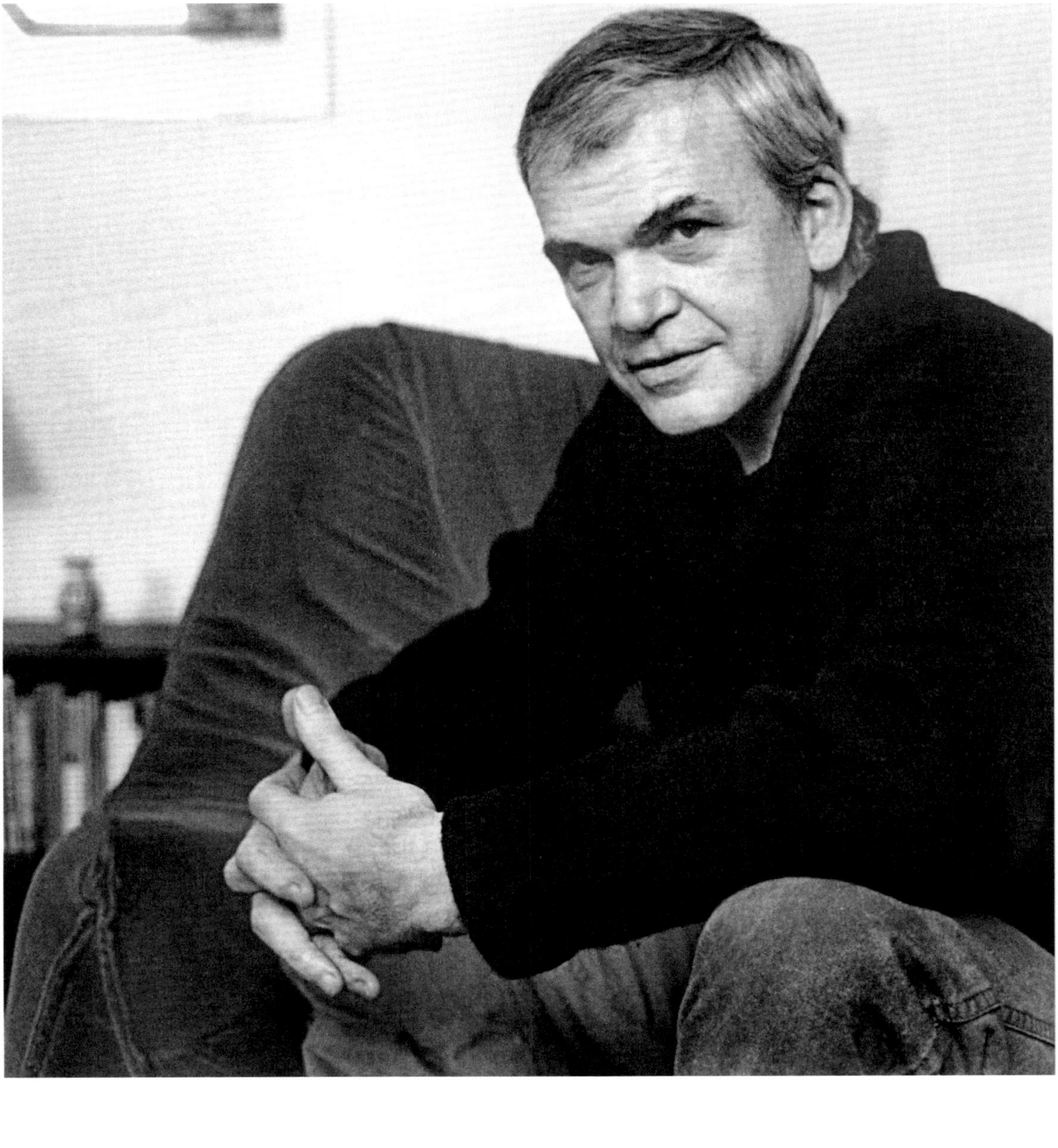

SELMA LAGERLÖF

born Sunne Municipality, Sweden, 1858; died Mörbacka, Sweden, 1940

unknown photographer

Mörbacka, Sweden c. 1928

In 1909, Selma Lagerlöf became the first woman to be awarded the Nobel Prize in Literature. Born in the Swedish region of Värmland, which appears in many of her novels, Lagerlöf drew on both her experience as a teacher at a girls' high school in Landskrona as well as her reading of the most popular novelists of the nineteenth century to develop her unique literary voice. She had an acute perception of the moral problems marked out by Protestantism, and her novels often portrayed a world of peasants and fishermen forced to confront the harshness of nature, basic instincts and human passions.

The historic settings of Lagerlöf's novels, with their extraordinary events and characters, are also intended to encourage the reader to recognize universal human dilemmas in his or her own experience. *The Saga of Gösta Berling* (1891), the novel that made her famous, was the colourful tale of a defrocked clergyman and the twelve cavaliers of Ekeby, a band of adventurers whose pursuit of freedom eventually clashes with the consequences of the radical choices they have made in both their private and public lives. Like the works of Charles Dickens or Victor Hugo, the novel was first published in instalments in a popular magazine. The legends recounted in her short-story collection *Invisible Links* (1894) focus on the collision of mundane and religious life; similar themes govern *The Miracles of Antichrist* (1897), which is set in Sicily and advocates the practice of socialism with a Christian framework as a defence against the illusions of materialism. *Jerusalem* (1902) portrayed a religious utopia beset by real problems; *The Emperor of Portugallia* (1914), which is written in an almost picaresque mood, is the story of a sweet-natured madness born out of the disillusionment that comes with human experience.

Finally, *The Wonderful Adventures of Nils* (1906), written for children, was a declaration of Lagerlöf's love of her nation and included her first-hand observations of Sweden's flora and fauna and descriptions of its regions and the surrounding sea to achieve a truly marvellous synthesis. In this work Lagerlöf emerges as the teacher who taught her fellow Swedes to love both their nation and themselves.

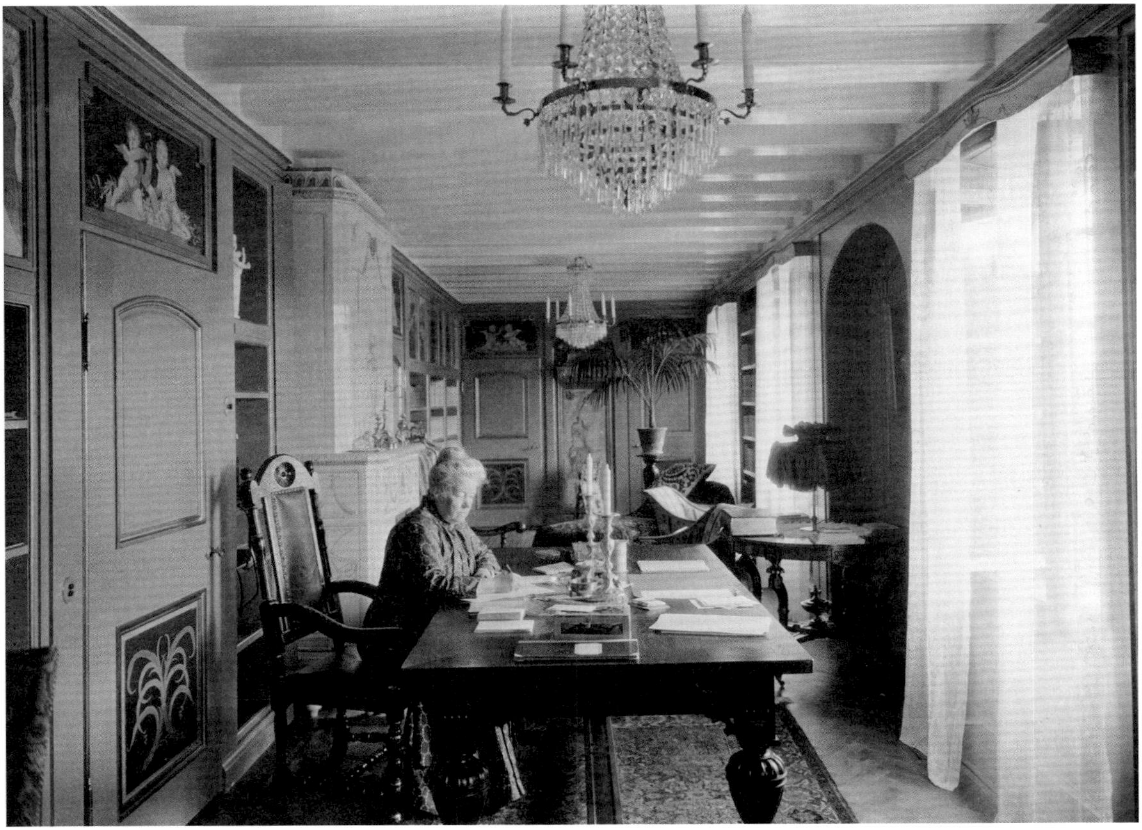

D. H. LAWRENCE

born Eastwood, Nottinghamshire, UK, 1885; died Vence, France, 1930

by Elliott & Fry

London, c. 1914

David Herbert Lawrence, the fourth of five children, was born into a coal-mining family. His father had worked in the mines from the age of ten, and continued to do so until he was sixty-six. His mother, determined to keep the young and often poorly Lawrence out of the mines, did much to encourage his studies, and at the age of twelve he won a scholarship to attend Nottingham High School. His close relationship with his mother, and her passion for literature, education and self-improvement, played a considerable role in Lawrence's subsequent career as a writer.

In 1912 Lawrence met Frieda Weekley (née von Richthofen), the wife of his former professor at Nottingham University College, where he had studied for a teacher's certificate. They fell in love and embarked on a passionate relationship, constantly on the move and often short of money. At first reluctant to leave her children, Frieda finally agreed to stay with Lawrence while the pair were living in Italy. He found himself exhilarated by their often fraught relationship; Frieda, he wrote, was 'the one possible woman for me, for I must have opposition – something to fight'.

In its sexual frankness and open criticism of society's norms, Lawrence's writing, notably his novels *The Rainbow* (1915) and *Women in Love* (1920), often attracted controversy. It was his final novel, *Lady Chatterley's Lover* (1928), however, that caused the greatest furore. Privileging love and sexual attraction over cultural and class distinctions, the book was first published privately in Italy in 1928 by Lawrence's good friend Pino Orioli, but it would be another thirty years before it was finally published in unexpurgated editions in the USA and UK, following unsuccessful prosecutions for obscenity that revealed the very class distinctions that Lawrence had intended to criticize.

This portrait of Lawrence was taken at Elliott & Fry, a photographic studio established in London in 1863. Among the many subjects who sat before its cameras were some of the greatest luminaries of the period, including writers, politicians, scientists, sportsmen and even aristocrats.

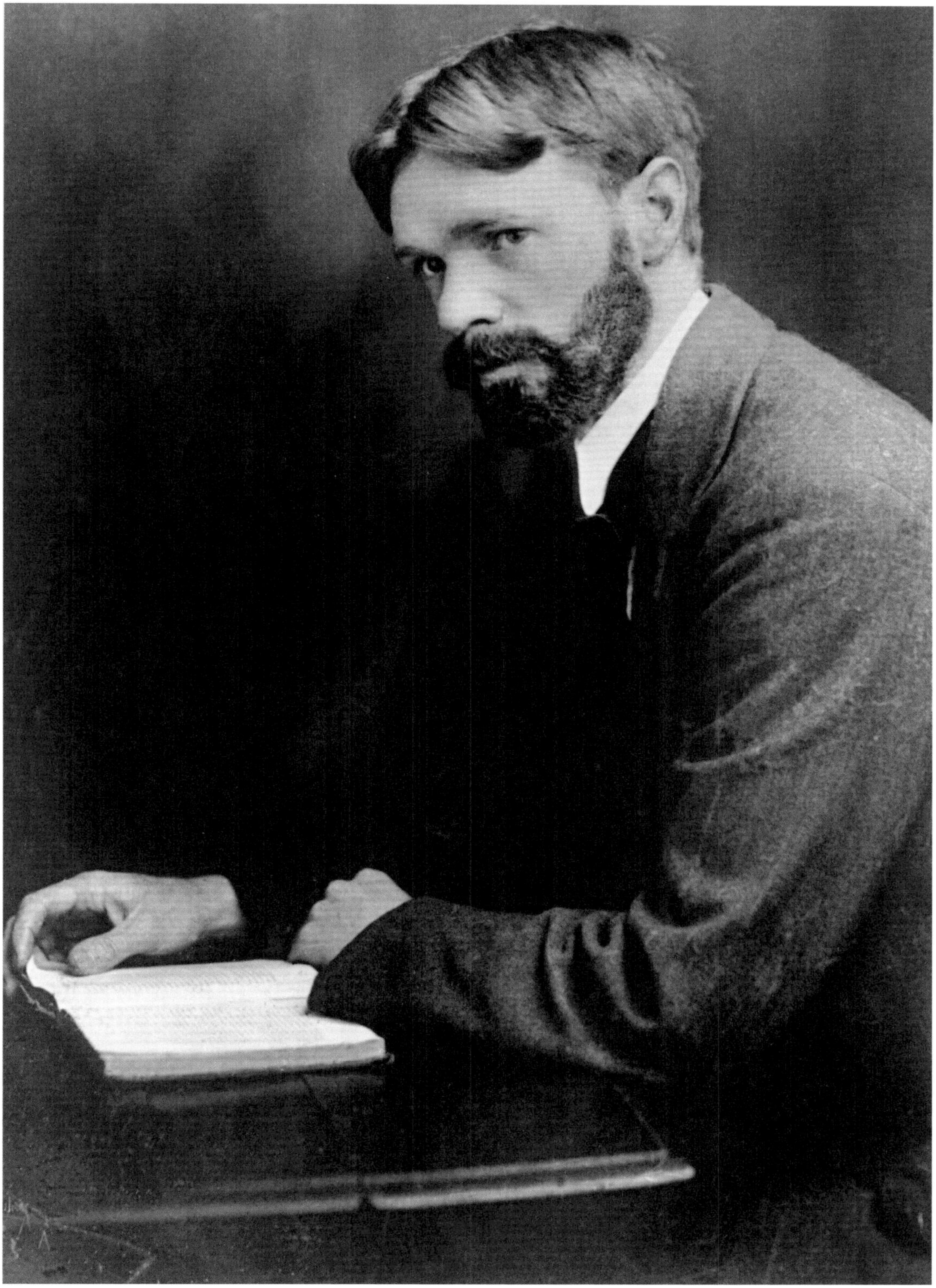

JOHN LE CARRÉ

[David John Moore Cornwell] born Poole, Dorset, UK, 1931

by Lord Snowdon

Loncon, 1989

George Smiley, John le Carré's fictional secret agent, is the anti-Bond, the polar opposite of Ian Fleming's sexy, physically robust and daring hero. He is short, tubby, shabbily dressed, a slave to rules and regulations, and just a little dull. It is his brain, in particular his extraordinary memory and his incredible capacity for concentration and logical thought, that wins him great respect, both inside and outside the 'Circus' – otherwise known as MI6, the British overseas intelligence agency, in which le Carré himself worked for several years.

Le Carré's career as an intelligence officer came to an end in 1964, following the betrayal of British agents' covers to the KGB by Kim Philby. Having already published *The Spy Who Came in from the Cold* (1963), le Carré took up writing full-time. Among the novels that followed was *Tinker, Tailor, Soldier, Spy* (1974), which drew on the events surrounding Philby's actions. From this period onwards le Carré produced a string of successful novels that cannot be dismissed as mere spy stories. Such books as *The Little Drummer Girl* (1983), *A Perfect Spy* (1986) and *The Night Manager* (1993) tackle complex issues and existential and philosophical questions that go far beyond the clichés of the genre.

Even for such a uniquely talented author, however, the end of the Cold War spelt the end of a remarkably rich source of material. Undismayed, le Carré ventured down new avenues, from his Graham Greene-influenced *The Tailor of Panama* (1996) to his novel exposing the deadly cynicism of pharmaceutical trials in Africa, *The Constant Gardener* (2001). The latter is a hard, intense and courageous book that demonstrated to the world that Smiley had not yet laid down his arms. Le Carré's novel of 2010, *Our Kind of Traitor*, focuses on the Russian mafia and the laundering of dirty money.

A rather shy and retiring individual, le Carré reveals a little about himself in a light-hearted 'self-interview' on his own website. Referring to his background, he says: 'I never knew my mother till I was twenty-one. I act like a gent but I am wonderfully badly born. My father was a confidence trickster and a gaol bird. Read *A Perfect Spy* [1986].'

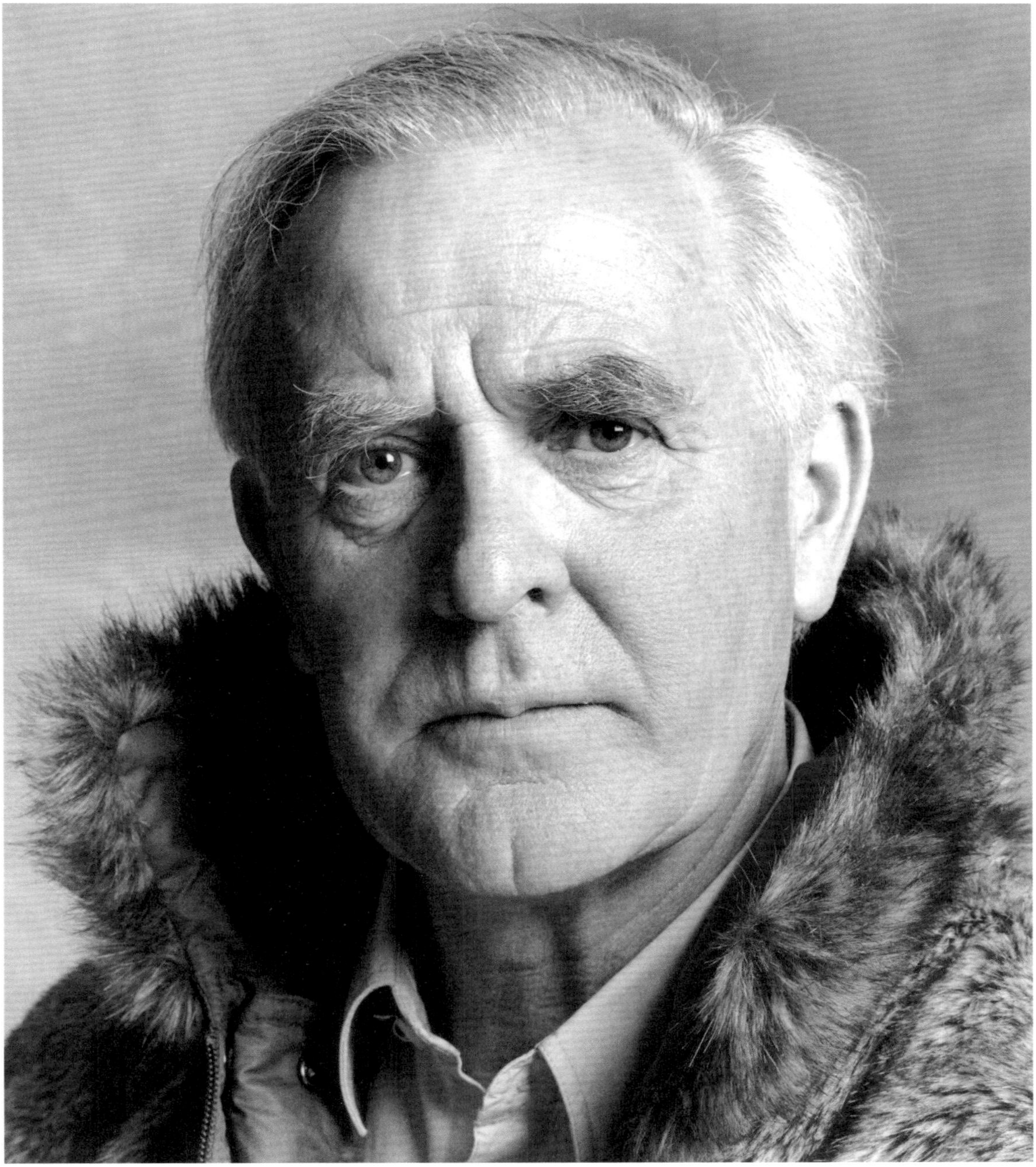

DORIS LESSING

[née Tayler] born Kermanshah, Iran, 1919

by Lord Snowdon

London, 2000

Portrayed by Lord Snowdon standing between the hedges of the garden surrounding her Hampstead home, Doris Lessing smiles directly at the camera. An imposing figure, the writer seems to interrupt this wall of plants, just as she pushed aside the barriers that she found intolerable in her own life – starting with those imposed by the tyranny of her mother's emotional grasp.

Doris May Tayler was born in Persia, modern-day Iran, to a British diplomat father and a mother who had trained as a nurse and had experienced a very Victorian upbringing. The family soon moved to Southern Rhodesia (now Zimbabwe), as her parents followed their dream of growing corn in the wilderness of Africa; however, Tayler refused to accept her destiny as a middle-class girl forced to live in the enclosed farming compounds. Filled with curiosity about the world, she ran away from home at the age of fifteen, abandoning her Catholic schooling to take charge of her own education by reading the great classics of literature. Later she would work as a telephone operator in Salisbury (Rhodesia's capital, now known as Harare), where she married and had two children, frequented various left-wing societies and became a member of Communist groups. She divorced her first husband in the middle of the Second World War and subsequently met and married German political activist Gottfried Lessing, adopting his surname as if to confirm her desire to divest herself of any sense of national allegiance.

Lessing made her debut in 1950 with *The Grass Is Singing*, a novel that was published in London but was set in her former African homeland during the 1940s. In 1962 she published *The Golden Notebook*, an intimate diary of a character called Anna Wulf, who tries to escape the hypocrisy and chaos of her own generation. This text is considered a feminist classic by many critics but not by the writer herself, who rejected any idea of her functioning as a guide for, or bearing witness to, a movement whose intransigent attitude towards the male sex she could not fully share. An eclectic writer impatient with any form of dogma, Lessing has moved freely in her texts from social to autobiographical themes, from Sufism to science fiction, blending different writing styles in her writing in a revolutionary, witty and visionary way. She won the Nobel Prize in Literature in 2007.

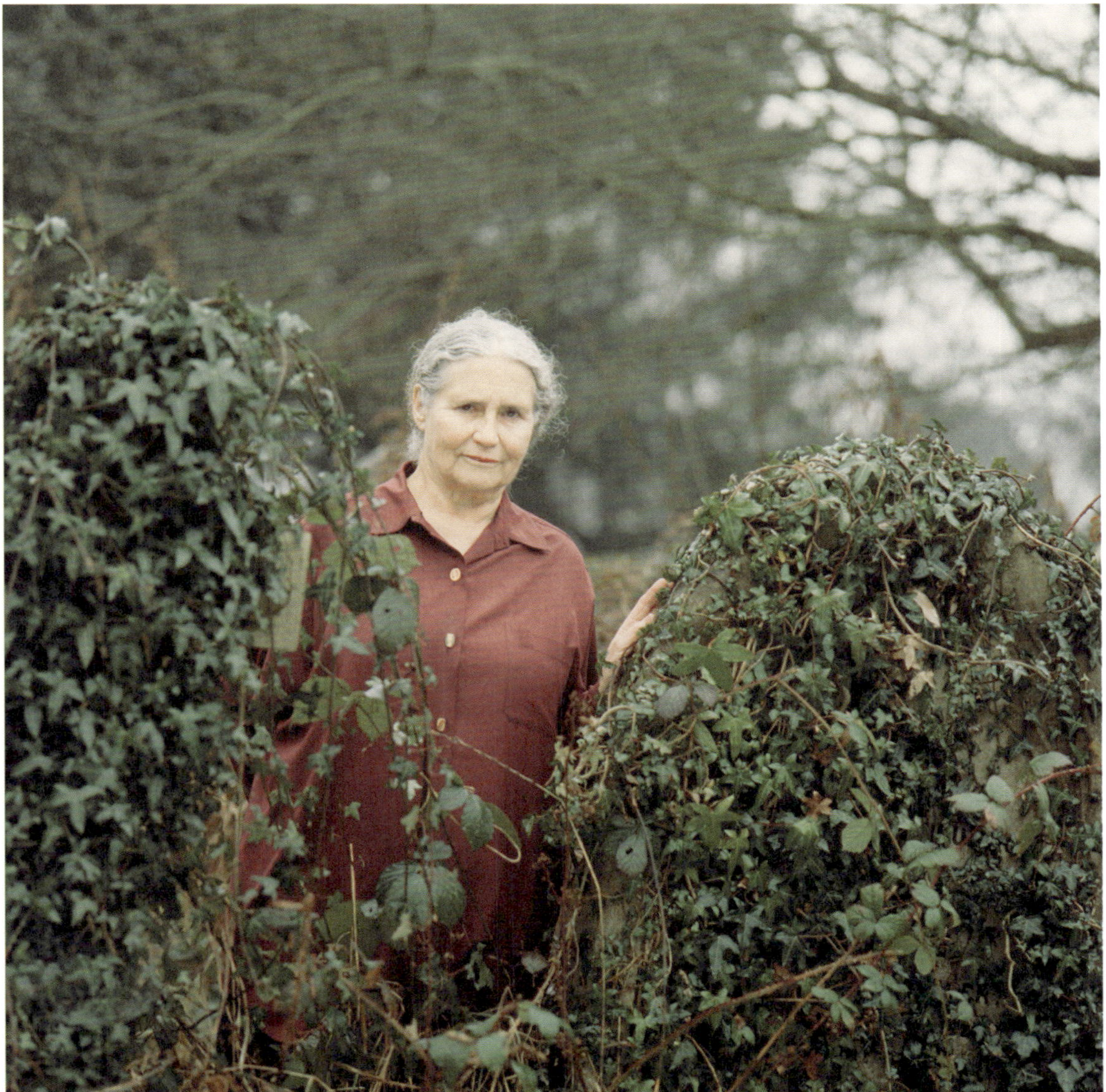

CARLO LEVI

born Turin, Italy, 1902; died Rome, 1975

by 'Chim' (David Seymour)

Rome, 1950

There were many sides to Carlo Levi. He grew up in Turin, the city-laboratory of liberal socialism, and took a medical degree, although he never practised professionally. His first true passion was painting, while his second was politics. In his Turin of an enlightened and progressive bourgeoisie, he struck up friendships with a variety of artists and intellectuals, including the Italian journalist Piero Gobetti, who for Levi remained a model of political activism. Both Turin and Paris were the axes around which Levi's initial education in art and life revolved.

Levi discovered his passion for writing only later, when he found himself living in a world profoundly different from the one he had previously known. In 1935 he was arrested for the second time for suspected anti-Fascist activity and sentenced to internal exile in a remote part of Lucania, an ancient district of southern Italy. He remained there for ten months, during which time he discovered the region's peasant society, a world set apart from history and the Italian state. It was as a result of this experience that he produced the work for which he is best known, *Christ Stopped at Eboli* (1945), an account of his time in exile that incorporates elements of fiction, reportage, memoir, travel writing and political analysis. In 1936 the Fascist regime pardoned Levi and he returned to Turin. His experience in southern Italy, however, remained at the heart of his work as a writer, painter and political activist, forming the basis not only of his peasant mythology but also of his battle for the reform of the region.

After the Second World War the desolate and magical land of southern Italy also attracted many photographers, including David Seymour, who in 1948 received a commission from UNICEF to document Europe's recovery from the destruction caused by the war. Seymour and Levi became close friends, and in this well-known photograph, the writer is shown engaged in painting – the longest lasting passion of his life. When Levi died in 1975 he was buried, as he had requested, in Aliano, the village that had been his home during his period of internment.

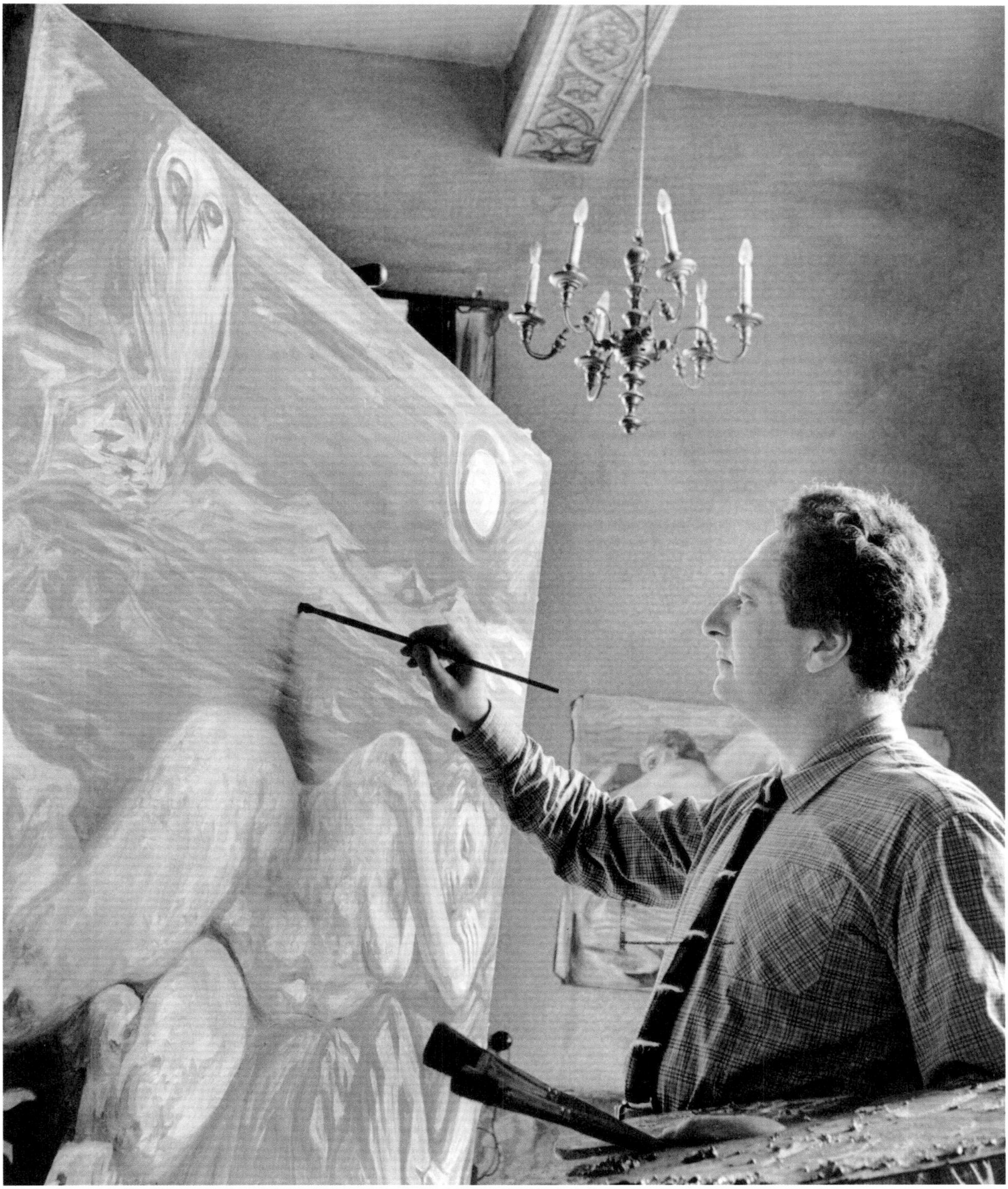

PRIMO LEVI

born Turin, Italy, 1919; died Turin, Italy 1987

by René Burri

Turin, Italy, 1985

There are certain books that serve as an essential outlet for controversial opinions or extreme emotions. *If This Is a Man* (1947), Primo Levi's account of his incarceration in Auschwitz, is one such book. As a trained chemist, Levi was able to secure a job in a chemical factory at the camp. In rare moments of solitude, he was also able to vent his emotions, to bear witness to the atrocities occurring all around him. It was on such occasions that he would take his pencil and notebook and write 'what I would never dare tell anyone'.

An Italian-Jewish anti-Fascist partisan, Levi arrived at the concentration camp on 22 February 1944, on a train packed with more than six hundred other Jews, and remained there for eleven months, until the camp was liberated by the Red Army. He finally arrived home nine months later, after a circuitous and arduous journey through Europe, the story of which is told in *The Truce* (1963). His need to write down everything he had experienced was so great that he wrote the manuscript for *If This Is a Man*, his first book, in one go. After being rejected by a number of major publishers, including Einaudi, it was eventually accepted by a small publishing house in 1947. The book did not sell well, however, and was temporarily forgotten. Gradually, the buried memories of a generation began to resurface, and in 1958 Einaudi republished it. Before long it was being hailed as a profound account of the extremes of human behaviour, from atrocious cruelty to survival and redemption.

Levi's experience in Auschwitz would define not only his life but also his writing. One of his last books was *The Drowned and the Saved* (1986), a collection of essays analysing the workings of the camp and the behaviour of both its guards and their prisoners. On 11 April 1987 Levi fell to his death from the landing of his third-storey apartment in Turin. Some believed that he had committed suicide, his mind still tormented by demons from the past. Others maintained that it was an accident, and that a chemist could have procured a much more foolproof method of suicide had that been his intention. Whatever the truth behind his death, the life and works of Primo Levi stand as a testimony to the courage and spirit of those whom the Nazi system failed to annihilate.

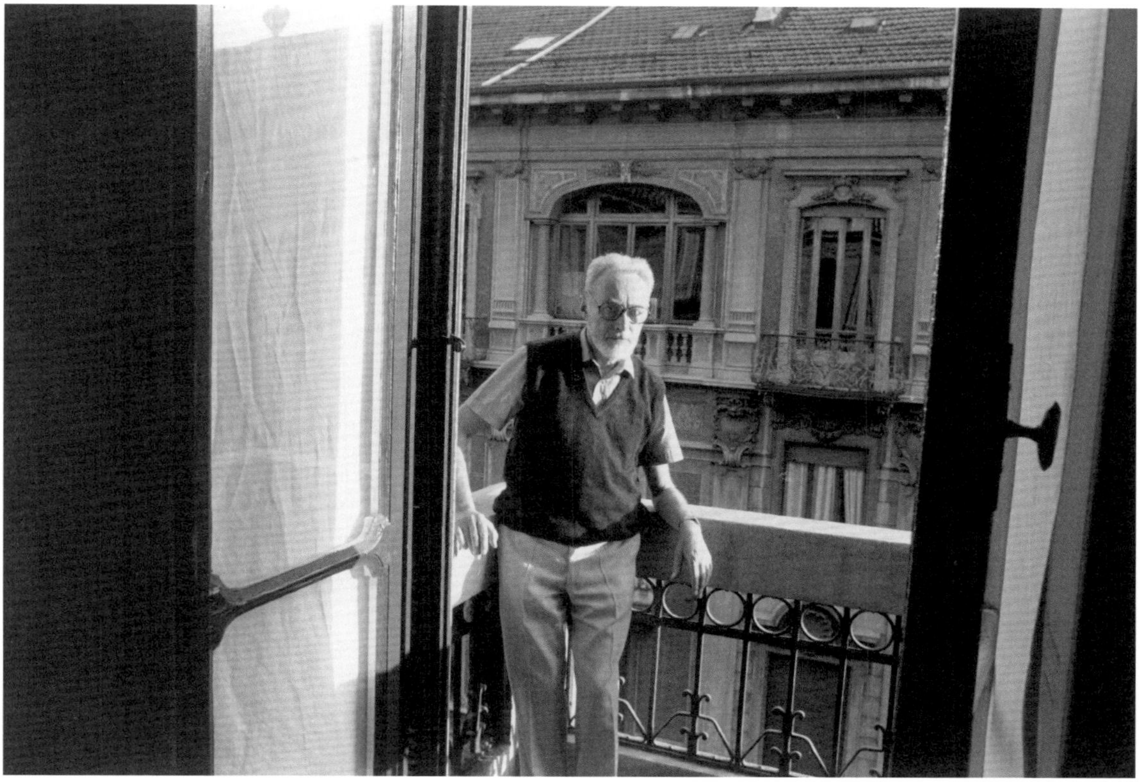

JOSÉ LEZAMA LIMA

born Havana, 1910; died Havana, 1976

by Iván Cañas

Havana, 1969

Possessed of a lively and curious mind, José Lezama Lima was a poet, an essayist, a novelist, an intellectual and the founder and driving force behind numerous revolutionary-minded literary magazines of the mid-twentieth century, including *Verbum*, *Espuela de Plata*, *Nadie parecía* and *Orígenes*. He made his literary debut in 1937 with 'The Death of Narcissus', a neo-baroque poem in which colours, flavours, scents and sounds are given a heightened reality. The Cuban Revolution complicated his life: in 1961 his two sisters moved to Miami while he remained in Cuba with his mother, who died three years later.

Lezama Lima's novel *Paradiso* was published in 1966. Although it brought him international notoriety, its homosexual content caused him difficulties in his own country. A coming-of-age novel, it tells the story of José Cemí (arguably the author's alter ego), focusing on his friendships and growing poetic sensibility. The subject of homosexuality, which triggered such criticism from the Cuban regime, earned Lezama Lima a tribute in *Strawberry and Chocolate* (1994), a film by Tomás Gutiérrez Alea and Juan Carlos Tabío based on 'The Wolf, the Forest and the New Man', a short story by Senel Paz. The film contains a scene in which the main character, Diego, invites his friend David to a 'Lezamanian lunch' and then presents him with a copy of *Paradiso*, telling him it is 'the best novel ever to have been written on the island'. A film adaptation of *Paradiso* by Tomás Piard, *El viajero inmovil* (The Immobile Traveller, 2008), paid him further homage.

Unfortunately, Lezama Lima saw none of these tributes in his lifetime. The final years before his death in 1976 were a difficult time for the author – despite the presence of such friends as the Argentine writer Julio Cortázar – due to both the Cuban regime's attitude to his work and the fact that his asthma was steadily worsening. Confined to his home, where he was able to take comfort from his writing, he began work on a sequel to *Paradiso*. *Oppiano Licario* (1977) remained incomplete when it was published after the author's death.

It was at Lezama Lima's home on the Calle Trocadero in the heart of Havana that the photographer Iván Cañas took this photo of the writer. Despite Lezama Lima's well-known aversion to photography, Cañas was able to shoot two rolls of film. However, Cañas left Cuba for the USA in 1992, and was only later able to recover his archive, which a friend had kept safe for him.

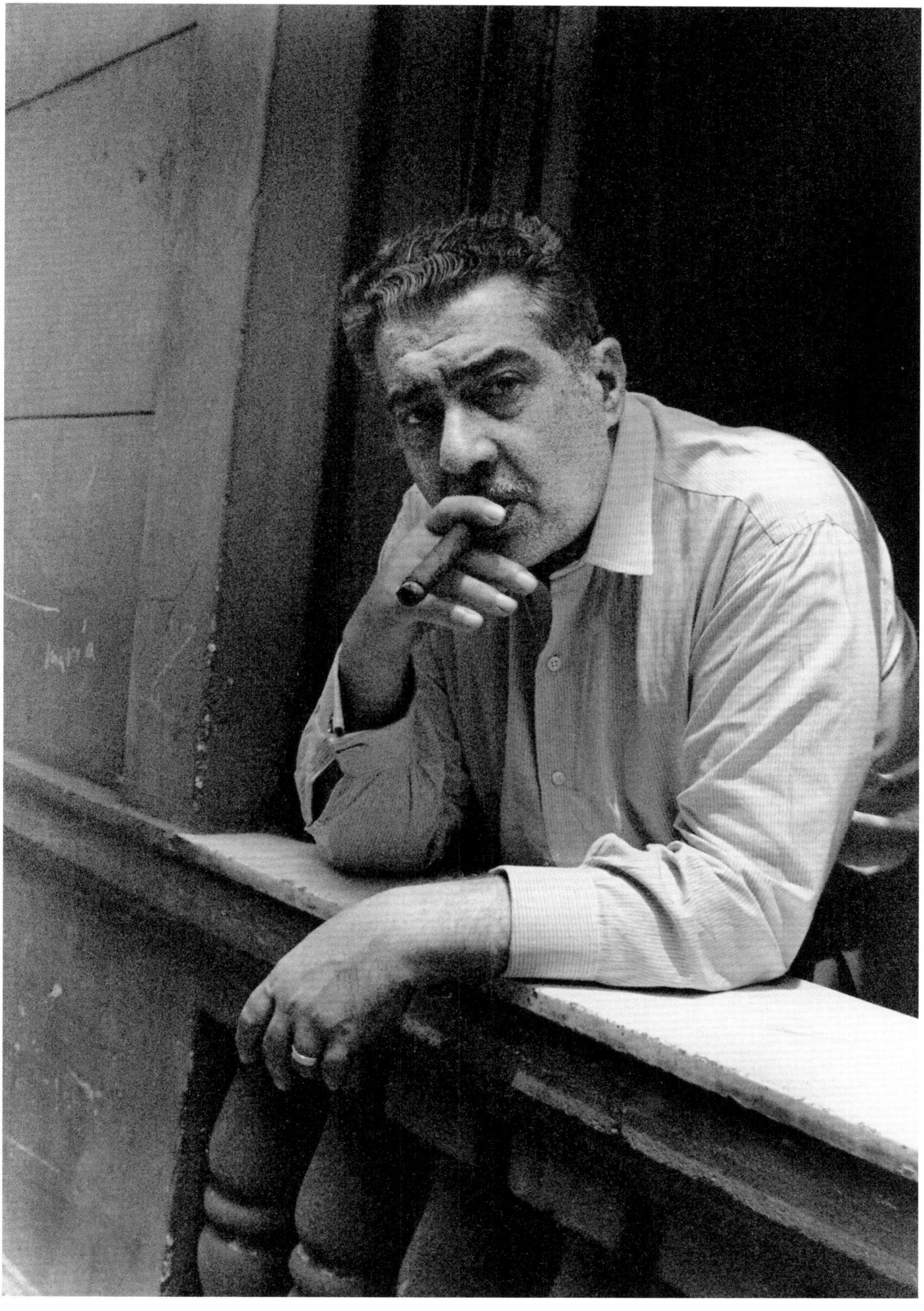

CLARICE LISPECTOR

born Chechelnik, Ukraine, 1920; died Rio de Janeiro, 1977

unknown photographer

Recife, Brazil c. 1936

In 1943, twenty-three-year-old Clarice Lispector's debut novel *Near to the Wild Heart* stunned the Brazilian literati. This young naturalized Brazilian writer employed a curt linguistic style that opened up new paths of expression and adapted them to the mental geography of the protagonist Joana. She is an elusive character who examines her life and her hopes of a much longed-for discovery that never happens.

Lispector's texts tell us that any attempted approach to happiness is slow and difficult. Her characters (predominantly female) seem to wallow in suffering, and almost fear they could one day be happy. The careful journeys she crafts often strive towards self-awareness and understanding. In the case of Martin, protagonist of *The Apple in the Dark* (1961), the journey is an allegorical one. After running away from the scene of a crime, disoriented and believing himself to be responsible, Martin relinquishes language, intelligence and social conventions, instead finding communion with nature and silence. He eventually regains understanding but is betrayed and arrested.

Lispector wielded her literary scalpel to probe the human soul and to confront it with evidence that it is not a thing apart. For her freedom does not come from solitude, but from sharing. As the editor of women's pages in various magazines, Lispector was able to promote views that went far beyond household economy and beauty tips: 'People who take pleasure in pain, who enjoy feeling unhappy and making others unhappy, can never take pride in their own beauty. Their ill humour, sense of frustration and bitterness all leave a mark on their physiognomy, extinguishing the light in their eyes, causing lines to appear on young faces and sometimes even making them ugly. These are the reasons why a woman who cares for her own beauty must force herself to be happy. Happiness is a state of mind; it is an atmosphere which does not depend on external facts or circumstances.'

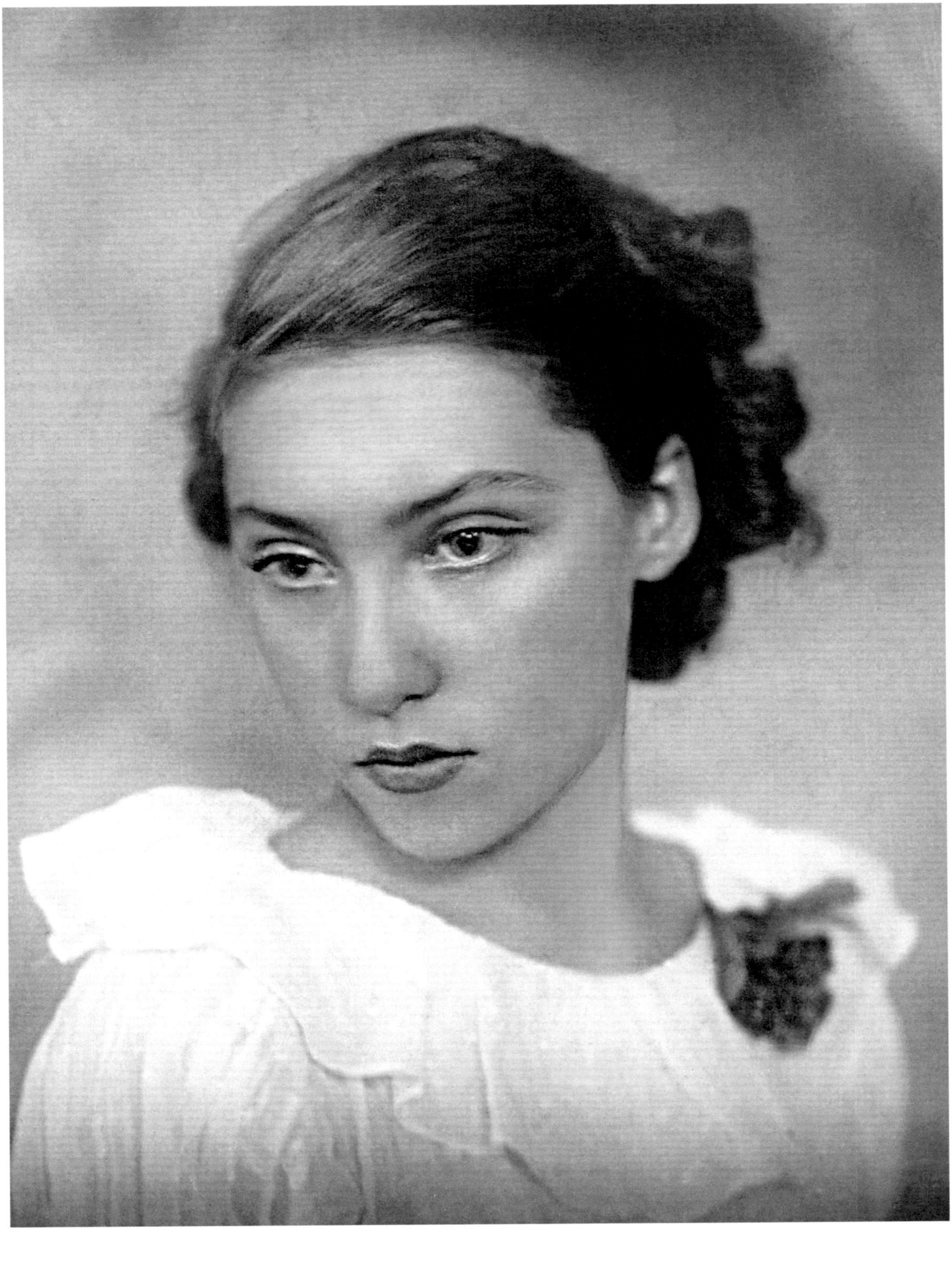

ANTÓNIO LOBO ANTUNES

born Lisbon, 1942

by Rodrigo Cabrita

Lisbon, 2010

The Carnation Revolution of 25 April 1974, which brought to an end nearly fifty years of dictatorship in Portugal, was still a very recent event in 1979. There was, however, a generation of writers, including António Lobo Antunes, ready to scrutinize the recent past and examine Europe's last colonial war, which Portugal had conducted in Africa between 1961 and 1974. In 1979 Lobo Antunes published two novels, *Elephant's Memory* and *The Land at the End of the World,* which were followed in 1980 by *Knowledge of Hell*. This deeply autobiographical trilogy drew on his experiences working as a psychiatrist with soldiers returning from the fighting in Angola. Almost immediately, Lobo Antunes's work came to represent Portugal's conscience: it loomed over the past and the present, and conducted a careful post-mortem examination of the country's recent history. This subjective and collective re-examination was a call not to forget the past, since memory, as Freud maintained, serves to record and process so that errors are not repeated.

In his writing about Portugal, Lobo Antunes has confronted a variety of issues, from the war and the *retornados* (the Portuguese citizens who fled Africa in a hurry only to arrive in a country that they did not recognize as their own) in *The Return of the Caravels* (1988) to post-colonial Africa in *The Splendour of Portugal* (1997) and *Good Evening to the Things From Here Below* (2003). Each of these works is characterized by a radical use of language, typography and punctuation. The author has frequently maintained that using such devices can help to overcome the difficulty of putting into words those elements that are hard to convey, such as deep emotion or fear. Adopting a subjective point of view, Lobo Antunes uses his stories' narratives to reflect the often chaotic mental states of his characters.

To follow a thought or an emotion, one must try to transcribe it. Such is the thinking behind Lobo Antunes's novels, which the reader must confront not only as an intellectual adventure but also as an emotional one, as he follows it through its phrases and deep ravines, loses himself in its labyrinths, falls into its traps, picks himself up again and carries on. The literature of Lobo Antunes is one that disturbs, that never leaves the reader untouched.

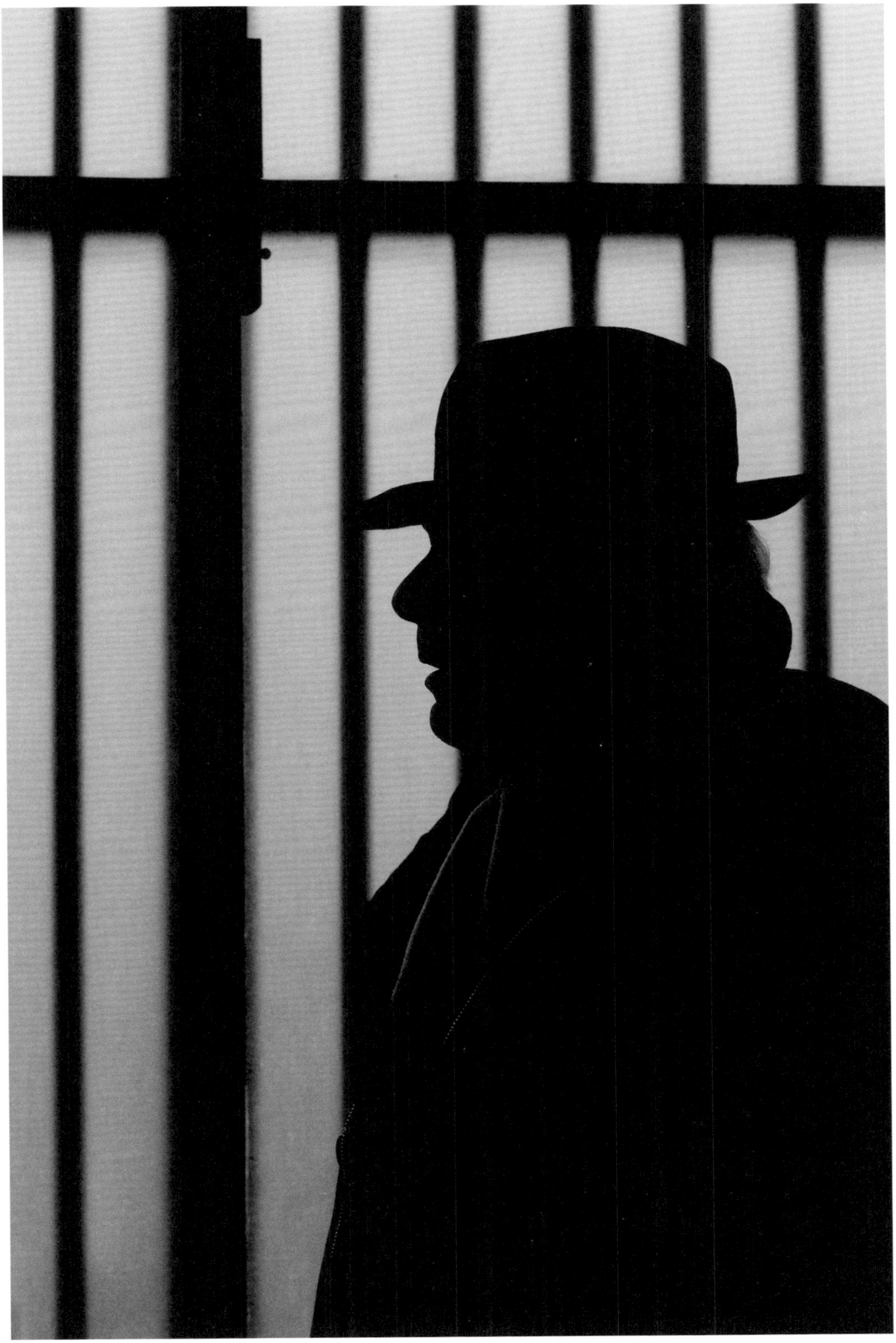

JACK LONDON

[John Griffith Chaney London] born San Francisco, California, 1876; died Glen Ellen, California, 1916

unknown photographer

Glen Ellen, California, 1916

To many people, Jack London's name means only rugged mountains, forests overrun by wolves, Klondike gold prospectors, blizzards and desolate landscapes in which man must fight for survival. However, London was born in San Francisco and spent most of his short life in California. He died in 1916 in his ultra-modern (but economically unviable) 'eco-ranch', which he had set up together with his second wife, Charmian.

London lived his life at a feverish pace, managing to fit several lifetimes' worth of experiences into forty years. His childhood was marked by poverty, and by an early age he was robbing oyster beds and working in a canning factory. At one stage he set sail for Japan on a seal hunt, but soon afterwards could be found travelling across the USA on trains as a hobo. He was struck by gold fever in 1897, and it was on his return from this particular adventure that he decided to become a writer. Over the course of his short career he produced a huge body of work, from novels and poetry to essays and short stories; some of his best-known fiction includes *The Call of the Wild* (1903), *White Fang* (1906), 'To Build a Fire' (1908) and the semi-autobiographical *Martin Eden* (1909). These and other works would make him one of the most widely read and best-loved American authors of all time.

London's success was immediate and extraordinary. However, his tendency to spend money faster than he could earn it meant that he was forced to write merely to make ends meet. In addition to being one of the masters of the adventure novel, London was a pioneer of political fantasy (*The Iron Heel* from 1908 is a terrifying prophesy of Fascism); with *The Road* (1907), he also provided the prototype for the quintessentially American road novel. As a journalist, he served as a war correspondent in Japan, commentated on boxing matches and reported on various natural disasters, including, famously, the San Francisco earthquake of 1904.

The exact nature of London's death remains uncertain. It appears that he died from an overdose of morphine, which he was taking to relieve his kidney pain. At the time, it was assumed that the overdose had been deliberate; however, recent scholarship has challenged this assumption, suggesting that it may have been accidental.

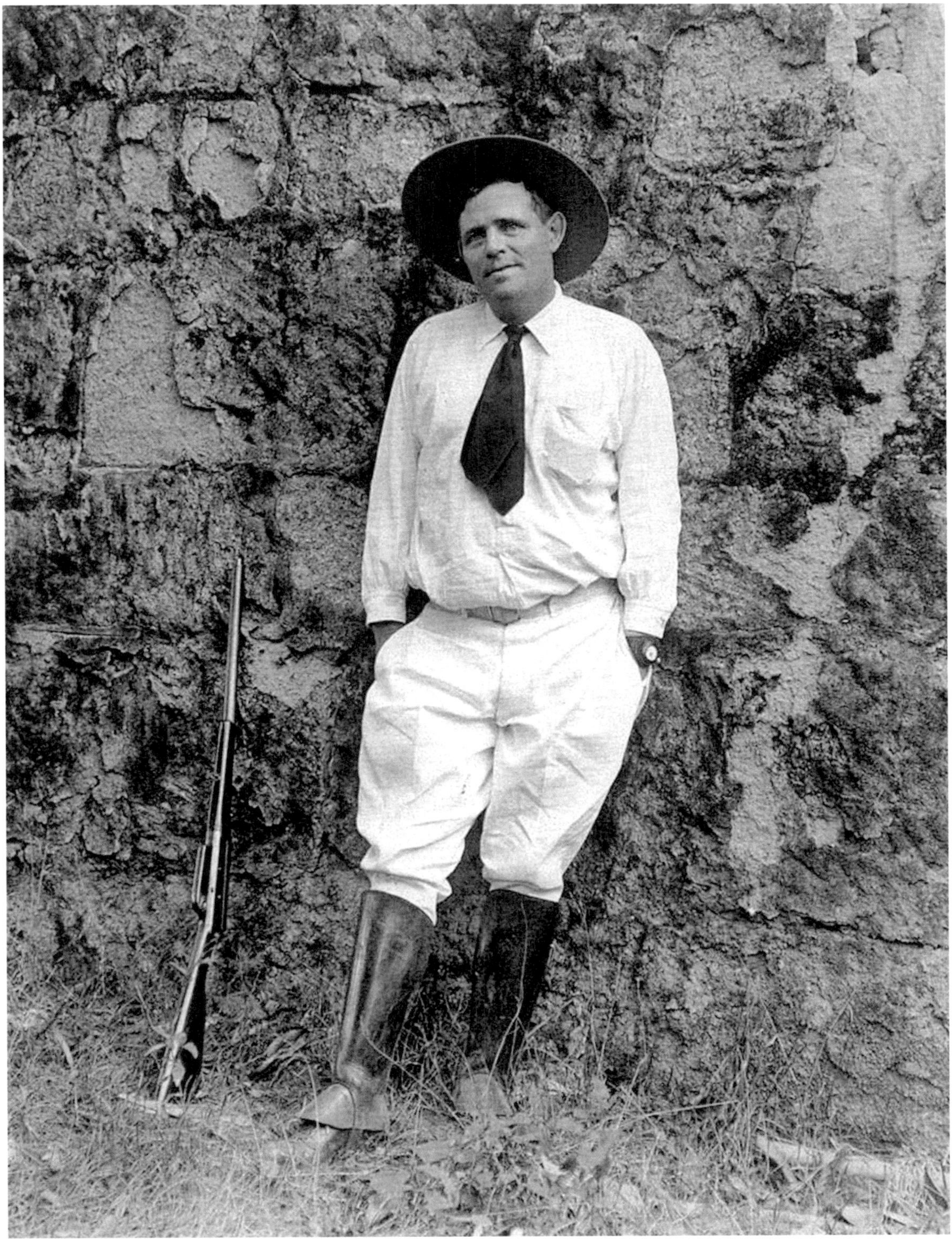

MALCOLM LOWRY

[Clarence Malcolm Lowry] born New Brighton, Merseyside, UK, 1909; died Ripe, East Sussex, UK, 1957

unknown photographer

Vancouver, 1946

In a cruel twist of fate, one of the greatest writers of the twentieth century was frequently unable to hold a pen. Lowry suffered from delirium tremens, and acute psychiatric problems. His method of writing was to stand, leaning his fists on the desk, whilst dictating everything to his wife.

Born into a wealthy family on the Wirral peninsula in 1909 and educated at the prestigious Leys School and the University of Cambridge, Lowry's path through life was nonetheless never easy or conventional. As a young lad he embarked on a boat for a five-month journey to China, following in the footsteps of his heroes Herman Melville, Joseph Conrad and Eugene O'Neill. At Cambridge a roommate committed suicide after Lowry refused his advances; the death haunted Lowry for the rest of his life. After graduating, he lived in Spain, France and New York and then spent nearly two years (1936–38) in Cuernavaca, Mexico. When his first wife left him for another man, he moved on to Los Angeles and then Vancouver, eventually living in a squatter's hut on the beach with Margerie Bonner, who became his second wife. He had always struggled to control his drinking, and by this stage he was an alcoholic. His fiery, alcohol-fuelled imagination erupted into *Under the Volcano* (1947), which became one of the most well-known novels of the post-war period. The nature of this masterpiece has been the subject of much discussion amongst the critics. It has been called a hymn of life, a hymn of death, a poem about feeling uprooted, or a primordial love-song. Lowry himself described it as follows: 'It can be regarded as a kind of symphony, or in another way as a kind of opera – or even a horse opera. It is hot music, a poem, a song, a comedy, a farce, and so forth. It is superficial, profound, entertaining, and boring, according to taste. It is a prophecy, a political warning, a cryptogram, a preposterous movie.'

The novel takes place within a single day, 2 November 1938. The alcoholic British consul Geoffrey Firmin is surprised by the return of his wife, who had left him a year before. He spends the day tormented by existential angst, before ending up shot dead after a scuffle with the Mexican police. It is a descent into hell along the lines of 'a drunken Divine Comedy', as Lowry put it. The character of Geoffrey Firmin is Lowry's alter ego in many respects. Aged only forty-eight, Lowry died in an English boarding house from an overdose of sleeping pills taken after a fight with his wife. Following his death, Margerie Bonner edited and published Lowry's substantial unfinished *oeuvre*, including the novels *Dark as the Grave Wherein my Friend Is Laid* (1968) and *October Ferry to Gabriola* (1970).

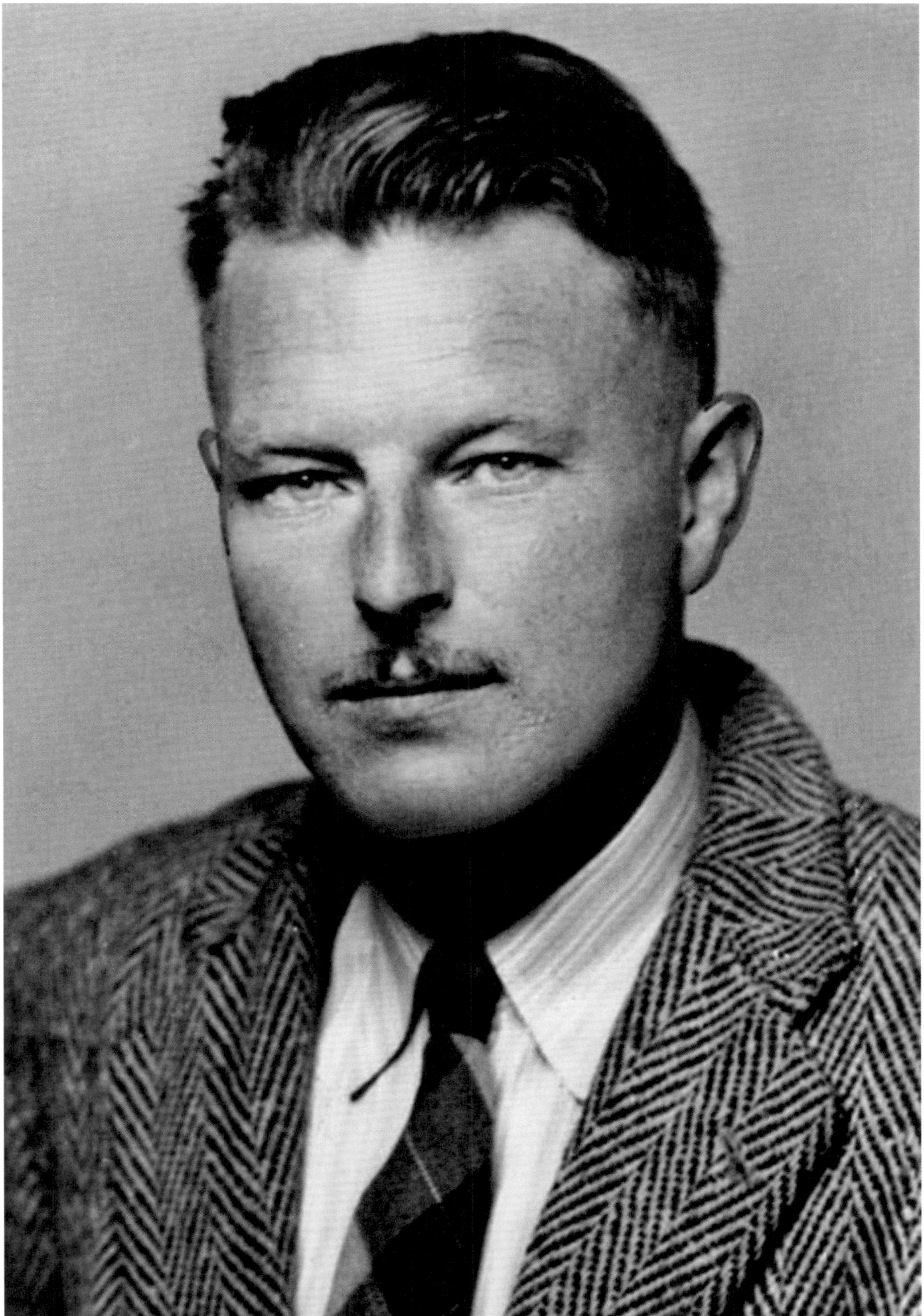

LU XUN

[Zhou Shuren] born Shaoxing, China, 1881; died Shanghai, 1936

unknown photographer

Shanghai, 1930

Lu Xun was one of the greatest Chinese writers of the twentieth century. Born in 1881, hislife coincided with some of the most significant and dramatic events in the history of his country: the collapse of Imperial China, the rise of the Chinese Communist Party, fierce internal fighting, the Japanese invasion and the intervention of Western colonial powers. But it was also a period of cultural ferment, in which for the first time China opened itself up to the philosophical and literary currents of other countries.

The first son of a well-educated and once wealthy family, Lu Xun was a diligent student, and in 1902 he was awarded a scholarship to study medicine at the University of Tokyo. He also immersed himself in the study of Western thought and Chinese culture. These studies led him to conclude that in order to save his country from its relative backwardness, it was necessary to change the way his compatriots thought. He thus became more interested in healing the mind than the body, and subsequently abandoned his medical studies in 1906. From then on he devoted himself to literature, education and militancy.

His short story 'A Madman's Diary' (1918), the first work to be written in vernacular rather than classical Chinese, would become the cornerstone of modern Chinese literature. The story describes the chilling realization of a madman that he is living in a society of cannibals. Through the voice of its protagonist, Lu Xun launches a ferocious attack on ancient dogmas and the feudal system, and calls for a new order of society. In 1921 he published the novella *The True Story of Ah Q*, another acknowledged masterpiece.

Lu Xun conceived of literature as a means of fighting a political and social battle, and he was the first author to give voice to those new currents of intellectual thought that would shape the development of modern China. Among his many admirers was Mao Zedong: 'As for Lu Xun's worth in China, he is in my view a Chinese sage of the first rank. If Confucius was the sage of feudal China, Lu Xun is the sage of modern China.'

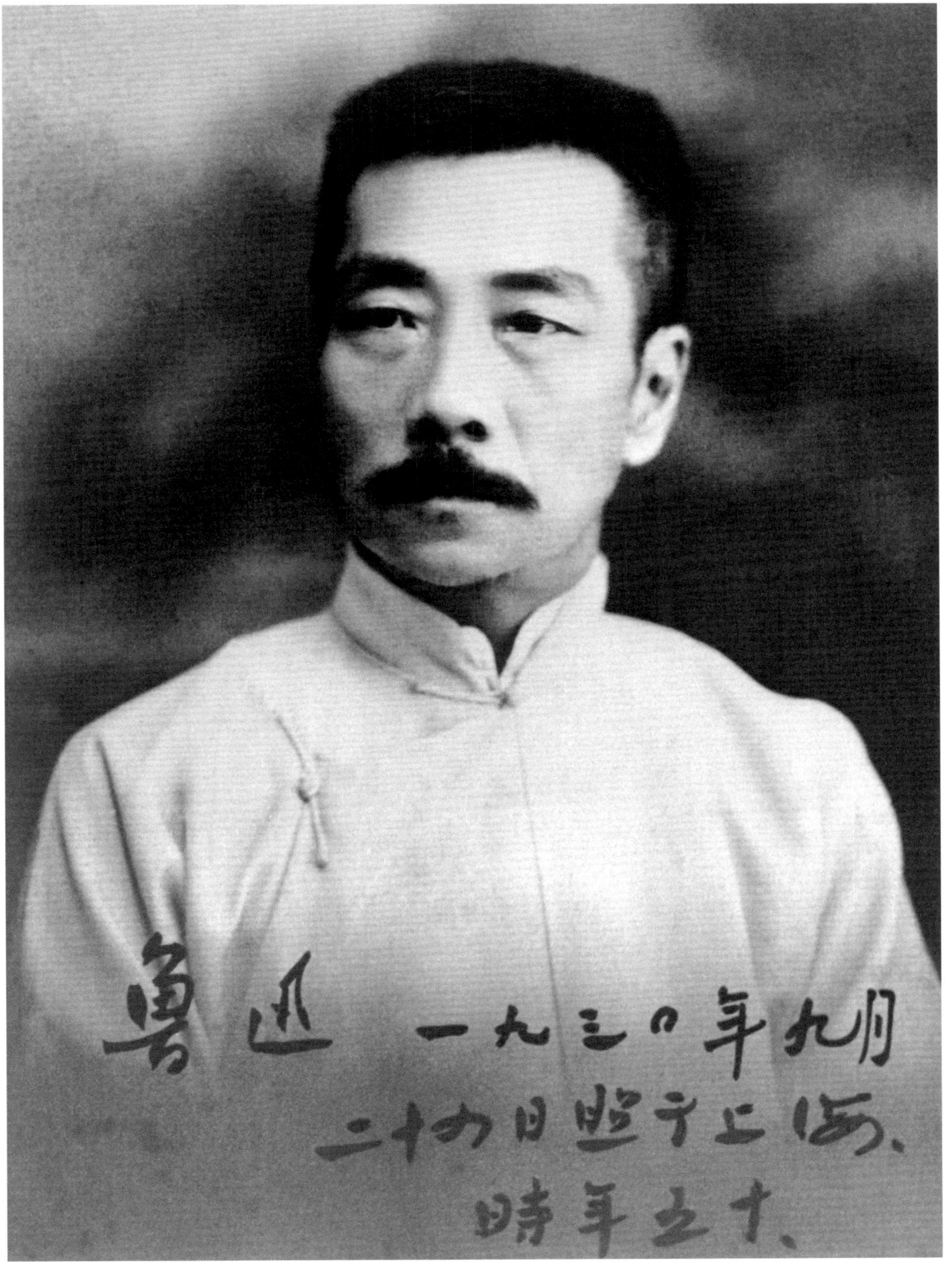
魯迅
一九三〇年九月
二十四日照于上海、
時年五十、

CORMAC MCCARTHY

[Charles McCarthy] born Providence, Rhode Island, 1933

by Gilles Peress

El Paso, Texas, 1992

Cormac McCarthy is among the most retiring, laconic and aloof of the great living American writers. The number of interviews he has consented to give could be counted on the fingers of one hand. McCarthy lives in New Mexico, where he draws inspiration for his hallucinatory descriptions of worlds in terminal decline from the desert landscapes.

It is rare that any event leads him to abandon his solitary independence, not even the enormous public response that followed the publication of *All the Pretty Horses* (1992). This, the first and most popular volume of his successful 'Border' trilogy, sold almost two hundred thousand copies in the first six months. *Blood Meridian* (1985), his first book set in the frontier era, is more radical in its depiction of violence and in its writing, with entire pages almost devoid of punctuation in a complex yet precisely worded story of scalp-hunters immersed in a savage, infernal landscape. *Suttree* (1979) is the only one of McCarthy's books to have any clear autobiographical qualities, portraying a man who is reduced to living on the periphery of society, among thieves, drunkards, whores and other marginal characters in Knoxville, Tennessee (where McCarthy himself lived for a long time). The rich, complex work has been compared to James Joyce's novel *Ulysses*.

In 2007 McCarthy won the Pulitzer Prize for *The Road*, which is the story of the peregrinations of a father and son through what remains of the world after an undefined global catastrophe. With its biblical overtones, its portrayal of the terror and mystical quality of the wilderness, its depiction of the cruelty and beauty of both nature and human beings, and its almost systematic rejection of any psychological introspection, the novel reveals McCarthy as a writer in the tradition of Ernest Hemingway or Jack London, with the stylistic density and visceral power of William Faulkner. For some critics, the style of McCarthy's books calls to mind works of Greek tragedy or medieval religious plays; others have read them as powerful allegories of a present from which there is no escape.

The great photographer Gilles Peress caught an echo of the atmosphere of McCarthy's dystopian landscapes by portraying him in El Paso's dazzling light, which is so bright that the black shadows it casts swallow up every detail.

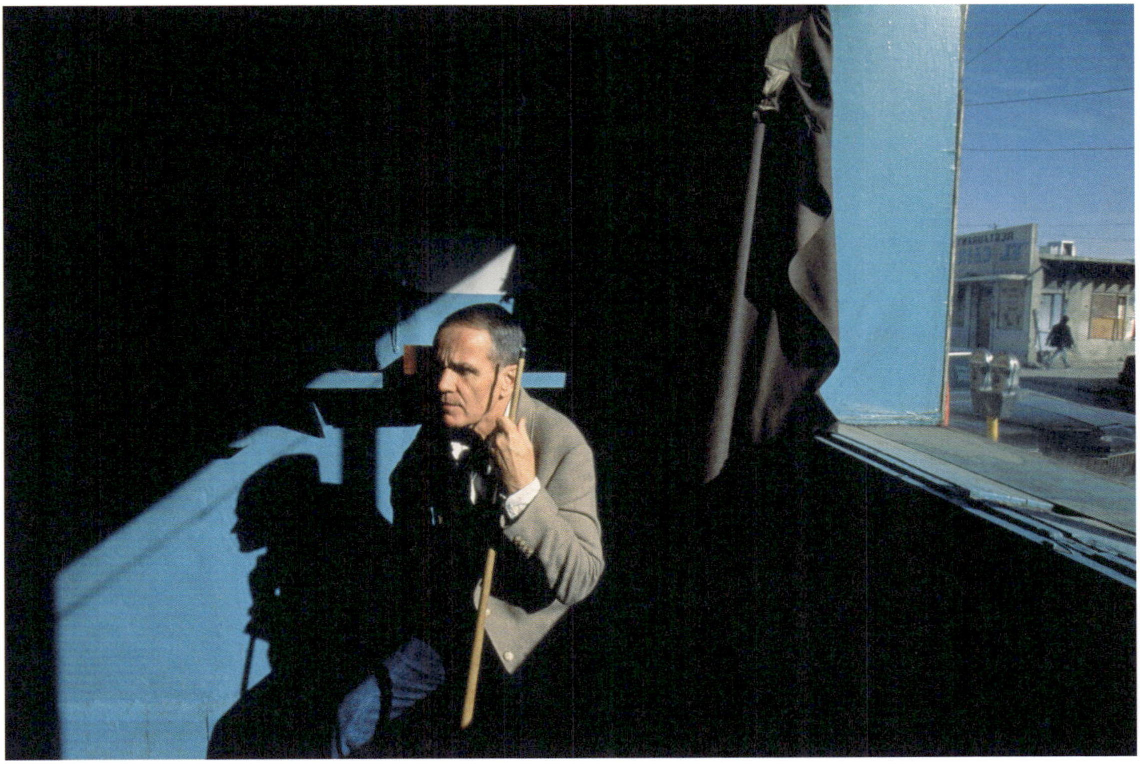

CARSON MCCULLERS

[Lula Carson Smith] born Columbus, Ohio, 1917; died Nyack, New York, 1967

by Henri Cartier-Bresson

New York, 1947

The opening lines of Charles Bukowski's poem 'Carson McCullers' (2001), although somewhat fictionalized, tell us much about the writer: 'she died of alcoholism / wrapped in a blanket / on a deck chair / on an ocean / steamer. / all her books of / terrified loneliness / all her books about / the cruelty / of loveless love / were all that was left / of her.' Both her life and her writing were woven from the same material: loneliness and suffering.

Born in Columbus, Georgia, in 1917, McCullers initially wanted to be a musician. Her ambitions were thwarted, however, by the first signs of a susceptibility to illness that would plague her for the rest of her life. Writing also fascinated her, and her first novel, *The Heart Is a Lonely Hunter* (1940), revealed the themes of isolation and profound loneliness around which she would build her literary career. In her later texts, such as *Reflections in a Golden Eye* (1941) and *The Ballad of the Sad Café* (1951), we find the same marginalized characters: misplaced, disorientated and sometimes grotesque individuals, for whom McCullers displayed great compassion. As she herself said, 'Everything which happens in my novels, happens to me.'

In 1937 she married James Reeves McCullers, with whom she had a troubled relationship marked by her alcohol dependency, bisexuality and depression; they divorced in 1941 but remarried four years later. Her principal torment, however, was her ailing body, and in 1948 she was left partly paralysed by a major stroke. That same year she tried to commit suicide while in hospital, but continued working thereafter. She died in 1967 from the effects of another serious stroke.

In Henri Cartier-Bresson's photo of McCullers, the writer is pictured with George Davis, then fiction editor of *Harper's Bazaar*. It was Davis who had conceived of the February House, a short-lived commune in Brooklyn Heights, New York, frequented by such artists and writers as McCullers, Benjamin Britten, W. H. Auden and Paul and Jane Bowles.

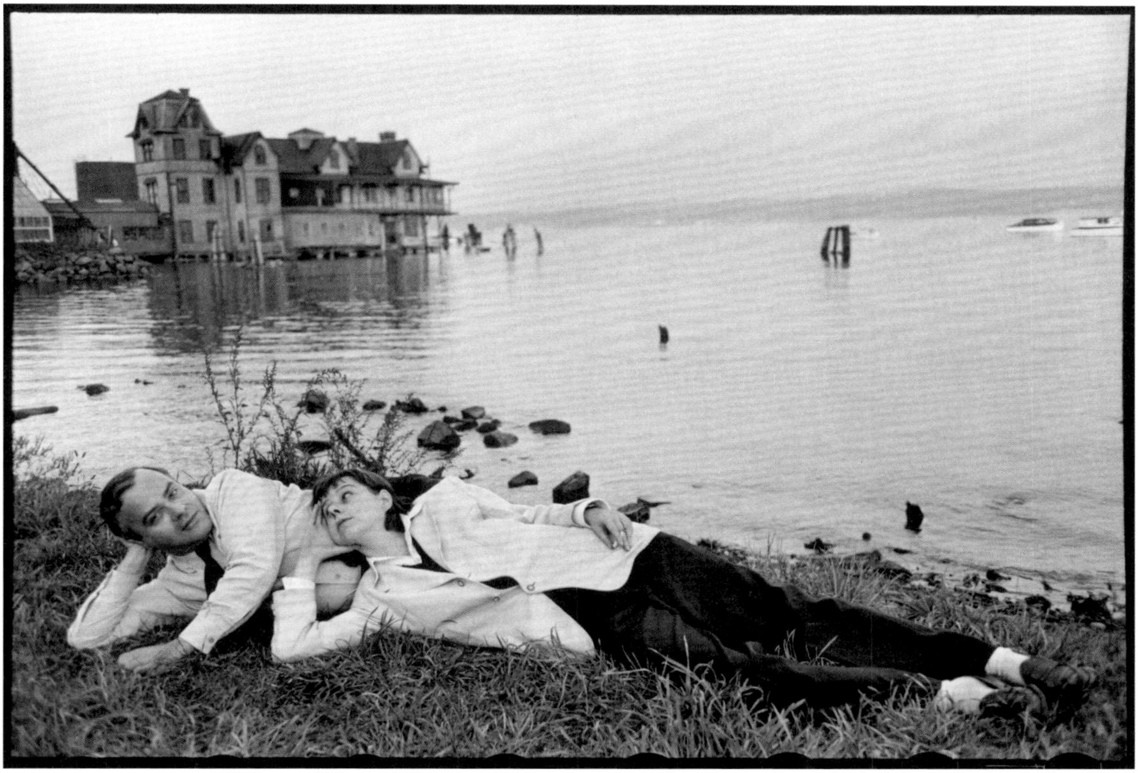

IAN MCEWAN

born Aldershot, Hampshire, UK, 1948

by Lord Snowdon

London, 1978

Born in the English county of Hampshire shortly after the Second World War, Ian McEwan spent much of his childhood overseas, living in the various countries to which his father, amajor in the British Army, had been posted. His first book, *First Love, Last Rites* (1975), a collection of short stories, caused something of a stir, winning the Somerset Maugham Award in 1976. This would prove to be the first of many such prizes and accolades.

With their dark and challenging themes, McEwan's first two novels, *The Cement Garden* (1978) and *The Comfort of Strangers* (1981), earned him the nickname 'Ian Macabre'; *Black Dogs* (1992), one of his most accomplished books, did nothing to dispel such associations. In 2002, in a turn of events not dissimilar to the plot developments that characterize his fiction, McEwan discovered that he had a brother, a bricklayer named David Sharp, who had been given up for adoption during the Second World War. His mother had become pregnant while having a wartime affair, and after her first husband was killed in combat, she married David's father. McEwan was born a few years later.

In 1998, having received several nominations for the award, McEwan was announced as the winner of the Man Booker Prize for *Amsterdam* (1998). Several of his books, most notably *The Comfort of Strangers*, *Enduring Love* (1997) and *Atonement* (2001), have been adapted into films. In recent years, McEwan has tried to shake off his reputation for being 'great but depressing', and, in comparison to some of his earlier novels, *Solar* (2010) and *Sweet Tooth* (2012) are written in a much lighter vein. In Lord Snowdon's photograph of the writer, a youthful McEwan gazes directly at the camera through a gap in a doorway. The picture was taken in 1978, the year in which McEwan made his debut as a novelist.

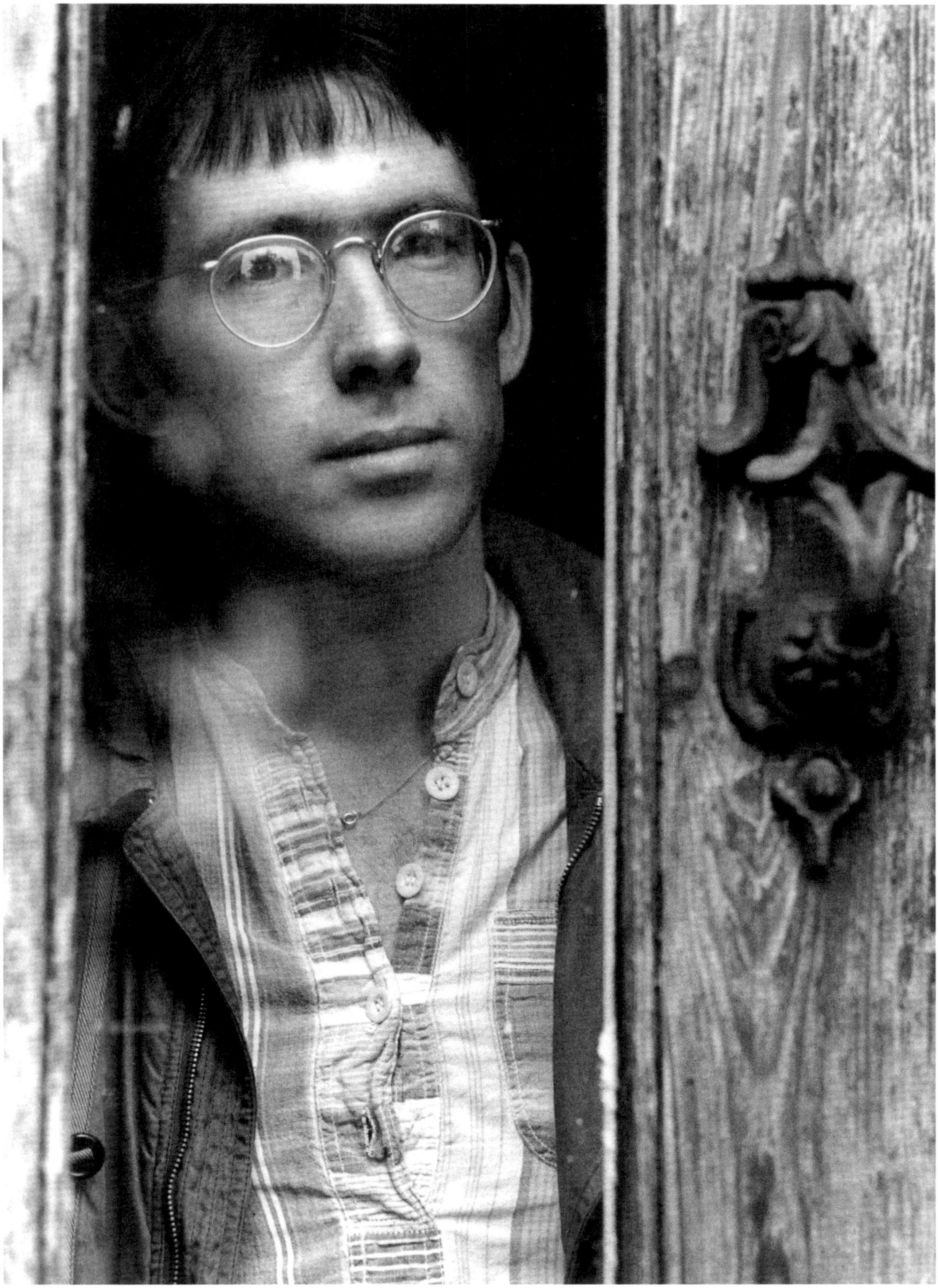

ANTONIO MACHADO

born Seville, 1875; died Collioure, France, 1939

by 'Alfonso' (Alfonso Sánchez García)

Madrid, 1933

Antonio Machado's first collection of poems, *Soledades* (Solitudes), was published in 1903. Its images were linked to Decadentism, which emphasized the individual's subconscious and instinct over scientific rationalism, and to nostalgia for childhood days. In an extended re-publication entitled *Solitudes, Galleries and Other Poems* (1907), he detached himself from the supremacy of form and his language became purposely simple and plain. These changes helped to instigate an intense dialogue between the writer and his times. Machado published his next collection, *Fields of Castile* (1912), after he had moved to Soria in Spain to teach. The intimate moods of *Soledades* had disappeared and the poet was now in a more lyrical mood, fired by the new landscape that surrounded him; however, just weeks after publication, the death of Machado's wife drove him to leave Soria.

By 1936, he had discovered a taste for prose writing and was authoring philosophical essays that he attributed to two heteronyms: Abel Martín and his disciple, Juan de Mairena. A collection of these 'apócrifos', *Epigrams, Maxims, Memoranda, and Memoirs of an Apocryphal Professor*, was published under Mairena's name in 1937, on the eve of the Spanish Civil War. During the war, Machado worked with the Republican newspaper *La Vanguardia* and also returned to creative writing with a cycle of war poems, including verse written on the death of his friend the great poet Federico García Lorca: 'They killed Federico / at the first glint of daylight. / The band of assassins / shrank from his glance.'

His political allegiance to the Republican side forced him to keep moving from place to place until he arrived in Barcelona, the ultimate Republican stronghold; however, in January 1939 he was forced to leave the city and cross the French border. By the time the poet reached Collioure in the Eastern Pyrenees he was tired and disillusioned, and would die just one month later. His coffin was draped with the Spanish flag and carried on the shoulders of the militia. Machado was buried in the cemetery of the little French town. The final lines of verse he wrote were a reminder that even in the face of war, his nostalgia for his childhood never faded: 'The blue of those days / that childhood of sun.'

This photograph of Machado seated at a table in the well-known Café de las Salesas in Madrid was taken by 'Alfonso' (Alfonso Sánchez García) a few years before the outbreak of the Spanish Civil War.

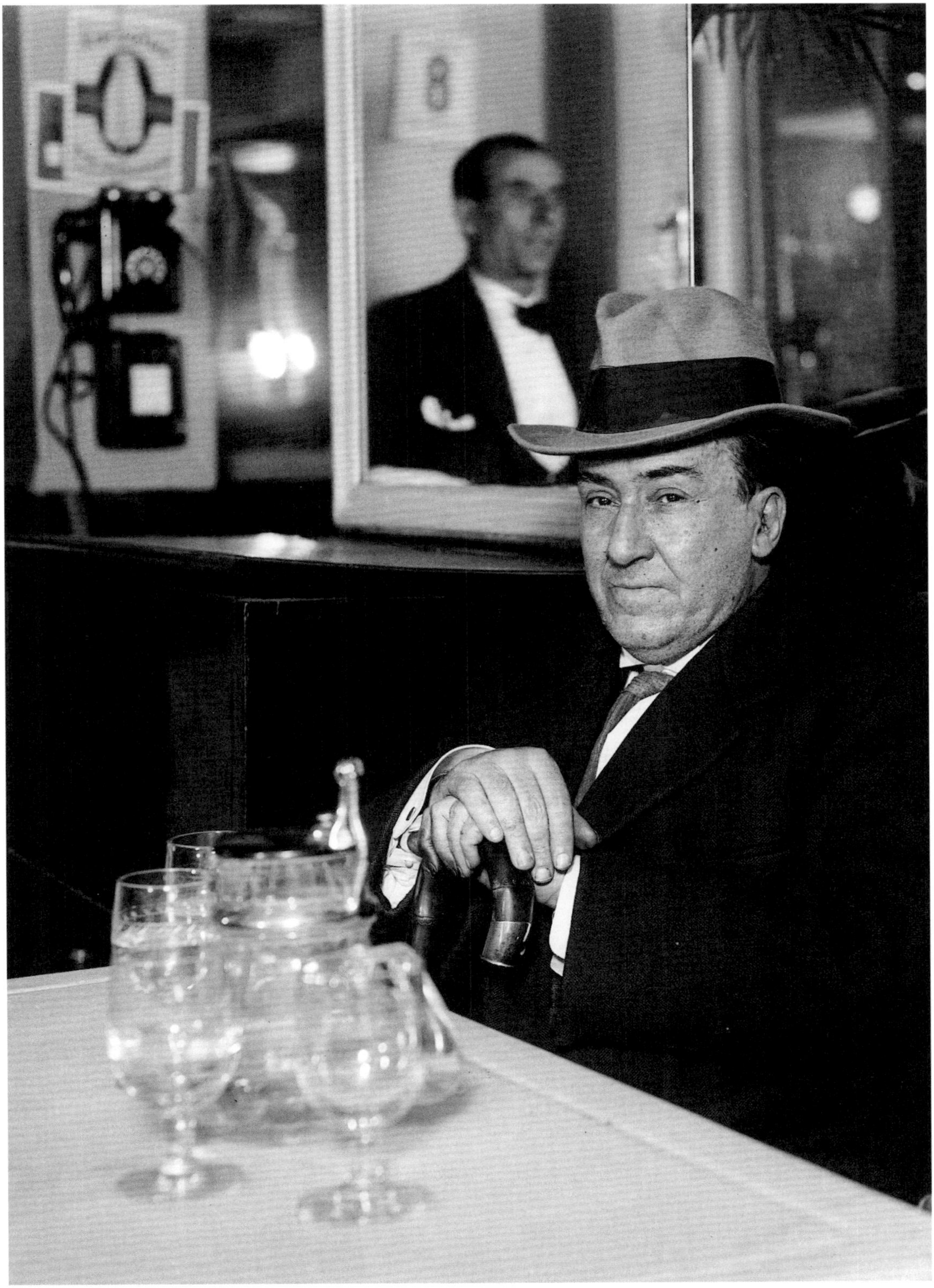

NAGUIB MAHFOUZ

born Cairo, Egypt, 1911; died Cairo, Egypt, 2006

by Chris Steele-Perkins

Cairo, Egypt, 1989

Naguib Mahfouz lived his entire life in Cairo, in the depths of the mysterious, dark maze of alleyways that constituted both his refuge and his window on the world. He did not leave the city even to receive his Nobel Prize, the first ever to be awarded to a writer whose native tongue is Arabic. Instead, he sent his two children and his fellow Egyptian writer and friend Mohamed Salmawy to the ceremony in December 1988. Mahfouz asked them to deliver a speech on his behalf, first in Arabic, then in English, part of which read: 'I would like you to accept my talk with tolerance. For it comes in a language unknown to many of you. But it is the real winner of the prize. It is, therefore, meant that its melodies should float for the first time into your oasis of culture and civilization.'

Although Mahfouz cast himself in the role of 'the man coming from the Third World', knowing full well that his name would be unfamiliar to most people, his literary vision transcended the borders of his homeland. He addressed with great clarity such contemporary issues as post-colonialism, corruption, social prejudice and religious fundamentalism. His inspiration came from his daily walks through the alleyways of Cairo, some of which gave their names to his early works, including: *Cairo Modern* (1945), *Khan al-Khalili* (1945), *Midaq Alley* (1947) and the novels of his 'Cairo' trilogy, *Palace Walk* (1956), *Palace of Desire* (1957) and *Sugar Street* (1957). As an advocate of a moderate Islam and an opponent of fundamentalism, Mahfouz began to attract the attention of the West, a fact that earned him many enemies at home. After the publication of *Children of Gebelawi* in 1959, the religious authorities accused him of blasphemy and the persecution of fundamentalists. The book was banned in Egypt and Lebanon, and Mahfouz received death threats.

The controversy surrounding Mahfouz intensified in the late 1980s following his acceptance of the Nobel Prize. In 1994, having been offered and refused police protection, he was attacked on his doorstep and had his throat cut. Miraculously he survived, and was determined to stay in his home regardless of the danger. Magnum photographer Chris Steele-Perkins took this portrait of the writer in 1989 during one of his local walks.

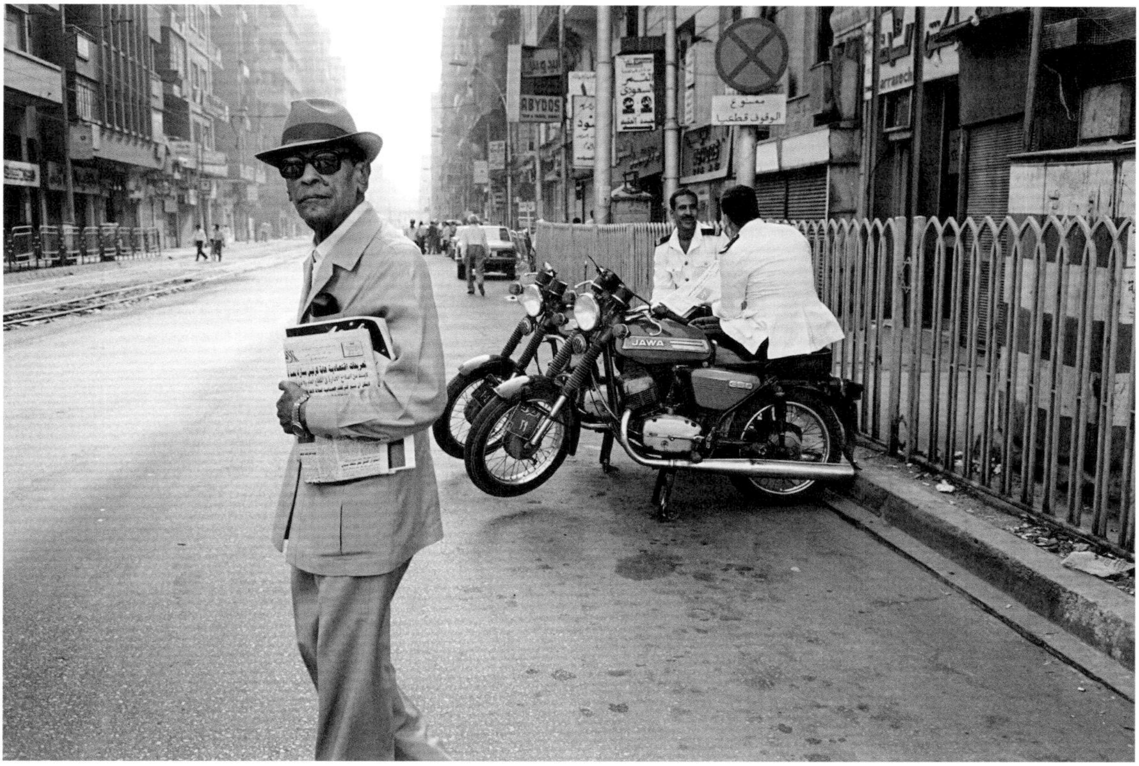
ABYDOS
ممنوع
الوقوف قطعيا
JAWA

NORMAN MAILER

born Long Branch, New Jersey, 1923; died New York, 2007

by Bob Peterson

New York, 1969

Despite his many wrangles with Norman Mailer, it is Gore Vidal who, in a review of Mailer's *Advertisement for Myself* (1959), provided one of the most frank and honest assessments of the writer: 'Mailer is forever shouting at us that he is about to tell us something we must know or has just told us something revelatory and we failed to hear him … each time he speaks he must become more bold, more loud, put on brighter motley and shake more foolish bells. … Yet of all my contemporaries I retain the greatest affection for Mailer as a force and as an artist. He is a man whose faults, though many, add to rather than subtract from the sum of his natural achievement.'

A colourful and controversial figure in both his private and his public life, Mailer burst on to the literary scene with *The Naked and the Dead* (1948), his semi-autobiographical novel about his experiences in the Pacific during the Second World War. Although clearly the work of an immature writer – Mailer himself admitted as much – it was a tremendous success. It catapulted him on to the international stage, where, thanks to both his artistic talents and his occasional behavioural excesses, he remained for the next sixty years.

As he confessed during an interview with *Paris Review* in 1963, Mailer had wanted to be a man of action, but ended up being a man of letters. In fact, his literary output was prodigious, with more than thirty books to his name, including novels, biographies (most famously of Marilyn Monroe) and collections of essays. Mailer was an exponent of New Journalism, which used unconventional literary techniques in the context of factual reporting, and was awarded two Pulitzer prizes, for *The Armies of the Night* (1968) and *The Executioner's Song* (1979); the former also won the National Book Award. In 1955 Mailer helped to launch the *Village Voice*, a Greenwich Village newspaper devoted to politics and the arts.

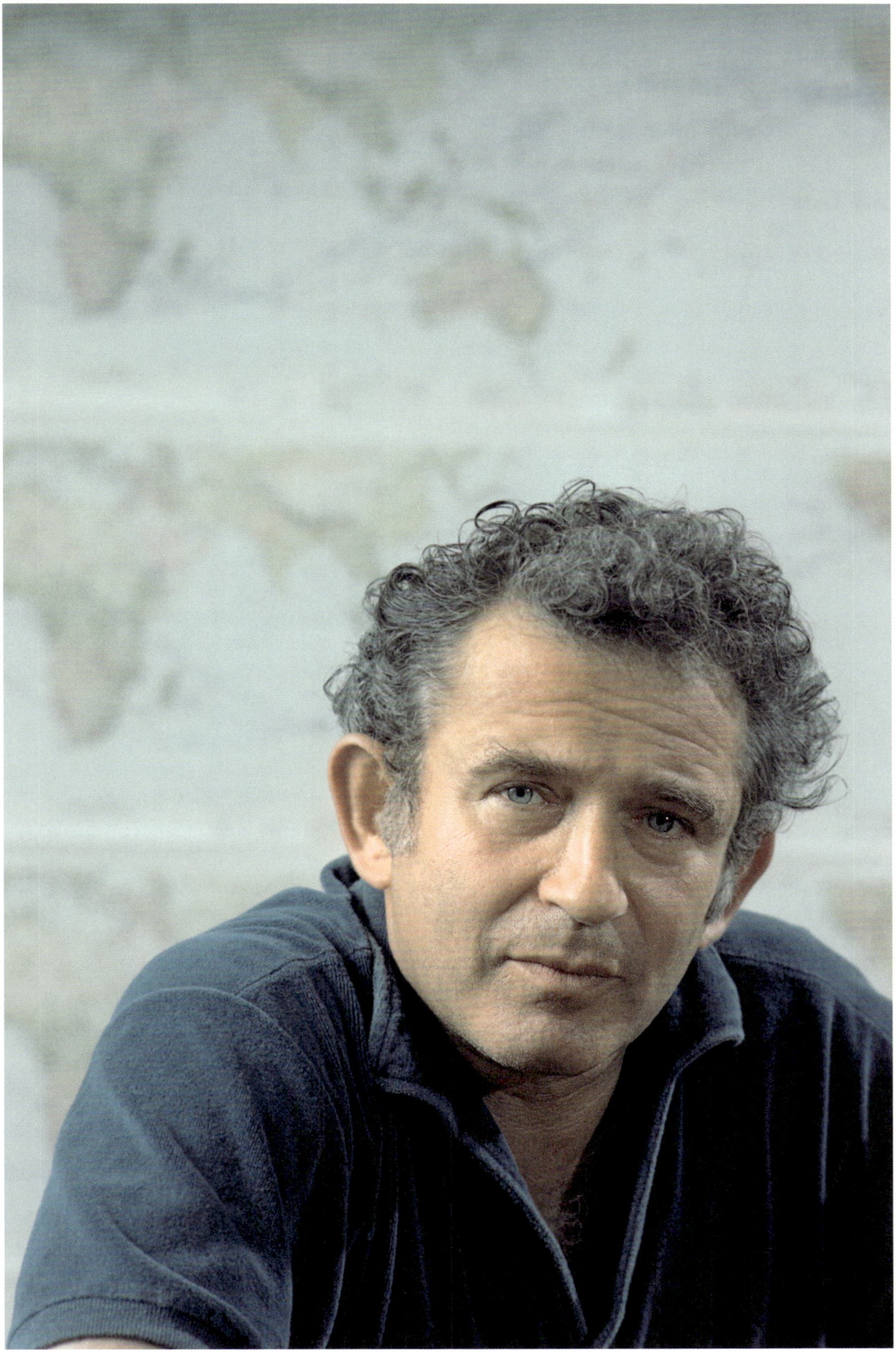

CURZIO MALAPARTE

[Kurt Erich Suckert] born Prato, Italy, 1898; died Rome, 1957

by Robert Doisneau

Paris, c. 1949

He defined himself and wished to be considered both 'antipathetic' and an 'arch-Italian', and he wanted to impress his controversial public personality on the successive generations who lived in the first half of a century dominated by destructive, larger-than-life figures. The models and rivals that Curzio Malaparte judged himself against were two of Italy's greatest exhibitionists: Benito Mussolini and Gabriele D'Annunzio – politician and bard, friends and enemies.

Malaparte fought in the First World War and published his early articles simultaneously in two magazines with contrary political allegiances: Mino Maccari's *Il Selvaggio* and Massimo Bontempelli's *900* (the first being a deeply patriotic journal, while the second promoted interaction with other nations). He became a journalist (and was a very good one, as can be seen from his correspondence from the Russian front); then a newspaper publisher; and he also tried his hand at diplomacy. In 1931 he wrote a curious and notable historico-political reflection entitled *Coup d'État: The Technique of Revolution*, which angered Mussolini, and earned Malaparte internal exile on the island of Lipari for a number of years.

Malaparte was also a writer of undoubted talent, the creator of highly coloured yet plausible stories. He specialized in tales 'taken from real life', inventing a literature of heightened reality, a style that would become enormously fashionable once again in the early years of the twenty-first century. He produced at least two great books: *Kaputt* (1944), a terrifying epic of Europe during World War Two, and *The Skin* (1949), an equally terrifying portrayal of Italy in defeat. Malaparte also worked in films (he directed the courageously anti-neo-Realist *The Forbidden Christ* in 1951); in the theatre he wrote the dramas *Du côté de chez Proust*, *The Women Lost the War Too* and *Das Kapital*, a portrait of Karl Marx; and he also proved himself to be a star performer in revue theatre. He was a man of both order and rebellion, both a Fascist and then an anti-Fascist. By the time of his death both the Vatican and the Communist Party had embraced him.

He pushed his way into twentieth-century Italian culture by playing on its provincial weaknesses, grossly exaggerating its tendencies and vices, but also managed to make it less insular. He was one of the few Italian writers who recognized the need to look to Paris, London, Berlin and Moscow, and much later towards the USA and even China (even if it was always from the perspective of the cocky, arrogant, 'accursed' region of Tuscany). Indeed, his final best-seller, a smug eulogy to his origins, was entitled *Those Cursed Tuscans* (1956).

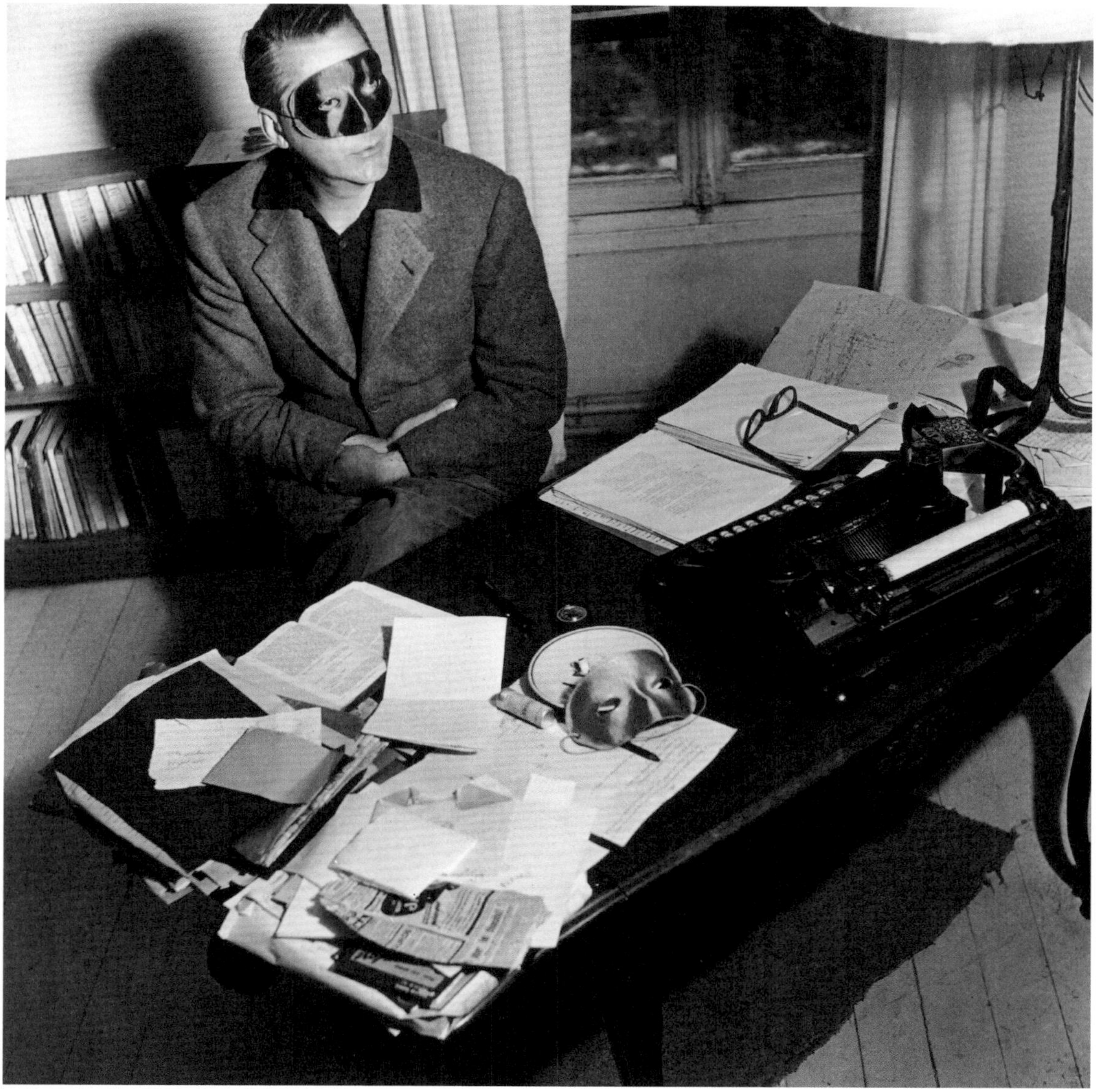

ANDRÉ MALRAUX

born Paris, 1901; died Créteil, France, 1976

by Philippe Halsman

Paris, 1934

In addition to photographing André Malraux in 1934, Philippe Halsman composed a second portrait of the writer using words: 'The two sides of his face were dissimilar – according to [Italian physician and psychiatrist] Cesare Lombroso, a sign either of genius or of criminality. Seen from the left, his profile had an aquiline nobility; from the right, however, it looked less romantic because his nose suddenly took on the shape of a duck's bill. Malraux's eyes fixed on my lens with an almost unbearable intensity and intelligence. Slowly, I moved slightly to the left to concentrate on the romantic side of his face.'

These two faces, that of the writer and that of the politician, reflect Malraux's entire being; his novels were the moment in which the zeal of his activism and his love of literature finally came together. His characters are often young revolutionaries, such as Kyo and Tchen, who, in his most famous novel, *Man's Fate* (1933), live in the turbulent city of Shanghai at the end of the 1920s. The author had spent time in China, and had experienced its civil war first hand, just as he would later take part in the Spanish Civil War and the French Resistance. After distancing himself from the Communist Party, he became one of Charles de Gaulle's closest friends and allies during the post-war period.

A highly enlightened figure and former student of archaeology, Malraux was twice appointed to positions in the French government: first in 1945, as Minister of Information, and secondly in 1958, as Minister of Cultural Affairs, a role in which he made culture a vital component of national policy. He explored numerous questions of aesthetics in his many essays and, at the same time, expended enormous efforts to ensure that French arts and letters were promoted throughout the world. It was his idea, for example, to have André Masson paint the ceiling of the Théâtre de l'Odéon, and for Marc Chagall to paint that of the Opéra de Paris. Malraux considered art to be humanity's only redeeming feature, its only chance of immortality, while the concepts of fraternity and humanism were for him key points for political and literary action: 'Humanism does not consist in saying: "No animal could have done what I have done," but in declaring: "We have refused what the beast within us willed to do, and we seek to reclaim man wherever we find that which crushes him"' (*The Voices of Silence*, 1951).

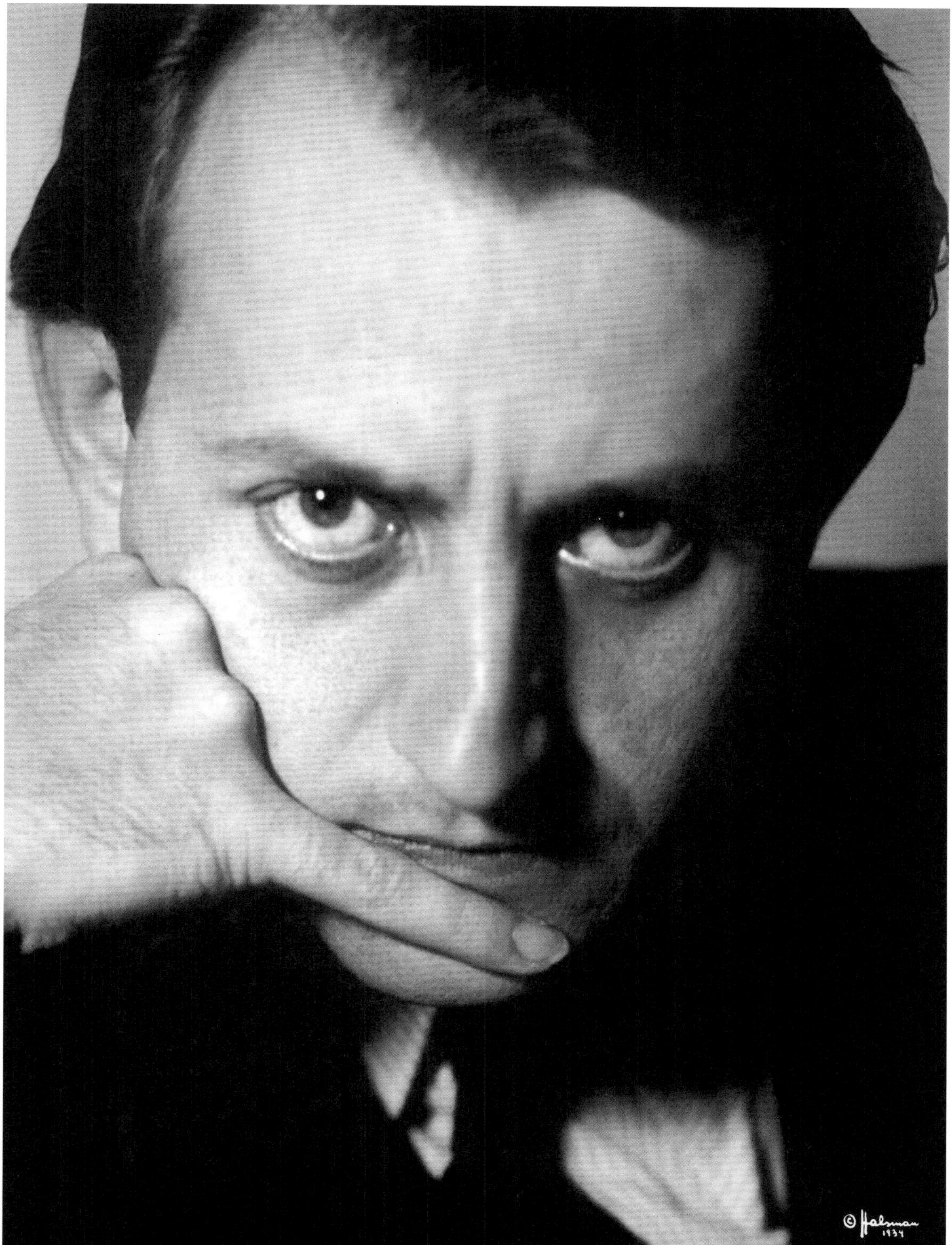
© Halsman
1934

THOMAS MANN

born Lübeck, Germany, 1875; died Zurich, 1955

by Carl Mydans

Princeton, New Jersey, 1939

In his youth, Thomas Mann was already something of an aesthete. He enjoyed the music of Wagner, and preferred the works of Schopenhauer, Goethe and Nietzsche to his school books. In 1894 he became a clerk in the office of an insurance company, a position he held only briefly before devoting all his time to writing. In 1901 he published the epic novel *Buddenbrooks*, which quickly made him famous and established his reputation as a writer of note.

At this stage in his career Mann's principal preoccupations included spirituality and art. He showed little interest in politics, even at the outbreak of the First World War, and in 1918 he published an essay entitled *Reflections of an Unpolitical Man*. Many people, including his brother, Heinrich, were never to forgive him for this apolitical stance, but for Mann, the label 'unpolitical' was one of intellectual merit. It took Germany's defeat in the Great War and the rise of Nazism in Germany to change his mind. In the meantime he had completed some of his best-known works, including *Tonio Kröger* (1903), *Death in Venice* (1912) and *The Magic Mountain* (1924). In 1929 he was awarded the Nobel Prize.

When the Nazis came to power in 1933, Mann was forced to leave his homeland and seek exile in Switzerland. In 1939 he emigrated to the USA, eventually settling in Pacific Palisades, a suburb of Los Angeles on the Pacific coast. During the Second World War he composed a series of radio messages for the German people, urging them to reject the evils of Nazism; the messages were recorded in the USA and then broadcast by the BBC in London. In a transmission from January 1942, he condemned the deportation of hundreds of Dutch Jews and their murder in the gas chambers of the concentration camps. The elegant, conservative and 'unpolitical' novelist thus became one of the first people publicly to denounce the evils of the Holocaust.

Carl Mydans took this photograph of Mann for *Life* magazine. It was taken in Princeton, at the university where Mann taught German literature from 1938 to 1941.

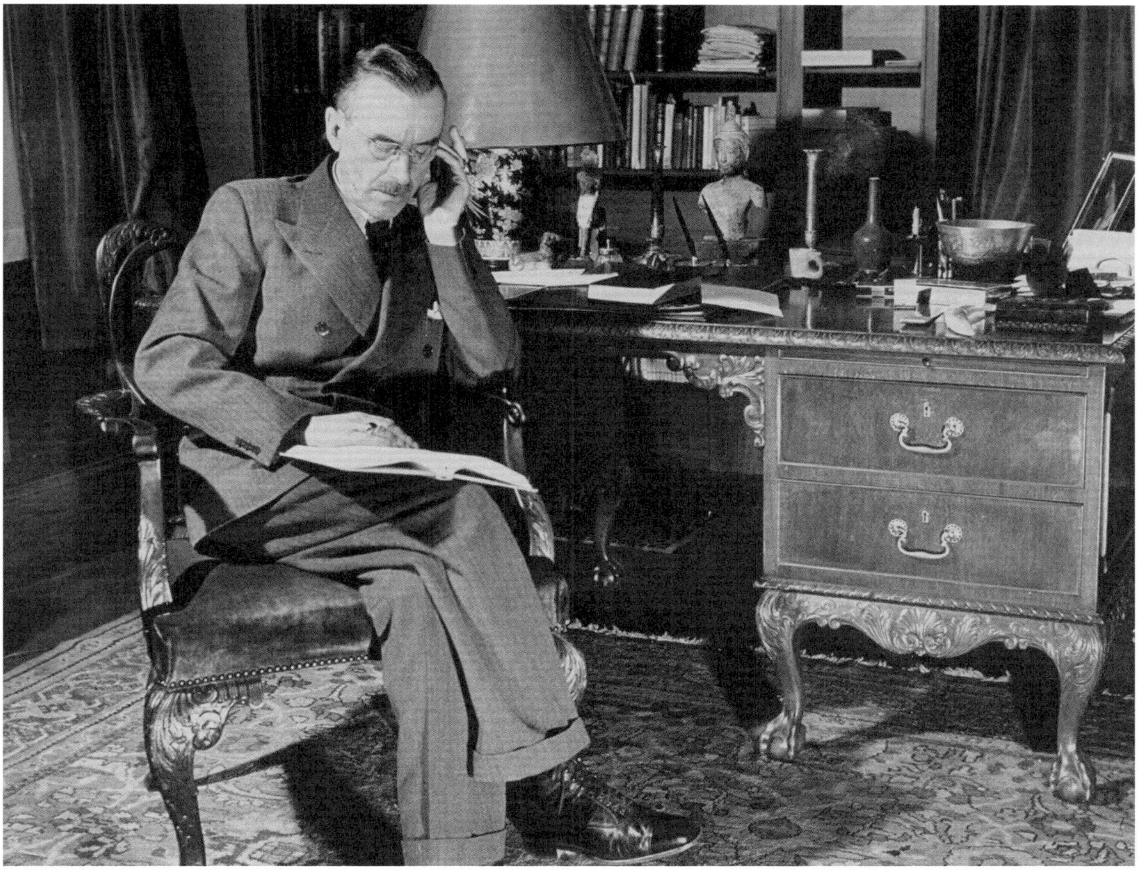

SÁNDOR MÁRAI

[Sándor Károly Henrik Grosschmied de Mára] born Košice, Slovakia, 1900; died San Diego, California, 1989

unknown photographer

Budapest, c. 1939

According to Hungarian writer Sándor Márai, who committed suicide at the age of eighty-nine, old age arrives a little at a time. It gradually creeps through the body and the soul; it makes itself felt through a sharpening sense of reality and becomes real and irreversible when, finally, every experience has become predictable, from the changing of the seasons to the occurrence of events. In Márai's work, expectation is a fundamental element of life, and even becomes a real protagonist in novels such as *Esther's Inheritance* (1939) or the more famous *Embers* (1942), which engages with the idea of friendship. Although widely read internationally only after Márai's death, this monumental and melancholy text caused him to be regarded as one of the twentieth century's most gifted storytellers.

Márai had been well-known in his own country since the 1930s, and no bookshelf belonging to any self-respecting middle-class Hungarian family was without his books. He left Hungary in 1948. As the Soviet domination of his country took hold, he had found himself denied the freedom to write. His long period in exile made him a citizen of the world. He spent time in Italy, living first in Naples where he got to know Benedetto Croce, with whom he shared a liberal philosophy, and in 1968 he moved to Salerno with his wife Lola, who was his inseparable companion for more than sixty years. He also spent time in Switzerland, and lived an itinerant life before eventually settling in New York in 1952. In 1934, when still a young man, he began writing his autobiography *Egy polgár vallmasai* (Confessions of a bourgeois, 1934–35), part of a collection of memoirs that he finally completed with his *Memoir of Hungary: 1944–48* (1972). In both texts, his personal memories are merged with the historical accounts of the catastrophic events that devastated Central Europe in the twentieth century.

Márai was posthumously awarded the prestigious Kossuth Prize in 1989 for his contribution to Hungarian literature. Despite his cosmopolitan outlook, he had always remained loyal to the Hungarian language, renouncing any chance of achieving greater fame by refusing to write in English – he believed that the language of his childhood was his only true homeland. Following his death, in the 1990s his books began to be published in French and English translation, reviving his literary reputation on an international scale.

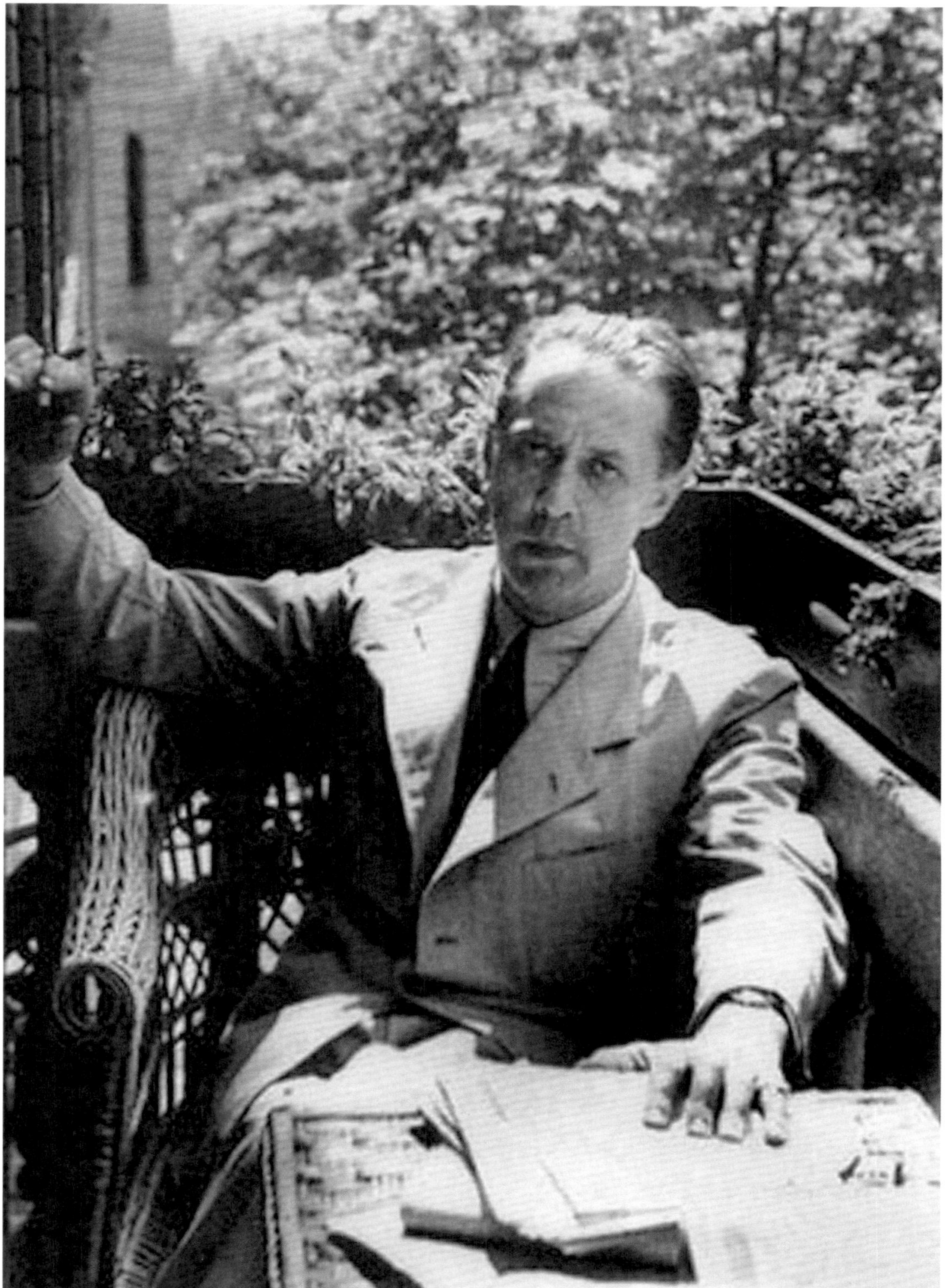

JAVIER MARÍAS

born Madrid, 1951

by Ferdinando Scianna

Madrid, 2005

Javier Marías is an important writer on the Spanish and international literary scenes. His complex novels explore the psychological confusion and dismay that ensue when an ordinary person discovers that appearance and reality are in fact totally different entities, and finds himself adrift in a world of uncertainty.

Marías's protagonists become anxious in the face of decisions and gripped by fear of the future as they encounter the complexity of the present. Although at times conscious of their existential dilemmas, they are nonetheless unable to break free from them. One such character is the central protagonist of *A Heart So White* (1992), an interpreter who, in the words of the author, is forced to renounce his own voice when exercising his profession. He struggles to make sense of his own recent marriage, the figure of his father, and his uncle who committed suicide after returning from his honeymoon. The characters created by Marías are acute observers, scrutinizing others in the vain hope of gaining an understanding of themselves, and imagining themselves living out different destinies. The harsh reality, however, is that there will be no moment of comforting enlightenment; human nature remains inscrutable and subject to a thousand different interpretations. Even those of purest character can become susceptible to vices to which they never dreamed themselves capable of succumbing.

Marías once said in an interview: 'If we believe that we could never denounce, betray or murder anyone, then that belief may well be put to the test. *Your Face Tomorrow* [the title of his trilogy, 2009] explores the idea that no one can ever know his face well today, let alone what it might look like tomorrow'.

As if in accord with this sentiment, the photograph of the author taken by Ferdinando Scianna shows only a part of his face; the rest remains resolutely hidden. Two delicate eyes peer out from behind a number of small figures, perhaps symbolizing humanity's various disguises.

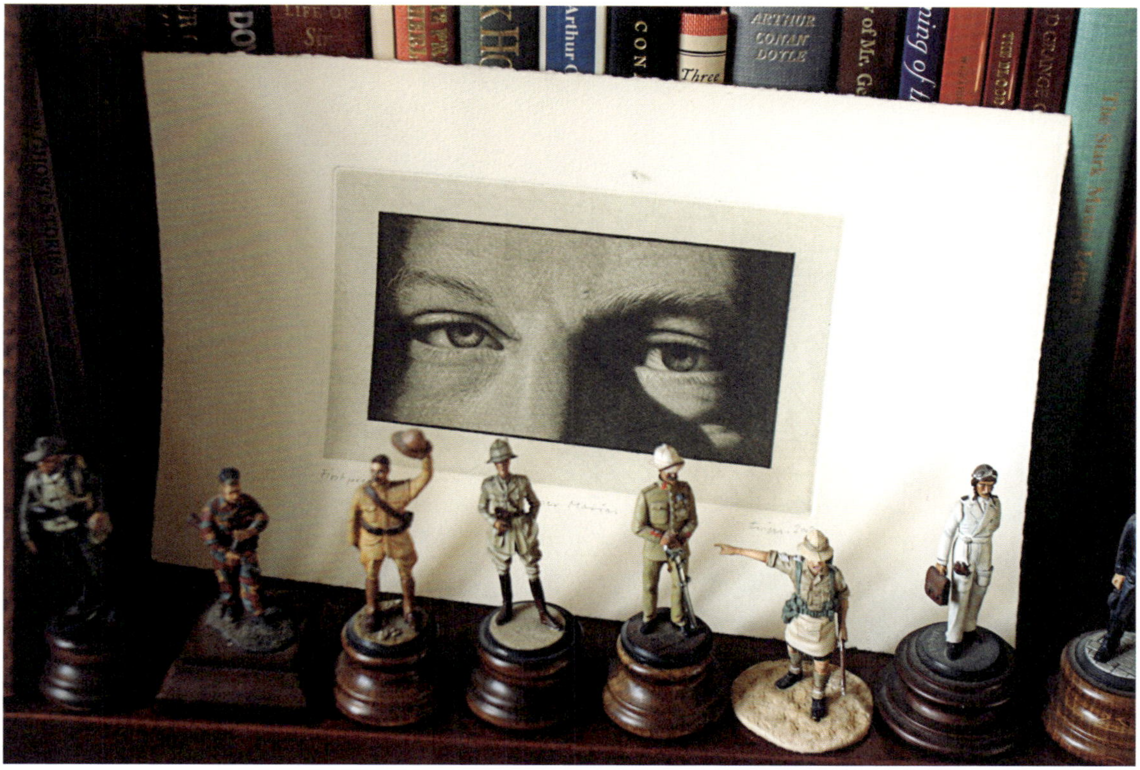
ARTHUR CONAN DOYLE

W. SOMERSET MAUGHAM

born Paris, 1874; died Saint-Jean-Cap-Ferrat, France, 1965

by Herbert List

Athens, 1950

Renowned for his sarcasm, which he reserved especially for women, William Somerset Maugham was not well liked by his peers. Noel Coward described him as the 'Lizard of Oz', while Virginia Woolf also compared him to a reptile. He probably would have followed in his father's footsteps and become a lawyer had he not been orphaned before he was ten years old. He was then sent to England to live with a bachelor uncle in Kent, who was a vicar and showed no affection to the boy. At school in Canterbury, Maugham was teased because of his French accent. He became increasingly withdrawn, developing a talent for making cutting remarks in self-defence. He went on to study medicine, but spent his evenings writing. He completed his first novel, *Liza of Lambeth* (1897), at the time of his graduation. It sold out in a few weeks, and he decided to return to Paris to dedicate himself to the world of letters.

In 1907 he had his first success as a playwright with *Lady Frederick*; before long he had four plays running simultaneously in London and Paris. Over the next few years he became one of the most prolific and popular writers of his generation. His writing is characterized by an objective view of the miseries of reality combined with a heavy dose of cynicism. The autobiographical novel *Of Human Bondage* (1915) is widely regarded as his masterpiece; other superlative works include *The Moon and Sixpence* (1919), *The Painted Veil* (1925) and *The Razor's Edge* (1948). His fame increased with the many successful film adaptations of his books.

During the First World War Maugham served as an agent for British intelligence; in the Second World War, having moved to the USA, he worked for the newly established Office of Strategic Services, later the CIA. These experiences would form the basis of his short stories about the fictional spy John Ashenden, a character said to have influenced Ian Fleming's James Bond. Maugham himself is said to have been inspired and intrigued by the wit and flamboyance of Oscar Wilde, while his writing had an impact not only on Fleming but also on Anthony Burgess, George Orwell and Paul Theroux, among others.

The German photographer Herbert List met Maugham at the elegant Hotel Grand Bretagne in Athens, where he took several photographs of the writer. The elegant pose and diagonal composition reinforce the expression of aloof disdain with which Maugham looks into the distance.

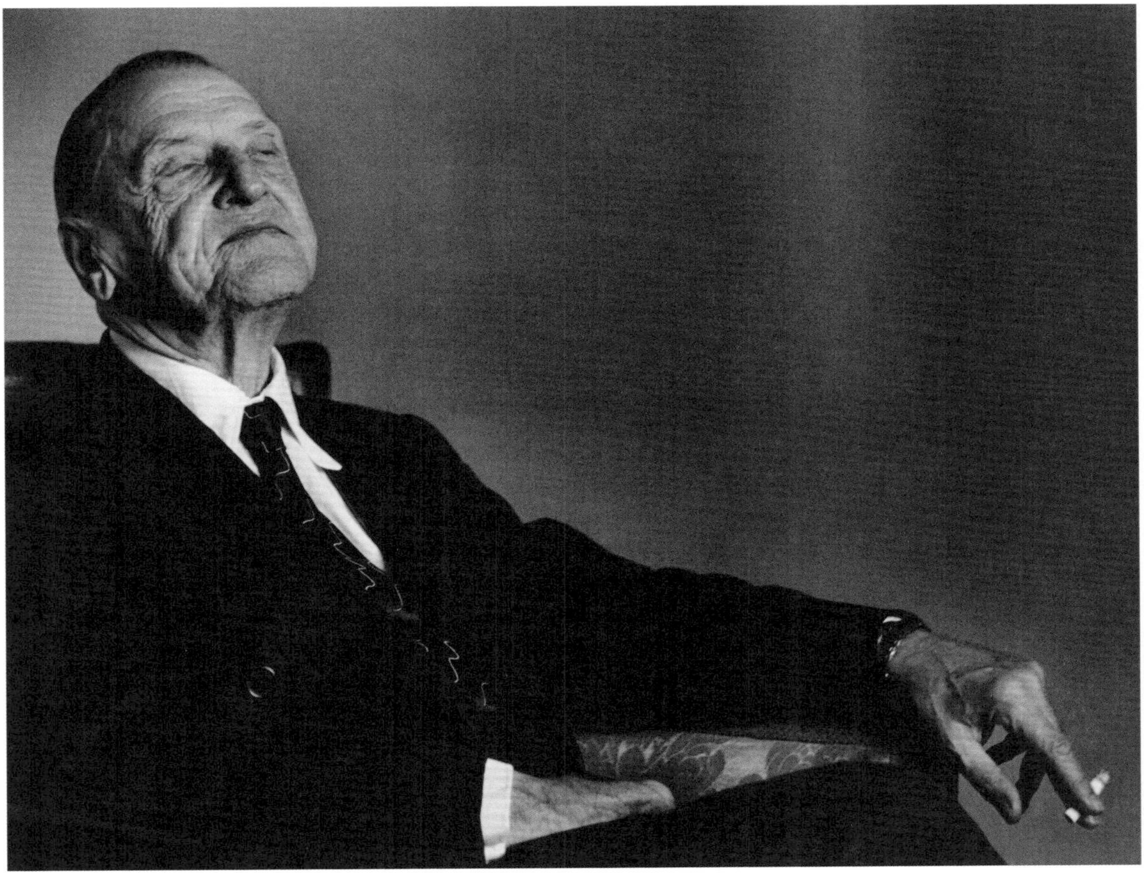

FRANÇOIS MAURIAC

born Bordeaux, 1885; died Paris, 1970

by Henri Cartier-Bresson

Paris, 1952

'I am a Catholic who writes novels.' This was how the French writer François Mauriac liked to define himself, emphasizing both the religious and moral inspiration that dominated his entire literary output.

His father died when he was young and his mother brought him up according to strict Catholic values. A central theme of his narrative work was the internal conflict that arises within human beings when they are torn – as the title of one of his many novels reminds us – between *God and Mammon* (1929). In his stories the painful search for God is often accompanied by the unmasking of hypocrisy and bourgeois conformism. Such is the case in *Thérèse Desqueyroux* (1927), in which Thérèse, a dark and fascinating protagonist, finds herself suffocated by social convention and her provincial life. After she attempts to poison her husband, Thérèse's family rallies around her in order to avoid a scandal; this leaves her even more tightly entrapped in her marriage however, and she abandons herself passively to her fate. Mauriac went on to construct an entire cycle of works around the figure of Thérèse.

His novels did not please Jean-Paul Sartre, who attacked him savagely in *What Is Literature?* (1948). Sartre claimed Mauriac played the role of a novelist–God who simply moves his characters around like mannequins. For Sartre, God was not an artist, and neither was Mauriac.

The harsh treatment he received from Sartre caused Mauriac to stop his creative activities for many years, but he did not abandon his typewriter completely. Instead, he went on to prove himself to be a deeply committed journalist: he argued against Franco's rule in Spain and against the Fascist campaign in Ethiopia, and he took part in the Resistance during the German occupation of France. During the Second World War he published underground newspaper *The Black Notebook* (anthologized in 1944) under the pseudonym 'Forez'. After the liberation he worked with both *L'Express* and the *Le Figaro littéraire*. Mauriac became a member of the Académie Française in 1933 and was awarded the Nobel Prize in 1952. He had returned to novel writing in the final years of his life.

In this portrait by Henri Cartier-Bresson, Mauriac has a melancholy air and holds a book inhis hands. It seems as if he has rediscovered his link with literature and would now like to retrace his past life as a writer.

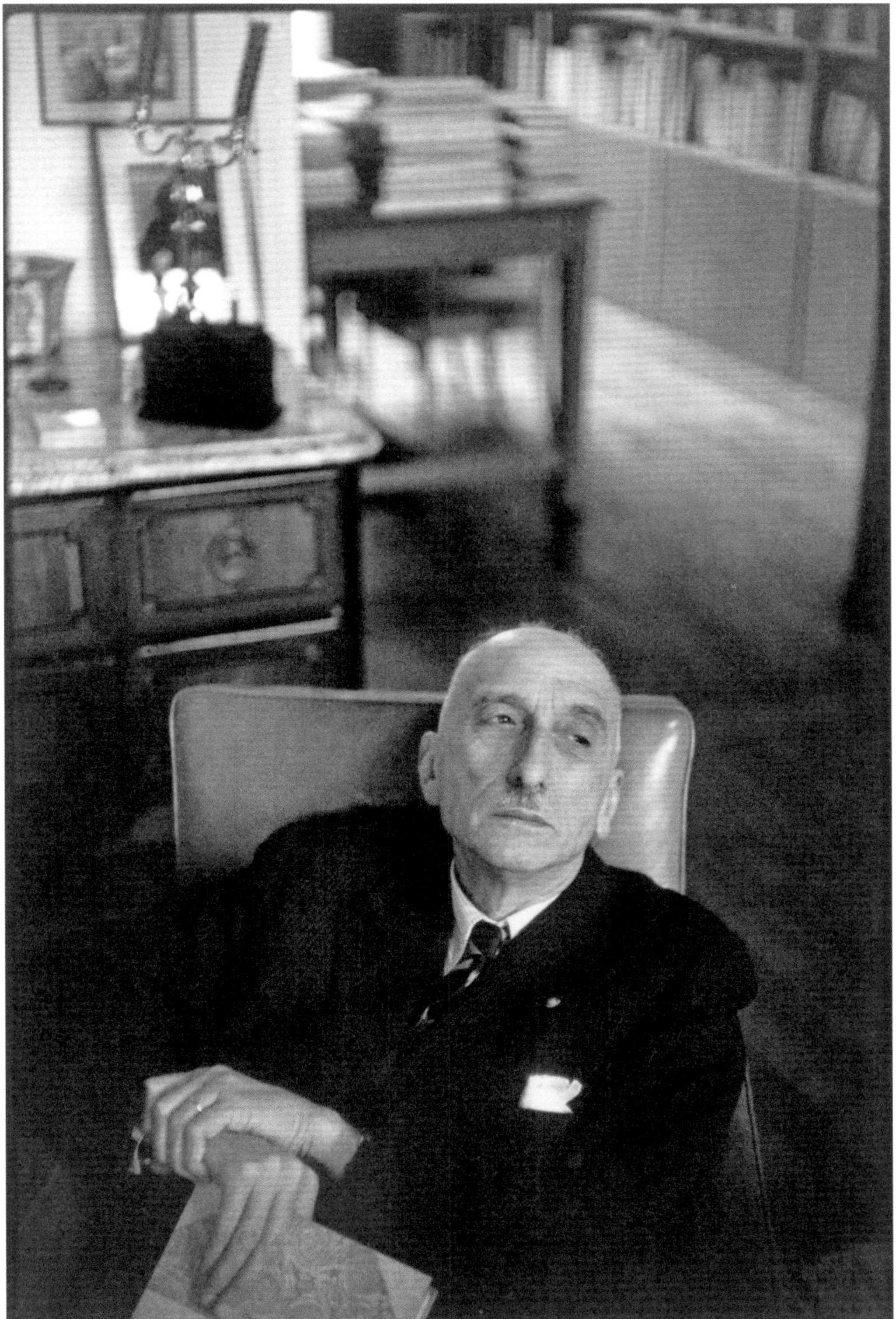

VLADIMIR MAYAKOVSKY

born Baghdati, Georgia, 1893; died Moscow, 1930

by Alexander Rodchenko

Moscow, 1924

Poet, playwright, artist, actor and revolutionary, Vladimir Mayakovsky was possessed of an unbridled energy and his short life was filled with activity. He was driven by the idea that a world built on socialist principles had to be reflected in a new kind of art – new subjects, new forms – and that neither art nor politics could progress without the other. Without understanding this view, it is impossible to comprehend the grandeur and audacity of Russian artistic expression in the first three decades of the twentieth century – a period that preceded a return to strict rules in both art and politics: the artistic rules of Socialist Realism and the iron rule of the Communist dictatorship.

Born in the final decades of the Russian Empire, in what is now Georgia, Mayakovsky was arrested many times by the Tsarist regime during his youth. In Moscow, with the assistance of David Burliuk and the friendship of Velimir Khlebnikov, he came into contact with radical artistic circles where – still wavering between restlessness and conviction; timidity and his characteristically generous and friendly brand of narcissism – he found himself mixing on equal terms with Sergei Eisenstein, Alexander Rodchenko, Roman Jakobson, Alexander Blok and Vsevolod Meyerhold. Meyerhold, a revolutionary figure in Russian theatre, staged Mayakovsky's irreverent, fantastical and provocative theatrical works – *The Bedbug* (1928) and *The Bathhouse* (1930), both of which, like his earlier play *Mystery-Bouffe* (1918), are set in the future, creating a perspective from which the old world and its vices could be judged, an artistic gesture that aroused the suspicions of the Stalinist regime.

Indeed, Mayakovsky was preoccupied with the future, and much of his poetry was written under the banner of Russian Futurism. He also tried his hand at writing and acting for the cinema and was a brilliant graphic artist who produced numerous propaganda posters, as well as editing the art journal *LEF*. His personal life was no less lively: he had numerous affairs and travelled widely. Above all, however, he wrote poetry. His poems were densely packed with images, unique associations and aggressive metaphors. He willingly declared himself to be a 'propagandist for Paradise' – a socialist, Soviet Paradise – and even wrote a poem in praise of Lenin (1925). Despite his growing public prominence, he felt most at ease among the lowest strata of society in the ramshackle taverns on the edge of the city.

The greatest poet of the Russian Revolution killed himself at the age of thirty-seven, betrayed by the very revolutionaries he had once supported. Mayakovsky and Rodchenko, who took this portrait, shared the same aesthetic ideals and activist beliefs and collaborated on many of their artistic projects. After his friend's early and dramatic death, Rodchenko abandoned the Constructivist avant-garde to dedicate himself entirely to photography.

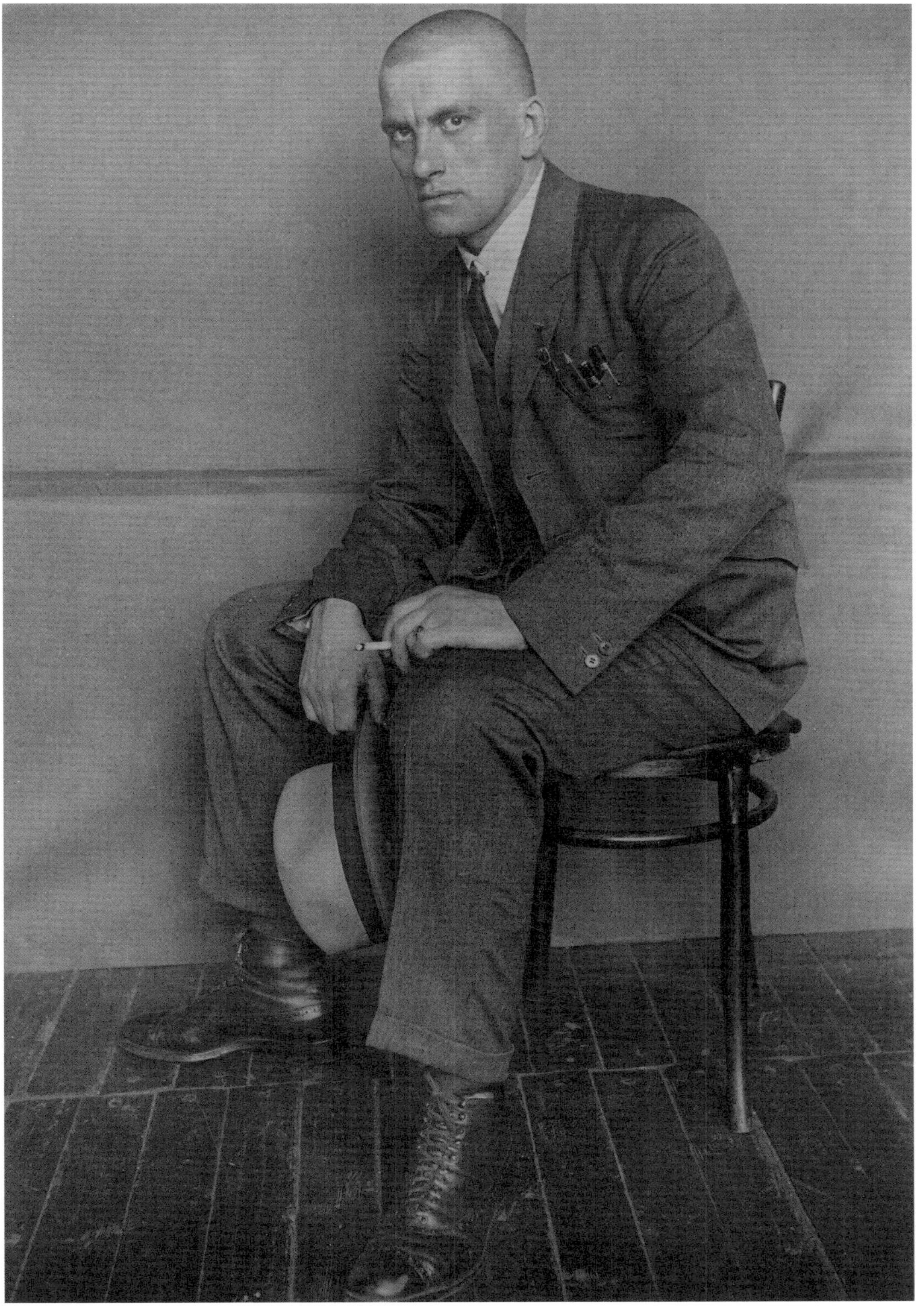

ARTHUR MILLER

born New York, 1915; died Roxbury, Connecticut, 2005

by Dennis Stock

New York, 1964

Arthur Miller was born in 1915 in New York to a well-to-do Jewish family whose fortunes then declined sharply during the Depression. He studied journalism and English literature at the University of Wisconsin. Even though his first Broadway play closed after only four performances, it was to his – and our – good fortune that Miller was willing to try again. Despite this inauspicious start, his subsequent works proved to be highly successful.

A pitiless analysis of conflict lies at the heart of his most celebrated theatrical works. In *All My Sons* (1947) Miller examines the conflict that exists between the generations, while in *Death of a Salesman* (1949) it is the personal and familial conflict encountered by an American Everyman, who dreams of being a self-made man, yet finds himself and his sons ineluctably inadequate. In an interview, Miller recalled that he wrote the first act of this play in single day and night, while the second act took him six weeks. It was through the depiction of failure that he established his extraordinary success.

Miller was also keen to write drama that engaged with contemporary political events, denouncing persecution, whether it be by the Nazis in *Incident at Vichy* (1964) or by McCarthyites in *The Crucible* (1953). Between the lines of *The Crucible* – his depiction of the trials of innocent people convicted of witchcraft in Salem, Massachusetts, and put to death in 1692 – could be seen clear references to the contemporary witch-hunt set in motion by US Senator Joseph McCarthy in the early 1950s to root out supposed Communist influence, activity and espionage.

In *A View from the Bridge* (1955) the conflict became internalized, with the protagonist Eddie Carbone experiencing a passion that contradicts his own moral principles and the best interests of those involved. A personal tragedy from the author's own life would provide the subject matter for *After the Fall* (1964). Between 1956 and 1961, Miller had an unhappy and tempestuous marriage to Marilyn Monroe, who in 1962 died from an overdose of barbiturates. The photographer Dennis Stock caught Miller's tension behind the scenes at the Lincoln Center Repertory Theater in New York while *After the Fall* (inspired by his relationship with Monroe) was being staged for the first time. Miller's next marriage, to Inge Morath, was a happy one. He remained with the Austrian photographer until her death in 2002.

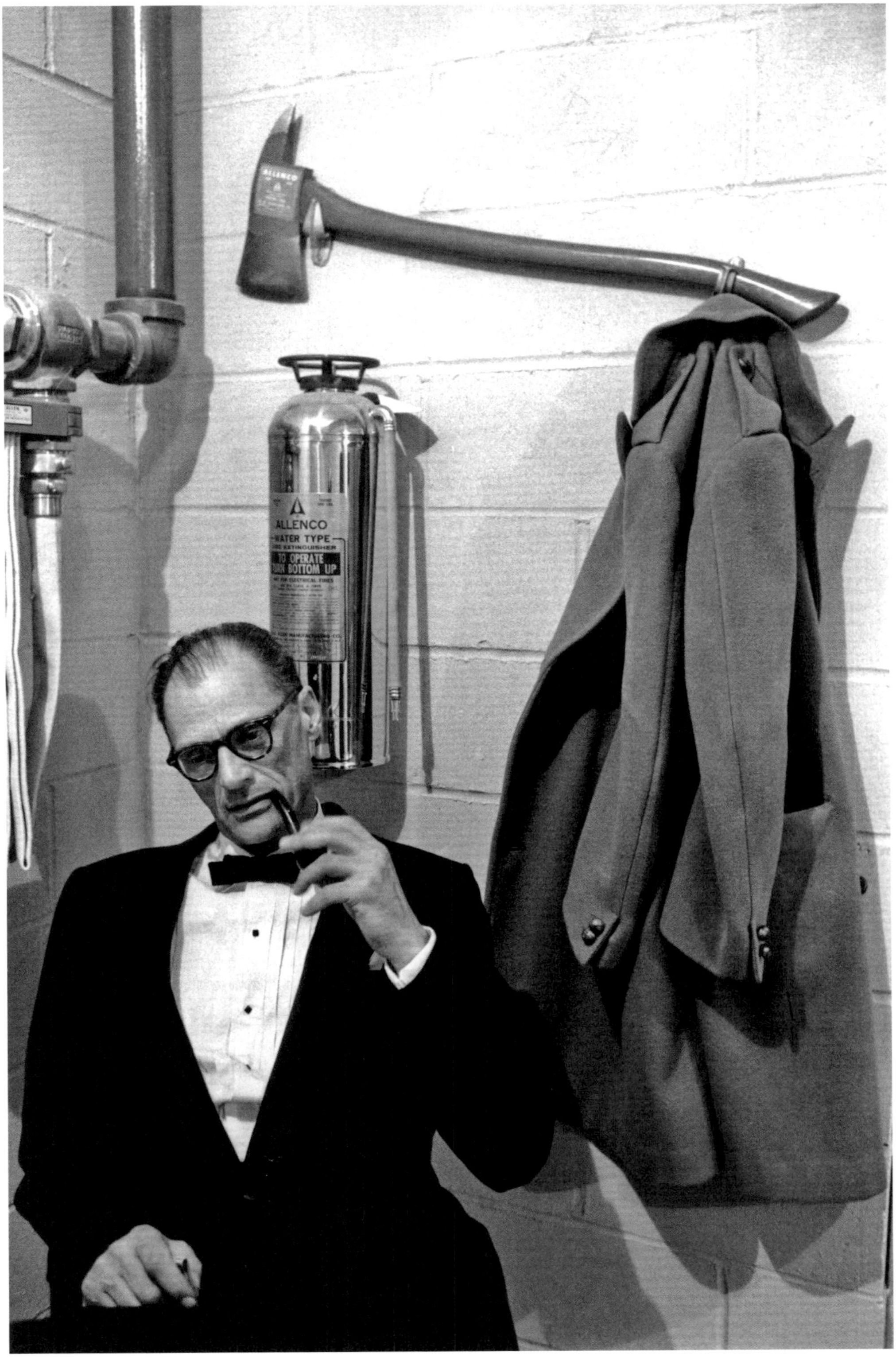
ALLENCO
WATER TYPE
TO OPERATE
TURN BOTTOM UP

HENRY MILLER

born New York, 1891; died Los Angeles, 1980

by Yukichi Watabe

Los Angeles, 1968

'From five to ten ... I lived in the street and acquired the typical American gangster spirit.' This is how Henry Miller – the son of a respectable family – proudly described his Brooklyn childhood. A natural-born rebel, he could not be held by academic life; after just a few months at college he ran off with a woman much older than himself. He did all sorts of jobs to support them and in 1920, when he had already embarked on his first marriage and had a daughter, he at last found a secure post with Western Union and could make his first attempts at writing; however, his early endeavours did not bring him success.

For that, he had to wait until he had married his second wife – the very beautiful and open-minded June Mansfield (who appeared in his novels as 'Mona' and 'Mara') in 1924 – and above all, until he had travelled to Europe and encountered Anaïs Nin in Paris in 1930. If five years on the streets of Brooklyn had been decisive in the education of Miller the man, then the period between 1924 and 1930 left its mark on him as a writer. It was June who convinced him to leave his job to dedicate himself to his art, and it was in the city of Paris that he found his inspiration and his true vocation: 'Paris is simply an obstetrical instrument that tears the living embryo from the womb and puts it in the incubator,' he said. It was in this incubator that his first extraordinary masterpieces emerged: *Tropic of Cancer* (1934), *Black Spring* (1936) and *Tropic of Capricorn* (1939); however, his works could not be published by his compatriots in the USA until 1963, when the Supreme Court ended the long-running controversy about the distinction between pornography and literature with a historic judgement in favour of *Cancer* and *Capricorn*. In the intervening years, Miller's novels circulated secretly, especially in intellectual Beat circles, where they were enormously influential.

Miller returned to the USA in 1942. He settled in California and went on to marry three more times, had two children, painted watercolours and worked on another great trilogy, 'The Rosy Crucifixion' – consisting of *Sexus* (1949), *Plexus* (1952) and *Nexus* (1959). He also wrote an imagined biography of his idol, Arthur Rimbaud, calling the book *The Time of the Assassins* (1956).

In this photograph we see him in his Californian home with his last wife, the young Japanese singer Hiroko 'Hoki' Tokuda. Miller was seventy-six when he fell in love with the cabaret singer, who was then just twenty-seven years old. The two married in 1967 and divorced ten years later. Miller's *Insomnia: or, The Devil at Large* (1974) was dedicated to her.

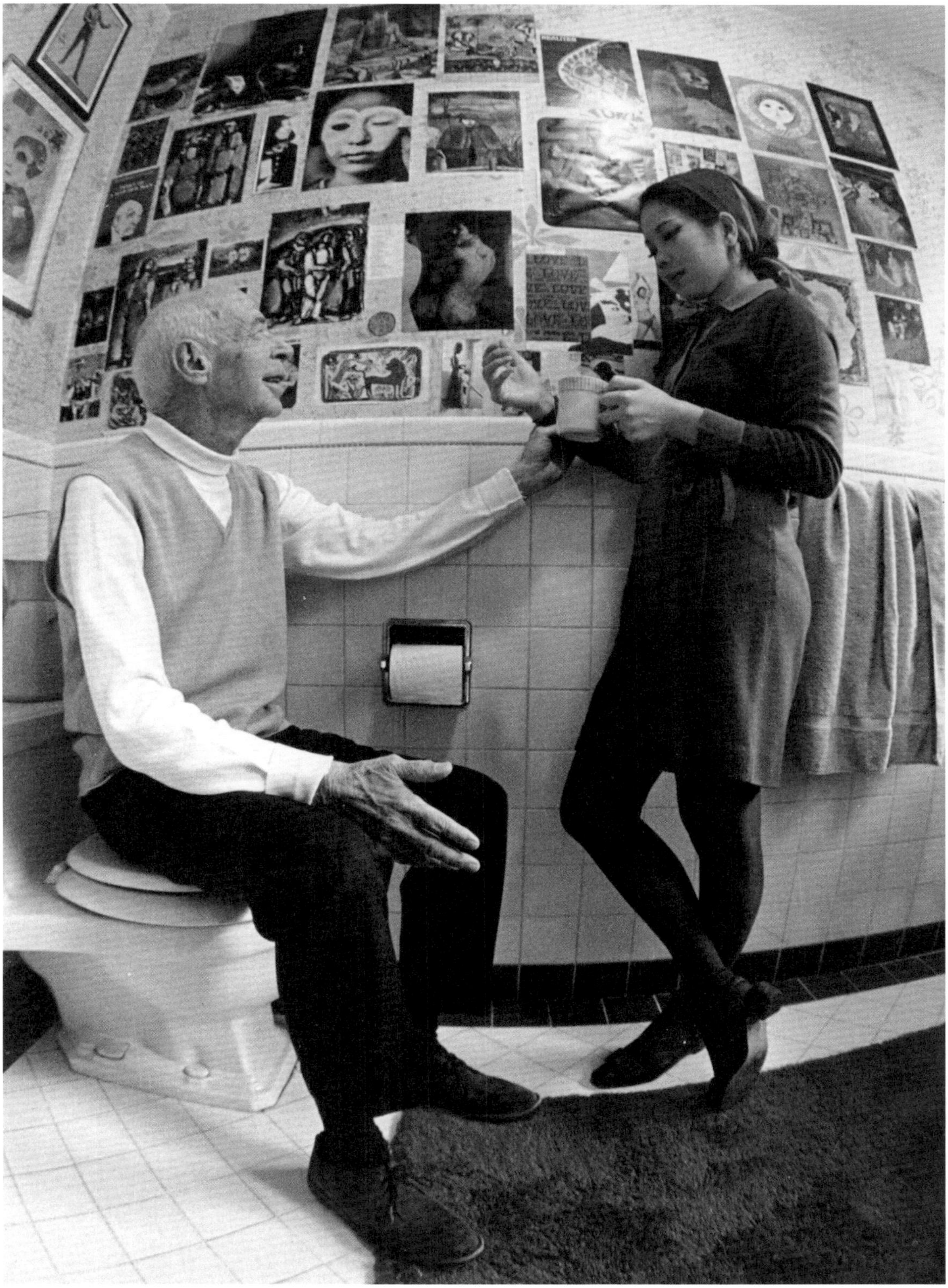

CZESŁAW MIŁOSZ

born Šeteniai, Lithuania, 1911; died Kraców, Poland, 2004

by Horst Tappe

Lugano, Switzerland, 1987

A Polish poet of Lithuanian origin, and a great fighter, Czesław Miłosz, like his own country, caught as it was between Nazi Germany and Communist Russia, lived through the worst events that Europe experienced in the twentieth century. He did so with intense suffering, but with an indomitable moral stubbornness in pursuit of justice and truth. His first poems (such as those, for example, in his collection *Trzy zimy* (Three winters, 1936) foreshadowed the coming catastrophe and were marked, like all his poetry, by the precision of his images and by a metaphysical tension. Throughout his life he continued to ponder the meaning of life, examining it through the mirror of the clash between history and culture.

One Italian writer said of his great poems that they make one feel one is listening to the 'sober chanting of a line of the song' that could also be 'etched with a sharpened stylus onto a tablet or stone'. Miłosz persuades us of the duty to resist the inertia typical of human beings in the face of history, and reminds us of the necessity for human dignity when confronted with a destiny that is both political and concretely historical. The poet espouses a way of confronting life in which the individual is not isolated from the larger community. The poet may make a distinction between these two poles, but he cannot actually isolate them from each other.

After the war, Miłosz sought to avoid being overwhelmed by his country's fate and, finding his freedom of thought and action had become impossibly restricted, chose to go into exile in France. There he was for many years the guiding spirit behind the journal *Kultura*, a mouthpiece for the most important Polish voices that was distributed clandestinely in his homeland. Much later he became a lecturer at the University of California in Berkeley.

The Captive Mind (1953) is a key text for assessing Soviet totalitarianism, while his *Native Realm* (1959) is a mixture of story and essay that helps to explain the history and culture of central Europe. Since Miłosz was awarded the Nobel Prize in 1980, many volumes of his poetry collections were republished, particularly in Kraców in the 1990s, and as abridged editions in other countries. Great Polish poets from Zbigniew Herbert to Wisława Szymborska owed him a great debt, and the determination with which the Polish tradition has tried to hold its ethics and worldview together has become a reference point for young poets in many countries in the new millennium.

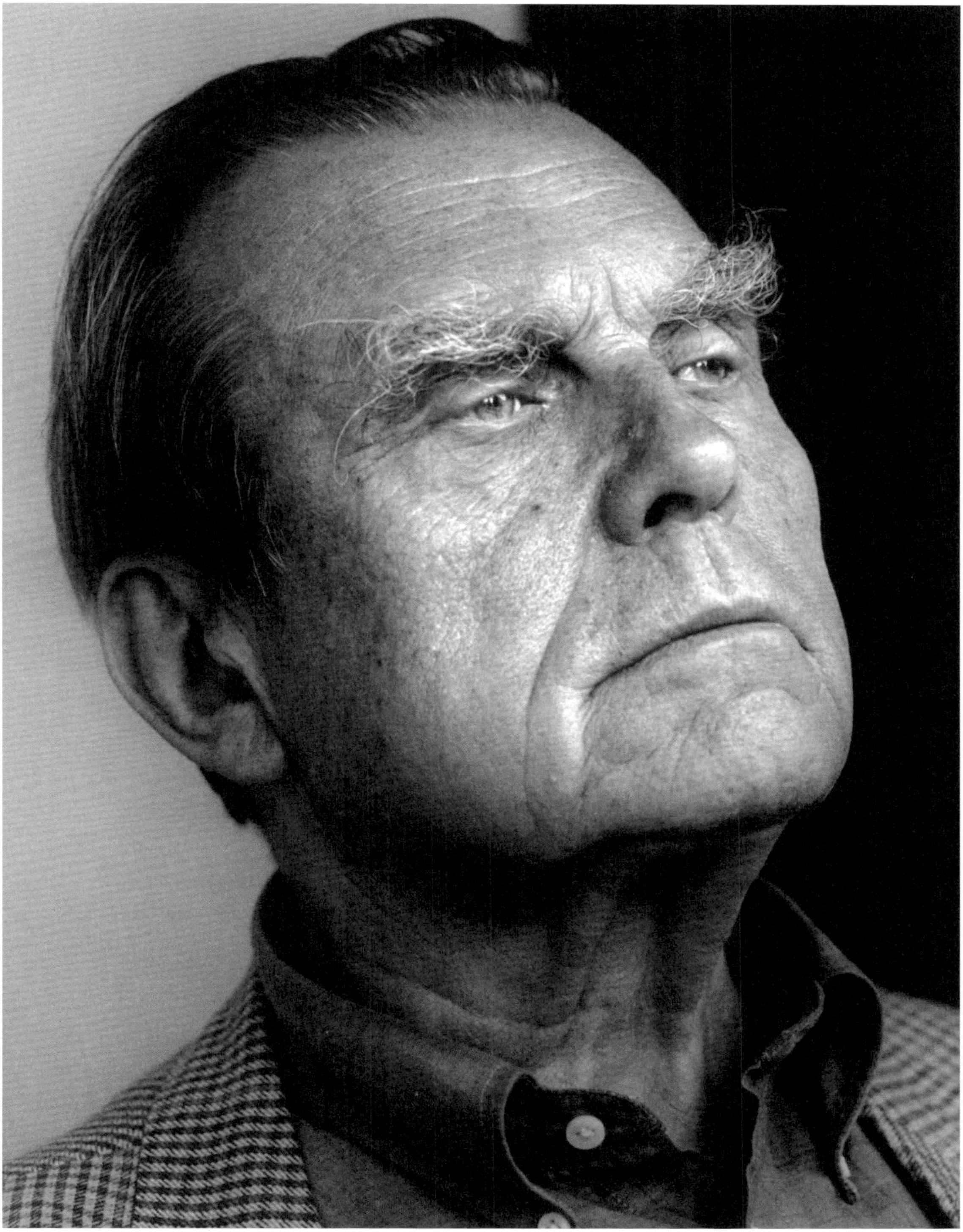

YUKIO MISHIMA

[Kimitake Hiraoka] born Tokyo, 1925; died Tokyo, 1970

by Elliott Erwitt

Tokyo, 1970

In 1970 Kimitake Hiraoka, who wrote under the pseudonym Yukio Mishima, killed himself in a dramatic *seppuku* ritual, following a failed attempt to start a right-wing coup to restore power to the Japanese emperor. Mishima was only forty-five years old and had just completed his series of four novels, *The Sea of Fertility* (1969–71), the apogee of his life's work. 'Words are not enough', he declared moments before committing the act, in a prepared speech delivered to the television news cameras from the balcony of the Tokyo military office that his paramilitary group had seized. Marguerite Yourcenar, in her book *Mishima: A Vision of the Void* (1980), commented that 'certainly Mishima's carefully premeditated death is part of his work.' With this final gesture, Mishima hoped to unite his own cult of the body, obsession with death and respect for Japanese tradition in a single, superior ideal.

A restless, scandalous personality, Mishima grew up under the overprotective control of his aristocratic grandmother, who separated him from his mother for several years and introduced him to art, as he later related in his autobiographical novel *Confessions of a Mask* (1949). He began writing short stories as a schoolboy, against the objections of his parents, and after a brief spell as a bureaucrat, left the civil service to write full-time, producing novels, serials, essays and traditional Japanese drama. Always interested in physical appearance, he worked occasionally as an actor and model and in his thirties developed an obsession with bodybuilding. In 1968 he founded a paramilitary organization called Tatenokai (Shield Society), a group of young men who set themselves up in symbolic opposition to Japan's political and military submissiveness after the end of the Second World War. His anti-conformism, martial fanaticism, Decadentism and struggle to revive the 'traditional spirit' of imperial Japan fascinated (and still fascinates) many with right-wing views, but his ambiguous worldview, which could not be reduced to labels or fitted into prevailing ideologies, also gained him the admiration of intellectuals such as Alberto Moravia and Pier Paolo Pasolini. Ironically, much of what Mishima attributed to the spirit of ancient Japan actually stemmed from European Romantic literature, making him one of the most Western of Japanese writers. He felt at home in the USA, visited Italy, loved the works of Charles Baudelaire, John Keats, Lord Byron, Oscar Wilde and Gabriele D'Annunzio, and was always keen for his own work to be recognized in the West. Mishima's hybrid and elusive nature also revealed itself in the way he used mass communication to transmit his messages and build up his own public personality, right up to the moment of his death.

Mishima's use of traditional Japanese iconography was part of his public persona. In this portrait by Elliott Erwitt, who visited Japan many times, the writer unsheathes a samurai sword in his studio; months later a similar weapon would be used in his ritual suicide.

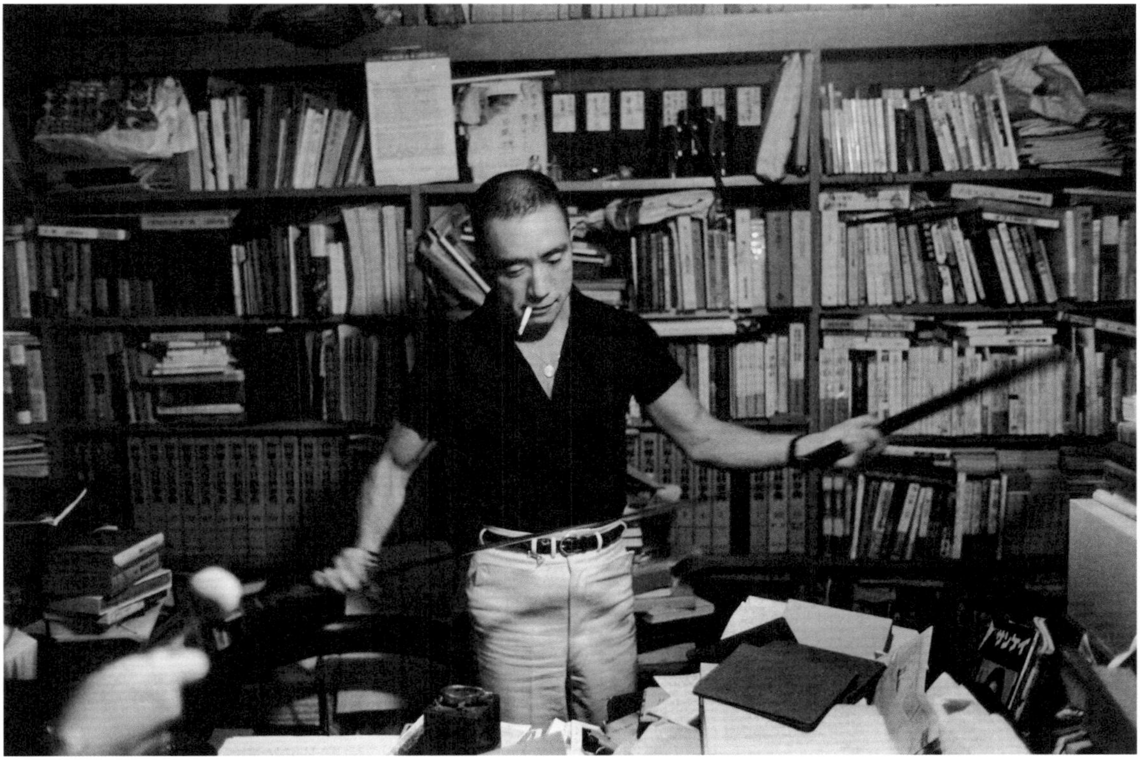
サンケイ

FERENC MOLNÁR

[Ferenc Neumann] born Budapest, 1878; died New York, 1952

by Carl Van Vechten

New York, 1941

In Billy Wilder's film *One, Two, Three* (1961), an unlikely collection of ambassadors, flighty housewives, uninhibited young women and improbable terrorists come together in a joyful blend of truth and fiction in post-war Berlin. In *The Guardsman* (1931), directed by Sidney Franklin, Alfred Lunt and Lynn Fontanne also blur the line between truth and fiction, with Lunt playing a husband who disguises himself as a guardsman in order to check up on his wife, thereby reawakening her fading passion for him. In Michael Curtiz's *A Breath of Scandal* (1960), the ups and downs of a beautiful Viennese princess's various love affairs and marriages are interwoven with affairs of state and hidden intrigues. And in *Liliom* (1934), Fritz Lang tells the story of a shiftless slacker and troublemaker who tries, even after his own death, to find redemption. These films have much in common: a knowing and well-constructed plot, a European setting, and classic *fin de siècle* comic situations in which no one is who he or she appears to be. These films are also, like many other classic products of Hollywood, all based on Ferenc Molnár's comic creations.

Molnár is widely remembered as the author of *The Paul Street Boys* (1907), an uplifting tale of education and high-minded sentiment that has become a classic of children's literature in Hungary. But perhaps his greatest legacy is his screenplays. Rich in irony, they are characterized by perfectly constructed plot twists that, despite their apparent innocence, are attempting to break down social and literary conventions – just like Billy Wilder's masterpieces. Molnár's personal life, however, was far from easy. He was divorced three times, and a loyal governess killed herself reportedly because of him. During the Second World War he was forced to flee his native country to escape persecution by the German authorities, finally settling in the USA, where he was known as Franz Molnár.

A writer himself, Carl Van Vechten bought his first camera in 1932 and soon found that his new passion overshadowed his work as a journalist and novelist. In addition to taking photographs of his fellow writers, actors, musicians and dancers, he had helped to promote the Harlem Renaissance, the cultural and artistic movement of the African American community that spanned the 1920s.

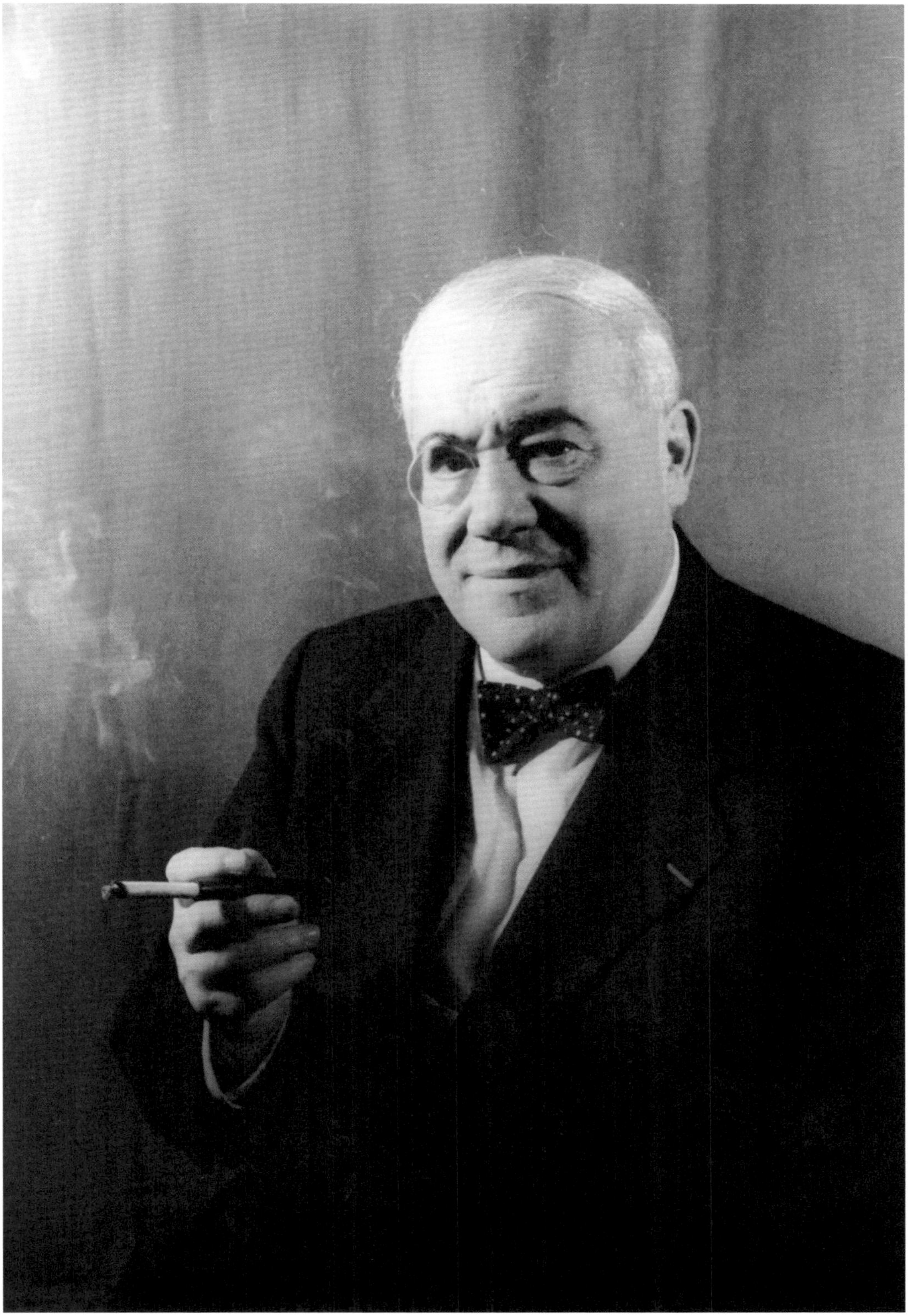

EUGENIO MONTALE

born Genoa, Italy, 1896; died Milan, Italy, 1981

by Ugo Mulas

Milan, Italy, 1970

'Do not ask us the word that may define our formless soul from every side.' In this opening line to one of the poems in *Cuttlefish Bones* (1925), Eugenio Montale's first collection of poetry, Montale warns the reader that it is impossible to find a word that will give meaning to everything, including our lives; rather, we are able to talk about only 'that which we are not, that which we do not want'.

Montale was born and grew up in Genoa, a city that, in the early twentieth century, teemed with poets. Despite the best intentions of his family, who were determined that he should finish school and enter the family business, he discontinued his studies and began to train as an opera singer. However, following the First World War and the death of his singing teacher, he concentrated his efforts on writing, especially poetry. His cultural interests were wide and numerous, from music and literature to art, and, after 1948, he became chief literary critic for Italy's primary newspaper, *Corriere della Sera*. His childhood summers had been spent in a villa in the Cinque Terre, and the countryside of the Ligurian Coast – the sea and the cliffs, the sun and the arid land – all play a powerful role in his poetry.

Montale's writing is characterized by a spare, lean style; he was not an extravagant stylist, but rather a sober, austere bearer of an image. Although he had little faith in the world, he still felt the need to define and to describe it. 'It was often the bad side of life that I encountered', he wrote; however, as the Italian writer Vittorio Sereni pointed out, Montale's poetic genius lay in the fact that despite all his doubts about existence, he was still passionate about life. In 1939 Montale published his second collection of poetry, *The Occasions*; this was followed, in 1956, by a third collection, *The Storm and Other Things*. It was for these two books, together with *Cuttlefish Bones*, that Montale was awarded the Nobel Prize in 1975.

In this portrait of Montale by Ugo Mulas, an Italian photographer renowned for recording Italian cultural and artistic life in the 1950s and 1960s, the writer is pictured face to face with a stuffed bird given to him by the Italian writer Goffredo Parise. It is a hoopoe, a bird whose reputation Montale defended in one of his best-loved poems.

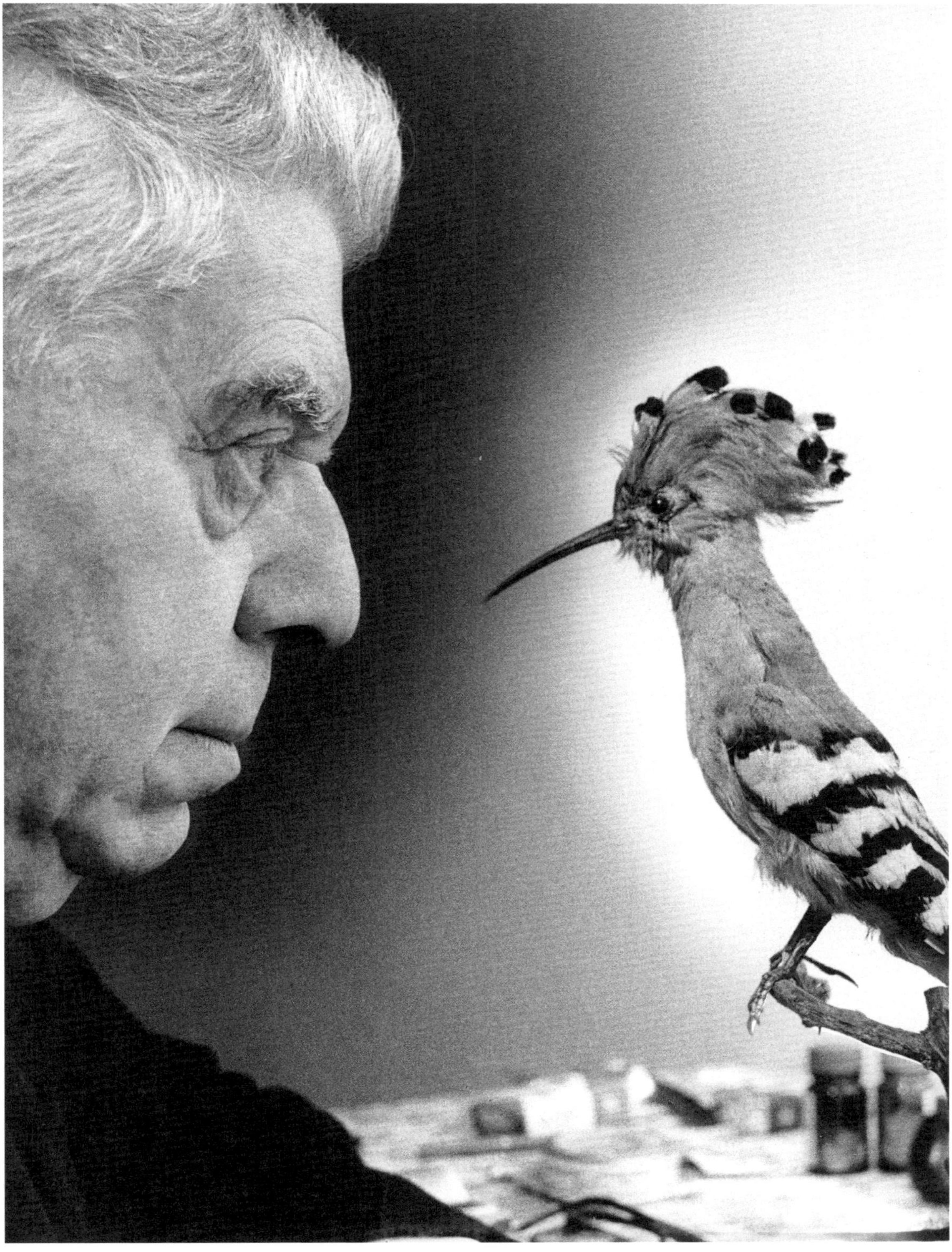

ELSA MORANTE

born Rome, 1912; died Rome, 1985

by Federico Garolla

Rome, 1956

As a girl, Elsa Morante began writing fables and stories for children just a little younger than herself. Her first book of short stories, *Il Gioco segreto* (The secret game), was published in 1941 and a second volume, *Lo Scialle Andalusso* (The Andalusian shawl), in 1963. But it was *House of Liars* (1948), a novel of visionary grandeur, that sealed her reputation. It recounted the story of a family in decline, told by its last heir and set in a magical and oppressive Palermo. In three other novels the author explored and extended the possibilities of the twentieth-century novel. *Arturo's Island* (1957), the story of a childhood spent on an island, confronts the tragedy of self-awareness and the discovery that paradise does not exist; *History* (1974), clearly influenced by her reading of Simone Weil, was both an epic canvas of Rome during the Second World War and a poetic work of maternal protectiveness written to alert the reader to the terrible harshness of history; *Aracoeli* (1982) described a son's frantic attempt to understand his sorrowful and unsatisfied mother.

Morante followed in the wake of the great writers of the past, from Miguel de Cervantes to Fyodor Dostoevsky, Anton Chekhov to Herman Melville. Her knowing literary constructions were filled with fascinating characters set against arcane backdrops, and were more religious than metaphysical in tone. She constantly interrogated the meaning of existence, investigated the beauty of creation and celebrated the joy of being alive, but she also examined the impossibility of achieving complete harmony between nature and society, a relationship she portrayed as being defeated both by human morality and by the violence perpetrated by an ever hostile history.

In 1968 she published a volume of poems, *Il Mondo salvato dai ragazzini* (The world saved by children). This was a declaration of faith in a kind of total revolution against all the fictions and cunning artifices of power; it was also a complex and extremely varied collection, liberated, fascinating and filled with a great variety of influences. Her vision was expressed in protest essays posthumously collected in *Pro o contra la bomba atomica e altri scritti* (For or against the atomic bomb, 1987), which stated that the poet must defend the city from unreality, from the violence inflicted by history, and from ideologies fostered by the fetishes of those in power.

Elsa Morante tried, unsuccessfully, to kill herself, but died a few years later of natural causes. Her message was that that the 'unreal' has conquered the 'real', and that paradise does not exist – we have been driven out of it forever.

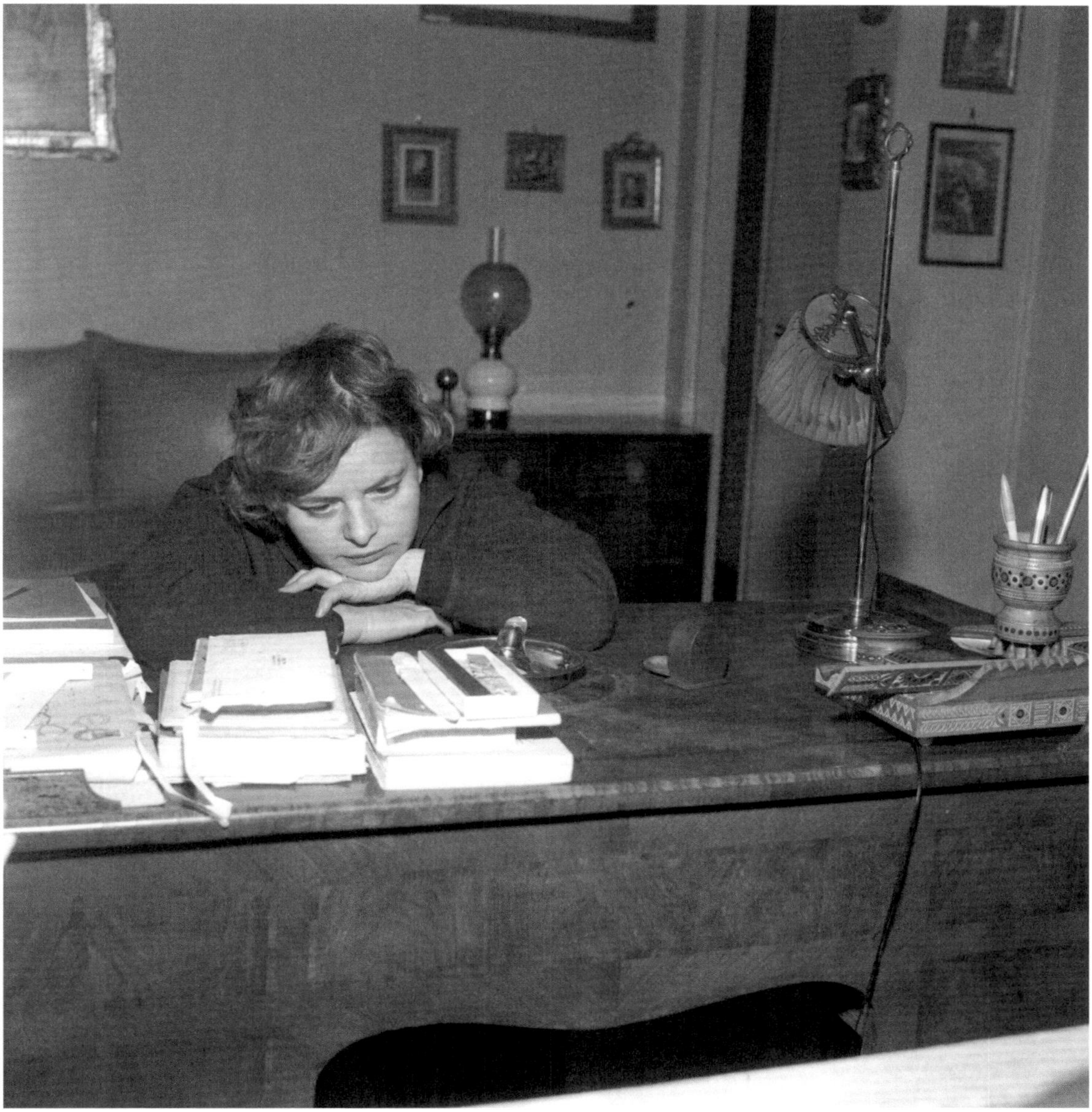

ALBERTO MORAVIA

[Alberto Pincherle] born Rome, 1907; died Rome, 1990

by Federico Garolla

Rome, 1956

Over the course of a career spanning some sixty years, Alberto Moravia addressed many of the issues faced by Italian society throughout the twentieth century. His numerous books, novels, stories, essays, articles, travelogues and plays all attest to his view that life is meant to be lived. When, in 1925, Moravia began writing his first novel, *The Time of Indifference* (1929), he was not quite eighteen years old. Italy was changing around him: the indignation provoked by the murder of socialist politician Giacomo Matteotti in 1924 had already been forgotten, and, in an atmosphere of general indifference, Benito Mussolini was successfully establishing his Fascist government.

Moravia narrates the events of just two days in *The Time of Indifference*, telling the story of stunted lives, an indolent and apathetic bourgeoisie, and a main character who is decaying internally and becomes a reflection of wider social decay. As a member of the bourgeoisie himself, Moravia was able to examine it from a privileged point of view: 'I wrote *The Time of Indifference* because I was inside the bourgeoisie and not outside it. If I had been outside it, as some people seem to think when they attribute various intentions of social criticism to me, I would have written another book. … That *The Time of Indifference* turned out to be an anti-bourgeois book is quite another matter. The fault or credit, above all, belongs to the bourgeoisie itself, to its Italian version in which very little or nothing is susceptible to being inspired. I do not say so admiringly, but rather with a more distant sympathy.'

The Time of Indifference was published to great acclaim, but it also attracted the attention of the Fascist government, which later seized Moravia's novel *The Fancy Dress Party* (1941), a violent satire about an imaginary South American dictatorship, and delayed the publication of *Two Adolescents* (1944). In the 1930s, in order to escape such scrutiny, Moravia travelled extensively as a correspondent for various journals, writing articles under the name 'Pseudo'. In the post-war period he became a major figure in Italian cultural life, known for his writing, his commitment to social issues, his intense friendships with other intellectuals such as Pier Paolo Pasolini, his love affairs with the writers Elsa Morante and Dacia Maraini, his arguments and polemics, and the film versions of some of his stories, including *Woman of Rome* (1954, directed by Luigi Zampa), *Two Women* (1960, Vittorio De Sica), *The Time of Indifference* (1964, Francesco Maselli) and *The Conformist* (1970, Bernardo Bertolucci).

The Italian photographer Federico Garolla photographed Moravia at his home in Rome. At the time the photograph was taken, the writer was having his portrait drawn by Ivy Nicholson, a successful model of the 1950s.

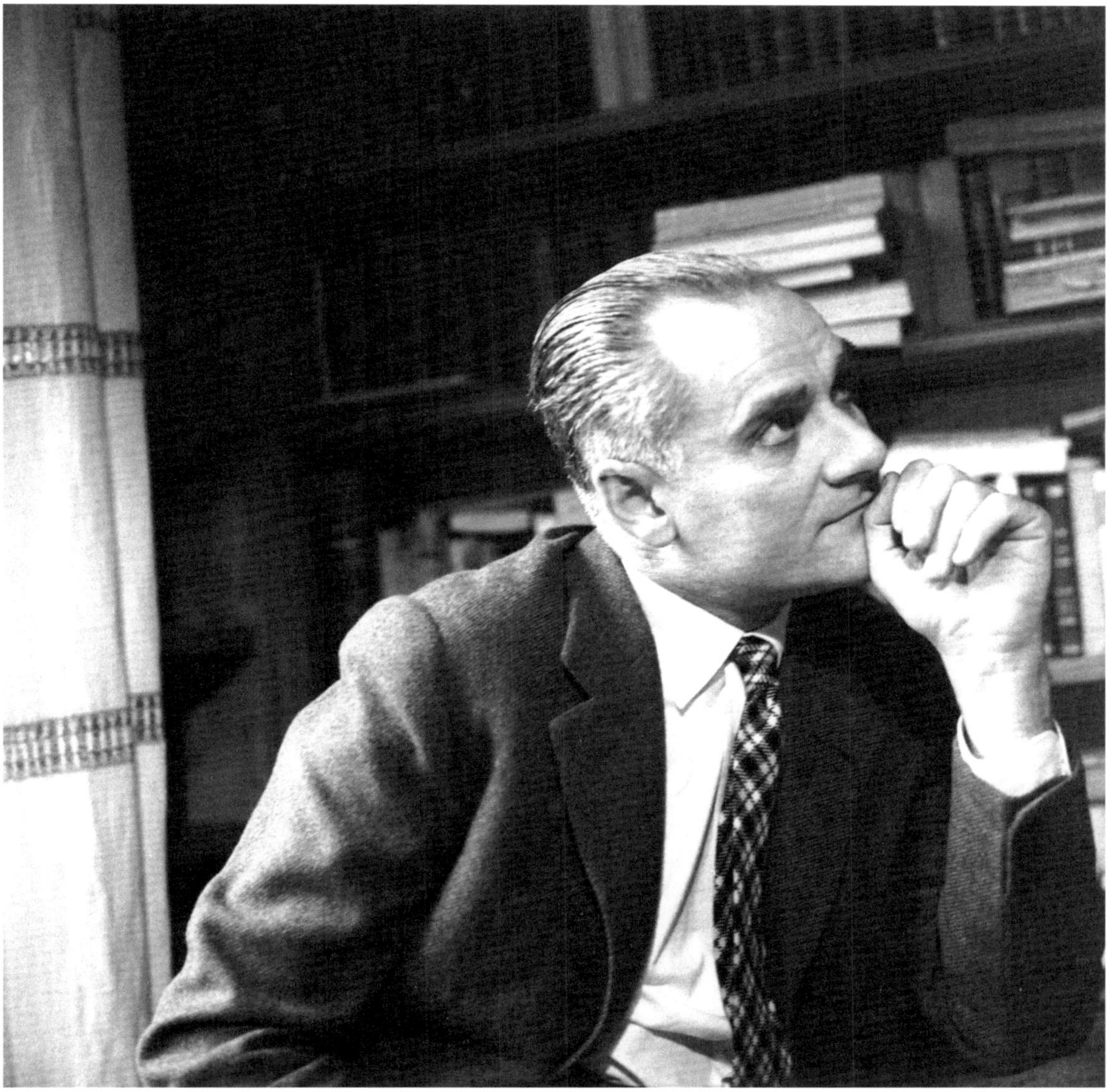

TONI MORRISON

[Chloe Ardelia Wofford] born Lorain, Ohio, 1931

by Eli Reed

Tarrytown, New York, 1993

As a young African American woman growing up in the racially segregated USA of the 1930s, Toni Morrison demonstrated a fierce determination to overcome obstacles, a determination that culminated in her being awarded the Nobel Prize in 1993. Born in a small town in Ohio, she went on to graduate from Howard University in Washington DC, and then from the prestigious Cornell University in New York. Still in her mid-twenties, she was offered a teaching post at Texas Southern University at a time when 'racial integration' had not even been heard of. She would later work as an editor for Random House and as a critic. In an interview given in 2008, she explained how her compulsion to write had emerged in the 1960s. As African Americans began to proclaim 'black is beautiful', she felt the need to remember the time when 'black was hurtful'.

Morrison's first novel, *The Bluest Eye* (1970), tells the story of a young black girl who dreams of having blue eyes like Shirley Temple's. When the time came to put her name to the book, she decided to combine her old nickname from school, 'Toni', with the surname of her ex-husband, the Jamaican architect Harold Morrison. *The Bluest Eye* was closely followed by *Sula* (1973), *Song of Solomon* (1977) and *Tar Baby* (1981). In these early works, Morrison uses a poetic narrative voice to tell of the various struggles for black identity, incorporating the oral tradition learned from her father when she was a girl. In 1988 her fifth novel, *Beloved*, won the Pulitzer Prize for fiction. One of the mostly highly acclaimed novels of the era, it tells the story of Sethe, a former slave who is haunted by the ghost of the young daughter she killed rather than see enslaved.

Eli Reed was the first black photographer to be employed by the Magnum photo agency. He has dedicated a large proportion of his work to photographing the black community, including for the volume *Black in America* (1997). This portrait of Morrison was taken at her home on the Hudson River in New York State.

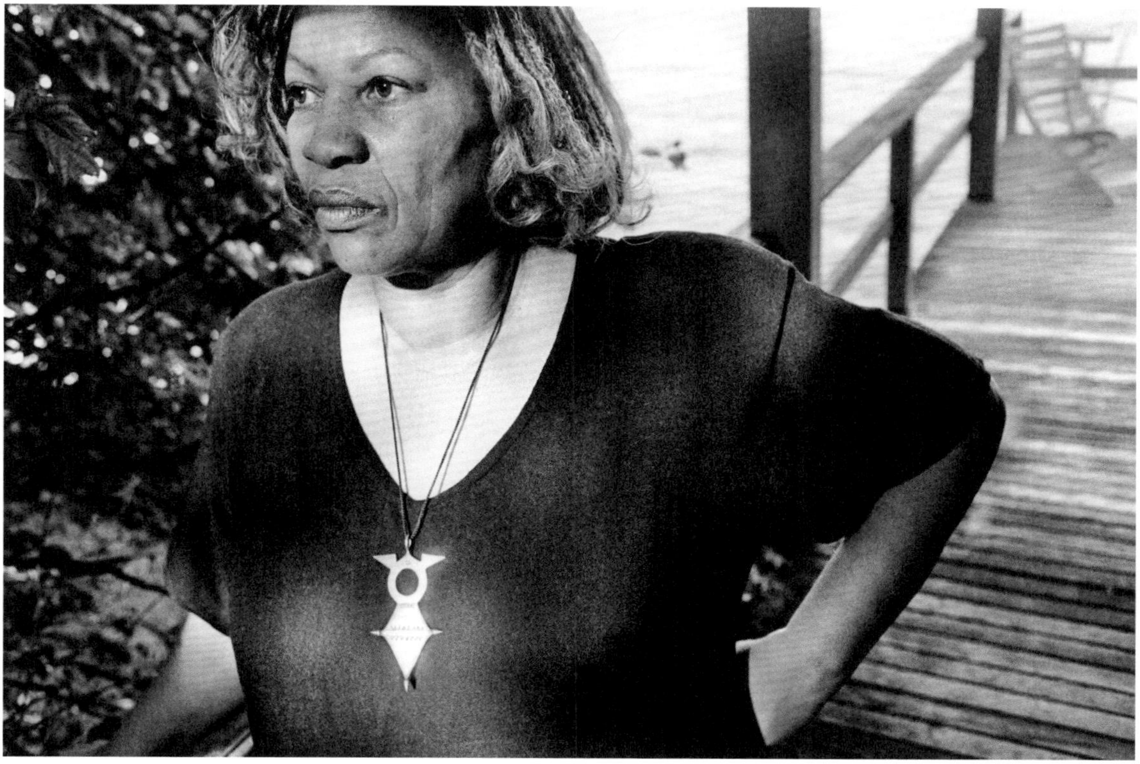

MO YAN

[Guan Moye] born Gaomi, China, 1955

by Günter Glücklich

Hamburg, Germany, 2009

In 2012 the Nobel Prize was awarded to one of the most influential writers ever to have emerged from rural China, Mo Yan (a pseudonym that translates as 'he who does not speak'). At the time of the award, he was still living in Gaomi, the village in which he was born, and which has shaped his literary world. The Swedish Academy awarded him the prize for his luxuriant prose, which 'with hallucinatory realism merges folk tales, history and the contemporary'.

The award, however, was not without controversy. As vice president of the pro-establishment China Writers' Association, Mo Yan has been criticized for not doing more to secure the release from prison of the literary critic, writer and human-rights activist Liu Xiaobo. Defending his position on the matter, Mo Yan explained: 'For a writer, the best way to speak is by writing. You will find everything I need to say in my works. Speech is carried off by the wind; the written word can never be obliterated.'

Certainly, Mo Yan's dense and unique style, rich in metaphor, provides an ideal vehicle for political themes. In the novel *Frog* (2009), he uses the story of a rural midwife to explore the Chinese government's contentious one-child family planning policy. The epic saga *Red Sorghum* (1987) chronicles the lives of three generations of the Shandong family, beginning in the 1930s amid the Japanese invasion of China; in 1987 the book was adapted into a film by Zhang Yimou. *Sandalwood Death* (2001) is the story of an act of rebellion, of passion for art and of the horrors of torture. It ends with a lengthy description of the wounds inflicted by an elderly executioner enjoying the last task of his gruesome career. Although the novel is set in China in the early twentieth century, the evocative power of Mo Yan's prose enables the issues of power and violence to resonate beyond the confines of the story.

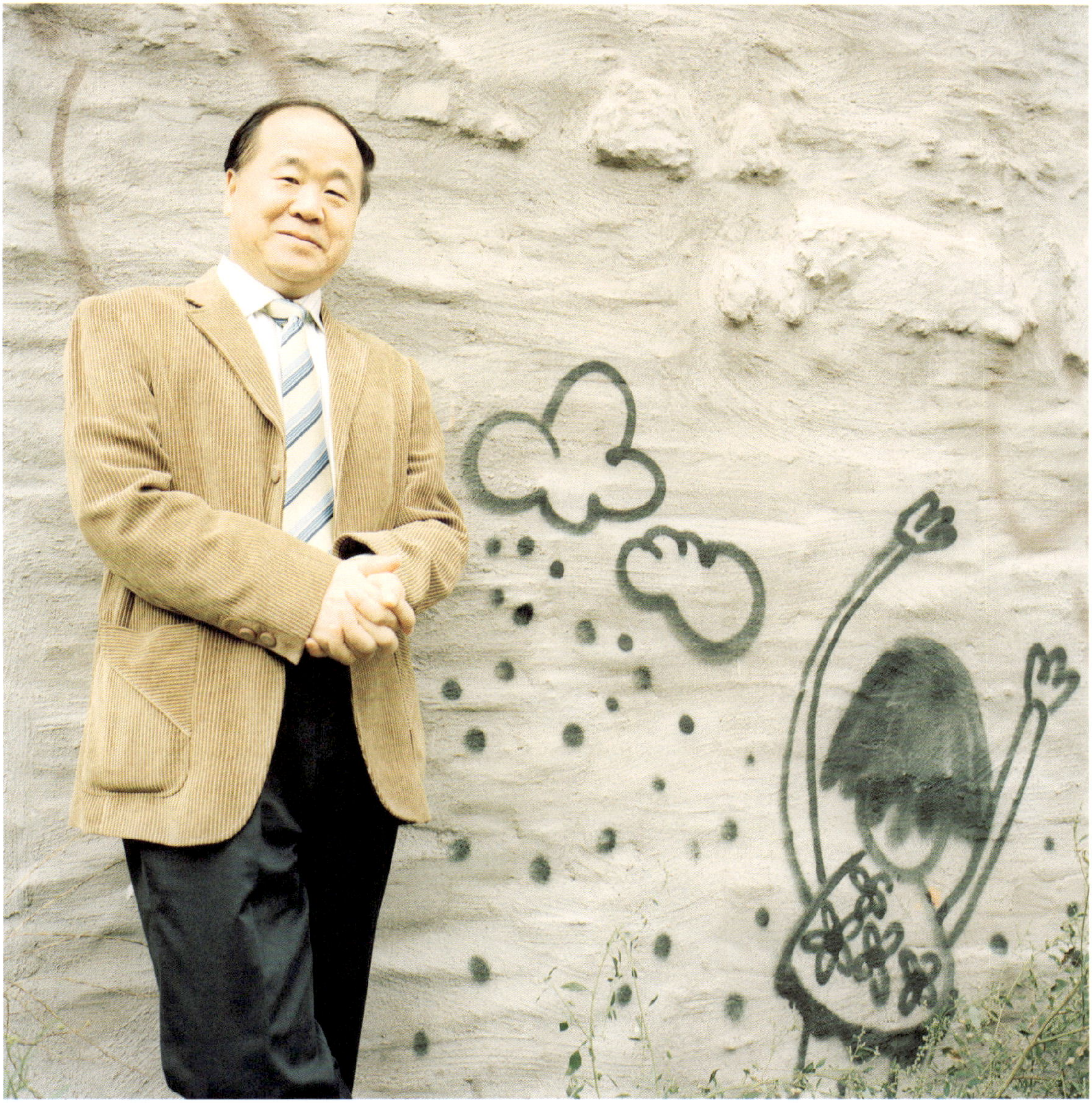

HERTA MÜLLER

born Nitchidorf, Romania, 1953

by Vincent Mentzel

Amsterdam, 2010

In her novel from 1989, *Travelling on One Leg*, Herta Müller tells the story of a once-deft acrobat and her search for a cultural and geographical identity. In common with her protagonist, Müller has performed a balancing act for much of her life, as a writer caught between two worlds: Romania and Germany, East and West.

Müller was born into a German-speaking family in the Banat, a former region of the Austro-Hungarian Empire that had become part of Romania in the wake of the First World War. She was just twelve years old when Ceauşescu took power in 1965, but her parents' experiences during the Second World War had already made her aware of the corrupting and destructive power of ideology (her father had volunteered for the Waffen SS, while her mother had been deported to the Soviet Union by Stalin's regime to perform five years of hard labour). From 1973 to 1976 Müller studied German and Romanian literature at the University of Timşoara, where she joined the Aktionsgruppe Banat, a group of dissident writers opposed to Ceauşescu's dictatorship.

As a result of her refusal to collaborate with the regime, and because she was both a German on Romanian soil and a writer 'at the margins', she was subjected to intimidation and violence. In 1979, while working as a translator, she was approached by the Securitate, the Romanian secret police, who asked her to become an informer; she refused, and subsequently lost her job. When, in 2004, she obtained the 914-page dossier that the Securitate had kept on her, she discovered that she had been labelled 'a dangerous enemy of the State who should be combated', and that her code name was 'Cristina'.

In 1987 Müller emigrated to West Germany. Her sense of being an outsider, however, remained. *The Foreign View, or Life Is a Fart in a Lantern* (1999) is told from the point of view of someone who feels as though he is being held hostage, far from home. For Müller, literature is a form of salvation, and she uses her own life as source material for what she calls her 'autofiction'. In many of her novels, such as *Nadirs* (1982), *The Land of Green Plums* (1993) and *The Appointment* (1997), Müller draws on not only her own story but also that of her country, her dry, pared-back style offset by a powerful and surprising use of metaphor and imagery. In 2009 Müller was awarded the Nobel Prize.

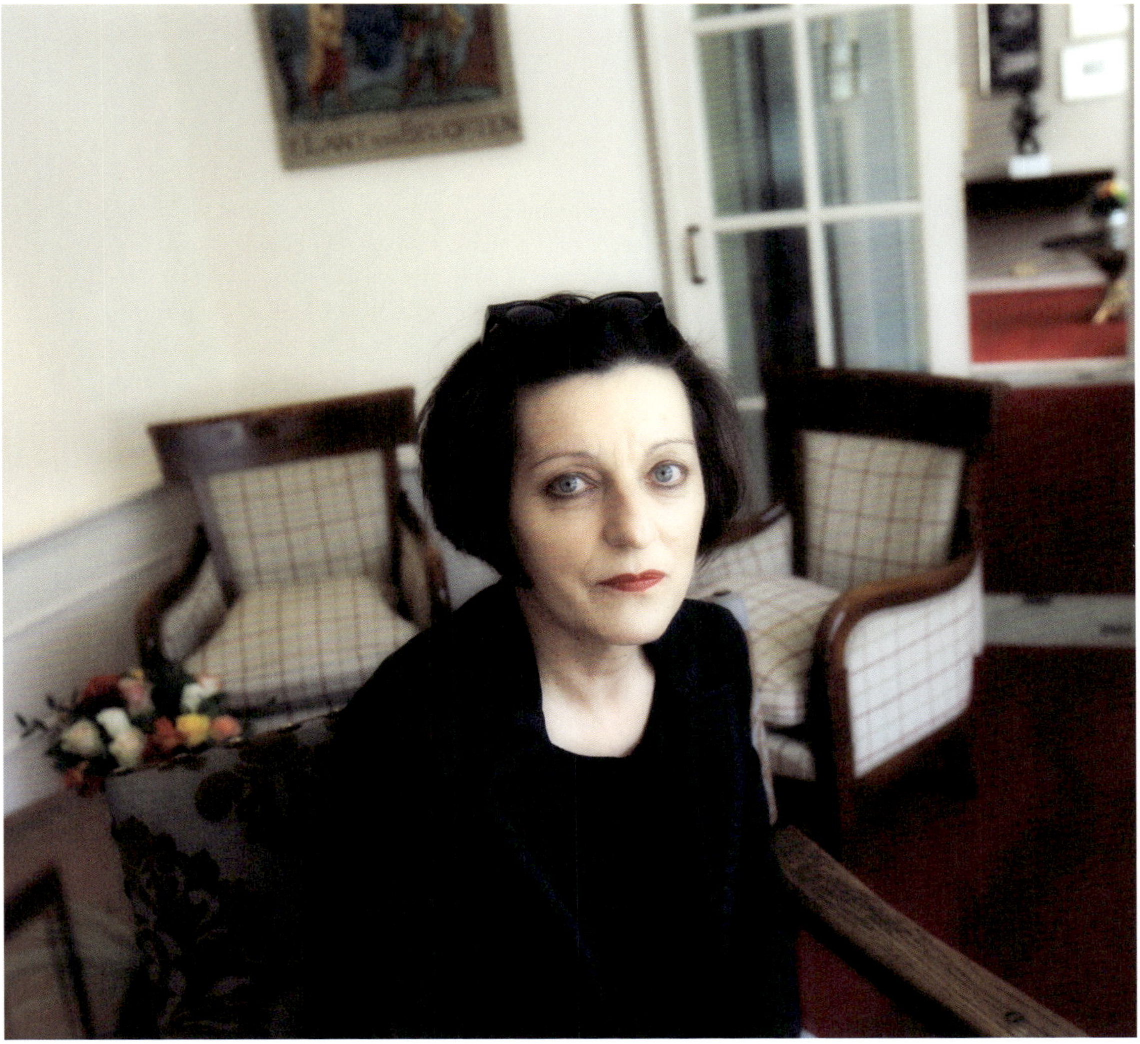

ANTONIO MUÑOZ MOLINA

born Úbeda, Spain, 1956

by Alberto Conti

Mantua, Italy, 2002

What is a generation such as Antonio Muñoz Molina's to do? A group born in the middle of the 1950s, who spent their youth in a reactionary and repressive country, who were then catapulted into the modern world during a period of suddenly accelerated progress? One reaction was to write, and, through writing, to attempt to link the present once again to the past in literature.

Until Franco's death, much of Spain's past was still taboo. The 'fratricidal' civil war could be interpreted from only one perspective, a perspective that devalued any version of events related by those who had been defeated. Muñoz Molina wrote *A Manuscript of Ashes* in 1986 as a direct contradiction to this historical monologue. His novel moves between the present and the past, overlapping individual and collective memory with the authoritarian (but not authoritative) diktat of history.

The novel's young protagonist, Minaya, flees from Francoist persecution and takes refuge in Mágina, an imaginary city. Muñoz Molina admits that 'I invented Mágina to tell myself the story of the events of my own life and those of my elders with a degree of intensity and the possibility of distance that only fiction could give me.' Once there, Minaya pursues the traces of the Republican poet Jacinto Solana, who was executed in 1947, over twenty years before. Solana is to be the subject of the young man's academic dissertation. In the course of Minaya's literary and historical investigations, the people he questions tell him their own versions of the poet's story: history is thus gradually deconstructed and becomes polyphonic. Halfway between fiction and essay, the novel rescues the past for the generations still to come: 'They, children of forgetting, were unaware that the pine groves and red-brick buildings they walked past had been a battlefield thirty years earlier.'

The city of Mágina reappears in his other novels, as does the Spanish Civil War *In the Night of Time* (2009). In this more recent novel the war is seen through the eyes of an architect from Madrid who, having been invited to work at an American university, chooses to remain there in exile. The theme of exile had already appeared Muñoz Molina's earlier novel, *Sefarad* (2001). In it, exiled characters watch the changing cartography of Europe in the 1930s and 1940s, as the old continent falls under the yoke of various totalitarian regimes. Their exile allows these events to be seen from afar with clarity and sometimes detachment, as well as providing a space for the events to be re-evaluated and take on new significances. In its journey beyond the borders of Spain, this novel reflects on the nature of power and highlights the risks still being run today by a 'civilized' world that carelessly continues to take things for granted.

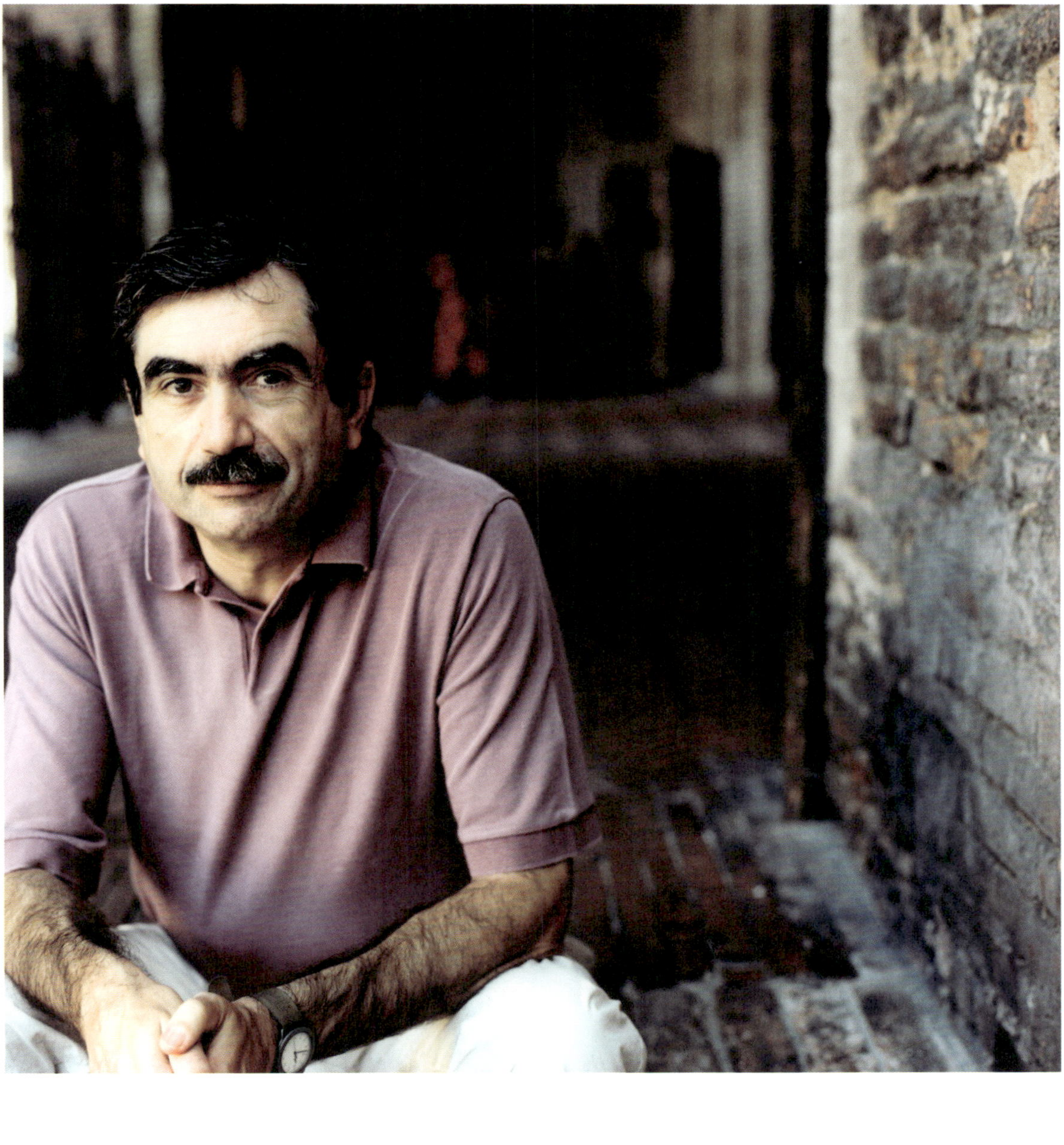

ALICE MUNRO

[née Laidlaw] born Wingham, Canada, 1931

by Peter Sibbald

Clinton, Canada, 1994

In this photo by Peter Sibbald, Alice Munro appears to us as a gentle and kindly middle-class woman, seated in the garden of her home, an expression of calm on her face. But it is this very quality, that of an inner contentment, which might take her readers by surprise.

Munro, a Canadian citizen from the rural province of Ontario, who has chosen to live in Clinton (a town of not more than three thousand inhabitants) in the house in which her second husband was born, seems very far removed from the stereotype of the cursed or blessed storyteller. Yet, in her apparently straightforward stories, life always unravels in an unexpected way, and the denouements are often so banally tragic that they take our breath away.

Even as a teenager Munro knew that she wanted to write, and, taking the great women authors of the past as her model, in particular Emily Brontë, she used every spare moment to write down her fantastical and eventful stories. She was still a young woman when she married a fellow student, James Munro, moved to Vancouver and became the mother of three daughters. But she never stopped writing, and in 1968 her first collection of short stories was published: *Dance of the Happy Shades*. Several other collections have followed since then, including *Something I've Been Meaning to Tell You* (1974), *The Moons of Jupiter* (1982)and *The Love of a Good Woman* (1998), as well as a novel, *Lives of Girls and Women* (1971). Her stories are mostly about young women in search of their own identity, and mothers suffocated by their complex and difficult daily lives – although she says she does not think of herself as a feminist writer per se. Her other subjects include divorce, loneliness and the effects of growing old and of time passing.

Munro's style has often rightly been compared to the kind of narrative progression found in Chekhov's stories. Her outwardly measured writing is able to pierce through seeming normality to reveal the darker aspects underneath. Nothing is predictable in her work, and if life is fundamentally absurd, then in Munro's writing the elements that make up our lives combine to create a powerful, if sometimes discordant, symphony.

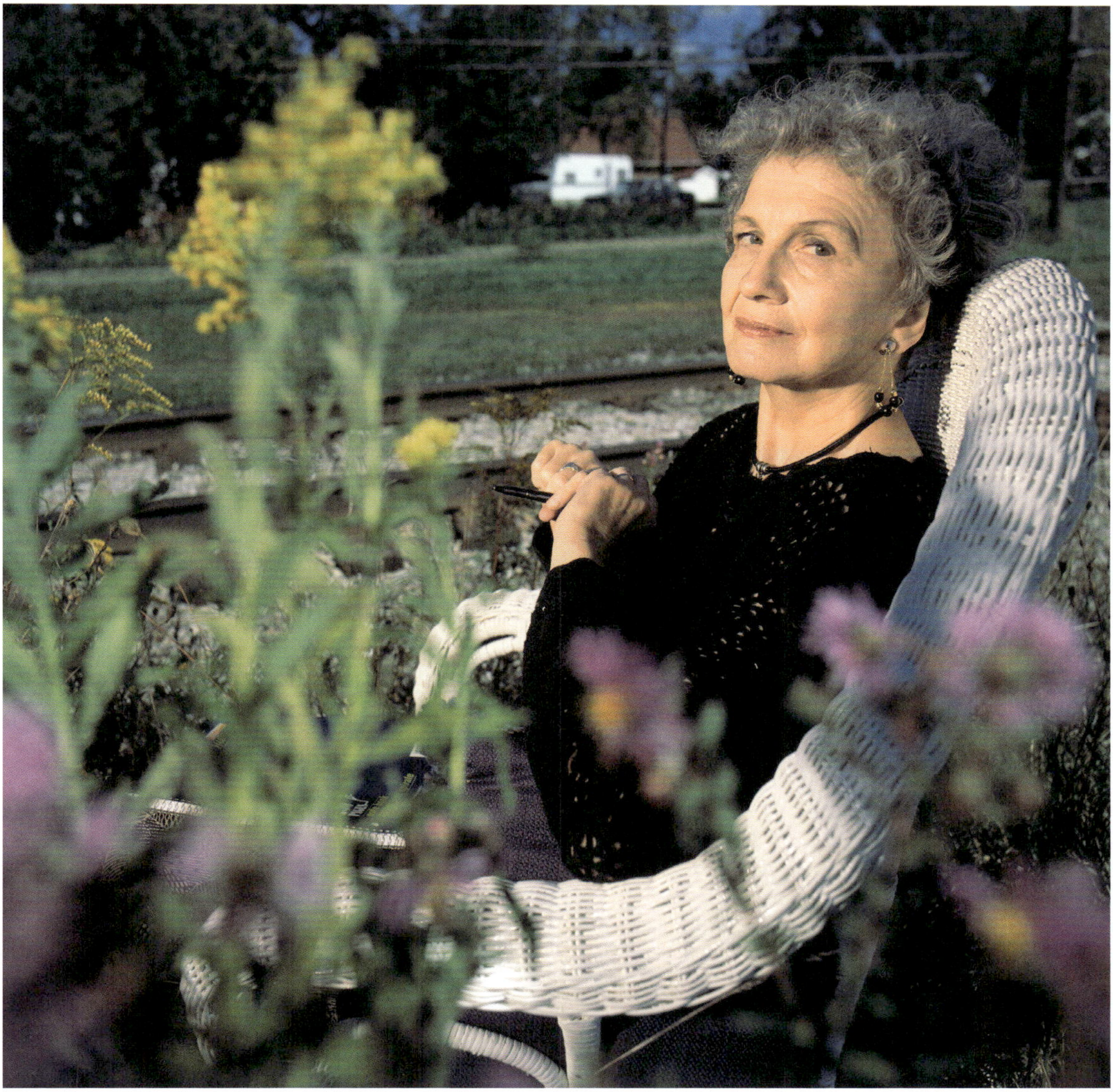

HARUKI MURAKAMI

born Kyoto, Japan, 1949

by Marion Ettlinger

New York, 1992

'I once had a girl, or should I say, she once had me.' So sang the Beatles in their hit song 'Norwegian Wood (This Bird Has Flown)' (1965), the title of which Haruki Murakami adapted for the title of one of his best-loved books. Published in 1987, *Norwegian Wood* soon became a literary sensation, achieving record sales. This story of impossible love between a young man and the fiancée of his best friend who has committed suicide, told through flashbacks and set against a background of the student protests of the late 1960s, brought an almost forty-year-old Japanese author to the world's attention. His refreshing style attracted considerable interest – both in Japan and further afield – and he quickly became a literary reference point for a transitional generation of young adults who not only recognized themselves in him but also identified with the sense of melancholy, uncertainty and social unease that permeates his stories.

Born in 1949 in Kyoto, Japan, Murakami has always tried to follow his own, sometimes anti-establishment path, thereby creating his own voice. He married his first wife before finishing university, against his parent's wishes, and, after completing his studies, opened a jazz bar, where he spent his time preparing drinks, reading books during quiet periods and observing other people. This somewhat unconventional apprenticeship helped to give rise to his signature style: a mix of edgy sensibility, affectionate irony and frequent references to music.

In each of his books, from his first novel, *Hear the Wind Sing* (1979), to *A Wild Sheep Chase* (1982), *The Wind-Up Bird Chronicle* (1994–95) and the best-selling trilogy *1Q84* (2009–10), Murakami's characters move through complex and highly structured plots. The books are also laced with literary quotations, European references and the necessities and yearnings of love – a state often portrayed by Murakami as the only one in which it is possible to endure the world.

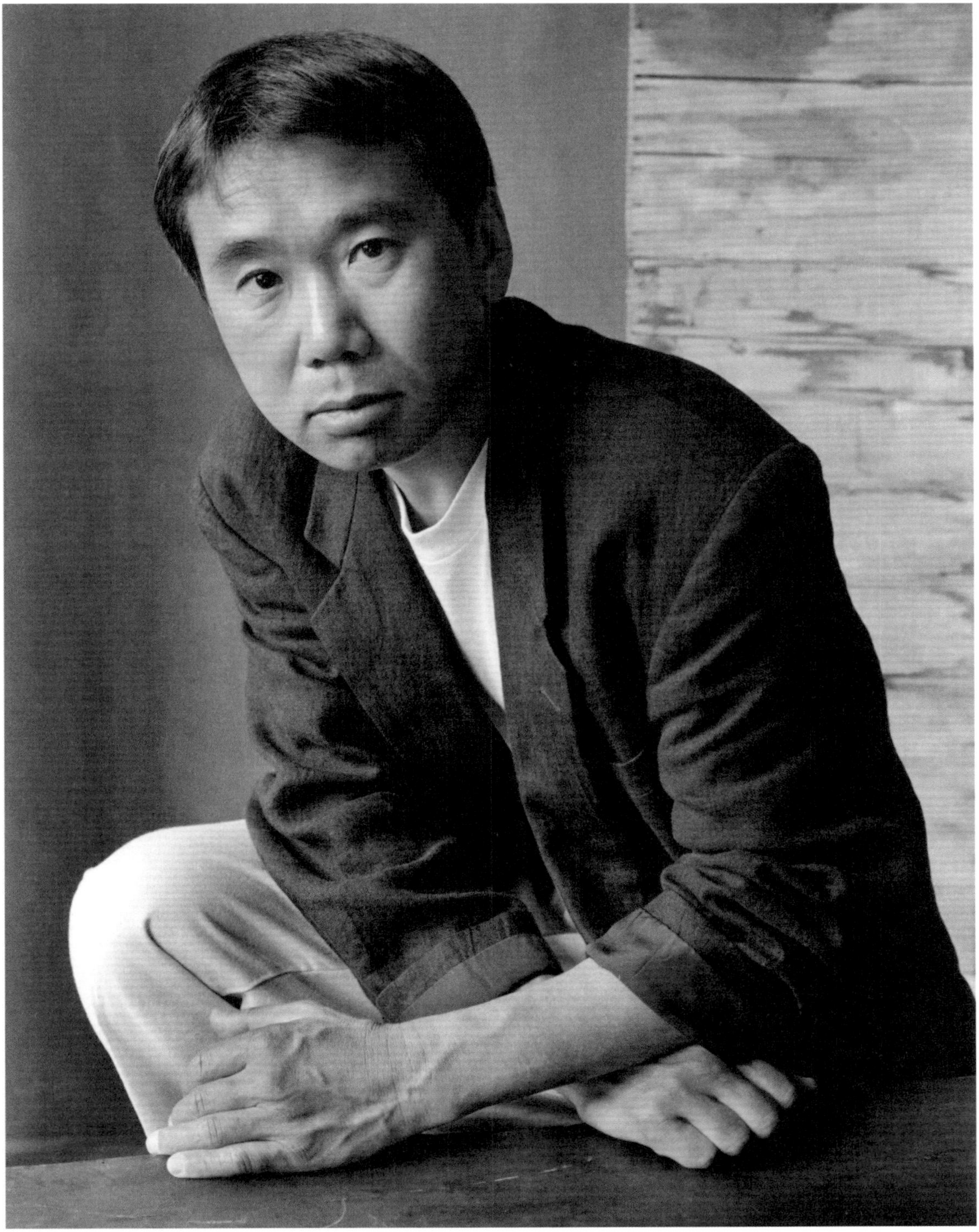

IRIS MURDOCH

born Dublin, 1919; died Oxford, UK, 1999

by Lord Snowdon

London, 1980

In July 1998, an edition of the *New Yorker* featured an article entitled 'Elegy for Iris'. Written by Iris Murdoch's husband, the British writer and academic John Bayley, it described, in both vibrant and moving prose, how Alzheimer's disease had caused such irreversible changes to the life he shared with his celebrated and much-loved wife.

Murdoch had been the prototypical intelligent, free-thinking writer; she was brilliant and non-conformist, attracted by philosophical thought and its potential power, and was someone who delighted in inventing stories that were both bitter and comic. Born in Dublin, she spent the majority of her life in England. In 1938 she won a scholarship to study at Somerville College, Oxford, where she read classics. She returned to academic life almost a decade later, this time to study philosophy at Newnham College, Cambridge, where she briefly met Ludwig Wittgenstein.

Murdoch's first book, the philosophical text *Sartre: Romantic Rationalist* (1953), and her first attempt at fiction, *Under the Net* (1954), appeared in print at almost the same time. This double debut reflects perhaps better than anything else Murdoch's rich and fascinating personality; indeed, it was her ability to move from philosophical investigation to storytelling that brought her to the public's attention. She created her plots by alternating between philosophical reflections and almost banal observations, mixing typical twentieth-century middle-class concerns with existential anxieties, all of which were powerfully informed by her own life. Her whole approach, which was seasoned by her taste for the ironic and her refined intelligence, had no equal.

After three years of increasing confusion and forgetfulness, Murdoch was diagnosed with Alzheimer's disease (as her mother had been before her) in 1997. She had initially hoped to use the disease to her advantage, by incorporating the chaos that had begun to take over her mind into one of her books, but her condition quickly deteriorated. Her husband's passionate eulogy is both a record of her tragic end and an aching love letter to his soulmate: 'Every day, we are physically closer; and Iris's little "mouse cry", as I think of it, signifying loneliness in the next room, the wish to be back beside me, seems less and less forlorn, more simple, more natural. She is not sailing into the dark: the voyage is over, and under the dark escort of Alzheimer's she has arrived somewhere. So have I.'

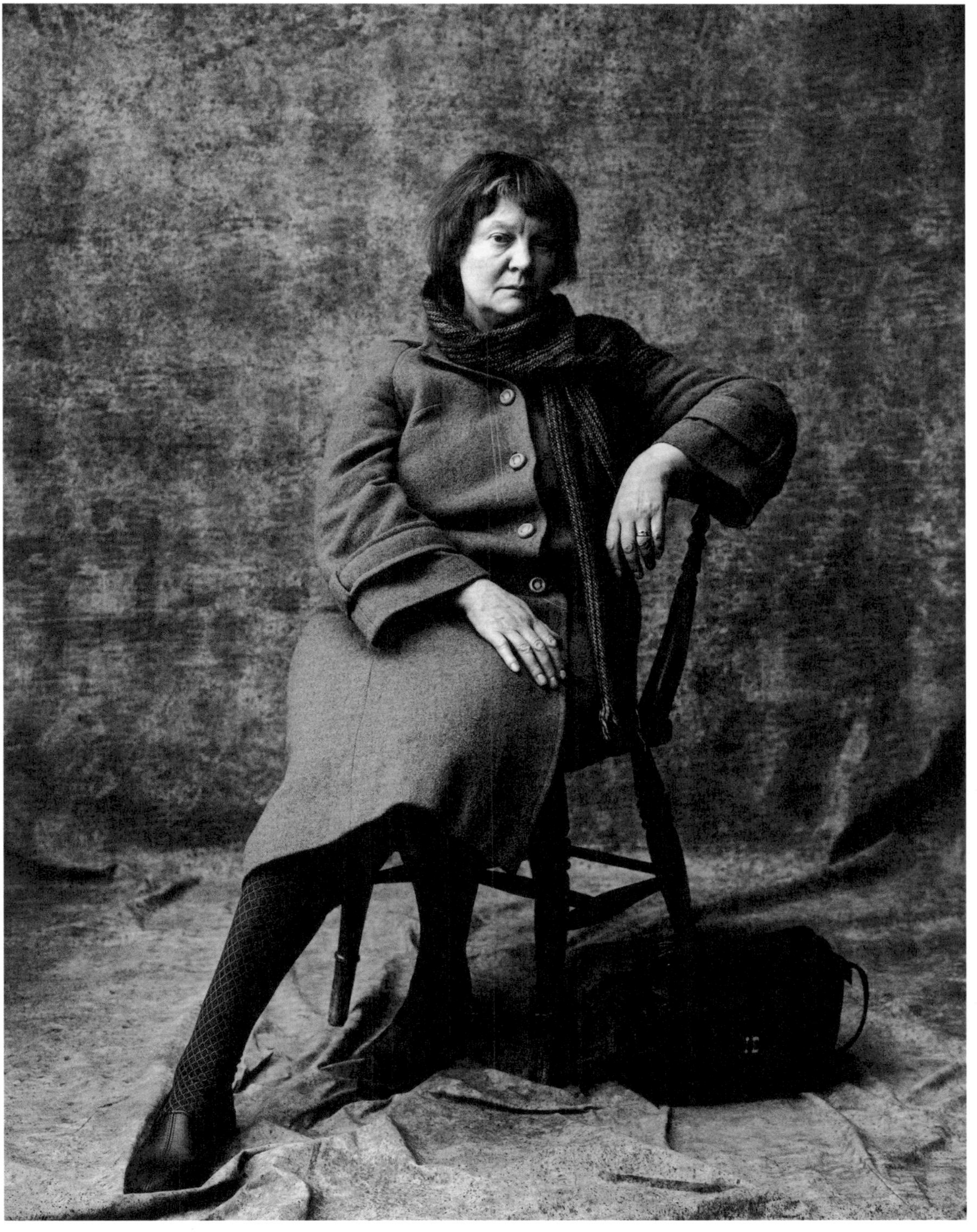

ROBERT MUSIL

born Klagenfurt, Austria, 1880; died Geneva, 1942

by Friedrich Rauch

unknown location, c. 1930

In 1932 the Prussian Academy decided to elect Gottfried Benn to its poetry section rather than Robert Musil, on the grounds that Musil was 'too intelligent to be a poet'. Elsewhere, in a letter to his friend Gershom Scholem, the German writer and philosopher Walter Benjamin quipped that Musil was 'a little more intelligent than necessary'. Such were some of the surprising indictments of a highly intelligent and thoughtful writer, a man who was arguably more of a philosopher than a storyteller. In many ways Musil resembles Ulrich, the main protagonist of his colossal, unfinished masterpiece, *The Man without Qualities* (1953–60). Consisting of three volumes and some seventeen hundred pages, this labyrinthine novel follows Ulrich as he attempts to reason his way through a precarious existence.

The son of an engineer, Musil followed a number of paths before becoming a writer. His family found the young Musil hard to control, and between the ages of twelve and seventeen he was sent to various military boarding schools, including the infamous military academy at Mährisch-Weisskirchen. Musil referred to his time at the academy as 'the year of the devil', and this and his other school experiences would form the basis of his first novel, *The Confessions of Young Törless* (1906). Abandoning any thoughts of a military career, Musil trained instead as a mechanical engineer. However, he soon became tired of engineering, and turned to the study of philosophy, psychology, mathematics and physics at the University of Berlin.

After completing his doctorate in 1909, Musil declined a position at the University of Graz so that he could concentrate on his writing, including his unfinished opus. Begun in 1921, *The Man without Qualities* would be the work of a lifetime, one that absorbed all his creative energy. As his hero Ulrich lived to think, Musil lived to write. For him, it was a necessary, open-ended and continuous process akin to an intellectual pilgrimage. It was also an attempt to make sense of a world that, with the collapse of the Austro-Hungarian Empire, was changing all around him.

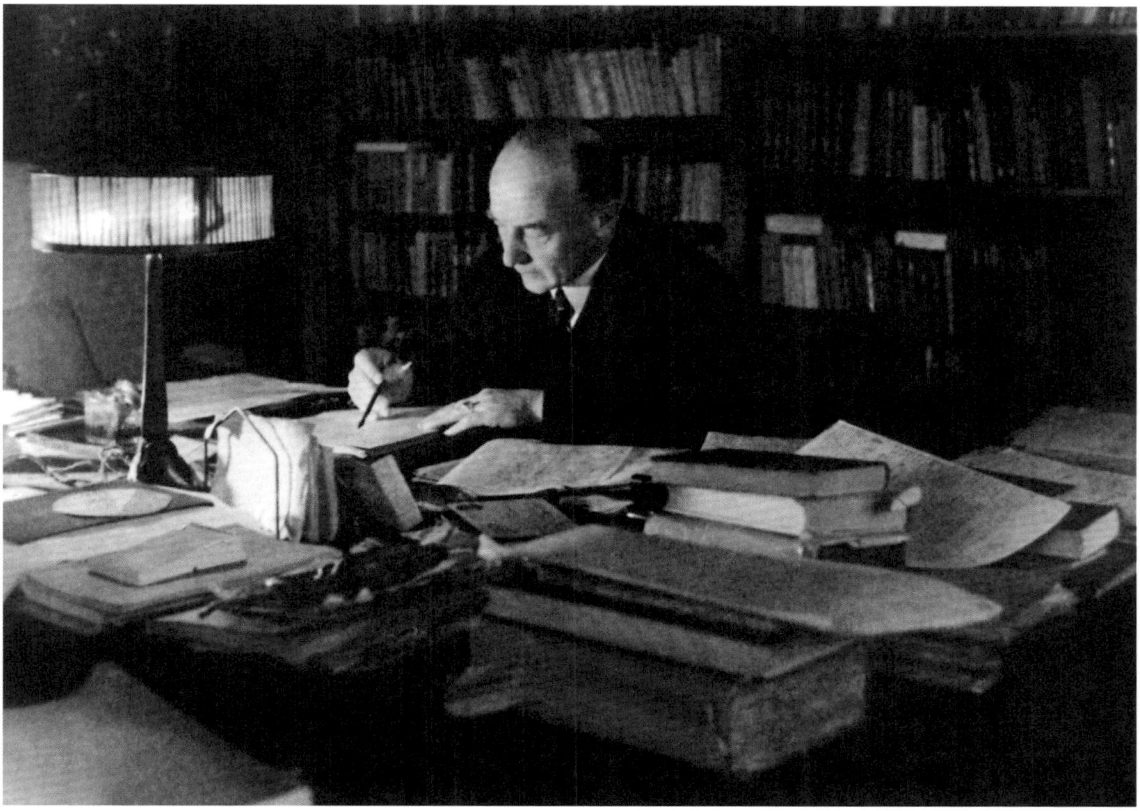

VLADIMIR NABOKOV

born St Petersburg, 1899; died Montreux, Switzerland, 1977

by Philippe Halsman

Montreux, Switzerland, 1966

In his book on the Russian writer and political dissident Eduard Limonov, French author Emmanuel Carrère explains the cool reception towards Nabokov among Russian exiles living in the USA at the end of the 1950s: 'Their bête noir was Nabokov, not because they were shocked by *Lolita* (well, just a little), but because he had stopped writing émigré novels for other émigrés, turning his broad back on their rancid little world.' To add insult to injury, he had also stopped writing in his native Russian.

Nabokov was born in St Petersburg at the turn of the twentieth century, into a cultured family of minor nobility. Brought up in a trilingual household, he learned to read and write in English before Russian. In 1919, in the wake of the October Revolution, the family went into exile, living briefly in England before settling in Berlin in 1920. Between 1919 and 1923 Nabokov studied at Trinity College, Cambridge, an experience that would later form the basis of his novel *Glory* (1932). In 1922 his father was assassinated in Berlin while attempting to protect the real target, a leader of a Russian political party in exile; this tragedy would reappear in a number of Nabokov's works, especially *Pale Fire* (1962). It was while living in Berlin that Nabokov first began to write, initially in Russian. His early novels were Symbolist in style, and bore a resemblance to those of Kafka and Dostoyevsky.

In 1940 Nabokov fled to the USA to escape the Nazis. While in Manhattan he made the acquaintance of the influential literary critic Edmund Wilson. In 1941 he began working as lecturer at Wellesley College, near Boston. The income from this post enabled him to spend time writing, studying and indulging in his favourite hobby: collecting butterflies. He became a renowned entomologist, and made many trips across the world with his wife, Véra, to collect specimens. It was during these travels that he wrote arguably his most accomplished work, *Lolita* (1955). Written in refined and complex English, it was deemed scandalous at the time owing to its portrayal of a relationship between a middle-aged man and a twelve-year-old girl. Nevertheless, it brought its author fame and financial success, and was followed shortly afterwards by the semi-autobiographical novel *Pnin* (1957). Nabokov's fame increased when Stanley Kubrick adapted *Lolita* into a film in 1962.

By this time Nabokov had returned to Europe and was living in Montreux. Philippe Halsman photographed him there in 1966, a butterfly net in his hand. He remained in Montreux until his death in 1977. As one of the most inventive and original stylists of the twentieth century, the author of not only novels and short stories but also poetry, drama and works of literary criticism, Nabokov exerted a profound influence on Western literature in the post-war era.

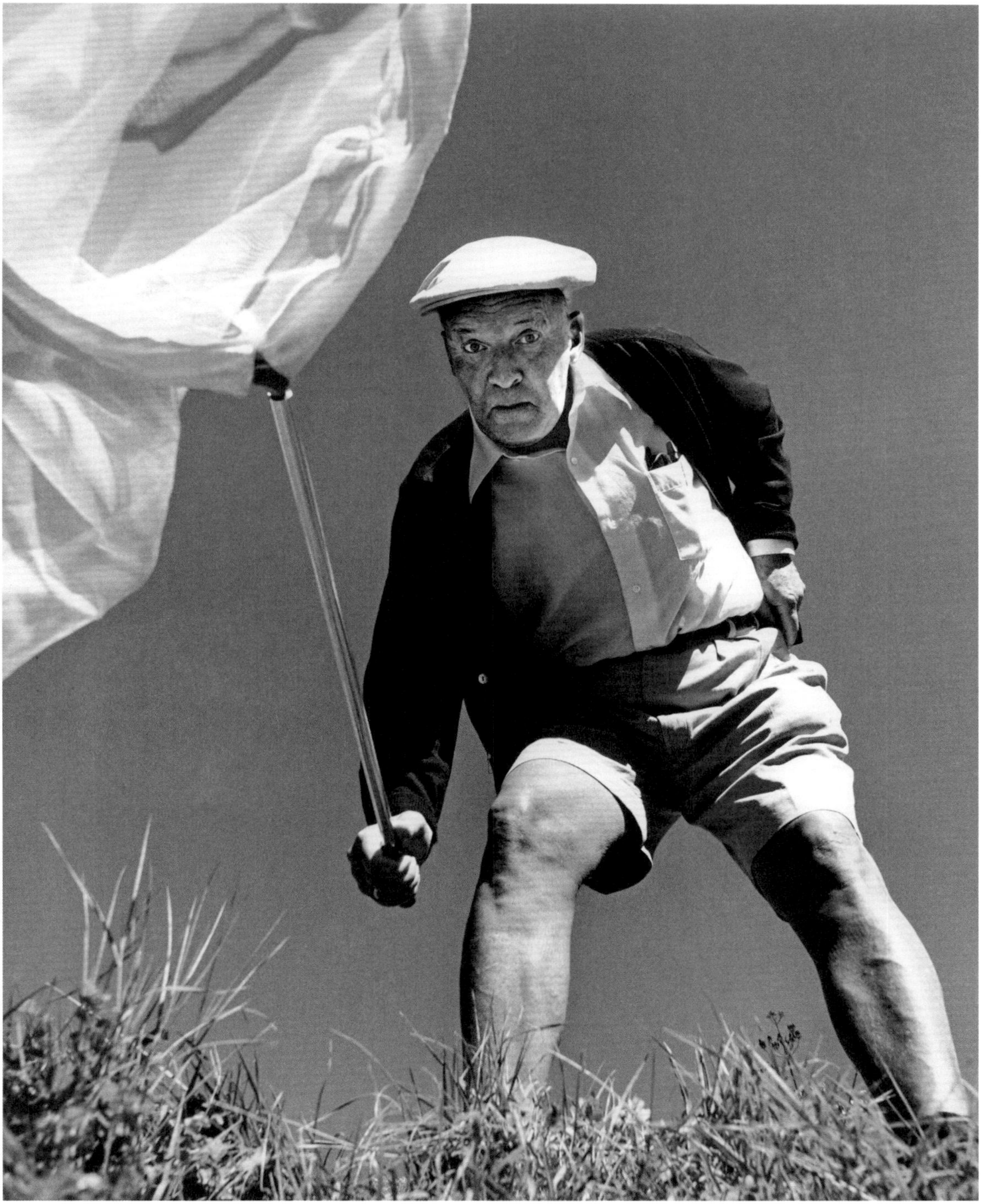

V. S. NAIPAUL

Chaguanas, Trinidad and Tobago, 1932

by Lord Snowdon

London, 1979

Born in Trinidad to parents of Indian descent, Vidiadhar Surajprasad Naipaul has been a major contributor to the post-colonial debate. A controversial writer, he has been heavily criticized for his radical interpretation of religious fundamentalism, while such books as *Among the Believers: An Islamic Journey* (1981) and *Beyond Belief: Islamic Excursions among the Converted Peoples* (1998) have led to accusations that he is anti-Islam. His books describing his travels in the developing world, especially in Africa, also contain contentious assertions regarding that continent's apparent lack of development. He has also been accused of misogyny, on account of certain public declarations he has made about women, and owing to aspects of his personal life. Naipaul is a complex figure, lauded by the South African writer J. M. Coetzee as 'a master of modern English prose', but attacked by many others, including the poet Derek Walcott, for his polemical ideas.

Naipaul has always distanced himself from politics, preferring to be thought of as an independent observer and literary man. To some extent his opinions have struck a chord with those in the West who are apprehensive of developments in the East, yet paradoxically he has also shown concern for the lost roots of societies that have been dominated by colonialism down the ages. His works are written from an unusual perspective, and his vision is fresh and penetrating. He has been hailed as one of the greatest British writers of the twentieth century, and in 2001 he was awarded the Nobel Prize 'for having united perceptive narrative and incorruptible scrutiny in works that compel us to see the presence of suppressed histories'. This is particularly true of the semi-autobiographical *Miguel Street* (1959), and of *A House for Mr Biswas* (1961), an autobiographical novel set in Trinidad, in which the main protagonist is based on his father.

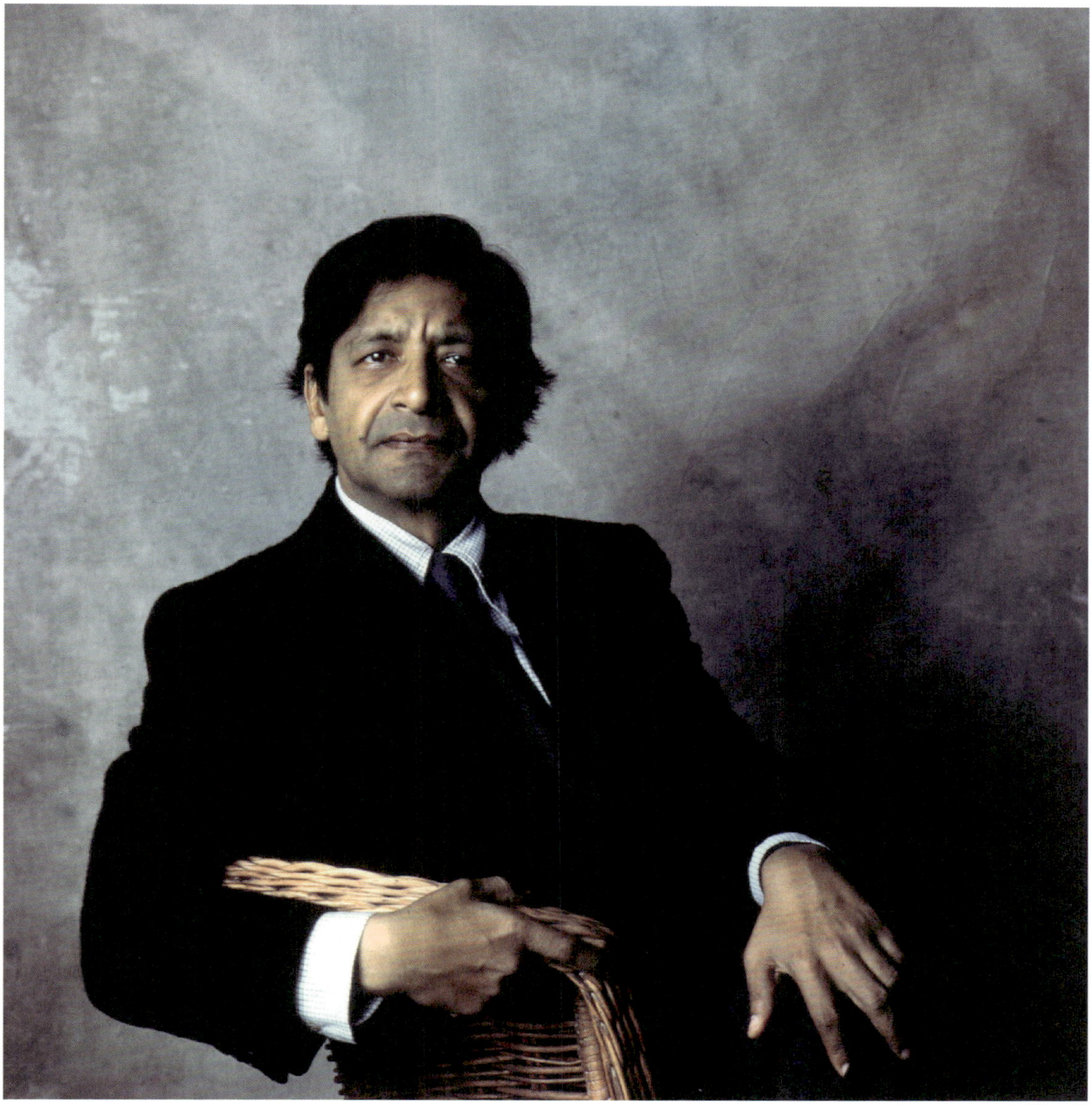

IRÈNE NÉMIROVSKY

born Kiev, Ukraine, 1903; died Auschwitz, Poland, 1942

by Albert Harlingue

Paris, 1938

David Golder was a businessman of Jewish descent who lived in France. Extremely rich and ruthless, he cultivated friendships for his own selfish ends and, up until the twilight of his life, he had thought of nothing but his business affairs. Golder is the cynical protagonist of a bitter story that revealed human nature in all its richness and misery. In 1929 the Paris-based publisher Grasset received the manuscript of this novel. There was just one problem: neither the name nor the address of the sender appeared anywhere on the text. Grasset was keen to publish it, but could find no trace of the author until six months later a twenty-six-year-old Russian woman introduced herself to him. She was Irène Némirovsky. 'I was pregnant,' she said, by way of explanation.

Born in Kiev, Irène Némirovsky was the daughter of a Tsarist Russian banker. The family sought refuge in France after the revolution in 1917, so she had spoken French since childhood, along with Russian, Polish, English, Basque, Finnish and a few words of Yiddish. *David Golder* (1929) was a resounding success, and was the first of a long and successful series of works that established their author as one of the greatest writers working in France. But she was also of Jewish origin, and was arrested on 13 July 1942 and deported to Auschwitz. She died in the concentration camp a month later. Her husband, Mikhail Epstein, made valiant attempts to save her but he, too, was interned at Auschwitz and killed soon after arrival.

In the meantime, their two daughters, thirteen-year-old Denise and five-year-old Elisabeth, whose care had been entrusted to a family friend, found themselves alone. They still remembered their father's last words of advice: take the suitcase that sits beside mama's writing desk and never part with it. The two young girls fled from Nazi persecution, taking the case with them as they moved from one hiding place to another. It took another sixty years to overcome the pain of their terrible experience enough to open the case. In it they discovered a time-yellowed notebook filled with their mother's closely written script. It was the 'Suite Française': Némirovsky's final, unfinished novel sequence, written during the period when she had taken refuge with her family in the countryside before her arrest.

Despite consisting of only two complete novels (of a planned five), the series has been compared with *War and Peace* for its sheer power and the complexity of its plot; it is an epic tale of German-occupied France, ranging from the entry of German troops into Paris to the fates of the city's evacuees in the French countryside. When it was published in France for the first time in 2004, it was hailed as the writer's masterpiece and became an instant literary phenomenon. This precious rediscovery, after such a long period of near-oblivion, revived the name of Irène Némirovsky.

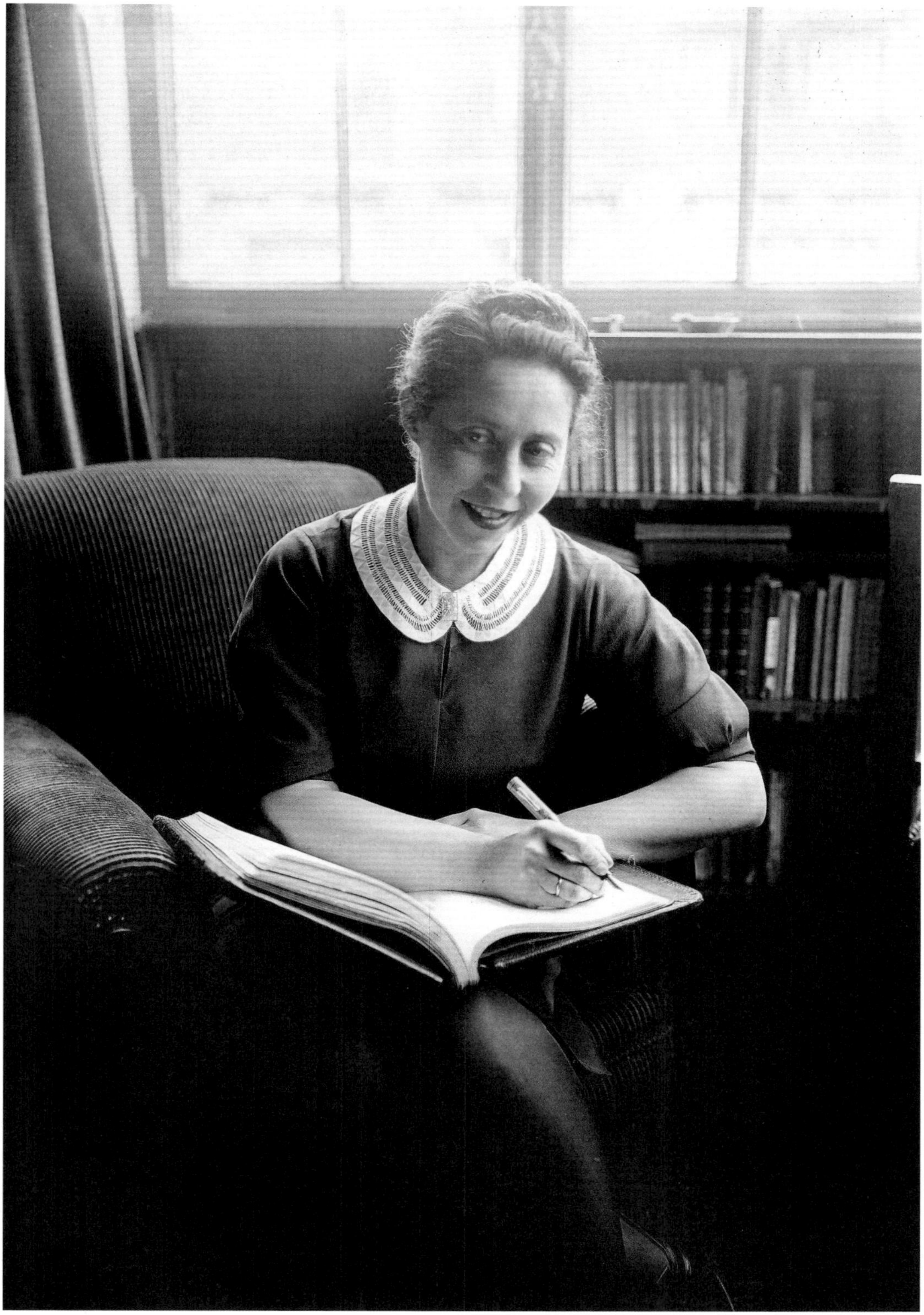

PABLO NERUDA

[Neftalí Ricardo Reyes Basoalto] born Parral, Chile, 1904; died Santiago, Chile, 1973

by Sergio Larrain

Isla Negra, Chile, 1957

Born in a small village in central Chile, Pablo Neruda was introduced to the world of letters by Gabriela Mistral, the first Latin American to win the Nobel Prize, who encouraged him to write poetry. His first volume of verse, *Crepusculario* (1923), was rooted in the modernist tradition but showed signs of the more expressive language that he would develop further in his next work, *Twenty Love Poems and a Song of Despair*, published the following year.

The outbreak of the Spanish Civil War in 1936 had a profound effect on Neruda's life. In 1937 he published *Spain in the Heart: Hymn to the Glories of the People at War*, a book of verse dedicated to the Republican cause and a lament for man's need to resort to conflict: 'Ah! If only a drop of poetry or of love were able to placate the wrath of the world, but this can only be done by battle and a decisive heart.' His experiences of both the Spanish Civil War and his time as a consul in Madrid, where he co-founded the revolutionary magazine *El Caballo verde para la poesía*, helped to shape his view of Spain as a colonial power. This resulted in the collection of poems entitled *Canto General* (1950), in which the story of Hispanic America is rewritten from the point of view of the oppressed. By giving a voice to those who would otherwise go unheard, to those who are often absent from the historical record, Neruda introduced a new form of historical poetry.

In 1971 Neruda was awarded the Nobel Prize, 'for a poetry that with the action of an elemental force brings alive a continent's destiny and dreams'. His health was already failing, however, and by the time of the Chilean military coup of 11 September 1973, in which President Salvador Allende was overthrown by forces led by Augusto Pinochet, he had been diagnosed with prostate cancer. With his hopes for a Marxist Chile finally dashed, Neruda died twelve days later. His memoirs were published the following year.

This photograph of Neruda, taken by the Chilean photographer Sergio Larrain, appeared in Larrain's *A House in the Sand* (1966), a collection of photographs dedicated to Neruda's much-loved house in Isla Negra on the Pacific coast.

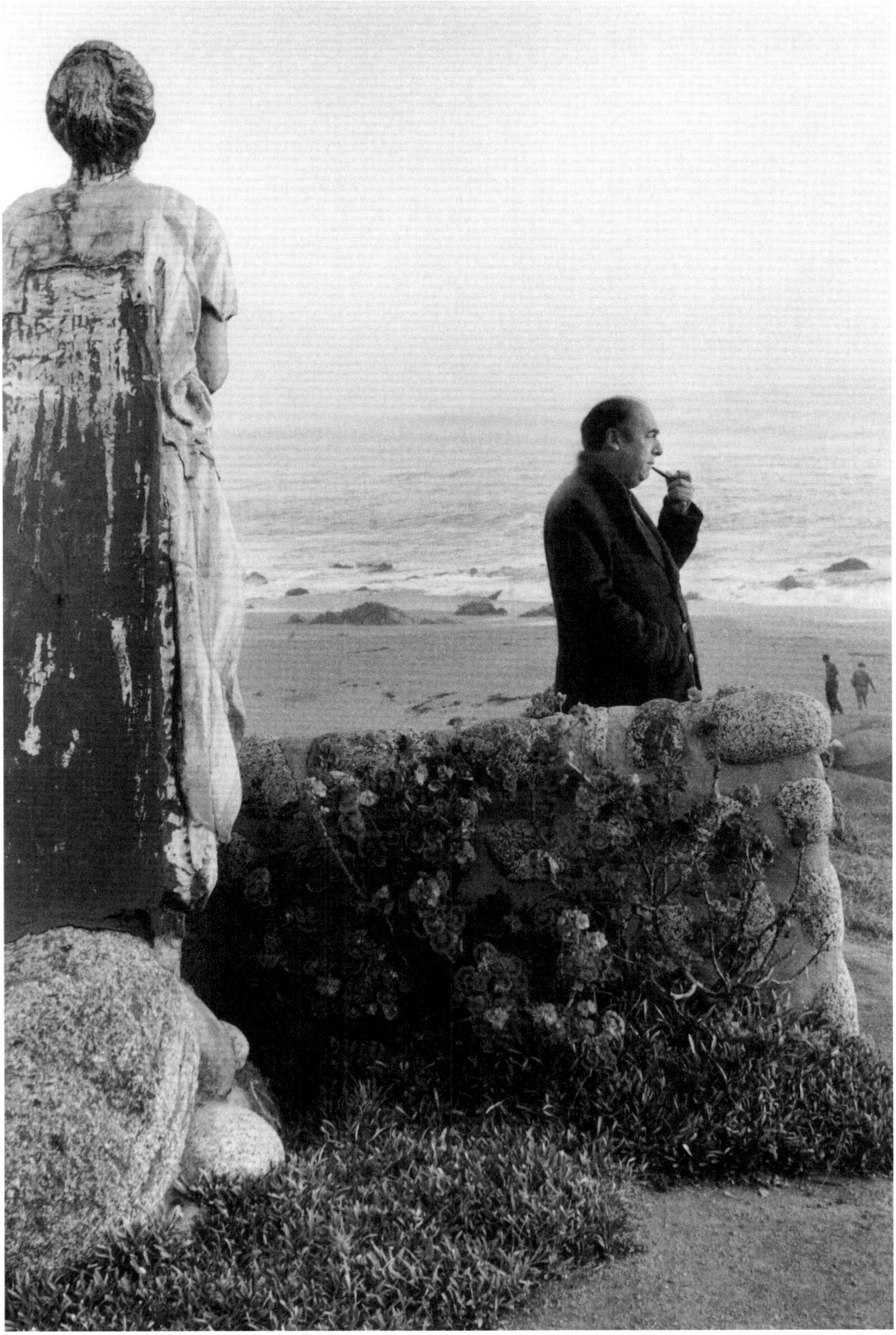

CEES NOOTEBOOM

born The Hague, 1933

by Tessa Posthuma de Boer

Amsterdam, 2002

Cees Nooteboom has always been willing to travel. He has spent a great deal of his life on the road, journeying throughout Asia and the Americas in search of adventure. It was no accident that he found himself in Budapest in 1956, in Paris in 1968 and in Berlin in 1989. He is similarly compelled to probe the lives of individuals, and the practice of literature with all of its cross-references, echoes, reversals, impossibilities, limits, openings and closings. It's no surprise that his work is characterized by a certain restlessness.

Nooteboom wrote his first novel, *Philip and the Others* (1955), an early European version of the road novel, at the age of twenty-two. Since then he has penned a number of books including *The Knight Has Died* (1963), constructed as a novel within a novel, *Rituals* (1980), *A Song of Truth and Semblance* (1981); and *Der Buddha hinter dem Bretterzaun* (The Buddha behind the fence, 1982), in which Buddha guides the narrator as he discovers the city of Bangkok.

Sometimes, as with many of the stories that make up *The Foxes Come At Night* (2009), his point of departure is an impossible dialogue with the dead, or the story of a deceased person, the memory of whom is perhaps stirred by a photograph, with time, memory and emotion woven together and unpicked. These meditations allow Nooteboom to pose questions, though not necessarily to find answers. Sooner or later Nooteboom's characters are challenged by the upheavals that confront us all, and by the inevitability with which relationships with fellow creatures, partners or friends are tarnished by time. With an irony that protects him from sentimentalism, Nooteboom explores and embraces the confines of fiction: he creates a narrator who confronts his characters, and characters who occasionally step out of the story to speak directly with the narrator, pointing out what might be changed. Nothing is left at rest.

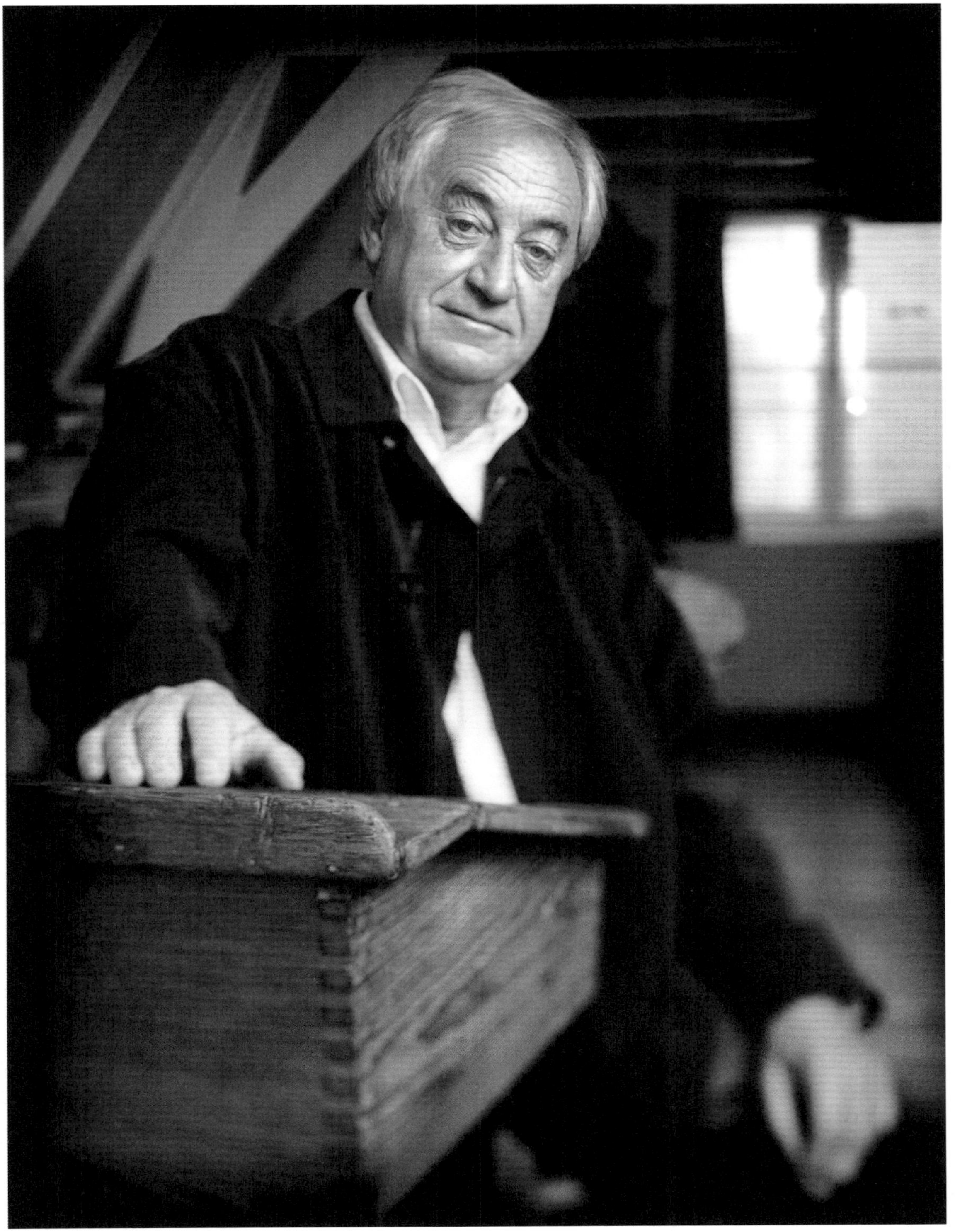

AMÉLIE NOTHOMB

[Fabienne-Claire Nothomb] born Kobe, Japan, 1967

by Beowulf Sheehan

New York, 2011

Amélie Nothomb writes in longhand every morning from four until eight, sipping a cup of tea as black as the enormous hats that she enjoys wearing when she appears in public. Her afternoons are spent answering letters. It's a fitting activity for a writer whose work is seen as a grand correspondence with her readers; indeed, *Life Form* (2010) was inspired by this ongoing written dialogue with her public. Nothomb surrounds herself with gastronomic passions, in particular, chocolate – the discovery of which she relates in *The Character of Rain* (2000) – and champagne, rivers of which flow through her books.

The daughter of a Belgian diplomat, she travelled the world, especially Asia, until the age of seventeen. On these journeys she learned about her father's professional duties and stored up material for future works, both autobiographical and fictional. Since then, her eccentricity has combined with a cult of personality, and the two mingle in her meta-fictional works.

Nothomb's particular infatuation with Japan, where she lived as a child, is described in her most successful book, *Fear and Trembling* (1999), which shared the Grand Prix du Roman de l'Académie Française and sold more than a million copies in France alone. In it she tells the story of returning to Japan to work as a translator for a large multinational company. Theincomprehensible Japanese corporate business ethic and a lack of humanity mean the story soon takes a dark turn. As is so often the case in her novels, Kafka-esque black humour is woven with an alienated romanticism.

Cerebral, grotesque, fantastical, self-mocking, even self-derisory, Nothomb is the most widely read Belgian – and possibly even French-language – writer in the world today. Her books have been published in over thirty languages. She describes herself as a graphomaniac (compulsive writer) and calculates that she writes 3.7 books a year. If she chooses to publish only one of them, that is because it is the one she is happy with.

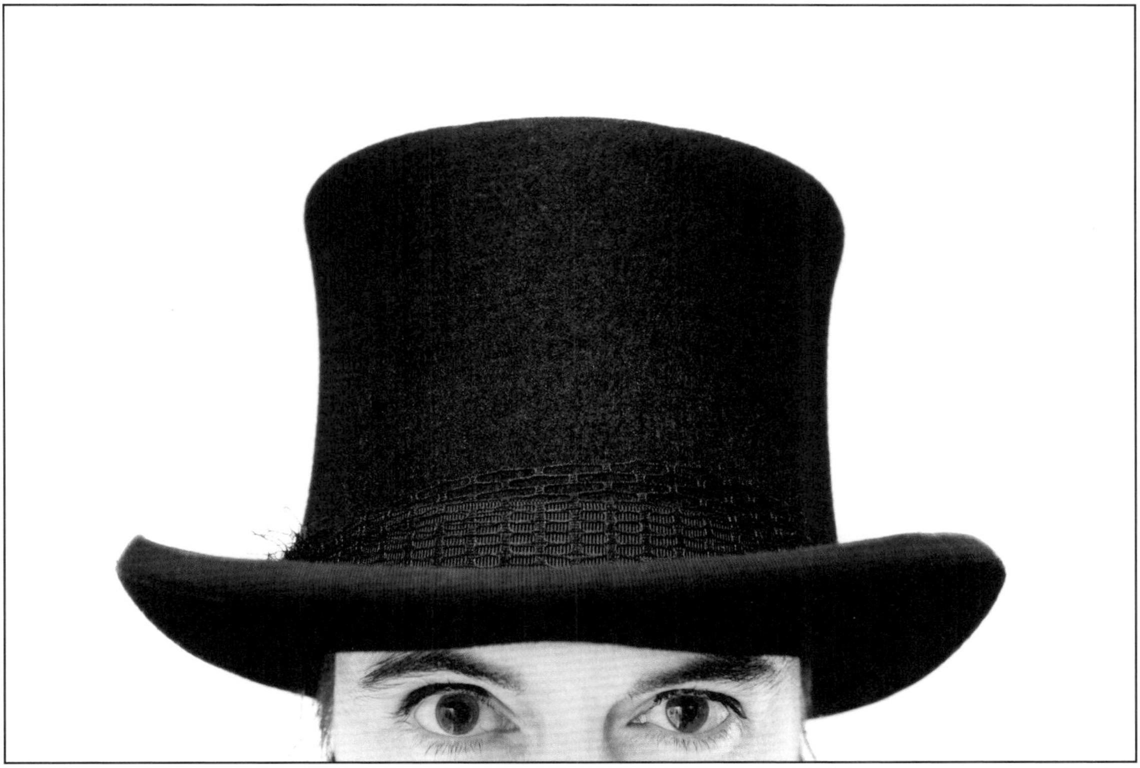

JOYCE CAROL OATES

born Lockport, New York, 1938

by Marion Ettlinger

Princeton, New Jersey, 1999

One should not be deceived by Joyce Carol Oates's somewhat fragile, ethereal appearance in Marion Ettlinger's portrait of her. Only a steely determination and tremendous strength of character could have produced such an impressive and varied body of work. She has written more than fifty novels since her debut, *With Shuddering Fall* (1964), as well as poetry, a large number of short stories, plays, various volumes of autobiography, essays and even children's books.

Oates's immense output stands as a testimony to her enduring interest in humanity, or, more specifically, in individuals and their stories of love, violence, alienation, fear and passion. The themes she has investigated in fifty years of writing are, in many ways, the themes of contemporary man. They are the concerns of the people whom Oates has known, or even simply interviewed, in the course of her life – people whose lives and relationships, fears and aspirations, vendettas and passions she has imagined.

In addition to writing under her own name, Oates has produced a number of books under the pseudonyms of Rosamond Smith and Lauren Kelly. However, her prolificacy has attracted the attention of those critics who believe that quantity has a detrimental effect on quality (the same cliché was applied to Anthony Burgess); Oates's response is simply that she works a lot. Indeed, she is far from being a slapdash writer, and spends a great deal of time in polishing, rewriting and revising her work. The excellence of her writing can be seen in such novels as *A Garden of Earthly Delights* (1967), *Them* (1969), *Black Water* (1992), *We Were the Mulvaneys* (1996) and *Mudwoman* (2012); in her fascinating essay about boxing, *On Boxing* (1987); and in her novelized biography of Marilyn Monroe, *Blonde* (2000). It is also reflected in her numerous award nominations and prizes, including the National Book Award for Fiction (1970, for *Them*) and the Norman Mailer Prize for Lifetime Achievement (2012).

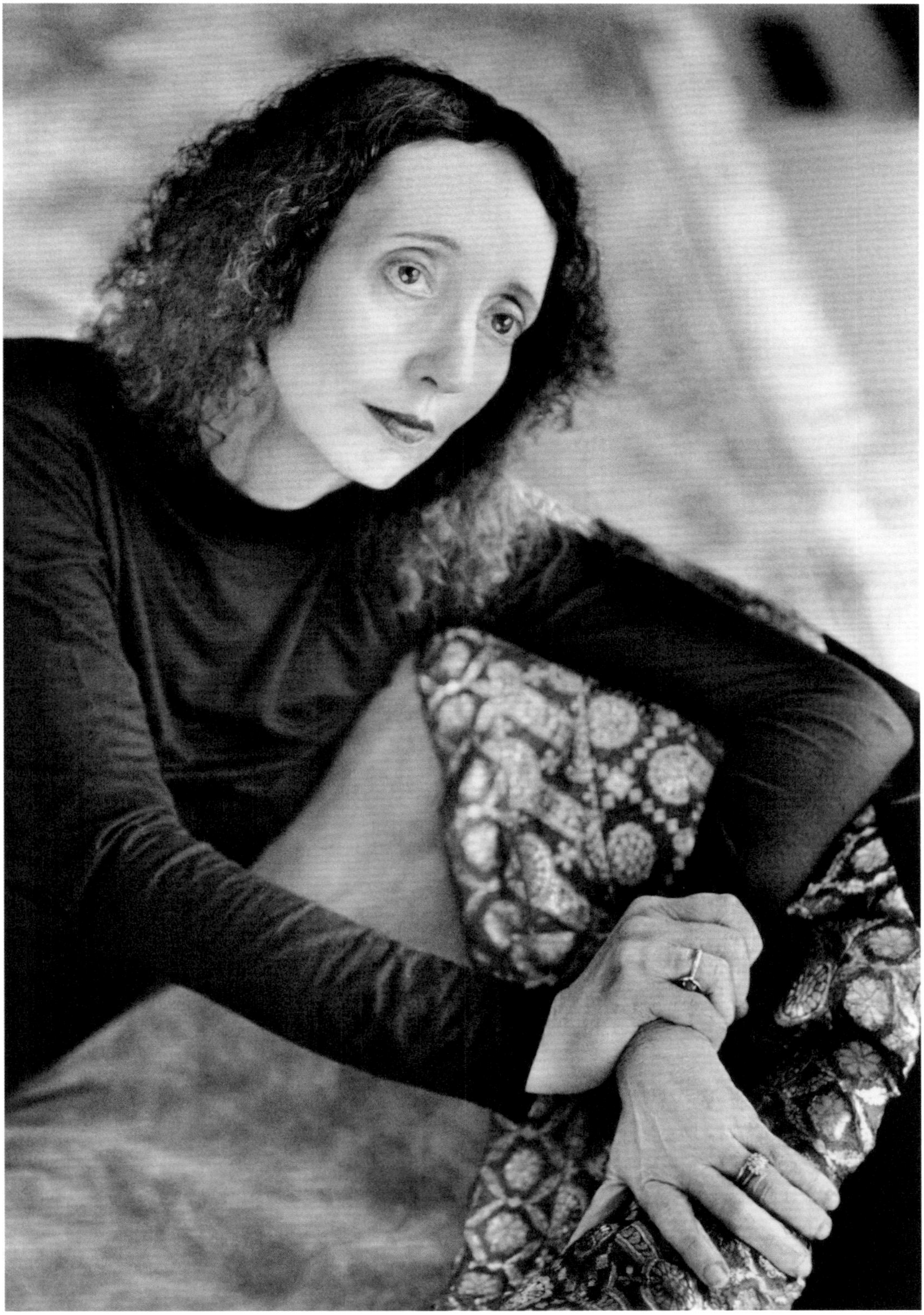

VICTORIA OCAMPO

[Ramona Victoria Epifanía Ocampo] born Buenos Aires, 1890; died Buenos Aires, 1979

by Gisèle Freund

Paris, 1939

Once described as the 'quintessential Argentine woman', Victoria Ocampo was one of the most important literary and cultural figures of the twentieth century. Born into a wealthy, aristocratic family, Ocampo was an ardent feminist, and in 1936 she was elected president of the Argentine Women's Union. In her book *La Mujer y su expresión* (Woman and her expression, 1935), she criticized the lack of recognition for women in a patriarchal society. She devoted numerous articles to authors such as Emily Brontë and Virginia Woolf, whose works she also translated. Ocampo was also a political activist, and in 1940 she published the magazine *Lettres Françaises* in Buenos Aires when it was banned in occupied France. An active opponent of the regime of Juan Domingo Perón, she was briefly imprisoned for her views.

Ocampo is perhaps best remembered as the founder in 1931 of the literary magazine *Sur*, which for more than forty years published the work of some of the most prestigious Latin American writers of the era, including Jorge Luis Borges, Julio Cortázar, Adolfo Bioy Casares, José Ortega y Gasset and Eduardo Mallea, as well as that of such European authors as André Malraux and Thomas Mann. The magazine significantly raised the profile of Latin American literature. In 1933 she founded a publishing house of the same name. Its first publication was an edition of Federico García Lorca's *Gypsy Ballads* (1928), followed by works by Jean-Paul Sartre, Carl Jung and Albert Camus, among others. The Mexican writer Octavio Paz described the importance of *Sur*, and of Ocampo herself, in the following terms: 'Victoria is something more: she is the founder of mental space. Because *Sur* is not only a journal or an institution; it is a state of mind.'

In 1976, at the age of eighty-six, she became the first woman ever to be admitted to the Argentine Academy of Letters. In her admittance speech she said: 'I congratulate you all because, of your own accord, you have overcome a prejudice, and that always requires effort. … The honour that I'm receiving today has fallen to me purely by chance, I suspect.' On the occasion of her death, her great friend Borges said: 'In a country and in an era in which women were generic, she had the merit of being an individual.' Her legacy includes a ten-volume work entitled *Testimonios* (Testimonies, 1935–77), a collection of essays on political, social and cultural aspects of Argentina, and a six-volume autobiography.

The photographer Gisèle Freund, who took this picture of Ocampo in 1939, described her as follows: 'She was very tall, exquisitely beautiful and extremely wealthy, having been born into one of the richest families in the country. She smiled a lot and laughed a lot; she had a great sense of humour. Her elegance – she wore clothes by Balmain and always had a flower in her buttonhole – was a topic of conversation in French literary circles.'

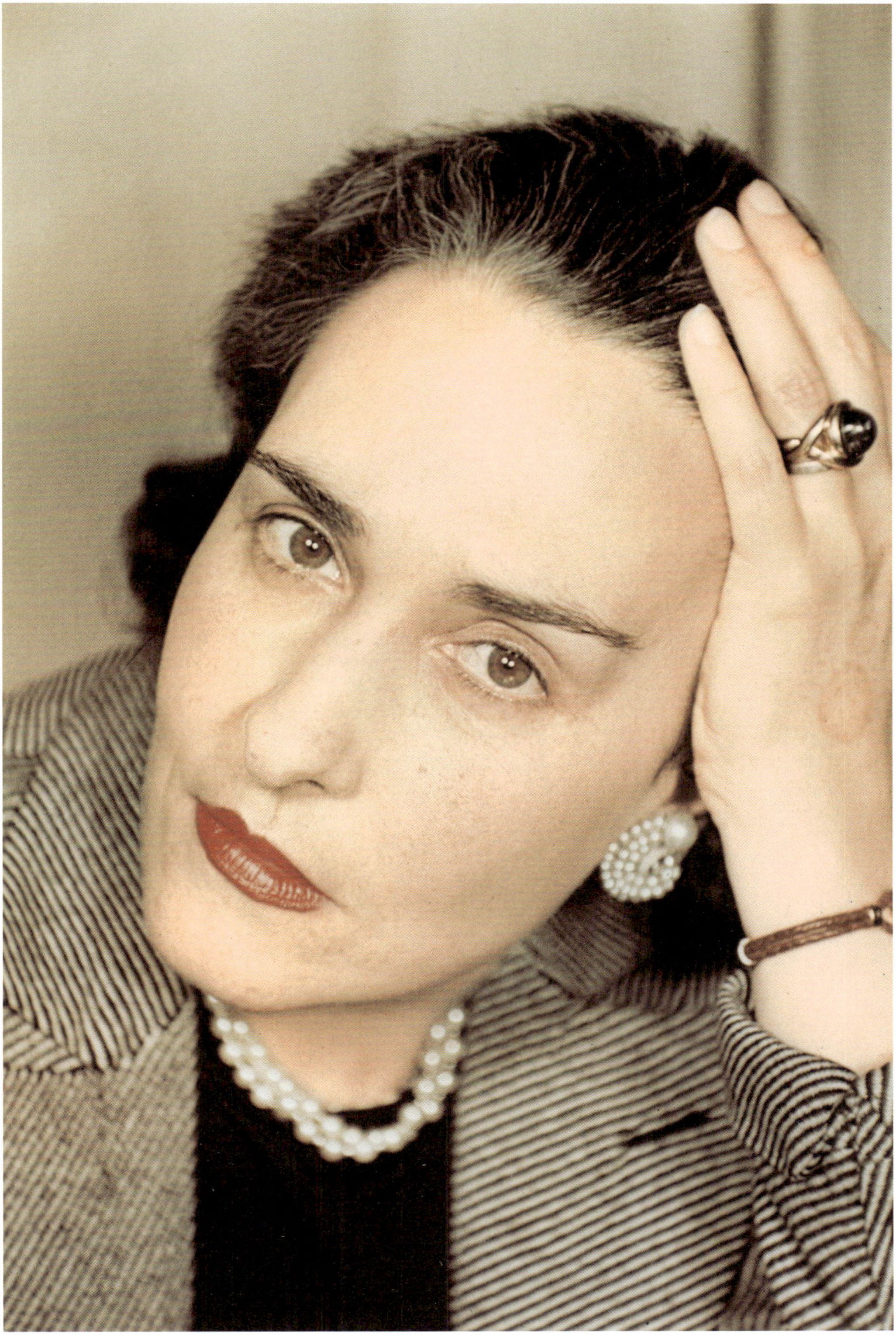

KENZABURO OE

born Uchiko, Japan, 1935

by Denis Allard

Paris, 2012

Kenzaburo Oe was ten years old when the atomic bomb was dropped on Japan, and grew up in the post-war generation. Raised in an isolated traditional village, he witnessed the atrocities of war inflicted on his country, and the sudden onset of modernization under the American occupation, which overturned the old values and systems.

Oe's *oeuvre* is steeped in Japanese folklore and history, and displays a unique blend of reality and invention, personal experience and imagination. *Hiroshima Notes* (1965), a searing journalistic reflection on the atomic bomb and its aftermath, is purely non-fiction, but Oe more frequently explores contemporary and personal events through the genre of fiction. The experience of having a mentally handicapped son influenced him profoundly: the novel *A Personal Matter* (1964) tells this story through a combination of autobiography and fiction. In *Rouse Up O Young Men of the New Age!* (1983), Oe continues the account, drawing on William Blake's imagery to portray his son's troubled journey to adulthood.

Although Oe has embraced many of the techniques of postmodernism in his writing, perhaps most prominently in *Routashi Anaberu ri souke dachitu mimakaritu* (The beautiful Annabel Lee was chilled and killed, 2007), which was partially inspired by Edgar Allan Poe's last poem, 'Annabel Lee', his works remain uniquely rooted in the real world. Oe has always considered himself to be a very Japanese writer, and his exploration of contemporary issues is typically conducted within the context of the history and social conditions of his own country. His early works, such as *Nip the Buds, Shoot the Kids* (1958) and *Seventeen* (1961), reflect the tensions of the 1950s and 1960s, and the tendency towards pessimism and disillusionment also explored by his contemporaries Kobe Abe in theatre and Nagisa Oshima in film. *Natsukashi tosi eno tegami* (Letters to my sweet bygone years, 1987), similarly interweaves Japanese myth and history, and autobiographical detail and fiction, in the story of a ten-year-old narrator (who resembles the young Oe) and his mentor Brother Gii, a troubled, visionary ex-convict who attempts to create a utopian village in the forest but eventually dies a brutal death at the hands of his community.

In 1994 Oe was awarded the Nobel Prize. The lecture he gave at the ceremony was entitled 'Japan, the Ambiguous and Myself' (published 1995). In it he addressed the ambiguity of contemporary life and criticized the deceptive nature of the media, urging the world, particularly Japan, to resist recourse to military intervention.

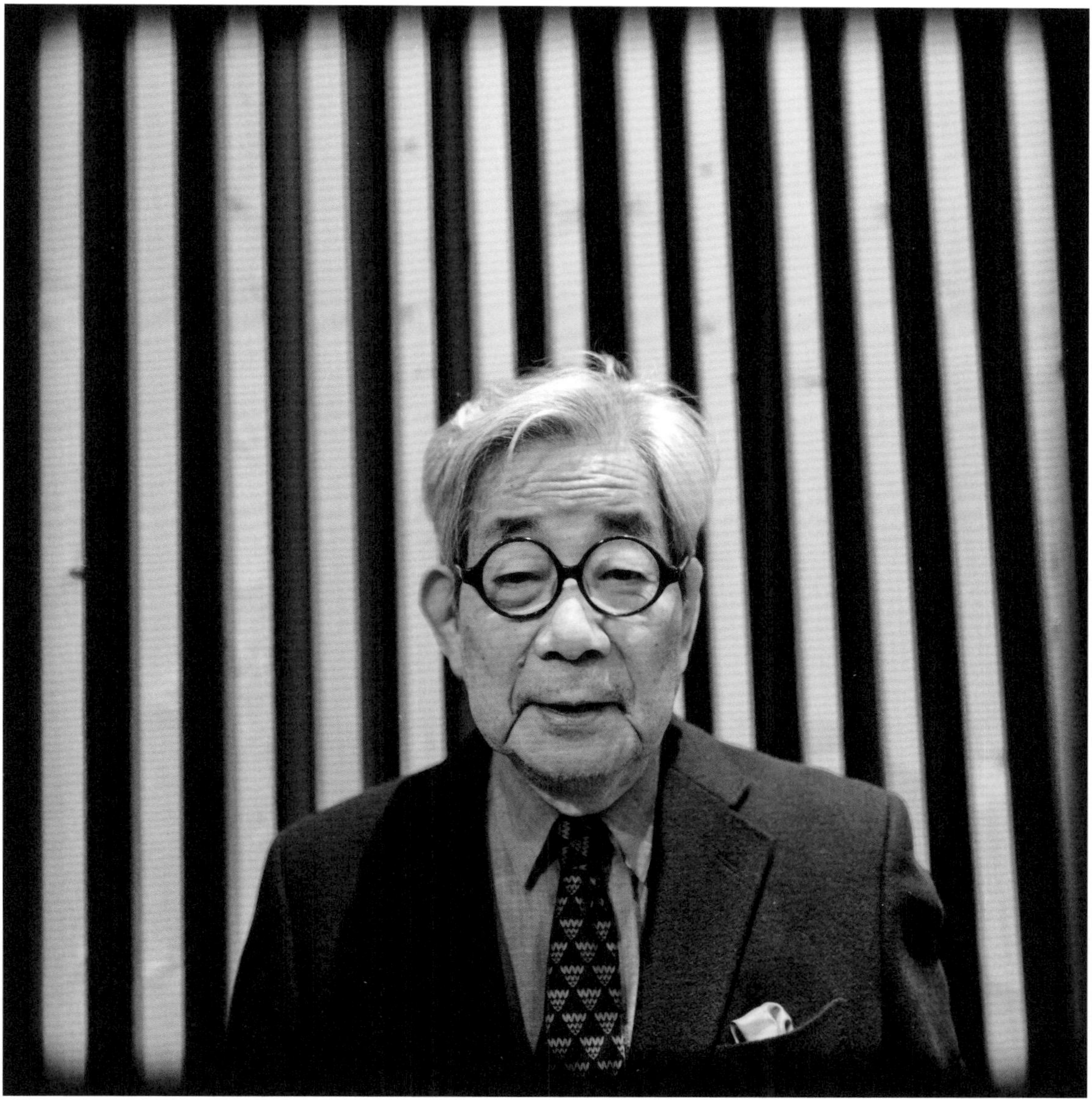

MICHAEL ONDAATJE

born Colombo, Sri Lanka, 1943

by Isolde Ohlbaum

Munich, 2007

Michael Ondaatje's face contains several clues to his ancestry. The intense blue of his piercing eyes, apparent even in this black-and-white photograph, is evidence of his Dutch heritage, while his otherwise Tamil features testify to a different culture and origin. He once described himself in the following terms: 'I am a mongrel of place. Of race. Of cultures. Of many genres.' Although now a Canadian citizen, he regards his roots in Sri Lanka (then Ceylon) as very important to his identity.

Ondaatje spent the early years of his childhood absorbing the rich oral traditions of Sri Lanka. At the age of eleven, however, he was put on a boat and forced to endure a three-week passage to London, where his mother, who had divorced his father and emigrated to England, was waiting for him. This traumatic experience forms the basis of his novel *The Cat's Table* (2011), in which events from his life are interwoven with elements of fiction. Ondaatje had previously explored the boundaries between fact and fiction in *Running in the Family* (1983), an evocative and fictionalized account of his return to Sri Lanka in the late 1970s. The novel immerses the reader in a chaotic jumble of the author's Tamil, Dutch and English roots.

In 1962 Ondaatje left England for Canada, where he studied at Queen's University in Ontario. It was there that he discovered his passion for writing. His first books were collections of poetry, including *The Dainty Monsters* (1967) and *The Man with Seven Toes* (1969). Subsequently he was seized with 'the curious desire to write prose', as he put it. His first success came in 1970 with *The Collected Works of Billy the Kid*, a virtuoso synthesis of poetry and prose based on the legendary anti-hero of the American West. International fame followed in 1992 with the publication of *The English Patient*, which won the Man Booker Prize and was later adapted into a multi-award-winning film directed by Anthony Minghella. Despite this success, Ondaatje remains in touch with his more playful, youthful self, as indicated by a quotation from Robert Frost that he carries in his wallet: 'What we do when we write represents the last of our childhood. We may for that reason practise it somewhat irresponsibly.'

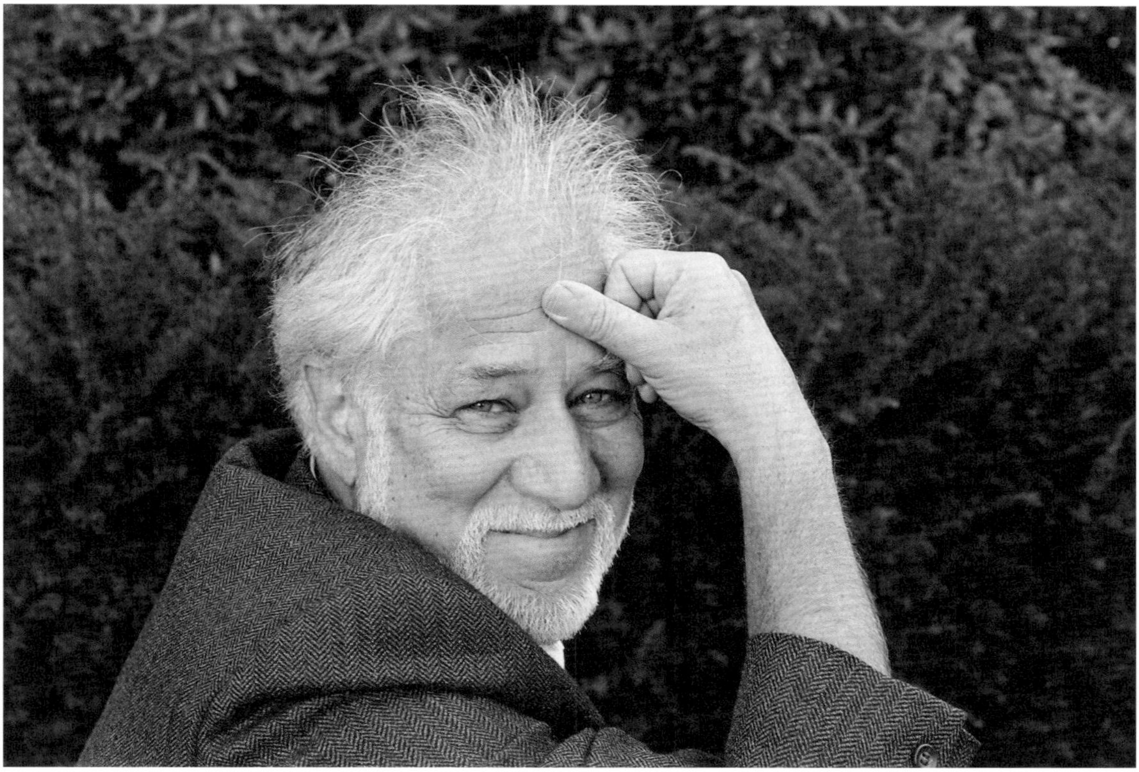

JUAN CARLOS ONETTI

born Montevideo, Uruguay, 1909; died Madrid, 1994

by Sigfrid Casals

Madrid, 1981

Shy, retiring and quiet, Juan Carlos Onetti spent most of his life as a recluse, reading and writing novels whose protagonists flee reality and seek refuge in fantasy. At the age of eighty Onetti described himself to a journalist in the following terms: 'Many times I have said to myself, without vanity, "My kingdom is not of this world." And it really is not. My world is the world that I invent, and this one in which I live exists solely because it provides me with material for the other one. … The fact that I use the events of this world to furnish my literary world means that I am very detached from this world.' This detachment is evident in this photograph of him taken by Sigfrid Casals at the ceremony in which he was awarded the Cervantes Prize in 1980. Onetti, the guest of honour, gives the impression of being there entirely by chance, a casual observer indifferently perched on a chair.

His works are typically set in enclosed spaces, within four walls, where a fantasy world provides the only real means of escape. In his most ambitious novel, *A Brief Life* (1950), fantasy merges with reality to the point that become indistinguishable. The main character, Juan María Brausen, is morally indifferent, like most of Onetti's protagonists, with a tendency to fantasize. On the verge of divorce and of being made redundant from his job with a publicity company, Brausen invents a fantasy existence as the protagonist of a screenplay he is writing. It is set in the fictitious town of Santa Maria, a location that reappears in Onetti's later works *The Shipyard* (1961) and *Body Snatcher* (1964). Brausen never finishes his screenplay, but the arrival next door of a prostitute and her pimp precipitates another level of fantasy. Intrigued by the voices next door, Brausen invents an alter-ego called Arce, an unpleasant character who he uses to get close to the prostitute.

As a writer, Onetti was fascinated by the imagination, and by the complex flights of fancy created by human beings. He found it hard to stay in one place, dividing his time between Montevideo and Buenos Aires prior to his exile in Spain. His self-examining vision influenced a new generation of writers, including Julio Cortázar, and revolutionized the hitherto provincial nature of Latin American literature. His major strength lies in his ability to render a nonexistent place so concrete that the reader becomes as convinced as the protagonist that it might actually provide a real place of escape.

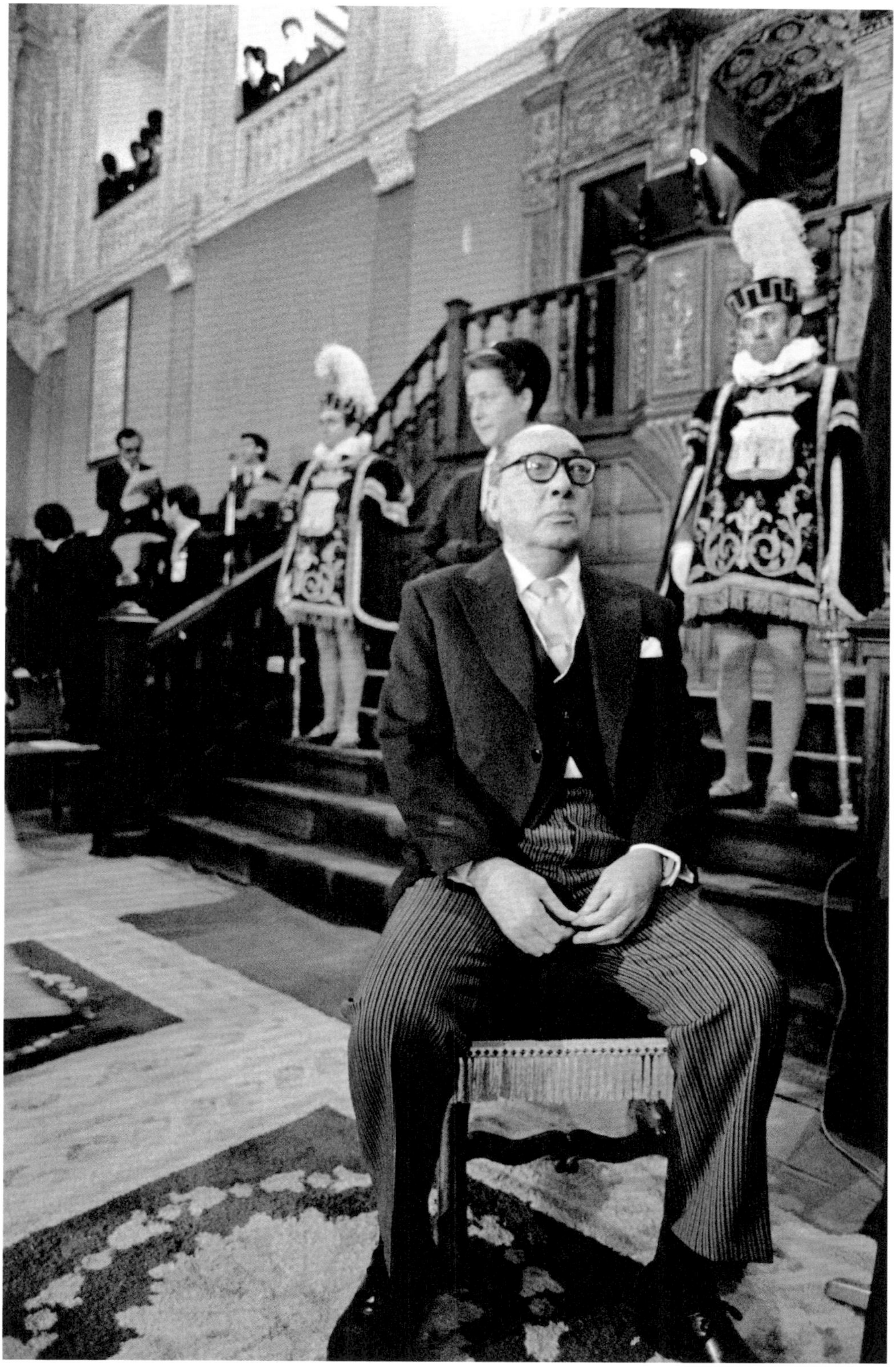

ANNA MARIA ORTESE

born Rome, 1914; died Rapallo, Italy, 1998

by Tullio Farabola

Milan, Italy, 1955

As with so many other great female writers in the twentieth century, it took some time for the high quality of Anna Maria Ortese's work to be recognized in the critical and academic spheres that in the twentieth century were still largely male dominated. This renewed appreciation for Ortese's work occurred first in her native Italy, and is ongoing in the rest of Europe.

A spiky personality, Ortese conceded very little to the demands of the culture industry. She gradually developed her own style, made non-conformist choices and, barely, scratched together a living through proofreading and journalism. Her memorable articles paid close attention to the lesser-known and little-talked-of subjects in Italy, the Soviet Union and Europe – places undergoing rapid change in the years after the Second World War.

Her debut collection of short stories, *Angelici dolori* (Angelic pains, 1937), published when she was just twenty-three years old, was promoted by the poet Massimo Bontempelli, who claimed it as an example of magic realism, a genre he had been instrumental in developing. Ortese went on to write *Il Mare non bagna Napoli* (The Sea does not reach Naples, 1953), which was somewhere between story, essay, investigative journalism and a harsh portrait of the misery of a city destroyed and corrupted by war. The novel also pointed out the inadequacies of its intellectual elite, exciting considerable debate and eliciting as much admiration as it did repulsion. In *Il Porto di Toledo* (The gate of Toledo, 1975), which some consider to be her masterpiece, the wounds of experience and knowledge are set against imaginary backdrops in which can be glimpsed Ortese's city of Naples. Naples can also be discerned in the novel that many years later would seal her reputation and capture the interest of a generation of new readers: *The Lament of the Linnet* (1993).

Despite the Ortese's habitually independent stance, her novel *Alonso e i visionari* (Alonso and the visionaries, 1996) appeared to be an attempt to clarify her inspiration, poetics and philosophy. Both testament and warning, the novel is directed to a world that – to Ortese – always appeared to be most cruel to children (especially young girls) and animals, its most defenceless creatures. She imagined these less powerful beings undergoing startling metamorphoses and, like the puma in *Alonso e i visionari*, being transformed into sacrificial or redeeming religious figures. Some commentators find Ortese's courageous and profound writing comparable to that of Etty Hillesum and Simone Weil, both great female literary figures of the twentieth century.

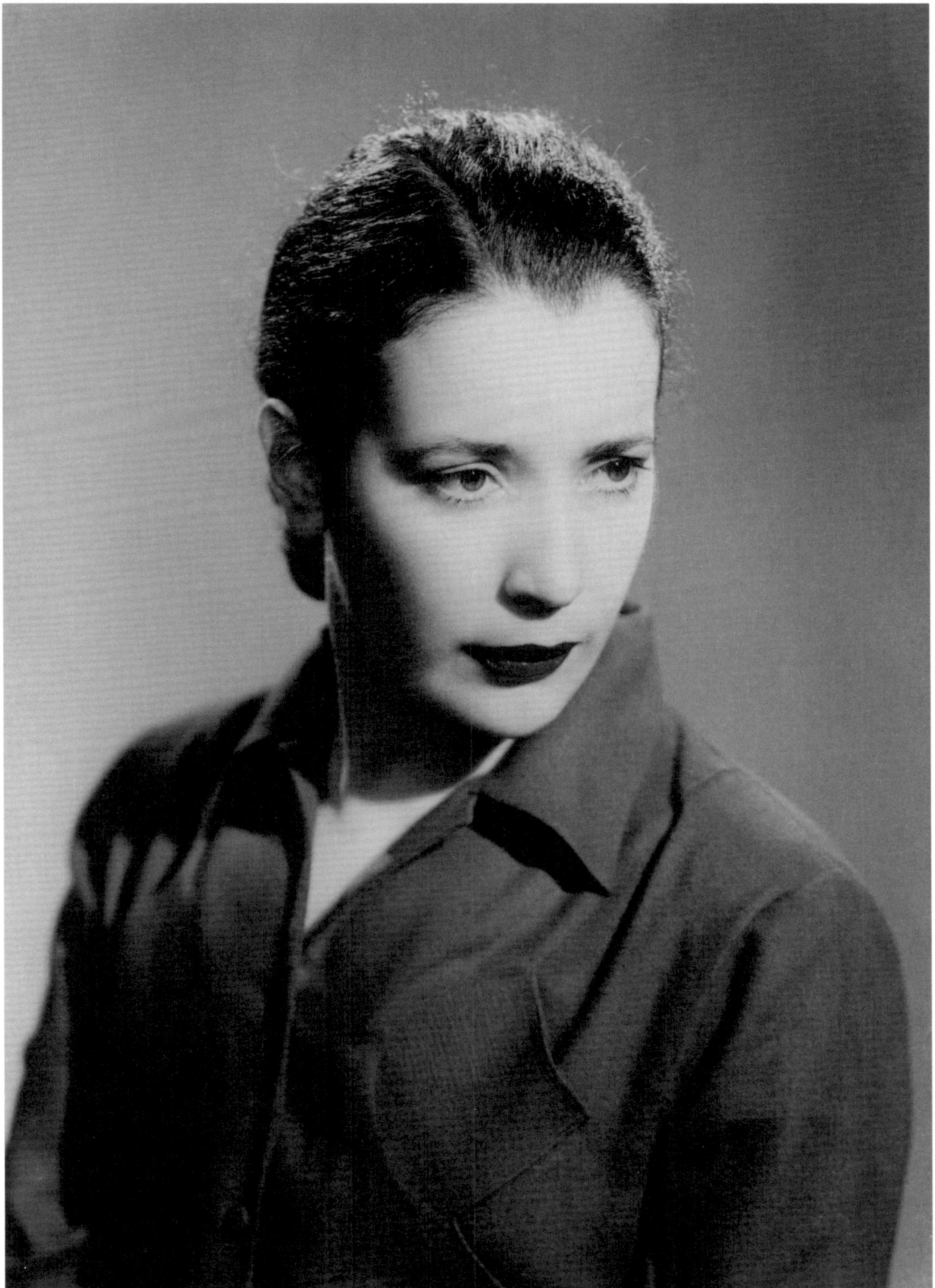

GEORGE ORWELL

[Eric Arthur Blair] born Motihari, India, 1903; died London, 1950

unknown photographer

London, c. 1941–43

Although George Orwell resolved to be a writer at an early age, it is said that he sometimes fought against his vocation. Although he analysed his calling with his characteristic cool and perceptive detachment, he was never able fully to explain it to himself. One of the most important political writers and essayists of the twentieth century, Orwell used these same powers of analysis and perception to produce a varied and memorable body of work, including *Homage to Catalonia* (1938), his first-person account of the Spanish Civil War; *Animal Farm* (1945), his satire on revolutionary and post-revolutionary Russia; and *Nineteen Eighty-Four* (1949), his dystopian masterpiece.

In a brilliant essay entitled 'Why I Write' (1946), Orwell pondered the motives behind his impulse to put pen to paper, explaining: 'All writers are vain, selfish, and lazy, and at the very bottom of their motives there lies a mystery. Writing a book is a horrible, exhausting struggle, like a long bout of some painful illness. One would never undertake such a thing if one were not driven on by some demon whom one can neither resist nor understand. For all one knows that demon is simply the same instinct that makes a baby squall for attention. And yet it is also true that one can write nothing readable unless one constantly struggles to efface one's own personality. ... I cannot say with certainty which of my motives are the strongest, but I know which of them deserve to be followed. And looking back through my work, I see that it is invariably where I lacked a political purpose that I wrote lifeless books and was betrayed into purple passages, sentences without meaning, decorative adjectives and humbug generally.'

In 1941, during the early years of the Second World War, Orwell, who had been left unfit for military duty by tuberculosis, was employed as a producer with the Far Eastern section of the BBC World Service. After its original home, Broadcasting House in London, had been badly damaged by aerial bombing, the World Service was transferred to Bush House, an impressive but rather sinister-looking building on Aldwych. Orwell, photographed there, sitting at a microphone, was entrusted with preparing broadcasts to India that were designed to counter Japanese and German propaganda. According to some accounts, both the canteen and the sinister Room 101 in *Nineteen Eighty-Four* were inspired by Orwell's time in Bush House, which came to an end in 1943.

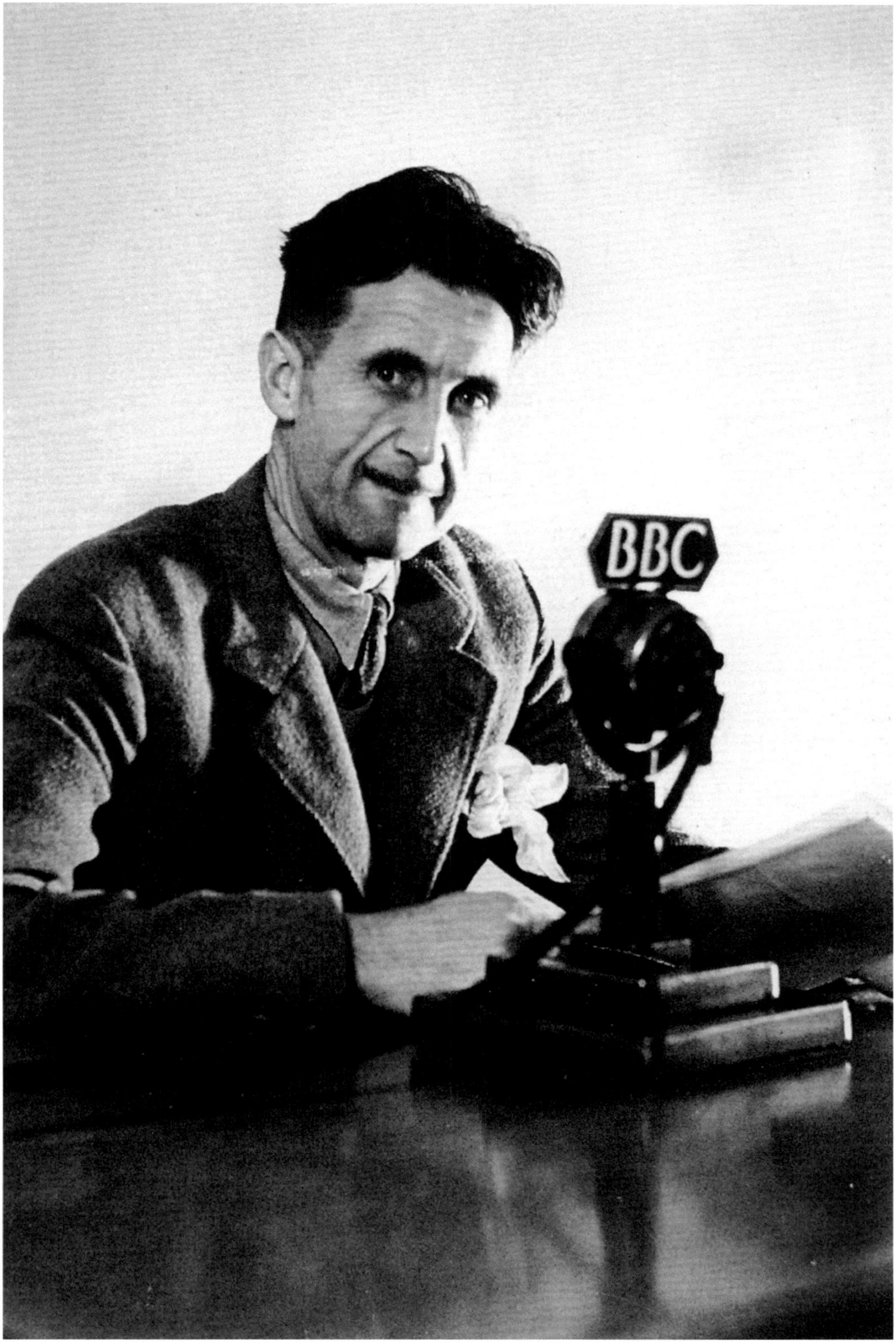
BBC

AMOS OZ

[Amos Klausner] born Jerusalem, 1939

by Micha Bar-Am

Arad, Israel, 2004

In Hebrew, Amos Oz's adopted surname means 'strength', and, for him, choosing such a name was a declaration of intent. Born in Jerusalem in 1939, Oz was severely tested in his early adolescence by the suicide of his mother, and later by a rift with his father. The latter was closely associated with the Israeli right wing, and, in order to distance himself from his father's politics, the young writer invented a new identity for himself, one that was no longer linked to the Klausner family.

In addition to being one of Israel's most powerful storytellers, Oz is a professor of literature, a committed journalist and an intellectual acutely aware of the problems faced by the country of his birth. Since the 1960s he has been an advocate of the two-state solution to the Arab–Israeli conflict, and in 1978 he co-founded the Peace Now movement, an Israeli organization calling for peace in the region. His writings, both fiction and non-fiction, address the difficulties, ambiguities, contradictions and everyday sufferings experienced by the Israeli people.

This image of the writer by Micha Bar-Am, a photographer of German origin who emigrated to Israel as a child, was taken in Arad, the settlement in which Oz has lived since 1986, in a house that overlooks the stony expanses of the Negev Desert. 'I wake at five each morning', recounts Oz, 'and walk for half an hour before the sun rises. I breathe in the silence. I look at the outline of the hills in the morning breeze. I walk for about forty minutes. I come home again and put on the radio and sometimes I hear politicians using words like "never" or "forever" or "for all eternity" – and I know that the outdoors, the stones of the desert, are laughing to themselves.'

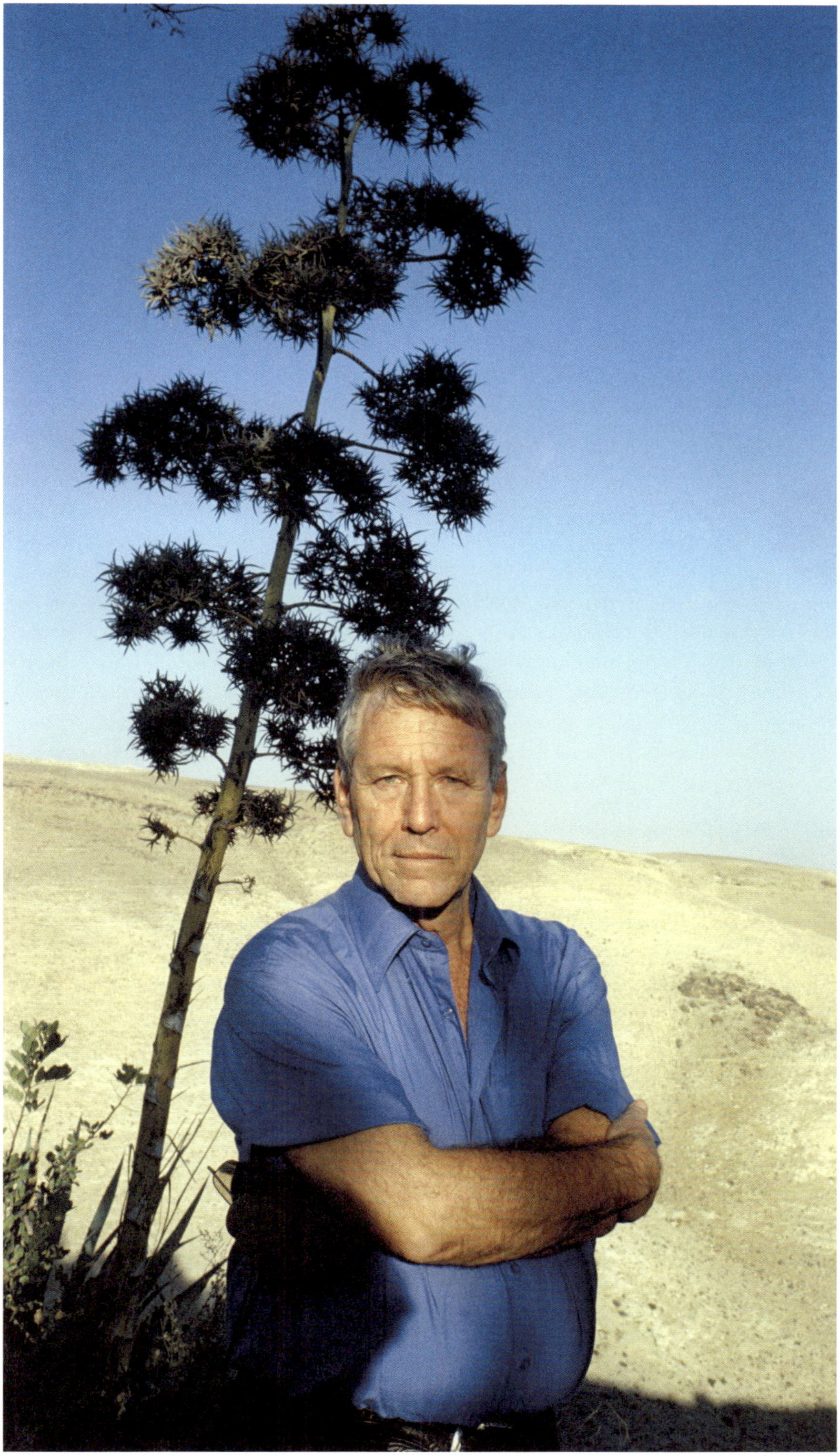

ORHAN PAMUK

born Istanbul, 1952

by Alex Majoli

Cannes, France, 2007

The themes that define the works of the Nobel Prize-winning author Orhan Pamuk are inextricably bound up with his homeland, Turkey. At the heart of his writing are the relationships between East and West, Islam and Christianity, and the past and the present.

Pamuk's career as a writer began in the late 1970s, but he first came to the world's attention in 2000 with the publication of the novel *My Name Is Red*. Set in sixteenth-century Turkey, the book revolves around a community of artists, and blends intrigue and romance with philosophical discussions on the country's future. He followed this work with *Snow* (2002), a novel set in the city of Kars in eastern Turkey, on the borders with Georgia and Armenia. The main character is a poet who, having returned to his native Turkey from exile in Germany, is stranded in a snow-bound Kars while investigating a series of suicides. Through the protagonist's encounters with some of the city's inhabitants, the book explores many of the religious, cultural and political events that have shaped modern-day Turkey. In 2005 Pamuk's comments regarding Turkey's treatment of its Armenian and Kurdish populations led to a criminal case being brought against him. However, the charges were dropped the following year after pressure from the international community.

Pamuk has explored many different styles in his writing, most radically in *The Black Book* (1990), which is often described as his postmodern novel. At the other end of the spectrum lies *Istanbul: Memories and the City* (2003), a complex and largely autobiographical analysis of the city and its inhabitants. Memories, stories and objects in particular are at the heart of *The Museum of Innocence* (2008), in which the story of an unhappy love affair becomes the setting for a wider reflection on the nature of love and obsession, including a longing for the past that manifests itself in the compulsive collection of objects. Pamuk has established an actual 'Museum of Innocence' based on the museum in the book. Located in Istanbul, it contains a collection of objects evocative of life in the city during the period in which the novel is set.

Italian photographer Alex Majoli took this photo of Pamuk in Cannes, as part of a body of work inspired by Philippe Halsman's famous 'Jump' series.

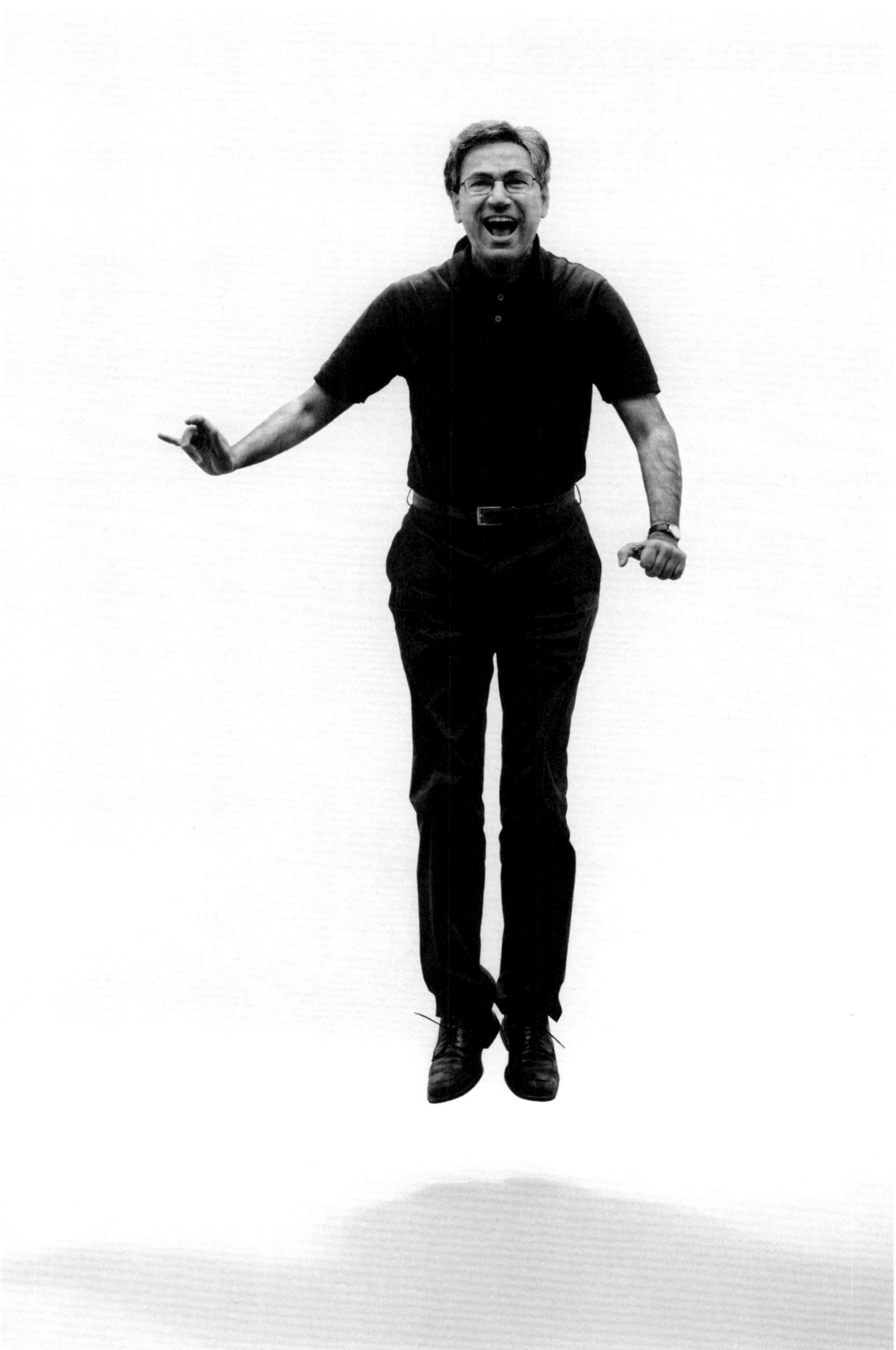

PIER PAOLO PASOLINI

born Bologna, Italy, 1922; died Ostia, Rome, 1975

by Federico Garolla

Rome, 1960

In 1949 a sexual scandal forced Pier Paolo Pasolini to leave the peaceful countryside of Friuli, the area of north-eastern Italy in which he had grown up. Aged twenty-seven, he fled to Rome with his mother, to lose himself in the anonymity of the big city. It would prove to be an event of great significance not only for Pasolini but also for Rome, the little-known underside of which he would later reveal to a wider world.

Initially, Pasolini lived in poverty on the outskirts of Rome, teaching in the schools of the notorious *borgate*, the housing communities where working-class immigrants lived in deprivation. It was here that he discovered the anti-bourgeois and alternative culture that would shape his political views. The reflective poetry written in his native Friulan gave way to the civic verses of *The Ashes of Gramsci* (1957) and *The Religion of My Time* (1961). He also wrote his first novels – *The Ragazzi* (1955), the story of a boy from the *borgate*, and *A Violent Life* (1959) – and directed what was to be the first of many films, *Accattone!* (1961).

For Pasolini, the inhabitants of the *borgate* were possessed of a potentially revolutionary energy. In the 1970s, however, he berated this generation for succumbing to bourgeois and conformist tendencies. By this time he had become more extreme and isolated in his views, and was an outspoken critic of consumerism, the degradation of culture, the hedonism of the masses and the violence of power. For many people, Pasolini's last work, the sexually explicit and sadistically violent film *Salò, or the 120 Days of Sodom* (1975), transgressed the bounds of what was deemed acceptable.

On 2 November 1975, Pasolini was found murdered on the beach in Ostia, on the outskirts of Rome. His friend and fellow Italian writer Alberto Moravia wrote: 'The manner of his death was violent, like his books, but he himself was not violent. It had announced itself already on the pages of his works, but he was not like his protagonists … He was a key figure in our culture, a poet and a chronicler of his time, a talented film director and an inexhaustible essayist.' Federico Garolla photographed Pasolini playing football with some of the boys from the Quarticciolo *borgate*, where he had spent his first years in Rome.

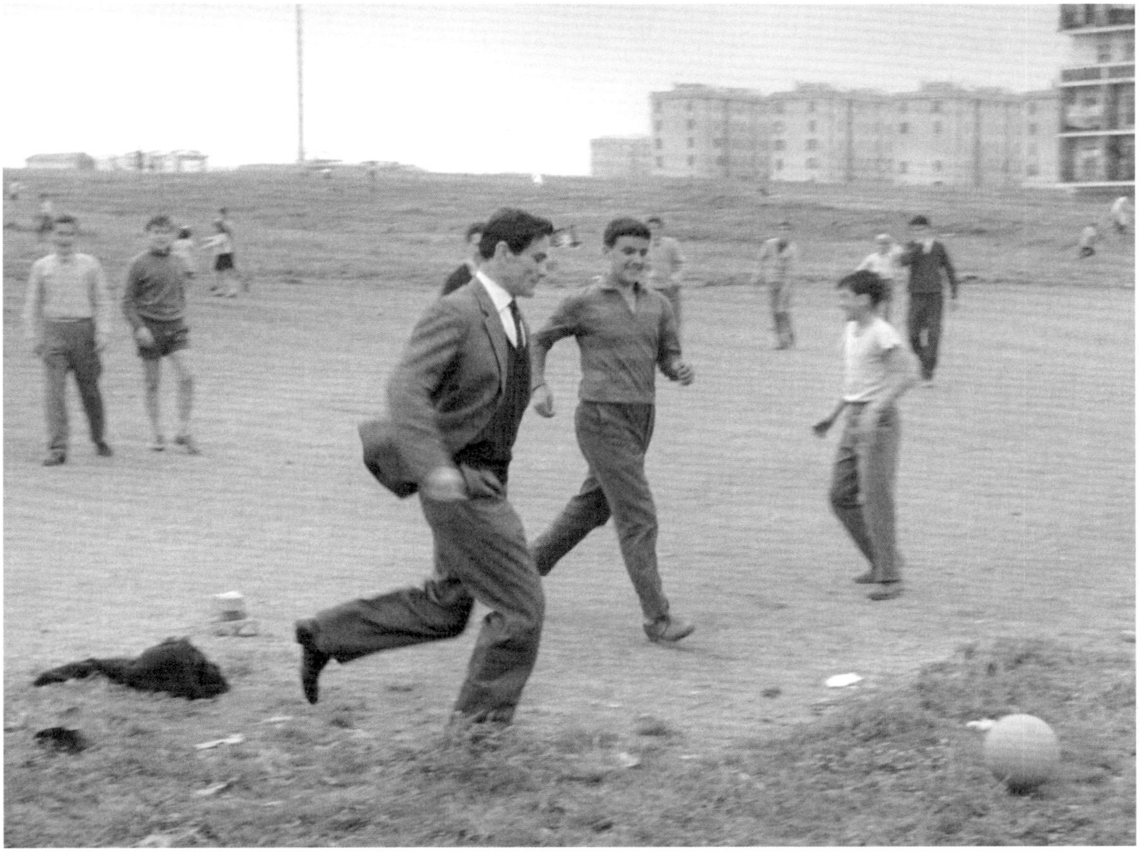

BORIS PASTERNAK

born Moscow, 1890; died Peredelkino, Russia, 1960

by Cornell Capa

Peredelkino, Russia, 1958

Despite spending his youth studying Immanuel Kant rather than Karl Marx, Boris Pasternak saw the possibility of the Russian Revolution resulting in a just society, and this conviction led him to embrace its cause. As a poet, he was attracted by the freedom celebrated by the Russian Futurists, although he was less appreciative of their declamatory fervour or their political obstinacy. He liked to sing of childhood and nature as well as history, and it is perhaps because of this that collections of his poems, such as *Poverkh baryerov* (Over the barriers, 1917), *My Sister, Life* (1922) and *Themes and Variations* (1923) still hold their fascination for readers today.

The poems 'The Year 1905' and 'Lieutenant Schmidt' (both written in 1927) tell the story of the Revolution in a tone that was very different from that used by the committed poets. The famous events are coloured by intimacy and presented through images of great power – without any trace of bombast or didacticism. His poetry from the Second World War and the post-war period took on a political engagement with the life of the people. Collections such as *Na rannikh poyezdakh* (On early trains, 1943) and *Zemnye prostory* (Wide spaces of the Earth, 1945) celebrated the power of resistance and of fundamental values. As well as being a great poet, Pasternak was also a writer of prose, although for him the divide between the two was not quite so clear-cut. The prose of his 1931 autobiographical study, *Safe Conduct*, often makes use of poetic language.

He achieved sudden international fame with the publication of one of the greatest novels of last century, *Doctor Zhivago* (1957). It was an unprejudiced vision of the history of the Revolution, told from the point of view of a doctor and Lara, the woman he loves. Both individuals are swept away by history, as are their family members and their persecutors. Along with Mikhail Bulgakov's *The Master and Margherita* (1967), Vasily Grossman's *Life and Fate* (1980) and the writings of Andrei Platonov, *Doctor Zhivago* is a masterpiece of literature that tells the story of the Russian Revolution and the regime that followed: its causes, contradictions and betrayals. The Soviet government detested the book and denounced it, but it won Pasternak the 1958 Nobel Prize. He would never collect the honour. Following threats that if he left the country he would be denied re-entry, he refused his medal.

Cornell Capa was in the Soviet Union when it was announced that Pasternak had won the Nobel Prize. He travelled at once to Pasternak's dacha near Moscow and photographed the celebrations for *Life* magazine. But Capa's favourite picture was taken just as he was leaving: it shows the writer looking rather distracted and melancholy, seated on a bench in the cherry orchard behind his house.

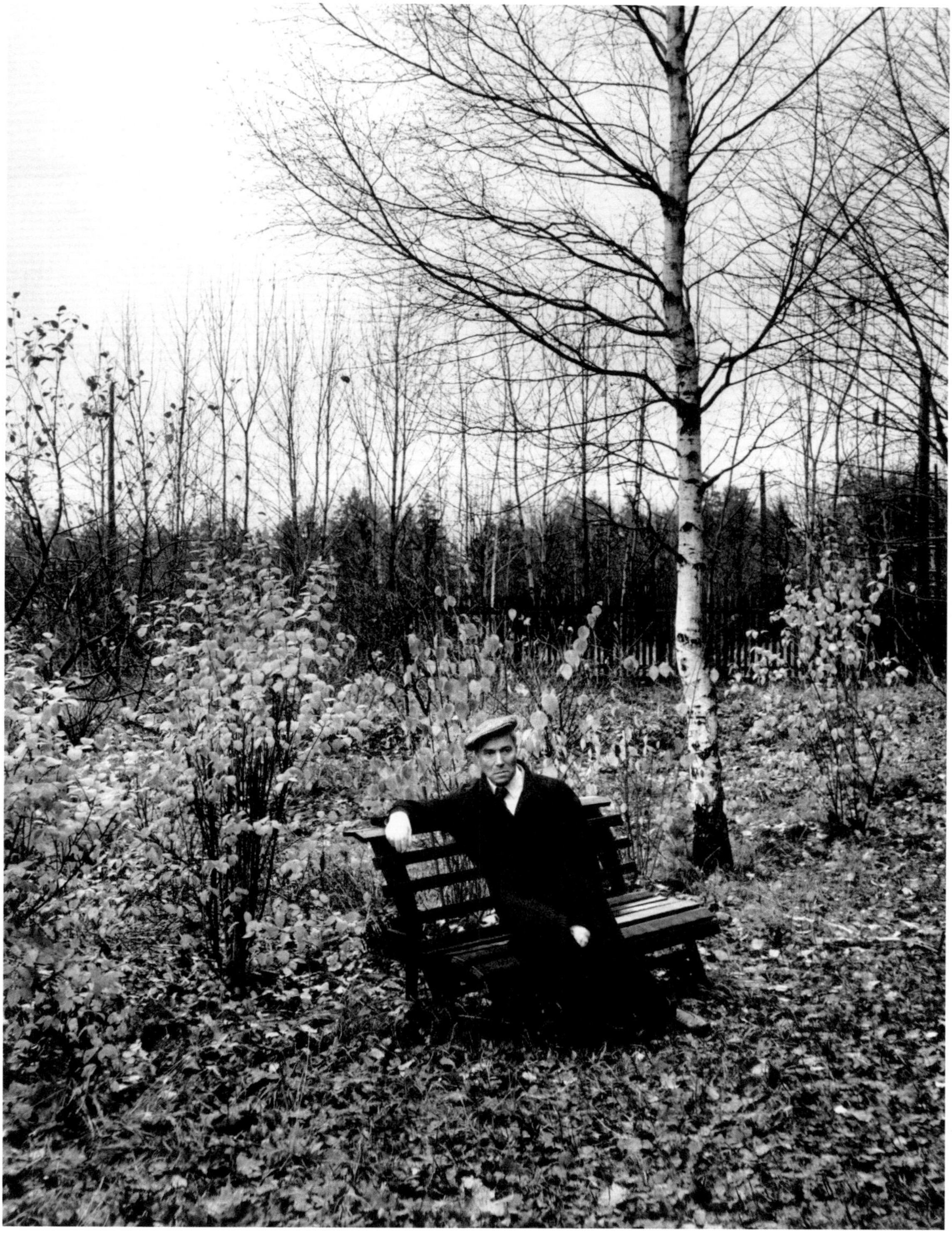

CESARE PAVESE

born Santo Stefano Belbo, Italy, 1908; died Turin, Italy, 1950

by Ghitta Carell

Milan, Italy, 1948

The countryside around Santo Stefano Belbo, a small town in the Piedmont region of Italy, provided the setting for Cesare Pavese's childhood. It also provided the location of his final novel, *The Moon and the Bonfires* (1950), whose protagonist returns to Santo Stefano Belbo after several years away. Turin, on the other hand, was the setting for Pavese's adult life and the various battles he experienced – personal, cultural (fought alongside his friend and publisher Giulio Einaudi) and political (between his fellow members of the Communist Party).

In 1935 Pavese was accused of anti-Fascist activities, arrested and sentenced to three years' internal exile in a Calabrian village. It was there that he began to keep a diary, published posthumously in 1952, as an antidote to his boredom and depression. The pages of this diary contain Pavese's reflections on life, dreams, memories and art, as well as his farewell to writing and to life: '16 August 1950. I have played my public part – as much as I was able to do. I have worked, given poetry to the people; I have shared the pain of many. … I cannot write any more.' Eleven days later, Pavese was found dead in a hotel room in Turin; he had taken an overdose of sleeping pills. His diary suggests that one of the reasons for his suicide was the failure of his relationship with the actress Constance Bowling. The next day, a folder was found containing the poems that would make up *Death Will Come and Will Have Your Eyes* (1951), which include some of the most intense and affecting love poems in the history of Italian literature.

This striking image of Pavese was taken by Ghitta Carell, a Hungarian photographer of Jewish origin who had moved to Italy in 1924. Many of the era's most influential personalities passed through her studio in Milan, where, in a carefully orchestrated ritual, she would welcome them with a cup of tea as she prepared for the shoot. She paid great attention to both the background and the light, for, as she was fond of saying, 'Each person has two faces; man is a product of both light and shade, and I am searching for the light.'

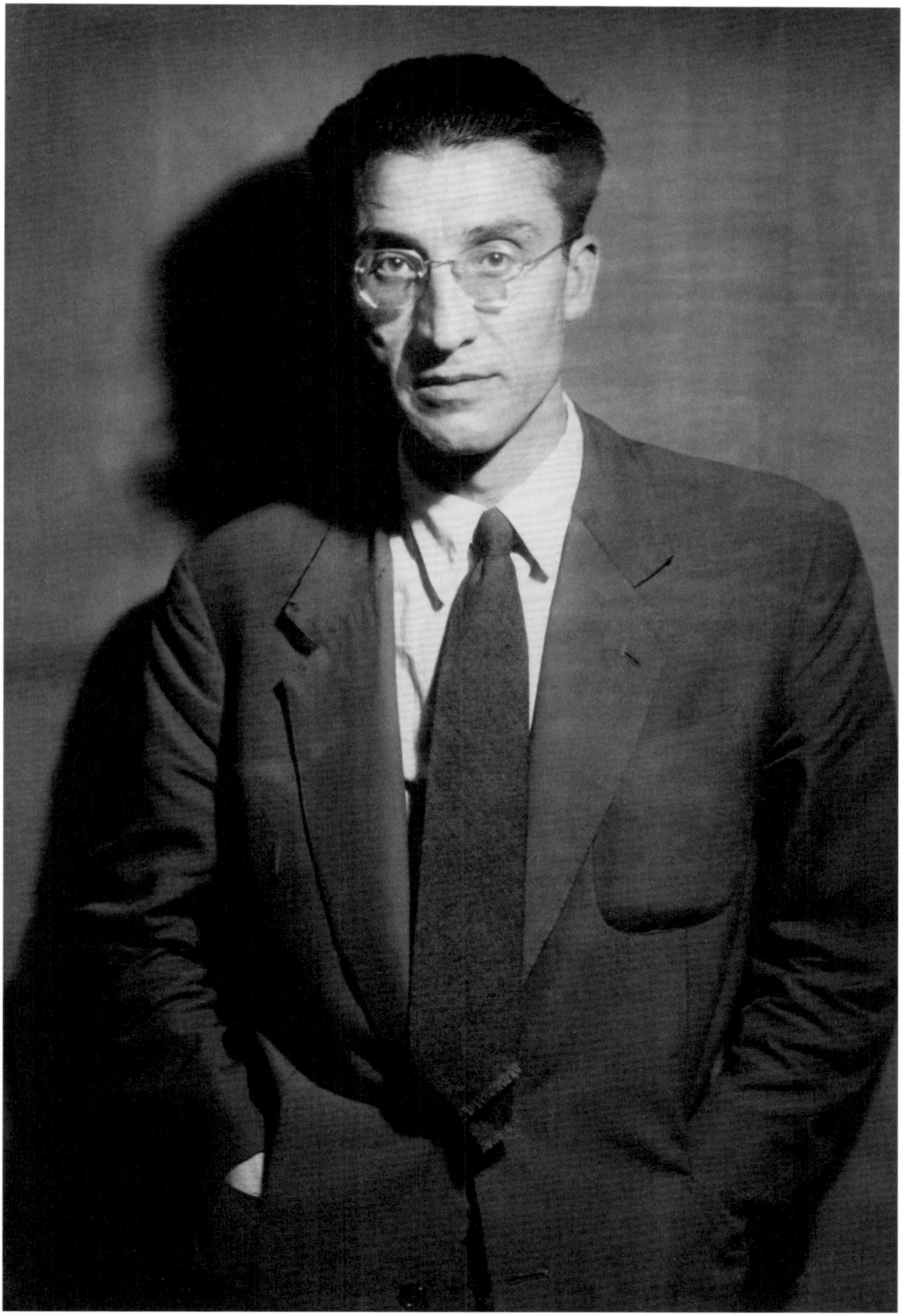

OCTAVIO PAZ

born Mexico City, 1914; died Mexico City, 1998

by Inge Morath

Mexico, 1959

Cosmopolitan poet and novelist Octavio Paz was born in Mexico City in 1914, during the Mexican Revolution. He was man of his time, and his life's work was devoted to reflecting on contemporary events. When was awarded the Nobel Prize in 1990, the speech he delivered at the ceremony was, characteristically, entitled 'In Search of the Present'.

In 1937 the twenty-three-year-old Paz travelled to Spain to express his solidarity with the Republicans opposing Fascism. In 1945 he entered the Mexican diplomatic service and was posted to Paris, where he affiliated himself with the Surrealists, with whom he shared a belief in 'the concrete exercising of liberty'. His work as a diplomat took him to Japan and Switzerland in 1952–53, and to India as the Mexican ambassador from 1962 to 1968. In 1968 he renounced his diplomatic role in protest at the massacre of students by police in Mexico City. He moved to the USA in 1970 and taught at various universities, including Harvard.

Paz published his first poems in 1933, but it was the collection *Libertad bajo palabra* (Liberty under oath, 1960), containing verse from 1935 to 1958, that brought international recognition for his unique poetic voice. For Paz, poetry functioned as an antidote to modernity, restoring the humanity of which man has been robbed. It should 'transform life into poetry rather than create poetry using life'.

In all aspects of his life Paz had the poet's capacity to turn any experience into gold. Inaddition to writing poetry, he worked as magazine editor and publisher, a translator and an essayist, remaining at the centre of artistic, social and cultural discourse in Mexico, and raising the profile of Mexican literature. Paz was praised for his non-fiction work as well as for his poetry: Mario Vargas Llosa called him a 'luxury prose writer'. His most famous prose work, *The Labyrinth of Solitude* (1950) is a collection of essays exploring Mexican identity, the story of how colonization has distanced the people from their own heritage, leaving them with a sense of alienation, adrift and alone in a zone where time seems suspended. Paz's goal, as outlined in his Nobel acceptance speech, was for Mexico to rediscover its pre-Columbian roots through renewed interest in myths, legends, popular arts and customs. Paz's 'philosophy of the present' required the full involvement of the past, in the hope of forging a reconciliation between the two.

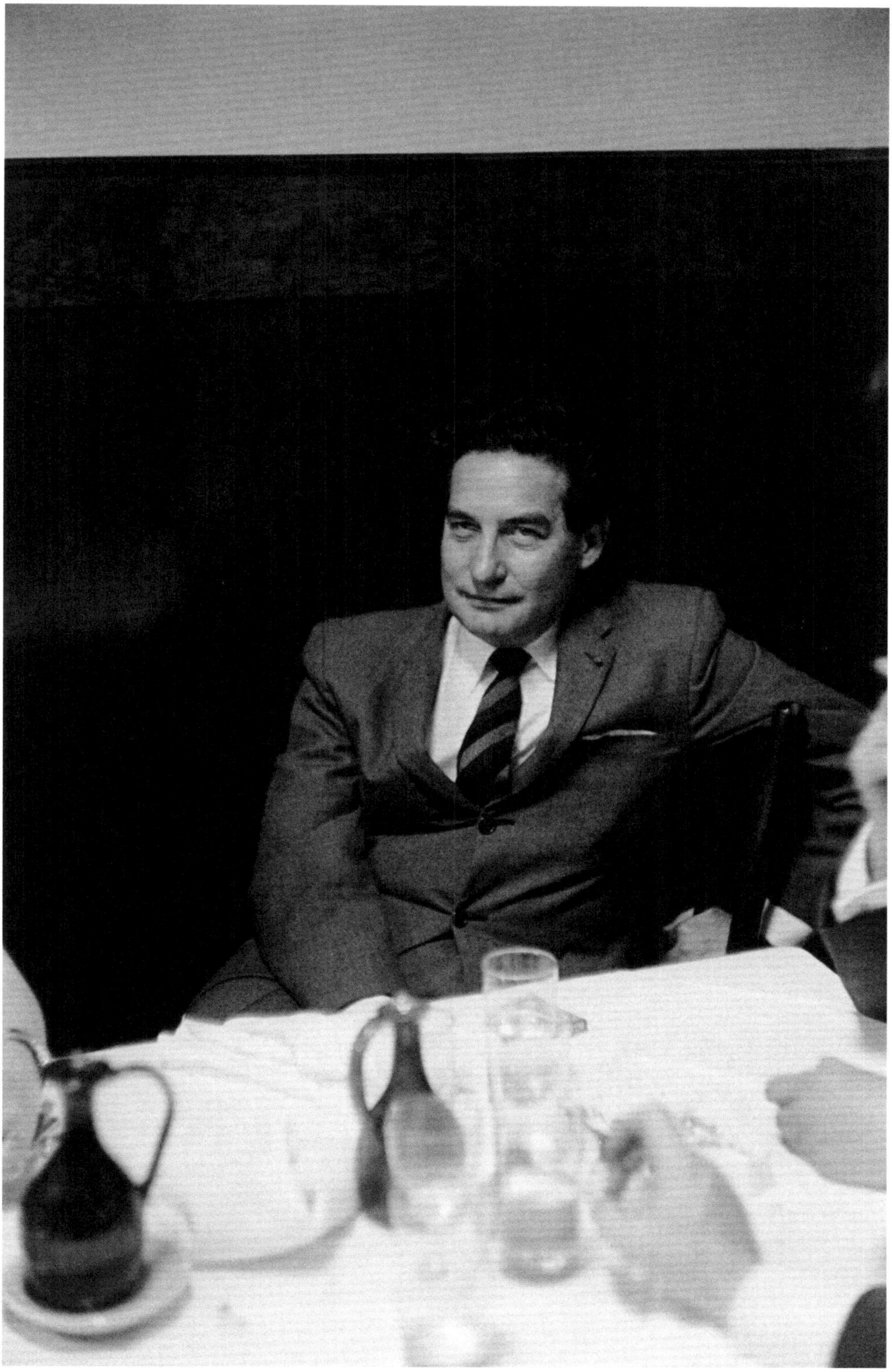

DANIEL PENNAC

[Daniel Pennacchioni] born Casablanca, Morocco, 1944

by Paolo Pellegrin

Paris, 2009

Portrayed here by Paolo Pellegrin on the streets of Paris, Daniel Pennac chose Belleville – a bustling, multi-ethnic part of the city, where he has lived for more than twenty years – as the setting for the surreal adventures of Benjamin Malaussène, a professional scapegoat and Pennac's most famous character. In a series of ironic and incisive novels, Monsieur Malaussène, who lives with his colourful family and epileptic dog, wanders the tiny streets of Belleville among its criminals, prostitutes, immigrants and nuns. The stories of his various mishaps, which are carefully balanced between comedy and something more serious, also touch on the theme of tolerance.

Pennac, a former teacher in a Parisian *lycée*, is an internationally acclaimed writer. A highly inventive author of stories for both adults and children, he also works in non-fiction. In *The Rights of the Reader* (1992), for example, he celebrates the very act of reading, offering the reader a series of witty suggestions and inalienable rights, such as the right to be able to skip some pages and to not finish a book; the right to read anything, anywhere; the right to dip in and out; and the right to read at the top of one's voice. Pennac is also interested in exploring children's experiences of school. In *School Blues* (2007), he tackles the subject from the perspective of what might be termed a dunce, an apparent slacker who never shines in any subject. Pennac, however, shows that every child, particularly those who struggle with traditional schooling, is equally deserving of the attentions of an understanding and inspiring teacher. Pennac himself was one such child: the youngest of four brothers (the others all graduated with top marks), he soon showed himself to be impervious to all teaching methods.

In his autobiographical reflections on French society, Pennac combines his professional experiences as a teacher with a glance over the other side of the fence in order to rediscover, in the young people of today, that insatiable thirst for learning that goes far beyond school reports and exam results: 'I've always believed that school meant teachers, first and foremost. Who was it that saved me from school, but three or four teachers?'

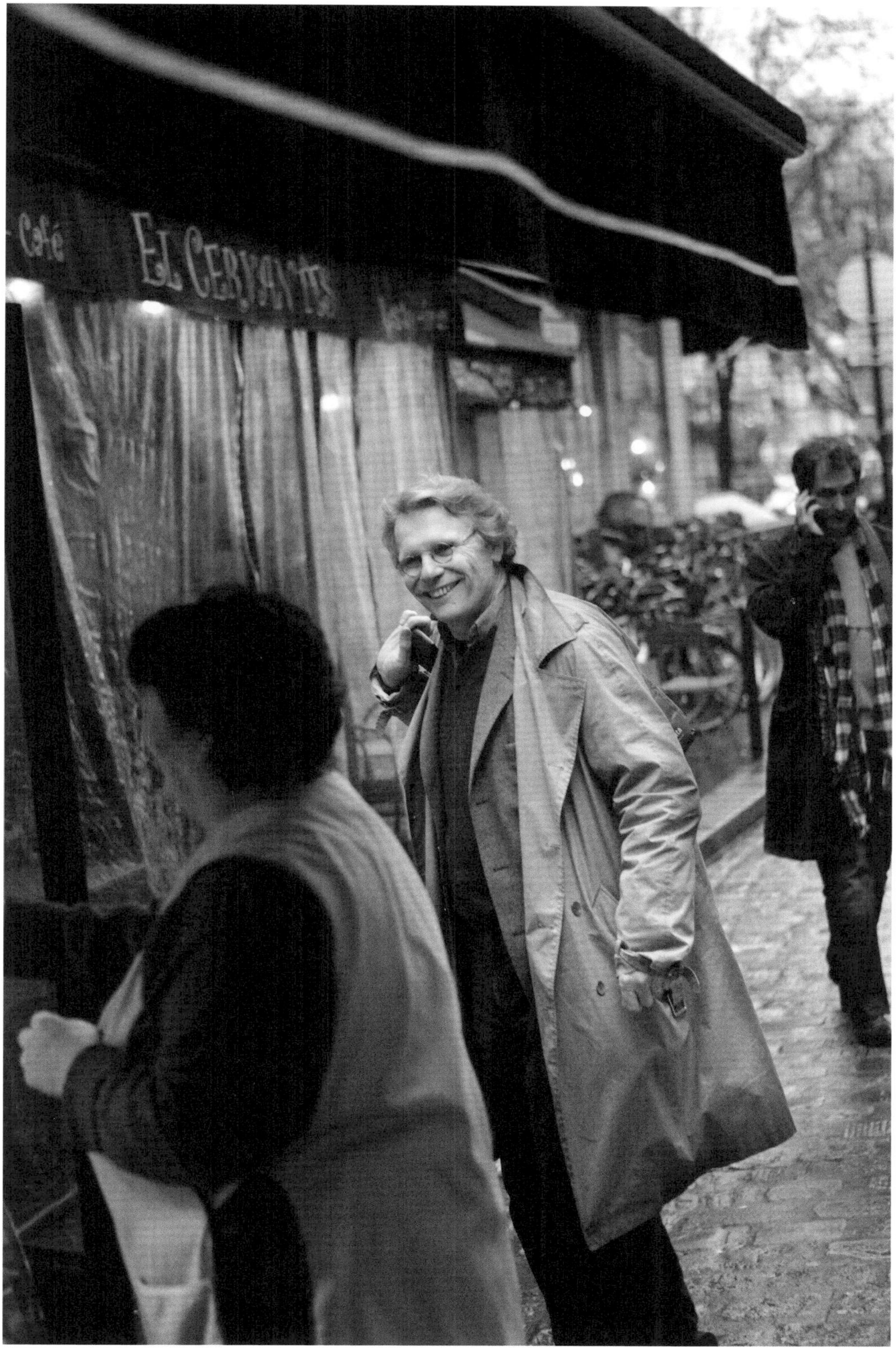
Café
EL CERVANTES

GEORGES PEREC

born Paris, 1936; died Ivry-sur-Seine, France, 1982

by Claude Schwartz

[centre] on the set for The Man Who Sleeps, Paris, 1973

The first-person narrator of the semi-autobiographical *W, or the Memory of Childhood* (1975) tells us that 'Perec' is derived from the ancient Hebraic name 'Peretz', meaning 'hole'. It could be said that the work of Georges Perec, who died at the age of forty-six leaving behind a large number of unfinished works, revolves around a similar void, created by the early loss of his mother and father (the latter, who had enlisted in the French Army during the Second World War, died from his wounds in 1940, while the former was deported from France and perished in Auschwitz three years later).

Perec is remembered as a writer who reinvented himself numerous times, writing in a variety of genres and styles (he also directed films, produced radio plays and worked as aphotographer and designer). He was determined never to write the same book twice, an ambition he achieved. His first novel, *Things: A Story of the Sixties* (1965), deals with theconsumer boom of that decade; seen by many as a sociological novel, it also won the approval of Roland Barthes. In *A Man Asleep* (1967), in which Perec adopts several of the stylistic features of the *nouveau roman* (new novel), he tells the story of a young student in Paris and his sudden withdrawal from life. Together with the French director Bernard Queysanne, Perec later turned the book into a film, *The Man Who Sleeps* (1974), which was awarded the Jean Vigo Prize in the year of its release and has since become a cult classic.

Perec's first masterpiece, however, was *W, or the Memory of Childhood*. It is a largely unclassifiable work, in which autobiography merges with an imaginary tale of an island whose population is principally involved in sport and competition, but where the Olympic ideal has evolved into the nightmare of life in a concentration camp. *Life: A User's Manual* (1978) is Perec's most ambitious 'novels', as it is described on the title page. Consisting of the interwoven stories of the inhabitants of a Parisian apartment block, the book is composed and structured around a set of rigorous self-imposed rules.

Perec's encounter in the late 1960s with Oulipo, a group of writers dedicated to exploring sophisticated linguistic and literary games, had a profound effect on his work. In Oulipo (an acronym of Ouvroir de Littérature Potentielle, or 'Workshop of Potential Literature') he was able to develop his idea of writing under certain constraints, of imposing highly restrictive rules of composition on the creative process. The most famous of his books produced in this way are the novel *A Void* (1969), which he wrote without ever using the letter 'e', and the complementary novella *The Exeter Text* (1972), in which the only vowel used is the one that was missing from its predecessor. In 1980 he published a poetry collection that contained a palindrome consisting of 1,247 words, at the time the longest in the world.

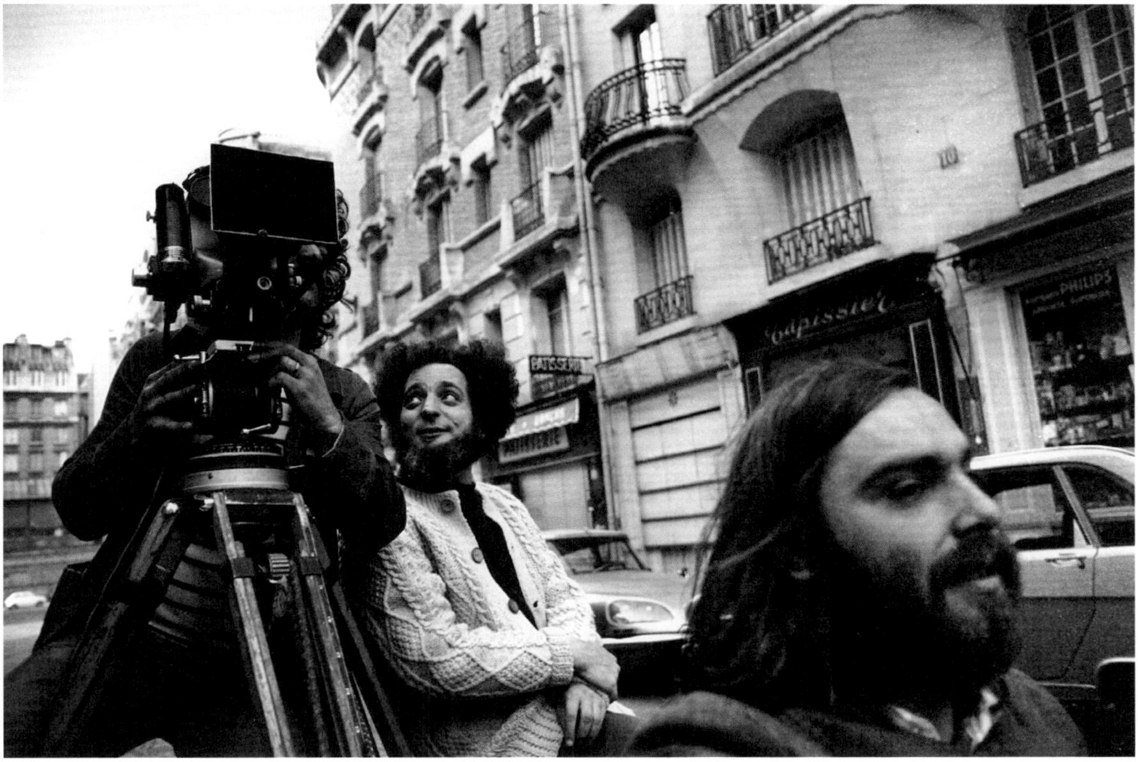
PHILIPS

FERNANDO PESSOA

born Lisbon, 1888; died Lisbon, 1935

unknown photographer

Lisbon, 1914

Many attempts have been made to define Fernando Pessoa, an apparently indefinable and elusive author. He was one person, nobody, a hundred thousand souls, a plural poet, a contradictory being. The enigma that is Pessoa is even reflected in his surname, which means 'person'. During his lifetime he created almost eighty literary alter egos, or to use his term, 'heteronyms', each of whom had a different style and world view. They included the Hellenist Ricardo Reis; the avant-garde artist Álvaro de Campos; the poet Alberto Caeiro; and the 'semi-heteronym' Bernardo Soares, author of *The Book of Disquiet*, which was published posthumously.

In the modest guise of a translator working for various import-export companies, Pessoa was responsible for an entire literary movement. Together with his heteronyms and the real characters that surrounded him, including the artist José de Almada Negreiros and the writer Mário de Sá-Carneiro, Pessoa helped to modernize Portuguese literature. He died having published very few books, although he had been extremely active as a journalist. Interest in Pessoa took off in Portugal in the 1940s following the discovery of a trunk containing his literary output, including that of his heteronyms, and soon spread to the rest of the world. Since then, previously undiscovered works have continued to be published.

The question of how to define Pessoa may never be fully resolved; indeed, the author himself once wrote, 'I am in great measure the very prose that I write … I've become a character in a book, a life already read.' Perhaps it is best left to one of his heteronyms, Alberto Caeiro, to answer: 'If, after my death, they want to write my biography / There's nothing simpler. / There are only two dates – that of my birth and of my death. / Between one and the other, all days are mine.'

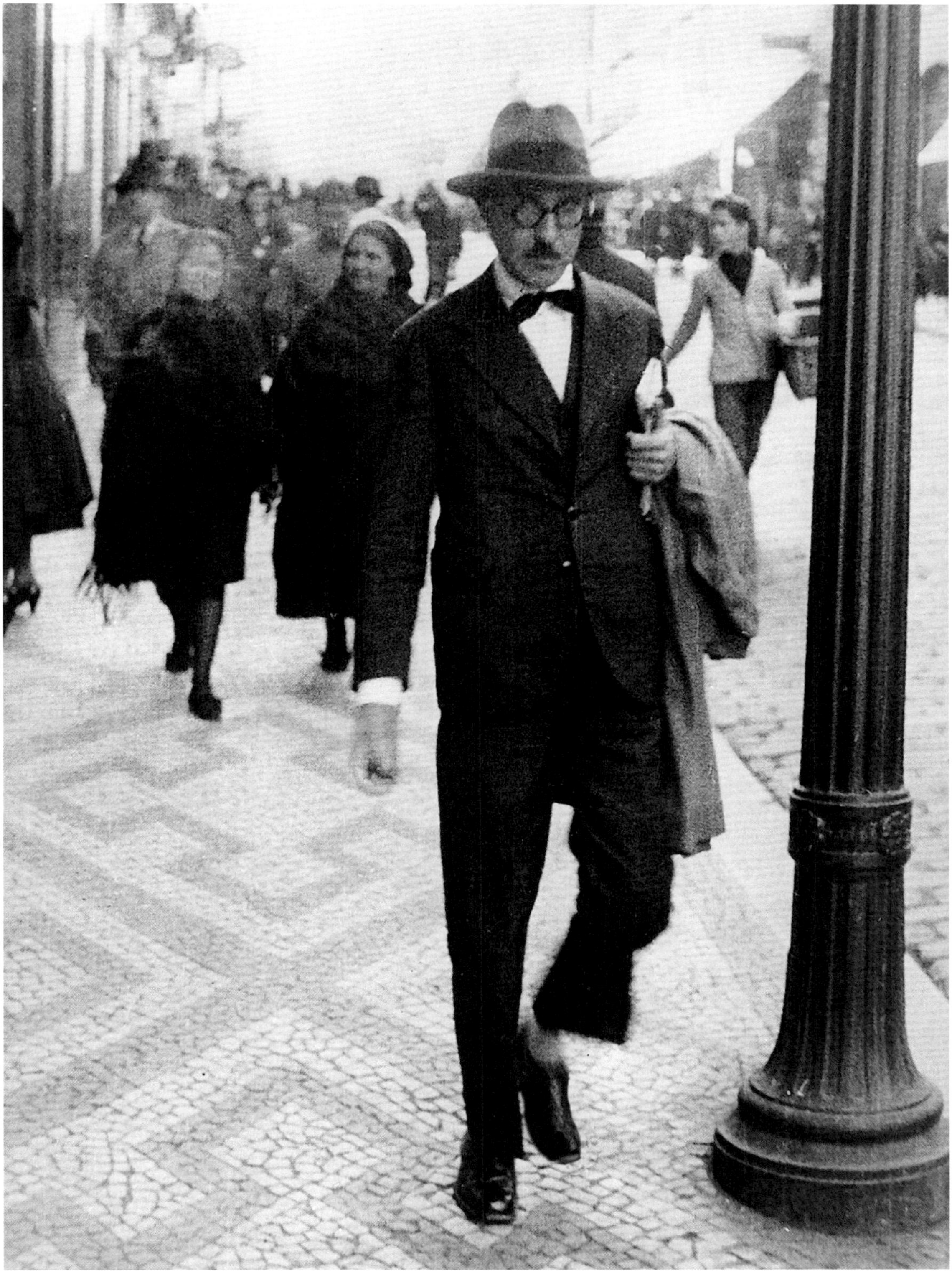

ALEJANDRA PIZARNIK

born Buenos Aires, 1936; died Buenos Aires, 1972

by Sara Facio

Buenos Aires, 1967

Born in Argentina, the daughter of Jewish immigrants from Ukraine, Alejandra Pizarnik always felt that she had been cut off from her roots. This agony of not belonging resonated through her poetry, and her first collection of verse was entitled *La Tierra más ajena* (The most alien land, 1955). The collections that followed, *La Última inocencia* (The last innocence, 1956) and *Las Aventuras perdidas* (The lost adventures, 1958), included themes such as the recovery of childhood as a golden age and the idea of the friendly night (as opposed to the menacing sun): 'Perhaps the night is life and the sun is death.'

Pizarnik combined romanticism – seen in her glorification of the night, solitude and death – with an obsessive effort to purify words and language: 'a stranger I have been / when close to faraway lights / I have treasured the purest words / to create new silences.' She felt that this continuous quest to find words worth treasuring offered security yet also kept her apart from life itself. 'I hide myself away in language / and the reason / is that I am afraid.' This metamorphosis into poetry – the struggle between words and silence, between a life lived and a life lived in verse – began to undermine her mental balance.

During a stay in Paris (1960–64), Pizarnik learned of a strange sixteenth-century Hungarian countess, Erzsébet Báthory, who sacrificed hundreds of young girls in an attempt to satisfy her desire for eternal youth. To her, Pizarnik dedicated an enigmatic prose poem, *The Bloody Countess* (1971), in which the writer seemed to reflect on the origin of evil by using language in an almost sterile way. After she left Paris, Pizarnik spent ever more frequent periods in psychiatric clinics. Her view of death as a liberation became firmer, and featured in her poetry: 'Words would have been able to save me but I am too much alive.' On 25 September 1972 she killed herself by taking an overdose of barbiturates.

Sara Facio, who took this portrait of her, remembered their meeting: 'She came to the studio to get to know me. She wanted me to make a portrait of her, but first she wanted to know what type of person I was … quite unusual, but it also told me that she was a very special person. She spoke with a Russian accent, pronouncing her words very slowly.' It was the unexpected arrival of Silvina Ocampo, a friend of the photographer and an object of veneration for the young poet, that caused Pizarnik to overcome any feelings of shyness. The photograph was taken a few days later in her father's home in a working-class district of Buenos Aires.

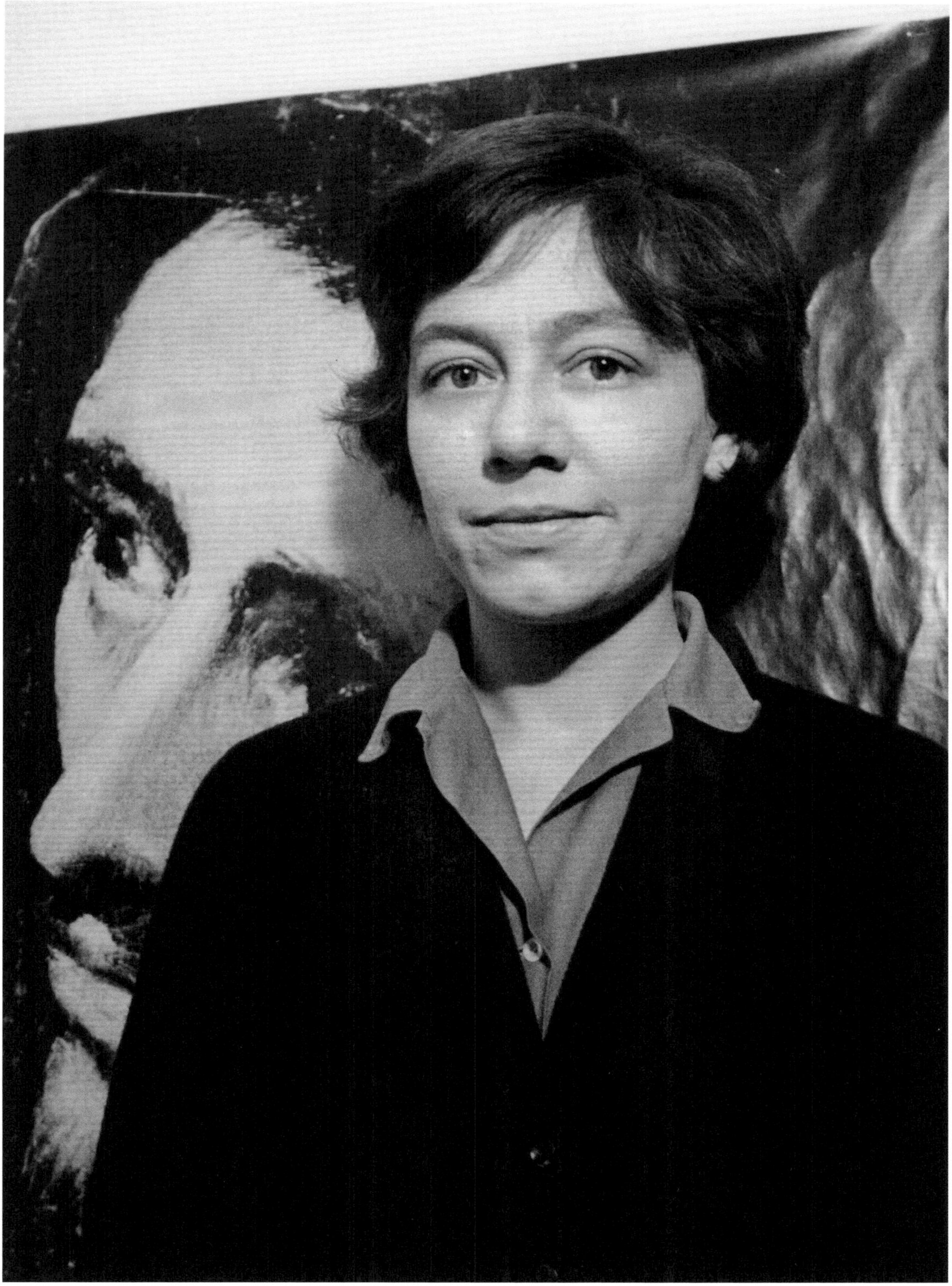

SYLVIA PLATH

born Boston, Massachusetts, 1932; died London, 1963

unknown photographer

Wellesley, Massachusetts, 1954

Sylvia Plath was born in Boston to a German father and an Austrian mother. As a young girl she was traumatized by both her troubled relationship with her father and his death when she was only eight years old. She was a precocious child, suffering depressive and perfectionist tendencies from a young age. In 1950 she attended Smith College in western Massachusetts, where she excelled academically. Following her graduation from Smith in 1955, she was awarded a Fulbright Scholarship to study at Newnham College, Cambridge. It was there that she met Ted Hughes.

Plath and Hughes were married in 1956. After teaching for a while in the USA, they returned to England for the birth of their first child, Frieda. Before the arrival of their second child, Nicholas, the two had separated following Plath's discovery of her husband's affair with Assia Wevill. Throughout these difficult years, Plath devoted herself to writing poetry. Her first collection of verse, *The Colossus*, was published in 1960; her second, *Ariel*, was published posthumously in 1965. The months immediately preceding her death were marked by an intense burst of creativity. Towards the end of 1962, however, Plath was suffering once again from depression, and in February 1963, one of the coldest for many years, she took her own life in her flat in London.

Plath died intestate, so it was Hughes, to whom she was still legally married at the time of her death, who inherited her literary estate. His decision to destroy Plath's final journal, and to withhold publication of some of her unseen work, attracted considerable criticism. Plath's only novel, *The Bell Jar* (1963), which deals with her first suicide attempt in 1953, was published shortly before her death. In 1982 *The Collected Poems* (1981), a collection of her verse with an introduction by Hughes, was awarded a Pulitzer Prize.

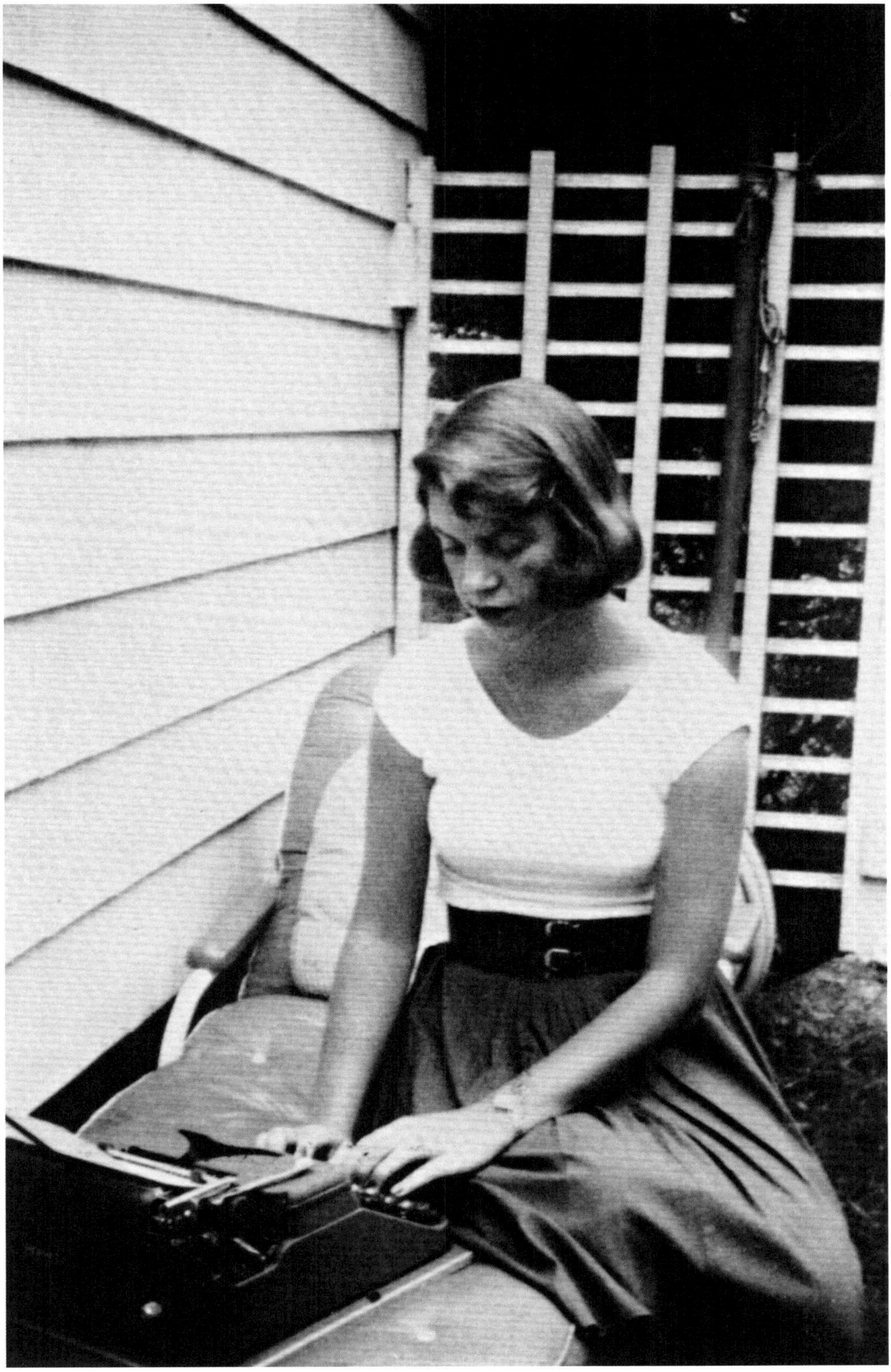

EZRA POUND

born Hailey, Idaho, 1885; died Venice, Italy, 1972

by Richard Avedon

Rutherford, New Jersey, 1958

Although he was born a child of the Midwest, in Hailey, Idaho, Ezra Pound proved to be the son and heir to a more ancient and refined global poetic culture. Pound first visited Europe while still a teenager, and soon decided that, before his thirtieth birthday, he would get to know ancient and modern poetry better than anyone else. Back in the USA, he studied hard and learned nine languages. Following a brief spell as a teacher in Indiana – a post from which he was asked to resign on account of his bohemian lifestyle – he returned to Europe in 1908, arriving in Italy. It was there that he published his first collection of verses, *A lume spento* (1908).

From Italy, Pound travelled to London, where he worked for several American literary magazines and established himself as a member of the literary avant-garde. In 1920 he moved to Paris, where he met Hemingway, who taught him how to box. Five years later Pound returned to Italy, a country chosen for its climate and for Mussolini's 'anti-Capitalist and anti-Marxist' social policy. Throughout this period he continued to compose verses in which his own poetry was interwoven with the lyrical echoes of the poets whose work he had absorbed so obsessively: from the troubadours and the love poetry of the thirteenth century to Dante, Homer and the Chinese poets whose work he had read and translated. He published several volumes of poetry during this time, including *Personae* (1909) and *Ripostes* (1912).

In 1945 Pound was arrested on charges of treason for broadcasting Fascist propaganda to America by radio. While being held in a military base in Pisa, he dedicated himself to his long-running and most ambitious work, the *Cantos,* producing *Pisan Cantos* (1948) as a result. On his return to the USA he was saved from being sentenced under martial law by a sympathetic psychiatric assessment, but was committed to St Elizabeths psychiatric hospital in Washington DC, where he was held until 1958. It was only the efforts of writers and poets from around the world that eventually secured his freedom.

Richard Avedon met Pound shortly after his release, in the house of the poet William Carlos Williams. Avedon's memorable portrait of Pound exemplifies his unique approach to photography: 'I've worked out of a series of no's. No to exquisite light, no to apparent compositions, no to the seduction of poses or narrative. And all these no's force me to the "yes". I have a white background. I have the person I'm interested in and the thing that happens between us.'

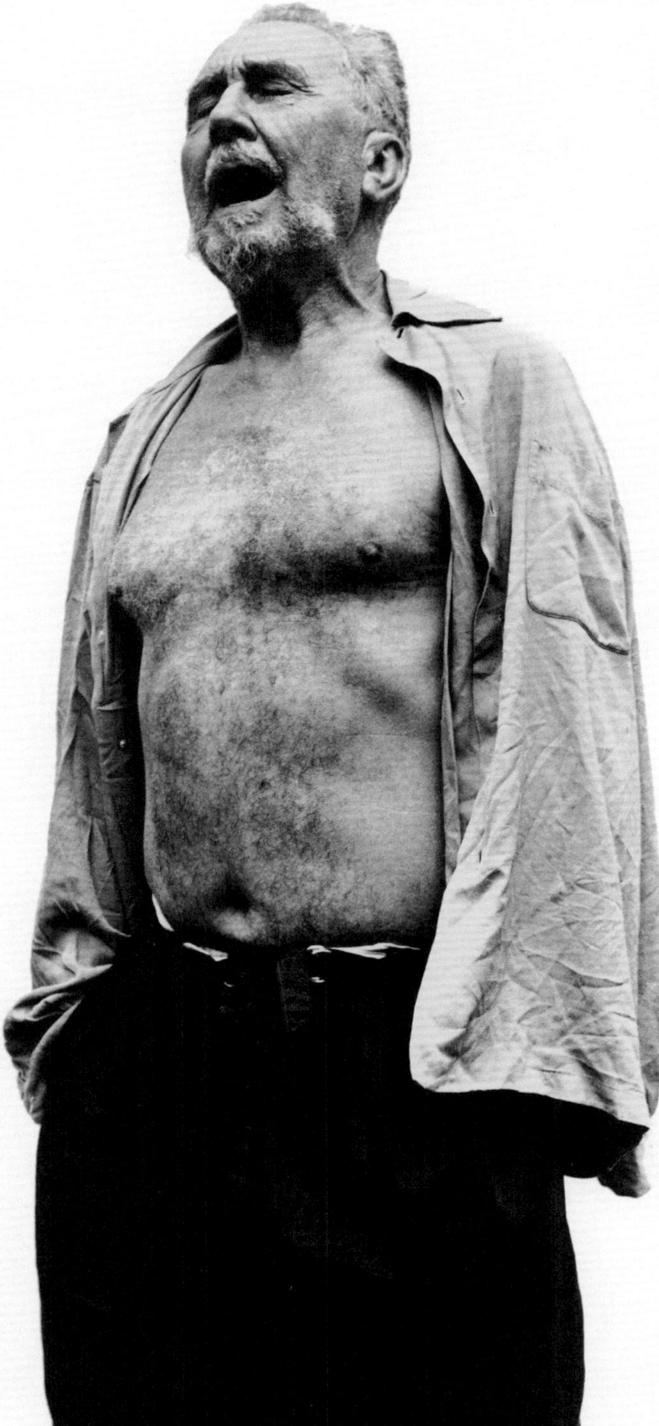

JACQUES PRÉVERT

born Neuilly-sur-Seine, France, 1900; died Omonville-la-Petite, France, 1977

by Robert Doisneau

Paris, c. 1955

Jacques Prévert and Robert Doisneau were great friends. 'When he works in a hurry', Prévert said of his photographer friend, 'it is with a fraternal sense of humour and without any kind of superiority complex that creates illusions and lays traps. And it is always the imperfect that his lens sees that allows him to conjugate the verb "to photograph".' Of his poet friend, Doisneau said: 'Jacques Prévert's elegance stems from the joy to be found in the way that he can make words dance.' It was the ability to recognize an impalpable and-playful dimension in everyday life – a dimension that encompassed games, affection and freedom – that these two French artists shared.

Everyday life in Prévert's work is closely associated with spoken language; it is dressed in a passionately authentic style that expresses to the very heart of existence. Love, liberty, satire directed against those in power and his loathing for social oppression are all expressed in an ironic and gentle manner, which may appear simple but is never banal.

The power and musical rhythm of his words are essential elements of his compositions, and it was no coincidence that for many years Prévert worked as a scriptwriter for the cinema, and also wrote lyrics for the great interpreters of French *chanson*, from Juliette Gréco to Yves Montand. Prévert also wrote the words for the well-known song *Les Feuilles mortes* (known in English as *Autumn Leaves*) for the soundtrack of Marcel Carné's 1946 film *Gates of the Night*.

Prévert was a major figure of Parisian cultural life, in which he had been surrounded by his artistic friends since the 1920s, when his apartment in Montparnasse became the Surrealists' favourite meeting place. And even when severe illness forced him to retire from public life, he carried on meeting with his dearest friends, such as Raymond Queneau.

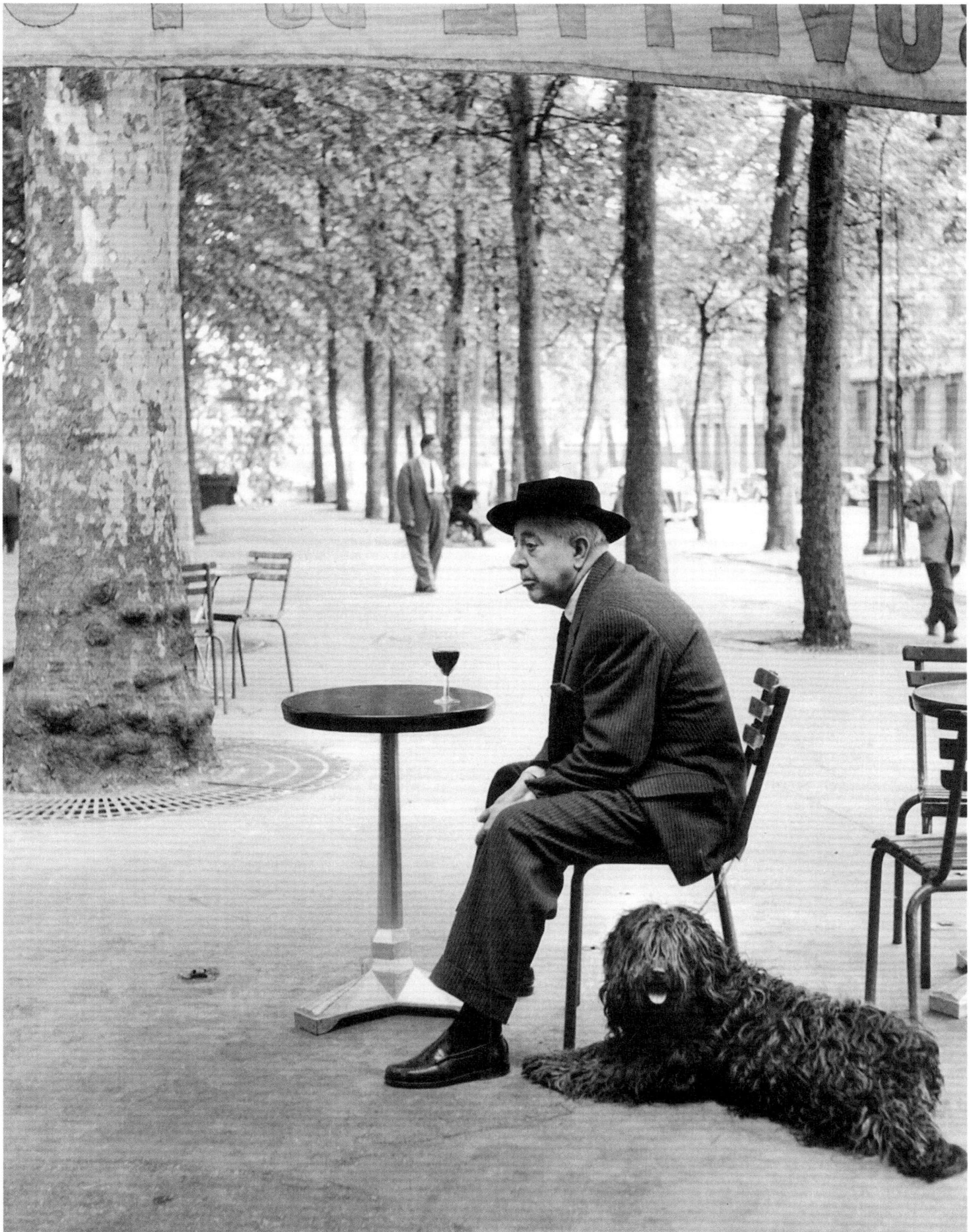

MARCEL PROUST

born Auteuil, France, 1871; died Paris, 1922

by Man Ray

Paris, 1922

At the heart of Marcel Proust's *In Search of Lost Time* (1913–27) is arguably one of the most famous foodstuffs in the whole of literature: the madeleine. In an early episode ofthe book, Proust uses this small, buttery, shell-shaped cake to illustrate his concept of 'involuntary memory', the process by which otherwise irretrievable memories of one's past can be conjured up by such sensory experiences as the taste of a madeleine dipped in a cup of tea.

Consisting of seven volumes, *In Search of Lost Time* was a new departure in the genre of the novel. Proust started the book in 1909 and continued to work on it for the rest of his life, closeting himself away in a room sound-proofed with cork tiles, so that no external noise could disturb his thoughts. It was an arduous and courageous undertaking for a man who had suffered from chronic asthma attacks since his childhood.

The book itself – a vast portrait of Parisian society, in which every character has an autobiographical element – constitutes a monumental exploration of the innumerable permutations and intricacies of human relations. In dense yet vivid prose, Proust records every nuance of the human psyche. He plumbs the depths of memory and emotion; analyses the effects of familial and social networks and of country and city living; and scrutinizes the role of different social classes in a constant search to find the human qualities that are not defined by a person's social status. Above all, Proust shows how human life is underpinned by memory. Not only does the past come alive in the key episode in which the narrator tastes the madeleine, but also it becomes a simultaneous and ongoing part of his present experience.

Proust was working on the book right up to his death from pneumonia in 1922. It was the author's brother who summoned Man Ray to take this final portrait of the writer on his deathbed, his calm features bearing little trace of the suffering he had experienced.

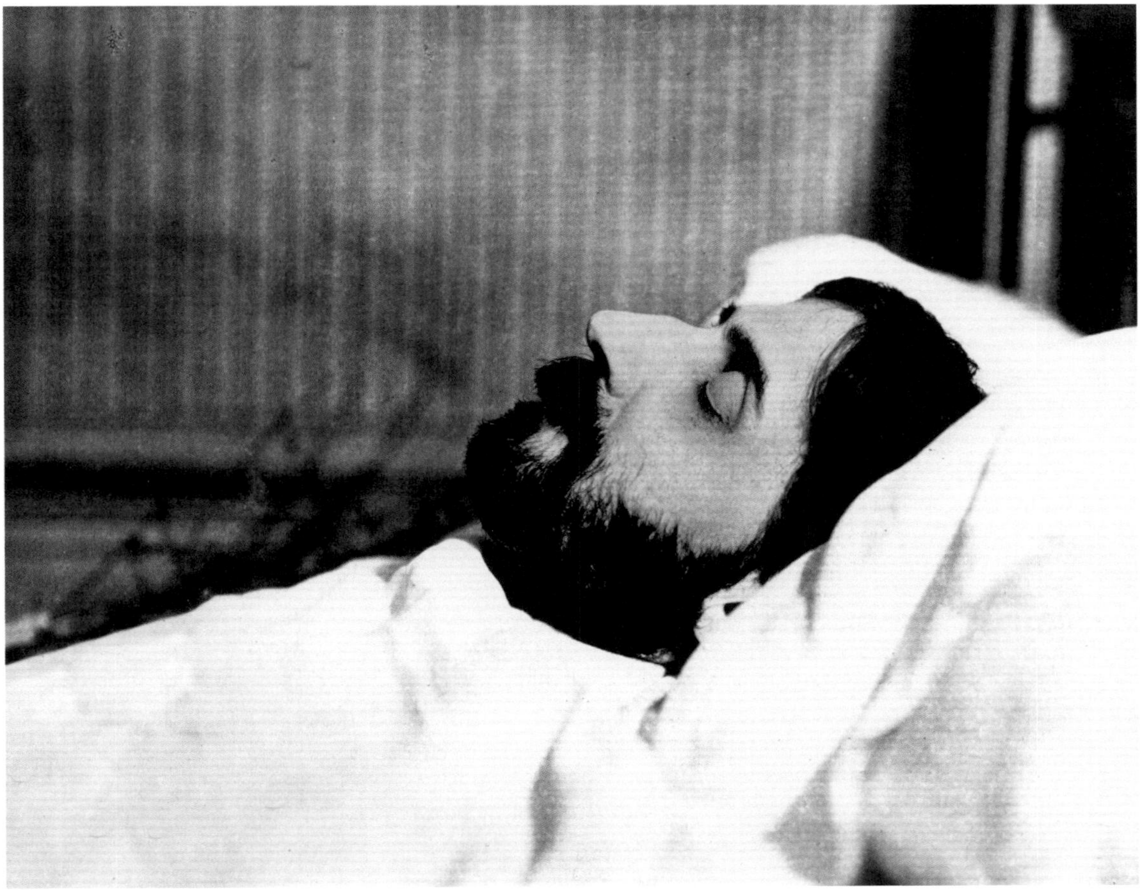

MANUEL PUIG

born General Villegas, Argentina, 1932; died Cuernavaca, Mexico, 1990

Deborah Feingold

unknown location, 1979

The works of Manuel Puig reflect the dominant themes of his life: his love of cinema, literature and theatre, as well as his own homosexuality. Puig was born in 1932 in the village of General Villegas, Argentina, set in the infinite expanse of pampas where there was little scenery, just 'an entirely blank screen'. As a child his one means of escape was to the only nearby cinema, which he visited almost every day with his mother. These trips nurtured his fascination with film, and in 1956 he won a scholarship to study at the Italian National Film School in Rome. Although this promised to be a dream come true, he found that the prevailing neo-Realism was not to his taste. A fan of Greta Garbo and Joan Crawford, for him cinema was the home of fantasy. He turned to writing, pouring his love of cinema into that medium.

In *Betrayed by Rita Hayworth* (1968) the protagonist escapes the reality of his daily life by imagining himself in a film. Puig was not only inventive in terms of plot, but also in the structure and technique of his novels. He incorporated cinematic montages, long dialogues and elements of popular literature such as serial stories, radio dramas, soap operas and tango lyrics. In his novel *Heartbreak Tango* (1969), he uses the lyrics of a famous tango song by Alfred Le Pera, 'Boquitas pintadas', not only as the Spanish title of the book, but also to punctuate the novel.

The Buenos Aires Affair (1973) was the last book he wrote during his Argentine period. In the mid-1970s he left the country after threats were made against him because of his political inclinations. His works were banned under the Perón regime and cinema became a political tool of the state. Puig never returned to his homeland, and spent the rest of his life exiled in Mexico, where he wrote his best-known novel, *Kiss of the Spider Woman* (1976), which was made into a film in 1985, directed by Héctor Babenco. The plot revolves around two cellmates in an Argentinian prison. Valentín is a militant from the extreme left; Molina is a homosexual who has been accused of 'corrupting a minor', and who is later revealed to have been sent by the authorities to spy on Valentín. The story is narrated by Molina, who recounts scenes from films as a form of escapism. The protagonists briefly become lovers and find their roles reversed when Valentín learns the power of the imagination as a weapon.

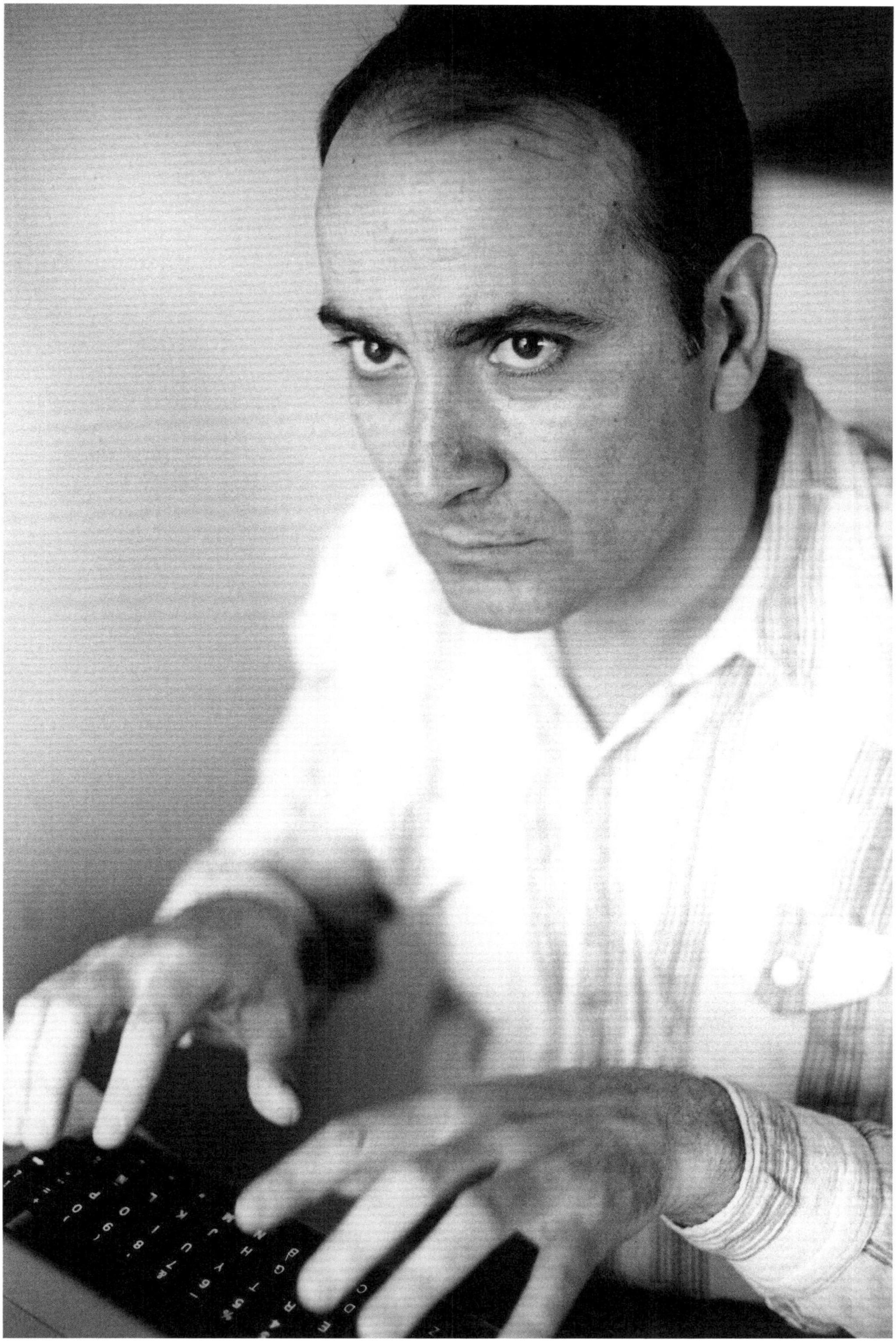

THOMAS PYNCHON

born Glen Cove, New York, 1937

passport photograph

Glen Cove, New York, 1955

In an interview for CNN in 1997, Thomas Pynchon reiterated his dislike of being filmed or photographed, and referred to his desire not to talk about his private life: 'My belief is that "recluse" is a code word generated by journalists ... meaning, "doesn't like to talk to reporters".' Indeed, little is known about this author, apart from the fact that he is descended from one of the first families to settle in the USA in 1630, and that he studied at Cornell University. It was there that he wrote his first short story, 'The Small Rain' (1959).

Pynchon later dismissed his youthful literary endeavours, and his first novel, *V*, was published in 1963. It was an experimental work, and was widely regarded as a milestone in postmodernist literature. Praised for its exaggerated elegance, cleverness, complexity and black humour, it won a William Faulkner Foundation Award for best debut novel, and was recommended for a National Book Award. The novel bears all the hallmarks of Pynchon's style: the plot, which exists on several different levels, is constructed like a puzzle, and the numerous characters appear in various incarnations; Stencil, one of the main protagonists, takes on at least eight different guises. Pynchon's stories often revolve around actual historical events that have been forgotten or overlooked (in the case of *V*, the Herero people of Namibia), often involve crime, and contain passing references to his interest in biology and mechanics. *The Crying of Lot 49*, published in 1966, takes the form of a riddle to be solved, not dissimilar to the assassination of John F. Kennedy. In 1973 Pynchon published his most celebrated novel, *Gravity's Rainbow*, which is set during the end of World War Two.

The publication of *Mason & Dixon* in 1997 saw Pynchon turn his hand to the historical novel. Set in the eighteenth century, it tells the story of the surveyors of the Mason–Dixon line in pre-revolutionary America. It is both meticulously researched and wildly inventive, and was widely acclaimed by the critics and the public alike. *Inherent Vice*, published in 2009, is a more mainstream work, a light-hearted detective novel. Yet even here, Pynchon does not completely abandon his apocalyptic undertones. Nor does he ignore the issues of freedom and repression that characterize many of his books.

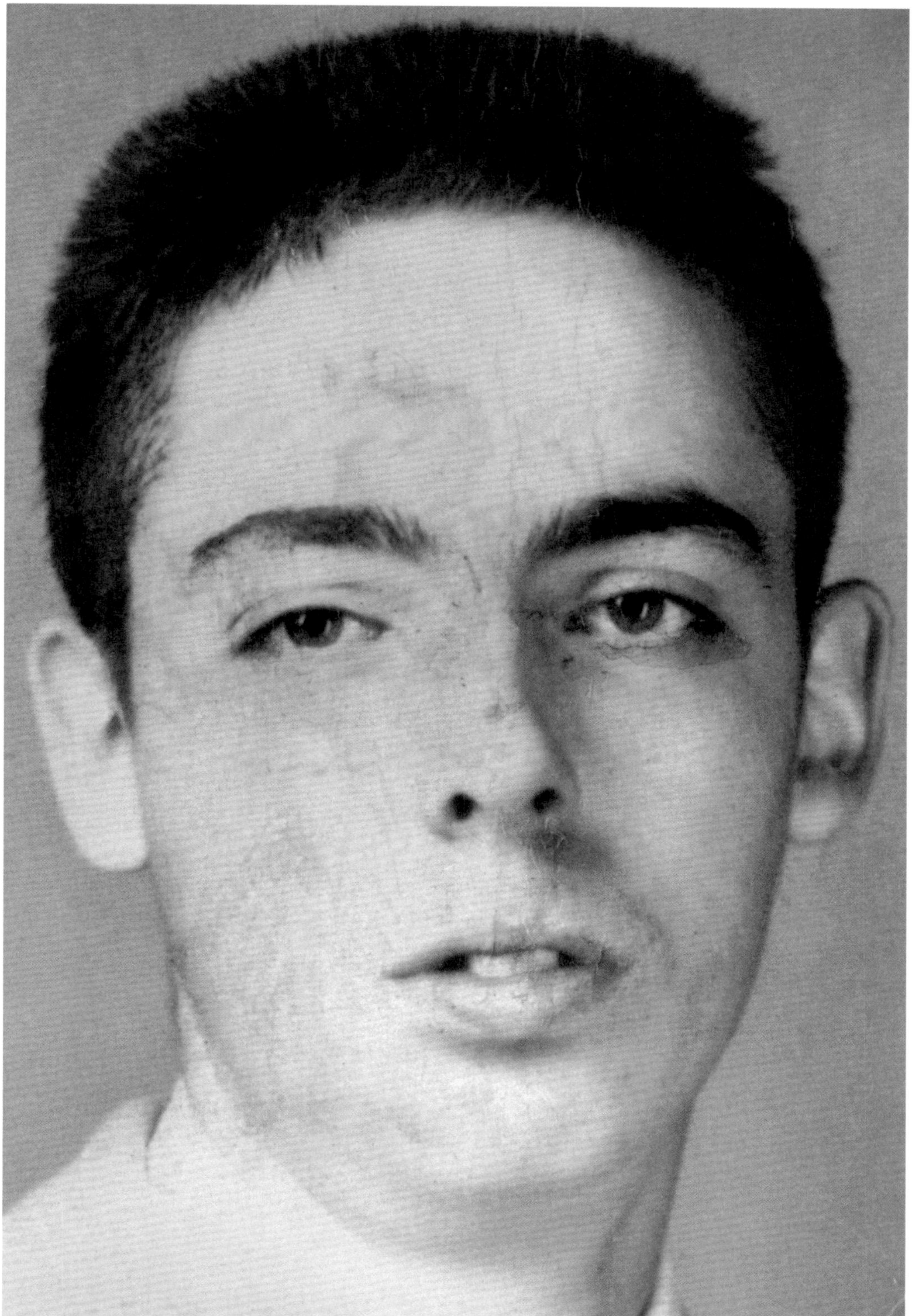

RAYMOND QUENEAU

born Le Havre, France, 1903; died Paris, 1976

by Robert Doisneau

Paris, 1956

According to the opening lines of Raymond Queneau's autobiographical verse novel, *Chêne et chien* (1937), the man who would go on to become one of the twentieth century's most influential and unclassifiable writers had a relatively simple start in life: 'I was born in Le Havre on the twenty-first of February / nineteen hundred and three. / My mother and my father were both haberdashers by trade.' Much of Queneau's work was devoted to those on the margins of life, to people of the provinces and to seemingly insignificant events. He played with the concepts of time, history and existence in a bold and surrealist manner (*The Blue Flowers*, 1965), and although he was a member of the Surrealist movement for a while, he never fully endorsed their methods. Indeed, his split with André Breton was due less to artistic reasons than to familial ones (Queneau was married to the sister of Breton's ex-wife).

Queneau's personality was perhaps too exuberant and multifaceted to submit to the rigid line dictated by the Surrealist leader. He was a man of science as well as letters, and from his youth had shown a keen interest in philosophy, history, sociology and mathematics. He spent much of his life working for the French publishing house Gallimard, and in 1956 was appointed director of its reference series *Encyclopédie de la Pléiade*. Possessed of a lively intellect, he applied his talents to eccentric spheres of research, the results of which included his 'Encyclopaedia of Inexact Sciences', a collection of nineteenth-century 'literary lunatics' and examples of their writing (unsurprisingly, it did not find a publisher). He wrote novels (*Children of Clay*, 1938) and poetry (*A Small Portable Cosmogony*, 1950), and explored the many different ways in which the same story can be told (*Exercises in Style*, 1947). He was also an obsessive compiler of lists and inventories, both within his works and in his own diaries.

Queneau was the creator of two particularly endearing female protagonists: the writer of *Le Journal intime de Sally Mara* (Sally Mara's Diary, 1950), and the young heroine of *Zazie in the Metro* (1959). In 1960 he co-founded Oulipo (an acronym of Ouvroir de Littérature Potentielle, or 'Workshop of Potential Literature') with his friend the mathematician François Le Lionnais. The group, whose members have included Georges Perec and Italo Calvino, was established to explore the use of constrained writing techniques based on mathematical patterns and structures.

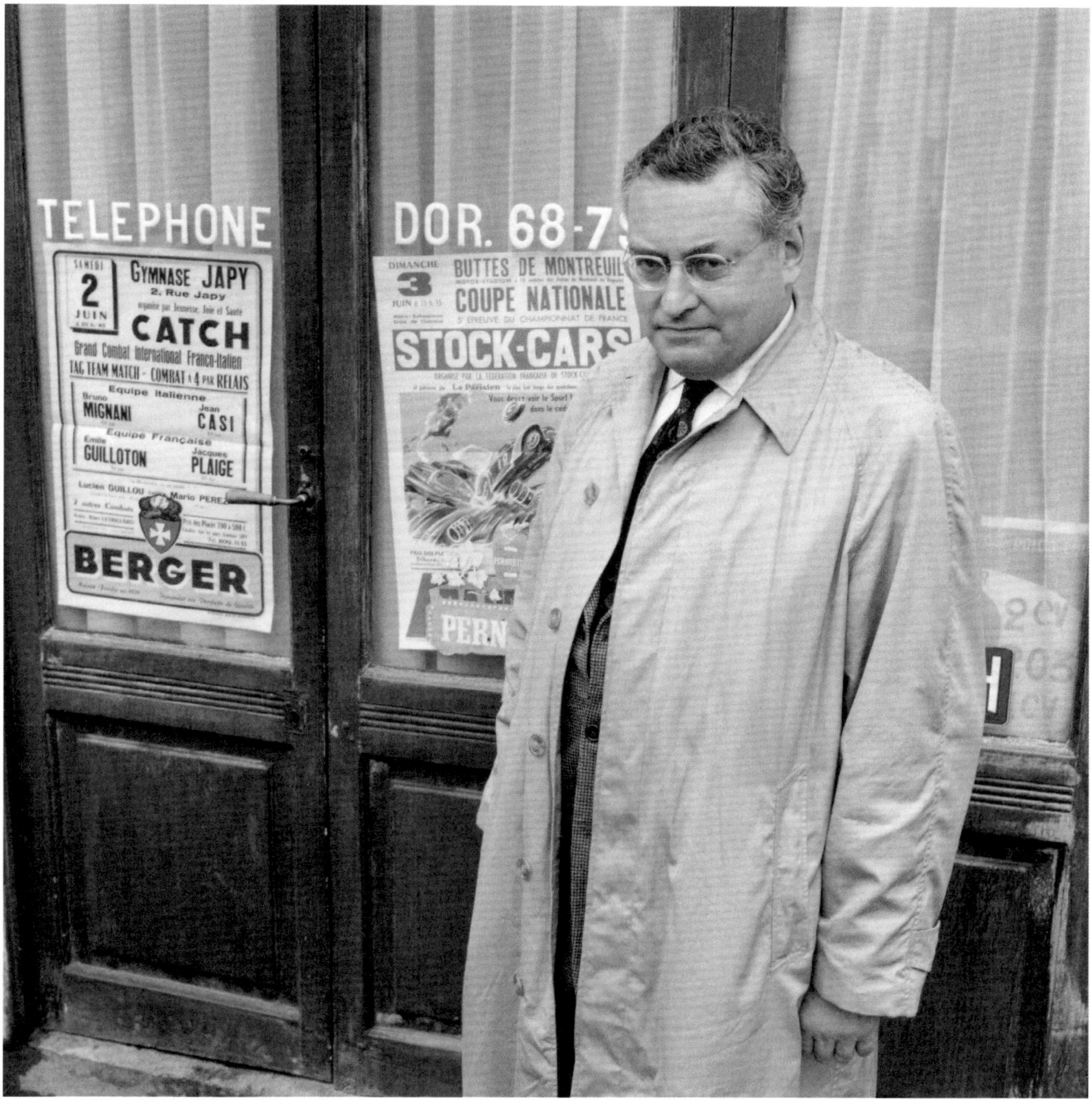
TELEPHONE
DOR. 68-7
SAMEDI
2
JUIN
GYMNASE JAPY
2, Rue Japy
CATCH
Grand Combat International Franco-Italien
TAG TEAM MATCH - COMBAT A 4 PAR RELAIS
Equipe Italienne
Bruno
MIGNANI
Jean
CASI
Equipe Française
Emile
GUILLOTON
Jacques
PLAIGE
Lucien GUILLOU
Mario PEREZ
BERGER
DIMANCHE
3
JUIN
BUTTES DE MONTREUIL
COUPE NATIONALE
5e EPREUVE DU CHAMPIONNAT DE FRANCE
STOCK-CARS
Le Parisien

RAINER MARIA RILKE

[René Karl Wilhelm Johann Josef Maria Rilke] born Prague, 1875; died Montreux, Switzerland, 1926

unknown photographer

Nyon, Switzerland, 1919

Rainer Maria Rilke is perhaps the writer who best embodies the existential anxiety of a world on the brink of change at the turn of the twentieth century. He was a charming conversationalist, popular with the ladies, aristocratic in style, a tireless traveller and a practised *flâneur*. He journeyed throughout Europe in a constant search for intellectual stimulation; he had nowhere he called home, and lived in the shadow of the impending First World War, which he knew would destroy the old world, and with it the certainties of life as he understood them.

Rilke was born in Prague, studied in Munich and Berlin, and travelled in Italy, Switzerland, France, Austria, Russia and North Africa. His first work of note was the prose poem *The Lay of the Love and Death of Cornet Christopher Rilke* (1906). Rilke felt an overwhelming need to write poetry, as both an act of faith and an act of conscience, and in his verses he explored the restlessness of modern man. In *The Notebooks of Malte Laurids Brigge* (1910), the protagonist – a young, foreign intellectual who wanders the streets of Paris – explains that in order to understand life, it is necessary to write, and in order to write ten good verses, it is necessary to live a whole life, for verses are formed not from sentiment, but from experience. Told in the form of a diary, the book is a semi-autobiographical work, with Malte serving as Rilke's alter ego.

Rilke lived in Paris from 1902 to 1910, during which time he became acquainted with such artists and writers as Rodin (about whom he wrote a monograph), Cézanne and André Gide. However, his restlessness propelled him to seek pastures new, and from 1911 to 1912 he lived in a castle at Duino, near Trieste, as a guest of Princess Marie of Thurn and Taxis. It was there that he began what would become one of his best-known works, the *Duino Elegies* (1923), poetical and philosophical reflections on the meaning of existence, the frailty of human life and the nature of death. In a letter to a friend, he wrote: 'We, let it be emphasized once more, in the sense of the Elegies, are the transformers of the earth; our entire existence, the flights and plunges of our love, everything qualifies us for this task (beside which there is, essentially, no other).'

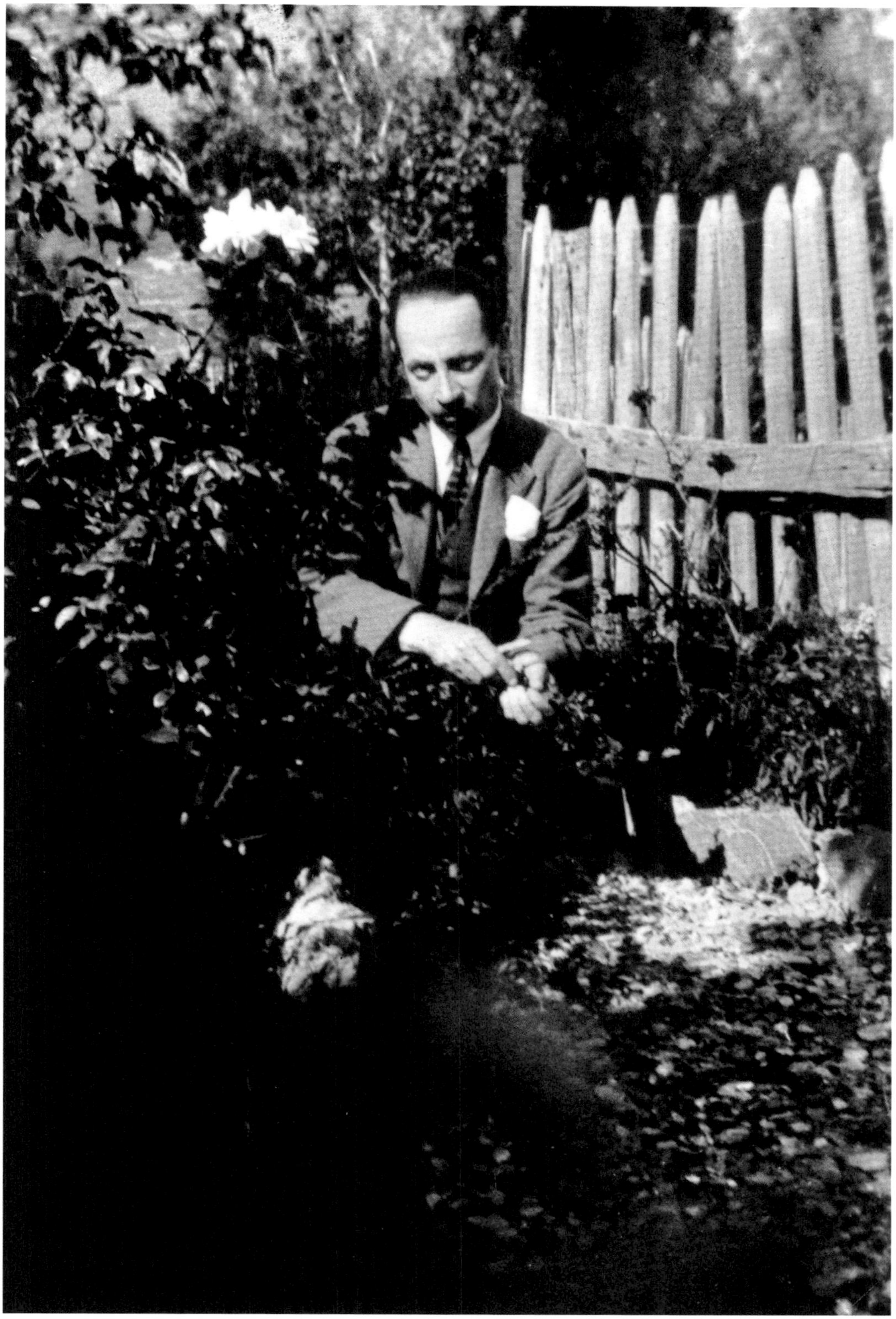

ALAIN ROBBE-GRILLET

born Brest, France, 1922; died Caen, France, 2008

by Henri Cartier-Bresson

[right] with the publisher Jérôme Lindon, Paris, 1961

'The world is neither meaningful nor absurd. It simply *is*.' Thus wrote Alain Robbe-Grillet in *Towards a New Novel* (1963), his polemic on the existentialism of Sartre and Camus, and a theoretical manifesto for the *nouveau roman* (new novel).

Between the late 1950s and early 1960s – albeit with varying degrees of willingness – such writers as the Nobel Prize-winner Claude Simon, Michel Butor, Marguerite Duras and Nathalie Sarraute rallied round Robbe-Grillet's pronouncements; even Samuel Beckett was enlisted in the cause. The purely visual, ice-cool descriptions in the most celebrated of Robbe-Grillet's *nouveaux romans* highlight his paring down of everything that *is*, and his radical rejection of the codes of novels from the past, including plot, the inner life of characters, a linear chronology and recognizable locations.

With such books as *The Erasers* (1953), *The Voyeur* (1955) *and Jealousy* (1957), Robbe-Grillet forged a reputation as French literature's last great transgressor of literary forms. This reputation helped him build a distinguished career as an intellectual and a respected, if controversial, cultural leader. It also led him to film-making and writing screenplays (in particular, for Alain Resnais's *Last Year in Marienbad* (1961), which Robbe-Grillet later published as a 'ciné-novel'), to working as a literary adviser for the publishing house Éditions de Minuit, to lecturing at universities (in the USA), and even, in 2005, to his being offered a chair in the Académie Française, which, in line with his polemical stance, he refused.

Henri Cartier-Bresson took this portrait of a seated Robbe-Grillet with Jérôme Lindon, then director of Éditions de Minuit, in 1961. The photographer's skilful use of black and white allowed him to create a cinematic atmosphere, which lends the image a mysterious, film noir-like quality.

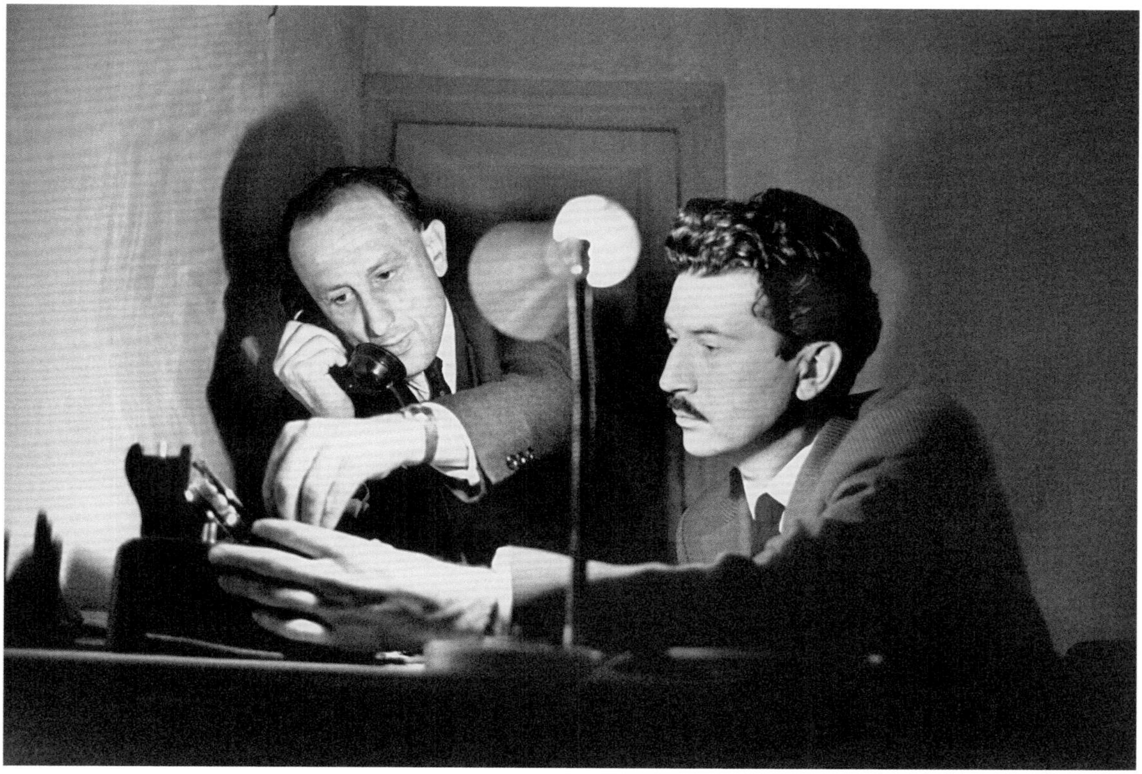

HENRY ROTH

born Tysmenytsia, Ukraine, 1906; died Albuquerque, New Mexico, 1995

by Chester Higgins Jr

Albuquerque, New Mexico, 1987

Together with J. D. Salinger (about whom it is said that he never stopped writing, he just stopped being published), Henry Roth is arguably one of the most striking figures in the history of American letters. Thirty years passed between the publication of his debut novel, *Call It Sleep* (1934), and its reissue in 1964. A further thirty years went by before *A Star Shines Over Mt Morris Park*, the first volume of his monumental series *Mercy of a Rude Stream* (1994–98), saw the light of day. And it would be another decade or so before the posthumous publication of his final novel, *An American Type* (2010).

Roth arrived in the USA when he was still a babe in arms, his parents having emigrated there from what is now the Ukraine. He grew up in the poverty-stricken Lower East Side of New York and then in Harlem, where he lived until 1927. It was then that he met the teacher and poet Eda Lou Walton, an emotional and intellectual encounter that opened his eyes to the world of poetry and letters. Walton introduced him to the work of Eliot and Joyce, gave him a copy of *Ulysses* smuggled in from Paris (the book was still banned in the USA) and supported him financially while he wrote *Call It Sleep*.

Despite poor sales, this largely autobiographical novel did not go unnoticed. Described by critics as 'the most accurate and profound study of an American slum childhood that has yet appeared', it was praised not only for its in-depth sociological analysis but also for the musicality of the writing, which echoed that of Joyce but was also personal and poetic. Roth's attempts to write a second novel attracted the attention of Maxwell Perkins, the famed literary editor at Charles Scribner's Sons, who offered him a contract for the book. However, it would not allow itself to be written, and Roth abandoned it soon afterwards. In 1938, while staying at Yaddo, the artists' colony in Saratoga Springs, New York, he met the pianist and composer Muriel Parker, who became his wife the following year, and would be a strongly supportive figure for the rest of his life.

In 1946 the couple moved to Maine, where Roth worked in a series of blue-collar jobs, including waterfowl farmer, labourer and attendant in a psychiatric hospital. In 1964 the reissue of *Call It Sleep* was met with extraordinary public and critical acclaim, generating demand for another book from both readers and publishers. However, although Roth produced some short fiction in this period, including 'The Surveyor' (1966), it was not until 1979 that he began to write seriously again, while the majority of his later works were published only after his death.

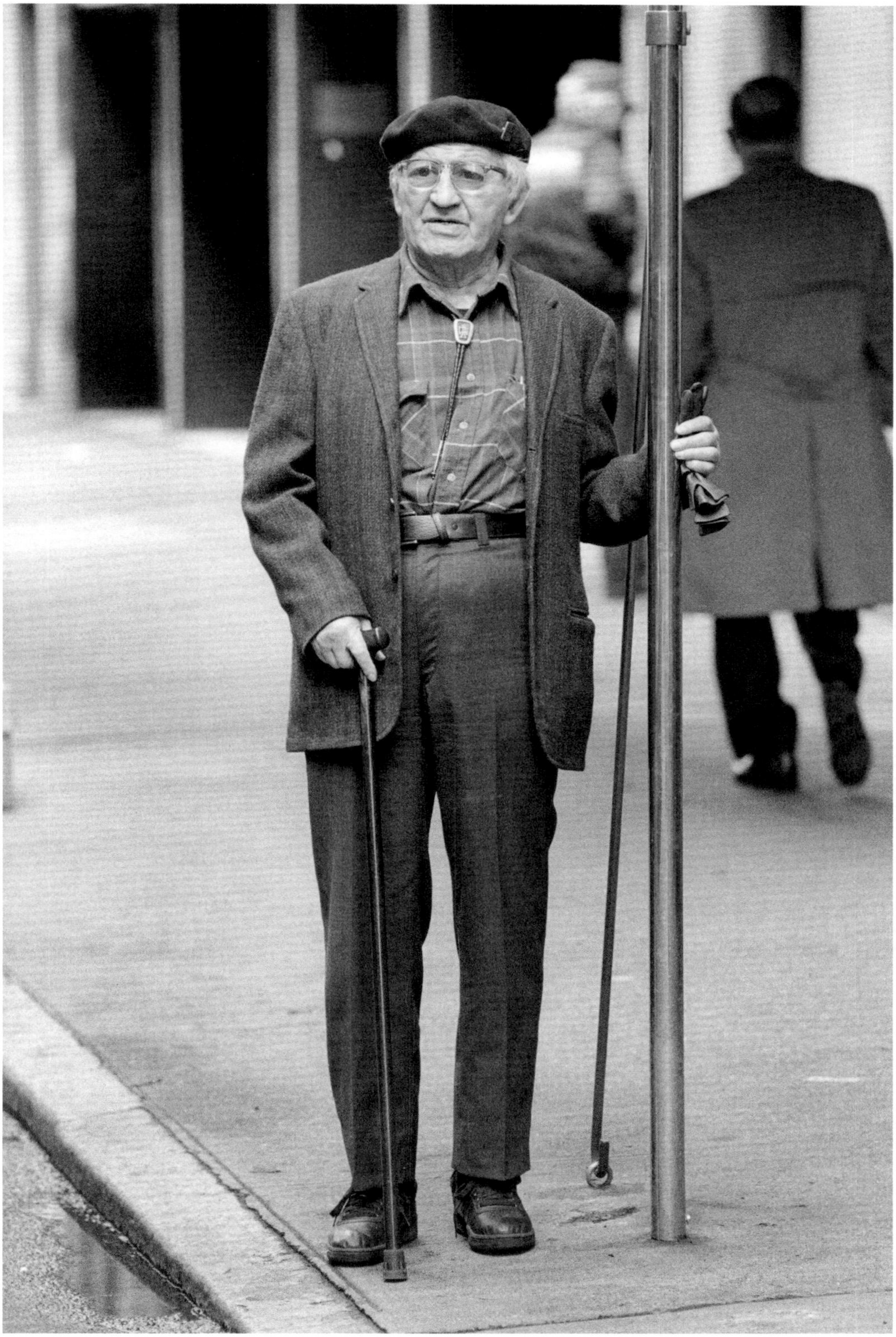

JOSEPH ROTH

born Brody, Ukraine, 1894; died Paris, 1939

photographer unknown

Ostend, Belgium, 1936

A recurrent theme lies at the heart of Joseph Roth's stories from the 1920s: his characters are survivors, people who have escaped from a terrible disaster. In many cases, like Roth himself, they are soldiers who have returned from war only to find that there is no longer a home for them to return to.

Roth was born into a Jewish family in the small town of Brody, which at that time was located in east Galicia, part of the Austro-Hungarian Empire. The First World War, in which Roth fought on the Eastern Front, brought about the dissolution of the empire and imbued the writer with a profound sense of homelessness. He spent much of his life working as a journalist, moving between Vienna, Paris and Berlin, and reporting from Russia, Poland, Albania and Italy, all the time living in hotels and writing his stories while sitting at tables in bars.

Although his narrative style was very much of the nineteenth century, his vision of the world was profoundly modern. The intimate drama of the loss of a homeland and of a society in which he recognized himself found its deepest expression in *Radetzky March* (1932), a hymn to the passing of an era and, on the eve of the Nazi Party's rise to power, an augury of much darker times to come.

Following Hitler's appointment as chancellor of Germany in 1933, Roth left Berlin for the hotels and bars of Paris, although he continued to travel extensively. He also continued to write, producing, among other works, *The Emperor's Tomb* (1938). However, his heavy drinking was taking its toll on his health, and despite various invitations to leave Europe, including one from Eleanor Roosevelt, he remained in Paris. In 1939 he became ill while staying at the Café Tournon and was moved to a poorhouse. He died shortly afterwards, aged just forty-four years old.

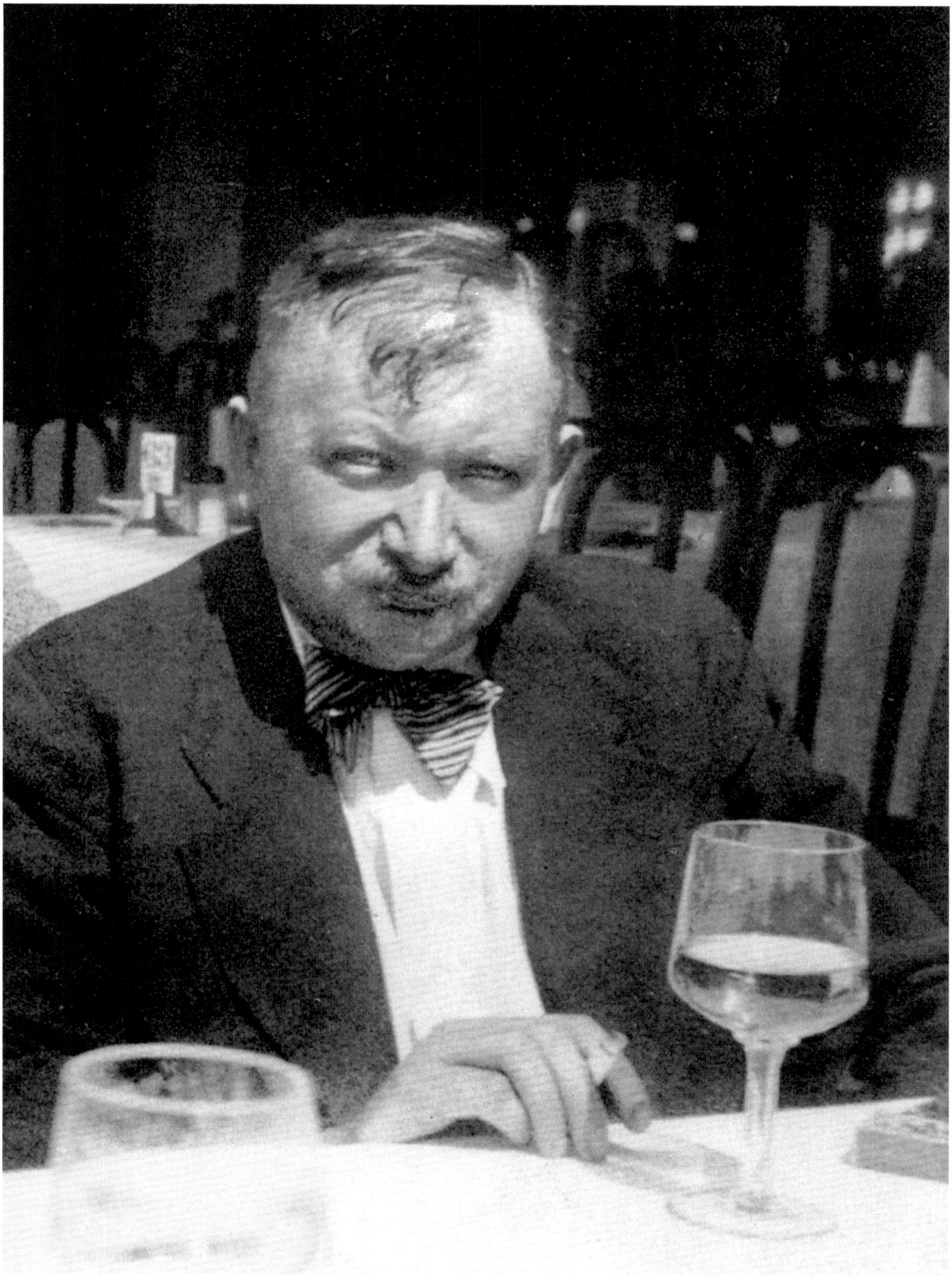

PHILIP ROTH

born Newark, New Jersey, 1933

by Elliott Erwitt

Connecticut, 1990

Philip Roth has officially retired from writing. His thirty-first book, *Nemesis* (2010), will be his last. In an interview with the French magazine *Les InRocks* in September 2012, he described how he had reached this decision after rereading his own novels: 'After this, I decided that I was done with fiction. I don't want to read any more of it, write any more of it, and I don't even want to talk about it anymore. I have dedicated my life to the novel: I have studied it, I have taught it, I have written it and I have read it. To the exclusion of almost everything else. It's enough. I no longer feel this dedication to write what I have experienced my whole life. The idea of struggling once more with writing is unbearable to me.'

To the thousands of Roth's fans around the world, this came as devastating news. The recipient of numerous literary awards, Roth has produced one of the most significant and influential bodies of work in the history of American literature. Among his many creations is a series of unforgettable protagonists, beginning with the notorious Alexander Portnoy in *Portnoy's Complaint* (1969), a novel that brought its author international fame and provoked a storm of controversy over its sexually explicit content. The tormented Nathan Zuckerman appears in at least six of Roth's novels, including *American Pastoral* (1997) and *Exit Ghost* (2007). His least salubrious protagonist is Mickey Sabbath in *Sabbath's Theater* (1995), while the character of Coleman Silk, the teacher in *The Human Stain* (2000), explores the themes of identity and racism in the USA. Under these various guises, Roth delves deep into the human psyche, revealing the emotional, psychological and sexual proclivities of modern man in an increasingly uncertain world.

Perhaps Roth will have second thoughts about putting down his pen. If not, his fans will have to make do with rereading his highly accomplished books.

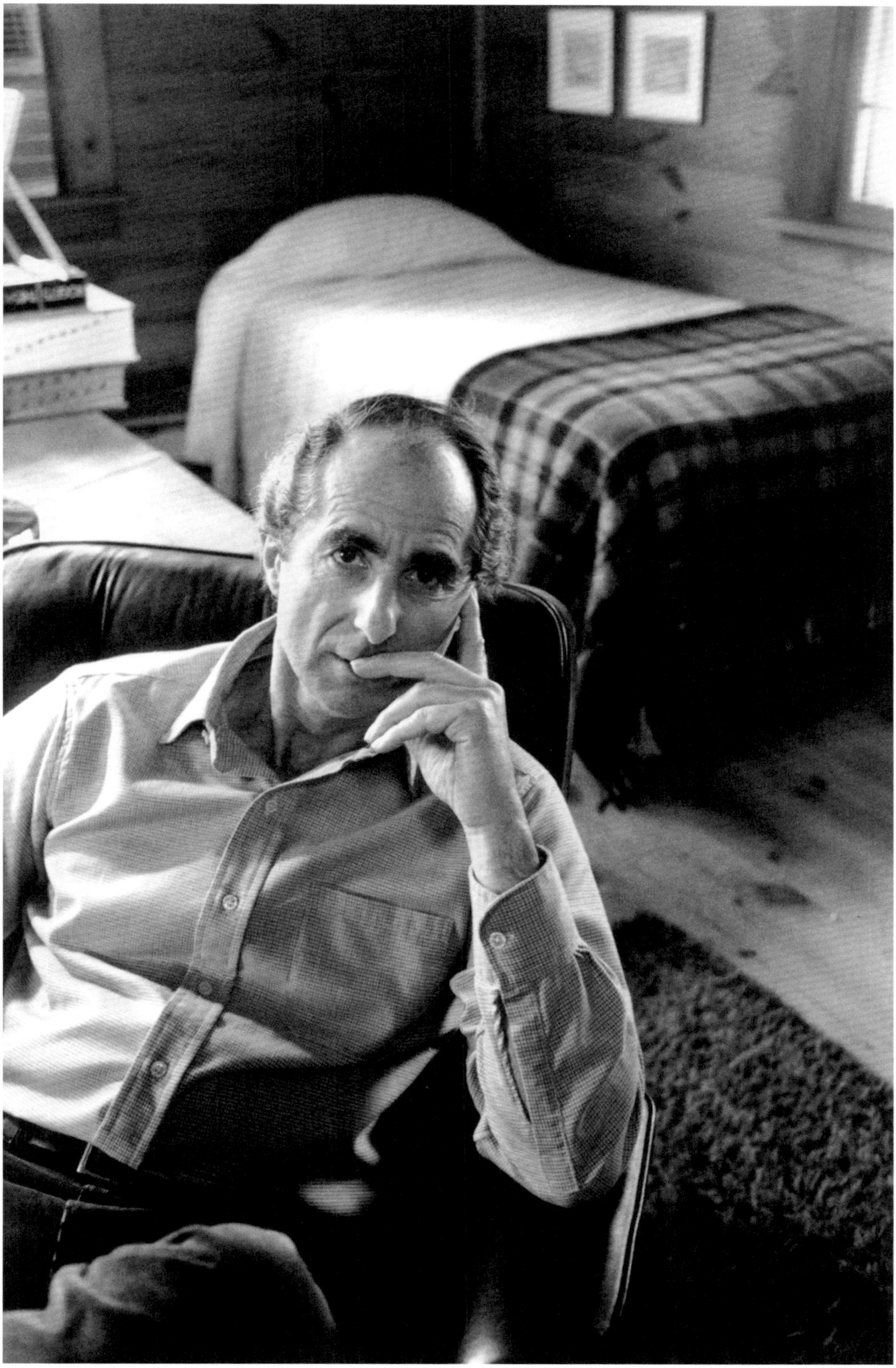

ARUNDHATI ROY

born Shillong, India, 1961

by Raghu Rai

Kerala, India, 1996

Is it possible to be considered a great novelist after completing just one book? This is what happened to Indian writer Arundhati Roy. *The God of Small Things* (1997), her first and only novel, is the fruit of four long years of work (from 1992 to 1996) into which the writer poured herself, her autobiography and a sensitive awareness of her beautiful, problematic,complex country.

Originally from the state of Kerala, Roy moved to New Delhi where she worked a number of part-time jobs and studied architecture. Her personal experiences from this period are echoed in the stories of the protagonists of her book, the twins Estha and Rahel. We read of their difficult transition into adulthood and the social problems of a country divided up into castes. Roy sets up a constant oscillation between the twins' individual affairs, their personal 'things' – those small, even minute, things that form part of every life – and the grander swell of history that towers over, swallowing everything. Cleverly interweaving narrative planes, Roy reconstructs not only a family but an entire nation, bringing them together in a rich and captivating narrative.

The great Indian photographer Raghu Rai photographed Roy the year her book was published. The young writer seems to have taken refuge in a corner of the image; she stays in the shadows, almost as if trying to hide from the light of celebrity. Although *The God of Small Things* was a true publishing success, Roy has put the writing of fiction aside (for the moment, at least) and spent recent years engaged in writing political and critical essays and pamphlets. The success and sales of her book have given Roy the opportunity to use her name and her writing to become the conscience of a country still dealing with the effects of imperialism, as well as freeing her to speak out against environmental destruction, globalization and nuclear weapons.

Roy has said that for her, storytelling can be as beautiful as dancing and singing. Given her writing's social and ethical significance, however, with so many crises still to be brought to light and announced to the world, Roy maintains that the moment in which she can allow herself to dance again has not yet arrived.

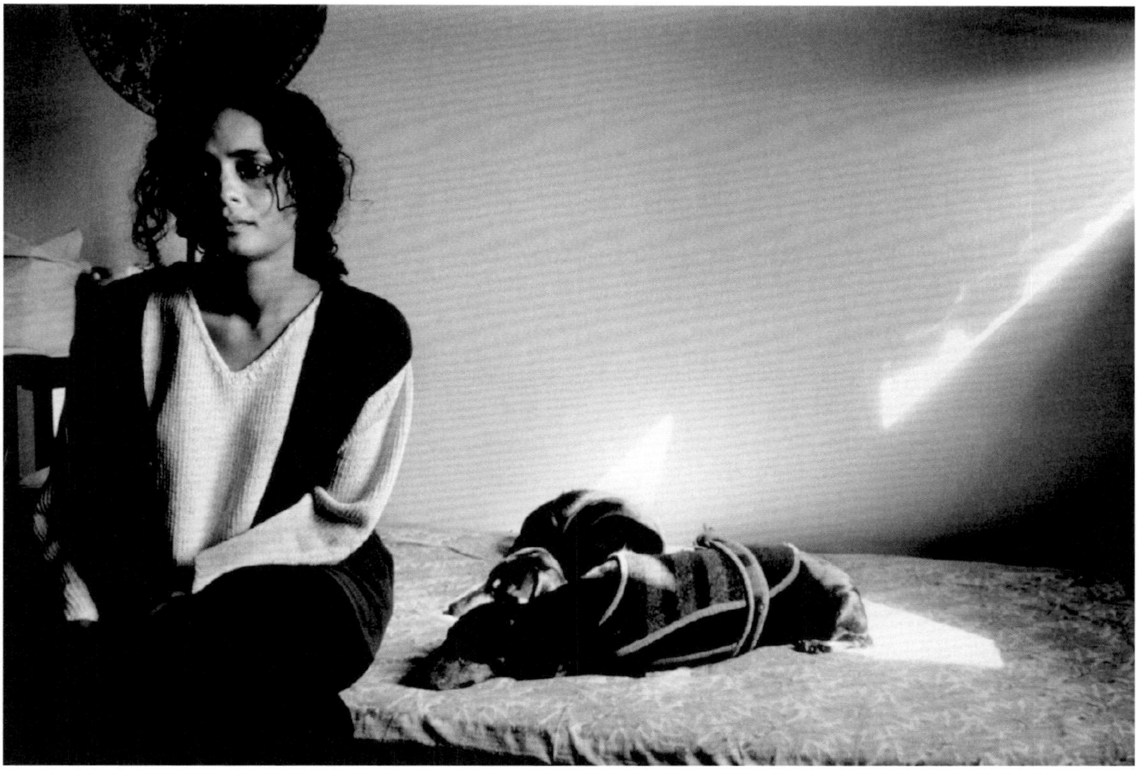

JUAN RULFO

born Sayula, Mexico, 1918; died Mexico City, Mexico, 1986

by Isolde Ohlbaum

Berlin, 1982

Despite the fact that he was the author of only two books, Juan Rulfo is considered to be one of the finest Latin American writers of the twentieth century and the founder of a new type of Latin American novel. His first book, *The Burning Plain*, a collection of seventeen short stories, appeared in 1953; his second, *Pedro Páramo*, followed two years later. In both works, Rulfo depicts the violent Mexico of his childhood, a period in which his father was killed and his country was turned upside down by the Cristero Rebellion (1926–29), a popular uprising against the anti-Catholicism of the ruling Mexican government. Everything is played out against a spectral landscape at the mercy of the elements, a world in which man faces a continuous struggle for survival.

Pedro Páramo is the story of a world of ghosts. Its protagonist, Juan Preciado, carries out his mother's dying wish and travels to the village of Comala (an early example of the Latin American literary tradition of mythical places, such as Gabriel García Marquez's Macondo) in search of his father, Pedro Páramo. Once there, he finds the town apparently abandoned, populated only by a series of tormented spirits whose stories, including that of Pedro, are revealed over the course of the novel. Told in both first- and third-person narration, it is a complex book composed of multiple voices and a highly fragmented, occasionally disorientating timeline.

Both Rulfo's books have received widespread critical acclaim. When the author was asked to explain why he had stopped writing, he answered that it was because his uncle Celestino, the true font of all his stories, had died. However, Rulfo used not only words to tell stories about Mexico, but also images. The more than six thousand negatives left behind by the writer suggest that, for him, photography and writing were two complementary means of exploring both his country and a people who seemed to embody its history.

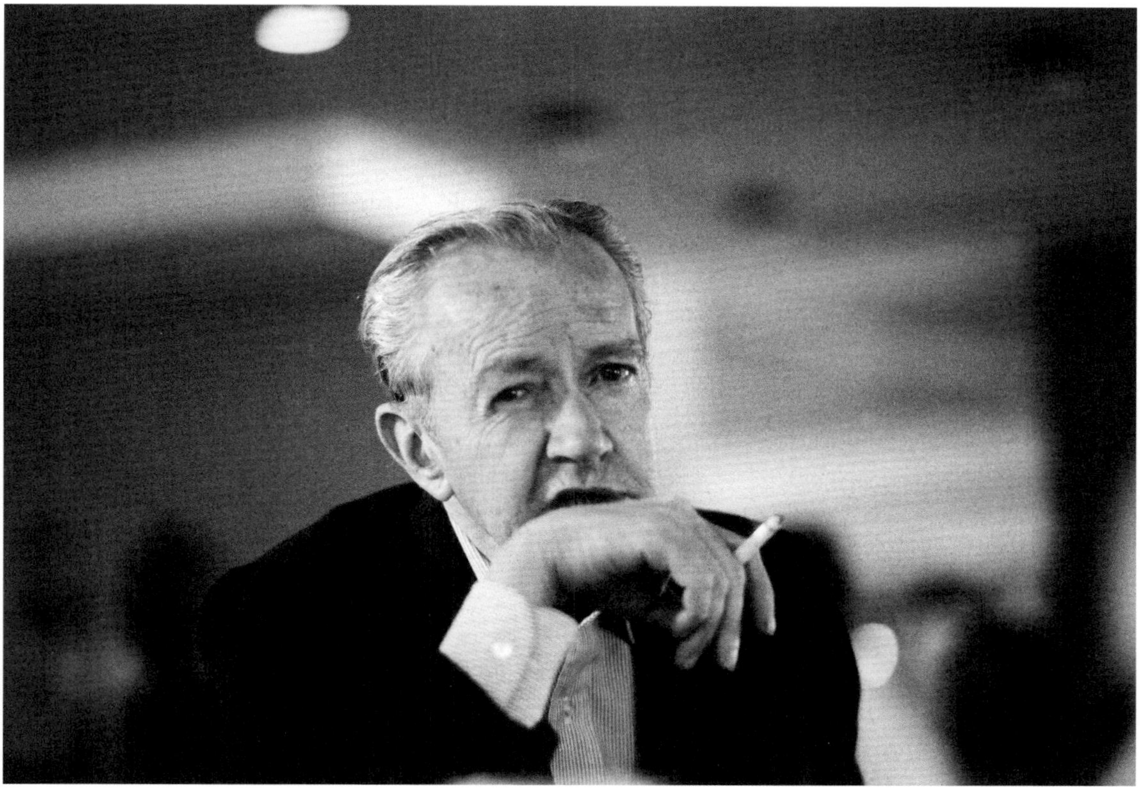

SALMAN RUSHDIE

born Mumbai, 1947

by David Hurn

Hay-on-Wye, Powys, UK, 1992

On 14 February 1989 the aged Ayatollah Khomeini, already close to death himself, issued a fatwa condemning Indian-born writer Salman Rushdie, the author of *The Satanic Verses* (2008), to death. The novel was guilty, in the eyes of this most intransigent of Islamists, of blasphemously portraying episodes in the history of Islam and the life of the Prophet Muhammed. The consequences were severe: the book's Japanese translator, Hitoshi Igarashi, was killed; its Norwegian publisher, William Nygaard, and its Italian translator, Ettore Capriolo, were wounded in assassination attempts; and Rushdie himself was forced to go into hiding in the UK for more than ten years. The Rushdie fatwa very quickly became a new 'Dreyfus Affair' touching off a highly sensitive debate about the global geopolitical balance, and governments' duty to protect the freedoms of artistic expression and the press. It also became a key diplomatic issue for the British government, and the subject of prolonged negotiations that have allowed the writer to live a normal life in recent years even though the fatwa was never formally lifted. In the meantime, Rushdie became one of the most famous living authors in the world.

Rushdie's literary reputation was established with *Midnight's Children* (1980), a narrative mosaic of modern India built around the life of Saleem Sinai and the thousand others who were born at midnight on 15 August 1947, the day on which Indian independence was declared. The novel was awarded the Man Booker Prize in 1981. *Shame* (1983), a family saga set in a fictionalized Pakistan, won the Prix du Meilleur Livre Étranger. Rushdie's style, which lies halfway between the fantastical and the believable, is often described as a distinctively Asian magic realism. He has also written collections of short stories, including *East, West* (1994) and two children's books: *Haroun and the Sea of Stories* (1990) and *Luka and the Fire of Life* (2010). His non-fiction works include *The Jaguar Smile: A Nicaraguan Journey* (1987), *Imaginary Homelands* (1992) and *Homeless by Choice* (1992).

In 2012 Rushdie published an autobiography entitled *Joseph Anton: A Memoir*, in which he recounted in the third person the story of his life starting from the day of the fatwa. The title was the pseudonym he chose when he had to go into hiding (it is taken from the first names of Joseph Conrad and Anton Chekhov). The book is an exceptional portrait of a man who is forced into the subterranean existence of a recluse, but who is still connected to the outside world through a dense web of emotional and professional ties. Although he is a high-profile media personality, he exists as a 'virtual' figure who can only rarely emerge from hiding to make public appearances under armed guard as, for instance, at the Hay-on-Wye literary festival in Wales in 1992, immortalized in this image taken by David Hurn.

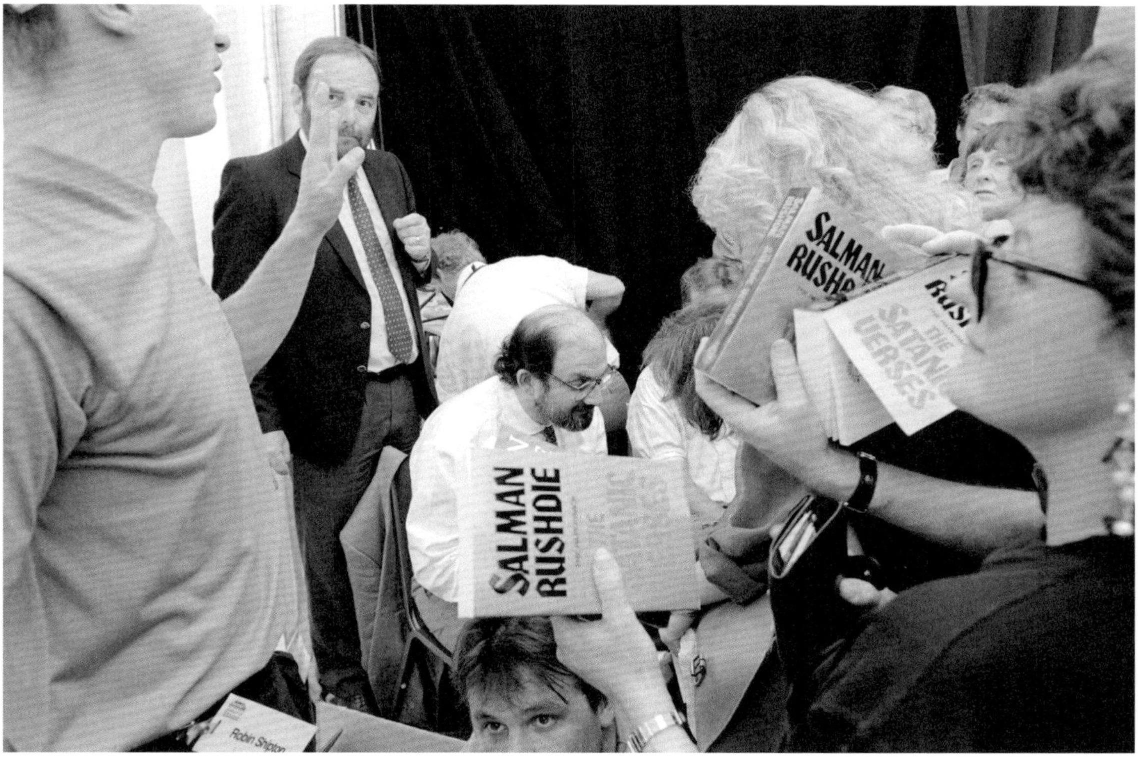
SALMAN RUSHDIE
Robin Shipton

ANTOINE DE SAINT-EXUPÉRY

born Lyon, France, 1900; died Mediterranean, south of Marseille, 1944

by John Phillips

Alghero, Italy, 1944

In common with the narrator of his most famous work, *The Little Prince* (1943), Antoine de Saint-Exupéry was a pilot by profession. He began his career at a time when aviation was still in its infancy. He later flew with the aviation company Aéropostale, and was one of the first pilots to transport letters and postcards by air. In 1935, while competing in an air race, Saint-Exupéry crashed in the Sahara, but was saved from certain death by local tribesmen. This experience and others would help to shape *The Little Prince*, which begins with a pilot being marooned in the desert. First printed in the USA, and since then translated into more than 250 languages, this much-loved book – the story of a stranded pilot and his friendship with a boy who has fallen to Earth – is a fable for both adults and children, a poetic exploration of the meaning of life.

Saint-Exupéry's love of flight is reflected in many of his other works, such as *Night Flight* (1931), *Wind, Sand and Stars* (1939) and *The Aviator* (published posthumously in 1956), which draw on his varied experiences at high altitude. In 1939 he joined the French Air Force, assuming command of an aerial reconnaissance squadron. After Germany's invasion of France in 1940, he fled to the USA, settling in New York. In 1943 he left America with US troops bound for Algiers, where, despite suffering the effects of his numerous accidents, and with the support of his friend the photographer John Phillips, he returned to flying an unarmed observation plane.

It was to Phillips that Saint-Exupéry dedicated his 'Letter to an American', written shortly before his disappearance and presumed death on 31 July 1944 during a reconnaissance mission off the coast of Saint Raphaél in southern France. There were many theories about the loss of his plane, including accident, pilot error and a German attack. His body was never found. Phillips had produced an entire series of photographs of the writer-aviator, but chose not to publish it, feeling guilty – wrongly, many would say – for having helped him fly again.

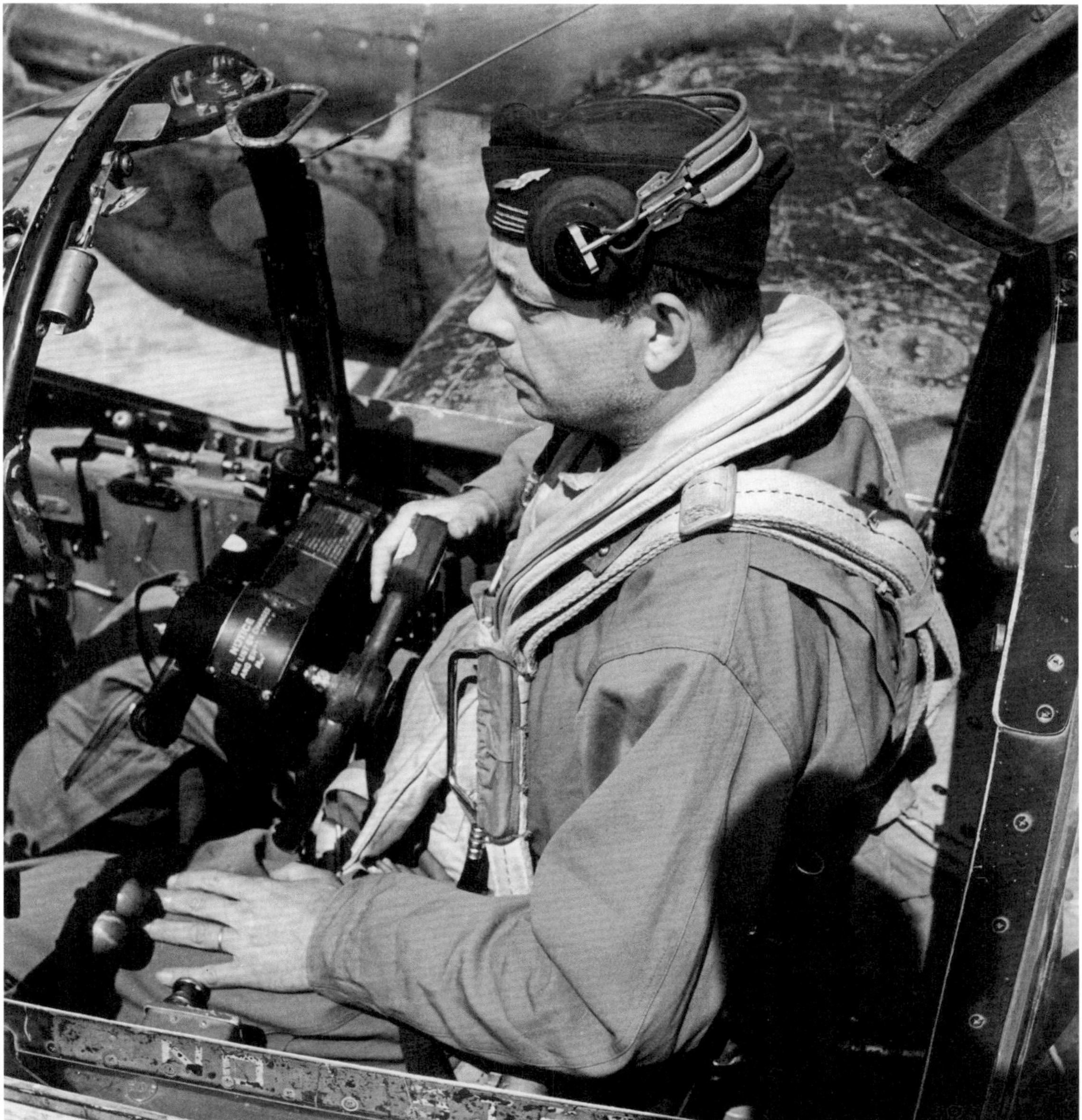

J. D. SALINGER

born New York, 1919; died Cornish, New Hampshire, 2010

by Antony di Gesu

New York, 1952

Despite his best efforts, Jerome David Salinger was unable to pass through life entirely unobserved. He received one of his first exposures to a wider audience during the Second World War, when, having been drafted into the US Army, he arranged to meet Ernest Hemingway in Paris, where the writer was working as a war correspondent. After reading some of Salinger's work, Hemingway, who was rarely kind to his fellow authors, commented: 'Jesus, he has a helluva talent!'

Salinger's wartime experience, in particular of being one of the first soldiers to enter a liberated concentration camp, affected him deeply; indeed, he was hospitalized for a few weeks to recover from the stresses of combat. The years immediately after the war were his most productive. In 1948 he sent the short story 'A Perfect Day for Bananafish' to the *New Yorker*, which accepted it immediately (it would later form the first story in his collection of 1953, *Nine Stories*). In fact, the *New Yorker* was already familiar with Salinger's work, from a number of short stories that the writer had unsuccessfully submitted to the magazine in the early 1940s, including one, which it had accepted but not published, entitled 'Slight Rebellion off Madison'. Some years later, its teenage protagonist, Holden Caulfield, would reappear in Salinger's best-known work, *The Catcher in the Rye* (1951). The story of a sensitive and unhappy young man with a complex and extremely nuanced personality, the book was an enormous success, thanks in part to the ease with which many readers were able to relate to its hero.

Although both the language, which was very uninhibited for the period, and the existential anxiety that permeated the novel shocked some people, they were greeted enthusiastically by the young. The book's success, however, was a surprise to its author. In order to continue writing, Salinger withdrew more and more from public life, which did nothing to satisfy the curiosity of either the publishing industry or the public (his most notable post-*Catcher* works include two stories about two members of the Glass family published as *Franny and Zooey*, 1961, and two stories narrated by Buddy Glass that had first appeared in the *New Yorker* and were later published together as *Raise High the Roof-Beam, Carpenters and Seymour: An Introduction*, 1963). But as William Faulkner declared in an interview, the tragedy of Holden (and his author) 'was not that he was, as he perhaps thought, not tough enough or brave enough or deserving enough to be accepted into humanity. His tragedy was that when he attempted to enter the human race, there was no human race there.'

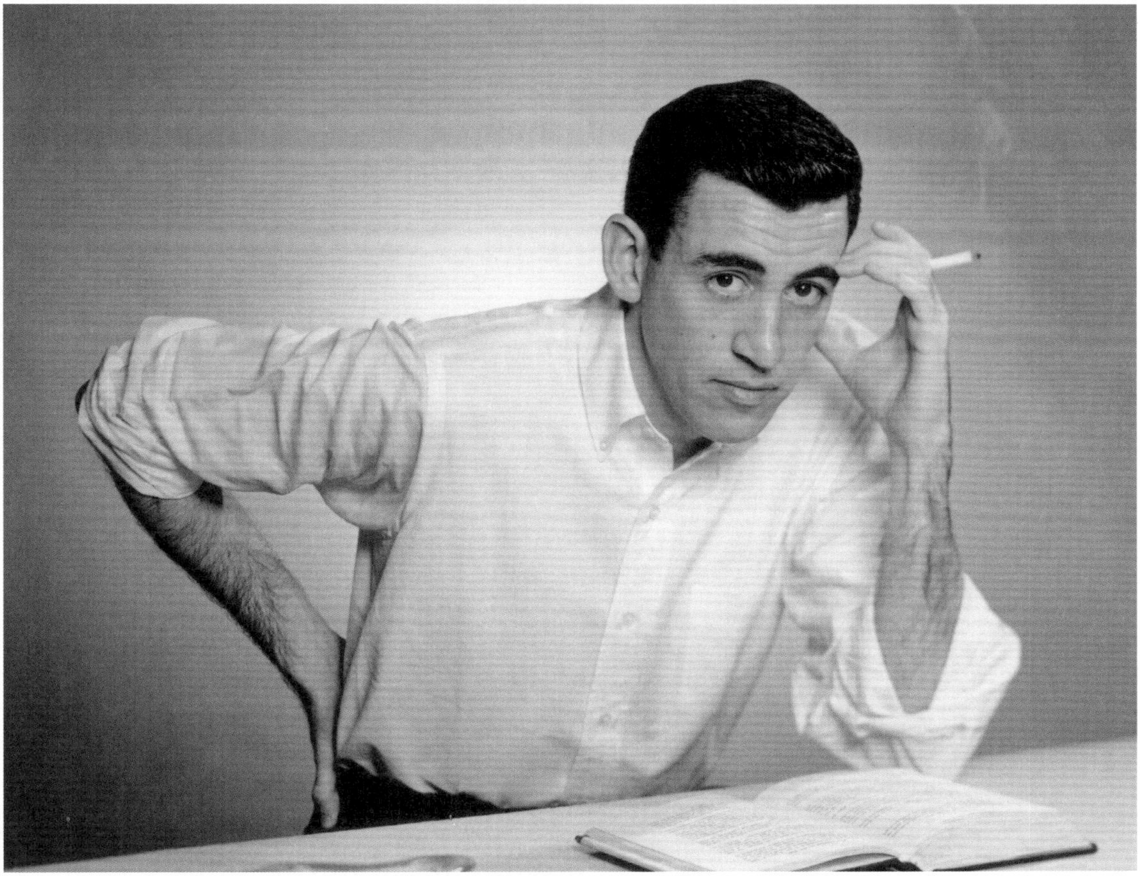

JOSÉ SARAMAGO

born Azinhaga, Portugal, 1922; died Tías, Canary Islands, 2010

by Sebastião Salgado

Lanzarote, Canary Islands, 1996

José Saramago first came to the world's attention with the publication of *Raised from the Ground* (1980), a novel whose key themes include a family with a name that is also a curse, Mau-tempo; a job that is also a prison sentence; and a land, the Alentejo in southern Portugal, that must be cultivated. Saramago's book blazed a trail for a new literary realism in which social needs, sophisticated plot structures, cutting irony and genuine pathos come together in engaging and often fast-moving narratives.

Saramago himself was born in the Alentejo, into a peasant family beset by various crises and economic hardships. The family's move to Lisbon was an attempt to extricate its members from such a harsh environment and its precarious means of making a living. Saramago's childhood, however, was far from easy, and before he was able to become a full-time writer, the family's straitened economic circumstances forced him to abandon his studies and to embark on a series of related jobs, including journalist, literary critic and editor.

Although Saramago wrote poetry, articles and plays, he is best remembered for his work within the tradition of the novel, a form that best suited his style of storytelling. It allowed him to create works of sweeping historical fiction (*Baltasar and Blimunda*, 1982), to revisit ancient myths and literary figures (*The Year of the Death of Ricardo Reis*, 1986), to explore universal metaphors (*Blindness*, 1995) and to investigate religious themes (*The Gospel According to Jesus Christ*, 1991). But Saramago also published political pamphlets and was unafraid to adopt radical positions, convinced as he was that, above all, the role of the intellectual was to reflect publically on both the events of the past and the possibilities of the future. In 1998 he was awarded the Nobel Prize, an honour that he dedicated to his family.

Saramago was linked to the Brazilian photographer Sebastião Salgado by a common language, by an awareness of social issues and by an interest in those communities that struggle to be heard. Salgado took this photograph of the writer in the volcanic landscape of Lanzarote in the Canary Islands, which Saramago had adopted as his home.

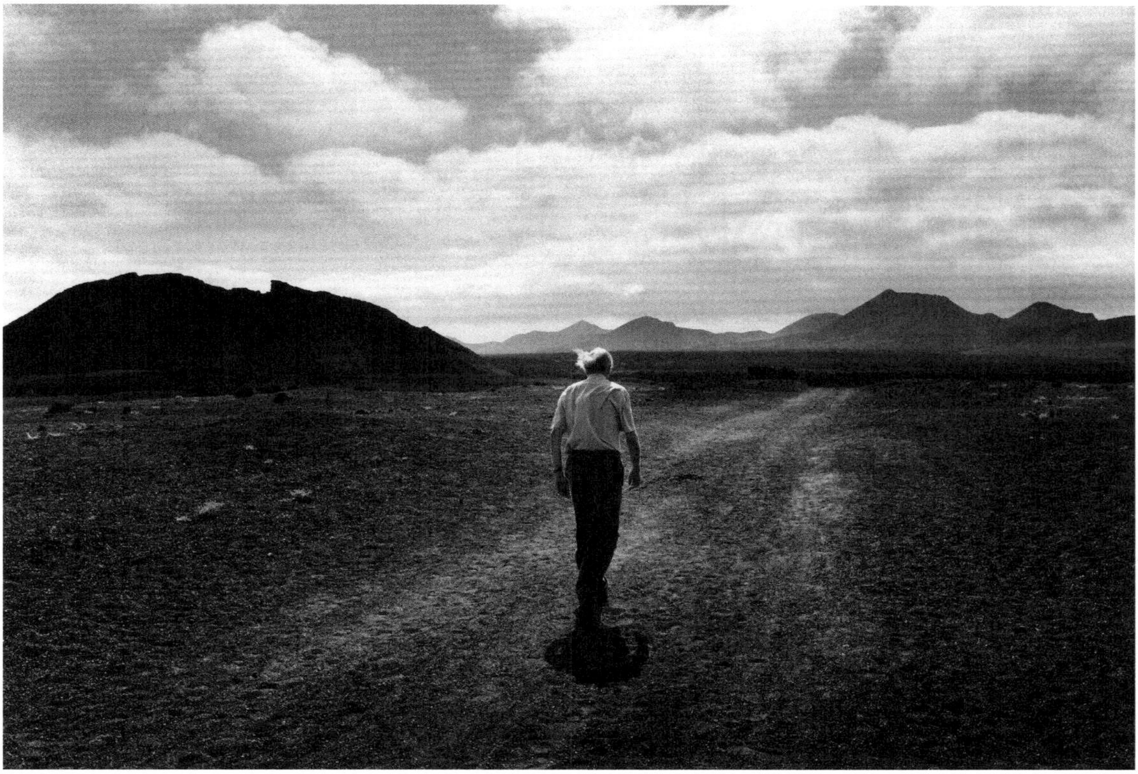

JEAN-PAUL SARTRE

born Paris, 1905; died Paris, 1980

by Henri Cartier-Bresson

Paris, 1946

Jean-Paul Sartre was perhaps the most incisive and influential figure of post-war French intellectual society. For more than thirty years his every act, declaration and philosophical position was counted as a point of reference or, at the very least, as grounds for argument. Rigorous and coherent in his political actions, he is remembered for his bitter disapproval of all forms of imperialism, from the French imperial adventure in North Africa to America's involvement in Vietnam, and for his protests against Soviet power and his definitive break with Communism after the military response to the Prague Spring of 1968. His leftism had its roots in his own background and, as he recounted in his autobiography, *Words* (1964), in the hatred he had developed from his earliest years of the bourgeois model of family life.

Sartre was a public and popular philosopher who was often to be found in the bars of the Saint-Germain-des-Prés area of Paris. He was also the standard-bearer of existentialism and an exemplar for an entire generation of young people. His novels and plays were artistic expressions of a mature philosophy, especially from the 1940s onwards, when he co-founded the literary review *Les Temps modernes* and published one of his most influential books, *Being and Nothingness* (1943).

Sartre sought to popularize his philosophy of responsibility and interpreted it, on an individual level, through many of his literary and theatrical characters. He would harangue workers in front of factories, and even came to argue in favour of violence as an instrument of political resistance. In 1964 he was awarded the Nobel Prize but rejected it by declaring, among other things, that 'no man deserves to be consecrated in his lifetime'. His relationship with the French writer and intellectual Simone de Beauvoir has taken on mythic proportions; Sartre himself, a man who throughout his life pursued his objective of autonomy and 'choice' in both the political and the private sphere, interpreted it as an anti-bourgeois model of uninhibited sexual love and emotional unconventionality.

Henri Cartier-Bresson captured a thoughtful Sartre on Paris's Pont des Arts. He is pictured with his friend Jean Pouillon, one of the founders of the Socialism and Freedom movement, which Sartre also helped to establish.

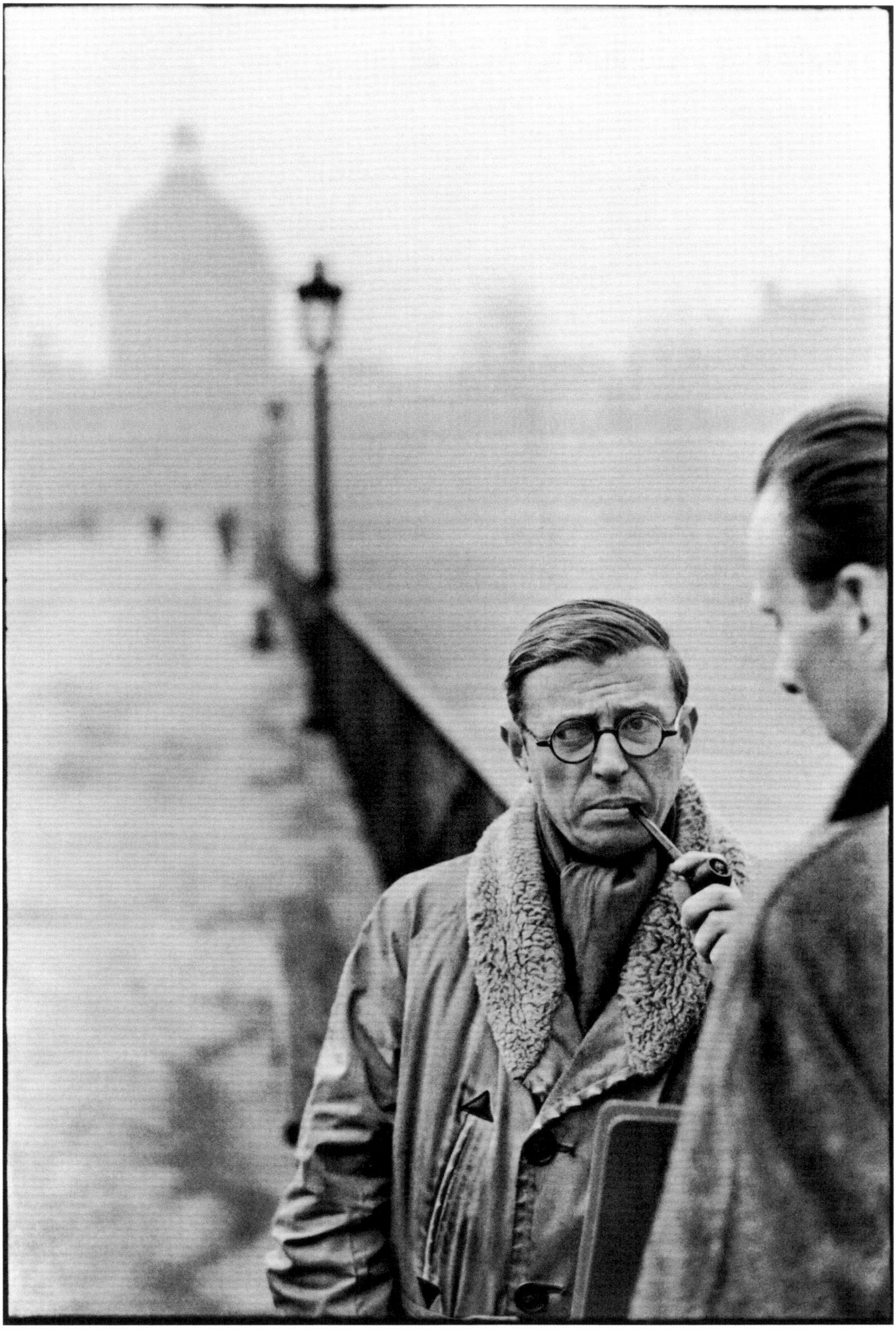

ROBERTO SAVIANO

born Naples, Italy, 1979

by Gianni Occhipinti

Hamburg, Germany, 2009

Gomorrah (2006), Roberto Saviano's long investigative report on the Neapolitan Camorra crime syndicate, opens with a dozen pages dedicated to the Mafia economy and includes extended descriptions of the apocalyptic landscape around Caserta that has been ruined by waste dumping carried out by organized crime. Truly no one could have imagined that such a text would be translated into fifty-two languages and sell ten million copies across the world in the course of just a few years, nor that it would become the Italian literary phenomenon par excellence of the early years of the twenty-first century. Least of all its author, who has been overwhelmed by the Mafia's threats of retribution, and then by his own sudden celebrity status, which has placed him on the front pages of countless national newspapers and as a guest on many high-profile television programmes.

Transformed in record time from a budding young journalist for *L'Espresso* and *La Repubblica* into one of the most authoritative and influential leaders of Italian national opinion, he now has an aura of heroism bordering on sanctity in the public imagination. With such a rock-star level of celebrity, it isn't easy for the author of *Gomorrah* to control his reputation, or the circumstances of his everyday life, which since 2006 have involved living in secret locations under twenty-four-hour police guard to protect him from the Camorra. Not that Saviano has shown any discomfort at his new high-profile identity: from the very beginning he has demonstrated great self-assurance in his television and other mass media appearances. He has also provoked almost visceral hatred in many, for reasons ranging from generalized envy at his success to more specific criticisms of the particular modes of communication that he has adopted with what is either naive or calculated confidence.

Aside from the controversy he has provoked, and taking into account the cultural phenomenon that he has become in Italy and in the rest of the world, it is very difficult to evaluate Saviano as a writer without taking his public image into account. Even in his debut work he has already clearly demonstrated a tendency to place himself in the foreground, a journalistic model that has reminded many critics of the militant egotism of Pier Paolo Pasolini and the histrionic style of Curzio Malaparte. Final judgment, however, awaits posterity and in particular the readers of Saviano's next book, *ZeroZeroZero* (2013) an examination of the international cocaine trade.

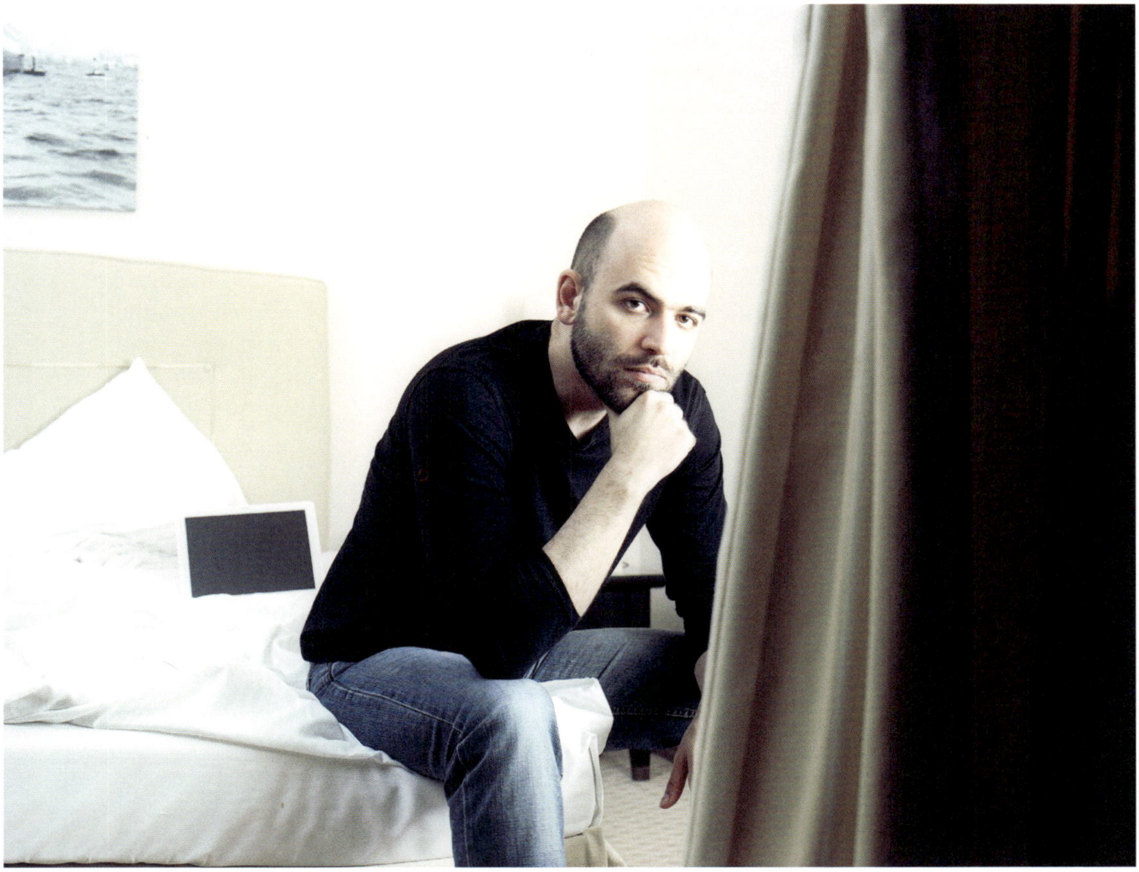

ALBERTO SAVINIO

[Andrea Francesco Alberto de Chirico] born Athens, 1891; died Rome, 1952

by Ghitta Carell

Milan, Italy, 1939

Alberto Savinio was a secular intellectual, a surrealist ahead of his time, an artist who was never limited by the rules of the genres in which he wrote. He was also a man of a thousand faces, with no homeland: stateless and nomadic; a man who never even accepted his own name, adopting instead that of a French literary figure, Albert Savin.

Born to Italian parents, Savinio grew up in his native Athens, where he developed a close relationship with his brother, Giorgio, in the cradle of Mediterranean culture and the land of those mythological characters (Clio, Hermes, Psyche, the Argonauts) whose stories he would later retell. He then spent time in Munich, immersing himself in a culture fostered by Nietzsche and influenced by psychoanalysis, before finally arriving in Paris, 'the heart and brain of the universe', where from 1910 he was associated with various avant-garde circles. It was out of this milieu that *The Songs of Half-Death* (1914), a piece of avant-garde theatre consisting of a free-form and groundbreaking collage of fragments, was born.

During the First World War, Savinio and his brother spent time in Italy, first in Ferrara, then in Rome and Milan. Savinio's nomadic lifestyle suited his character: he was multilingual with a highly eclectic mind, and travelling was his guarantee of independence from the idea of an absolute truth. In his battle against all types of authoritarianism and rhetoric, Savinio employed play, paradox, fun, humour, duality and dilettantism; *Hermaphrodite* (1918), his first novel, is the epitome of such multiplicity. As a musician, writer, painter and playwright, Savinio took his anti-conformism to heart. Between 1940 and 1945 he fought quite different battles from those of the Second World War, publishing his novel *The Childhood of Nivasio Dolcemare* (1941), as well as his surreal and, to use his term, 'supercivic' stories: *Casa 'la Vita'* (The House of 'Life') and *Tutta la vita* (All life long) (both 1943).

Each of Savinio's works is highly radical, even those that at first glance seem fairly conventional, such as *Tell, Men, Your Story* (1942) and *Listen to Your Heart, City* (1943). In his writing, as in his paintings, a procession of surreal figures and situations seems to emerge from the depths of his subconscious. Savinio played with his imagination and with language, overturning certainties and morals; he also produced his own encyclopaedia, pushed his prose to its absolute limits and, through play, challenged ossified meaning.

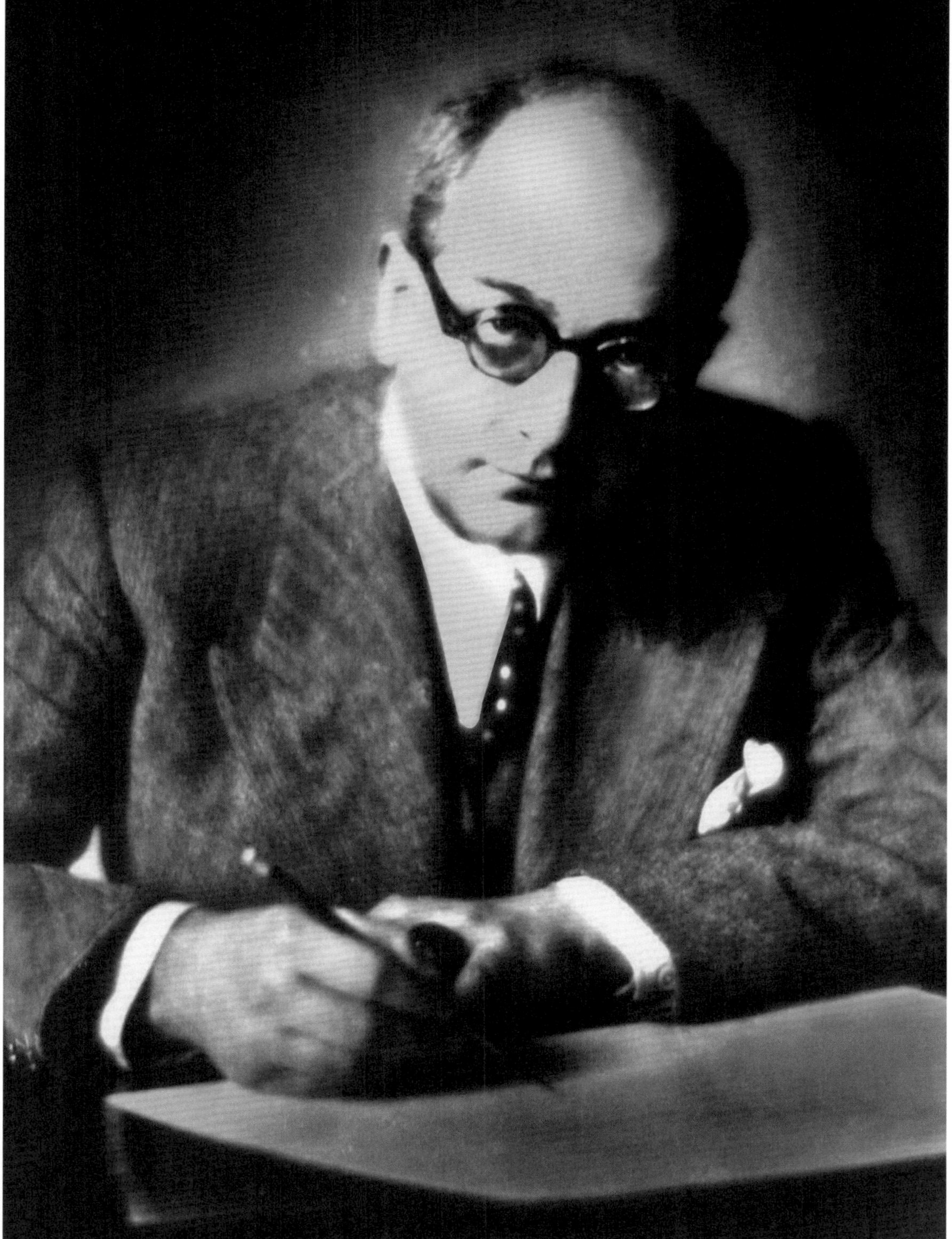

LEONARDO SCIASCIA

born Racalmuto, Italy, 1921; died Palermo, Italy, 1989

by Ferdinando Scianna

Racalmuto, Italy, 1964

Ferdinando Scianna met Leonardo Sciascia when the photographer was a young man. In 1963 Scianna had mounted an exhibition of his photographs of Sicilian religious festivals in his hometown of Bagheria; Sciascia happened to visit the exhibition and left his card there. Sometime after the exhibition, Scianna visited the writer at his country house at Racalmuto. Scianna describes the meeting as being 'like a bolt of lightning. I had discovered a key person in my life. … I was impetuous, as twenty-year-olds are, and he seemed to like this, as he liked all those with an appetite for life. He was more intellectual, and although equally capable of vehemence, this was reserved for and resolved in his writing.' Out of this encounter, both an artistic collaboration and a lifelong friendship were born.

At the time of Sciascia's visit to Scianna's exhibition, the writer had already produced what was to become his most famous work, *The Day of the Owl* (1961), a crime novel set in the world of the Mafia. In common with many of his fellow intellectuals, Sciascia felt a sense of belonging as a Sicilian yet also felt himself to be an outsider. Although rooted in the philosophy of the Enlightenment, he showed a deep appreciation for the mysteries of life. In *To Each His Own* (1966), another detective novel, an unsuspecting village chemist receives an anonymous death threat, and, together with his hunting partner, is found dead the following day. In an attempt to solve the double murder, a local academic is murdered himself after becoming involved in web of corruption.

In addition to detective fiction, which also included *Death of an Inquisitor* (1964), Sciascia wrote poetry, plays, short stories and essays. Many of his stories start with an element of truth, often something from his own life, but then move into the realms of fiction, touching on such subjects as aesthetics and ethics along the way. In *Sicily as Metaphor*, an autobiographical work based on a series of conversations he had with the French journalist Marcelle Padovani, Sciascia says: 'Of me as an individual – an individual who, incidentally, wrote books – I'd like people to say, "He was contradictory and self-contradictory," as a way of saying that I was alive in the midst of so many "dead souls", so many people who weren't contradictory and who never contradicted themselves.'

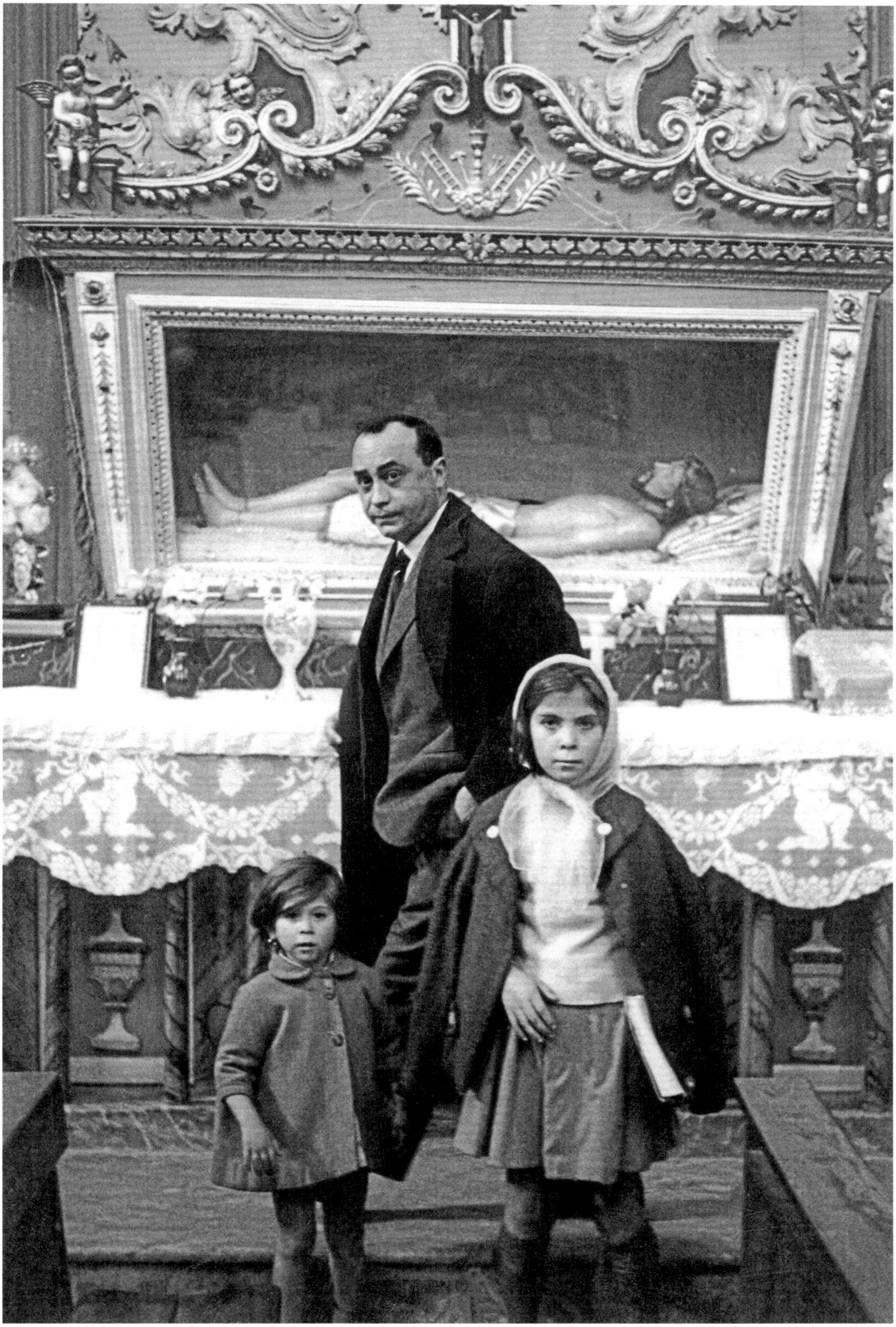

W. G. SEBALD

[Winfried Georg Maximilian Sebald] born Wertach, Germany, 1944; died Norfolk, UK, 2001

by Francesco Gattoni

Paris, c. 2000

The works of W. G. 'Max' Sebald, considered by many to be the most important German writer of the last few decades, were discovered by the wider world only after his death in a car accident, aged only fifty-seven. His final novel, the melancholic wartime narrative *Austerlitz* (2001), contains the same blend of fact and fiction, philosophical reflections and autobiographical allusions that had characterized his earlier books, including *Vertigo* (1990), *The Emigrants* (1992) and *The Rings of Saturn* (1995).

One of four children, Sebald was born in the final years of the Second World War. His father had joined the German Army in 1929 and remained in the service after the Nazis came to power. While Sebald was at grammar school, his class was shown footage of the concentration camps. He recalls being struck by the fact that no one knew what to say or think, and much of his subsequent writing would be informed by the search for an adequate response to the Holocaust. In 1970 he took a lectureship in German at the University of East Anglia, where he researched the work of such writers as Adalbert Stifter and Gottfried Keller. In an interview, he notes how he sought to emulate their carefully constructed prose in his own writing.

Abandoning the conventional idea of a plot, Sebald took an innovative approach to the format of his novels, particularly *Austerlitz*, leaving the reader uncertain as to place and time within the flow of events, recollections and digressions. His books often involve journeys and pilgrimages, in which the more traumatic and violent events of European history are seen through the eyes of real or imaginary characters. In an essay entitled *On the Natural History of Destruction* (1999), Sebald tackles the difficult subject of the Allied bombing of Germany, and the inability of German literature to broach the issue. In his collection of posthumously published essays, *A Place in the Country* (2013), he explores the works of some of his favourite writers. One of the hallmarks of his style was his use of photography alongside narrative, a device that has since had many imitators. However, none has been able to match the intensity and power of his prose.

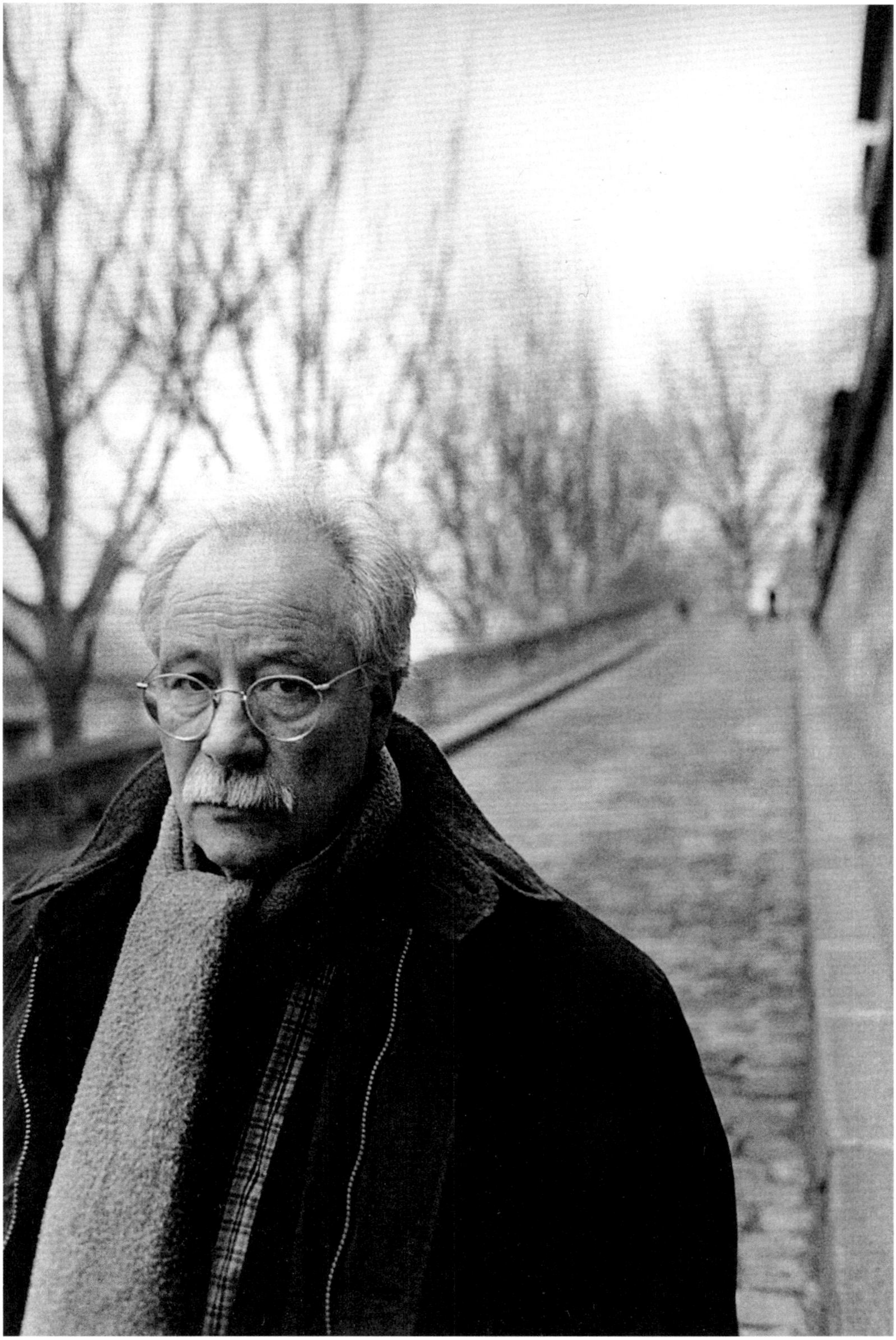

LÉOPOLD SÉDAR SENGHOR

born Joal, Senegal, 1906; died Verson, France, 2001

by Thomas Hoepker

Dakar, 1970

Léopold Sédar Senghor was one of the most important African cultural figures of the twentieth century. An intellectual, poet and politician, he invented the concept of 'negritude', which he described as the totality of the cultural values of the black world. Although his ideas had their critics, they influenced generations of African writers, and black writers all over the world, including many in the USA. He was a regular contributor to the journal *Présence Africaine,* founded by Alioune Diop in 1947. Other contributors included leading French intellectuals such as André Gide, Michel Leiris, Jean-Paul Sartre, Albert Camus and Emmanuel Mounier, and black intellectuals and artists from across the globe, including the American author Richard Wright. 'Negritude' was rooted in the notion of a universal black identity and a diverse black culture. Senghor maintained that it was a cultural movement rather than a political one, aimed at encouraging the world to embrace a universal vision of diversity rather than superiority, and to celebrate humanity's common heritage.

Senghor was the author of collections of poetry written in French, such as *Hosties noires* (Black hosts, 1948) and *Élégies majeures* (Major elegies, 1948). They are predominantly rhythmic and sonorous in style. He was also one of the first to circulate Francophone African poetry, with his *Anthologie de la nouvelle poésie nègre et Malgache de langue Française* (The anthology of new black and Malagasy poetry in the French language, 1948). He published numerous collections of interviews and articles, including the five volumes of *Liberté* (Liberty, 1964–92). In *La Poésie de l'action* (The poetry of action, 1980) he explores the complimentary roles of poetry and political action.

In 1946 Senghor was elected to the Assemblée Nationale Française, and two years later he founded the Bloc Démocratique Sénégalais. He believed that the political and social progress of Africa was inextricably linked with its cultural development. He was an important mediator between Africa and the Western world, although his desire to maintain friendly relations with the West was criticized by some young Africans. In 1960 he became the first President of the Republic of Senegal and remained in office until 1980, presiding over the post-colonial conflicts of his country without losing his fervent humanism and his optimistic vision of Africa's future. This photograph shows him and his wife, Colette Hubert, watching a fly-past during a military parade.

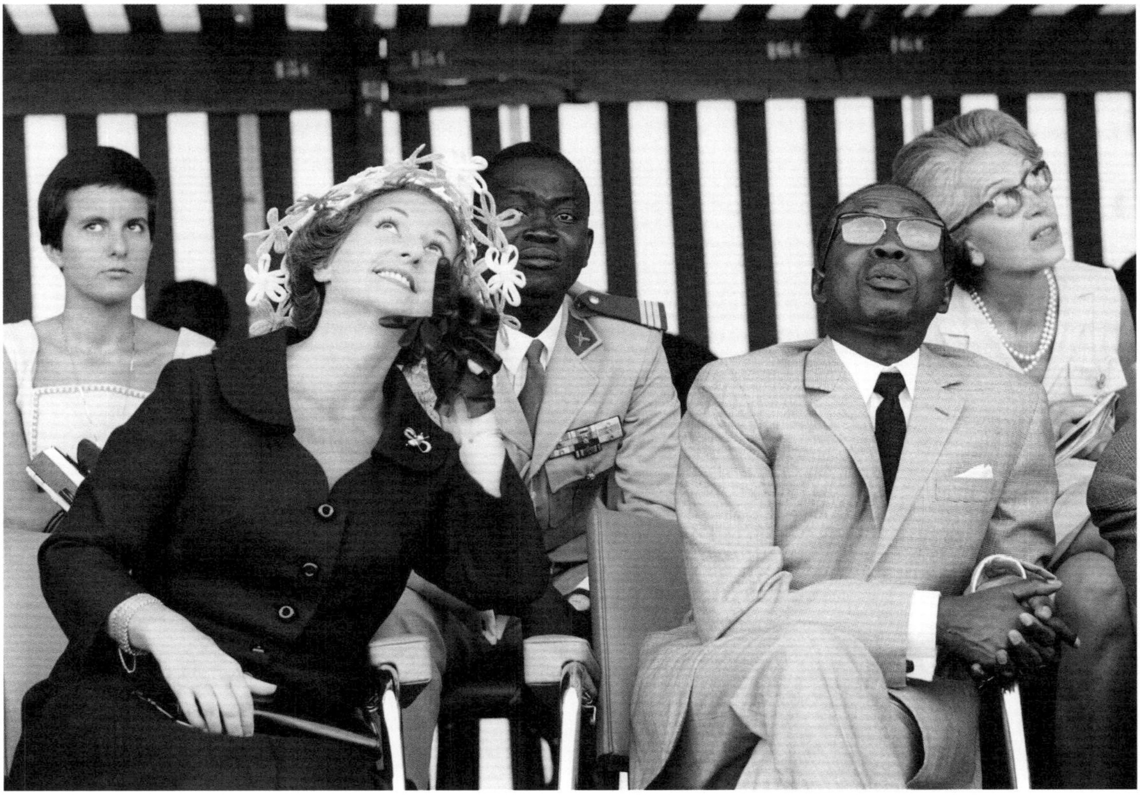

GEORGE BERNARD SHAW

born Dublin, 1856; died Ayot St Lawrence, Hertfordshire, UK, 1950

by Yousuf Karsh

London, 1943

George Bernard Shaw was a man of many interests and abilities. He was, among other things, a socialist, a supporter of women's rights, a great admirer of Ibsen, a vegetarian and an enthusiastic pioneer of photography and of photographic criticism (he bought himself a camera in 1898 and never stopped taking pictures). He is perhaps best remembered, however, as a dramatist and as a prolific writer, a virtual graphomaniac: aside from the plays that made his name, several novels and a selection of works of criticism, he also wrote at least 250,000 letters.

Shaw was born in Dublin but moved to London when he was about twenty years old to join his estranged mother. Between 1879 and 1883 he dedicated himself to writing his first novels: *An Unsocial Socialist* (1884), *Cashel Byron's Profession* (1885–86), *The Irrational Knot* (1886–87), *Love Among the Artists* (1900) and *Immaturity* (1930–31). He was an active member of the Fabian Society, which promoted a reformist version of socialism, and, in 1885, co-founded the London School of Economics. He met Stalin on his first journey to the Soviet Union and kept faith with the dictator for the rest of his life, even defending him internationally with strongly worded speeches and writing articles in favour of the Soviet Union. Many of his plays, such as *Mrs Warren's Profession* (1898), *The Devil's Disciple* (1901) and his celebrated *Pygmalion* (1913), were inspired by political and philosophical themes.

Blessed with a highly acute and versatile intelligence, Shaw was animated by a radical ethical and counter-cultural drive. He was always ready to lend his weight to causes that he believed in, and was impatient with the idea of rosettes, prizes and profits; following his acceptance of the Nobel Prize in 1925, he used the prize money to finance the translation of some Swedish texts into English. Shaw is also remembered for his biting aphorisms and famous one-liners, to which perhaps only Winston Churchill was able to respond appropriately. When Shaw sent Churchill an invitation with the words, 'I am enclosing two tickets to the first night of my new play; bring a friend ... if you have one', Churchill replied, 'Cannot possibly attend first night, will attend second ... if there is one.'

Yousuf Karsh, who photographed Shaw in the final decade of the writer's life, later recalled his encounter with the great man: 'Shaw came bursting into the room with the energy of a young man, though he was almost ninety years old. His manner, his penetrating old eyes, his flashing wit, and his bristling beard were all designed to awe me; in the beginning they succeeded. He obviously loved to act, and assumed the role of harmless Mephistopheles.'

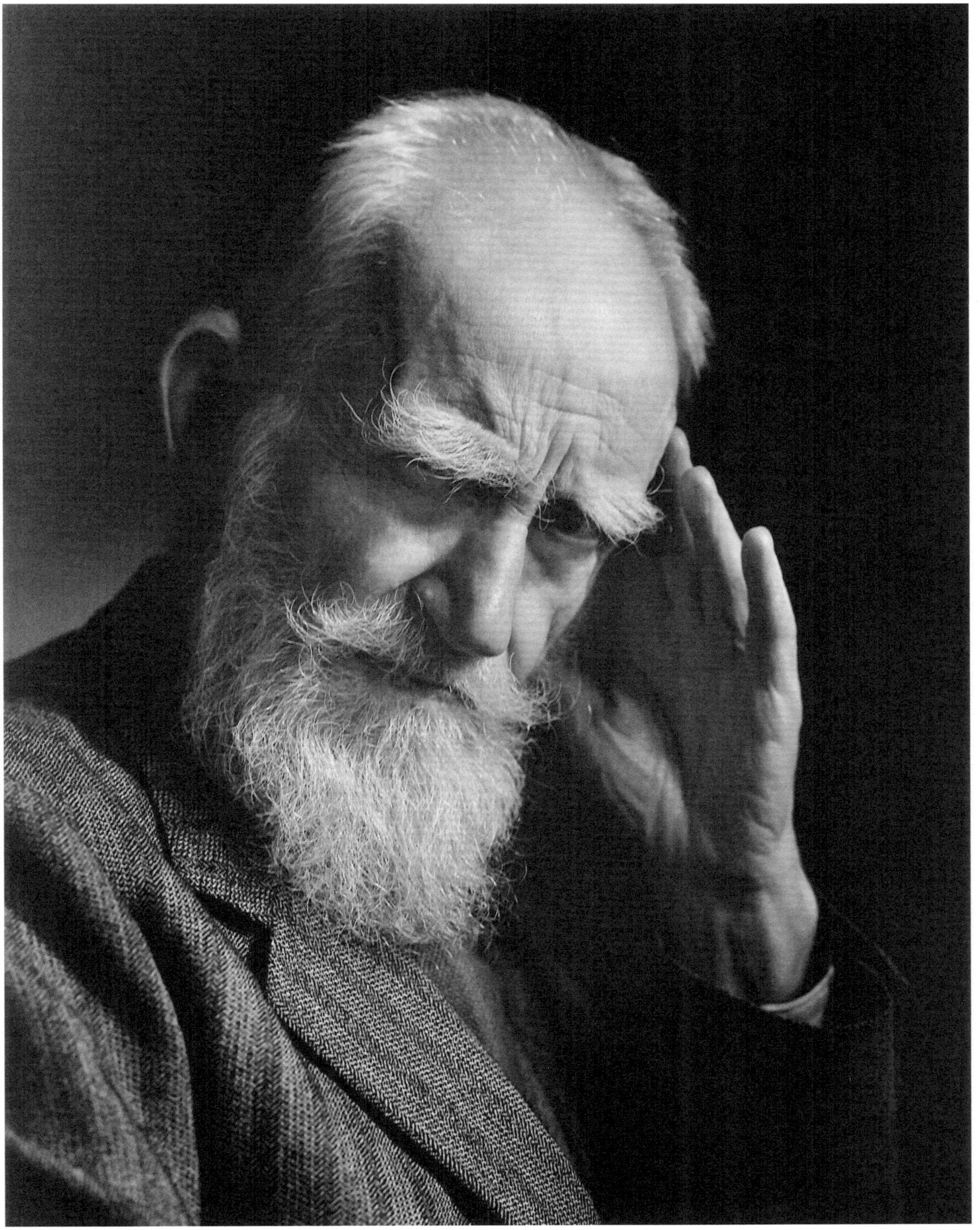

GEORGES SIMENON

born Liège, Belgium, 1903; died Lausanne, Switzerland, 1989

by Robert Doisneau

unknown location, c. 1962

Commissaire Maigret – physically robust with a friendly appearance, a man of few words who never carried a gun but always had a pipe in his mouth – was the most popular character to emerge from the pen of Georges Simenon. Indeed, since his first appearance in the early 1930s, he has become synonymous with the type of detective fiction in which an apparently sleepy community is disrupted by an unexpected and shocking event. Simenon's impact on the detective novel stems, in fact, from his decision to focus on the question of why a crime has been committed as opposed to that of who was responsible, as the classic English detective story had always done.

Born in Belgium but a French citizen by adoption, Simenon was a prolific writer. He could produce more than eighty pages a day and was the author of almost two hundred novels, an equally large quantity of pulp fiction written under various pseudonyms, several autobiographical works and numerous articles; the majority of his output, however, was detective fiction. Simenon explored a wide variety of social contexts in his writing, from small provincial towns to the suburbs of big cities. Using simple, terse language that was nonetheless capable of conveying drama and emotion, he was also able to create highly convincing scenarios in which the fate of his characters was reflected in their surroundings. The advice given to him by the French novelist Colette regarding one of his first collections of short stories – 'Look, it is too literary, always too literary' – clearly had an effect.

In addition to being the creator of the celebrated *commissaire*, Simenon was a complex, tortured author of great personal charm. We get a sense of this complexity in such novels as *The Man Who Watched the Trains Go By* (1938), *Marie of the Port* (1938) and *Dirty Snow* (1948), which are suffused with a palpable sense of anguish and loneliness.

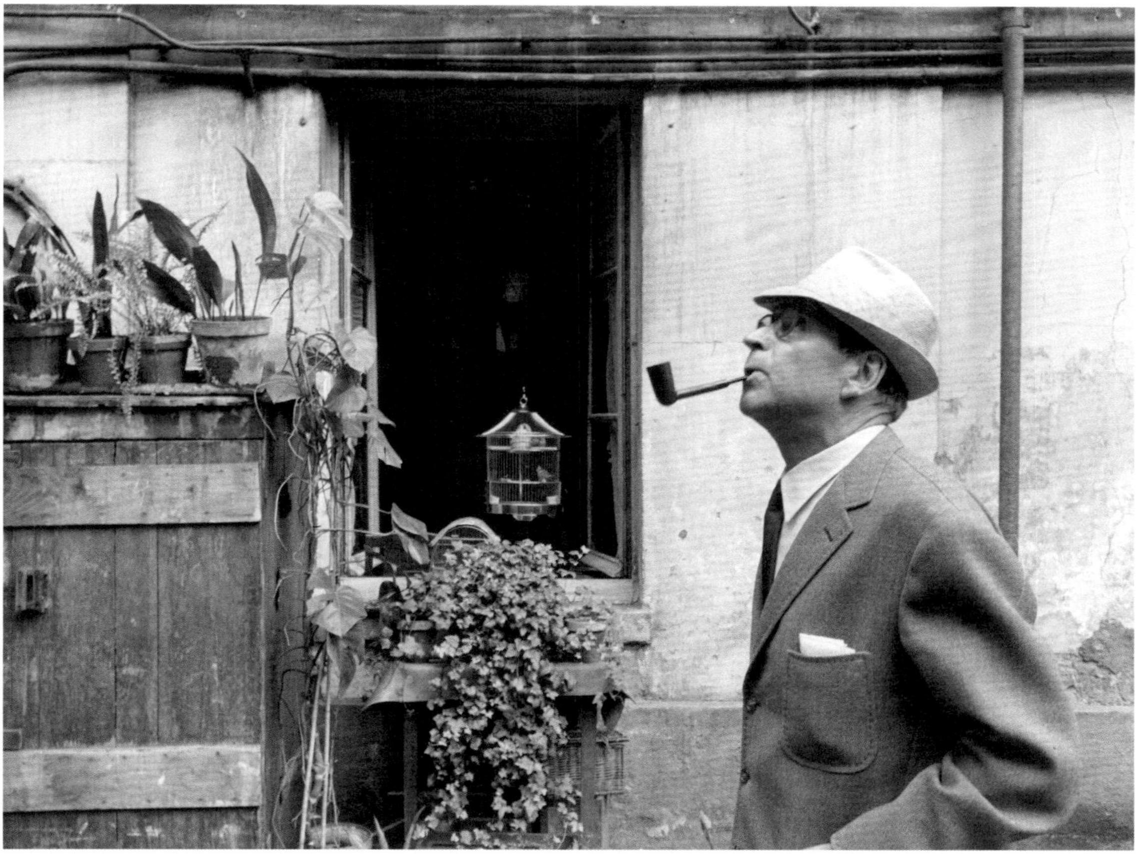

ISAAC BASHEVIS SINGER

born Leoncin, Poland, 1902; died Miami, 1991

by Bruce Davidson

New York, 1975

When a family has a tradition of telling stories, it is hardly surprising if its children go on to become writers. Isaac Bashevis Singer was born into one such family – strictly observant Polish Jews who cultivated the art of storytelling and passed it on from one generation to another. Indeed, Singer's life was dominated by his pursuit of stories, both lived and invented. He even reinvented his date of birth: born in 1902, he maintained that he had in fact been born in 1904, possibly in an attempt to escape conscription during the First World War.

Singer lived a full and varied life, from his childhood in a poor and over-populated quarter of Warsaw to his studies at the Rabbinical seminary in Tachkemoni, his first translations offoreign authors, his work as a journalist in the interwar years, his arrival in the USA in 1935 and his many literary accomplishments, for which he was awarded the Nobel Prize in 1978. The author of numerous novels, children's books, essays, articles, reviews and short stories, Singer wrote and published almost everything in Yiddish; he would then rework it before translating it into English (his 'second first language', as he liked to call it). He was assisted in this task by friends, translators and other advisers, all of whom would help to shape the new text.

Singer's fiction has its roots in variety of traditions. His novel *Satan in Goray* (1935), for example, is written in the style of the medieval Yiddish chronicles, while the stories in *Gimpel the Fool* (1957) combine the fantastical with the everyday, the astonishing with the trivial, ancient legends with religion, and passion with harsh reality. His heroes, from thetitle character in *The Magician of Lublin* (1960) to the family in *The Manor* (1967) and the lovelorn Haron in *Shosha* (1978), live in an atmosphere of melancholia, irony and suppressed tragedy, where changes to their lives threaten their very identities. A committed vegetarian (he described life for animals as an eternal Treblinka), Singer was also horrified by the effect of time on memory, on history and on people: 'Time is also a Hitler. It too destroys everything.'

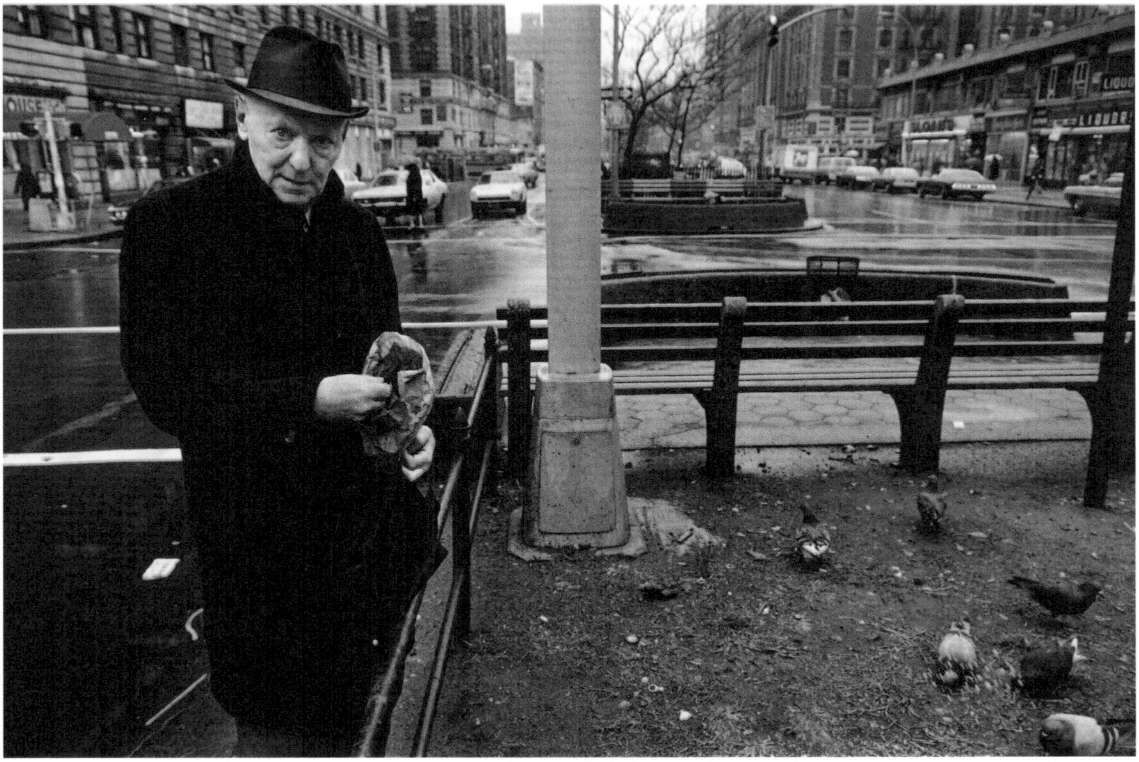

ZADIE SMITH

born London, 1975

by Eamonn McCabe

London, 2005

Zadie Smith started writing her first novel while she was still a student at King's College, Cambridge. Following an auction among publishers to secure the rights to the book, it was finally published in 2000. *White Teeth* is a lively and original portrait of multicultural London, told through the story of three ethnically diverse families. It was an immediate success, winning both the *Guardian* First Book Award and the Whitbread First Novel Award, and Smith was hailed as the voice of the new millennium. In 2003 she was named by *Granta* magazine as one of twenty 'Best of Young British Novelists'.

Born to a Jamaican mother and an English father, Smith has admitted to struggling with writer's block during the creation of her second novel, *The Autograph Man* (2002), which was followed by the more mature *On Beauty* (2005). A gap of seven years passed before the appearance of her fourth novel, *NW* (2012), which she describes as 'the first book that I've really written as an adult'. It is a more complex and experimental work, which reverts to the themes of cultural and ethnic differences. Smith has also published a work of non-fiction about writing, *Fail Better* (2006), and a collection of essays, *Changing My Mind: Occasional Essays* (2009). In 2010 she became a tenured professor of fiction at New York University.

Smith remains humble about her achievements and realistic about the writing process: 'I was very young, and I thought everybody felt the way that I did, as you do when you are young. As I met writers (I had never met any writers before in my life), you realize there are plenty of writers who just adore their work and think that every word they write is absolutely fantastic and will defend it to their dying day. Some writers feel that way; I just can't find that confidence in myself. At the same time, there is not much point in talking about it all the time because people think you are being falsely modest. But to me, writing is a very painful experience. And I hope it will stop being so painful as I get older, but it doesn't seem to be getting any better.'

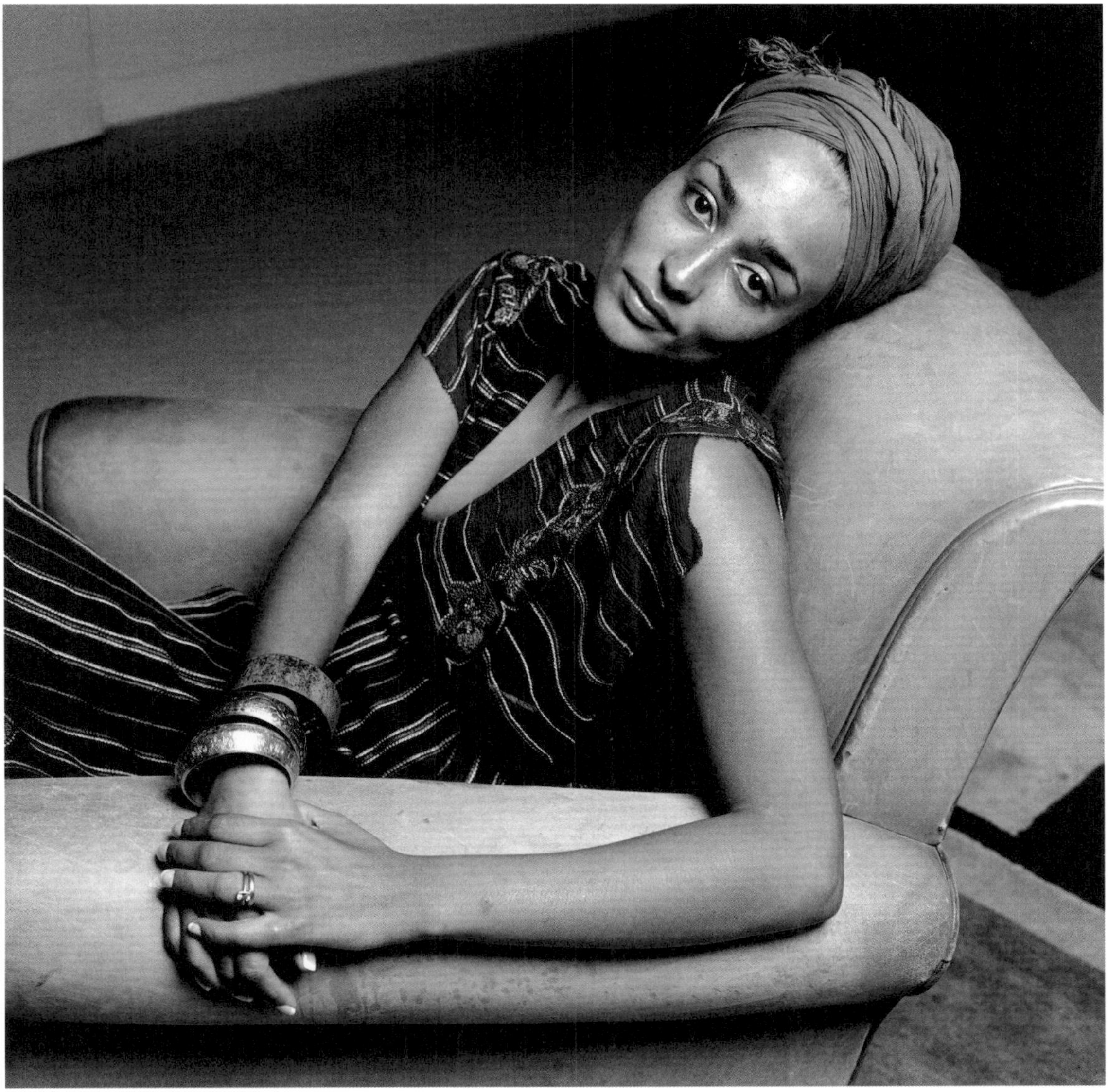

ALEKSANDR SOLZHENITSYN

born Kislovodsk, Russia, 1918; died Moscow, 2008

by Steve Liss

Vermont, 1989

In 1962, the publication of *One Day in the Life of Ivan Denisovich* – a short novel by the then unknown author Aleksandr Solzhenitsyn – in the Moscow literary journal *Novy Mir* was an event of extraordinary historic significance. The story of the courageous struggle for survival of a Russian peasant interned in a gulag, it revealed the horror of Stalin's work camps to the world for the first time.

The knowledge came first hand. In 1945, Solzhenitsyn had been condemned to eight years correctional hard labour for having criticized Stalin's military strategy in a letter to a friend. He survived with the intention of writing about his experiences, so that nothing should ever be forgotten, but it never entered his head that this work would be published during his lifetime; however, in 1961, at the XXII Congress of the Communist Party of the Soviet Union, premier Nikita Khrushchev gave permission for the novel to be published. Khrushchev had gone to lengths to distance himself from Stalin's policies, and hoped the publication would help shake off his predecessor's long shadow. The novel achieved great success when it was published and 800,000 copies were printed in just a few months. The writer went on to describe life in the camp at much greater length in *The Gulag Archipelago* (1973).

When Khrushchev's policies and the Soviet thaw came to an end, Solzhenitsyn soon found that the freedom he had enjoyed was increasingly restricted: he became the object of a defamatory campaign by the KGB and was expelled from the Soviet Union of Writers for not having observed the aesthetic criteria of socialist realism in his works. When he was awarded the Nobel Prize in 1970 he did not travel to Sweden to receive it, fearing he would not be allowed to return home.

He was expelled from the Soviet Union in 1974 and became the point of reference for Soviet dissidence, while at the same time retained strong links with 'Great Mother' Russia. His exile lasted twenty years, and during this period he searched for traces and memories of the country of his birth, even in the woods around his new home in Cavendish, Vermont. America could never replace his homeland. He returned to Russia in 1990 and lived there with his family in a dacha to the west of Moscow.

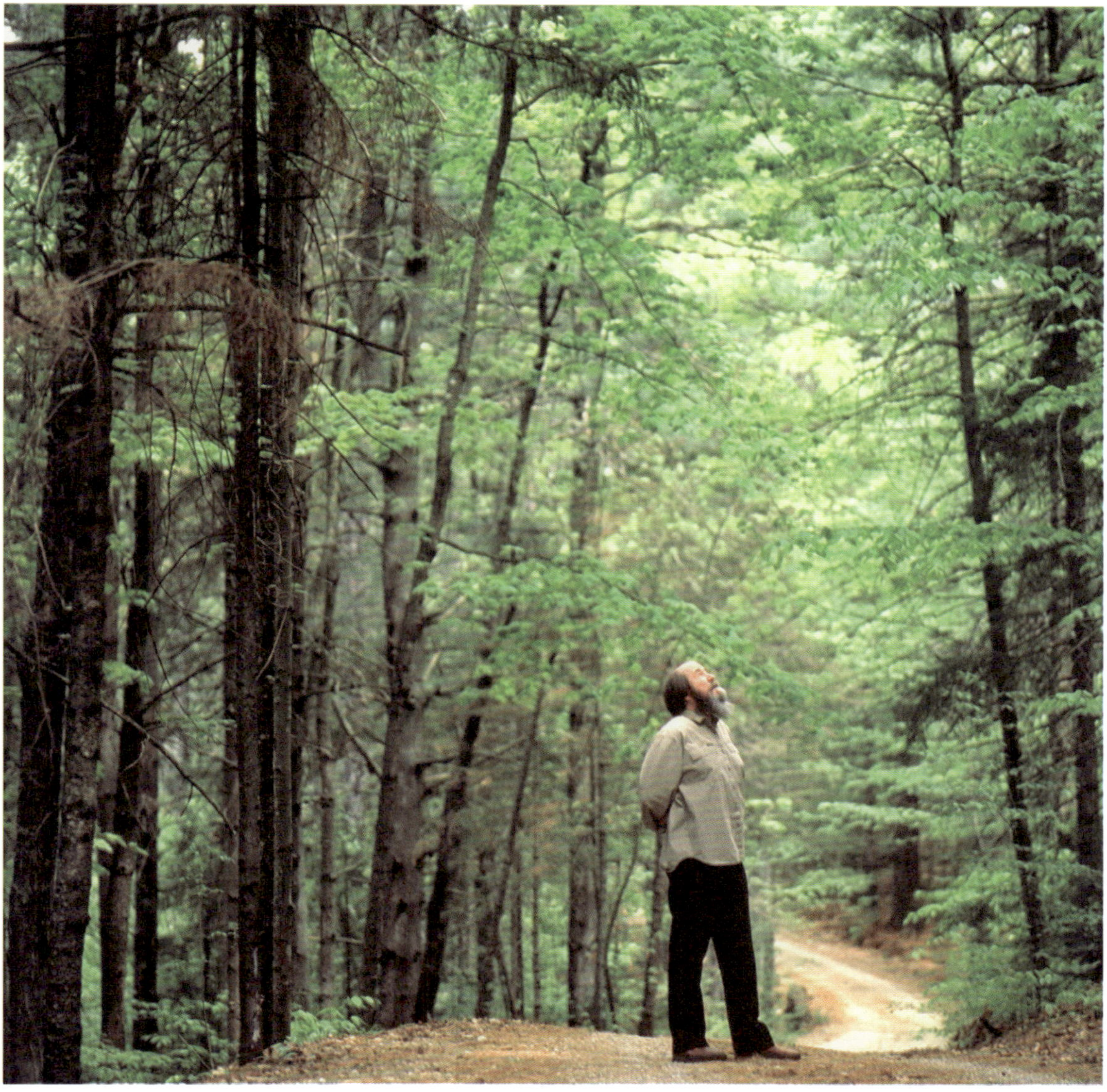

OSVALDO SORIANO

born Mar del Plata, Argentina, 1943; died Buenos Aires, 1997

by Ulf Andersen

Paris, 1991

Osvaldo Soriano was a passionate man: passionate about football ('I believe that football is like a war without deaths, but with conflict'); cinema, especially Laurel and Hardy films ('a metaphor for ingenuity and spirit in the face of the powerful'); and hard-boiled detective fiction, in particular the works of Raymond Chandler ('I don't think I could have written a credible dialogue without having first read *The Long Goodbye*. I have become an aficionado of Chandler and his characters'). It was these passions, together with a love of boxing and tango, that Soriano brought to his writing.

Soriano left Argentina following the military coup of 1976, and returned only once democracy had been restored. Before leaving, he had succeeded in publishing his first novel, *Sad, Lonely and Final* (1973), in which a character named Osvaldo Soriano combines forces with thefictional detective Philip Marlowe, a character created by Chandler, to investigate the artistic decline of Stan Laurel. The work constitutes a delicate blend of melancholy, parody and humour. While living in exile, first in Brussels then in Paris, Soriano continued to analyse and comment on the country of his birth. *A Funny Dirty Little War* (1979) and *Winter Quarters* (1981) are both set in the fictional town of Colonia Vela in the province of Buenos Aires. The former recounts the events leading up to the coup of 1976, while the latter is set during the military dictatorship.

Soriano was particularly skilled in illustrating universal truths and finding the absurd in everything. In *A Lion Laid at His Feet* (1988), the title of which is taken from the lyrics of Argentina's former national anthem, he moves away from making direct references to his homeland in a story inspired by the Falklands War of 1982. *A Shadow You Soon Will Be* (1990), which takes its title from the famous 'Caminito' tango, tells the story of a man wandering the pampas with no ultimate destination. Along the way, he encounters several other lost souls, including a banker and an astrologist, as well as stopping off at Colonia Vela.

In common with his fellow Argentine author Manuel Puig, Soriano wrote in a fast, furious and action-packed style, with much emotion but little introspection. It is a style that seems to pay homage to one of Soriano's many passions, Raymond Chandler.

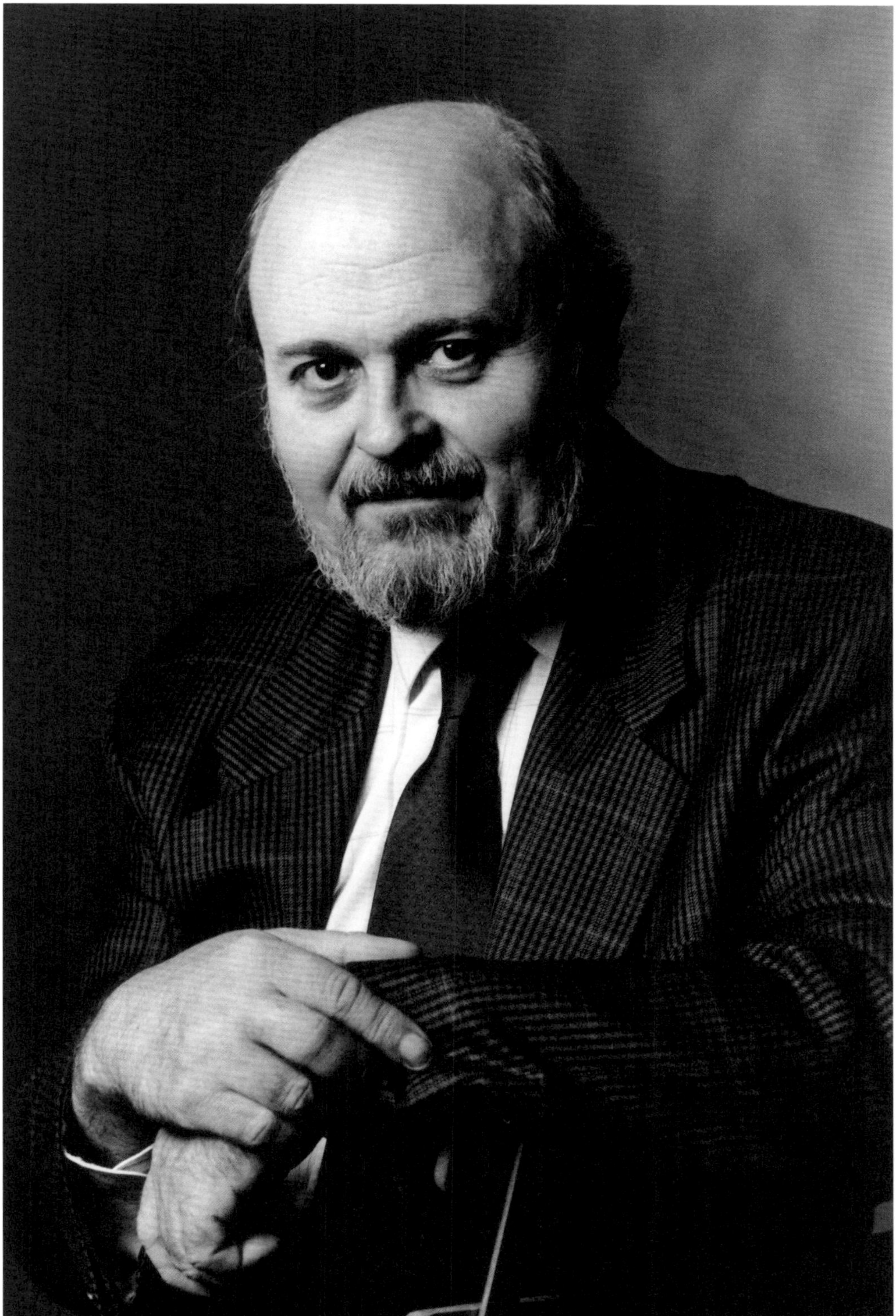

WOLE SOYINKA

[Akinwande Oluwole Soyinka] born Abeokuta, Nigeria, 1934

by David Hurn

Hay-on-Wye, Powys, UK, 2007

In 1986, Wole Soyinka, a Nigerian writer of Yoruba heritage who writes in English, became the first African, as well as the first black writer, to be awarded the Nobel Prize in Literature. Soyinka's novels, memoirs, poetry, essays and, above all, plays, portray the deleterious effects of post-colonial meddling by foreign governments on native African cultures. He has been sharply critical of both the indiscriminate adoption of Western political models by post-colonial African governments and the purist illusions and chauvinism in the concept of 'Negritude' promoted by the Senegalese poet and politician Léopold Sédar Senghor. Instead, Soyinka has advocated for a progressive syncretism, through which African cultures can engage in a dialogue of mutual exchange with European cultures. This approach is reflected in his own literary works, in which Nigerian folklore, European modernism, Yoruba myths, classical Greek references and Christian cultural elements intersect in an extremely original and expressive manner. His debut novel, *The Interpreters* (1964) a semi-autobiographical tale of his departure from and return to his native country, is among his best-known works, along with numerous plays such as *The Road* (1965), *Kongi's Harvest* (1968), *Death and the King's Horseman* (1975) and *King Baabu* (2001), a satirical portrayal of African dictators. He also also produced a translation of Euripides's classical Greek play in *The Bacchae of Euripides* (1969). His many essays move easily between literary theory in *Myth, Literature and the African World* (1976) and political-cultural analysis of globalization in *A Climate of Fear* (2004).

Soyinka has been actively engaged in regional politics ever since Nigeria became independent from Britain in 1960. His public criticism of corruption in African political practices led to him spending a period of time in prison in the 1960s, a story that he later recounted in his memoir *The Man Died* (1971). In 1994 he was forced to flee Nigeria for the USA following the military coup by General Sani Abacha, and was subsequently accused of treason and condemned to death in absentia by the regime, which had already executed the Nigerian playwright Ken Saro-Wiwa. Although Soyinka was eventually able to return to Nigeria when civilian rule resumed in 1999, he has since worked in universities in both Europe and the USA, and has continued to denounce what he sees as the increasingly barbarous nature of African politics, the spread of religious fundamentalism in sharp contrast with the spirit of the native African religions, and the prejudiced representations of Africa in the Western media.

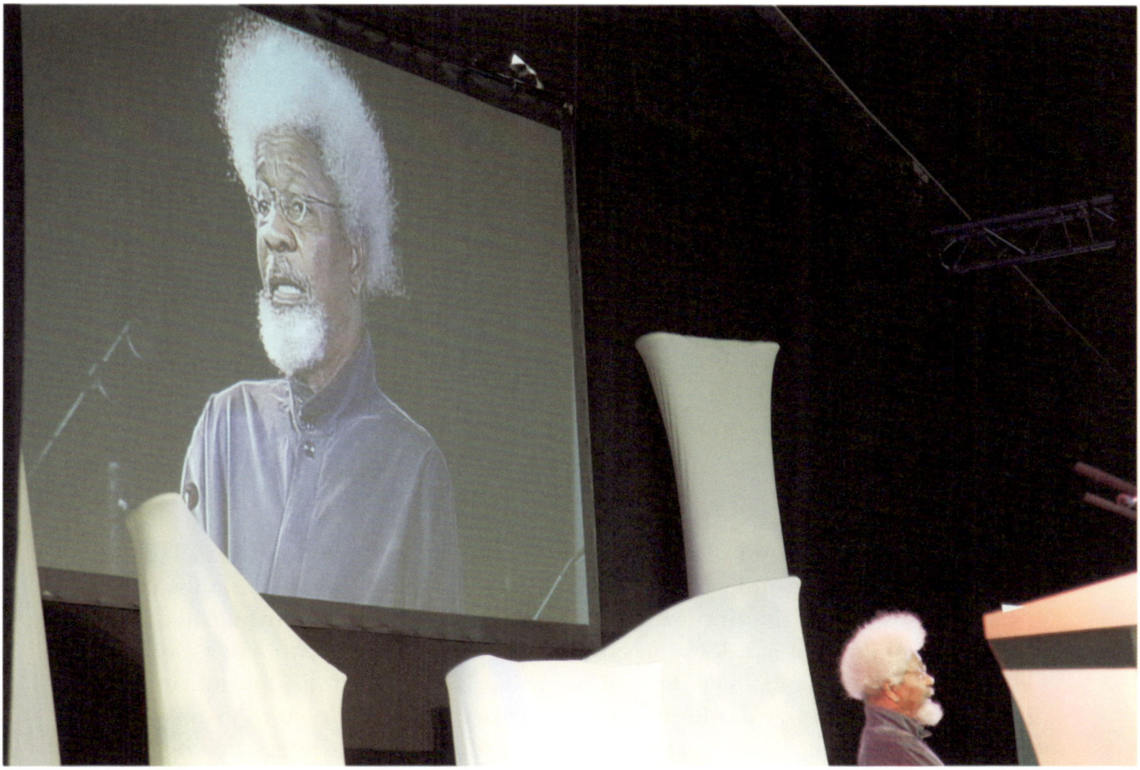

MURIEL SPARK

[née Camburg] born Edinburgh, UK, 1918; died Florence, Italy, 2006

by Ian Berry

London, 1965

Muriel Spark did not find her literary voice until relatively late in life, and not until she had experienced a series of personal crises. Her first novel, *The Comforters*, was published in 1957 when she was thirty-nine years old, shortly after her recovery from a complete breakdown. In 1944 she had returned to Britain from Rhodesia following the break-up of her marriage, and was living scarcely above the poverty line on the margins of London's literary community. Despite having a job at the Poetry Society, where she served as editor of the *Poetry Review* from 1947 to 1949, she could not afford regular meals and took diet pills to stave off her hunger. In 1954, however, unable to maintain such a lifestyle, she suffered a physical and emotional collapse.

Spark had been born to a Jewish father and a Christian mother, and it was her conversion to Catholicism in the mid-1950s that paved the way for her recovery; indeed, this conversion was to have a profound effect on both her life and her work. During this period she was supported financially by Graham Greene, who sent her money and red wine, but on the strict condition that she never prayed for him. From the late 1950s to the mid-1970s her output was prolific, resulting in almost one novel every year, as well as short stories, poetry collections and works of non-fiction.

The year 1961 saw the publication of one of Spark's most famous novels, *The Prime of Miss Jean Brodie*, the disturbing story of a charismatic Edinburgh schoolmistress and her group of favoured pupils. The novel was a resounding success, and was later adapted for film, television and stage. In 1963, now financially secure, Spark left England for good, living first of all in New York, then in Rome and finally in Tuscany, where she lived until the end of her life. In many of her novels and short stories, Spark explored the relationship between power and personality, in each case employing her characteristically lively and ironic narrative voice. Her own devout faith did not prevent her from also exposing aspects of the church and state to satire and humour.

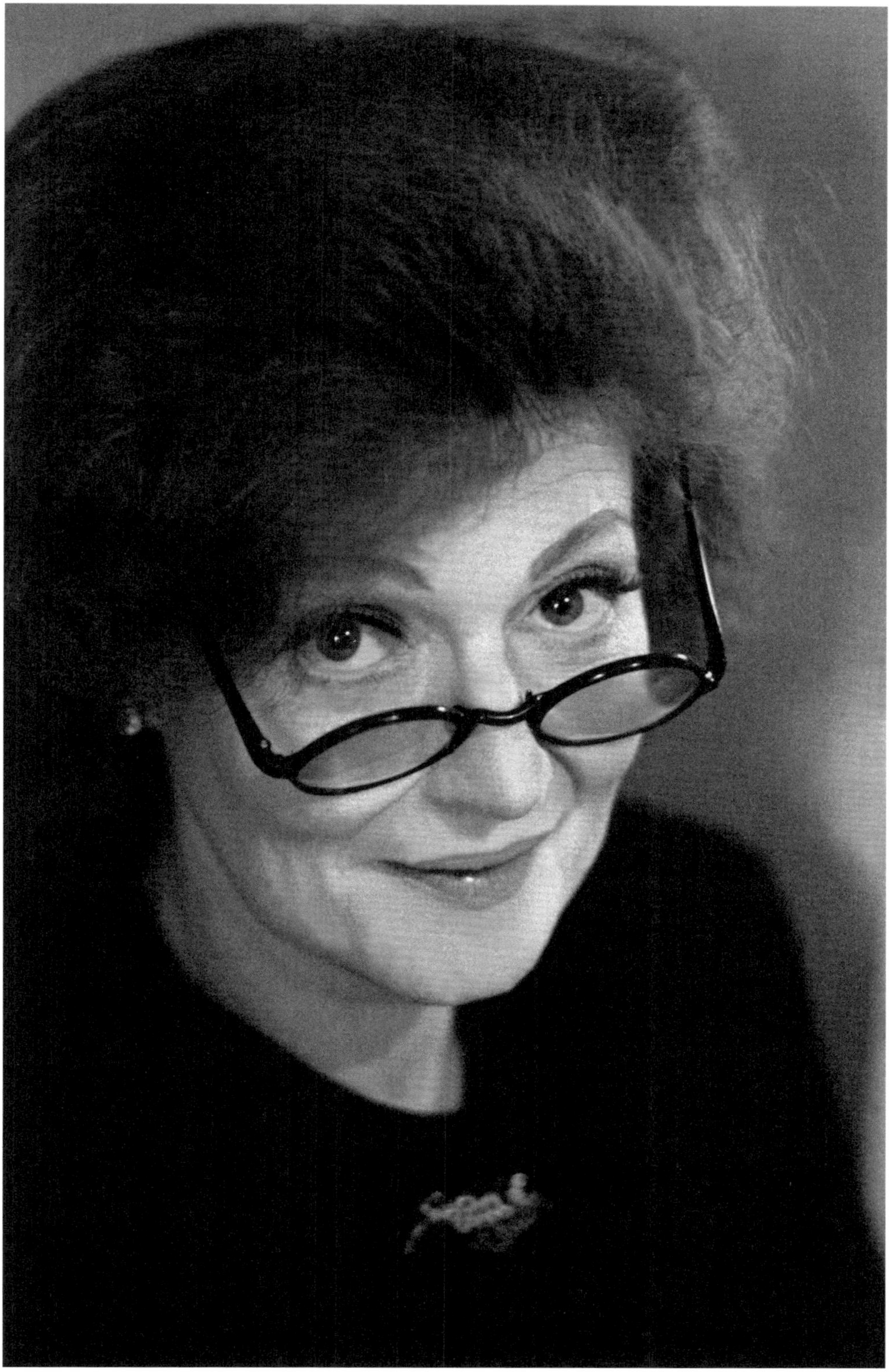

CHRISTINA STEAD

born Rockdale, Australia, 1902; died Sydney, 1983

by Jacqueline Mitelman

Melbourne, 1981

Christina Stead's first novel, entitled *Seven Poor Men of Sydney* (1934), follows a group of poor, working-class men in Sydney, just after the First World War. They are trapped by unemployment, mental and emotional instability, and the impossibility of finding opportunities of any kind. In the author's pitiless and acute vision of reality, nothing is spared or hidden. Hers was a superb portrait of a country still oppressed by a prevailing colonial attitude that had created injustices of class, race and other social inequalities.

Stead was born in the suburbs of Sydney and the story of her life is one of stubborn determination to carve out her own, very different, destiny. Her mother died when Stead was only two years old, and her father then remarried and had six children with his new wife. He was a despotic and tyrannical man, at least according to the stories Stead later told about him in her novels. She worked as a teacher and secretary, and in the 1930s fled from both her father and her country with the money she had managed to save. Stead sought a new life and new opportunities in Europe, beginning in London. There she had hopes of joining W. G. K. Duncan, a postgraduate student at the London School of Economics and formerly a tutor at the University of Sydney. The match did not come off, but she soon met William J. Blake (born Wilhelm Blech) with whom she shared her life, work, ideological passions and political commitment. They married in 1949 and moved to Paris, Spain and, much later, to the USA.

Her works are unflinching examinations of the problems of living as a woman in a world filled with many forms of discrimination. She examined the relationships between the sexes in *The Beauties and Furies* (1936); the capitalist system of the banks, which only a Communist uprising would bring to an end, in *House of All Nations* (1938); the suffocating and reactionary conventions of family life in what was perhaps her most famous novel, *The Man Who Loved Children* (1940); and, above all, the necessity of women finding ways of expressing themselves and discovering an identity that transcended the prevailing sexist attitudes and economic prejudices in *For Love Alone* (1944). Her writing has been esteemed by generations of feminists.

Stead also worked as a scriptwriter in Hollywood, although she was blacklisted for her Communist views during the years of McCarthyite persecution. After Blake died, Stead returned to Australia, where she remained from 1974 until her death in 1983. It was during those later years that Australia's 'lost' writer was rehabilitated as one of her country's most important voices and newly appreciated by readers elsewhere for her clear and innovative vision.

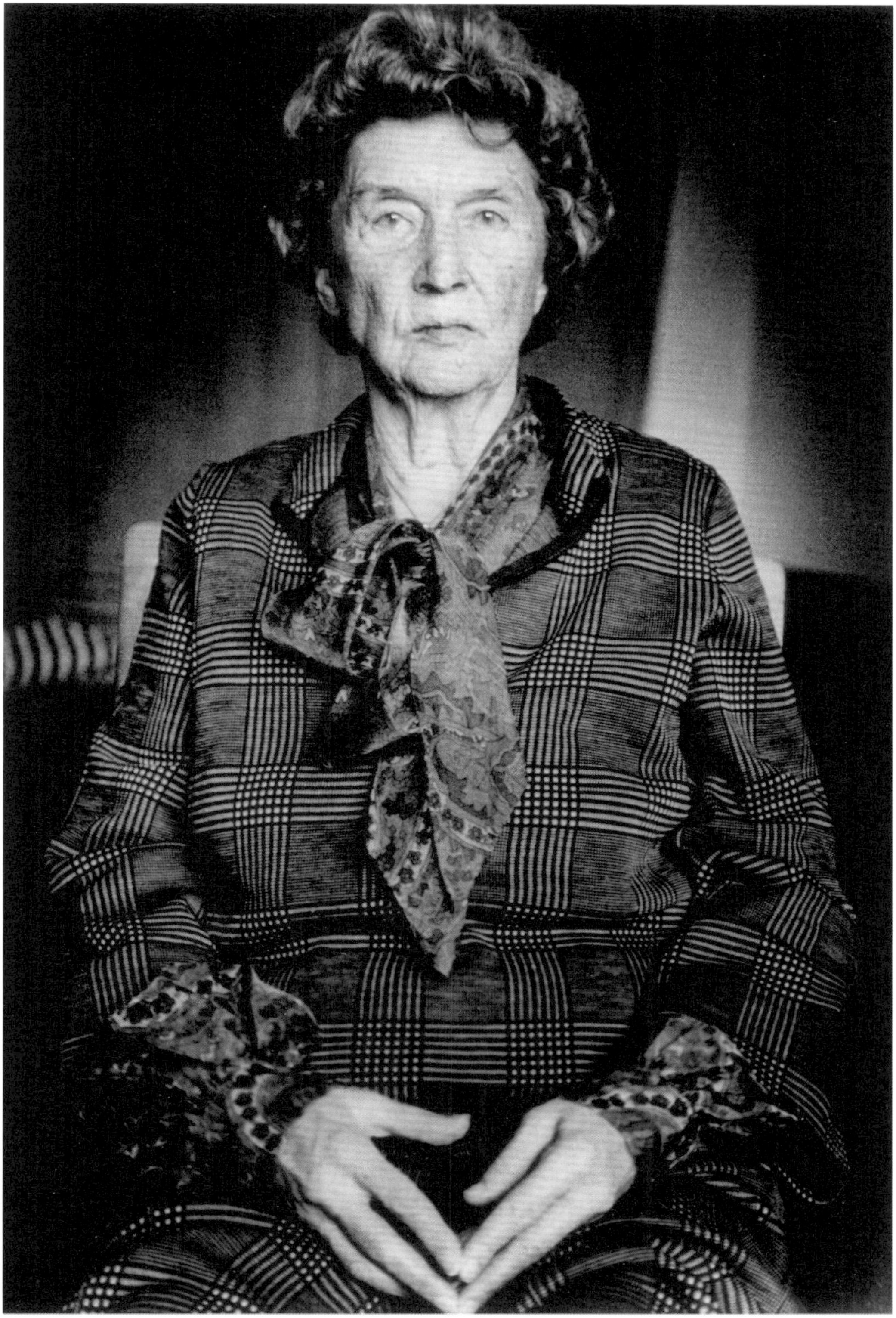

GERTRUDE STEIN

born Allegheny, Pennsylvania, 1874; died Neuilly-sur-Seine, France, 1946

by Carl Mydans

[left] with Alice B. Toklas, Culoz, France, 1944

Gertrude Stein's fate is a curious one. Although she is remembered primarily for her literary and artistic friendships, and for being a highly influential collector and patron of the arts, she was also an avant-garde writer in her own right. Indeed, one of the most quoted, copied and now clichéd lines in all literature, 'Rose is a rose is a rose is a rose', is hers.

Known as the mother of the Lost Generation – a group of expatriate American writers living in Paris after the First World War, many of whom would gather at her literary salon – Stein was born in Pennsylvania in 1874. She visited both Vienna and Paris before her tenth birthday, and had lost both her parents before her twentieth. After studying psychology at Radcliffe College, where she was a student of the philosopher and psychologist William James (brother of Henry), she studied brain anatomy at Johns Hopkins University. In 1902 she moved to Paris with her brother, Leo. There, free of any financial constraints, she and Leo set up home in Montparnasse (they were joined in 1909 by Stein's secretary and friend, Alice B. Toklas, with whom she formed one of the most openly gay partnerships of the twentieth century). The Steins' famous apartment at 27, rue de Fleurus was soon filled with paintings and the men who had painted them: Gauguin, Cézanne, Matisse, Renoir, Braque and Picasso. It was also frequented by such artists, writers, poets and musicians as Apollinaire, Eric Satie, Ernest Hemingway, Ezra Pound, Sherwood Anderson, F. Scott Fitzgerald, Jean Cocteau and Man Ray.

Stein wrote in a wide variety of form and genres, from poetry and essays to novels and comedies. Much of her writing anticipated the themes and styles of both modernism and postmodernism, and although she had an impact on the literature of the period, her own work achieved very little public recognition – with the exception, perhaps, of her memoir, *The Autobiography of Alice B. Toklas* (1933). However, this lack of commercial success did not seem to worry Stein, assured as she was of her own worth: 'The Jews have produced only three originative geniuses: Christ, Spinoza, and myself.'

In the summer of 1940 Stein and Toklas left occupied Paris for the Rhône-Alpes region of France, finding refuge first in Bilignin and later in Culoz. She was able to remain in Culoz incognito until September 1944, when she was sought out by Carl Mydans, a correspondent for *Life* magazine attached to the Allied armies. Sometime later, *Life* published Mydans's photograph of Stein, Toklas and their dog, Basket, under the title 'The Liberation of Gertrude Stein'.

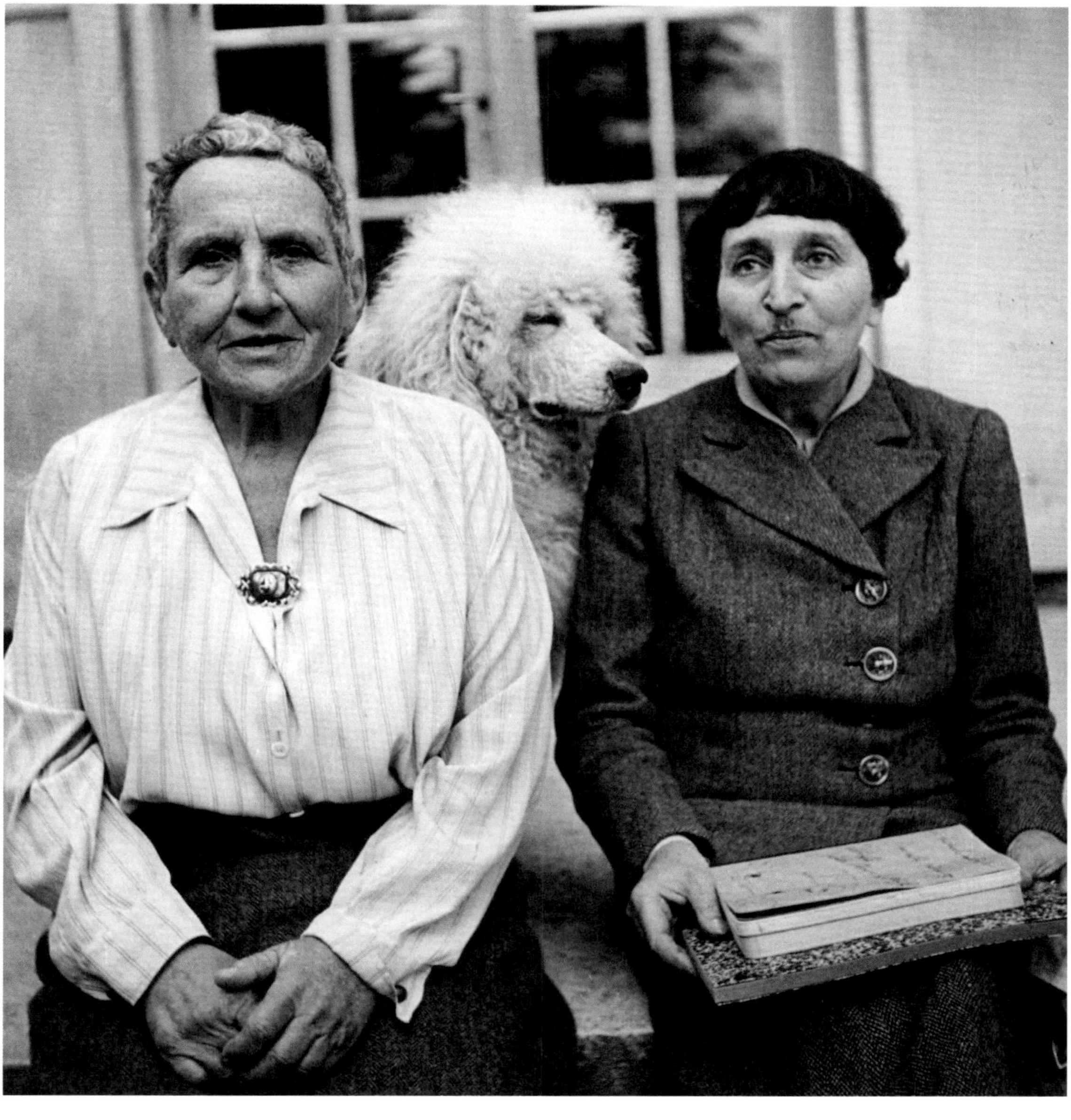

JOHN STEINBECK

born Salinas, California, 1902; died New York, 1968

by Philippe Halsman

New York, 1953

'If there is a magic in story writing, and I am convinced there is, no one has ever been able to reduce it to a recipe that can be passed from one person to another. The formula seems to lie solely in the aching urge of the writer to convey something he feels important to the reader.' John Steinbeck spoke these words to an audience of young writers in 1963. They encapsulate the sentiments that informed all his writing, with the possible exception of his début novel, *Cup of Gold* (1929), which tells the colourful life story of the pirate Henry Morgan. Certainly the urge to communicate 'something ... important' is tangible in *The Pastures of Heaven* (1932) and in all his subsequent works up to and including *Travels with Charley* (1962). Steinbeck writes with fervour about the lives of the peons of Salinas and Monterey, California, the daily struggles of the common people, their search for employment, the hypocrisy of the bourgeois and the lack of social justice in the USA.

Steinbeck was born into a modest family in Salinas. Supporting himself by means of various jobs, he managed to gain a place at prestigious Stanford University, but failed to graduate. His first success as a writer came with *Tortilla Flat* (1935), and this success was confirmed when *Of Mice and Men* was published in 1937. The two foreshadowed many of the themes found in *The Grapes of Wrath* (1939), one of the quintessential American novels to be set 'on the road', a motif to which he would return later in his career with *Travels with Charley*. *The Grapes of Wrath* is set in the era of the Great Depression, during the period of severe drought in the 1930s that transformed many rich farming areas of the American heartland into a desolate waste nicknamed 'the Dust Bowl'. Thousands of families (called 'Okies') were forced to flee their homes in Oklahoma and travel to California in search of a better existence. The book proved to be controversial. Steinbeck describes the Okies' plight with ruthless honesty and compassion, which led to him being branded both a propagandist and a socialist. He was also criticized for using vulgar language. Despite the controversy, the book won the Pulitzer Prize and the National Book Award. The publication of *The Grapes of Wrath* marked the pinnacle of Steinbeck's writing career, and although he continued to write popular novels, such as *East of Eden* (1952), none was as successful. In 1962 he was awarded the Nobel Prize in Literature.

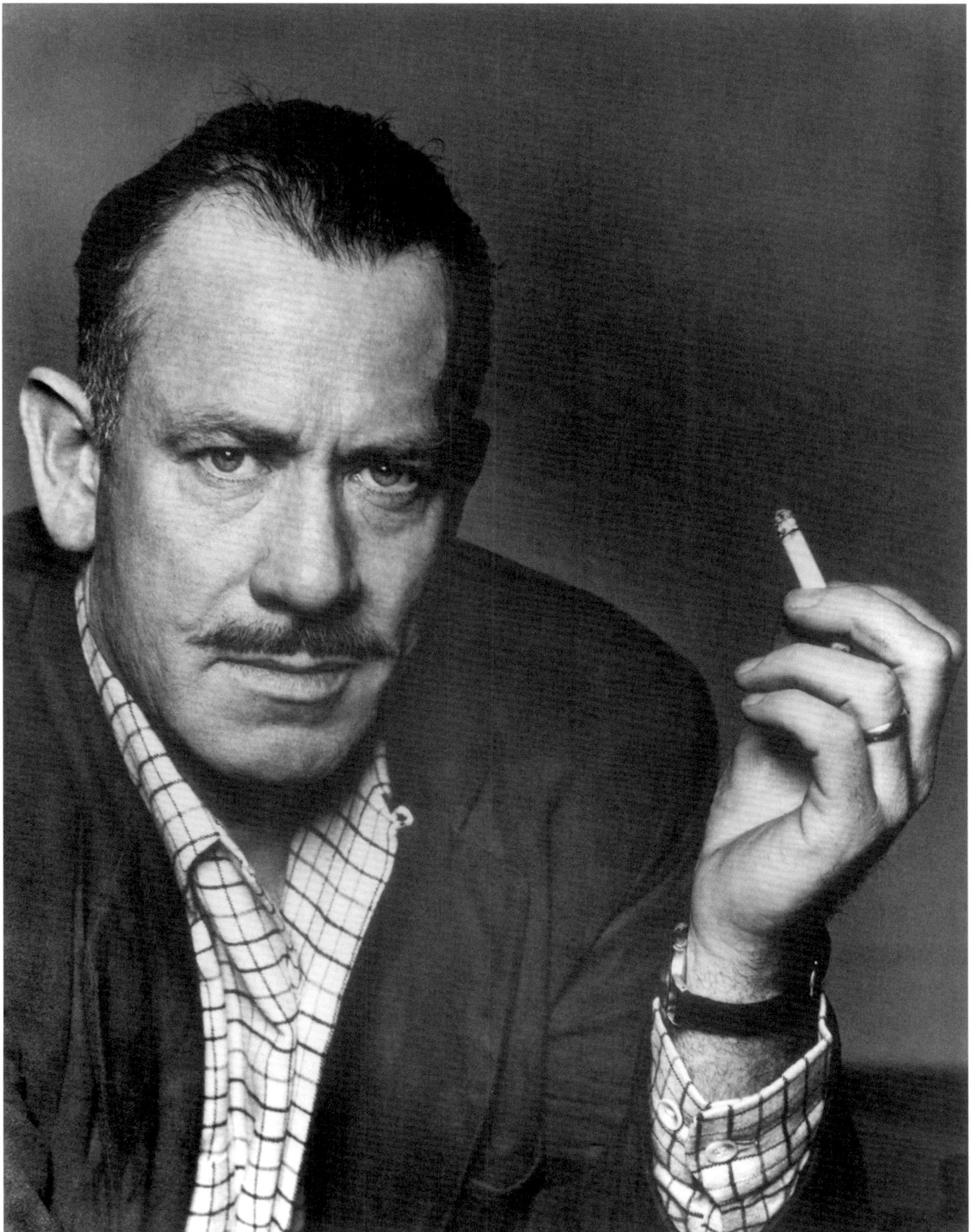

ITALO SVEVO

[Ettore Schmitz] born Trieste, Italy, 1861; died Motta di Livenza, Italy, 1928

unknown photographer

Trieste, Italy, 1892

As a pseudonym, 'Italo Svevo' (literally, Italian Swabian) was a statement of identity. Born in the Italian border town of Trieste to Jewish Italo-German parents, Svevo received a German education and was initially an office worker. He later met Freud, Joyce and Kafka, and spent much of his literary career – as he had his childhood – situated between two worlds: the nineteenth and twentieth centuries, naturalism and modernism, nationalism and socialism, and Marxism and psychoanalysis. He had much in common with Kafka: they were both clerks of Jewish descent who lived middle-class lives, and they were both interested in exploring the brave new world of the twentieth century through their fiction.

Svevo's professional life began in 1880, in a bank, where he worked for the next eighteen years. His spare time was taken up with his literary activities, which initially resulted in the publication of a few short stories. His first novel, *A Life* (the manuscript of which can be seen tucked beneath the writer's arm in the photograph opposite), appeared in 1893. Originally titled *A Good-for-Nothing*, it tells the story of Alfonso Nitti, whose fate is determined by a series of poor life choices that culminate in his suicide. The first of a series of memorable characters, Nitti was followed a few years later, in *As a Man Grows Older* (1898), by Emilio Brentani, and then, in *Confessions of Zeno* (1923), by Zeno Cosini. The first two books of this quasi-trilogy received almost no attention, and Svevo, apparently having set his literary activities aside, had begun to work for his father-in-law's company.

It was in 1907, while attending English classes in Trieste, that Svevo met Joyce, who happened to be teaching there. After reading some of his earlier work, Joyce later helped Svevo with the publication of *Confessions of Zeno*. Told in the form of a diary written by Zeno but published by his former psychiatrist, the book offers an analysis of the modern world as seen through the eyes of its protagonist. It is a complex work in which time and point of view are relative, and where the positivist and rationalist nineteenth century is a thing of the past: 'Contemporary life', says Zeno, 'is polluted down to its roots.' And, suggests Svevo at the end of the novel, it may be that only a disaster can save us.

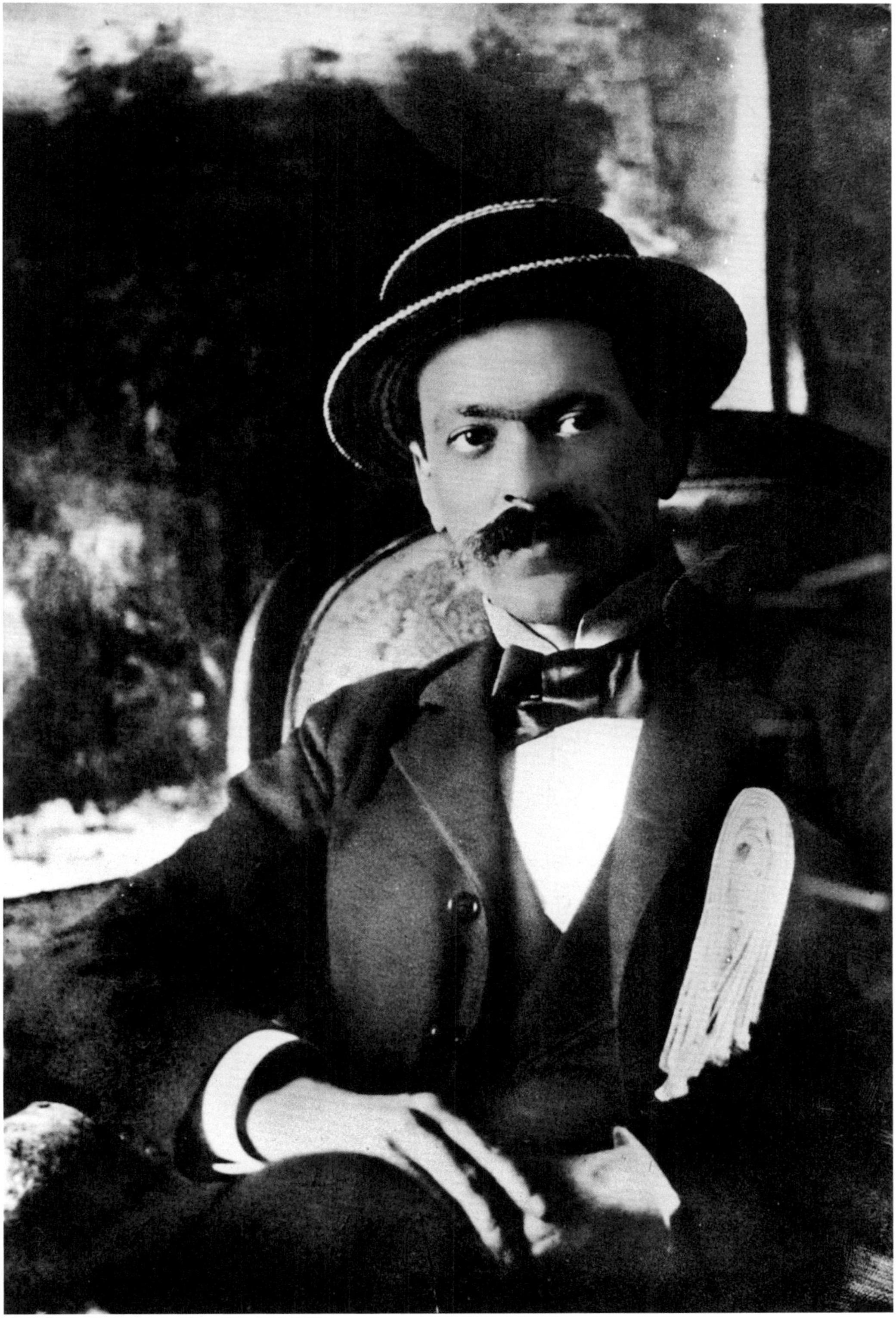

WISŁAWA SZYMBORSKA

born Bnin, Kórnik, Poland, 1923; died Kraców, Poland, 2012

by Zak Andre

Kraców, Poland, 1966

'After each war / somebody has to clear up, / put things in order, / by itself it won't happen.' These are the opening lines of Wisława Szymborska's poem 'The End and the Beginning' (1993), which Joseph Brodsky translated into English for *The Times Literary Supplement*, as he considered it to be one of the hundred finest poems of the century.

Yet three years later, there were still surprised reactions when the Nobel Prize was awarded to a Polish poet who was virtually unknown to most readers. In her acceptance speech, Szymborska explained that for her a poet was a semi-clandestine being, who in public would only unwillingly admit to being a poet, 'as if they were a little ashamed of it'. She went on to say that a poet's work has nothing photogenic about it and there are no teachers of poetry, because poets have a short but simple motto: 'I don't know.' After that, the almost unknown Szymborska was transformed, presumably against her will, into a cult writer. She published only twelve volumes in the span of fifty years.

Szymborska made her literary debut in 1945, when she published a poem in the weekly magazine *Walka*. Her life, like that of so many of her compatriots, was marked by great initial enthusiasm for the Communist experiment, followed by swift disillusionment. Always staying away from the limelight, she was a diminutive figure with an intelligent, smiling face. She constructed a poetic diction based on oral forms of expression, without any hint of artificiality, enriched by her keen sense of irony. Hers was a poetry that overturned clichés and conventions, and that awakened a simple yet rare sense of astonishment. Yet it was the world itself, rather than language, that she found amazing: it was said that she had a rare talent for telling stories about the ordinary miracles of life. The grace and levity that she brought to bear on every detail was striking, whether describing the layers of an onion or the first photograph of Adolf Hitler. Accordingly, Szymborska ended her Nobel acceptance speech by saying, 'Granted, in daily speech, where we don't stop to consider every word, we all use phrases like "the ordinary world", "ordinary life", "the ordinary course of events". ... But in the language of poetry, where every word is weighed, nothing is usual or normal. Not a single stone and not a single cloud above it. Not a single day and not a single night after it. And above all, not a single existence, not anyone's existence in this world. It looks like poets will always have their work cut out for them.'

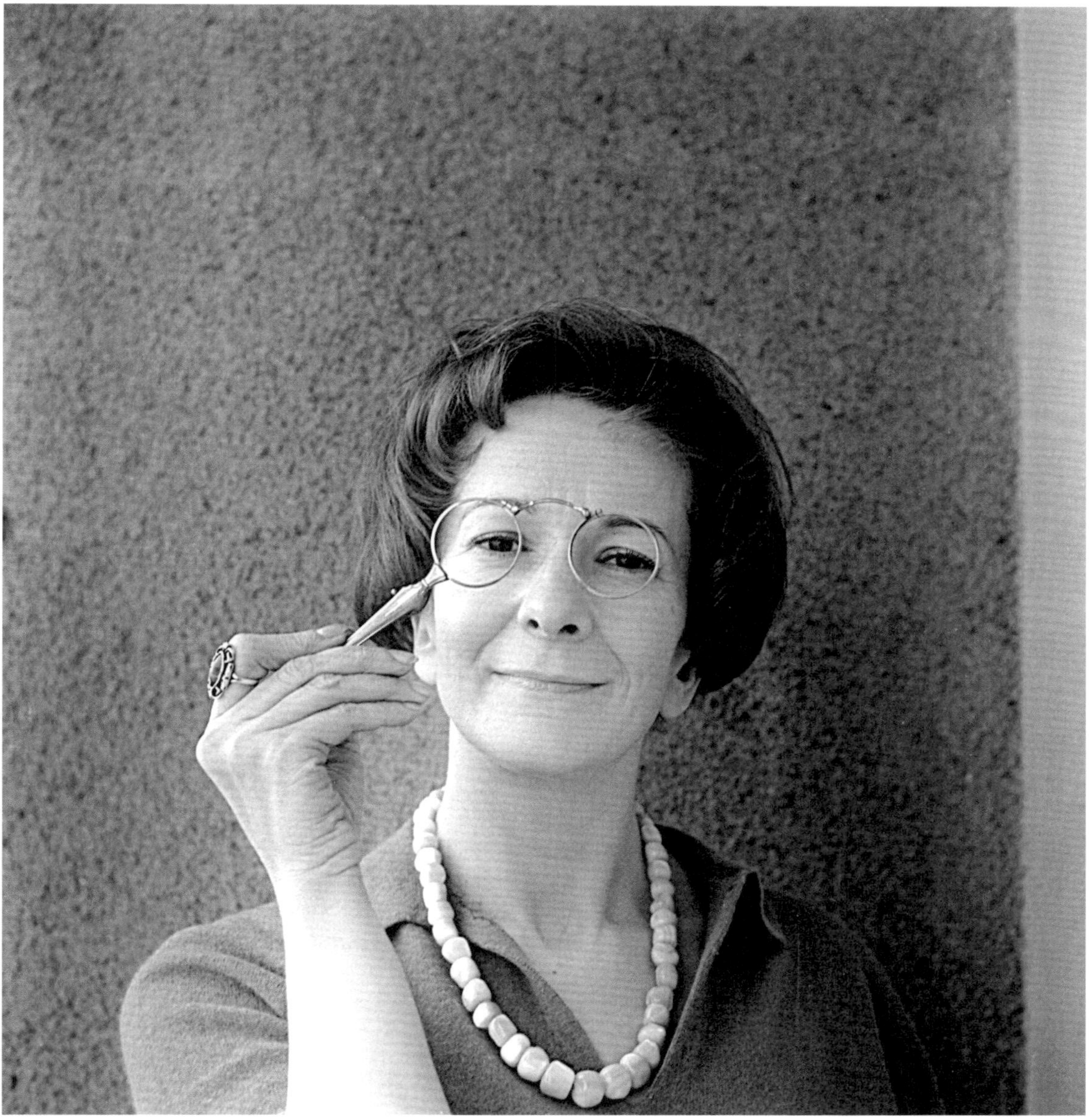

ANTONIO TABUCCHI

born Pisa, Italy, 1943; died Lisbon, 2012

by Giuseppe Pino

Milan, Italy, 1985

It sometimes happens that the celebrity conferred by a single work obscures an author's entire *oeuvre*. This is what happened, in part, to the novels of Antonio Tabucchi. While the success of *Indian Nocturne* (which took the Prix Médicis in France in 1987) was still that of an elegant writer addressing a select readership, the extraordinary success Tabucchi experienced in 1994 with *Pereira Maintains* was overwhelming. The novel found favour with a mass audience and was quickly translated into a dozen languages and turned into a film.

Pereira Maintains follows a modest and unassuming journalist in Lisbon who, during the Salazar dictatorship, decides to oppose the regime with an extreme gesture of revolt. The storyline reflected Tabucchi's own political and social commitment. Publication took place in the same year that Silvio Berlusconi arrived on Italy's political stage, and opponents of the controversial figure greeted the book as a rallying cause. Tabucchi himself went on to take an active public role in the Italian political and media scenes. The novel showed that Tabucchi could no longer be considered a provincial writer – indeed, Cesare Segre has called him 'the most cosmopolitan of Italian writers', although he has also found some appreciation beyond his native land.

Pereira Maintains was not the sole reason that during his life Tabucchi came to be considered one of the greatest Italian writers of recent decades. The writer spent his time conjuring up atmospheres replete with nostalgia and charm, writing about travel, dreams and disappearances and even creating sophisticated anti-monumentalist reconstructions ofhistorical events. Literary gems such as *Vanishing Point* (1986) and *The Flying Creatures of Fra Angelico* (1987) bear witness to this. Even after the breakthrough of *Pereira Maintains*, Tabucchi carried on producing unconventional texts brimming with originality and inventiveness, for example, his peculiar epistolary novel *It's Getting Later All the Time* (2001) his historical monologue *Tristano Muore* (Tristano dies, 2004) and the beautiful stories from one of his final works: *Il tempo invecchia in fretta* (Time ages in a hurry, 2009).

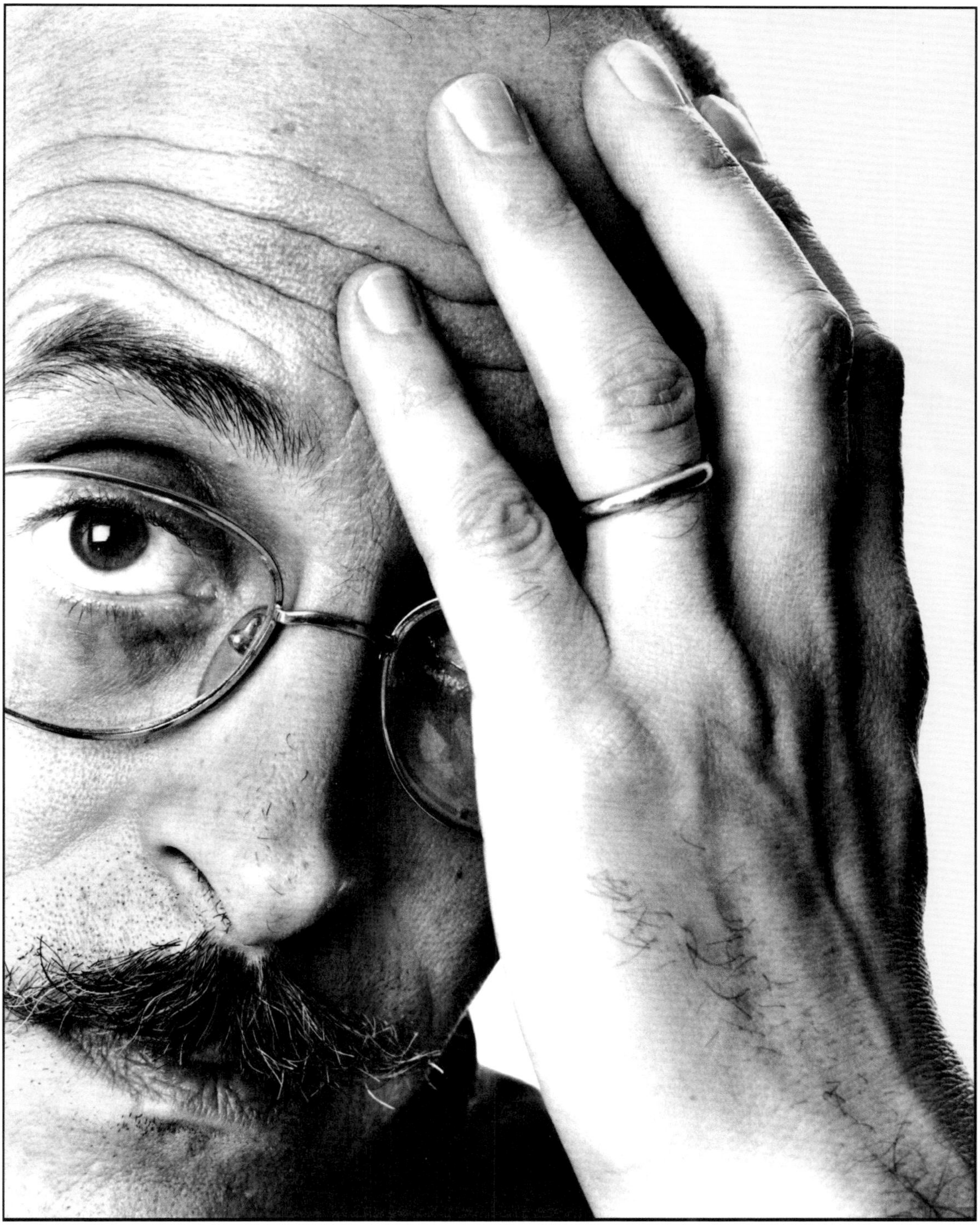

RABINDRANATH TAGORE

born Calcutta, India, 1861; died Santiniketan, India, 1941

by E. O. Hoppé

London, 1920

To use a Western metaphor, Rabindranath Tagore was a Renaissance man par excellence. One of the finest lyric poets and interpreters of his culture, he also wrote novels and plays, composed music, studied philosophy, took up painting late in life and engaged actively in the social needs of his country, particularly in the area of education. It seems that there was no aspect of modern Indian life in which he did not participate.

Tagore was born into a wealthy and artistic family of Bengali Indians. His grandfather was Dwarkanath Tagore, known as the 'Prince' for his magnificence. It was Dwarkanath who had financed the Brâhmo Sâmâj, an institution that tried to combine elements of the Hindu, Islamic and Christian traditions, and which campaigned against all forms of prejudice and superstition. The house of Tagore's childhood was full of freethinkers, religious mystics, poets, musicians and dancers. It was a spiritual, liberated and profoundly Indian environment. If Gandhi was the key figure of Indian nationalism, then Tagore was the key figure in the cultural dialogue between East and West. He travelled and worked tirelessly, translating many of the great European poets into his native tongue, and translating his own works into English and other languages.

Tagore is best known for his poetry, which he liberated from classical models, introducing new forms and the use of colloquial language. Much of it is spiritual, focusing on the divine and a sense of universal, brotherly love, but he also wrote with passion of the beauties of the physical world. His verses are rhythmic and musical, reflecting his talents as a composer of songs and other musical works. His role was that of a modern poet-troubadour, his verses indicating the pathway to a better life. In 1913 he was awarded the Nobel Prize.

The German-born English photographer E. O. Hoppé left an impressive archive of historically valuable photographs. The subjects of his portraits taken between 1907 and 1939 include members of the British royal family, various stars of the Russian ballet, and famous writers and politicians. This portrait of Tagore was taken in London in 1920. Hoppé was also an early exponent of travel photography, and in 1929 Tagore invited him to India, to take pictures of the school that he had founded in Santiniketan. The ethos of the school was based on an equality and harmony between teacher and pupil, in close affinity with nature. Tagore himself taught there, and wrote the motto for the school: *Yatra visvam bhavatyekanidam* (Where the world makes a home in a single nest).

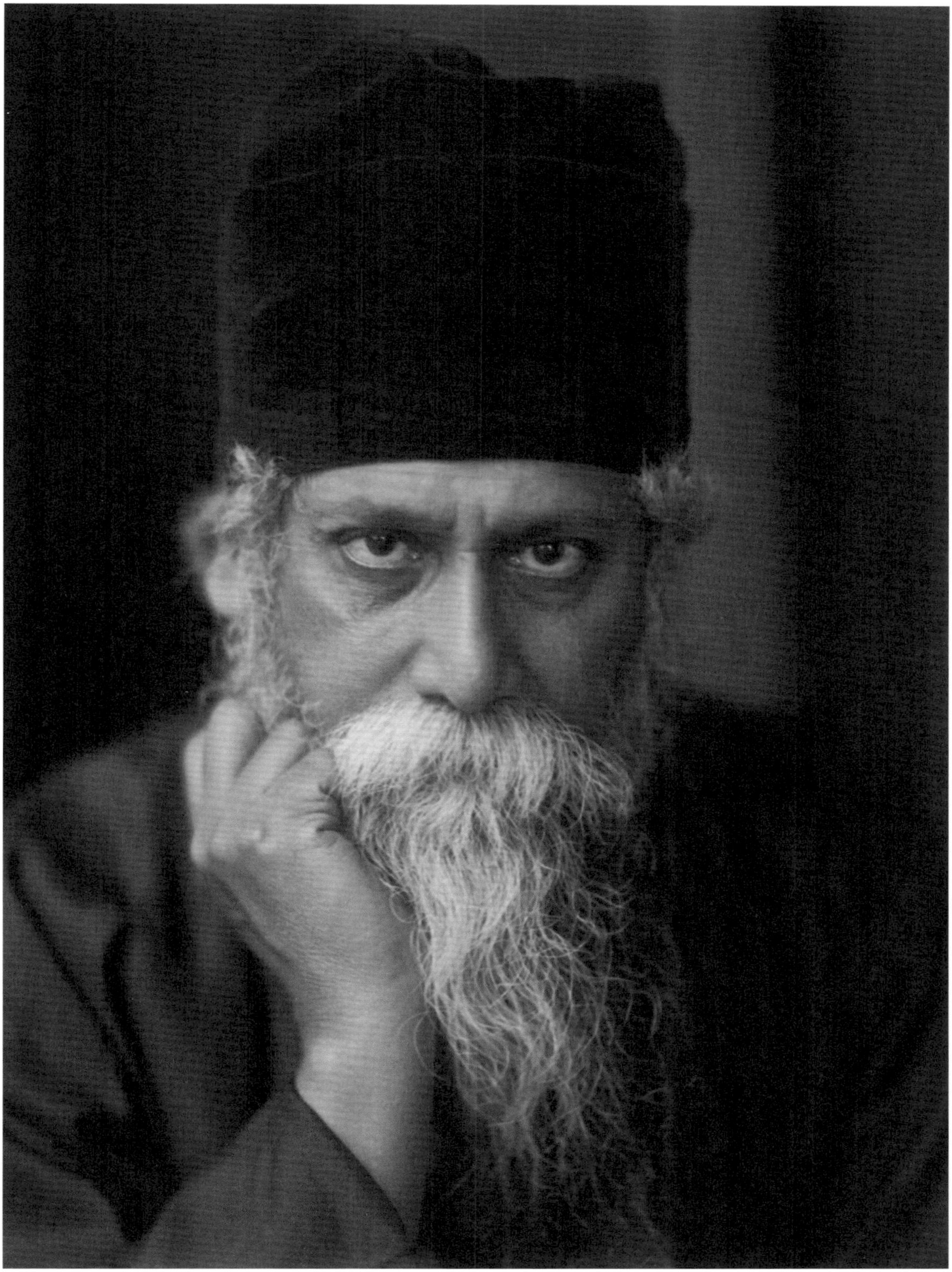

JUNICHIRO TANIZAKI

born Tokyo, 1886; died Yugawara, Kanagawa, Japan, 1965

unknown photographer

Atami, Japan, 1950s

Junichiro Tanizaki's works can be read as eulogies for traditional oriental values and culture in the face of Western modernization. Among the most well-known is a short essay, *In Praise of Shadows* (1933), an elegy for Japanese aesthetics, which he celebrates as subtle, nuanced and 'shadowy', yet comforting, in contrast to the dazzling brashness of Western culture: 'I do not want the memory of the shadowy world we have left behind to be extinguished; I would like to lower the blinds, dilute the colours on the walls, hide the objects which are too visible, and strip all the excess ornamentation from this palace they call Literature. Let's start by switching off the lights. Then we'll see.'

Tanizaki was born into a wealthy family of merchants in Tokyo in 1886, and enjoyed a privileged childhood at a time when European and American values were in the ascendant in Japan. His life changed dramatically when his childhood home and many historic buildings were destroyed in the Kanto earthquake of 1923. Devastated by the loss, he moved to the ancient city of Kyoto, and from then on his work became characterized by a morbid eroticism and a sense of the gulf between young and old; modernity and tradition. Some of his novels, such as *Naomi* (1924), *The Secret History of the Lord of Musah* (1935), *The Key* (1956) and *Diary of a Mad Old Man* (1961), explore his erotic obsessions. In these works the pursuit of pleasure becomes a metaphor that reflects the collision between cultures. A similar clash of cultures underlies his frequent portrayal of two contrasting types of women: the traditional geisha, who is statuesque, inhibited and silent, and the emancipated woman who asserts herself and wears modern clothes. Tanizaki's writings explored the erotic fantasies of men in their reactions to these two very different representations of womanhood with sensuality, irony and sophistication.

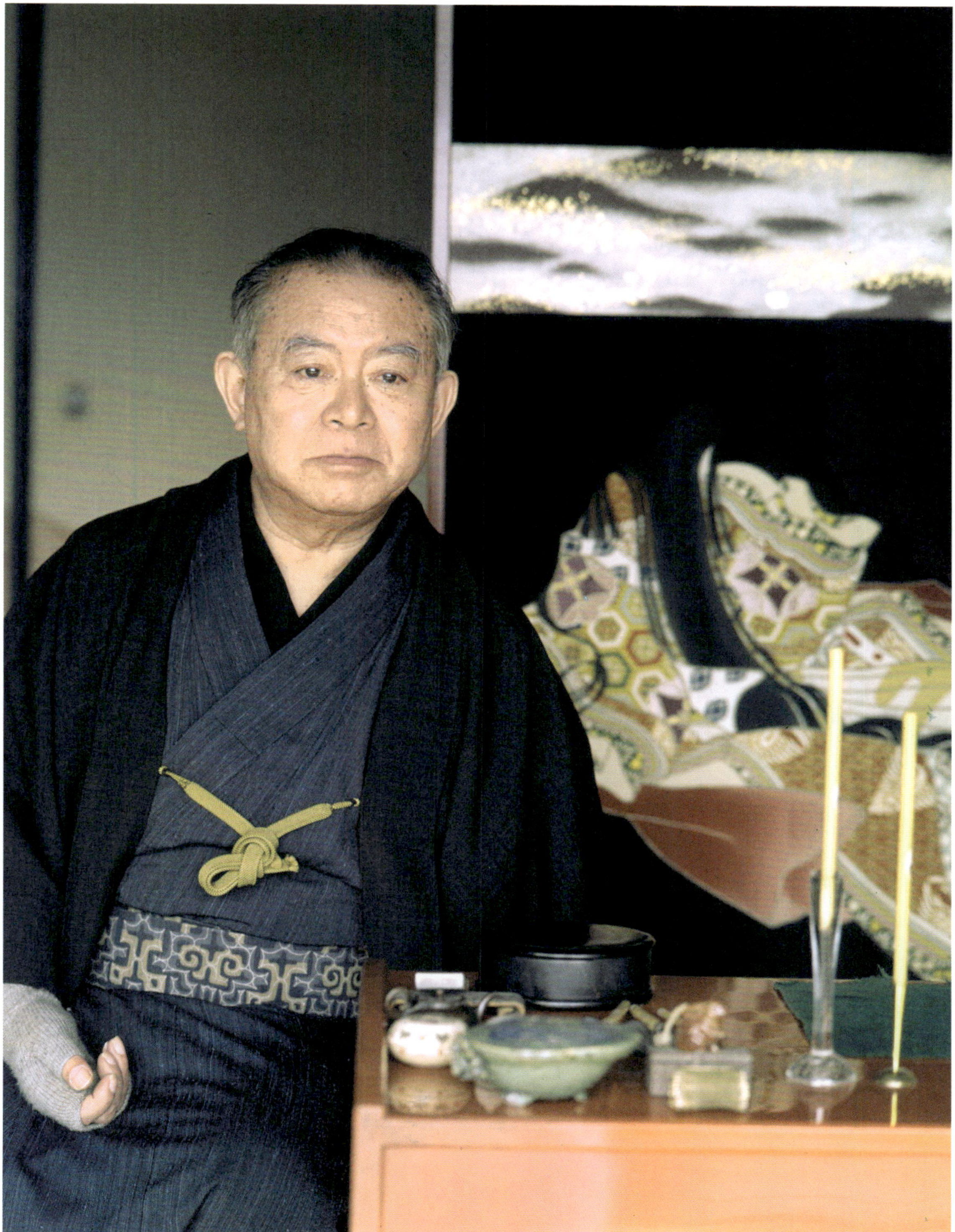

DYLAN THOMAS

born Swansea, UK, 1914; died New York, 1953

by Francis Reiss

Oxford, UK, 1946

Even judging from his usually rumpled appearance, and not just from what we know about his life and his death, one could certainly say that Dylan Thomas had drunk a few beers too many. He said of himself: 'One: I am a Welshman; two: I am a drunkard; three: I am a lover of the human race, especially of women.' This makes it tempting to label the self-professed 'Welsh Rimbaud' as the black sheep of British poetry. But if his life – his stormy relationship with his wife Caitlin, his drinking and his death before the age of forty – appears to be a succession of clichés, his poetry defies all labels.

'I make one image', he said in a letter, 'though "make" is not the right word; I let, perhaps, an image be "made" emotionally in me and then apply to it what intellectual and critical forces I possess – let it breed another, let that image contradict the first, make, of the third image bred out of the other two together, a fourth contradictory image, and let them all, within my imposed formal limits, conflict.' This bundling up of images, soaked in lyricism and emotional intensity, never detracted from the sonority of his words or the structure of his verses.

A true literary prodigy, Thomas said that he had first become aware of poetry while listening to the nursery rhymes his mother recited to him when he was a baby. These were English lullabies, as the family did not speak Welsh at home. Under the influence of the classic works of Thomas Hardy, Gerard Manley Hopkins and Edgar Allan Poe, as well as those contemporary writers such as D. H. Lawrence and W. B. Yeats, Thomas was still a teenager when he decided to dedicate himself entirely to writing poetry. One of his most famous compositions, 'And Death Shall have No Dominion' (1932), was published in England when he was just eighteen years old, and his early works soon attracted the attention of T. S. Eliot and Stephen Spender, among others. His most important collection, *18 Poems*, was published in 1934 (Thomas's twentieth year), and immediately achieved enormous success.

When he died in New York in rather dubious circumstances, Thomas left behind an important body of poetry, as well as a collection of somewhat Joycean short stories, *Portrait of the Artist as a Young Dog* (1940) and, above all, his play for voices, *Under Milk Wood* (posthumously published in 1954), which describes a single night in the life of a village and the intense dream world of its inhabitants. This visionary, Freudian work was considered by many to be his masterpiece.

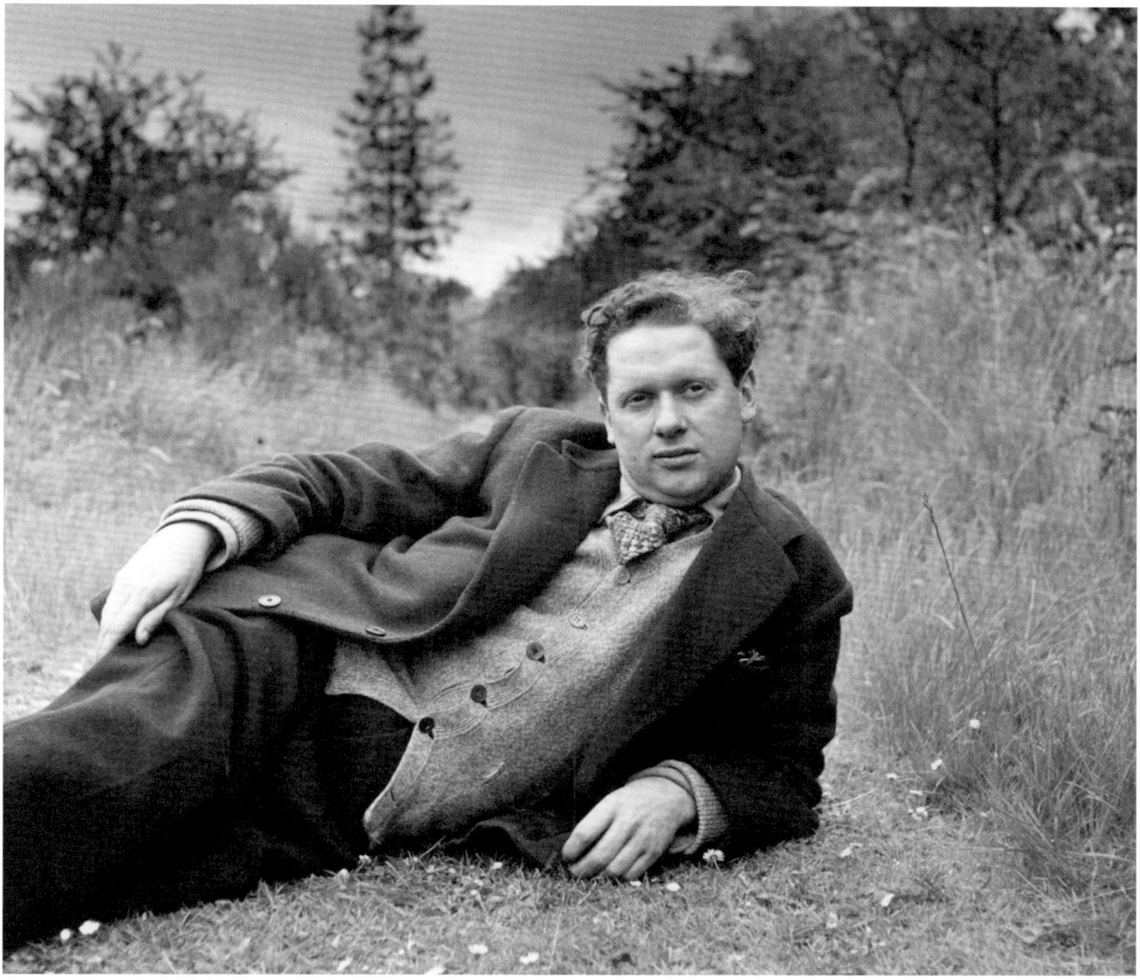

MARINA IVANOVNA TSVETAEVA

born Moscow, 1892; died Yelabuga, Russia, 1941

by Max Voloshin

Koktebel, Russia, 1911

Marina Tsvetaeva was a poet and a nonconformist, a woman desperately in search of the truth. She led an extraordinarily turbulent life in which poetry was both her destiny and her armoury. She began to write verse when she was only six years old. Her first collection, *Evening Album* (1910), containing poetry she had written between the ages of fifteen and seventeen, established her reputation as a poet. An independent and rebellious spirit, she cut her hair short, smoked cigarettes, travelled unaccompanied to Paris, and had passionate love affairs with both men and women. When she was nineteen, she met Sergei Efron, a student at the Military Academy who was also a writer. The couple got married and stayed together for the rest of their lives, although they were forced to spend much of that time apart.

Tsvetaeva was in Moscow when the October Revolution occurred in 1917. Her husband joined the White Army, and she did not see him again for three years. She suffered one hardship after another: she was left alone with two small children; her house was sacked and burned; and her youngest daughter died of starvation during the Moscow famine. Tsvetaeva remained strong and courageous throughout, and her determination in the face of adversity was admired by Boris Pasternak, with whom she maintained a long and intense correspondence. In 1922 she left Russia and joined her husband in Czechoslovakia, where she wrote *Craft* (1923), 'Poem of the End' (1924) and *The Ratcatcher* (1925–26). She then moved with him to Paris where they lived in extreme poverty. During the day sheworked as a cleaner, writing poetry at night. *After Russia* (1928) is her best-known work from this period, during which she also wrote verse dramas, including the classically inspired *Phaedra* (1928). Her poems contain swift changes in rhythm and syntax, and encompass both the shamanistic heritage of poetry and the modern obsession with form. She drove all her energy, passion and suffering into her written words.

There was still worse hardship to come, however. Her husband, who had started to work for the Soviet secret police, was accused of murder and fled to Moscow with their surviving daughter, Alya. After two years on her own, in 1939 Tsvetaeva decided to go back to Moscow with her son, Mur. It was a decision that was to prove fatal. All doors proved closed to her in Moscow. Her husband and daughter were sent to a concentration camp, and he was later shot. In 1941, as the German army threatened to advance on Moscow, she was evacuated to Yelabuga in north-central Russia, where she lived in desperate poverty, isolated from her friends and family. One Sunday in August 1941 she hanged herself, leaving a farewell note expressing her love for her children. She was forty-nine years old.

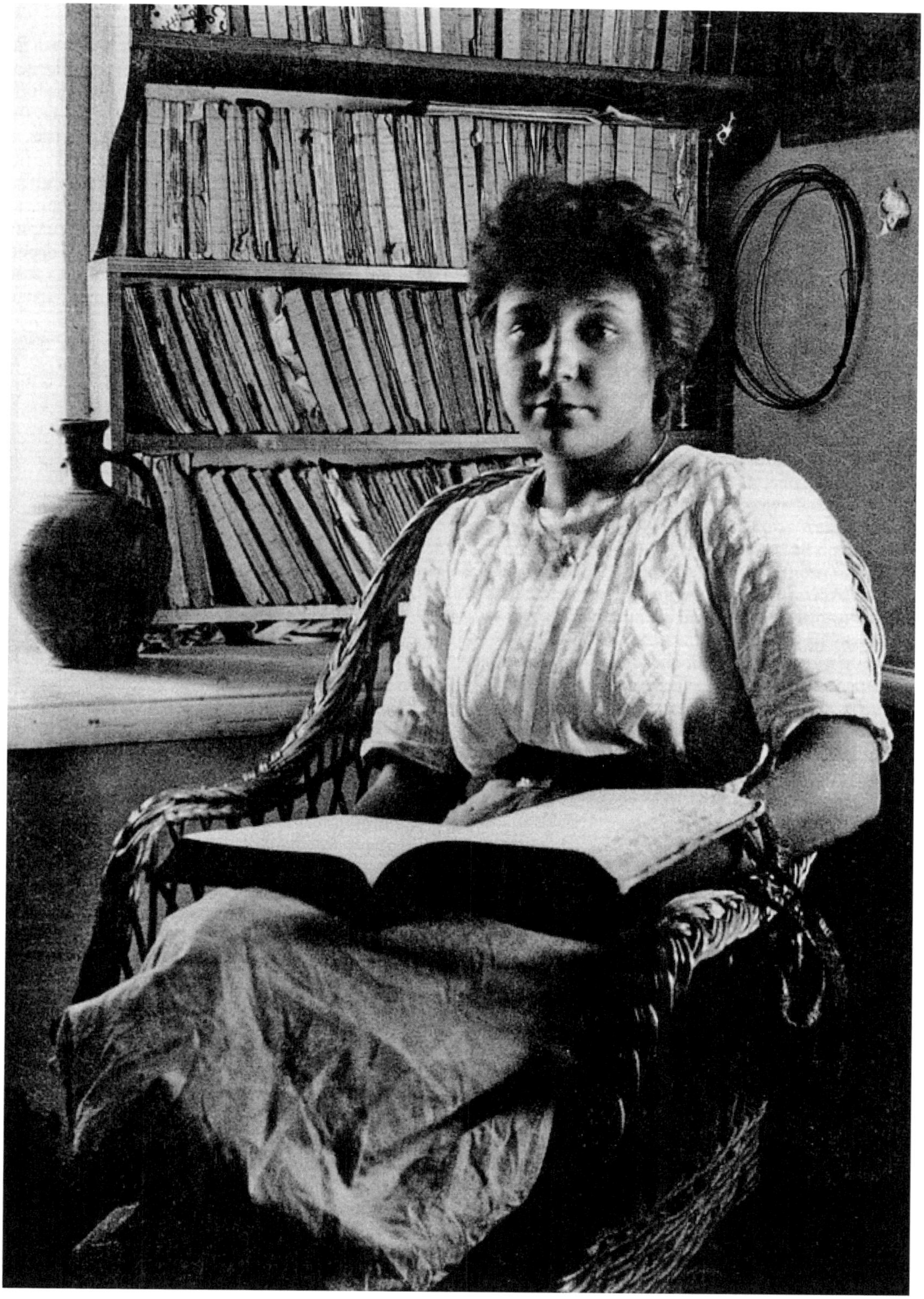

GIUSEPPE UNGARETTI

born Alexandria, Egypt, 1888; died Milan, Italy, 1970

by Gianni Berengo Gardin

Venice, Italy, 1968

Giuseppe Ungaretti's first collection of poetry, *The Buried Port*, published in 1916 in the middle of the First World War, was a dazzling debut. His was a pure, immediate poetry, set among the dirt and mud of the trenches. Born in the Egyptian city of Alexandria to Italian parents, Ungaretti was something of an outsider. He did not set foot in Italy until he was twenty-four years old, when he enlisted voluntarily in the Italian Army, driven, perhaps, by the kind of patriotism that is often felt by those separated from their perceived homeland.

Ungaretti published a further volume of war poetry, *The Joy of Shipwrecks*, in 1919, believing that words were the medium through which he could reaffirm his own dignity and humanity following the catastrophe of war. In the preface to the 1931 edition of his collection *Joy* (first published 1914–15), he wrote: 'This old book is a diary. The author has no other ambition. ... His poetry thus represents his formal torments, but he would like it to be recognized just this once that the form tormented him only because of the demands caused by the changes wrought in his soul, and, if he has made any progress as an artist, he would also like to point out that he has achieved this perfection as a man. He became a grown man in the midst of extraordinary events, which have never left him since.'

Ungaretti lived the rest of his life as both a poet and a citizen of the world, with a vitality that he retained into old age. He is seen here, in a photograph by Gianni Berengo Gardin, greeting demonstrators at the 1968 Venice Biennale with a generous wave and a warm and lively smile. He had reached his eightieth birthday that year, but remained defiantly young at heart – almost 'madly' so, as he described himself.

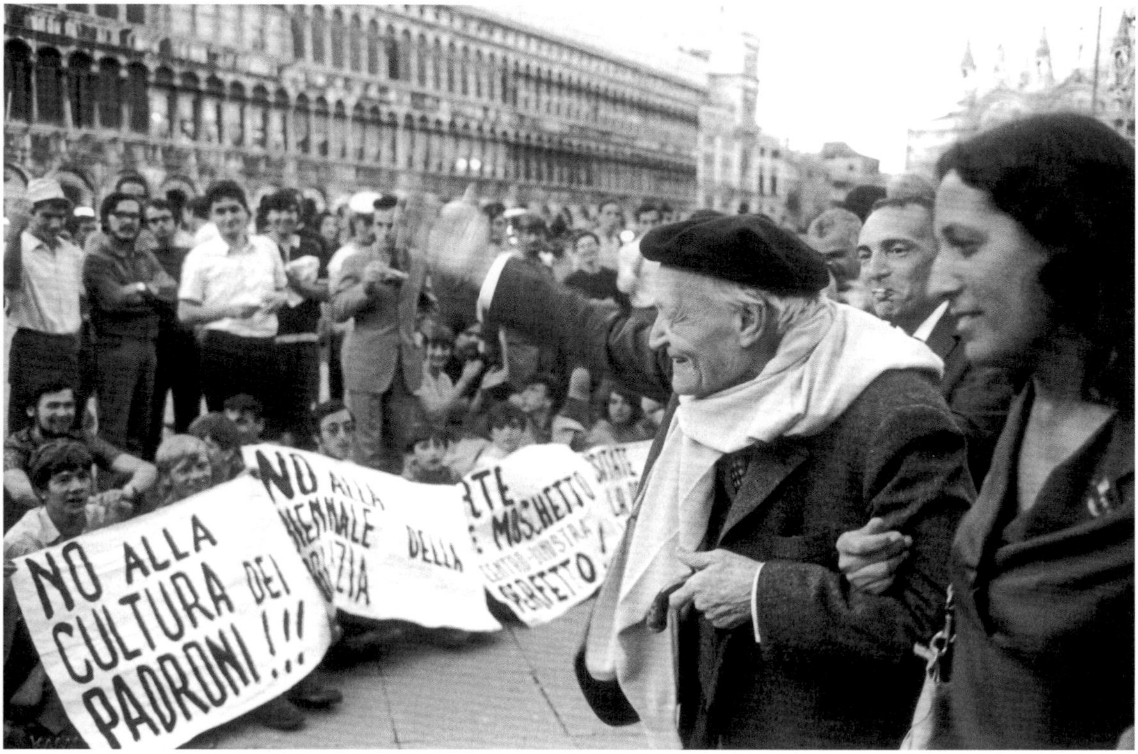
NO ALLA
CULTURA DEI
PADRONI !!!

PAUL VALÉRY

born Sète, France, 1871; died Paris, 1945

by Philippe Halsman

Paris, 1936

Paul Valéry was born to an Italian mother and a Corsican father in the town of Sète in the south of France and grew up in Montpelier. His ability to distill the spirit of the bustling Mediterranean ports into the transcendental purity of Parisian rationality brought him into contact with some of the most influential figures of French thought and letters, such as Henri Bergson, André Gide and Stéphane Mallarmé.

If Valéry is regarded today as one of the twentieth century's greatest intellectuals, as the archetypal modernist thinker, philosopher and man of letters, it is not due to the pile ofofficial titles and honours that he accumulated, but to his multifaceted literary work of rigorous precision and unmatched pithiness. Lucid expression and aesthetic beauty were one and the same for Valéry. In poems that are now considered his classic works, such as 'The Young Fate' (1917) and 'The Graveyard by the Sea', from *Charmes* (1922), he draws directly on Mallarmé's formalism, as well as on an ideal of intuitive power and sense of the sublime. Valéry had a boundless capacity for discrimination and imagination; characteristics celebrated in his *Introduction to the Method of Leonardo da Vinci* (1895) and in the eponymous hero of Monsieur Testé (1896), an ascetic who directs his intelligence towards the mystical revelation of the 'laws of the mind'. Valéry enthusiastically supported closer links between science and literature. His eccentric and polymorphic thought processes were demonstrated with great vividness and impressive analytical depth in the notebooks that he wrote in every morning for more than fifty years. Published posthumously, his *Notebooks* (1973–87) remain one of his most important works.

Valéry's literary career did not follow the conventional pattern. Saddened by the death of his mentor Mallarmé, he ceased to write for nearly twenty years, resuming only in 1917. He spent most of his working life as a government bureaucrat and began writing full-time only in 1920, when he was in his late forties. After his election to the Académie Française in 1925 he became a celebrated public speaker and academic, founding the Collège International de Cannes and holding posts at the University of Nice and the Collège du France until he was sidelined professionally for declining to support the Vichy government. He died in 1945 and was buried in the same cemetery in Sète that had inspired 'The Graveyard by the Sea'.

Latvian photographer Philippe Halsman moved to Paris in 1930 to dedicate himself to photography. His passion for portraiture led him to develop his skill in capturing what he described as 'the mystery of each human being', overturning the traditional rules of the genre. He photographed intellectuals and artists including André Malraux, Marc Chagall, Jean Giraudoux, André Gide and Le Corbusier for the most prestigious journals of the age.

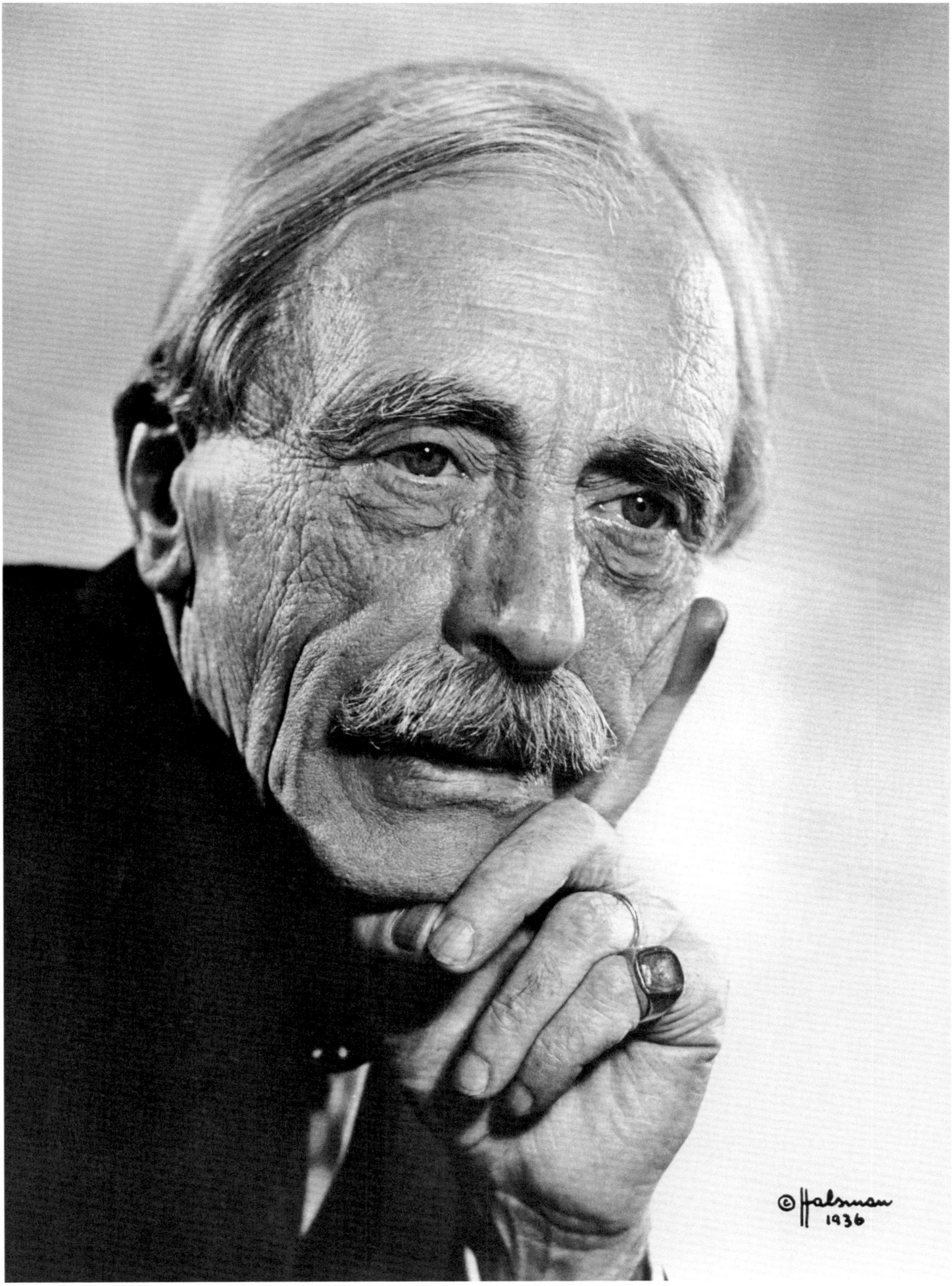

© Halsman
1936

RAMÓN DEL VALLE-INCLÁN

born Villanueva de Arosa, Spain, 1866; died Santiago de Compostela, Spain, 1936

by René Dazy

unknown location, c. 1930

The events of Ramón del Valle-Inclán's early life were not unlike those of his dramas. He was born into an impoverished aristocratic family in a rural village in Galicia, Spain. After studying law in Santiago de Compostela, he moved to Madrid, where his extravagant lifestyle and incisive opinions soon made him welcome on the literary scene. It was in Madrid that he lost his left arm following a fight with a critic, after which he became known as 'the second cripple of Spanish literature' (the first being Cervantes). In an ironic twist of fate, the creator of *esperpento* – a distorted and satirical style of writing used by Valle-Inclán to criticize Spain – had himself become deformed, regarded as an oddity.

Although primarily a dramatist, Valle-Inclán was also a novelist, a poet, a journalist and a historian. His writing is characterized by a sense of decadence and the use of symbolism. Politically subversive, he despised literary realism and deemed it inadequate to express the demise of his country from 1898, when it lost the last of its colonies, through to the aftermath of the First World War. This sense of pessimism and irony permeated his writing, resulting in the creation of *esperpento*. While this style was new to Spanish literature, it had already been evident in the works of the Spanish artist Francisco de Goya, particularly in his *Caprichos* (1799), a set of prints satirizing the follies of Spanish society.

In 1920 Valle-Inclán published perhaps his best-known drama, *Bohemian Lights*, which bears many of the hallmarks of *esperpento*. It was a decisive break with the past, with naturalism, with social conventions and with the prevailing culture of the time. But behind the grotesque and sometimes comical satire was Valle-Inclán's conviction that his country was plunging into the abyss. His caustic narrative revolves around Spain, but his liberal ideas and forms of protest are of universal relevance.

Valle-Inclán's plays were so complex and demanded so many special effects that they were difficult to stage. In many ways, his style of drama was the precursor of modern theatre. Valle-Inclán died in 1936, shortly before the outbreak of the Spanish Civil War. He was thereby spared the experience of a tragedy that even he might have found difficult to turn into farce.

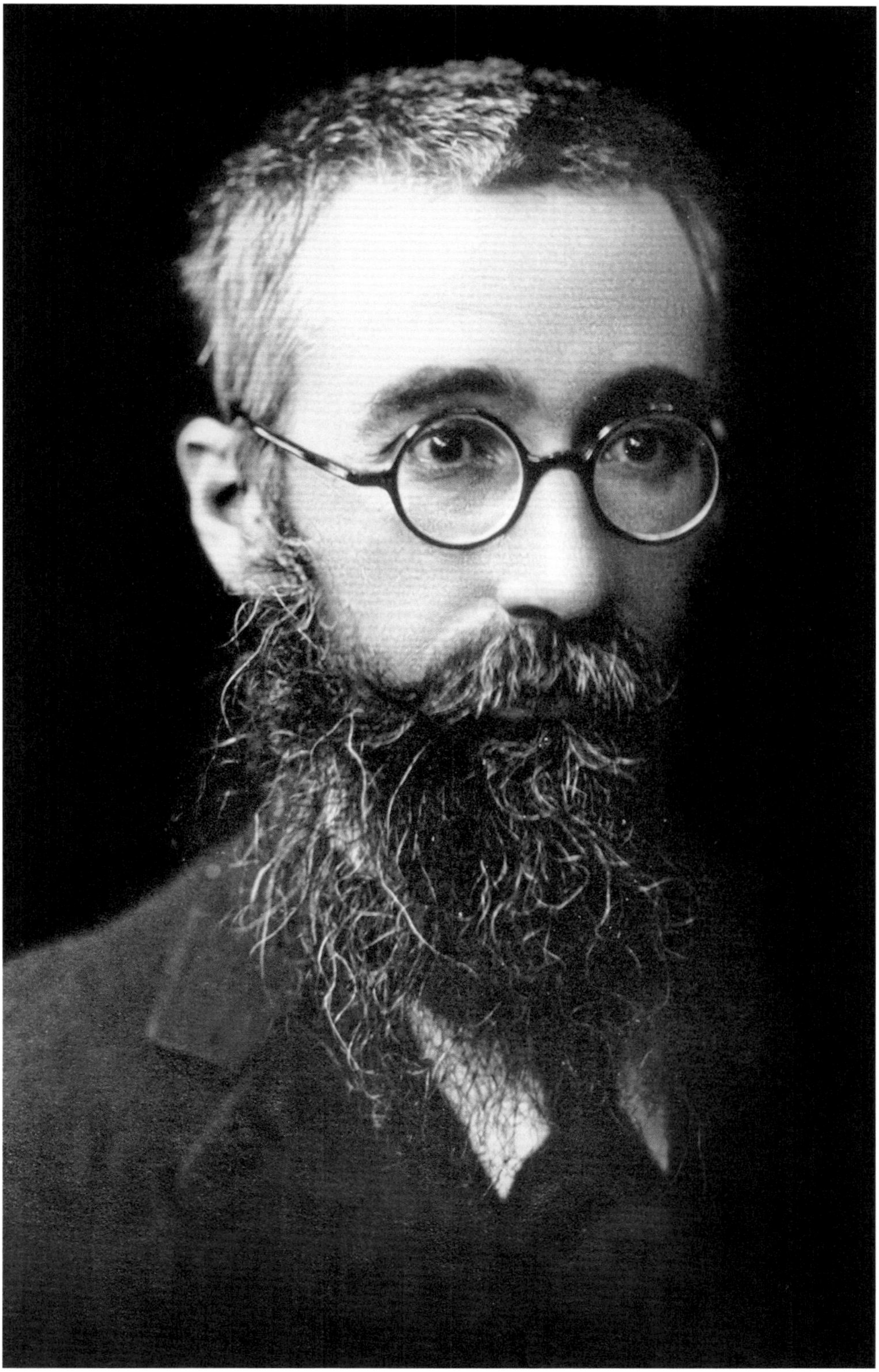

CÉSAR VALLEJO

born Santiago de Chuco, Peru, 1892; died Paris, 1938

by Juan Domingo Córdoba Vargas

Versailles, France, 1929

'I was born on a day / when God was sick.' These are the repeating lines of 'Exergasia', the poem that concludes Vallejo's first collection, *The Black Heralds* (1919), a milestone ofavant-garde Peruvian poetry. He followed it with *Trilce* (1922), which is considered one of the most radical books in the Spanish language. Vallejo's life did indeed have its share oftroubles – love affairs, scandals, escapes, returns, even a spell in prison – before he made the decision to leave Peru. He spent time as an expatriate in Spain and Russia but chose to make Paris his home. It was there that he died in 1938.

Vallejo enjoyed subverting language by inventing words (such as 'trilce' itself), by exhuming vocabulary that had sunk into oblivion and by adopting scientific terminology, creating a new poetic language that occasionally bordered on the hermetic. But this was no mere rhetorical game. Through his innovations, Vallejo was attempting to give voice to his own state of mind. As he wrote in a letter to Antenor Orrego: 'The book is born in a great vacuum. I am responsible for the book. I assume full responsibility for its aesthetics. Today, as never before perhaps, I feel weighing upon me a hitherto unknown and most sacred obligation, as a man and as an artist. That of being free!'

Perhaps it was in search of that freedom that he travelled to Europe, setting sail for Paris in 1923, although from that moment onwards he published very little. In 1931, while assisting in the birth of a new Spanish republic in Madrid, he published *Tungsten*, a novel about a dispute in the Andean mines that achieved a moderate success. This revolutionary phase of Vallejo's life gave rise to *Human Poems* and *Spain, Take This Cup From Me*, both collections published by his widow a year after his death in 1938. In these two collections (selected, respectively, from the periods 1923–29 and 1931–37), we can see his return to a more accessible use of language in order to be closer to the people, and perhaps a developing sympathy with the Marxist approach he had grown closer to in France and during his journeys in the Soviet Union.

This later verse possessed a more dramatic style, and in it communal suffering became a uniting factor that represents an invitation to solidarity and action. *Spain, Take This Cup From Me* was written with the Republicans fighting in the Spanish Civil War in mind. In the words chosen for the collection's title, the atheist poet echoes the words of Christ as he prayed in the garden of Gethsemane: 'Father, if You are willing, take this cup from me.'

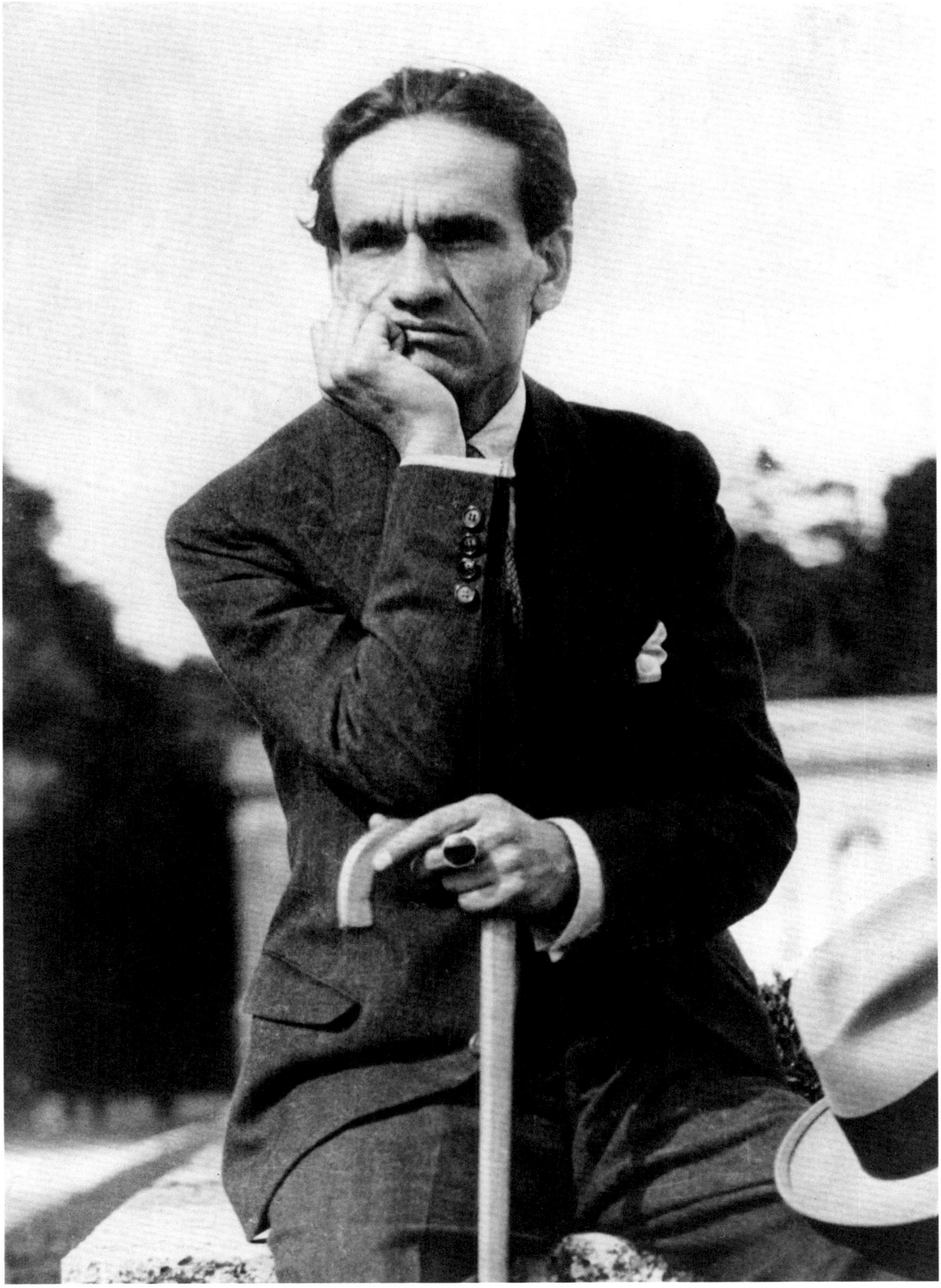

MARIO VARGAS LLOSA

born Arequipa, Peru, 1936

by Peter Marlow

London, 2002

The works of Mario Vargas Llosa are predominantly concerned with the use and abuse of power. Vargas Llosa, one of Latin America's most significant writers, was educated at Leoncio Prado Military Academy, an institution whose heavy-handed discipline he later criticized in his novel *The Time of the Hero* (1963). Political power was the subject of his fourth novel, *Conversation in the Cathedral* (1969), a portrayal of Peru under the dictatorship of Peruvian president Manuel Odría in the 1950s. Set largely in a bar known as 'The Cathedral', the book is centred around a conversation between a journalist named Santiago Zavala, whose father had collaborated with Odría's regime, and an old black man named Ambrosio, who had been Zavala's father's chauffeur.

Vargas Llosa's writing takes on a much lighter tone in *Captain Pantoja and the Special Service* (1973), in which the unsuspecting captain is sent on a mission to supply prostitutes to a garrison of soldiers stationed in the Peruvian jungle. The book was twice made into a film, first in 1975, by the author and José María Gutiérrez Santos, and again in 2000, by Francisco José Lombardi.

In *Aunt Julia and the Scriptwriter* (1977), Vargas Llosa tells the semi-autobiographical story of a turbulent love affair between a young man, Mario, and an older woman, Julia; Mario works at a radio station, and his relationship with Julia is echoed in the radio dramas of one of the book's other characters, Pedro Camacho. Vargas Llosa returned to the subject of the abuse of power with *The War of the End of the World* (1981), which is based on an actual event from the history of Brazil, the War of Canudos (1896–97). The book tells the story of a large number of destitute beggars who, having established a utopian-style community in north-eastern Brazil, are brutally massacred by government troops.

In 2000 Vargas Llosa published *The Feast of the Goat*. Set in the Dominican Republic, it describes the assassination of the Dominican dictator Rafael Trujillo and its aftermath, but from two different moments in time: one in 1961, during and immediately after the event, and the other in 1996. *The Dream of the Celt* (2010) is based on the life of the Irish nationalist Roger Casement, who, in the early 1900s, was the first person publicly to denounce the injustices committed by the colonial powers in Africa. This accomplished and acclaimed novel won Vargas Llosa the Nobel Prize, 'for his cartography of structures of power and his trenchant images of the individual's resistance, revolt and defeat'.

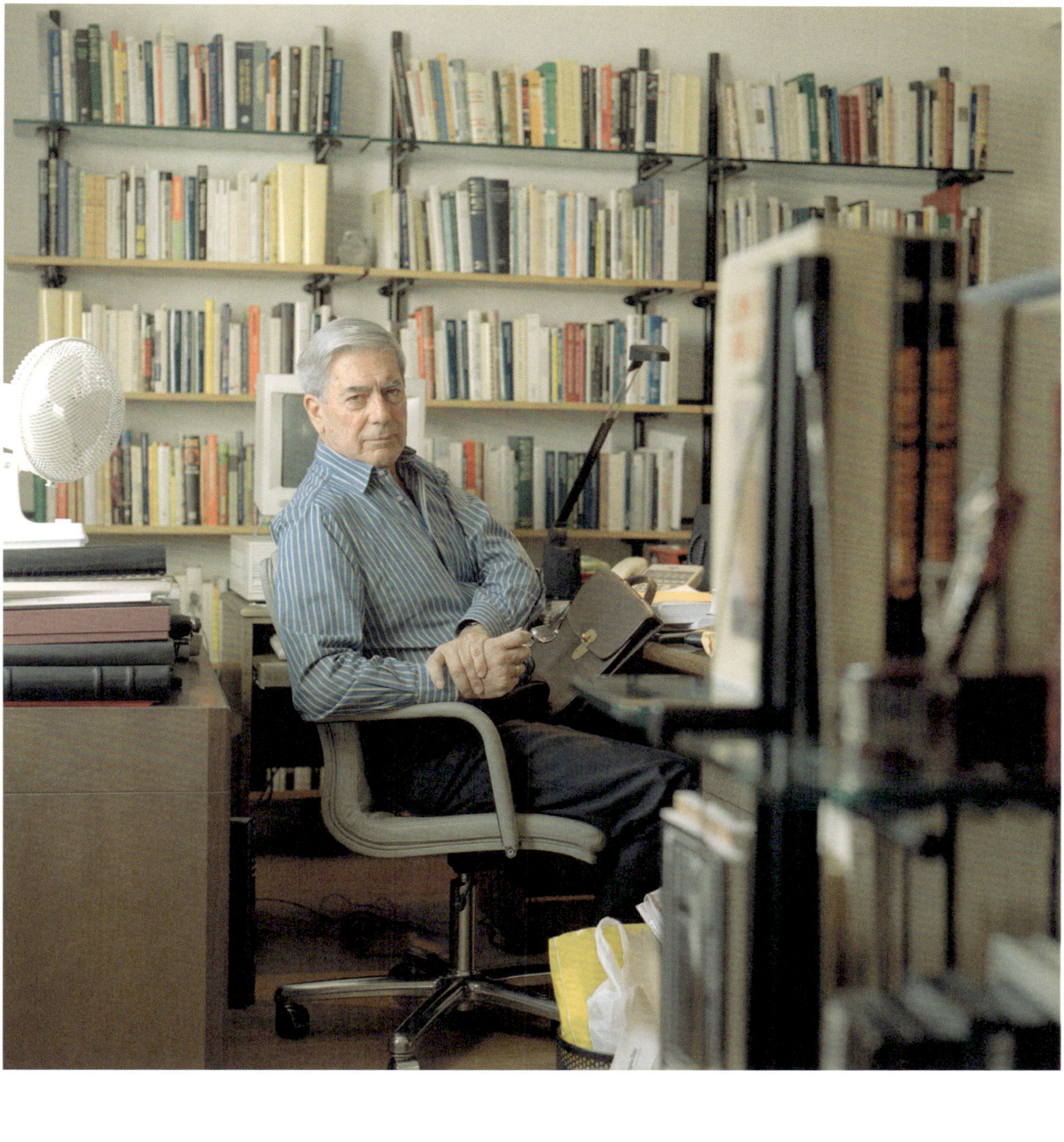

GIOVANNI VERGA

born Catania, Italy, 1840; died Catania, Italy, 1922

self-portrait

Catania, Italy, 1887

In 1966 a total of 448 photographic negatives – 327 glass plates and 121 celluloid slides – were found in Giovanni Verga's former home in Catania. These negatives, which had been left to moulder in dark cupboards and chests of drawers, had been taken by the writer from 1878 onwards. Photography, as he himself acknowledged, was Verga's secret passion. He had been born at the same time as this new art, just a year after Daguerre's discovery had been announced in 1839, and it changed not only how he looked at the world but also the words he used to describe it.

Together with Luigi Capuana and Federico de Roberto, Verga was one of the foremost proponents of *verismo*, a realist movement akin to Naturalism, and all three writers considered photography to be a powerful medium with which to observe life close up. Among the many photos of Verga's friends and family, one can find numerous images of the hunters and peasants who worked on the Verga family estate. Wearing white shirts and with handkerchiefs tied round their necks, they stare fixedly into the camera with the curious expression of someone who is trying to fathom the workings of a new machine.

Many of Verga's images feature landscapes, glimpses of houses and deserted Sicilian country roads, which evoke the closed and immutable world of Verga's stories. But he also portrays the rural settings of his own properties and the bondsmen and field hands who work them, their coarsened faces marked by the sun and hard physical labour. Thus we see not only rural and domestic scenes but also the men and women whose stories fill Verga's realist universe, including his novella *The Life of the Fields* (1880); his saga of the downtrodden, *The House by the Medlar Tree* (1881); and his story of an ambitious master stone-mason, *Master Don Gesualdo* (1889), translated into English by D. H. Lawrence.

Although Verga took great pleasure in pointing a camera at the world, he was less keen on having it turned on himself. In a letter to his partner, Dina di Sordevolo, dated 4 October 1919, Verga expresses his dislike of being a photographic subject: 'I am not sending you the latest photograph which you asked me for because I have made neither a first or last one nor will I be making one. That way I don't have to see myself or make anyone else look at this ugly mug.' Nevertheless, he did succeed in taking several self-portraits, one of which is shown here.

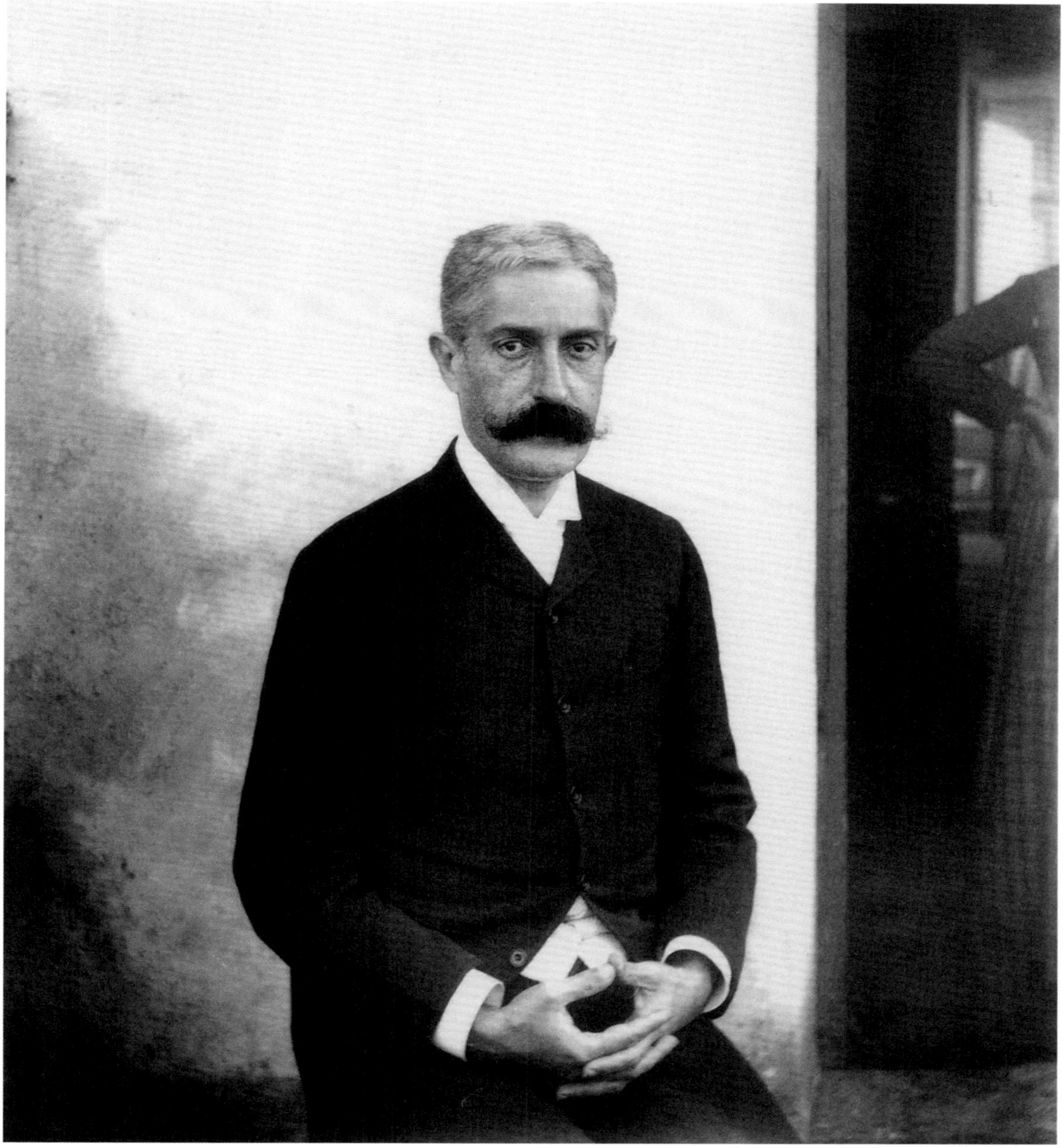

GORE VIDAL

[Eugene Louis Vidal] born West Point, New York, 1925; died Hollywood Hills, California, 2012

by Jerry Cooke

New York, 1947

He was born Eugene Louis Vidal in the hospital of the the famous West Point military academy and grew up in the political world of Washington DC. His father, who had been both a military- and civil-aviation pioneer, held various important positions in President Franklin D. Roosevelt's administration and was also distantly related by marriage to the Kennedy family. Vidal's grandfather, Thomas Gore, was an influential senator for Oklahoma. As Senator Gore was blind, Vidal soon began to accompany him everywhere and to read for him. His grandfather's strong isolationist perspective remained with the writer throughout his life.

His passion for history, his love of truth, his hatred of imperialism and his courage in battling for his own ideas had all been deeply rooted characteristics since his childhood. Indeed, he might well have followed in his grandfather's political footsteps had he not suffered, when still very young, the horrible experience of war. What affected him above all was the death of his dearly loved companion Jimmie Trimble during the landing of American forces at Iwo Jima. 'My other half', Vidal would later describe him in the memoir *Palimpsest* (1994).

When Vidal returned home from the war he started to write. By the age of twenty-two he had already published two novels. In 1948 he published – against his editor's advice – *The City and the Pillar*, in which he told the story of the passion of a sturdy, young all-American boy for another young man. The enormous scandal that it provoked stemmed not just from his explicit treatment of homosexuality but from his refusal to reduce his gay protagonist to an oddball, or to a languid and decadent aesthete. This book meant that a large proportion of the literary pages of various magazines became closed to him (for a long time the *New York Times* refused even to review his books), but he carried on writing, using his own name and various pseudonyms, producing detective stories, comedies, historical novels, essays and biographies, as well as screenplays for Hollywood.

From the 1960s onwards he began to cultivate his passion for Italy (he set up house first in Rome and then later in Ravello) and for history. In between his study of the Roman Empire, *Julian* (1964), and concluding his examination of the rise of the USA in the 'Narratives of Empire' heptalogy – which included *Washington, D.C.* (1967), *Lincoln* (1984) and *Empire* (1987) – he dashed off the short novel *Myra Breckinridge* (1968) in just a month. Both caustic and mocking in tone, this work was a pitiless satire of the world of Hollywood, but above all it also sounded the death knell for traditional gender roles. According to the critic Dennis Altman, the novel was part of that 'major cultural assault on the assumed norms of gender and sexuality which swept the Western world in the late 1960s and early 1970s.'

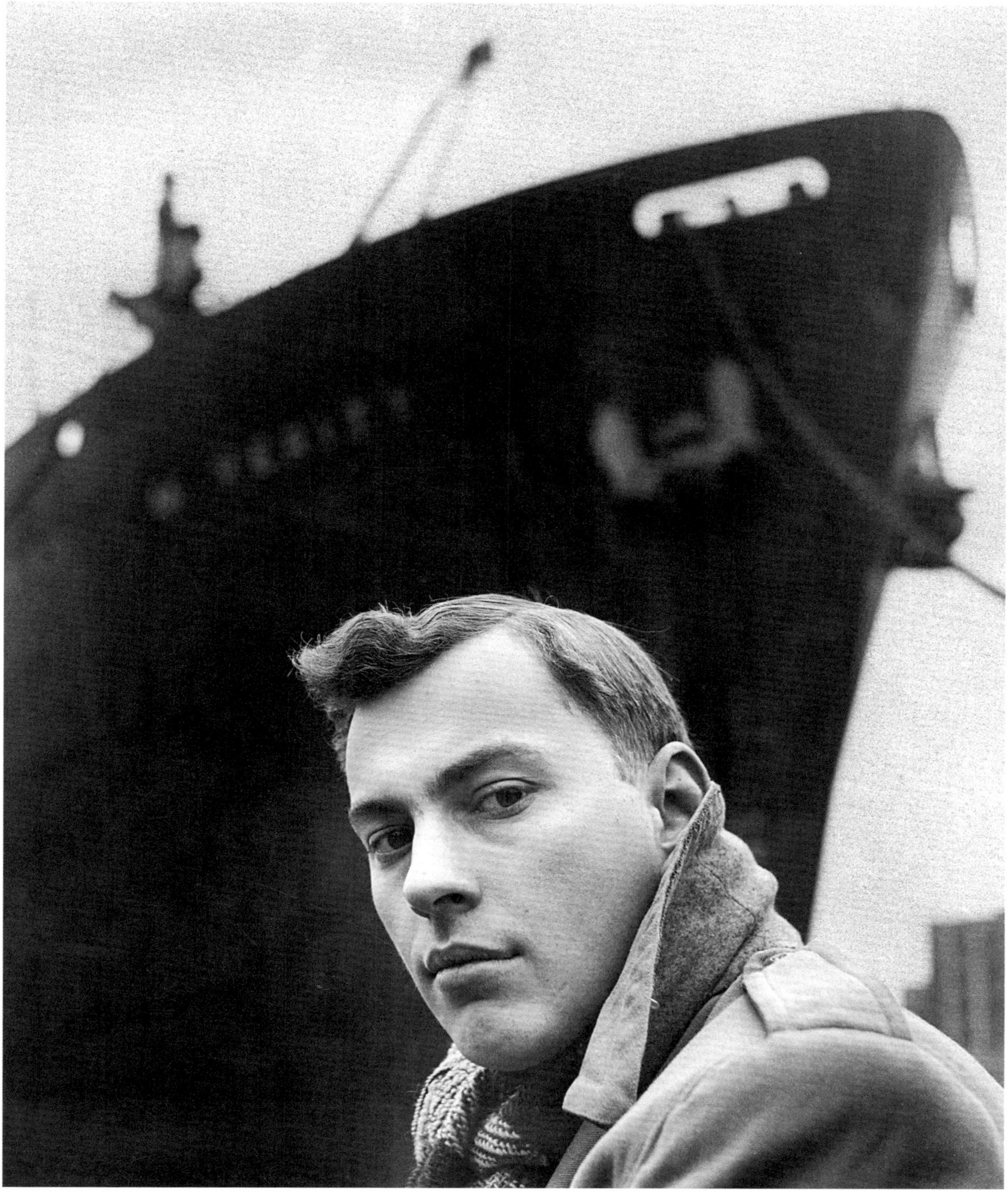

ENRIQUE VILA-MATAS

born Barcelona, Spain, 1948

by Oscar Elias

Barcelona, Spain, 2007

Right from his early literary works, such as *La Asesina ilustrada* (The illustrated murderess, 1977), Enrique Vila-Matas seems to have entered into literature in order to disrupt it, adopting every instrument available to him to bewilder the reader. In this novella, Vila-Matas draws heavily on the tradition begun by Jorge Luis Borges: he creates labyrinths, mirrors, imaginary writers and stories-within-stories, and places all the tricks of literature and literary criticism in the service of a Dark Lady.

It was with *Historia abreviada de la literatura portátil* (A short history of portable literature, 1985), that the game began in earnest. The book tells the story of a conspiracy that included Francis Picabia, Federico García Lorca and Alberto Savinio (among others) and had been instigated by the secret 'Shandy' society. The name paid homage to Laurence Sterne's great work but was also an acronym of Si Hablas Alto Nunca Digas Yo (which literally translates as 'If you talk loudly never say I'); not to mention also being a British drink made from beer topped up with lemonade or ginger beer. There were two key principles: members had to have produced a work that could fit into a valise, echoing Duchamp's *boîte-en-valise*, and had to adhere to an *esprit de corps* that celebrated nomadism, sensuality and insolence. Later the society came to celebrate speed and transience – 'heroes of the lost battle that is life' – but also, and especially, a brevity and lightness of touch exemplified by the work of Italo Calvino.

In Vila-Matas's work, the borders between reality and fantasy, and literature and reality become blurred. *Suicidios ejemplares* (Exemplary suicides, 1991) presents us with twelve different ways of ending our lives, which Vila-Matas justifies with the maxim: 'What makes life bearable is the idea that we can choose when to escape.' The idea behind *Bartleby & Co.* (2000) is also associated with escape. The protagonist is a civil servant who studies the 'Bartleby syndrome' in literature – writers who have taken Herman Melville's character to heart, and renounced literature. It is conceived like an eccentric tracking shot in which well-known names appear alongside those who have been forgotten or perhaps never even existed. This is the game that Vila-Matas plays: he leads the reader on various literary perambulations, or inserts nonexistent characters or quotations intended to mislead. His intention is to force the reader to explore the abyss of suicide, death and failure. In essence, as he himself has declared, he considers literature to be 'a plot against reality', an invitation to draw up our own *Perder teorías* (Losing theories, 2010).

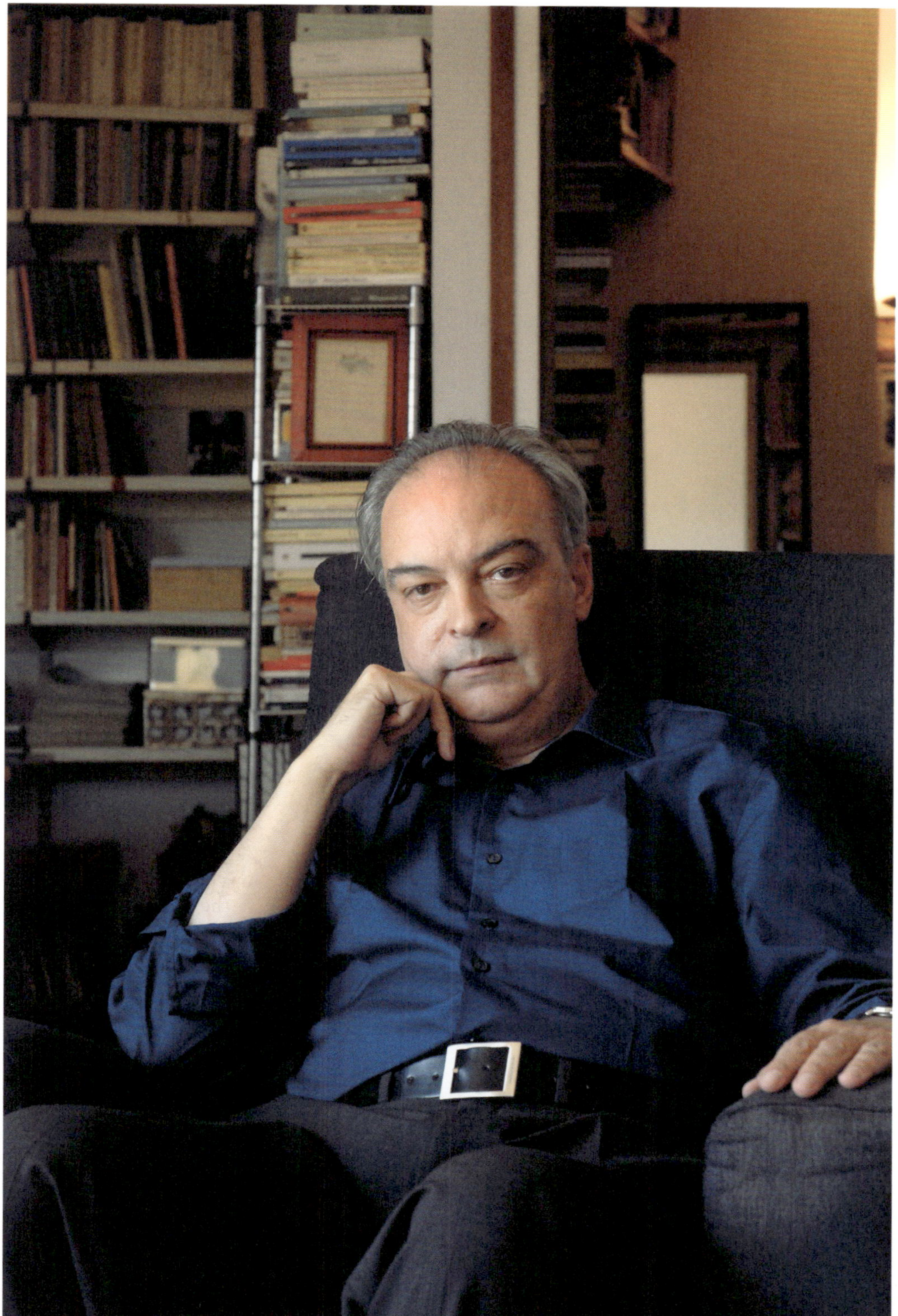

KURT VONNEGUT

born Indianapolis, Indiana, 1922; died New York, 2007

by Oliver Morris

New York, 1980s

Kurt Vonnegut's life was marked by a number of dramatic events that affected him profoundly. During the Second World War, he was on leave at home when his mother took an overdose of barbiturates and committed suicide. When he returned to the front, he was taken prisoner and incarcerated in the infamous 'Slaughterhouse-Five' in Dresden, Germany, where he survived the blanket firebombing that razed the city to the ground. It would be years before he could recount this episode, albeit within the framework of a science fiction story, resulting in the novel *Slaughterhouse-Five* (1969). In 1958 his sister Alice and his brother-in-law James Adams died within weeks of each other, she of cancer and he in a rail accident. They left behind four small children, the older three of whom Vonnegut adopted and brought up alongside his own four children. Had all these tragedies been invented in a story, the author would have been criticized for its implausibility, yet Vonnegut experienced all of them, retaining his integrity and compassion throughout. His ability to respond to horrific events with touches of humour and irony became the hallmark of his style throughout his literary career.

Like J. G. Ballard and Philip K. Dick, Vonnegut was an exponent of 'interior' science fiction, which, rather than focusing on travel through space and time, explored the infinite possibilities and destinies of the human psyche. For this reason, as well as quality of his writing, Vonnegut escaped being labelled as a mere 'science fiction author', and was regarded as a writer of depth and gravitas. This reaction was as true of his début novel *Player Piano* (1952) as it was of his later masterpieces *Cat's Cradle* (1963), *God Bless You, Mr Rosewater* (1965) and *Breakfast of Champions* (1973). The 1960s and 1970s represented the pinnacle of his success as a writer of fiction, and thereafter his interests diversified. He spent less time writing and devoted more time to his talent as a graphic artist (he had already designed the illustrations for *Breakfast of Champions*). He also became politically active, campaigning against George W. Bush and the Iraq War. Although less prolific, his later years still saw the publication of significant works such as *Jailbird* (1979), *Galapagos: A Novel* (1985) and his last novel, *Timequake* (1997).

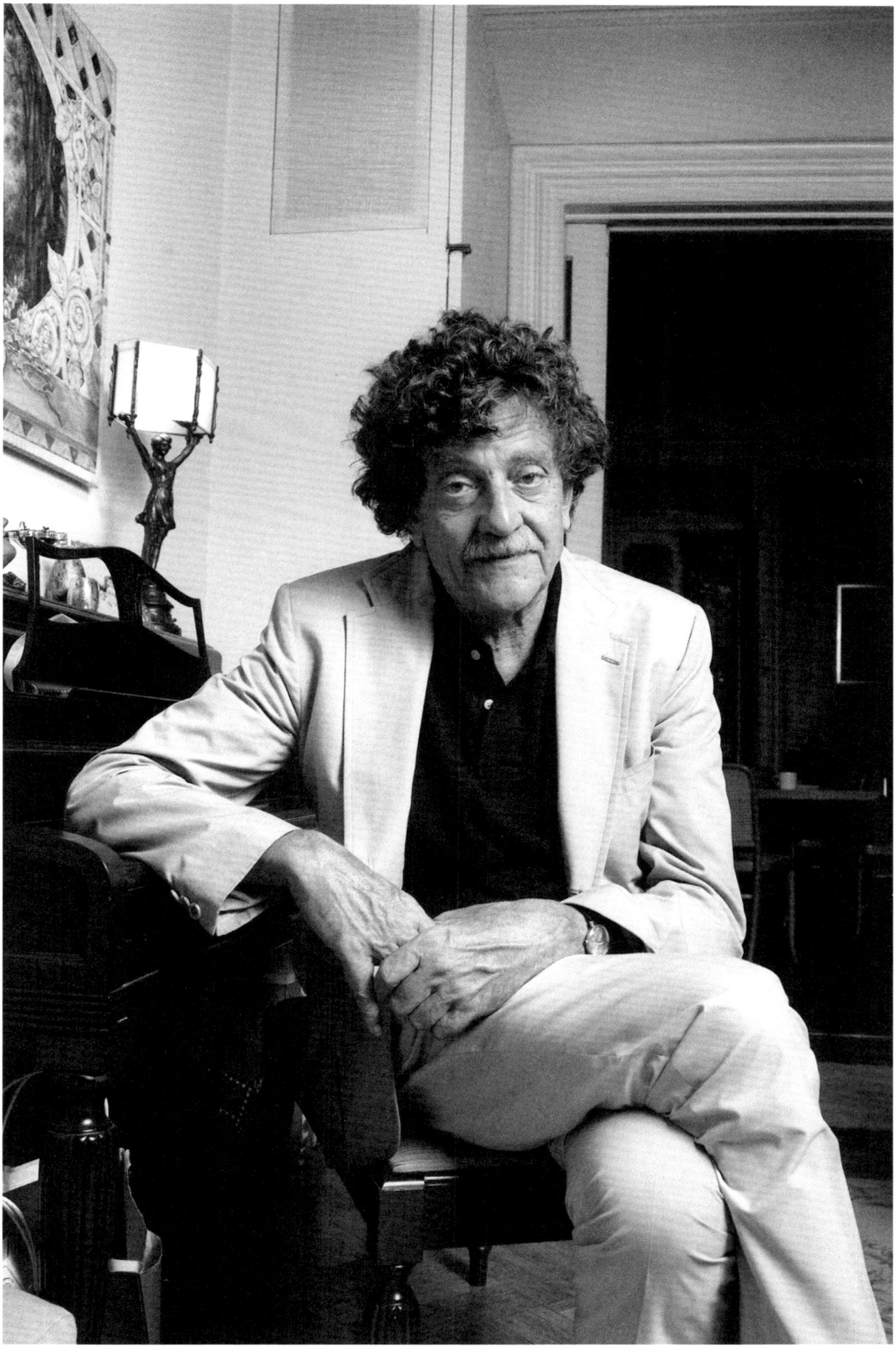

DEREK WALCOTT

born Castries, St Lucia, 1930

by Micheline Pelletier

St Lucia, 2005

A native of the Caribbean island of St Lucia, Derek Walcott is renowned for his lengthy and inspired lyrical compositions, as well as for being a successful playwright. He published his first collection of poetry, *25 Poems* (1948), when he was still in his teens, using money borrowed from his mother. Walcott's gift for poetry was soon recognized, and not only on his native island. With the aid of a scholarship, he studied at the University of the West Indies in Kingston, Jamaica. After graduation he moved to Trinidad, and later relocated to the USA, where he began teaching at a number of American universities. It was while living in America that he became friends with the poets Seamus Heaney and Joseph Brodsky.

Despite being internationally acclaimed for his writing – he was awarded the Nobel Prize in 1992 – Walcott has never abandoned the land of his birth, to which he returns as often as he can, and which also provides inspiration for his poetry. *Omeros* (1990), for example, often cited as Walcott's major achievement, is an epic poem of some eight thousand verses that reimagines the Trojan War as the story of the Caribbean people. Here, Achilles, Hector and Helen are not only demigods but also fishermen, taxi drivers and housemaids; they are the humble inhabitants of a country that is hard and unforgiving but incredibly beautiful, who live by the sea that surrounds and dominates them all.

In his narrative poem 'The Schooner Flight' (1979), Walcott, through the poem's narrator, Shabine, defines himself as the product of a unique blend of cultural influences. It is precisely in this union of contrasting elements that the mystery and essence of the Caribbean identity resides: 'I'm just a red nigger who love the sea, / I had a sound colonial education, / I have Dutch, nigger, and English in me, / and either I'm nobody, or I'm a nation'.

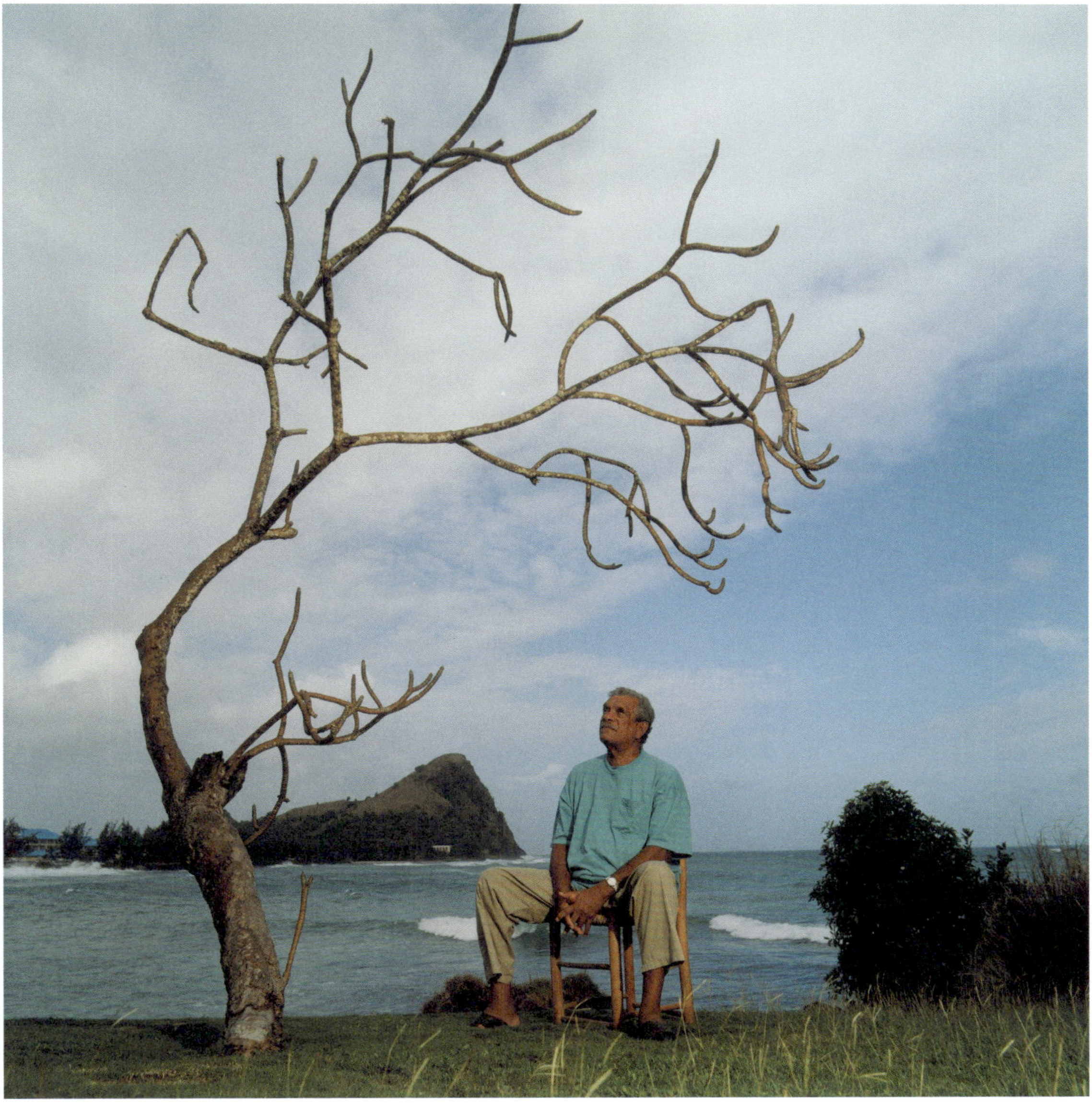

ALICE WALKER

born Eatonton, Georgia, USA, 1944

by Eamonn McCabe

London, 1998

Fighting spirit is in Alice Walker's blood. It comes partly from her parents, who worked as sharecroppers on a plantation in Putnam County, Georgia, USA, at a time when that state imposed racist laws virtually indistinguishable from those of Apartheid-era South Africa. Her parents, despite their almost starvation-level income, battled to send their eight children to school. When the plantation owner put pressure on them, hoping to force the children to work in the fields, Alice's mother, Minnie Lou Walker, told him: 'You might have some black children somewhere, but they don't live in this house. Don't you ever come around here again talking about how *my* children don't need to learn how to read and write.'

Her mother also taught her the necessity of beauty. After a long day of back-breaking work in the fields or as a housemaid Minnie Lou still found the strength to take care of the minuscule garden attached to their house. This instilled the love of order and beauty Walker recalled in her celebrated essay 'In Search of Our Mothers' Gardens' (1983). Another formative experience occurred at the age of eight, when an accident caused her to lose the sight in her right eye. She says that the accident helped her begin 'really to see people and things, really to notice relationships and to learn to be patient enough to care about how they turned out.'

Walker's love of stories began in her childhood. She enjoyed listening to her grandfather's tales, and began writing work of her own at just eight years old. This pastime led to a career as a journalist and editor, as well as to published books of poems and short stories. She had already written *The Third Life of Grange Copeland* (1970) and *Meridian* (1976), when in 1983 her third novel, *The Color Purple* (1982), won the Pulitzer Prize and the American National Book Award. She was the first black woman to win either.

Long before her literary success, Walker's social commitment and passion for politics were confirmed in 1962 by a decisive meeting with Coretta Scott King in the home she shared with her husband Martin Luther King Jr. Walker's subsequent interventions and struggles on behalf of the oppressed in racist, sexist societies are as memorable as her writings, and inseparable from them.

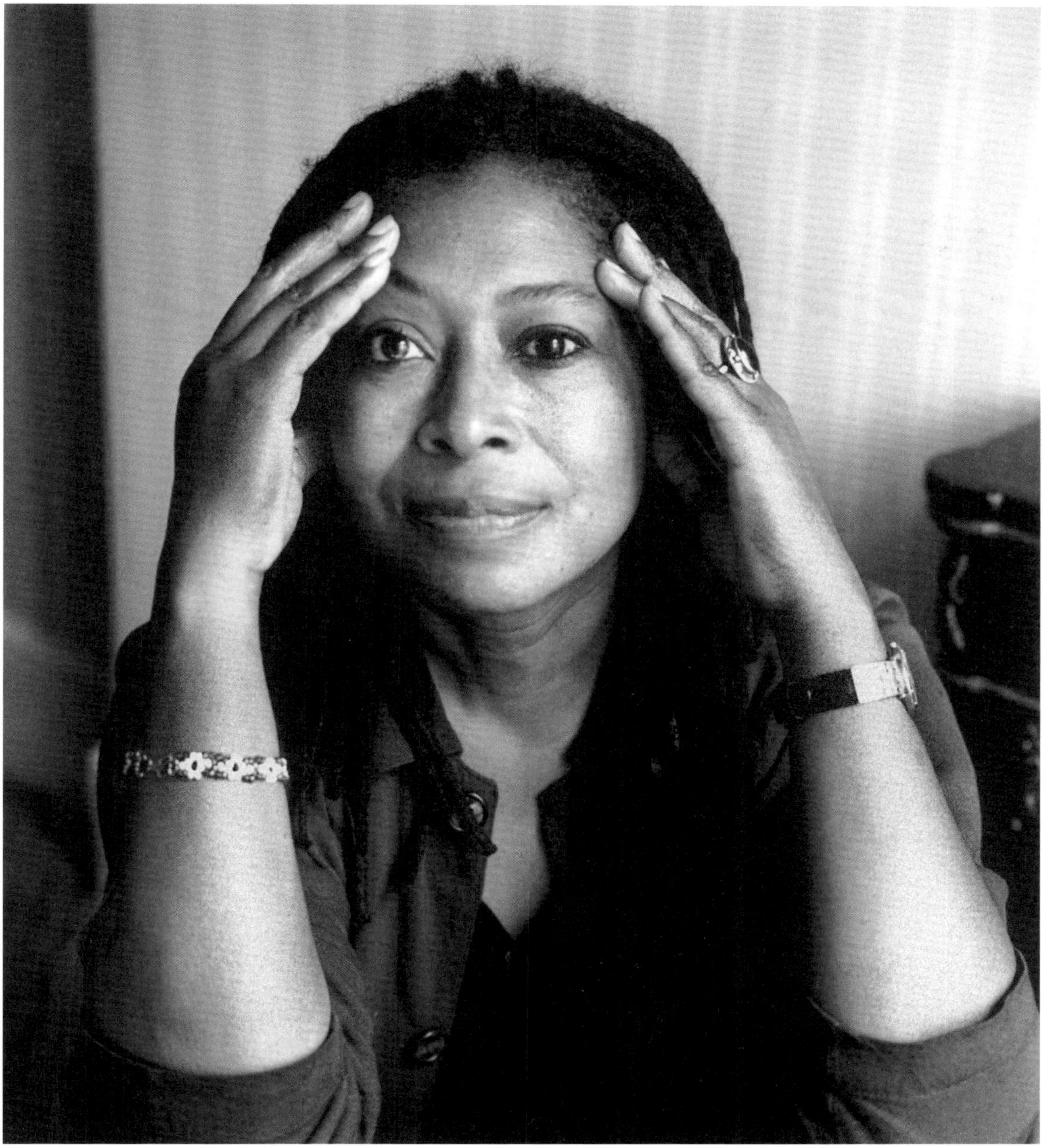

DAVID FOSTER WALLACE

born Ithaca, New York, 1962; died Claremont, California, 2008

by Marion Ettlinger

Bloomington, Indiana, 2001

No book by 'the most tedious, overrated, tortured, pretentious writer of my generation', as Bret Easton Ellis described him, ever achieved the popularity of *American Psycho,* but David Foster Wallace, especially after his suicide in 2008, succeeded in generating a wave of admiration that, as it spread out from American university campuses, became a true cult phenomenon. Wallace's writing is characterized by a fierce intelligence, a stylistic virtuosity and an irrepressible interest in the most diverse spheres of life. *A Supposedly Fun Thing I'll Never Do Again* (1997), a collection of essays, gained him a considerable following for its incisiveness, originality and irony; in his long, flowing, labyrinthine novels, as in his collections of short stories, we are confronted with thousands of variations on the theme of contemporary unease.

It is in Wallace's profound and painful awareness of his own complicity in the disorientation he talks of that we recognize his sincerity and the reason why his characters appear so human, despite the accumulation of words, digressions and linguistic manipulations to which he subjects them. It is reasonable to speculate that only a small percentage of the readers who bought *Infinite Jest*, his lengthy and complex novel from 1996, actually enjoyed it; by that time, Wallace had gone from being a writer's writer to a fashionable author surrounded by an aura of veneration. But his uniqueness is clear in each of his works – in their density and lightness of touch, in the intelligence and emotionality of his voice, and, perhaps most significantly, in his ability to combine all these qualities.

Marion Ettlinger, an American photographer specializing in author portraits, refers to the state in which the photographer is able to go beyond appearances and peer behind their subject's mask as 'an atmosphere of consensus'. Her portrait of Wallace, who seems lost in his thoughts and apparently unaware of the photographer's presence, his hands in his pockets and his gaze lowered, was clearly taken in such an atmosphere.

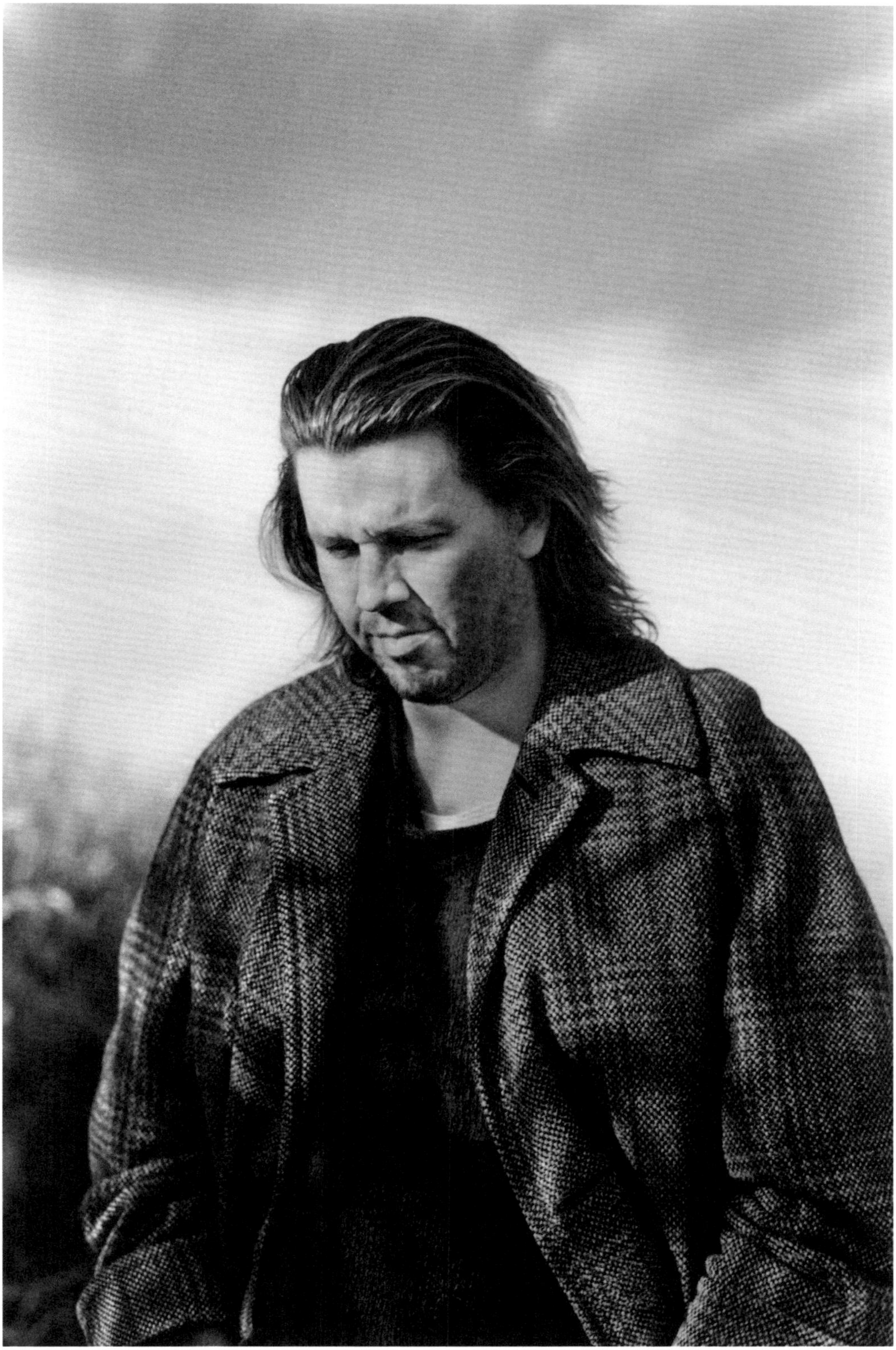

ROBERT WALSER

born Biel, Switzerland, 1878; died Herisau, Switzerland, 1956

by Carl Seelig

Herisau, Switzerland, 1939

The body of the Swiss writer Robert Walser was found on Christmas Day, 1956, lying in the snow not far from the nursing home in the Swiss Alps where he had lived for more than twenty years. He was seventy-eight and had died of heart failure. The young men who discovered his body said that he had looked very peaceful: his trips into the mountains were the only excursions to enliven the silence of his literary and physical isolation. Walser, the son of a bookbinder from Biel, Switzerland, had been diagnosed with schizophrenia and voluntarily institutionalized in 1929 after his career as a professional writer began to decline; shorty thereafter he ceased to write. Although mental illness severely affected more than one generation of Walser's family – his mother suffered from chronic depression; one brother killed himself and another died after a period in a psychiatric clinic in Waldau – there is still some doubt as to the degree of illness that Walser actually suffered, especially with regard to his long stay in Herisau, to which he was forcibly transferred in 1933. The Swiss writer Fleur Jaeggy commented: 'He was a poet and simply didn't know where else to go.'

The desire to limit his own presence in the world is discernible in all of Walser's books, in the lightness of his writing; and also in the many modest occupations that he held – bank clerk, butler – before he began writing full-time. The semi-autobiographical *Jakob von Gunten* (1909), the novel that was perhaps closest to his heart, tells the story of an impish young man training at a school for servants who receives an initiation into humility as a way of life. Walser's legendary passion for walking, attributed to his provincial reserve and need for solitude, was immortalized repeatedly in non-fictions, sketches and short stories such as *The Walk* (1917; revised 1920) that comprise his most significant literary output. Many of Walser's late works were destroyed by the author, but a significant number survived as handwritten manuscripts that were discovered and deciphered only after his death.

Wanderungen mit Robert Walser (Wandering with Robert Walser, 1957), written by Carl Seelig, who was the curator of Walser's work as well as his friend and walking companion, has given us a unique and moving portrait of the writer's personality. With reference to the day on which this image was taken, Seelig wrote: 'As usual, Robert had his umbrella with him; and his hat was looking even more battered than ever. The ribbon had fallen to pieces, but he just didn't want a new one. … We took three-and-a-half hours to get from Herisau to Wil, talking all the way. It was as if he were wearing skates, he could walk so fast. Sometimes Robert would draw my attention to an exceptionally lovely meadow, over which a cloud shaped like a baroque palace might be passing. He even let me photograph him without protest. I was astonished.'

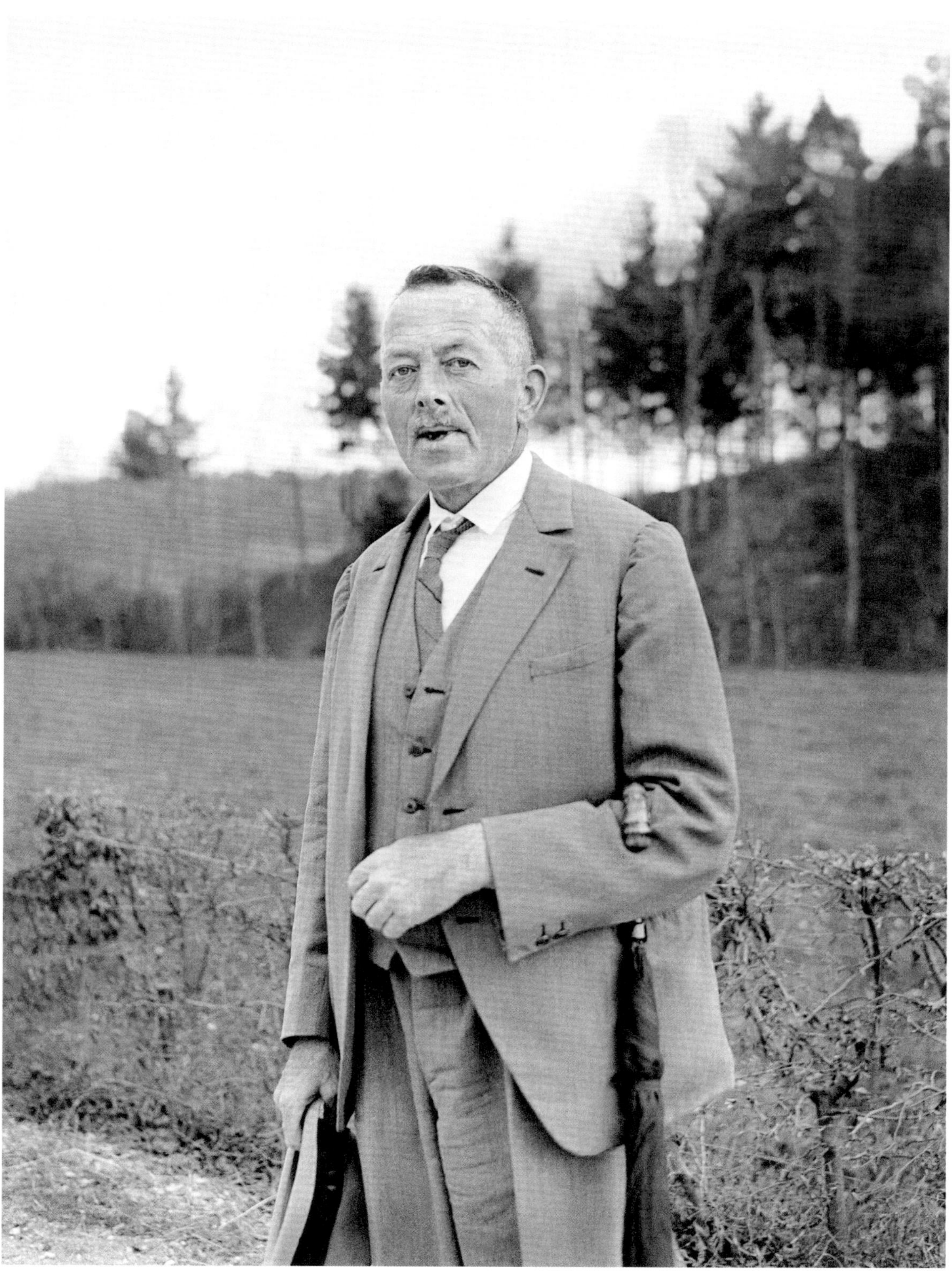

H. G. WELLS

[Herbert George Wells] born Bromley, Kent, UK, 1866; died London, 1946

by Alvin Langdon Coburn

London, 1905

H. G. Wells is seen, along with Jules Verne, as one of the founders of modern science fiction, and was also a progressive figure in many fields. Although he grew up in very modest family circumstances, Wells was a bright young man (in 1884 he won a scholarship to the Normal School of Science in London, where he studied biology) and he was able to make a living by teaching and doing odd jobs. In the meantime, he cultivated his passion for writing and managed to publish a few stories.

His *annus mirabilis* came in 1895. At this time, Wells, who had already been married to his cousin Isabel for a few months, managed to obtain an annulment and married Amy Catherine Robbins – one of his pupils. Despite Wells's innumerable 'digressions', the marriage lasted until her death. That year also saw the publication of his first great success, *The Time Machine*. Thereafter, Wells continued to produce novels that were destined to leave their mark on the history of literary science fiction: *The Island of Dr Moreau* (1896), *The Invisible Man* (1897) and *The War of the Worlds* (1898) are some of his best-known titles. Elements of his tales were even borne out as prophesy years later. A virtual Leonardo da Vinci of letters, Wells anticipated the atomic bomb, genetic engineering (long before the discovery of DNA), robotics, laser beams, tanks and even automatic doors. His main intent, however, was not to imagine possible future technologies but to invent better social models, models in which science – provided it remained under the control of human intelligence – must play a functional role.

After the great success of his science fiction, Wells dedicated himself to other literary forms but is best remembered today for the daring adaptation of his novel as a radio play, aired in 1938, which took the form of news bulletins describing an invasion from Mars. Orson Welles's broadcast – part-hoax, part-performance – triggered panic in Middle America. This stunt boosted the fame of both Wells and Welles. When commenting on the episode later, Wells joked that perhaps one should be put in prison for such a prank, but instead one ended up in Hollywood.

Alvin Langdon Coburn, a key figure in the American pictorial tradition, photographed Wells and other famous writers for various magazines and, in particular, for *Camera Work*. This photographic journal had been created by Alfred Stieglitz and was considered to be the bible of art photography.

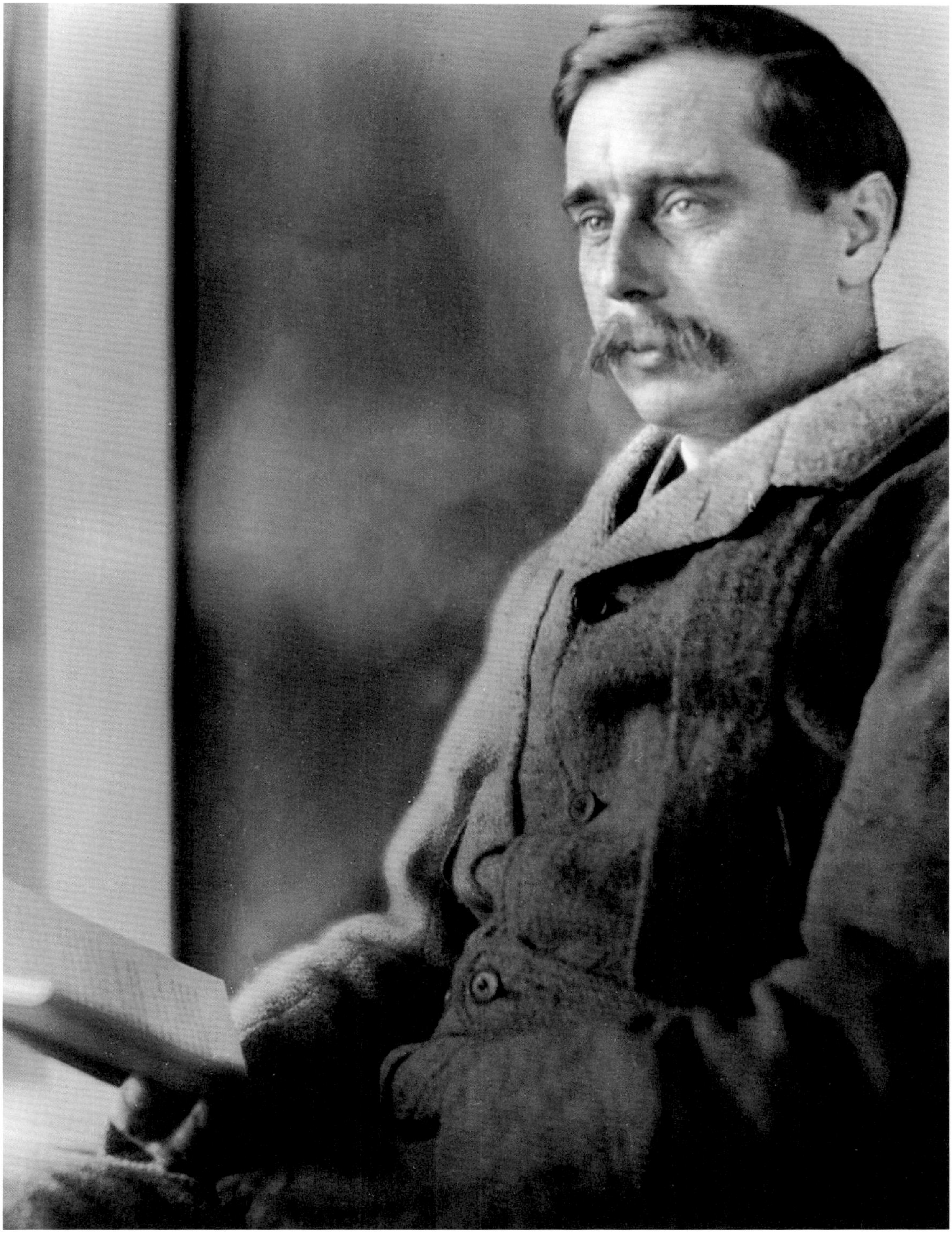

IRVINE WELSH

born Leith, Edinburgh, UK, 1958

by Martin Hunter

Edinburgh, UK, 2009

Society's outcasts, drug addicts, misfits, hooligans, ravers and post-punk layabouts: these are the characters who appear in Irvine Welsh's popular debut novel, *Trainspotting* (1993), with their strong working-class Edinburgh dialects faithfully rendered phonetically.

The details of Welsh's own youth could have been drawn from one of his novels; indeed, some suggest that Welsh has changed or exaggerated some elements of his official biography to stay in character with his books. After his astonishingly successful debut in 1993 (a success rekindled in 1996 when the film *Trainspotting* was released), many people were willing to bet that Welsh would remain the writer of only one book, even if it was a book that was destined to leave its mark on cult literature.

Two collections of short stories and another novel, *Marabou Stork Nightmares* (1995), hardly caused a ripple when they appeared. It was with *Filth* (1998) – which many consider to be his best book – that Welsh made his triumphant return. This novel was anything other than conventional, both in its storyline and in its narrative technique: the protagonist's stream of consciousness is in places typographically obscured by the interior monologue of a tapeworm lodged in his gut. Other novels soon followed, such as *Glue* (2001), *Porno* (2002) and *Crime* (2008), along with more short-story collections, including *If You Liked School, You'll Love Work* (2007). In 2012 it was the turn of *Skagboys*, a prequel to his first novel. Welsh had not simply given in to the fashion for prequels – many critics considered it to be as good as, perhaps even better than, his debut. One thing is certain: twenty years on, the writer has proved the prophets of doom wrong: Irvine Welsh is the writer of more than one great book.

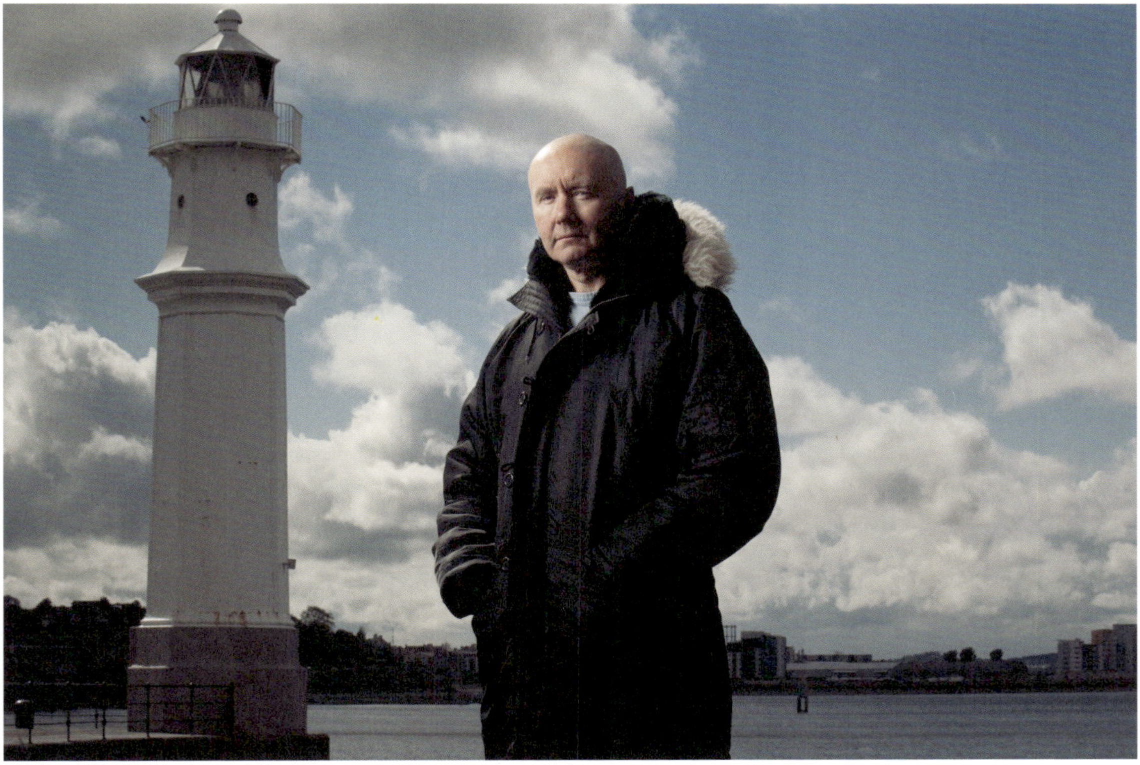

EUDORA WELTY

born Jackson, Mississippi, 1909; died Jackson, Mississippi, 2001

self-portrait

Jackson, Mississippi, 1930s

The links between photography and writing are strong. The narrative thread of photographic 'stories' often takes on the dimension of a written story or a novel, and photographs have inspired works of writers. Some authors – among them Eudora Welty – have even made alternating use of the camera and the pen. Welty understood how a land, a time and a whole society could be investigated through both photography and writing.

Welty knew the places through which she travelled well. She was born in Jackson, Mississippi, in 1909, and for her the southern states were a territory to be analysed and from which to draw inspiration. It was here that she found stories to tell about the relationships between individuals and the communities at large, communities where the machinery of social convention had the power to suffocate the passions and ambitions of its individual members.

Welty dabbled in photography without achieving any great success, and establishing herself in the literary world took some time. Her first published short story, 'Death of a Traveling Salesman', was printed in the literary magazine *Manuscript* in 1936. Then, in 1941, she published 'Why I Live at the P.O.', in which the narrator tells the story of why she has chosen to live in the post office, far away from the small irritations and petty tyrannies of family life. This tale was reputed to have been inspired by a picture of a woman, busily ironing in the backroom of a post office, one of the images Welty took as part of her great photographic documentation of Depression-era America. Her first novella, *The Robber Bridegroom*, appeared in 1942. After the war she slowly gained recognition and was awarded a Guggenheim Fellowship, followed by the Pulitzer Prize for *The Optimist's Daughter* (1972).

Hers is a large and varied body of work. Welty's writing draws us in and presents us with very precise observations without sacrificing warmth of heart. Her gaze was compassionate, as we can also see from her photographs. While these often tell of desolation and difficulties, they also often point to potential salvation for both the observer and the observed.

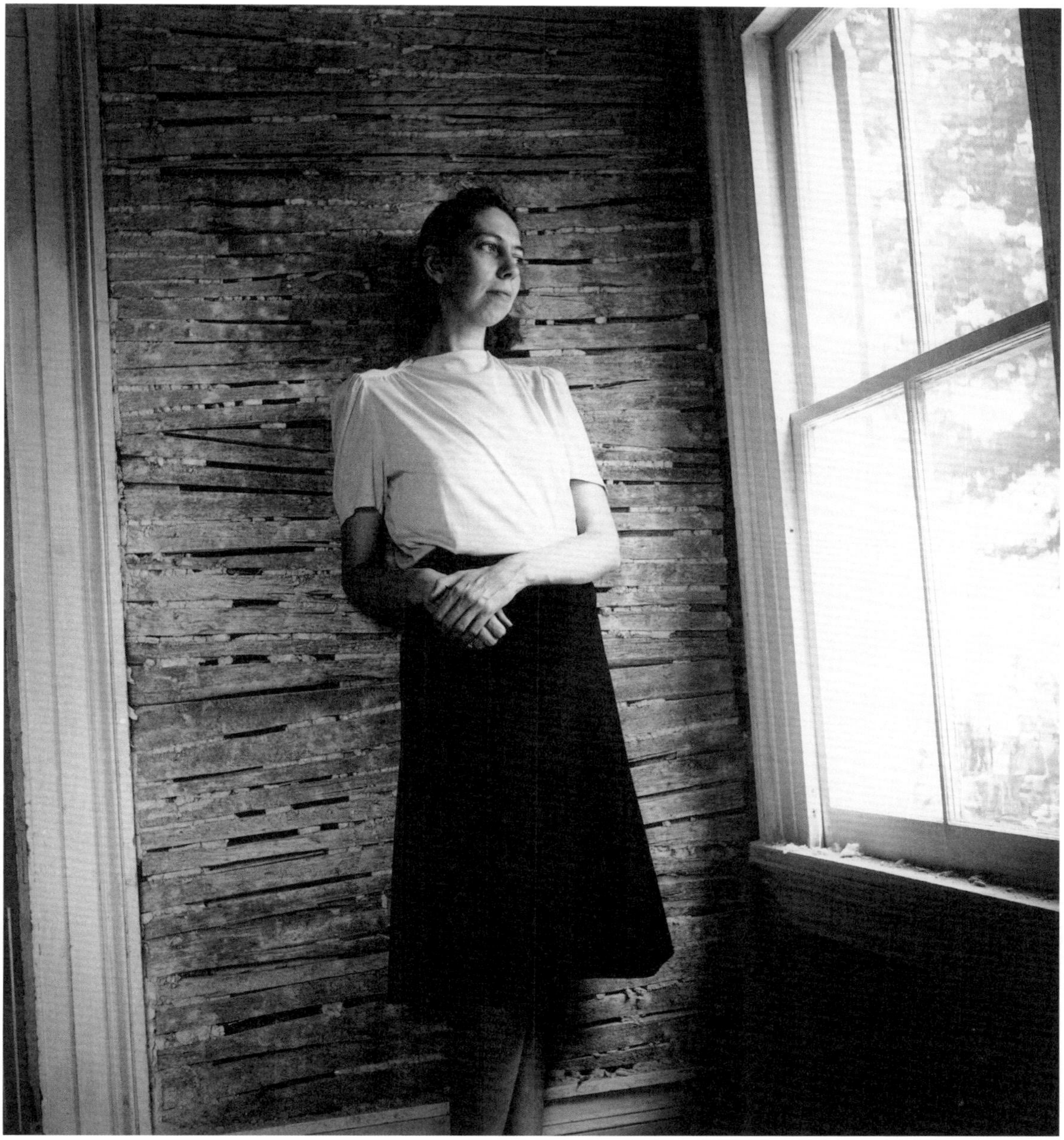

NATHANAEL WEST

[Nathan Weinstein] born New York, 1903; died El Centro, California, 1940

unknown photographer

California, 1930s

Nathan Weinstein was born in New York, into a middle-class Jewish family originally from Lithuania. As a boy he was rebellious and lazy at school. He dropped out of school and forged a transcript to gain admittance to Tufts College. Although he was expelled when the deception was discovered, he then managed to get into Brown University using the transcript of another boy at Tufts who had the same name. At university he studied little but read much. He was fascinated by the unusual, the absurd and the unconventional. Although he continued to do badly in his exams, he started to design comic strips, and wrote Surrealist short stories, which were later published in a collection called *The Dream Life of Balso Snell* (1931). He managed to scrape through with a degree, and left university under a new name, Nathanael West.

Due to the impoverished circumstances of his family, West had to renounce his dream of living in Paris. He worked odd jobs, including one as a night manager in a hotel, which suited him perfectly. During the long, quiet night shifts he wrote *Miss Lonelyhearts* (1933), a sarcastic, caustic and highly original novel about a newspaper columnist. West described it as 'a comic without cartoons'. By 1933 West considered himself a fully-fledged writer, albeit with little success to speak of, and managed to procure a job as a scriptwriter forColumbia Pictures. While in Hollywood he wrote film scripts, including a screenplay for Alfred Hitchcock's *Suspicion*, although in the end the script was not used. He also completed his most famous work, *The Day of the Locust* (1939), whose characters are outcasts on the fringes of the Hollywood dream, many of them drawn from West's life.

West married Eileen McKenney, sister of the writer Ruth McKenney, and inspiration behind the play *My Sister Eileen*, which later became a television sitcom. On 22 December 1940 West and his wife were returning from a trip in Mexico when West drove through a stop sign and the couple was struck and killed by an oncoming vehicle. West's friend F. Scott Fitzgerald had died the previous day, and it is possible that grief at learning the news had distracted him. It was to take many years for West's works to achieve the success and critical recognition they deserve.

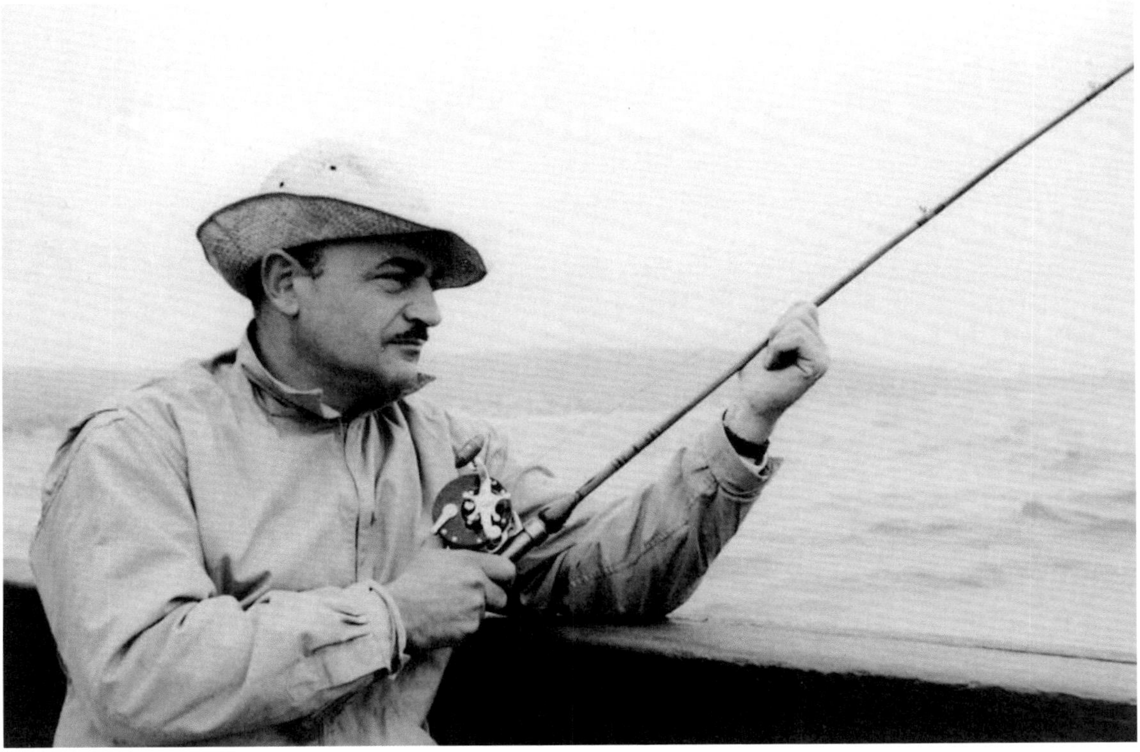

CHRISTA WOLF

[née Ihlenfeld] born Gorzów Wielkopolski, Poland, 1929; died Berlin, 2011

by Isolde Ohlbaum

Berlin, 1979

'The past is not dead; it is not even past. We cut it off from ourselves and pretend we are strangers.' So begins *A Model Childhood*, Christa Wolf's autobiographical novel from 1976, in which a woman in her early forties (as was Wolf when she was writing the book) recalls her childhood as she travels to her native city. Wolf's childhood and adolescence had coincided with the rise of National Socialism, and the book depicts a terrible period in history in which ordinary life and unimaginable horror existed side by side. It left an indelible mark on Wolf's life, as did the other great event of the twentieth century: the end of the socialist dream.

Wolf was born in 1929 in the Province of Brandenburg, now part of Poland, and grew up under Nazi rule. Following the end of the Second World War, her family found themselves living in the state of Mecklenburg, in the newly created German Democratic Republic, otherwise known as East Germany. Wolf became a fervent Communist, a young activist and a socially committed writer. The act of writing was her chosen instrument for interpreting the past; it was also her way of being politically active in a society that soon revealed itself to be extremely closed.

Wolf's literary output, which included novels, short stories and essays, was often highly autobiographical. Her breakthrough novel, *Divided Heaven* (1963), was inspired by the period she spent working in a factory making railway carriages; *What Remains*, written in 1979, is an account of an East German woman living under the watchful eye of the Stasi. This later book, published in 1990 just a few months after the fall of the Berlin Wall and the East German Communist regime, attracted much personal and political criticism: accusations of opportunism poured in from the West, and Wolf was accused of wanting to present herself as a victim. The political debate was further inflamed when, in 1992, it was revealed that she had in fact collaborated with the secret police. It subsequently became clear that Wolf had been interviewed only three times, and that the information she had provided had been so insignificant that the Stasi had broken off the relationship; furthermore, she and her husband had themselves been the subjects of surveillance.

Wolf's highly imaginative writing, which could conjure up entire worlds in the space of a single phrase, constantly questioned her relationship with society. *Cassandra* (1983), her reworking of the story of the tragic figure from Greek mythology, remains an unforgettable book, an allegory of the unheard female voice and the oppression and censorship Wolf experienced in East Germany.

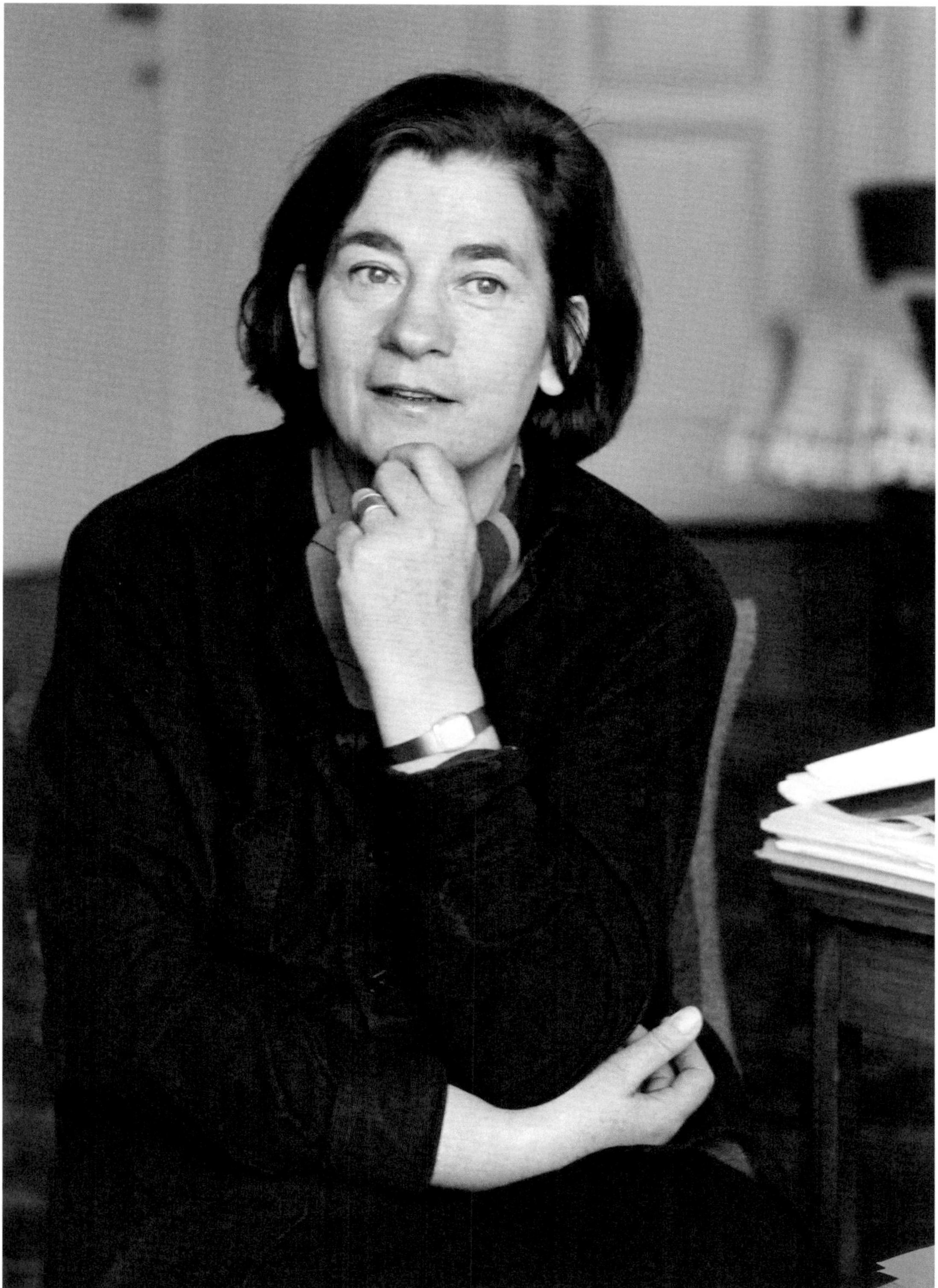

VIRGINIA WOOLF

[née Stephen] born London, 1882; died Rodmell, East Sussex, UK, 1941

by Gisèle Freund

London, 1939

Virginia Woolf grew up in a house near London's Hyde Park, surrounded by books belonging to her father, the author and historian Sir Leslie Stephen. Her childhood home was a lively one, frequented by artists and writers, but the young Virginia was traumatized by the unexpected deaths of her mother and, shortly afterwards, her half-sister, Stella Duckworth Hills. These early tragedies precipitated the onset of the mental illness that would plague her throughout her life. After the death of her father in 1904, she and her siblings, Vanessa, Thoby and Adrian, bought a house in Bloomsbury. It would soon become home to the most famous intellectual circle of the era, the Bloomsbury Group, an unconventional, avant-garde collection of writers, artists, historians, poets and economists. After the stifling atmosphere of the Victorian salon, it was a breath of fresh air for its members.

Lytton Strachey, famous biographer of the Victorians and an active homosexual, was one such member. In 1909, beguiled by the dynamism of the group, he proposed to Virginia and was accepted; the engagement, however, was quickly aborted (although their platonic relationship would continue, resulting in a lifelong correspondence). Subsequently, in 1912, Virginia married another member of the group, the writer Leonard Woolf. Despite the marriage being a happy and supportive one, Virginia continued to suffer prolonged bouts of depression. In 1941, having moved out of London with Leonard to their country home in Rodmell, East Sussex, to escape the Blitz, she decided she could go on no longer. She filled her pockets with stones and waded into the River Ouse. As one of the principal exponents of modernism, she left behind her a highly significant and influential body of work, including the novels *Mrs Dalloway* (1925), *To the Lighthouse* (1927) and *The Waves* (1931).

Gisèle Freund took this photograph of Woolf as part of her series of photographs of some of the most prominent writers of the era. Her impression of the author was of a 'frail, luminous' woman, 'the very incarnation of her prose'. In her diaries, Virginia wrote that she considered posing for the camera a 'violation of her purity'.

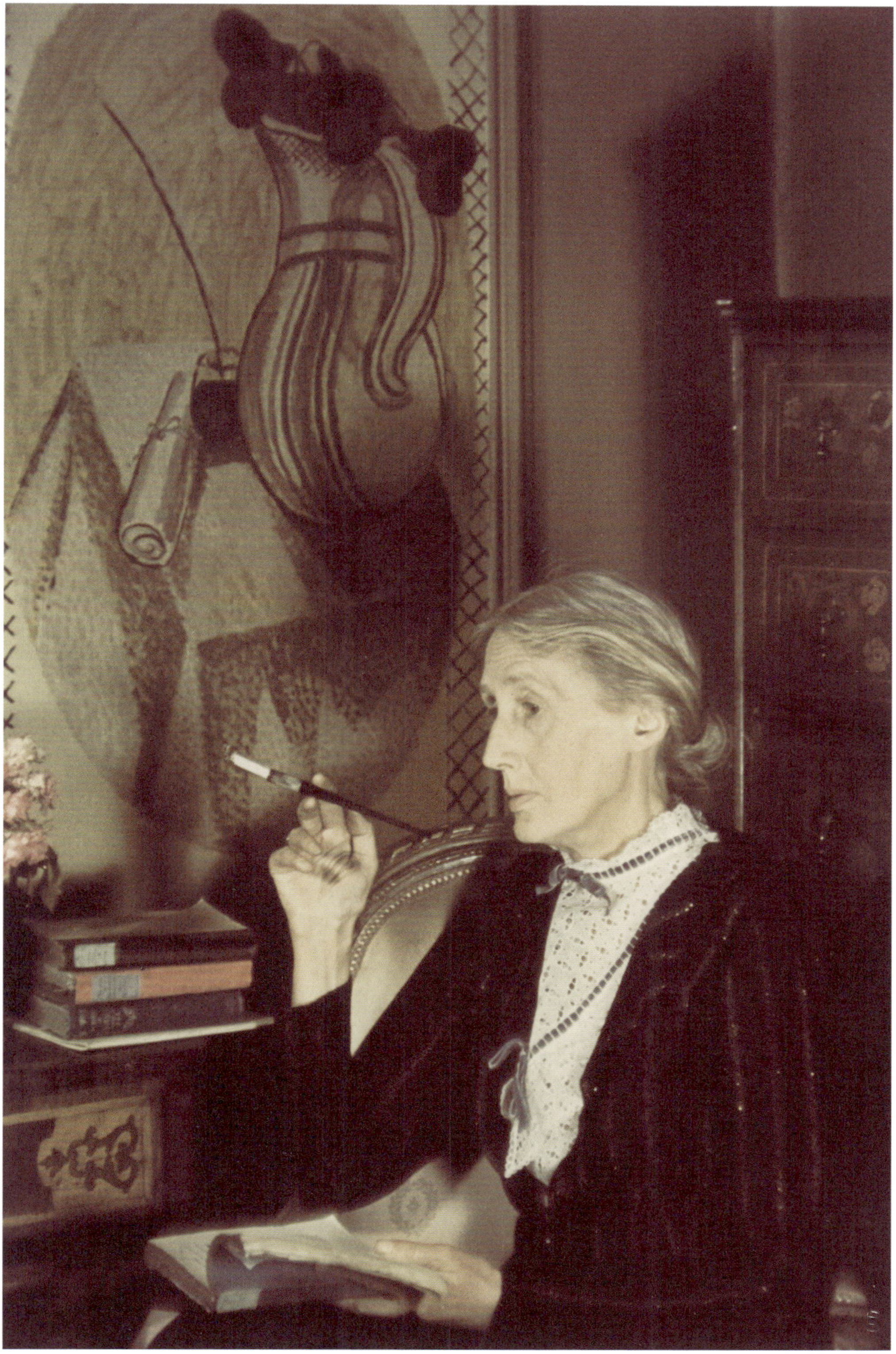

KATEB YACINE

[Yacine Kateb] born Zighoud Youcef, Algeria, 1929; died Grenoble, France, 1989

by Nathalie Blandin

Paris, 1956

Yacine's given name was Yacine Kateb ('Kateb' means 'writer' in Arabic, so he made it the first element of his pen name). He was born in a village on the outskirts of Constantine, one of the most historic cities in Algeria and the ancient capital of Numidia. On 8 May 1945, when he had just turned sixteen, he participated in a nationalist demonstration in his city that ended in the massacre of thousands. was arrested and imprisoned for two months, during which time his determination to become a writer increased. Two great and enduring passions emerged from his imprisonment, revolution and poetry: 'A true poet ... must express his opposition. If he cannot express himself freely, he will suffocate. This is his function. He creates his own revolution within the political revolution; he is at the centre of the agitation and he is the eternal agitator. His is the voice of the revolution; he must swim against the tide. The poet is in essence the revolution; he is a continuous, unending explosion.' His first collection of poems, *Soliloquies*, was published in 1946.

Yacine's literary reputation was established by his first novel, *Nedjma* (meaning 'star' in Arabic), which was published in 1956, in the middle of the Algerian War of Independence. The book was an immediate sensation that changed the face of Maghribi literature. Nedjma, the heroine, does not dominate the action, but remains in the background, an idealized, elusive personification of the quintessential oriental woman, loved by four different men. She also represents the country of Algeria, which has yet to take shape and assert itself. Yacine's second major work was the experimental *Le Polygone étiolé* (The etiolated polygon, 1966), a mosaic of poetry, prose and fragmentary drama exploring themes of exile and cultural identity. In 1987 he was awarded the French Grand Prix National des Lettres.

Kateb travelled extensively and lived for long periods abroad. Educated in the language of the colonial rulers, he initially wrote in French, 'to tell the French that I am not French', describing the French language as 'the trophy of war'. When he returned to Algeria in the early 1970s, after a long period in Europe and South East Asia, he abandoned French in favour of Arabic in order to reach a wider local audience. He founded a theatrical company, Action Culturelle des Travailleurs (ACT), and started to write plays in the Algerian vernacular, rather than in French or the Classical Arabic that was the new official language only understood by the privileged few. For Kateb, such aesthetic choices were inextricably bound up with politics. He remained 'the eternal agitator' until the end of his days, fighting against colonialism, but also against the post-war dictatorship and religious fanaticism. He firmly believed that poetry had the power to 'revolutionize the revolution', and to open up another dimension of reality.

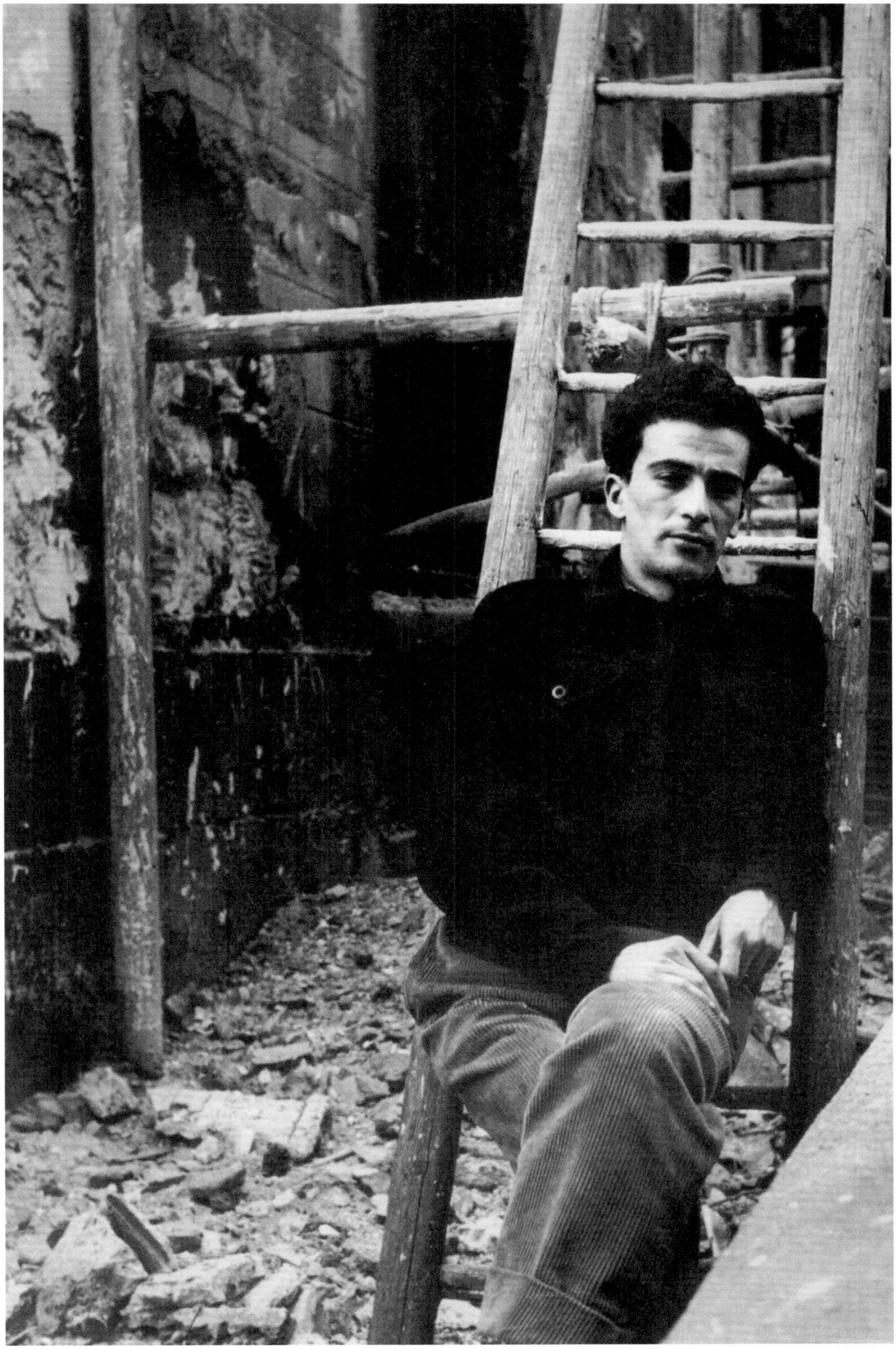

W. B. YEATS

born Dublin, 1865; died Roquebrune-Cap-Martin, France, 1939

by Alvin Langdon Coburn

London, 1908

Born in Dublin, William Butler Yeats spent much of his childhood in the small town of Sligo on the north-west coast of Ireland, even after he and his family had moved to London when he was two years old. Together with the Celtic legends and folklore imparted to him by his mother, Sligo would inspire his imagination and creativity throughout his life. Both the place and the memories associated with it took on an almost mystical, metaphorical significance for the poet.

Yeats was heavily involved in hermeticism, spiritualism and mysticism. In 1885 he helped to establish the Dublin Hermetic Society. He later joined the Theosophical Society co-founded by the Russian-German occultist Helena Blavatsky, and was admitted to the Hermetic Order of the Golden Dawn. He also became an acolyte of the Swedish mystic Emanuel Swedenborg, who promoted dialogue between Eastern and Western philosophies, and was an avid reader of the poetry of the Indian writer Rabindranath Tagore. In 1937 Yeats helped to compile and translate a selection of the Upanishads, the sacred texts of Hinduism.

Yeats's own poetry is characterized not only by spiritualism and esotericism but also by his passion for his homeland and his interest in Irish folklore. Between 1913 and 1916 he was assisted in his work by the American poet Ezra Pound, who also helped to disseminate his work in the USA. In 1917, having unsuccessfully pursued the Irish patriot Maud Gonne – as well as, briefly, her daughter Iseult – Yeats married Bertha Georgie Hyde-Lees (known as George), who shared his interest in spiritualism and encouraged him in the use of mediums. In 1923 Yeats was awarded the Nobel Prize, and he continued to write until his death. The late collection of verse entitled *The Tower* (1928) contains some of his most famous poems.

In 1913 Alvin Langdon Coburn published this photograph of Yeats in his book *Men of Mark*, a collection of thirty-three portraits of such men of distinction as Henri Matisse, Auguste Rodin, Henry James, Mark Twain and Theodore Roosevelt. In his preface to the book, Coburn wrote: 'To make satisfactory photographs of persons it is necessary for me to like them, to admire them, or at least to be interested in them. It is rather curious and difficult to exactly explain, but if I dislike my subject it is sure to come out in the resulting portrait.'

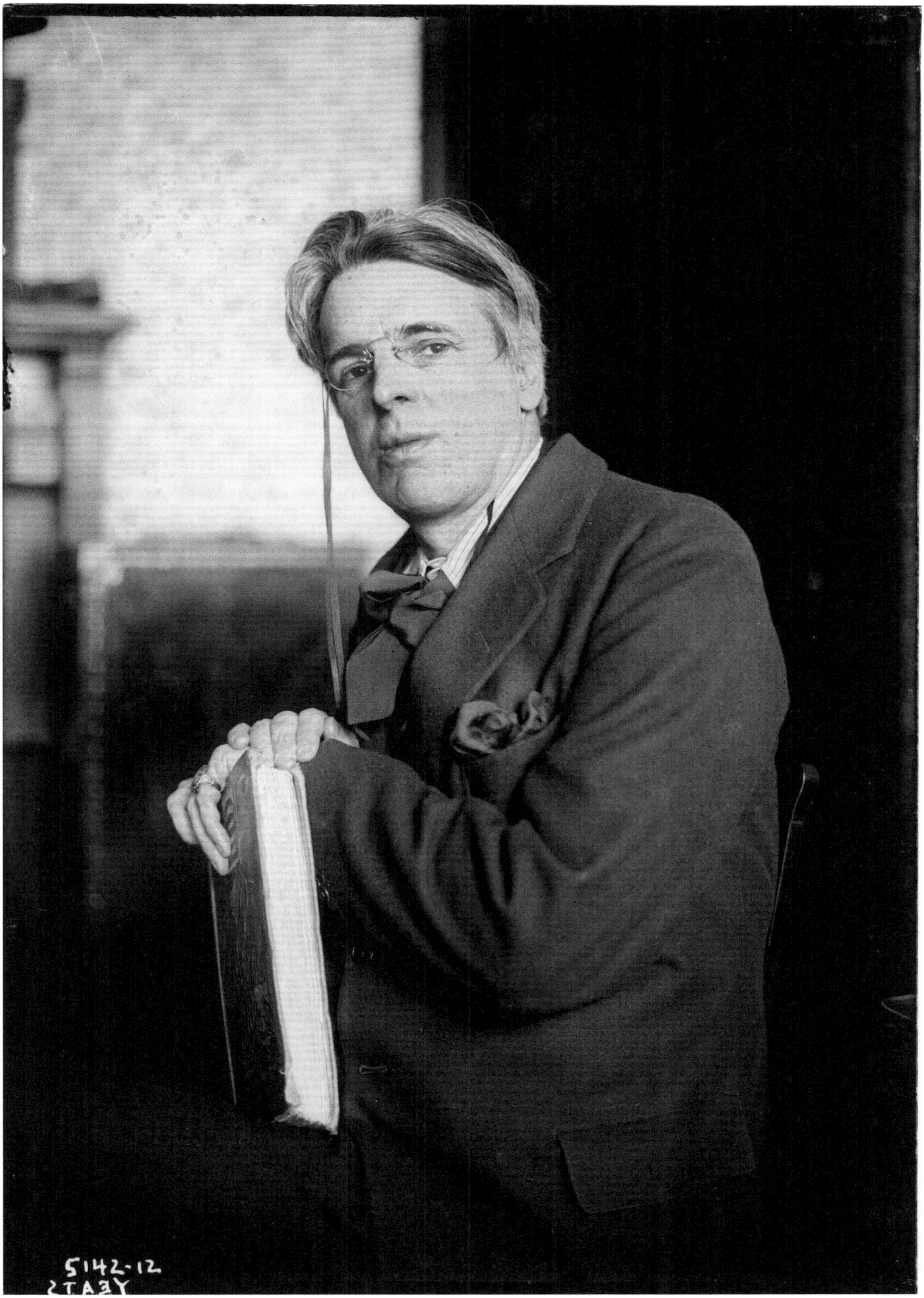
5142-12

A. B. YEHOSHUA

born Jerusalem, 1936

by Gianni Giansanti

Haifa, Israel, 2005

Together with Amos Oz and David Grossman, Abraham B. ('Bulli') Yehoshua, seen here in a portrait by Gianni Giansanti, is one of a number of Israeli authors who have long been committed to the search for a peaceful solution to the Arab–Israeli conflict. Several of his works, both novels and essays, are dedicated to examining the state of Israel's troubled relationship with the Palestinian people.

Born in Jerusalem in 1936 into a Sephardic family, Yehoshua now lives in Haifa, where he lectures in comparative and Hebrew literature at the city's university. His tireless exploration of the political and military problems of the region also includes an investigation of similar forms of misunderstanding – albeit less extreme but just as tangled – within families and marriages, and between the generations.

Such instances of miscommunication can be found in one of Yehoshua's best-known novels, *The Lover* (1977), which was made into a film, *The Lost Lover* (1999), by Italian director Roberto Faenza. In the book, the multiple-narrative structure signals the difficulties experienced by the characters in gaining access to one another's inner lives. However, although the author is engaged in analysing the difficulties encountered in the course of human relations, he does not exclude the possibility of the different worlds represented by each character eventually coming together. This faith in the possibility of overcoming the lack of understanding between the characters in the story can be interpreted as a broader desire for dialogue between Israelis and Palestinians.

Yehoshua's novel of 2013, *The Retrospective*, is dedicated to the visual world, including the cinema and painting. Its protagonist, an elderly film director (arguably the author's alter ego), retraces his career by examining his views on art, the creative process and its intellectual possibilities. As he rediscovers the symbolic and visionary language of his youthful stories, he finds the imagination to be the most effective way of deconstructing reality.

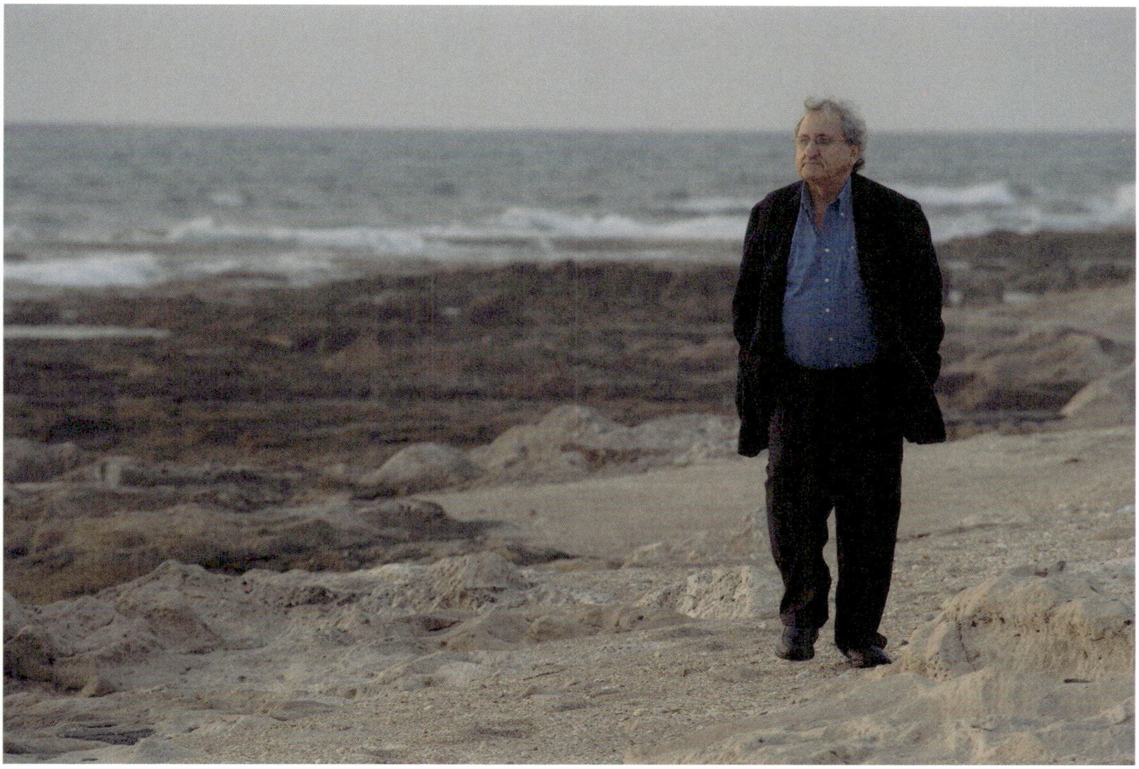

MARGUERITE YOURCENAR

[Marguerite Cleenewerck de Crayencour] born Brussels, 1903; died Northeast Harbor, Maine, 1987

Robert Doisneau

Paris, 1955

In 1948 an important trunk was unloaded in the USA. It had travelled all the way from Europe, and the name written on the side of the trunk was Marguerite de Crayencour. The trunk's owner, whose pen-name was Marguerite Yourcenar, opened it up eagerly and began to sift through the piles of letters, postcards and papers. She came across a single torn-off sheet starting with the words 'My dear Mark…'. It was the beginning of an idea she had abandoned years before, and on rereading it she was seized with the desire to complete the work that was to become her masterpiece, *Memoirs of Hadrian* (1951). It is the story of a mature man who, sensing that the end of his life may not be far, writes a long and passionate letter to his eighteen-year-old nephew narrating the events of his life, and his personal philosophy. But this is no ordinary story, for the mature man is none other than the Roman emperor Hadrian, and his nephew is Marcus Aurelius. The novel portrays a complex and courageous man who struggles with insecurity and doubt. Yourcenar pieces together the elements that comprise the public and private life of the man, his loves, his passions, his youthful enthusiasm and his fear of the onset of senility.

As an adolescent, Yourcenar developed a passion for the classics, reading Virgil in Latin and Homer in Greek. Her mother died soon after she was born, so she was brought up by her father, who she followed on his travels around the world. She was educated by private tutors, and amassed a vast knowledge of humanist culture. At the age of sixteen she wrote a verse drama entitled *Le Jardin des chimères* (The garden of chimeras, 1921) and in 1929 she published her first novel, *Alexis*, which tells the story of a musician who leaves his wife in order to follow his homosexual desires.

Homosexuality was an integral part of both Yourcenar's life and literary works. She made no secret of her own bisexuality and her unconventional lifestyle caused a stir in conservative circles. By the time she published *Memoirs of Hadrian* she was living in the USA with her long-term partner Grace Frick after fleeing the Second World War in Europe. Here she taught art history and French literature and wrote numerous essays and novels, including *The Abyss* (1968), which was awarded the Prix Femina. She also wrote three volumes of copious memoirs, which she edited meticulously. This account of her life from the vantage point of advanced age is reminiscent of her most famous protagonist, Hadrian. In 1980 she became the first woman to be admitted to the Académie Française.

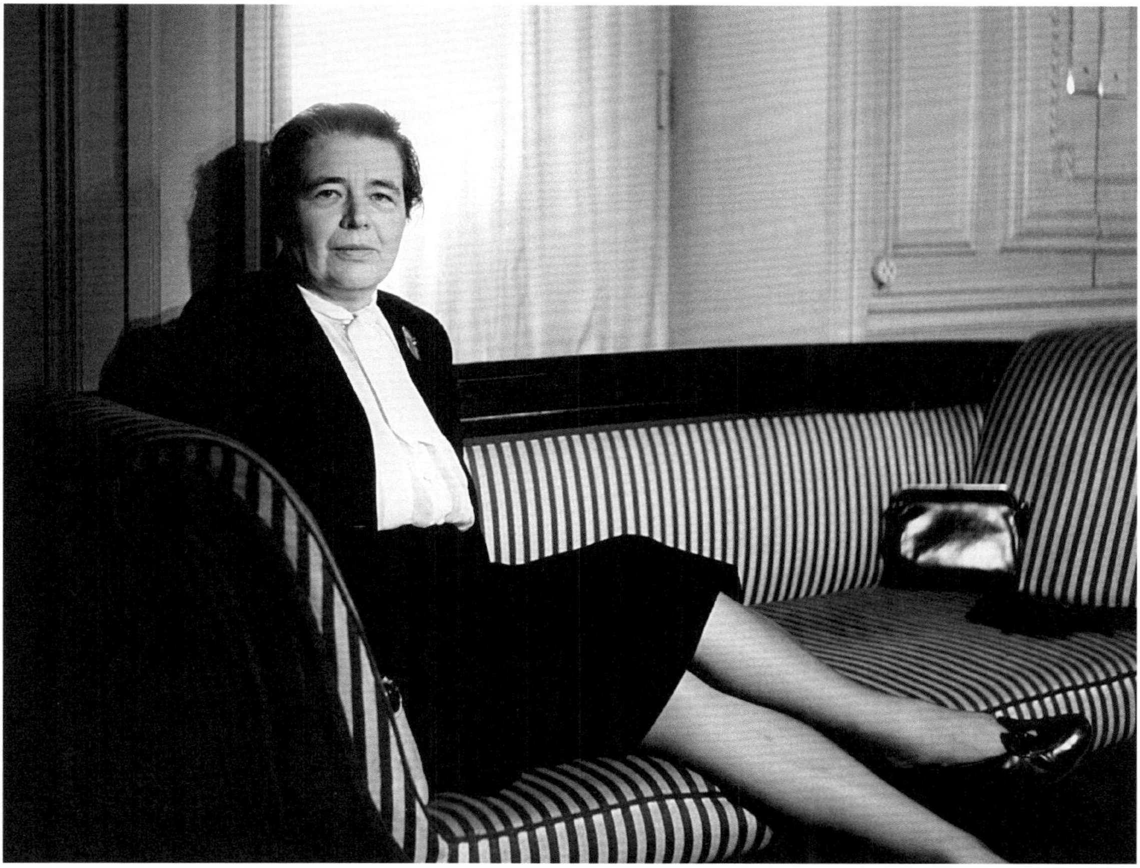

ANDREA ZANZOTTO

born Pieve di Soligo, Italy, 1921; died Conegliano, Italy, 2011

by Isolde Ohlbaum

Munich, 2000

Andrea Zanzotto was born and grew up in Pieve di Soligo, a village located in the shadow of the Alps in the Veneto region of Italy. His relationship with the area was as passionate and exclusive as any love affair. Throughout his life Pieve di Soligo remained his chosen hideaway, a kind of refuge. However, as the poet himself declared, this refuge was made up of 'burrows', which could lead out to the open or to a dead end, depending on what kind of shelter one sought.

Zanzotto inherited his social conscience from his anti-Fascist art-teacher father. He recalled the time in 1929 when, in the run-up to the plebiscite intended by Mussolini to provide the necessary consensus for his Fascist state, his school teacher put a ballot paper up on the blackboard with the word 'yes' written on it so that the children could copy it down. However, remembering what he had learned at home, Zanzotto wrote 'no' instead. He was just eight years old. In addition to developing a social awareness during his childhood, he discovered a love for the hidden music of language: lullabies, nursery rhymes and short verses all exerted a powerful influence over him.

Zanzotto took part in the anti-Fascist resistance, and was a member of the anti-Fascist Justice and Liberty movement. He also continued with his studies, receiving a degree in Italian literature. After a short stay in Switzerland and France, he returned to his village in 1947 and devoted himself to teaching. Throughout his life he was both poet and teacher, as he saw both roles as integral to combating what he perceived to be the growing barbarism of society. For him, poetry and even individual words were key elements of identity and civilization.

By the time of the publication of his poetry collection *IX Ecloghe* (1962), Zanzotto's language had become extremely rarefied. Another collection, *Beauty*, followed in 1968, an eclectic accumulation of phonemes, incoherencies, Latin phrases, technical terms, neologisms and colloquialisms. His was a language suffused with history and all its uncertainties: 'I still think that there is no more precise historiography than poetry, if it is interpreted correctly, because all the sharpest realities of history seep into its "ectoplastic" body and express themselves there, even (and perhaps especially) in its formal aspects.'

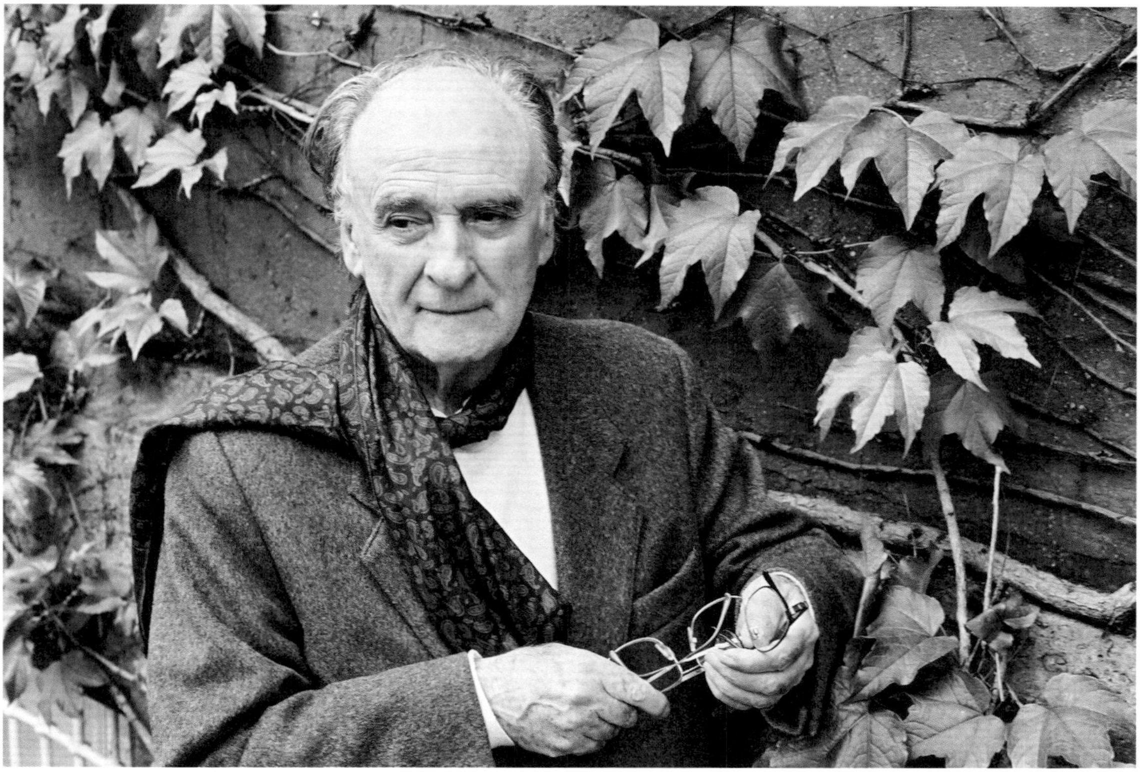

SOURCES OF ILLUSTRATIONS

Abbas/Magnum Photos, p. 15

Bob Adelman/Magnum Photos, p. 99

Adoc-Photos, p. 391

Alfonso (Sánchez García)/Archivio General de la Administración, Madrid © by SIAE 2013, p. 277

Denis Allard/REA, p. 347

Ulf Andersen/Getty Images, pp. 215, 435

Zak Andre/Sipa Press/Olycom, p. 449

John Angerson/Camera Press, p. 215

Archivio Bettmann/Corbis, pp. 247, 269, 387

Archivio GBB/Contrasto, pp. 151, 235, 377

Richard Avedon © The Richard Avedon Foundation, p. 29 W. H. Auden, poet, St Mark's Place, New York, 3 March 1960; p. 93 Truman Capote, New York, 10 October 1955; p. 179 Allen Ginsberg, poet, New York, 30 December 1963; p. 379 Ezra Pound, poet, at the home of William Carlos Williams, Rutherford, New Jersey, 30 June 1958

Helmut Baar/Getty Images, p. 57

Micha Bar Am/Magnum Photos, p. 357

Bruno Barbey/Magnum Photos, p. 55

Sophie Bassouls/Sygma/Corbis, pp. 119, 175, 181, 223

Jerry Bauer, p. 161

Jerry Bauer/Luz Photo, p. 63

Gianni Berengo Gardin/Contrasto, p. 461

Ian Berry/Magnum Photos, p. 439

Nathalie Blandin/Opale/Luz Photo, p. 499

Pierre Boulat/Getty Images, p. 59

René Burri/Magnum Photos, pp. 17, 149, 189, 257

Larry Burrows/Time&Life Pictures/Getty Images, p. 191

Rodrigo Cabrita/4SEE, p. 263

Iván Cañas, p. 259

Cornell Capa/Magnum Photos © International Center of Photography, p. 363

Robert Capa/Magnum Photos © International Center of Photography, p. 203

Ghitta Carell/Fondazione 3M, pp. 365, 417

Henri Cartier-Bresson/Magnum Photos, pp. 25, 47, 49, 89, 133, 155, 219, 273, 295, 393, 413

Sigfrid Casals/Getty Images, pp. 53, 351

Centro de Estudios Juanramonianos, Fundación Zenobia-Juan Ramón Jiménez, Moguer (Huelva) España, p. 227

Alvin Langdon Coburn/ George Eastman House/Getty Images, p. 487

Alvin Langdon Coburn/George Grantham Bain Collection/LOC/Writer Pictures, p. 501

Alberto Conti/Contrasto, p. 321

Jerry Cooke/Time&Life Pictures/Getty Images, p. 473

Juan Domingo Córdoba Vargas, p. 467

Alberto Cristofari/A3, p. 11

Bruce Davidson/Magnum Photos, pp. 31, 429

René Dazy/Rue des Archives/Writer Pictures, p. 465

DeA Picture Library, concesso in licenza ad Alinari, p. 447

Anthony Di Gesu/Getty Images, p. 409

Robert Doisneau/Gamma Rapho/Getty Images, pp. 131, 145, 283, 381, 389, 427, 505

Jillian Edelstein/Camera Press, p. 41

Oscar Elias/Album, p. 475

Elliott & Fry/Getty Images, p. 249

Elliott Erwitt/Magnum Photos, pp. 239, 305, 399

Marion Ettlinger, pp. 163, 325, 343, 483

Sara Facio, pp. 95, 115, 375

Courtesy Victoria Cohen Fante, p. 153

Tullio Farabola/Archivi Farabola, p. 353

Deborah Feingold/Corbis, p. 385

Giorgia Fiorio/Contrasto, p. 77

Foto Fine Art/Heritage Images/Scala, Firenze, p. 185

Martine Franck/Magnum Photos, pp. 67, 81, 209, 213

Leonard Freed/Magnum Photos, pp. 121, 173

Gisèle Freund © RMN-Grand Palais/Paris, Musée National d'Art Moderne-Centre Pompidou, Fond MCC/IMEC, riproduzioni di P. Migeat p. 177, G. Meguerditchian p. 229, B. Prévost p. 345, G. Carrard p. 497

Gisèle Freund/Science Photo Library, p. 207

Federico Garolla/Contrasto, pp. 311, 313, 361

Francesco Gattoni/Writer Pictures, p. 421

Getty Images, pp. 75, 117, 157, 397

Gianni Giansanti/Contrasto, pp. 87, 503

Bruce Gilden/Magnum Photos, p. 143

Burt Glinn/Magnum Photos, p. 73

Günter Gluecklich/Laif, p. 317

Ara Güler/Magnum Photos, p. 35

Philippe Halsman/Magnum Photos, pp. 127, 217, 285, 331, 445, 463

Albert Harlingue/Roger-Viollet/Archivi Alinari, p. 335

Chester Higgins Jr/Redux, p. 395

Thomas Hoepker/Magnum Photos, p. 423

E. O. Hoppé/Hulton/Getty Images, p. 225

E. O. Hoppé/Corbis, p. 453

Martin Hunter/Camera Press, p. 489

Debra Hurford Brown/Camera Press, p. 139

David Hurn/Magnum Photos, pp. 405, 437

Graham Jepson/Writer Pictures, p. 183

Richard Kalvar/Magnum Photos, p. 231

Yousuf Karsh/Camera Press, pp. 237, 425

Roberto Koch/Contrasto, pp. 39, 135

Sergio Larrain/Magnum Photos, p. 337

Cato Lein/Writer Pictures, p. 193

David Levenson/Getty Images, p. 37

Geraint Lewis/Writer Pictures, p. 103

Bernard Lipnitzki/Roger-Viollet/Archivi Alinari, p. 101

Steve Liss/Time&Life Pictures/Getty Images, p. 433

Herbert List/Magnum Photos, pp. 33, 109, 113, 125, 293

Man Ray/Getty Images, p. 383

Alex Majoli/Magnum Photos, p. 359

Peter Marlow/Magnum Photos, p. 469

Eamonn McCabe/Camera Press, pp. 431, 481

Vincent Mentzel/Hollandse Hoogte, p. 319

Jacqueline Mitelman/National Portrait Gallery, Canberra, p. 441

Inge Morath/Magnum Photos © The Inge Morath Foundation, pp. 165, 367

Oliver Morris/Getty Images, p. 477

Ugo Mulas © Eredi Ugo Mulas. Tutti i diritti riservati, p. 309

Carl Mydans/Time&Life Pictures/Getty Images, pp. 287, 443

Moisei Nappelbaum/Adoc Photos, p. 61

Moisei Nappelbaum/Archivio GBB, p. 13

Sandy Nicholson/Redux, p. 27

Giovanni Occhipinti, p. 415

Isolde Ohlbaum/Laif, pp. 65, 85, 91, 147, 243, 349, 403, 495, 507

Olycom, pp. 79, 355

Oronoz/Album, p. 43

Gordon Parks © The Gordon Parks Foundation, Courtesy The Gordon Parks Foundation, p. 141

Paolo Pellegrin/Magnum Photos, p. 369

Micheline Pelletier/Corbis, p. 479

Gilles Peress/Magnum Photos, p. 271

Véronique Pestoni, p. 23

Bob Peterson/Time&LifePictures/Getty Images, p. 281

John Phillips/Time&LifePictures/Getty Images, p. 407

Pablo Picasso/Rue des Archives/Writer Pictures, p. 21

Giuseppe Pino/Contrasto, p. 451

George Platt Lynes/Condé Nast Archive/Corbis, p. 105

George Platt Lynes © Estate of George Platt Lynes/Scala, Firenze, p. 221

Tessa Posthuma de Boer/Hollandse Hoogte, p. 339

Raghu Rai/Magnum Photos, p. 401

Friedrich Rauch/Writer Pictures, p. 329

Steye Raviez/Hollandse Hoogte, p. 111

Eli Reed/Magnum Photos, p. 315

Francis Reiss/Picture Post/Getty Images, p. 457

Peter Rigaud/Laif, p. 159

Alexandr Rodchenko/The Museum of Modern Art, New York/Scala, Firenze, © by SIAE 2013, p. 297

Mario Ruiz/Time&Life Images/Getty Images, p. 83

René Saint Paul/Rue des Archives/Writer Pictures, p. 45

Sebastião Salgado/Amazonas Images, p. 411

Lise Sarfati/Magnum Photos, p. 97

Claude Schwartz/Corbis, p. 371

Ferdinando Scianna/Magnum Photos, pp. 51, 69, 245, 291, 419

Carl Seelig/Robert Walser Stiftung/Keystone, p. 485

Davis Seymour/Magnum Photos, pp. 71, 169, 205, 255

Beowulf Sheehan/Writer Pictures, pp. 9, 341

Peter Sibbald/Redux, p. 323

Eugenio Silva, p. 195

Lord Snowdon/Camera Press, pp. 19, 107, 137, 251, 253, 275, 327, 333

Chris Steele Perkins/Magnum Photos, p. 279

Isabel Steva Hernández/Colita/Corbis, pp. 171, 187

Dennis Stock/Magnum Photos, p. 299

Niki Sublime/http://flickr.com/photos/18113405@N00/221259238, p. 123

Horst Tappe/Lebrecht Music & Arts, p. 303

Ted Thai/Time&Life Pictures/Getty Images, p. 241

Top Foto/Archivi Alinari, p. 455

Carl Van Vechten/Library of Congress Washington, pp. 129, 307

Giovanni Verga/Fondazione 3M, p. 471

Marx Voloshin, p. 459

Patrick Zachmann/Magnum Photos, p. 201

Yukichi Watabe/Camera Press, p. 301

Eudora Welty/Corbis, p. 491

Anders Beer Wilse/Norsk Folkemuseum, p. 199

Writer Pictures, pp. 167, 197, 233, 265, 289

INDEX OF WRITERS AND PHOTOGRAPHERS